THE LOEB CLASSICAL LIBRARY
FOUNDED BY JAMES LOEB

EDITED BY
G. P. GOOLD

PREVIOUS EDITORS

T. E. PAGE	E. CAPPS
W. H. D. ROUSE	L. A. POST
E. H. WARMINGTON	

VIRGIL
II

LCL 64

VIRGIL

AENEID VII–XII
THE MINOR POEMS

WITH AN ENGLISH TRANSLATION BY

H. RUSHTON FAIRCLOUGH

HARVARD UNIVERSITY PRESS
CAMBRIDGE, MASSACHUSETTS
LONDON, ENGLAND

First published 1918
Reprinted 1922, 1925, 1929, 1930 (3 times)
New and revised edition 1934
Reprinted 1937, 1940, 1942, 1950, 1954,
1960, 1966, 1969, 1978, 1986, 1996, 1998

LOEB CLASSICAL LIBRARY® is a registered trademark
of the President and Fellows of Harvard College

ISBN 0-674-99071-4

*Printed in Great Britain by St Edmundsbury Press Ltd,
Bury St Edmunds, Suffolk, on acid-free paper.
Bound by Hunter & Foulis Ltd, Edinburgh, Scotland.*

CONTENTS

THE AENEID
BOOK VII	2
BOOK VIII	60
BOOK IX	112
BOOK X	170
BOOK XI	234
BOOK XII	298

THE MINOR POEMS
INTRODUCTION	368
CULEX	370
CIRIS	404
COPA	448
MORETUM	452
DIRAE	462
LYDIA	472
PRIAPEA	480
CATALEPTON	486

APPENDIX	511
INDEX	543

THE AENEID
BOOKS VII–XII

AENEIS

LIBER VII

Tu quoque litoribus nostris, Aeneia nutrix,   MPR
aeternam moriens famam, Caieta, dedisti;
et nunc servat honos sedem tuus, ossaque nomen
Hesperia in magna, si qua est ea gloria, signat.
  At pius exsequiis Aeneas rite solutis,   FMPR
aggere composito tumuli, postquam alta quierunt   6
aequora, tendit iter velis portumque relinquit.
adspirant aurae in noctem, nec candida cursus
Luna negat, splendet tremulo sub lumine pontus.
proxima Circaeae raduntur litora terrae,   10
dives inaccessos ubi Solis filia lucos
adsiduo resonat cantu, tectisque superbis
urit odoratam nocturna in lumina cedrum,
arguto tenuis percurrens pectine telas.
hinc exaudiri gemitus iraeque leonum   15
vincla recusantum et sera sub nocte rudentum,
saetigerique sues atque in praesepibus ursi
saevire, ac formae magnorum ululare luporum,

---

    ² famam moriens $P^1\gamma^1$.   ⁴ signant $MP\gamma^1$.
    ⁷ portus $P\gamma$.   ⁸ cursum R.
    ¹³ nocturno in lumine M.   ¹⁵ exaudire P.
    ¹⁶ saeva P.

THE AENEID

BOOK VII

Thou, too,[1] Caieta, nurse of Aeneas, hast by thy death given deathless fame to our shores; and still thine honour guards thy resting-place, and in great Hesperia, if such glory be aught, thy name marks thy dust.

[5] But good Aeneas, when the last rites were duly paid and the funeral mound was raised, soon as the high seas were stilled, sails forth on his way and leaves the haven. Breezes blow on into the night, and the Moon, shining bright, forbids not the voyage; the sea glitters beneath her dancing beams. Closely they skirt the shores of Circe's land,[2] where the rich daughter of the Sun thrills her untrodden groves with ceaseless song, and in her stately halls burns fragrant cedar to illuminate the night, as with shrill shuttle she sweeps the fine-spun web. Hence could be heard the angry growls of lions chafing at their bonds and roaring in midnight hours, the raging of bristly boars and encaged bears, and howls from shapes of monstrous wolves; whom with her potent

[1] As well as Misenus (vi. 234) and Palinurus (vi. 381). Caieta gave her name to Gaeta and the Gulf of Gaeta.

[2] Circeii, a promontory of Latium, but once an island, is identified by Virgil with Homer's island of Aeaea, the home of Circe.

3

VIRGIL

quos hominum ex facie dea saeva potentibus herbis
induerat Circe in voltus ac terga ferarum. 20
quae ne monstra pii paterentur talia Troes
delati in portus, neu litora dira subirent,
Neptunus ventis implevit vela secundis,
atque fugam dedit, et praeter vada fervida vexit.

Iamque rubescebat radiis mare, et aethere ab alto 25
Aurora in roseis fulgebat lutea bigis:
cum venti posuere omnisque repente resedit
flatus, et in lento luctantur marmore tonsae.
atque hic Aeneas ingentem ex aequore lucum
prospicit. hunc inter fluvio Tiberinus amoeno 30
verticibus rapidis et multa flavus harena
in mare prorumpit. variae circumque supraque
adsuetae ripis volucres et fluminis alveo
aethera mulcebant cantu, lucoque volabant.
flectere iter sociis terraeque advertere proras 35
imperat, et laetus fluvio succedit opaco.

Nunc age, qui reges, Erato, quae tempora rerum,
quis Latio antiquo fuerit status, advena classem
cum primum Ausoniis exercitus appulit oris,
expediam, et primae revocabo exordia pugnae. 40
tu vatem, tu, diva, mone. dicam horrida bella,
dicam acies actosque animis in funera reges,
Tyrrhenamque manum, totamque sub arma coactam
Hesperiam. maior rerum mihi nascitur ordo,
maius opus moveo.

     Rex arva Latinus et urbes 45
iam senior longa placidas in pace regebat.
hunc Fauno et Nympha genitum Laurente Marica

---

[37] tempora rerum *as punctuated in* M^2P^2 *and by Servius:*
tempora, rerum *Peerlkamp.*

AENEID BOOK VII

herbs Circe, cruel goddess, had changed from the likeness of men, clothing them in the features and frames of beasts. But lest the good Trojans should suffer such monstrous fate, should enter the haven or draw near the cursed shore, Neptune filled their sails with favouring winds, and gave them escape, and bore them past the seething shallows.

25 And now the sea was reddening with the rays of dawn, and from high heaven saffron-hued Aurora shone in roseate car, when the winds fell, and every breath sank suddenly, and the oar blades strive amid the sluggish calm of waters. Then lo! Aeneas, gazing forth from the flood, sees a mighty forest. Through its midst the Tiber, with pleasant stream, leaps forth to sea in swirling eddies and yellow with plenteous sand. Around and above, birds of varied plumes, that haunt the banks and river-channel, charmed the sky with song, and flitted amid the forest. He bids his comrades change their course and turn their prows to land, and joyfully enters the shady river.

37 Awake now, Erato! Who were the kings, what was the tide of events, how stood ancient Latium, when first that stranger host beached its barques on Ausonia's shore—this will I unfold; and the prelude of the opening strife will I recall. Thou, goddess, do thou prompt thy bard! I will tell of grim wars, will tell of battle array, and princes in their valour rushing upon death—of Tyrrhenian bands, and all Hesperia mustered in arms. Greater is the story that opens before me; greater is the task I essay.

45 King Latinus, now old, ruled over lands and towns in the calm of a long peace. He, we are told, was sprung of Faunus and the Laurentine nymph,

VIRGIL

accipimus: Fauno Picus pater, isque parentem
te, Saturne, refert, tu sanguinis ultimus auctor.
filius huic fato divum prolesque virilis 50
nulla fuit, primaque oriens erepta iuventa est.
sola domum et tantas servabat filia sedes,
iam matura viro, iam plenis nubilis annis.
multi illam magno e Latio totaque petebant
Ausonia.   petit ante alios pulcherrimus omnes 55
Turnus, avis atavisque potens, quem regia coniunx
adiungi generum miro properabat amore;
sed variis portenta deum terroribus obstant.
laurus erat tecti medio in penetralibus altis, MPR
sacra comam multosque metu servata per annos, 60
quam pater inventam, primas cum conderet arces,
ipse ferebatur Phoebo sacrasse Latinus,
Laurentisque ab ea nomen posuisse colonis.
huius apes summum densae (mirabile dictu),
stridore ingenti liquidum trans aethera vectae, 65
obsedere apicem et pedibus per mutua nexis
examen subitum ramo frondente pependit.
continuo vates "externum cernimus," inquit,
"adventare virum et partis petere agmen easdem
partibus ex isdem et summa dominarier arce." 70
praeterea, castis adolet dum altaria taedis
et iuxta genitorem adstat Lavinia virgo,
visa, nefas, longis comprendere crinibus ignem,
atque omnem ornatum flamma crepitante cremari,
regalisque accensa comas, accensa coronam 75
insignem gemmis; tum fumida lumine fulvo
involvi ac totis Volcanum spargere tectis.
id vero horrendum ac visu mirabile ferri:
namque fore inlustrem fama fatisque canebant
ipsam, sed populo magnum portendere bellum. 80

[53] in plenis *P*.
[71] dum] cum *Nonius*.

AENEID BOOK VII

Marica. Faunus' sire was Picus, and he boasts thee, O Saturn, as his father; thou art first founder of the line. To him by Heaven's decree was no son or male descent, cut off, as it was, in the spring of early youth. Alone, to preserve the house and noble home, was a daughter, now ripe for a husband, now of full age to be a bride. Many wooed her from wide Latium and all Ausonia, yet goodliest above all other wooers was Turnus, of long and lofty ancestry, whom the queen-mother yearned with wondrous passion to unite to her as son. But divine portents, with manifold alarms, bar the way. In the midst of the palace, in the high inner courts, stood a laurel of sacred leafage, preserved in awe through many years, which lord Latinus himself, 'twas said, found and dedicated to Phoebus, when he built his first towers; and from it he gave his settlers their name Laurentes. Atop of this tree, wondrous to tell, settled a dense swarm of bees, borne with loud humming across the liquid air, and with feet intertwined hung in sudden swarm from the leafy bough. Forthwith the prophet cries: "I see a stranger draw near; from the self-same quarter a troop seeks the same quarter, and reigns in the topmost citadel!" Moreover, while with hallowed torch he kindles the altars, and at her father's side stands the maiden Lavinia, she was seen (O horror!) to catch fire in her long tresses, and burn with crackling flame in all her headgear, her queenly hair ablaze, ablaze her jewelled coronal; then wreathed in smoke and yellow glare, she scattered fire throughout the palace. That indeed was noised abroad as an awful and wondrous vision; for she, they foretold, would herself be glorious in fame and fortune, yet to her people she boded a mighty war.

VIRGIL

At rex sollicitus monstris oracula Fauni,
fatidici genitoris, adit lucosque sub alta
consulit Albunea, nemorum quae maxima sacro
fonte sonat saevamque exhalat opaca mephitim.
hinc Italae gentes omnisque Oenotria tellus   85
in dubiis responsa petunt: huc dona sacerdos
cum tulit et caesarum ovium sub nocte silenti
pellibus incubuit stratis somnosque petivit,
multa modis simulacra videt volitantia miris
et varias audit voces fruiturque deorum   90
conloquio atque imis Acheronta adfatur Avernis.
hic et tum pater ipse petens responsa Latinus
centum lanigeras mactabat rite bidentis,
atque harum effultus tergo stratisque iacebat
velleribus: subita ex alto vox reddita luco est: 95
" ne pete conubiis natam sociare Latinis,
o mea progenies, thalamis neu crede paratis:
externi venient generi, qui sanguine nostrum
nomen in astra ferant quorumque ab stirpe nepotes
omnia sub pedibus, qua Sol utrumque recurrens   100
aspicit Oceanum, vertique regique videbunt."
haec responsa patris Fauni monitusque silenti
nocte datos non ipse suo premit ore Latinus,
sed circum late volitans iam Fama per urbes
Ausonias tulerat, cum Laomedontia pubes   105
gramineo ripae religavit ab aggere classem.

Aeneas primique duces et pulcher Iulus

⁸⁴ saevum *M.*   ⁹⁵ subito *M.*
⁹⁸ veniunt *preferred by Servius.*

AENEID BOOK VII

⁸¹ But the king, troubled by the portent, visits the oracle of Faunus, his prophetic sire, and consults the groves beneath high Albunea, which, mightiest of forests,[1] echoes with hallowed fountain, and breathes forth from her darkness a deadly vapour. Hence the tribes of Italy and all the Oenotrian land seek responses in days of doubt; hither the priestess brings the offerings, and as she lies under the silent night on the outspread fleeces of slaughtered sheep and woos slumber, she sees many phantoms flitting in wondrous wise, hears voices manifold, holds converse with the gods, and speaks with Acheron in lowest Avernus. Here then, also, King Latinus himself, seeking an answer, duly slaughtered a hundred woolly sheep, and lay couched on their hides and outspread fleeces. Suddenly a voice came from the deep grove: "Seek not, O my son, to ally thy daughter in Latin wedlock, and put no faith in the bridal-chamber prepared. Strangers shall come, to be thy sons, whose blood shall exalt our name to the stars, and the children of whose race shall behold, where the circling sun looks on either ocean,[2] the whole world roll obedient beneath their feet." This answer of his father Faunus, and the warning he gave in the silent night, Latinus keeps not shut within his own lips; but Rumour, flitting far and wide, had already borne the tidings through the Ausonian cities, when the sons of Laomedon moored their ships to the river's grassy bank.

¹⁰⁷ Aeneas, and his chief captains and fair Iülus,

[1] Albunea is here identified with the forest. Situated at or near Laurentum, this must be different from the Albunea of Horace, *Carm.* I. 7, 12, which is a cascade at Tibur.

[2] *i.e.* in East and West; the Ocean being conceived as flowing round the earth.

VIRGIL

corpora sub ramis deponunt arboris altae
instituuntque dapes et adorea liba per herbam
subiciunt epulis (sic Iuppiter ipse monebat)   110
et Cereale solum pomis agrestibus augent.
consumptis hic forte aliis, ut vertere morsus
exiguam in Cererem penuria adegit edendi
et violare manu malisque audacibus orbem
fatalis crusti patulis nec parcere quadris: 115
"heus! etiam mensas consumimus," inquit Iulus,
nec plura adludens.   ea vox audita laborum
prima tulit finem primamque loquentis ab ore
eripuit pater ac stupefactus numine pressit.
continuo "salve fatis mihi debita tellus   120
vosque," ait, "o fidi Troiae, salvete, penates:
hic domus, haec patria est.   genitor mihi talia namque
(nunc repeto) Anchises fatorum arcana reliquit:
'cum te, nate, fames ignota ad litora vectum
accisis coget dapibus consumere mensas,   125
tum sperare domos defessus ibique memento
prima locare manu molirique aggere tecta.'
haec erat illa fames, haec nos suprema manebat,
exitiis positura modum.
quare agite et primo laeti cum lumine solis,   130
quae loca, quive habeant homines, ubi moenia gentis,
vestigemus et a portu diversa petamus.
nunc pateras libate Iovi precibusque vocate
Anchisen genitorem, et vina reponite mensis."

[110] ipse] ille M^2, *known to Servius*.
[125] ambesis *R*.   [128] manebant *R*.

---

[1] The round cakes, like our hot cross-buns, were scored by cross-lines into four quarters (*quadrae*).

AENEID BOOK VII

lay their limbs to rest under the boughs of a high tree, and spread the feast; they place cakes of meal along the sward beneath the viands—Jove himself inspired them—and they crown the wheaten base with fruits of the field. Here, haply, when the rest was consumed, and the scantness of fare drove them to turn their teeth upon the slender cakes—to profane with hand and daring jaw the fateful circles of crust, and spare not the broad loaves[1]: "Ha! we eat our tables too!" quoth Iülus, jesting; this and no more. That cry,[2] when heard, first brought an end of toil; and as it first fell from the speaker's lips, his father caught it up and held it fast,[3] awestruck at Heaven's will. Straightway, "Hail, O land," he cries, "destined as my due! and hail to you, ye faithful gods of Troy! Here is our home, here our country! For my father Anchises—now I recall it—bequeathed me this secret of fate: 'My son, when, wafted to an unknown shore, hunger shall compel thee, as food fails, to devour thy tables, then in thy weariness hope for a home, and there be mindful first to set up thy dwellings with thy hand and bank them with a mound.' This was that hunger foretold, this the last strait awaiting us, that should set an end to our deadly woes! Come then, and, gladly with the sun's first beams, let us explore what lands these are, what people here dwell, where is the city of the nation, and let us fare forth from the harbour in divers ways. Now pour your cups to Jove, and call in prayer on my sire Anchises, and set the wine again upon the board."

---

[2] *cf.* III. 255, where, however, the prophecy is uttered by Celaeno, not by Anchises.

[3] Others render "stopped his utterance"; sc. *vocem*.

VIRGIL

Sic deinde effatus frondenti tempora ramo   135
implicat et geniumque loci primamque deorum
Tellurem nymphasque et adhuc ignota precatur
flumina, tum Noctem Noctisque orientia signa
Idaeumque Iovem Phrygiamque ex ordine Matrem
invocat et duplicis caeloque Ereboque parentis.   140
hic pater omnipotens ter caelo clarus ab alto
intonuit radiisque ardentem lucis et auro
ipse manu quatiens ostendit ab aethere nubem.
diditur hic subito Troiana per agmina rumor,
advenisse diem, quo debita moenia condant.   145
certatim instaurant epulas atque omine magno
crateras laeti statuunt et vina coronant.

Postera cum prima lustrabat lampade terras
orta dies, urbem et finis et litora gentis
diversi explorant: haec fontis stagna Numici,   150
hunc Thybrim fluvium, hic fortis habitare Latinos.
tum satus Anchisa delectos ordine ab omni
centum oratores augusta ad moenia regis
ire iubet, ramis velatos Palladis omnis,
donaque ferre viro pacemque exposcere Teucris.   155
haud mora, festinant iussi rapidisque feruntur
passibus.   ipse humili designat moenia fossa
moliturque locum primasque in litore sedes
castrorum in morem pinnis atque aggere cingit.
iamque iter emensi turris ac tecta Latinorum   160
ardua cernebant iuvenes muroque subibant.
ante urbem pueri et primaevo flore iuventus
exercentur equis domitantque in pulvere currus
aut acris tendunt arcus aut lenta lacertis

¹⁴³ manum *M*¹.   ¹⁶⁰ et *M*¹γ. Latini *M (late)*.
¹⁶³ exercetur *P*γ¹.

12

AENEID BOOK VII

¹³⁵ So speaking, he straightway wreaths his temples with leafy bough and prays to the genius of the place, and Earth, first of gods; to the nymphs and the streams yet unknown; then to Night and Night's rising signs, and to Jove of Ida and the Phrygian Mother, each in order, and his twain parents, in heaven and in the world below. At this, the almighty Father thundered thrice aloft from a clear sky, and with his own hand shook forth to view from heaven a cloud ablaze with shafts of golden light. Then suddenly through the Trojan band runs the rumour, that the day has come to found their promised city. Emulously they renew the feast, and cheered by the mighty omen set on the bowls and wreathe the wine.

¹⁴⁸ On the morrow, soon as the risen day was lighting the earth with her earliest torch, by separate ways they search out the city[1] and boundaries and coasts of the nation. This, they learn, is the pool of Numicius' fount; this the Tiber river; here dwell the brave Latins. Then Anchises' son commands a hundred envoys, chosen from every rank, to go to the king's stately city, o'er-shaded all by the boughs of Pallas, to bear gifts for the hero, and to crave peace for the Trojans. They linger not, but hasten at his bidding and move with rapid steps. Aeneas himself marks out his walls with a shallow trench, toils o'er the ground, and encircles this first settlement on the coast, after the fashion of a camp, with mound and battlements. And now his band had traversed their way; they were in sight of the towers and steep roofs of the Latins, and drew near to the wall. Before the city, boys and youths in their early bloom are a-training in horsemanship, or break in teams amid the dust, or bend eager bows, or hurl

[1] *i.e.* Lavinium.

VIRGIL

spicula contorquent cursuque ictuque lacessunt,   165
cum praevectus equo longaevi regis ad auris
nuntius ingentis ignota in veste reportat
advenisse viros.   ille intra tecta vocari
imperat et solio medius consedit avito.

   Tectum augustum, ingens, centum sublime
      columnis,   170
urbe fuit summa, Laurentis regia Pici,
horrendum silvis et religione parentum.
hic sceptra accipere et primos attollere fasces
regibus omen erat, hoc illis curia templum,
hae sacris sedes epulis, hic ariete caeso   175
perpetuis soliti patres considere mensis.
quin etiam veterum effigies ex ordine avorum
antiqua e cedro, Italusque paterque Sabinus
vitisator, curvam servans sub imagine falcem,
Saturnusque senex Ianique bifrontis imago,   FMPR
vestibulo adstabant aliique ab origine reges   181
Martiaque ob patriam pugnando volnera passi.
multaque praeterea sacris in postibus arma,
captivi pendent currus curvaeque secures
et cristae capitum et portarum ingentia claustra 185
spiculaque clipeique ereptaque rostra carinis.
ipse Quirinali lituo parvaque sedebat
succinctus trabea laevaque ancile gerebat
Picus, equum domitor; quem capta cupidine coniunx
aurea percussum virga versumque venenis   190
fecit avem Circe sparsitque coloribus alas.

   [182] Martia qui *F¹M*.

AENEID BOOK VII

with their arms tough darts, and challenge to race or boxing bout—when, galloping up, a messenger brings word to the aged monarch's ears that mighty men are come in unknown attire. The king bids them be summoned within the halls, and takes his seat in the midst on his ancestral throne.

170 Stately and vast, towering with a hundred columns, his house crowned the city, once the palace of Laurentian Picus, awe-inspiring with its grove and the sanctity of olden days. Here 'twas auspicious for kings to receive the sceptre, and first uplift the fasces; this shrine was their senate-house, this the scene of their holy feasts; here, after slaughter of rams, the elders were wont to sit down at the long line of tables. Yea, and in order are images of their forefathers of yore, carved of old cedar—Italus and father Sabinus, planter of the vine, guarding in his image the curved pruning-hook, and aged Saturn, and the likeness of two-faced Janus—all standing in the vestibule; and other kings from the beginning, and they who had suffered wounds of war, fighting for their fatherland. Many arms, moreover, hang on the sacred doors, captive chariots, curved axes, helmet-crests and massive bars of gates; javelins and shields and beaks wrenched from ships. There sat one, holding the Quirinal staff[1] and girt with short robe, his left hand bearing the sacred shield—even Picus, tamer of steeds, whom his bride Circe, smitten with love's longing, struck with her golden rod, and with drugs changed into a bird with plumes of dappled hue.

---

[1] Quirinus (*i.e.* Romulus) was Rome's first augur, and as such carried the augur's badges of office—the *lituus*, or curved staff, and the *ancile*, or sacred shield—while he wore the purple striped toga, or *trabea*.

15

VIRGIL

Tali intus templo divum patriaque Latinus
sede sedens Teucros ad sese in tecta vocavit,
atque haec ingressis placido prior edidit ore:
"dicite, Dardanidae (neque enim nescimus et urbem
et genus, auditique advertitis aequore cursum), 196
quid petitis? quae causa rates aut cuius egentis
litus ad Ausonium tot per vada caerula vexit?
sive errore viae seu tempestatibus acti,
qualia multa mari nautae patiuntur in alto, 200
fluminis intrastis ripas portuque sedetis,
ne fugite hospitium neve ignorate Latinos
Saturni gentem, haud vinclo nec legibus aequam,
sponte sua veterisque dei se more tenentem.
atque equidem memini (fama est obscurior annis) 205
Auruncos ita ferre senes, his ortus ut agris
Dardanus Idaeas Phrygiae penetravit ad urbes
Threiciamque Samum, quae nunc Samothracia fertur.
hinc illum Corythi Tyrrhena ab sede profectum
aurea nunc solio stellantis regia caeli 210
accipit et numerum divorum altaribus auget."

Dixerat, et dicta Ilioneus sic voce secutus:
"rex, genus egregium Fauni, nec fluctibus actos
atra subegit hiems vestris succedere terris,
nec sidus regione viae litusve fefellit: 215
consilio hanc omnes animisque volentibus urbem
adferimur, pulsi regnis, quae maxima quondam
extremo veniens Sol aspiciebat Olympo.
ab Iove principium generis, Iove Dardana pubes

²⁰⁷ penetrarit *R.*
²¹¹ numerom *P*¹: numero *P*²γ¹. addit γ¹.
²¹² dictum *M*¹.

AENEID BOOK VII

¹⁹² Such was the temple of the gods wherein Latinus, seated on the throne of his fathers, summoned the Teucrians to his presence in the halls, and as they entered greeted them thus with gentle mien: "Tell, O Sons of Dardanus—for your city and race we know, and not unheard of is your journey over the deep—what seek ye? What cause, or what need, hath borne you to the Ausonian shore o'er so many dark-blue waters? Whether straying from your course, or driven by storms (for such things oft do sailors suffer on the high seas), ye have entered the river banks and lie in haven, shun not our welcome, and be not unaware that the Latins are Saturn's race, righteous not by bond or laws, but self-controlled of their own free will and by the custom of their ancient god. And in truth I remember, though time has dimmed the tale, that Auruncan elders told how that in this land sprang Dardanus,[1] and hence passed to the towns of Phrygian Ida and Thracian Samos, that men now call Samothrace. 'Twas hence, from the Tuscan home of Corythus, he came, and now the golden palace of the starry sky admits him to a throne, and he increases the number of altars of the gods."

²¹² He ceased, and Ilioneus followed thus: "O King, illustrious seed of Faunus, no black storm hath tossed us on the waves and driven us to seek shelter in your lands, nor hath star or shore misled us in our course. Of set purpose and with willing hearts do we draw near to this thy city, exiled from a realm once the greatest that the sun beheld as he journeyed from the uttermost heaven. From Jove[2] is the origin of our race; in Jove, as ancestor, the sons of

[1] *cf.* III. 167.
[2] Jupiter was father of Dardanus.

VIRGIL

gaudet avo, rex ipse Iovis de gente suprema: 220
Troius Aeneas tua nos ad limina misit.
quanta per Idaeos saevis effusa Mycenis
tempestas ierit campos, quibus actus uterque
Europae atque Asiae fatis concurrerit orbis,
audiit et si quem tellus extrema refuso 225
summovet Oceano et si quem extenta plagarum
quattuor in medio dirimit plaga Solis iniqui.
diluvio ex illo tot vasta per aequora vecti
dis sedem exiguam patriis litusque rogamus
innocuum et cunctis undamque auramque patentem.
non erimus regno indecores, nec vestra feretur 231
fama levis tantique abolescet gratia facti,
nec Troiam Ausonios gremio excepisse pigebit.
fata per Aeneae iuro dextramque potentem,
sive fide seu quis bello est expertus et armis: 235
multi nos populi, multae (ne temne, quod ultro
praeferimus manibus vittas ac verba precantia)
et petiere sibi et voluere adiungere gentes;
sed nos fata deum vestras exquirere terras
imperiis egere suis. hinc Dardanus ortus, 240
huc repetit, iussisque ingentibus urget Apollo
Tyrrhenum ad Thybrim et fontis vada sacra Numici.
dat tibi praeterea fortunae parva prioris
munera, reliquias Troia ex ardente receptas.
hoc pater Anchises auro libabat ad aras, 245
hoc Priami gestamen erat, cum iura vocatis

[221] mittit *F.*   [224] concurritur *Pγ¹*: concurreret *R.*
[226] quam *R.*   [232] tantive *R.*
[237] vittasque precantia verba *F²*: verba precantum *R.*

AENEID BOOK VII

Dardanus glory; of Jove's supreme race is our king himself, Trojan Aeneas, who has sent us to thy doors. How fierce the storm that burst from cruel Mycenae and passed o'er the plains of Ida; how, driven by fate, the two worlds of Europe and Asia clashed—has come to the ears of all, whom the farthest land where Ocean is flung back keeps far away, and of all whom the zone of the tyrannous sun, stretched midmost of the four, severs from us.[1] From that deluge have we sailed o'er many waste seas, and now crave a scant home for our country's gods, a harmless landing-place, and air and water free to all. We shall be no shame to the realm, nor shall your renown be lightly told or the grace of such a deed grow faint, nor shall Ausonia repent of having welcomed Troy to her breast. By the fortunes of Aeneas I swear, and by his strong right hand, whether in loyalty or in war and arms it has been proved, many are the peoples, many the nations—scorn us not, that of ourselves we proffer garlands with our hands and address to you words of suppliance—who have sought us for themselves and craved our alliance; but the will of heaven has forced us by its behests to seek out your shores. Hence was Dardanus sprung and hither he returns;[2] while with high decrees Apollo urges us to Tuscan Tiber and the sacred waters of the Numician spring. Further, to thee our king offers these poor tokens of his former fortune—relics snatched from burning Troy. With this gold did his father Anchises pour libation at the altars; this was Priam's array when after his wont

[1] Those who dwell farthest away on Atlantic shores, and those beyond the tropics, alike have heard.

[2] *i.e.* in the person of his descendants. Others make *Apollo* the subject of *repetit*.

19

VIRGIL

more daret populis, sceptrumque sacerque tiaras
Iliadumque labor vestes." FMPRV

Talibus Ilionei dictis defixa Latinus
obtutu tenet ora soloque immobilis haeret, 250
intentos volvens oculos. nec purpura regem
picta movet nec sceptra movent Priameia tantum,
quantum in conubio natae thalamoque moratur,
et veteris Fauni volvit sub pectore sortem:
hunc illum fatis externa ab sede profectum 255
portendi generum paribusque in regna vocari
auspiciis, huic progeniem virtute futuram
egregiam et totum quae viribus occupet orbem.
tandem laetus ait: "di nostra incepta secundent
auguriumque suum! dabitur, Troiane, quod optas; 260
munera nec sperno. non vobis, rege Latino,
divitis uber agri Troiaeve opulentia deerit.
ipse modo Aeneas, nostri si tanta cupido est,
si iungi hospitio properat sociusque vocari,
adveniat, voltus neve exhorrescat amicos: 265
pars mihi pacis erit dextram tetigisse tyranni.
vos contra regi mea nunc mandata referte.
est mihi nata, viro gentis quam iungere nostrae
non patrio ex adyto sortes, non plurima caelo
monstra sinunt; generos externis adfore ab oris, 270
hoc Latio restare canunt, qui sanguine nostrum
nomen in astra ferant. hunc illum poscere fata
et reor et, si quid veri mens augurat, opto."

Haec effatus equos numero pater eligit omni FMPR
(stabant ter centum nitidi in praesepibus altis); 275

---

[254] volvens F^1.   [262] Troiaeque $P^2\gamma$.
[264] sociusve FRV.

AENEID BOOK VII

he gave laws to the assembled nations—the sceptre, the sacred diadem, and the robes wrought by Ilium's daughters."

249 At these words of Ilioneus Latinus holds his face fixed in steady gaze downward, rolling the while his earnest eyes. Nor is it so much that the embroidered purple or the sceptre of Priam moves the king, as that he broods o'er his daughter's wedlock and bridal bed, and revolves in his breast the oracle of ancient Faunus. "This," he thought, "must be he who, coming from a stranger's home, is predestined by the fates as my son, and called to sovereignty with equal power; hence must come the offspring, glorious in valour, whose might is to master all the world." At last, in gladness, he speaks: "May the gods prosper our intent and their own prophecy! Trojan, thy wish shall be granted; nor do I spurn thy gifts. While Latinus is king, ye shall not lack the bounty of a fruitful soil, nor Troy's abundance. Only let Aeneas, if so he longs for us, if he be eager to join us in amity and be called our ally, let him come in person and shrink not from friendly eyes. To me it shall be a term of the peace to have touched your sovereign's hand! Do ye now in turn take back to the king my answer: I have a daughter whom oracles from my father's shrine and countless prodigies from heaven suffer me not to unite to a bridegroom of our race; sons shall come from shores of strangers—such destiny, they foretell, awaits Latium—whose blood shall exalt our name to the stars. That this is he on whom fate calls, I both think, and, if my soul forebodes aught of truth, him I choose."

274 With these words the old king picks out horses from all his number—three hundred stood sleek in

VIRGIL

omnibus extemplo Teucris iubet ordine duci
instratos ostro alipedes pictisque tapetis FMR
(aurea pectoribus demissa monilia pendent,
tecti auro fulvum mandunt sub dentibus aurum),
absenti Aeneae currum geminosque iugalis 280
semine ab aetherio, spirantis naribus ignem,
illorum de gente, patri quos daedala Circe
supposita de matre nothos furata creavit.
talibus Aeneadae donis dictisque Latini
sublimes in equis redeunt pacemque reportant. 285

Ecce autem Inachiis sese referebat ab Argis
saeva Iovis coniunx aurasque invecta tenebat,
et laetum Aenean classemque ex aethere longe
Dardaniam Siculo prospexit ab usque Pachyno.
moliri iam tecta videt, iam fidere terrae, 290
deseruisse rates: stetit acri fixa dolore.
tum quassans caput haec effundit pectore dicta:
"heu stirpem invisam et fatis contraria nostris
fata Phrygum! num Sigeis occumbere campis,
num capti potuere capi? num incensa cremavit 295
Troia viros? medias acies mediosque per ignis
invenere viam. at, credo, mea numina tandem
fessa iacent, odiis aut exsaturata quievi.
quin etiam patria excussos infesta per undas
ausa sequi et profugis toto me opponere ponto: 300
absumptae in Teucros vires caelique marisque.
quid Syrtes aut Scylla mihi, quid vasta Charybdis

²⁸¹ flagra(n)tis *F*; *so Sabb.*   ²⁸³ longo *M*.
²⁹⁵ nunc capti *M*.   ²⁹⁸ aut] haud *M*¹γ².

AENEID BOOK VII

their high stalls. At once for all the Teucrians in order he commands them to be led forth, fleet of foot and caparisoned with purple and embroidered housings. Golden are the chains that hang drooping from their breasts, of gold are their trappings, and yellow gold they champ with their teeth. For the absent Aeneas he chooses a car and twin coursers of ethereal seed, breathing fire from their nostrils, and sprung from the stock of those steeds which cunning Circe, stealing them from her sire, bred bastard from the mare she had mated.[1] With such words and gifts from Latinus, the sons of Aeneas, mounted on their horses, return carrying back peace.

286 But lo! the fierce wife of Jove was faring back from Argos, city of Inachus, holding her airy flight; and from the sky afar, even from Sicilian Pachynus, she espied the rejoicing Aeneas and his Dardan fleet. She sees them already building a home, already trusting in the land, their ships deserted. She stopped, pierced with sharp grief; then, shaking her head, pours forth from her breast these words: "Ah! hated race, and Phrygian fates, that cross my own! Could they perish on the Sigean plains? Could they, captured, suffer captivity? Did the fires of Troy consume them? Lo! through the midst of armies, through the midst of flames, they have found a way. But, methinks, my power at last lies outworn; or my wrath is sated, and I rest! Nay more, when they were hurled forth from their country, with my vengeance I dared to follow the exiles through the waves and confront them o'er all the deep: against the Teucrians has been spent all the power of sea and sky. Yet what have the Syrtes availed me, or Scylla,

[1] Circe was daughter of the Sun, whose horses were immortal, while her mare was of mortal stock.

VIRGIL

profuit? optato conduntur Thybridis alveo,
securi pelagi atque mei.   Mars perdere gentem
immanem Lapithum valuit, concessit in iras   305
ipse deum antiquam genitor Calydona Dianae,
quod scelus aut Lapithas tantum aut Calydona merentem?
ast ego, magna Iovis coniunx, nil linquere inausum
quae potui infelix, quae memet in omnia verti,
vincor ab Aenea.   quod si mea numina non sunt   310
magna satis, dubitem haud equidem implorare quod usquam est.
flectere si nequeo superos, Acheronta movebo.
non dabitur regnis, esto, prohibere Latinis,
atque immota manet fatis Lavinia coniunx:
at trahere atque moras tantis licet addere rebus,   315
at licet amborum populos exscindere regum.
hac gener atque socer coeant mercede suorum.
sanguine Troiano et Rutulo dotabere,. virgo,
et Bellona manet te pronuba.   nec face tantum
Cisseis praegnas ignis enixa iugalis,   320
quin idem Veneri partus suus et Paris alter,
funestaeque iterum recidiva in Pergama taedae."

Haec ubi dicta dedit, terras horrenda petivit;
luctificam Allecto dirarum ab sede dearum
infernisque ciet tenebris, cui tristia bella   325
iraeque insidiaeque et crimina noxia cordi.   FMRV
odit et ipse pater Pluton, odere sorores
Tartareae monstrum: tot sese vertit in ora,

---

³⁰⁷ Capithis *M*¹: Lapithas *M*². Calydone *M*¹*R*: Calydo *F*¹ merentes *M*¹: merente *R*γ²: *Servius and Priscian prefer the ablatives.* ³¹⁰ vincar *M*¹.
³¹¹ est *omitted by M*¹. ³¹⁷ hac] at *M*. ³²⁴ sororum *M*²*R*γ².

24

AENEID BOOK VII

what yawning Charybdis? They find shelter in Tiber's longed-for channel, careless of ocean and of me. Mars could destroy the Lapiths' giant race; the very father of the gods yielded ancient Calydon to Diana's wrath;[1] though for what heinous sin did Lapiths or Calydon merit such penalty? But I, Jove's mighty consort, who have endured, alas! to leave naught undared, who have turned me to every shift, I am worsted by Aeneas! But if my powers be not strong enough, surely I need not be slow to seek succour wherever it may be; if Heaven I cannot bend, then Hell I will arouse! Not mine will it be—I grant it—to keep him from the crown of Latium, and by fate Lavinia abides immovably his bride; yet to put off the hour and to bring delay to such great issues—that may I do; yet may I uproot the nation of either king. At such price of their people's lives be father and son-in-law united! Blood of Trojan and Rutulian shall be thy dower, maiden, and Bellona awaits thee as thy bridal matron. Nor did Cisseus' daughter alone conceive a firebrand and give birth to nuptial flames.[2] Nay, Venus has the like in her own child, a second Paris, another funeral torch for reborn Troy."

323 These words uttered, she with awful mien passed to earth, and calls baleful Allecto from the home of the Dread Goddesses and the infernal shades —Allecto, whose heart is set on gloomy wars, passions, plots and baneful crimes. Hateful is the monster even to her sire Pluto, hateful to her Tartarean sisters; so many are the forms she assumes, so savage

[1] The wild boar of Calydon ravaged the land because Oeneus, the king, had neglected sacrifice to Diana.
[2] Hecuba, before bearing Paris, dreamed that she would give birth to a firebrand.

25

VIRGIL

tam saevae facies, tot pullulat atra colubris.   329
quam Iuno his acuit verbis ac talia fatur: MRV
"hunc mihi da proprium, virgo sata Nocte, laborem,
hanc operam, ne noster honos infractave cedat
fama loco, neu conubiis ambire Latinum
Aeneadae possint Italosve obsidere finis.
tu potes unanimos armare in proelia fratres   335
atque odiis versare domos, tu verbera tectis
funereasque inferre faces, tibi nomina mille,
mille nocendi artes. fecundum concute pectus,
disice compositam pacem, sere crimina belli;
arma velit poscatque simul rapiatque iuventus."   340
  Exim Gorgoneis Allecto infecta venenis
principio Latium et Laurentis tecta tyranni
celsa petit, tacitumque obsedit limen Amatae,
quam super adventu Teucrum Turnique hymenaeis
femineae ardentem curaeque iraeque coquebant.   345
huic dea caeruleis unum de crinibus anguem
conicit, inque sinum praecordia ad intima subdit,
quo furibunda domum monstro permisceat omnem.
ille inter vestis et levia pectora lapsus
volvitur attactu nullo fallitque furentem,   350
vipeream inspirans animam; fit tortile collo
aurum ingens coluber, fit longae taenia vittae,   MR
innectitque comas et membris lubricus errat.
ac dum prima lues udo sublapsa veneno
pertemptat sensus atque ossibus implicat ignem,   355
necdum animus toto percepit pectore flammam,
mollius et solito matrum de more locuta est,
multa super natae lacrimans Phrygiisque hymenaeis:

<small>³³⁰ verbis] dictis *R*γ.   ³³⁷ -que *omitted by V*.
³⁵¹ spirans *MV*.   ³⁵⁷ est *omitted by M*γ¹.   ³⁵⁸ nata *R*γ².</small>
26

AENEID BOOK VII

their aspect, so thick her black upsprouting vipers.[1] Her Juno inflames with these words, speaking thus: "Grant me, maiden daughter of Night, this service, a boon all my own, that my honour and glory yield not o'ermastered, that the sons of Aeneas be not able to cajole Latinus with wedlock or beset the borders of Italy. Thou canst arm for strife brothers of one soul, and overturn homes with hate; thou canst bring under the roof the lash and funeral torch; thou hast a thousand names, a thousand means of ill. Rouse thy fertile bosom, shatter the pact of peace, sow seeds of wicked war! In the same hour let the men crave, demand, and seize the sword!"

341 Thereon Allecto, steeped in Gorgonian venom, first seeks Latium and the high halls of the Laurentine king, and sits down before the silent threshold of Amata, who, with a woman's distress, a woman's passion, was seething with frenzy over the Teucrian's coming and Turnus' marriage. On her the goddess flings a snake from her dusky tresses, and thrusts it into her bosom, into her inmost heart, that maddened by the pest she may embroil all the house. Gliding between her raiment and smooth breasts, it winds its way unfelt, and, unseen by the frenzied woman, breathes into her its viperous breath. The huge snake becomes the collar of twisted gold about her neck, becomes the festoon of the long fillet, entwines itself into her hair, and slides smoothly over her limbs. And while first the taint, stealing on in fluent poison, thrills her senses and wraps her bones with fire, nor yet her soul has caught the flame throughout her breast, softly, and as mothers are wont, she spoke, shedding many a tear over her daughter's and the Phrygian's wed-

[1] The Furies are commonly represented with snakes for hair.

27

VIRGIL

"exsulibusne datur ducenda Lavinia Teucris,
o genitor? nec te miseret gnataeque tuique? 360
nec matris miseret, quam primo Aquilone relinquet
perfidus alta petens abducta virgine praedo?
an non sic Phrygius penetrat Lacedaemona pastor
Ledaeamque Helenam Troianas vexit ad urbes?
quid tua sancta fides? quid cura antiqua tuorum 365
et consanguineo totiens data dextera Turno?
si gener externa petitur de gente Latinis
idque sedet, Faunique premunt te iussa parentis,
omnem equidem sceptris terram quae libera nostris
dissidet, externam reor et sic dicere divos. 370
et Turno, si prima domus repetatur origo,
Inachus Acrisiusque patres mediaeque Mycenae."

His ubi nequiquam dictis experta Latinum
contra stare videt, penitusque in viscera lapsum
serpentis furiale malum totamque pererrat, 375
tum vero infelix, ingentibus excita monstris,
immensam sine more furit lymphata per urbem.
ceu quondam torto volitans sub verbere turbo,
quem pueri magno in gyro vacua atria circum
intenti ludo exercent (ille actus habena 380
curvatis fertur spatiis; stupet inscia supra
inpubesque manus, mirata volubile buxum;
dant animos plagae), non cursu segnior illo
per medias urbes agitur populosque ferocis.
quin etiam in silvas, simulato numine Bacchi, 385

³⁶³ at non *R*γ.   ³⁷⁰ dicere] poscere *M*¹γ².   ³⁸⁵ silvis *M*¹.

---

[1] Paris was brought up as a shepherd on Mount Ida.
[2] Turnus was descended from the kings of Argos through the daughter of Acrisius, Danaë, who came to Italy, founded

AENEID BOOK VII

lock: "Is it to exiled Teucrians Lavinia is given as wife, O father? and hast thou no pity on thy daughter and thyself? no pity on her mother, whom with the first North wind the faithless pirate will desert, steering for the deep with a maid as booty? Or, was it not thus that the Phrygian shepherd[1] entered Lacedaemon and bore off Leda's Helen to Trojan towns? What of thy solemn pledge? What of thine old love for thine own, and the hand so oft pledged to Turnus, thy kin? If for Latins a son be sought of strangers' stock, and if that be fixed, and the commands of thy sire Faunus weigh upon thee, then I hold that every land, free and separate from our rule, is strange, and that such is the word of the gods. Turnus, too, if the first origin of his house be traced back, has ancestry in Inachus and Acrisius and midmost Mycenae."[2]

373 When, after such vain trial with words, she sees Latinus stand firm against her—when the serpent's maddening venom has glided deep into her veins and courses through her whole frame—then, indeed, the luckless queen, stung by monstrous horrors, in wild frenzy rages from end to end of the city. As at times a top, spinning under the twisted lash, which boys intent on the game drive in a great circle through an empty court—urged by the whip it speeds on round after round; the puzzled, childish throng hang over it in wonder, marvelling at the whirling box-wood; the blows give it life: so, with course no slacker, is she driven through the midst of cities and proud peoples. Nay, feigning the spirit of Bacchus, essaying a greater sin and launching a

Ardea, and married Pilumnus. Mycenae is regarded as in the centre of Greece.

VIRGIL

maius adorta nefas maioremque orsa furorem,
evolat et natam frondosis montibus abdit,
quo thalamum eripiat Teucris taedasque moretur,
euhoe Bacche fremens, solum te virgine dignum
vociferans; etenim mollis tibi sumere thyrsos, 390
te lustrare choro, sacrum tibi pascere crinem.
fama volat, furiisque accensas pectore matres
idem omnis simul ardor agit nova quaerere tecta.
deseruere domos, ventis dant colla comasque;
ast aliae tremulis ululatibus aethera complent 395
pampineasque gerunt incinctae pellibus hastas.
ipsa inter medias flagrantem fervida pinum
sustinet ac natae Turnique canit hymenaeos,
sanguineam torquens aciem, torvumque repente
clamat: "io matres, audite, ubi quaeque, Latinae: 400
si qua piis animis manet infelicis Amatae
gratia, si iuris materni cura remordet,
solvite crinalis vittas, capite orgia mecum."
talem inter silvas, inter deserta ferarum   MRV
reginam Allecto stimulis agit undique Bacchi. 405

Postquam visa satis primos acuisse furores
consiliumque omnemque domum vertisse Latini,
protinus hinc fuscis tristis dea tollitur alis
audacis Rutuli ad muros, quam dicitur urbem
Acrisioneis Danae fundasse colonis, 410
praecipiti delata Noto. locus Ardea quondam
dictus avis: et nunc magnum manet Ardea nomen,
sed fortuna fuit. tectis hic Turnus in altis
iam mediam nigra carpebat nocte quietem.

---

³⁹¹ choros $M^2R\gamma^2$.   ³⁹⁵ illae M^2.
⁴¹² tenet M^2R, *Servius*.   ⁴¹³ hic tectis V.

AENEID BOOK VII

greater madness, forth she flies to the forest, and hides her daughter in the leafy mountains, thereby to rob the Teucrians of their marriage and delay the nuptial torch. "Evoe Bacchus!" she shrieks. "Thou alone," thus she shouts, "art worthy of the maiden! For thee, in truth, she takes up the waving thyrsus, to thee she pays honour in the dance, for thee she grows her sacred tresses." Fame flies abroad, and the matrons, their breasts kindled with fury, are driven on, all by the same frenzy, to seek new dwellings. They have left their homes, and bare neck and hair to the winds, while some fill the sky with tremulous shrieks and, clad in fawn-skins, carry vine-bound spears. Herself in the centre, the infuriate queen uplifts a blazing brand of pine and sings the marriage-song of her daughter and Turnus, rolling the while blood-shot eyes; then of a sudden she fiercely shouts: "Ho! mothers of Latium, give ear, where'er ye be! If in your loyal hearts still lives affection for unhappy Amata, if care for a mother's rights stings your souls, doff the fillets from your hair, join the revels with me!" Such is the queen, as amid woods, amid wild beasts' coverts, Allecto drives her far and wide with Bacchic goad.

[406] Soon as she deemed that she had whetted enough the first shafts of frenzy, and had upturned the purpose and all the palace of Latinus, forthwith the gloomy goddess flies hence on dusky wings to the walls of the bold Rutulian, the city which, Danaë, they say, thither borne by the headlong South, built with her Acrisian settlers.[1] The place was once called Ardea by our sires, and still stands Ardea, a mighty name, but its fortune is fled. Here, in his high palace, Turnus, at dead of night, was in

[1] *cf.* 372 and note.

31

VIRGIL

Allecto torvam faciem et furialia membra 415
exuit, in voltus sese transformat anilis
et frontem obscenam rugis arat, induit albos
cum vitta crinis, tum ramum innectit olivae;
fit Calybe Iunonis anus templique sacerdos,
et iuveni ante oculos his se cum vocibus offert: 420
"Turne, tot incassum fusos patiere labores,
et tua Dardaniis transcribi sceptra colonis?
rex tibi coniugium et quaesitas sanguine dotes
abnegat, externusque in regnum quaeritur heres.
i nunc, ingratis offer te, inrise, periclis; 425
Tyrrhenas, i, sterne acies, tege pace Latinos.
haec adeo tibi me, placida cum nocte iaceres,
ipsa palam fari omnipotens Saturnia iussit. FMRV
quare age et armari pubem portisque moveri [FMR
laetus in arma para, et Phrygios qui flumine pulchro
consedere duces pictasque exure carinas. 431
caelestum vis magna iubet.   rex ipse Latinus,
ni dare coniugium et dicto parere fatetur,
sentiat et tandem Turnum experiatur in armis."

Hic iuvenis, vatem inridens, sic orsa vicissim 435
ore refert: "classis invectas Thybridis undam
non, ut rere, meas effugit nuntius auris;
ne tantos mihi finge metus; nec regia Iuno
immemor est nostri.
sed te victa situ verique effeta senectus, 440
o mater, curis nequiquam exercet, et arma
regum inter falsa vatem formidine ludit.
cura tibi divum effigies et templa tueri;
bella viri pacemque gerent, quis bella gerenda."

⁴²⁰ arva *Peerlkamp*: iube *M*; *so Sabb.*   ⁴³⁶ undam] albeo *M (late)*: alveo *MRγ²*.   ⁴⁴⁴ gerant *M*.

AENEID BOOK VII

the midst of slumbers. Allecto puts off her grim features and fiendish limbs, transforms herself to an old dame's face, furrows her loathly brow with wrinkles, assumes hoary locks and fillet, next entwines them with an olive spray, and becomes Calybe, aged priestess of Juno and her temple, then, with these words, presents herself to the young man's eyes: "Turnus, wilt thou brook all these toils poured forth in vain, and thy sceptre transferred to Dardan settlers? The king denies thee thy bride and the dower thy blood has won, and a stranger is sought as heir to thy throne. Go now, confront thankless perils, thou scorned one: go, lay low the Tuscan ranks; shield the Latins with peace. This it was that, in very presence, Saturn's almighty daughter bade me say to thee, as thou wert lying in the stillness of night. Rise then, and gladly make ready the arming of thy youth, and their march from the gates to battle. Consume the Phrygian chiefs, who are anchored in our fair stream, and burn their painted ships. The mighty force of the gods commands. Let King Latinus himself, unless he consent to give thee thy bride, and stand by his word, know of it, and at last make proof of Turnus as a foe."

[435] Hereon, the youth, mocking at the seer, thus in turn takes up the speech: "That a fleet has entered Tiber's waters, the tale has not, as thou deemest, escaped my ear—feign not for me such terrors—nor is Queen Juno unmindful of me. But thee, O mother, old age, enfeebled by decay and barren of truth, frets with vain distress, and amid the feuds of kings mocks thy prophetic soul with false alarms Thy charge it is to keep the gods' images and temples; war and peace men shall wield, whose work war is."

VIRGIL

Talibus Allecto dictis exarsit in iras. 445
at iuveni oranti subitus tremor occupat artus,
deriguere oculi : tot Erinys sibilat hydris
tantaque se facies aperit. tum flammea torquens
lumina cunctantem et quaerentem dicere plura
reppulit et geminos erexit crinibus anguis, 450
verberaque insonuit rabidoque haec addidit ore
"en ego victa situ, quam veri effeta senectus
arma inter regum falsa formidine ludit.
respice ad haec: adsum dirarum ab sede sororum,
bella manu letumque gero." 455
Sic effata facem iuveni coniecit et atro
lumine fumantis fixit sub pectore taedas.
olli somnum ingens rumpit pavor, ossaque et artus
perfundit toto proruptus corpore sudor.
arma amens fremit, arma toro tectisque requirit; 460
saevit amor ferri et scelerata insania belli,
ira super: magno veluti cum flamma sonore
virgea suggeritur costis undantis aëni
exsultantque aestu latices, furit intus aquai
fumidus atque alte spumis exuberat amnis, 465
nec iam se capit unda, volat vapor ater ad auras.
ergo iter ad regem polluta pace Latinum
indicit primis iuvenum et iubet arma parari ;
tutari Italiam, detrudere finibus hostem,
se satis ambobus Teucrisque venire Latinisque. MR
haec ubi dicta dedit divosque in vota vocavit, 471
certatim sese Rutuli exhortantur in arma.
hunc decus egregium formae movet atque iuventae,
hunc atavi reges, hunc claris dextera factis.

⁴⁵¹ rapido $F\gamma^1$.
⁴⁵⁹ perfudit M. praeruptus $F\gamma^1$.
⁴⁶⁴ aquae vis $FK\gamma^2$, *Macrobius:* aquai, *according to Servius, was introduced by Tucca and Varius for the original* aquae amnis.

34

AENEID BOOK VII

⁴⁴⁵ At such words Allecto blazed forth in fury. But even as the youth spoke, a sudden tremor seized his limbs, and his eyes were set in fear; so many are the Fury's hissing snakes, so monstrous the features that unfold themselves. Then, rolling her flaming eyes, she thrust him back, as he faltered and was fain to say more, reared two snakes from her tresses, sounded her whip, and spoke further with rabid lips: "Behold me, enfeebled by decay, whom old age, barren of truth, amid the feuds of kings, mocks with vain alarm! Look on this! I am come from the home of the Dread Sisters, and in my hand I bear war and death."

⁴⁵⁶ So saying, she hurled at the youth a torch, and fixed in his breast the brand, smoking with lurid light. A monstrous terror broke his sleep, and the sweat, bursting forth from all his frame, drenched bone and limb. For arms he madly shrieks; arms he seeks in couch and chamber; lust of the sword rages in him, the accursed frenzy of war, and resentment crowning all: even as when flaming sticks, loud crackling, are heaped under the ribs of a billowing cauldron, and the waters dance with the heat; within seethes the liquid flood, steaming and bubbling up high with foam; and now the wave contains itself no longer, and the black smoke soars aloft. Therefore, profaning peace, he orders his chief warriors to march upon Latinus, and bids arms be made ready. "Defend Italy," he cries, "drive the foe from her bounds; I come, a match for both Teucrians and Latins." When thus he spake, and called the gods to hear his vows, the Rutuli vie in exhorting one another to arms. One is moved by the peerless beauty of his form and youth, one by his royal ancestry, another by the glorious deeds of his hand.

35

VIRGIL

Dum Turnus Rutulos animis audacibus implet, 475
Allecto in Teucros Stygiis se concitat alis.
arte nova speculata locum, quo litore pulcher
insidiis cursuque feras agitabat Iulus.
hic subitam canibus rabiem Cocytia virgo
obicit et noto naris contingit odore, 480
ut cervum ardentes agerent; quae prima laborum
causa fuit belloque animos accendit agrestis. MRV
cervus erat forma praestanti et cornibus ingens,
Tyrrhidae pueri quem matris ab ubere raptum
nutribant Tyrrhusque pater, cui regia parent 485
armenta et late custodia credita campi. FMRV
adsuetum imperiis soror omni Silvia cura
mollibus intexens ornabat cornua sertis,
pectebatque ferum puroque in fonte lavabat.
ille, manum patiens mensaeque adsuetus erili, 490
errabat silvis rursusque ad limina nota
ipse domum sera quamvis se nocte ferebat.

Hunc procul errantem rabidae venantis Iuli
commovere canes, fluvio cum forte secundo
deflueret ripaque aestus viridante levaret. 495
ipse etiam, eximiae laudis succensus amore,
Ascanius curvo direxit spicula cornu;
nec dextrae erranti deus afuit actaque multo
perque uterum sonitu perque ilia venit harundo.
saucius at quadrupes nota intra tecta refugit 500
successitque gemens stabulis, questuque cruentus
atque imploranti similis tectum omne replebat.
Silvia prima soror, palmis percussa lacertos,
auxilium vocat et duros conclamat agrestis.
olli (pestis enim tacitis latet aspera silvis) 505

⁴⁸¹ malorum M^2.   ⁴⁸⁶ lati $F^1M^1RV\gamma^2$.
⁴⁹⁰ manu FM^1.   ⁴⁹⁷ derexit $F^1R\gamma^1$.
⁴⁹⁸ dextra M.   ⁵⁰² replevit $RV\gamma^2$.

AENEID BOOK VII

⁴⁷⁵ While Turnus fills the Rutuli with daring courage, Allecto on Stygian wing speeds toward the Trojans, with new wiles spying out the place, where, on the shore, fair Iülus was hunting wild beasts with nets and steeds. Here the hellish maid flings upon his hounds a sudden frenzy, and touches their nostrils with the well-known scent, so that in hot haste they course a stag. This was the first source of ill; this first kindled the rustic spirit to war. There was a stag of wondrous beauty and mighty antlers, which, torn from the mother's breast, the sons of Tyrrhus nurtured, and Tyrrhus, their sire, controller of the royal herds, and charged with care of pastures near and far. Their sister Silvia had trained him to obey, and with constant love she adorned him, twining his horns with soft garlands, combing the wild thing's coat, and laving him in the crystal spring. He, patient of her hand, and accustomed to his master's board, roved the woods, and of his own accord betook himself home again to the well-known door, howe'er late the night.

⁴⁹³ While far afield the stag was straying, the maddened hounds of the huntsman Iülus started him, as haply he floated down stream and cooled his heat on the grassy bank. Ascanius himself, too, fired with longing for chiefest honour, aimed a shaft from his bent bow, nor did the goddess fail his faltering hand; the reed sped with a loud whiz, and pierced belly and flank alike. But the wounded creature fled under the familiar roof, and moaning crept into his stall, where, bleeding and suppliant-like, he filled all the house with his plaints. First Silvia the sister, beating her arms with her hands, calls for help and summons the hardy country-folk. They—for the fell fiend lurks in the silent woods—

VIRGIL

improvisi adsunt, hic torre armatus obusto,
stipitis hic gravidi nodis; quod cuique repertum
rimanti, telum ira facit.   vocat agmina Tyrrhus, FMR
quadrifidam quercum cuneis ut forte coactis
scindebat, rapta spirans immane securi.   MR
 At saeva e speculis tempus dea nacta nocendi   511
ardua tecta petit stabuli et de culmine summo
pastorale canit signum cornuque recurvo
Tartaream intendit vocem, qua protinus omne
contremuit nemus et silvae insonuere profundae;   515
audiit et Triviae longe lacus, audiit amnis
sulpurea Nar albus aqua fontesque Velini,
et trepidae matres pressere ad pectora natos.
tum vero ad vocem celeres, qua bucina signum
dira dedit, raptis concurrunt undique telis   520
indomiti agricolae, nec non et Troia pubes
Ascanio auxilium castris effundit apertis.
derexere acies.   non iam certamine agresti,
stipitibus duris agitur sudibusve praeustis,
sed ferro ancipiti decernunt atraque late   525
horrescit strictis seges ensibus aeraque fulgent
sole lacessita et lucem sub nubila iactant:
fluctus uti primo coepit cum albescere vento,
paulatim sese tollit mare et altius undas
erigit, inde imo consurgit ad aethera fundo.   530
hic iuvenis primam ante aciem stridente sagitta,
natorum Tyrrhi fuerat qui maximus, Almo,
sternitur; haesit enim sub gutture volnus et udae
vocis iter tenuemque inclusit sanguine vitam.

---

[510] scindebant M^1.   [511] nancta R.
[514] incendit M^1R^2.   [523] direxere $R\gamma$.
[528] vento γ^1: ponto $MR\gamma^2$.

AENEID BOOK VII

came unlooked for, armed one with seared brand, one with heavy-knotted stick; what each can find in his quest, wrath makes a weapon. Tyrrhus summons his bands, snatching up an axe and breathing savage rage,—for then by chance he was cleaving an oak in four with inward driven wedges.

511 But the cruel goddess, espying from her watch-tower the moment of mischief, seeks the steep farm-roof, and from the topmost ridge sounds the shepherds' call, and on the twisted horn strains her hellish voice, whereat forthwith every grove trembled, and the woods echoed to their depths. It was heard by Trivia's lake afar,[1] heard by Nar with his white sulphurous water, and by the springs of Velinus; and startled mothers clasped their children to their breasts. Then indeed, hurrying to the sound, wherewith the dread clarion gave the signal, the wild husbandmen snatch up their weapons and gather from all sides; no less the Trojan youth pour through the camp's open gates their succour for Ascanius. The lines are ranged: not now do they contend in rustic quarrel with heavy clubs or seared stakes, but with two-edged steel they try the issue; far and wide bristles a dark harvest of drawn swords, while brass shines at the challenge of the sun and flings its light to the clouds: as when a billow begins to whiten under the wind's first breath, little by little the sea swells and lifts its waves higher, till at last it rises to heaven from its lowest depths. Here in the front rank, young Almo, who had been eldest of Tyrrhus' sons, is laid low by a whistling arrow; for the wound was fixed beneath his throat, choking with blood the path of liquid

[1] The famous and beautiful Lago di Nemi, beside which was a grove of Diana.

corpora multa virum circa seniorque Galaesus, 535
dum paci medium se offert, iustissimus unus
qui fuit Ausoniisque olim ditissimus arvis:
quinque greges illi balantum, quina redibant
armenta, et terram centum vertebat aratris.

Atque ea per campos aequo dum Marte geruntur,
promissi dea facta potens, ubi sanguine bellum 541
imbuit et primae commisit funera pugnae,
deserit Hesperiam et caeli conversa per auras
Iunonem victrix adfatur voce superba:
"en, perfecta tibi bello discordia tristi! 545
dic, in amicitiam coeant et foedera iungant,
quandoquidem Ausonio respersi sanguine Teucros.
hoc etiam his addam, tua si mihi certa voluntas:
finitimas in bella feram rumoribus urbes,
accendamque animos insani Martis amore, 550
undique ut auxilio veniant; spargam arma per agros."
tum contra Iuno: "terrorum et fraudis abunde est.
stant belli causae, pugnatur comminus armis,
quae fors prima dedit, sanguis novus imbuit arma.
talia coniugia et talis celebrent hymenaeos 555
egregium Veneris genus et rex ipse Latinus.
te super aetherias errare licentius auras
haud pater ille velit, summi regnator Olympi
cede locis. ego, si qua super fortuna laborum est,
ipsa regam." talis dederat Saturnia voces: 560
illa autem attollit stridentis anguibus alas,
Cocytique petit sedem, supera ardua linquens.
est locus Italiae medio sub montibus altis,
nobilis et fama multis memoratus in oris,

⁵⁴³ conversa *M¹:* convexa *M²Rγ, Donatus, Servius.*
⁵⁶² super *MR.*

AENEID BOOK VII

speech and the slender breath. Around him lie many dead, and among them old Galaesus, slain as he throws himself between to plead for peace—he who was of all men most righteous and erstwhile wealthiest in Ausonia's fields; for him five flocks bleated, five herds came back from pasture, and a hundred ploughs upturned the soil.

540 While thus o'er the plains they fight in even warfare, the goddess, her promise fulfilled, when once she has stained with blood and opened with death the first encounter, quits Hesperia, and turning away through the air of heaven, addresses Juno in haughty tones of triumph: "Lo, at thy will, discord is ripened into gloomy war. Bid them unite in friendship and join alliance, seeing that I have sprinkled the Teucrians with Ausonian blood. Moreover, this will I add, if I am assured of thy wish: with rumours I will draw bordering towns to battle, and will kindle their minds with lust of maddening war, that from all sides they may come to aid; I will sow the land with arms." Then Juno, in answer: "Enough of alarms and treachery; sure are the causes of war; man with man they fight in arms, and the arms that chance first brought, fresh blood now stains. Such be the alliance, such the bridal they solemnize—this peerless son of Venus, and this great king Latinus! That thou shouldst roam too freely in the upper air, the mighty sire, sovereign of high Olympus, would not suffer. Give place; whatsoever may yet chance in the struggle, that I myself will sway." So spake Saturn's daughter; but the other raises her serpent-hissing pinions, and leaving the heights above, seeks her home in Cocytus. There is a place in the heart of Italy, beneath high hills, renowned and famed in

VIRGIL

Ampsancti valles; densis hunc frondibus atrum 565
urget utrimque latus nemoris, medioque fragosus
dat sonitum saxis et torto vertice torrens.
hic specus horrendum et saevi spiracula Ditis
monstrantur, ruptoque ingens Acheronte vorago
pestiferas aperit fauces, quis condit Erinys 570
invisum numen, terras caelumque levabat.

   Nec minus interea extremam Saturnia bello
imponit regina manum. ruit omnis in urbem
pastorum ex acie numerus caesosque reportant
Almonem puerum foedatique ora Galaesi, 575
implorantque deos obtestanturque Latinum.
Turnus adest medioque in crimine caedis et igni
terrorem ingeminat : Teucros in regna vocari,
stirpem admisceri Phrygiam, se limine pelli.
tum, quorum attonitae Baccho nemora avia matres 580
insultant thiasis (neque enim leve nomen Amatae)
undique collecti coeunt Martemque fatigant.
ilicet infandum cuncti contra omina bellum,
contra fata deum, perverso numine poscunt.
certatim regis circumstant tecta Latini : 585
ille velut pelagi rupes immota resistit,   MRV
ut pelagi rupes magno veniente fragore,
quae sese, multis circum latrantibus undis,
mole tenet ; scopuli nequiquam et spumea circum
saxa fremunt laterique inlisa refunditur alga. 590
verum ubi nulla datur caecum exsuperare potestas
consilium, et saevae nutu Iunonis eunt res,
multa deos aurasque pater testatus inanis :   [FMRV
"frangimur heu! fatis," inquit, "ferimurque procella.

---

⁵⁶⁵ ampsancti γ.   Ampsacti *M*: Amfracti *R*: amsancti *b*, *Servius.*
⁵⁷⁰ condit *M*γ, *known to Servius*; condita *R, commonly read.*
⁵⁷¹ levavit *R.*
⁵⁸¹ *In M ll.* 581-615 *are by a strange, though ancient hand.*
⁵⁸⁹ et *omitted M(late)V.*   ⁵⁹² consilio *M*².
⁵⁹³ testatur *MR*γ.

42

AENEID BOOK VII

many lands, the Vale of Ampsanctus. On either hand a forest's fringe, dark with dense leafage, hems it in, and in the centre a roaring torrent resounds o'er the rocks in swirling eddies. Here is shown an awful cavern, and a breathing-place of horrid Dis; and a vast gorge, whence Acheron bursts forth, opens its pestilential jaws. Herein the Fury hid her loathed power, relieving earth and heaven.

[572] No less meanwhile does Saturn's royal daughter put a final hand to the war. From the battle-field there pours into the city the whole company of shepherds, bearing back the slain—the boy Almo, and Galaesus with mangled face—calling on the gods and adjuring Latinus. Turnus is there, and amid the outcry at the slaughter, and fire of passion, redoubles terror: "Teucrians are called to reign; a Phrygian stock mingles its taint; I am spurned from the door!" Then they, whose matrons, frenzied by Bacchus, tread the pathless woods in dancing bands (for of no light weight is Amata's name) draw together from every side, and importune the War-god. Straightway, one and all, despite the omens, despite the oracles of gods, with will perverse, clamour for unholy war. With emulous zeal they swarm round Latinus' palace. He, like an unmoved ocean-cliff, resists; like an ocean-cliff, which, when a great crash comes, stands steadfast in its bulk amid many howling waves; in vain the crags and foaming rocks roar about, and the sea-weed, dashed upon its sides, is whirled back. But when no power is given him to quell their blind resolve, and all goes as cruel Juno wills, then with many an appeal to the gods and the voiceless skies, "Alas!" cries the father, "we are shattered by fate, and swept away by the storm! Ye yourselves, my wretched children,

VIRGIL

ipsi has sacrilego pendetis sanguine poenas, 595
o miseri.   te, Turne, nefas, te triste manebit
supplicium votisque deos venerabere seris.
nam mihi parta quies, omnisque in limine portus;
funere felici spolior."   nec plura locutus
saepsit se tectis rerumque reliquit habenas. 600

Mos erat Hesperio in Latio, quem protinus urbes
Albanae coluere sacrum, nunc maxima rerum
Roma colit, cum prima movent in proelia Martem,
sive Getis inferre manu lacrimabile bellum
Hyrcanisve Arabisve parant, seu tendere ad Indos 605
Auroramque sequi Parthosque reposcere signa:
sunt geminae Belli portae (sic nomine dicunt),
religione sacrae et saevi formidine Martis;
centum aerei claudunt vectes aeternaque ferri
robora, nec custos absistit limine Ianus. 610
has, ubi certa sedet patribus sententia pugnae,
ipse Quirinali trabea cinctuque Gabino   FMR
insignis reserat stridentia limina consul,
ipse vocat pugnas; sequitur tum cetera pubes
aereaque adsensu conspirant cornua rauco. 615
hoc et tum Aeneadis indicere bella Latinus
more iubebatur tristisque recludere portas.
abstinuit tactu pater aversusque refugit
foeda ministeria, et caecis se condidit umbris.

⁶⁰⁵ Hyrcaniisque *F*¹.   ⁶⁰⁶ deposcere *R*.
⁶¹¹ haec *M* (*late*).   ⁶¹² Sabino *F*.
⁶¹⁴ tunc *M*.   ⁶¹⁵ adversus γ.

---

¹ A much debated passage. The rendering given follows Servius, *securitas omnis in promptu est*. Others explain thus: "for to me rest is won, and it is when wholly on the threshold of life's haven that I am robbed of a happy death" (Page).

AENEID BOOK VII

with your impious blood shall pay the price of this! Thee Turnus, thee the guilt and its bitter punishment shall await, and too late with vows shalt thou adore the gods. For me, my rest is won, and my haven is full at hand; 'tis but of a happy death I am despoiled.[1]" And saying no more he shut himself in the palace, and let drop the reins of rule.

[601] A custom there was in Hesperian Latium, which thenceforth the Alban cities held holy, as now does Rome, mistress of the world, what time they first rouse the war-god to battle, be it Getae or Arabs or Hyrcanians against whom their hands prepare to carry tearful war, or to march on India's sons[2] and pursue the Dawn, and reclaim their standards from the Parthian:—there are twin gates[3] of War (so men call them), hallowed by religious awe and the terrors of fierce Mars: a hundred brazen bolts close them, and the eternal strength of iron, and Janus their guardian never quits the threshold. Here, when the sentence of the Fathers is firmly fixed on war, the Consul, arrayed in Quirinal robe[4] and Gabine cincture, with his own hand unbars the grating portals, with his own lips calls forth war; then the rest of the warriors take up the cry, and brazen horns blare out their hoarse accord. With such custom then, too, Latinus was bidden to proclaim war on the sons of Aeneas, and to unclose the grim gates. But the father withheld his hand, shrank back from the hateful office, and buried him-

---

[2] Used of the East generally.
[3] The Temple of Janus was opened in time of war, and closed in peace.
[4] *cf.* l. 187 above, with note. The "Gabine cincture" refers to a special way of wearing the toga, one part of which was folded round the waist, leaving the arm free.

VIRGIL

tum regina deum caelo delapsa morantis 620
impulit ipsa manu portas, et cardine verso
Belli ferratos rumpit Saturnia postis.
ardet inexcita Ausonia atque immobilis ante;
pars pedes ire parat campis, pars arduus altis
pulverulentus equis furit; omnes arma requirunt. 625
pars levis clipeos et spicula lucida tergent
arvina pingui subiguntque in cote securis;
signaque ferre iuvat sonitusque audire tubarum.
quinque adeo magnae positis incudibus urbes
tela novant, Atina potens Tiburque superbum, 630
Ardea Crustumerique et turrigerae Antemnae.
tegmina tuta cavant capitum flectuntque salignas
umbonum cratis; alii thoracas aënos
aut levis ocreas lento ducunt argento;
vomeris huc et falcis honos, huc omnis aratri 635
cessit amor; recoquunt patrios fornacibus ensis.
classica iamque sonant; it bello tessera signum.
hic galeam tectis trepidus rapit, ille frementis
ad iuga cogit equos, clipeumque auroque trilicem
loricam induitur fidoque accingitur ense. 640

Pandite nunc Helicona, deae, cantusque movete,
qui bello exciti reges, quae quemque secutae
complerint campos acies, quibus Itala iam tum
floruerit terra alma viris, quibus arserit armis: [FMPR
et meministis enim, divae, et memorare potestis;
ad nos vix tenuis famae perlabitur aura. 646

Primus init bellum Tyrrhenis asper ab oris MPR
contemptor divum Mezentius agminaque armat.

⁶²² rupit *FR*.   ⁶²⁸ iuvant *R*: iubet *M*.
⁶³³ rapidus *M*¹.   trementis *FM*¹*R*γ¹.
⁶⁴¹ monete *F(late)*γ², *known to Servius*.

46

AENEID BOOK VII

self in blind darkness. Then the queen of the gods, gliding from the sky, with her own hand dashed in the lingering doors, and on their turning hinges Saturn's daughter burst open the iron-bound gates of war. All ablaze is Ausonia, erstwhile sluggish and unmoved. Some make ready to march o'er the plains afoot, some, on high steeds mounted, storm amid clouds of dust: all cry out for arms. Some with rich fat burnish shields smooth and javelins bright, and whet axes on the stone; they joy to bear the standards, and hear the trumpet call. Nay, five mighty cities set up anvils and forge new weapons—strong Atina and proud Tibur, Ardea and Crustumeri and turreted Antemnae. They hollow helms to guard the head, and weave the wicker-frame of shields; others beat out breastplates of bronze, or polished greaves from pliant silver. To this is come all pride in share and sickle, all passion for the plough; they retemper in the furnace their fathers' swords. And now the clarion sounds; the password goes forth, the sign for war. One in wild haste snatches a helm from his home; another couples his snorting steeds to the yoke, dons his shield and coat of mail, triple-linked with gold, and girds on his trusty sword.

⁶⁴¹ Now fling wide Helicon, ye goddesses, and wake your song—what kings were roused to war, what hosts, in the train of each, filled the plains, with what manhood even then kindly Italy bloomed, with what arms she was aglow; for ye, divine ones, remember, and can recount; to us scarcely is wafted some scant breath of fame.

⁶⁴⁷ First, from Tuscan coasts, fierce Mezentius, scorner of the gods, enters the war and arms his

VIRGIL

filius huic iuxta Lausus, quo pulchrior alter
non fuit, excepto Laurentis corpore Turni, 650
Lausus, equum domitor debellatorque ferarum,
ducit Agyllina nequiquam ex urbe secutos
mille viros, dignus patriis qui laetior esset
imperiis et cui pater haud Mezentius esset.

Post hos insignem palma per gramina currum 655
victoresque ostentat equos satus Hercule pulchro
pulcher Aventinus, clipeoque insigne paternum
centum anguis cinctamque gerit serpentibus Hydram;
collis Aventini silva quem Rhea sacerdos
furtivum partu sub luminis edidit oras, 660
mixta deo mulier, postquam Laurentia victor
Geryone exstincto Tirynthius attigit arva,
Tyrrhenoque boves in flumine lavit Hiberas.
pila manu saevosque gerunt in bella dolones, MPRV
et tereti pugnant mucrone veruque Sabello. 665
ipse pedes, tegimen torquens immane leonis,
terribili impexum saeta, cum dentibus albis
indutus capiti, sic regia tecta subibat,
horridus Herculeoque umeros innexus amictu.

Tum gemini fratres Tiburtia moenia linquunt, 670
fratris Tiburti dictam cognomine gentem,
Catillusque acerque Coras, Argiva iuventus,
et primam ante aciem densa inter tela feruntur:
ceu duo nubigenae cum vertice montis ab alto
descendunt Centauri, Homolen Othrymque nivalem
linquentes cursu rapido; dat euntibus ingens 676
silva locum et magno cedunt virgulta fragore.

Nec Praenestinae fundator defuit urbis,
Volcano genitum pecora inter agrestia regem

⁶⁴⁹ hunc *M*¹.   ⁶⁵⁴ Medientius *P*.
⁶⁵⁵ palmam *R*.   ⁶⁶⁹ innixus *PR*.
⁶⁷¹ de nomine *P*.   ⁶⁷⁵ discendunt *M*.   nivali *V*.
⁶⁷⁶ liquentes *R*.
⁶⁷⁷ et *written above in* P.   caedunt *M*.   ⁶⁷⁸ deficit *R*.

48

AENEID BOOK VII

array. At his side, goodliest of form save Laurentine Turnus, is his son Lausus,—Lausus, tamer of steeds and vanquisher of beasts. From Agylla's town he leads a thousand men, that followed him in vain;[1] one worthy to be happier in a father's rule, and to have other than Mezentius for sire!

655 Next to these, Aventinus, beauteous son of beauteous Hercules, displays on the sward his palm-crowned chariot and victorious steeds, and on his shield bears his father's device—a hundred snakes and the Hydra, girt with serpents. Him, in the wood of the Aventine hill, Rhea the priestess brought in secret birth up into the borders of light—a woman mated with a god—when the Tirynthian victor, having slain Geryon, reached the Laurentian fields and bathed his Iberian kine in the Tuscan stream.[2] In their hands the men carry to battle javelins and grim pikes, and fight with the tapering sword and Sabellian dart. Himself, he went on foot, swinging a huge lion's skin, unkempt with terrifying mane, its white teeth crowning his head; in such guise he entered the royal halls, shaggy-rough, his shoulders enveloped in the garb of Hercules.

670 Next twin brethren leave the walls of Tibur, and the folk called from the name of their brother Tiburtus—Catillus and brave Coras, Argive youths. On they come in the front ranks amid the thronging spears, as when two cloud-born Centaurs descend from a mountain's high peak, leaving Homole or snowy Othrys in swift course; the mighty forest yields place as they go, and the thickets give way with loud crash.

678 Nor was the founder of Praeneste's city absent, —Caeculus, the king who, as every age has believed,

[1] Because they could not save him from his fate.
[2] The Tiber.

VIRGIL

inventumque focis omnis quem credidit aetas, 680
Caeculus. hunc legio late comitatur agrestis,
quique altum Praeneste viri quique arva Gabinae
Iunonis gelidumque Anienem et roscida rivis
Hernica saxa colunt, quos dives Anagnia pascit,
quos, Amasene pater. non illis omnibus arma, 685
nec clipei currusve sonant; pars maxima glandes
liventis plumbi spargit, pars spicula gestat
bina manu, fulvosque lupi de pelle galeros
tegmen habent capiti; vestigia nuda sinistri
instituere pedis, crudus tegit altera pero. MPR

At Messapus, equum domitor, Neptunia proles, 691
quem neque fas igni cuiquam nec sternere ferro,
iam pridem resides populos desuetaque bello
agmina in arma vocat subito ferrumque retractat.
hi Fescenninas acies Aequosque Faliscos, 695
hi Soractis habent arces Flaviniaque arva
et Cimini cum monte lacum lucosque Capenos.
ibant aequati numero regemque canebant:
ceu quondam nivei liquida inter nubila cycni,
cum sese e pastu referunt et longa canoros 700
dant per colla modos; sonat amnis et Asia longe
pulsa palus.
nec quisquam aeratas acies ex agmine tanto
misceri putet, aëriam sed gurgite ab alto
urgeri volucrum raucarum ad litora nubem. 705

Ecce Sabinorum prisco de sanguine magnum
agmen agens Clausus magnique ipse agminis instar,

---

681 late legio *M*.
689 tegmina *P*γ[1]. capitis *M*[2].
696 Flaminia *P*[2].

686 currusque *R*.
690 pedes *M*[2].
699 flumina *P*γ[1].

AENEID BOOK VII

was born to Vulcan among the rural herds, and found upon the hearth. Him, in loose array, a rustic legion attends: they who dwell in steep Praeneste, and the fields of Gabine Juno, by the cold Anio and the Hernican rocks with their dewy streams; they whom rich Anagnia nurtures, and thou, father Amasenus. Not all of these have armour, or shields, or sounding chariots. The most part shower bullets of livid lead; part wield in the hand two darts, and have for head-gear tawny caps of wolf-skin. Bare is the left foot as they plant their steps; a boot of rawhide shields the other.

691 But Messapus, tamer of horses, the seed of Neptune, whom none may lay low with fire or steel, suddenly calls to arms tribes long inert and bands unused to war, and again grasps the sword. These hold the ranks of Fescennium and of Aequi Falisci; these Soracte's heights and Flavinian fields, Ciminus' lake and hill and the groves of Capena. In measured time they marched and sang their king: as ofttimes snowy swans amid the moist clouds, when they return from feeding, and from their long throats utter their tuneful strains; afar the river echoes, and the smitten Asian mead.[1] Nor would one think that mail-clad ranks were massed in that vast array, but that high in air, a cloud of hoarse-voiced birds was pressing shoreward from the deep gulf.

706 Lo! Clausus,[2] of the ancient Sabine blood, leading a mighty host, and equal to a mighty host himself;

[1] Referring to the valley of the Cayster in Lydia.
[2] *cf.* Livy, II. 16, where we learn that the Claudian tribe was founded by Attus Clausus, who seceded from the Sabines in 506 B.C. and was received as a citizen in Rome. Virgil, however, refers the founding of the Claudian *gens* to the earlier day when Romulus formed a treaty with the Sabines under T. Tatius.

VIRGIL

Claudia nunc a quo diffunditur et tribus et gens
per Latium, postquam in partem data Roma Sabinis.
una ingens Amiterna cohors priscique Quirites,   710
Ereti manus omnis oliviferaeque Mutuscae,
qui Nomentum urbem, qui Rosea rura Velini,
qui Tetricae horrentis rupes montemque Severum
Casperiamque colunt Forulosque et flumen Himellae,
qui Tiberim Fabarimque bibunt, quos frigida misit 715
Nursia et Ortinae classes populique Latini,
quosque secans infaustum interluit Allia nomen:
quam multi Libyco volvuntur marmore fluctus,
saevus ubi Orion hibernis conditur undis,
vel cum sole novo densae torrentur aristae   720
aut Hermi campo aut Lyciae flaventibus arvis.
scuta sonant pulsuque pedum conterrita tellus.

Hinc Agamemnonius, Troiani nominis hostis,
curru iungit Halaesus equos Turnoque ferocis
mille rapit populos, vertunt felicia Baccho   725
Massica qui rastris, et quos de collibus altis
Aurunci misere patres Sidicinaque iuxta
aequora, quique Cales linquunt, amnisque vadosi
accola Volturni, pariterque Saticulus asper
Oscorumque manus. teretes sunt aclydes illis   730
tela, sed haec lento mos est aptare flagello;
laevas cetra tegit, falcati comminus enses.

Nec tu carminibus nostris indictus abibis,
Oebale, quem generasse Telon Sebethide nympha
fertur, Teleboum Capreas cum regna teneret,   735
iam senior; patriis sed non et filius arvis

⁷⁰⁸ e quo M^1. ingens M. ⁷¹² Rosa M: Roscia $P^2\gamma$.
⁷¹³ amnem $P\gamma^1$. ⁷¹⁵ Fabarum P^1R. ⁷²² cursu M.
⁷²⁵ veniunt R. ⁷²⁷ senes M^2. ⁷³⁶ armis R.

52

AENEID BOOK VII

from whom now is spread through Latium the Claudian tribe and clan, since Rome was shared with the Sabines. With him came Amiternum's vast cohort, and the ancient Quirites,[1] the whole band of Eretum and olive-bearing Mutusca; they who dwell in Nomentum's city and the Rosean country by Velinus, on Tetrica's rugged crags and Mount Severus, in Casperia and Foruli, and by Himella's stream; they who drink of Tiber and Fabaris, they whom cold Nursia sent, the Ortine squadrons, the Latin peoples, and they whom Allia, ill-boding name, severs with its flood; as many as the waves that roll on the Libyan main, when fierce Orion sinks in the wintry waves; or thick as the corn-ears that are scorched by the early sun in the plain of Hermus or the yellow fields of Lycia. The bucklers clang, and the earth trembles under the tramping feet.

723 Next, Agamemnon's son, foe of the Trojan name, Halaesus, yokes his steeds to the car, and in Turnus' cause sweeps along a thousand warlike tribes, men who turn with mattocks the wine-rich Massic lands; whom Auruncan sires sent from their high hills, and the Sidicine plains hard by; those who leave Cales, and the dweller by Volturnus' shallow river, and by their side the rough Saticulan and the Oscan bands. Shapely javelins are their weapons, but these it is their wont to fit with a pliant thong. A targe shields their left side; for close combat are their curved swords.

733 Nor shalt thou, Oebalus, pass unhonoured in our songs—thou whom, 'tis said, the nymph Sebethis bare to Telon, when he reigned o'er Teleboan Capreae, now stricken in years; but, not content with his

---

[1] The inhabitants of Cures.

VIRGIL

contentus late iam tum dicione tenebat
Sarrastis populos et quae rigat aequora Sarnus,
quique Rufras Batulumque tenent atque arva
    Celemnae,
et quos maliferae despectant moenia Abellae,   740
Teutonico ritu soliti torquere cateias;
tegmina quis capitum raptus de subere cortex,
aerataeque micant peltae, micat aereus ensis.

   Et te montosae misere in proelia Nersae,
Ufens, insignem fama et felicibus armis;   745
horrida praecipue cui gens adsuetaque multo
venatu nemorum, duris Aequicula glaebis.
armati terram exercent semperque recentis
convectare iuvat praedas et vivere rapto.

   Quin et Marruvia venit de gente sacerdos,   750
fronde super galeam et felici comptus oliva,
Archippi regis missu, fortissimus Umbro,
vipereo generi et graviter spirantibus hydris
spargere qui somnos cantuque manuque solebat,
mulcebatque iras et morsus arte levabat.   755
sed non Dardaniae medicari cuspidis ictum
evaluit neque eum iuvere in volnera cantus
somniferi et Marsis quaesitae montibus herbae.
te nemus Angitiae, vitrea te Fucinus unda,
te liquidi flevere lacus.   760

   Ibat et Hippolyti proles pulcherrima bello,
Virbius, insignem quem mater Aricia misit,
eductum Egeriae lucis umentia circum

    [737] premebat $R\gamma^2$.   [738] qua $R\gamma^2$.
    [740] Bellae *MSS.*, *Servius, who, however, mentions the reading* Abellae.
    [755] feras *P*.   [757] in] ad M^2. volnere M^1: vulnere *R*.
    [758] in montibus M^2.

AENEID BOOK VII

ancestral fields, his son even then held in his sway far and wide the Sarrastian tribes, and the plains watered by Sarnus, those who dwell in Rufrae and Batulum and Celemna's fields, and those on whom look down the battlements of Abella, rich in apples. In Teuton fashion these were wont to hurl their darts;[1] their head-gear was bark stripped from the cork-tree; bronze flashes on their shields, flashes with bronze their sword.

744 Thee, too, Ufens, mountainous Nersae sent forth to battle, of noble fame and success in arms—whose clan, on the rough Aequian clods, was rugged above all others, and inured to hard hunting in the woods. In arms they till the earth, and 'tis ever their joy to bear away fresh booty, and to live on plunder.

750 Yea, and from the Marruvian race, sent by King Archippus, there came a priest, his helm decked with leaves of the fruitful olive, most valiant Umbro, who with charm and touch was wont to shed slumber on the viperous brood and watersnakes of baneful breath, soothing their wrath and curing their bites by his skill.[2] Yet he availed not to heal the stroke of the Dardan spear-point, nor against wounds did slumbrous charms aid him, or herbs culled on Marsian hills. Thee Angitia's grove wept, thee Fucinus' glassy wave, thee the limpid lakes!

761 Likewise went to war Hippolytus' son, Virbius, most fair, whom his mother Aricia sent forth in his glory. In Egeria's groves was he reared round the

---

[1] The *cateia* is an unknown weapon, probably a dart, similar to one used by the wild German tribes.
[2] The Marsians were skilled in magic and incantations.

VIRGIL

litora, pinguis ubi et placabilis ara Dianae.
namque ferunt fama Hippolytum, postquam arte
    novercae   765
occiderit patriasque explerit sanguine poenas
turbatis distractus equis, ad sidera rursus
aetheria et superas caeli venisse sub auras,
Paeoniis revocatum herbis et amore Dianae.
tum pater omnipotens, aliquem indignatus ab umbris
mortalem infernis ad lumina surgere vitae,   771
ipse repertorem medicinae talis et artis
fulmine Phoebigenam Stygias detrusit ad undas.
at Trivia Hippolytum secretis alma recondit
sedibus et nymphae Egeriae nemorique relegat,   775
solus ubi in silvis Italis ignobilis aevum
exigeret versoque ubi nomine Virbius esset.
unde etiam templo Triviae lucisque sacratis
cornipedes arcentur equi, quod litore currum
et iuvenem monstris pavidi effudere marini.   780
filius ardentis haud setius aequore campi
exercebat equos curruque in bella ruebat.

  Ipse inter primos praestanti corpore Turnus
vertitur arma tenens et toto vertice supra est.
cui triplici crinita iuba galea alta Chimaeram   785
sustinet, Aetnaeos efflantem faucibus ignis;
tam magis illa fremens et tristibus effera flammis
quam magis effuso crudescunt sanguine pugnae.
at levem clipeum sublatis cornibus Io
auro insignibat, iam saetis obsita, iam bos,   790
(argumentum ingens), et custos virginis Argus

₇₆₉ Paeonis *M*¹.
₇₇₃ Poenigenam *MR*γ². ad] in γ². undis *P*¹.
₇₇₆ ibi *M*¹.   ₇₉₀ insignitam *R*.

AENEID BOOK VII

marshy shores, where stands Diana's altar, rich and gracious. For they tell how that Hippolytus, when he fell by his stepdame's craft, and slaked a sire's vengeance in blood, torn asunder by frightened steeds—came again to the starry firmament and heaven's upper air, recalled by the Healer's herbs and Diana's love. Then the Father omnipotent, wroth that any mortal should rise from the nether shades to the light of life, himself with his thunder hurled down to the Stygian waters the finder of such healing-craft, the Phoebus-born.[1] But Trivia, kindly goddess, hides Hippolytus in a secret dwelling, and sends him away to the nymph Egeria and her grove, that there alone, amid Italian woods, he might live out his inglorious days, and take the altered name of Virbius. Hence, too, hoofed horses are kept far from Trivia's temple and hallowed groves, for that they, affrighted by ocean-monsters, strewed chariot and youth along the shore. None the less, his son was driving his fiery steeds on the level plain, and speeding charioted to war.

783 Himself too, amid the foremost, moves Turnus, of wondrous frame, holding sword in hand, and by a whole head o'ertopping all. His lofty helmet, crested with triple plume, upbears a Chimaera, breathing from her jaws Aetnean fires, lo! raging the more, and the madder with baleful flames, the more blood is outpoured and the fiercer waxes the fight. But, on his polished shield, Io with uplifted horns was emblazoned in gold,[2]—Io, wondrous device, already o'ergrown with bristles, already a heifer,— and Argus the maiden's warder, and father Inachus

[1] Aesculapius, son of Apollo (the Healer).
[2] A figure of Io, wrought in gold, formed the device on the iron shield.

VIRGIL

caelataque amnem fundens pater Inachus urna.
insequitur nimbus peditum clipeataque totis
agmina densentur campis, Argivaque pubes
Auruncaeque manus, Rutuli veteresque Sicani   795
et Sacranae acies et picti scuta Labici;
qui saltus, Tiberine, tuos sacrumque Numici
litus arant Rutulosque exercent vomere collis
Circaeumque iugum, quis Iuppiter Anxurus arvis
praesidet et viridi gaudens Feronia luco;   800
qua Saturae iacet atra palus gelidusque per imas
quaerit iter vallis atque in mare conditur Ufens.

  Hos super advenit Volsca de gente Camilla,
agmen agens equitum et florentis aere catervas,
bellatrix, non illa colo calathisve Minervae   805
femineas adsueta manus, sed proelia virgo
dura pati cursuque pedum praevertere ventos.
illa vel intactae segetis per summa volaret
gramina nec teneras cursu laesisset aristas,
vel mare per medium fluctu suspensa tumenti   810
ferret iter celeris nec tingueret aequore plantas.
illam omnis tectis agrisque effusa iuventus
turbaque miratur matrum et prospectat euntem,
attonitis inhians animis, ut regius ostro
velet honos levis umeros, ut fibula crinem   815
auro internectat, Lyciam ut gerat ipsa pharetram
et pastoralem praefixa cuspide myrtum.

⁸¹⁴ inhians] haesere $P\gamma^1$, cf. v. 529.

AENEID BOOK VII

pouring his stream from an embossed urn.[1] Behind him comes a cloud of infantry, and shielded columns throng all the plain, Argive manhood and Auruncan bands, Rutulians and old Sicanians, the Sacranian lines and Labicians with painted bucklers; they who till thy glades, O Tiber, and Numicius' sacred shore, whose ploughshare moves the Rutulian hills and Circe's ridge[2]; o'er whose fields Jupiter of Anxur reigns, and Feronia rejoicing in her greenwood; where lies Satura's black marsh, and cold Ufens winds his way through the valley-depths and sinks into the sea.

[803] To crown the array comes Camilla, of Volscian race, leading her troop of horse, and squadrons gay with brass,—a warrior-maid, never having trained her woman's hands to Minerva's distaff or basket of wool, but hardy to bear the battle-brunt and in speed of foot to outstrip the winds. She might have flown o'er the topmost blades of unmown corn, nor in her course bruised the tender ears; or sped her way o'er mid sea, poised above the swelling wave, nor dipped her swift feet in the flood. All the youth, streaming from house and field, and thronging matrons marvel, and gaze at her as she goes; agape with wonder how the glory of royal purple drapes her smooth shoulders; how the clasp entwines her hair with gold; how her own hands bear a Lycian quiver and the pastoral myrtle tipped with steel.

---

[1] The river Inachus is represented by a figure of the river-god, pouring water from an urn.   [2] cf. 10 above.

LIBER VIII

Ut belli signum Laurenti Turnus ab arce MPR
extulit et rauco strepuerunt cornua cantu,
utque acris concussit equos utque impulit arma,
extemplo turbati animi, simul omne tumultu
coniurat trepido Latium saevitque iuventus 5
effera. ductores primi Messapus et Ufens
contemptorque deum Mezentius undique cogunt
auxilia et latos vastant cultoribus agros.
mittitur et magni Venulus Diomedis ad urbem,
qui petat auxilium, et Latio consistere Teucros, 10
advectum Aenean classi victosque Penates
inferre et fatis regem se dicere posci
edoceat, multasque viro se adiungere gentis
Dardanio et late Latio increbrescere nomen. [MPRV
quid struat his coeptis, quem, si Fortuna sequatur,
eventum pugnae cupiat, manifestius ipsi 16
quam Turno regi aut regi apparere Latino.
   Talia per Latium. quae Laomedontius heros
cuncta videns magno curarum fluctuat aestu
atque animum nunc huc celerem, nunc dividit illuc 20
in partisque rapit varias perque omnia versat:

   ² sonuerunt P^1.   ¹⁰ considere (d *in rasura*) P.
   ²⁰⁻²¹ = IV. 285, 286.

60

BOOK VIII

SOON as Turnus raised up the flag of war from the
Laurentine citadel, and the horns rang with their
hoarse notes, soon as he roused his fiery steeds and
clashed his arms, straightway men's hearts were
troubled; all Latium at once is leagued in startled
uprising, and her sons rage madly. The chief cap-
tains, Messapus and Ufens, with Mezentius, scorner
of the gods, from all sides muster forces and strip
the wide fields of husbandmen. Venulus too is sent
to mighty Diomede's city[1] to seek aid, and announce
that Teucrians set foot in Latium; that Aeneas is
come with his fleet, bringing to them his vanquished
gods, and proclaiming himself a king summoned by
Fate; that many tribes are joining the Dardan hero
and his name spreads far and wide in Latium.
What end he compasses with these beginnings, what
outcome of the feud he craves, should Fortune attend
him, would be more clearly seen by Diomede's self
than by King Turnus or King Latinus.[2]

[18] Thus it was throughout Latium. And the hero
of Laomedon's line, seeing it all, tosses on a mighty
sea of troubles; and now hither, now thither he
swiftly throws his mind, casting it in diverse ways,
and turning it to every shift;[3] as when in brazen

[1] Argyripa or Arpi, in Apulia.
[2] Knowing the Trojans as he did, Diomede could judge
best as to their plans and aspirations.
[3] *cf. Aen.* IV. 285, 286.

VIRGIL

sicut aquae tremulum labris ubi lumen aënis
sole repercussum aut radiantis imagine lunae
omnia pervolitat late loca iamque sub auras
erigitur summique ferit laquearia tecti. 25
Nox erat et terras animalia fessa per omnis
alituum pecudumque genus sopor altus habebat,
cum pater in ripa gelidique sub aetheris axe
Aeneas, tristi turbatus pectora bello,
procubuit seramque dedit per membra quietem. 30
huic deus ipse loci fluvio Tiberinus amoeno
populeas inter senior se attollere frondes
visus (eum tenuis glauco velabat amictu
carbasus et crinis umbrosa tegebat harundo),
tum sic adfari et curas his demere dictis: 35
"O sate gente deum, Troianam ex hostibus urbem
qui revehis nobis aeternaque Pergama servas,
exspectate solo Laurenti arvisque Latinis,
hic tibi certa domus, certi (ne absiste) Penates;
neu belli terrere minis; tumor omnis et irae   MPR
concessere deum. 41
iamque tibi, ne vana putes haec fingere somnum,
litoreis ingens inventa sub ilicibus sus
triginta capitum fetus enixa iacebit,
alba, solo recubans, albi circum ubera nati. 45
[hic locus urbis erit, requies ea certa laborum.]
ex quo ter denis urbem redeuntibus annis
Ascanius clari condet cognominis Albam.
haud incerta cano. nunc qua ratione quod instat
expedias victor, paucis, adverte, docebo. 50
Arcades his oris, genus a Pallante profectum,
qui regem Euandrum comites, qui signa secuti,
delegere locum et posuere in montibus urbem

²⁹ pectore M^1.   ⁴³⁻⁴⁶ = III. 390-393.
⁴⁶ *omitted by* $MP\gamma^1a^1$, *not noticed by Servius*.
⁵⁰ expediam $M^2P^2\gamma^1$.

AENEID BOOK VIII

bowls a flickering light from water, flung back by the sun or the moon's glittering form, flits far and wide o'er all things, and now mounts high and smites the fretted ceiling of the roof aloft.

²⁶ It was night, and over all lands deep sleep held wearied creatures, birds and beasts alike, when father Aeneas, his heart troubled by woeful war, stretched him on the bank under the sky's chill cope, and let late sleep steal over his limbs. Before him the very god of the place, Tiberinus of the pleasant stream, seemed to raise his aged head amid the poplar leaves; thin lawn draped him in mantle of grey, and shady reeds crowned his hair. Then thus he spake to him, and with these words took away his cares:

³⁶ "O seed of a race divine, thou who from foemen's hands bringest back to us our Trojan city,[1] and preservest her towers for ever, thou long looked for on Laurentine ground and Latin fields, here thy home is sure—draw not back—and sure are thy gods! Nor be scared by threats of war; all the swelling wrath of Heaven has abated. Even now, lest thou deem these words the idle feigning of sleep, thou shalt find a huge sow lying under the oaks on the shore, just delivered of a litter of thirty young, the mother reclining on the ground white—white, too, the young about her teats. By this token in thirty revolving years shall Ascanius found a city, Alba of glorious name. Not doubtful is my prophecy. Now on what wise thou mayest make thy triumphant way through this present ill, in few words—pay thou heed—I will explain. On these coasts Arcadians, a race sprung from Pallas, who were the company of King Evander and followed his banner, have chosen a site and set their city on the hills, from their forefather Pallas

[1] Dardanus came from Italy.

63

VIRGIL

Pallantis proavi de nomine Pallanteum.
hi bellum adsidue ducunt cum gente Latina; 55
hos castris adhibe socios et foedera iunge.
ipse ego te ripis et recto flumine ducam,
adversum remis superes subvectus ut amnem.
surge age, nate dea, primisque cadentibus astris
Iunoni fer rite preces iramque minasque 60
supplicibus supera votis.   mihi victor honorem
persolves.   ego sum, pleno quem flumine cernis
stringentem ripas et pinguia culta secantem,
caeruleus Thybris, caelo gratissimus amnis.
hic mihi magna domus, celsis caput urbibus exit." 65
  Dixit, deinde lacu fluvius se condidit alto,
ima petens; nox Aenean somnusque reliquit.
surgit et aetherii spectans orientia solis
lumina rite cavis undam de flumine palmis
sustinet ac talis effundit ad aethera voces: 70
" Nymphae, Laurentes Nymphae, genus amnibus
        unde est,   FMPR
tuque, o Thybri tuo genitor cum flumine sancto,
accipite Aenean et tandem arcete periclis.
quo te cumque lacus miserantem incommoda nostra
fonte tenet, quocumque solo pulcherrimus exis, 75
semper honore meo, semper celebrabere donis,
corniger Hesperidum fluvius regnator aquarum.
adsis o tantum et propius tua numina firmes."
sic memorat, geminasque legit de classe biremis
remigioque aptat, socios simul instruit armis. 80

[56] foedere $P\gamma$, *known to Servius.*
[63] pinguia] singula M^1.   [65] magna] certa $P\gamma^1$.
[67] relinquit R.   [75] tenent FR.
[78] proprius P^1, *known to Servius.*

AENEID BOOK VIII

called Pallanteum. These wage war ceaselessly with the Latin race; these do thou take to thy camp as allies, and join with them in league. I myself will guide thee along the banks straight up the stream, that so, impelled by thy oars, thou mayest o'ercome the opposing current. Up, arise, goddess-born, and, as the stars first set, duly offer prayers to Juno, and with suppliant vows vanquish her wrath and her threats. To me thou shalt pay thy tribute when victorious. I am he whom thou seest laving my banks with full flood and cleaving the rich tilth,—the blue Tiber, river best beloved of Heaven. Here is my stately home; amid lofty cities flows forth my fountain-head.[1]"

"So spake the River, then plunged into his deep pool, seeking the lowest parts; night and sleep left Aeneas. He arises, and gazing toward the eastern beams of the celestial sun, in due form uplifts water from the stream in his hollow palms, and pours forth to Heaven this prayer: "Ye Nymphs, Laurentine Nymphs, from whom rivers have their being, and thou, O father Tiber, thou and thy hallowed stream— receive Aeneas, and at last shield him from perils. In whatsoever springs thy pools contain thee, who pitiest our travails, from whatsoever soil thou flowest forth in all thy beauty, ever with my offerings, ever with my gifts, shalt thou be graced, thou horned stream, lord of Hesperian waters. Only be thou with me, and more surely confirm thy will!" So he speaks, and choosing two galleys from his fleet mans them with crews, and withal equips his comrades with arms.

---

[1] The Tiber rises in Etruria. This verse, of doubtful meaning, is rendered thus by some: "Here rises my great home, the head of mighty cities," the "home" being either the river-god's palace under the water, or the city of Rome.

VIRGIL

Ecce autem subitum atque oculis mirabile
  monstrum,
candida per silvam cum fetu concolor albo
procubuit viridique in litore conspicitur sus.
quam pius Aeneas tibi enim, tibi, maxima Iuno,
mactat sacra ferens et cum grege sistit ad aram.   85
Thybris ea fluvium, quam longa est, nocte tumentem
leniit et tacita refluens ita substitit unda,
mitis ut in morem stagni placidaeque paludis
sterneret aequor aquis, remo ut luctamen abesset.
ergo iter inceptum celerant rumore secundo: 90
labitur uncta vadis abies; mirantur et undae,
miratur nemus insuetum fulgentia longe
scuta virum fluvio pictasque innare carinas.   FMPRV
olli remigio noctemque diemque fatigant
et longos superant flexus, variisque teguntur   95
arboribus viridisque secant placido aequore silvas.
sol medium caeli conscenderat igneus orbem,
cum muros arcemque procul ac rara domorum
tecta vident, quae nunc Romana potentia caelo   MPRV
aequavit, tum res inopes Euandrus habebat.   100
ocius advertunt proras urbique propinquant.

Forte die sollemnem illo rex Arcas honorem
Amphitryoniadae magno divisque ferebat
ante urbem in luco.   Pallas huic filius una,
una omnes iuvenum primi pauperque senatus   105
tura dabant, tepidusque cruor fumabat ad aras.
ut celsas videre rates atque inter opacum

[90] peragunt *R, Macrobius.*   Rumone *M¹, known to Servius.*
[92] mirantur *Fγ¹.*   [102] sollemne *PR.*

AENEID BOOK VIII

⁸¹ But lo ! a portent, sudden and wondrous to see
Gleaming white amid the wood, of one colour with
her milk-white brood, lay outstretched on the green
bank before their eyes—a sow: her good Aeneas
offers in sacrifice to thee, even thee, most mighty
Juno, and sets with her young before thine altar
All that night long Tiber calmed his swelling flood,
and flowing back with silent wave stayed thus, so
that like a gentle pool or quiet mere he smoothed his
watery plain, that the oars might know no struggle.
Therefore with cheering cries they speed the voyage
begun : over the waters glides the well-pitched pine ;
in wonder the waves, in wonder the unwonted woods
view the far gleaming shields of warriors and the
painted hulls floating on the stream. They with
their rowing give night and day no rest, pass the
long bends, are shaded with diverse trees, and cleave
the green woods in the peaceful water.[1] The fiery
sun had scaled the mid arch of heaven, when afar
they see walls and a citadel, and scattered house-
roofs, which to-day Rome's empire has exalted to
heaven, but then Evander ruled, a scant domain.
Quickly they turn the prows to land, and draw near
the town.

¹⁰² It chanced that on that day the Arcadian king
paid wonted homage to Amphitryon's mighty son [2]
and the gods in a grove before the city. With him his
son Pallas, with him all the foremost of his people
and his humble senate were offering incense, and
the warm blood smoked at the altars. Soon as
they saw the high ships, saw them gliding up

---

[1] Thus Servius, who is doubtless right in supposing that Virgil refers to the reflected woods. Otherwise, "on" for "in."
[2] Hercules. Virgil doubtless has in mind the rites connected with the *Ara Maxima* in the Forum Boarium.

VIRGIL

adlabi nemus et tacitis incumbere remis,
terrentur visu subito cunctique relictis
consurgunt mensis. audax quos rumpere Pallas 110
sacra vetat raptoque volat telo obvius ipse,
et procul e tumulo : " iuvenes, quae causa subegit
ignotas temptare vias ? quo tenditis ? " inquit.
" qui genus ? unde domo ? pacemne huc fertis an
    arma ? "
tum pater Aeneas puppi sic fatur ab alta 115
paciferaeque manu ramum praetendit olivae:
"Troiugenas ac tela vides inimica Latinis,
quos illi bello profugos egere superbo.
Euandrum petimus. ferte haec et dicite lectos MPR
Dardaniae venisse duces, socia arma rogantis." 120
obstipuit tanto percussus nomine Pallas :
" egredere o quicumque es," ait, " coramque parentem
adloquere ac nostris succede penatibus hospes ; "
excepitque manu dextramque amplexus inhaesit.
progressi subeunt luco fluviumque relinquunt. 125

  Tum regem Aeneas dictis adfatur amicis :
"optume Graiugenum, cui me Fortuna precari
et vitta comptos voluit praetendere ramos,
non equidem extimui, Danaum quod ductor et Arcas
quodque a stirpe fores geminis coniunctus Atridis ; 130
sed mea me virtus et sancta oracula divum,
cognatique patres, tua terris didita fama,
coniunxere tibi et fatis egere volentem.
Dardanus, Iliacae primus pater urbis et auctor,
Electra, ut Grai perhibent, Atlantide cretus, 135
advehitur Teucros ; Electram maximus Atlas

       [108] tacitis γ^2c^2, *Servius :* tacitos $MPR\gamma^1bc^1$.
       [115] fatus $PR\gamma^1$.   [123] ac] et M^1, *Nonius.*

AENEID BOOK VIII

between the shady woods and plying noiseless oars, they are affrighted by the sudden sight, and all rise up, quitting the feast. But Pallas, undaunted, forbids them to break off the rites, and seizing his spear, flies himself to meet the strangers, and from a mound afar cries: "Warriors, what cause has driven you to try unknown paths? Whither fare ye? Of what race are ye? From what home? Is it peace or war ye bring hither?" Then father Aeneas speaks thus from the high stern, outstretching in his hand a branch of peaceful olive: "Men born of Troy thou seest, and arms hostile to Latins—men whom they have driven to flight by insolent warfare. We seek Evander: bear ye this message, and say that chosen captains of Dardania are come, suing for alliance in arms." Smitten with amaze was Pallas at that mighty name. "Come forth," he cries, "whoe'er thou art; speak to my father face to face, and pass, a guest, beneath our roof!" And with a grasp of welcome he caught and clung to his hand. Advancing, they enter the grove and leave the river.

[126] Then with friendly words Aeneas addresses the king: "Noblest of the sons of Greece, to whom Fortune has willed that I make my prayer, and offer boughs decked with fillets, I feared not because thou wert a Danaan chief, an Arcadian and linked by blood with the twin sons of Atreus; but my own worth and Heaven's holy oracles, our ancestral kinship, and thy fame spread through the world, have bound me to thee, and brought me Fate's willing follower. Dardanus, first father and founder of Ilium's city, born (as Greeks relate) of Atlantean Electra, came to the Teucrians; Electra was begotten

VIRGIL

edidit, aetherios umero qui sustinet orbis.
vobis Mercurius pater est, quem candida Maia
Cyllenae gelido conceptum vertice fudit ;
at Maiam, auditis si quicquam credimus, Atlas,   140
idem Atlas generat, caeli qui sidera tollit.
sic genus amborum scindit se sanguine ab uno.
his fretus non legatos neque prima per artem
temptamenta tui pepigi ; me, me ipse meumque
obieci caput et supplex ad limina veni.   145
gens eadem, quae te, crudeli Daunia bello
insequitur ; nos si pellant, nihil afore credúnt,
quin omnem Hesperiam penitus sua sub iuga mittant,
et mare, quod supra, teneant, quodque adluit infra.
accipe daque fidem.   sunt nobis fortia bello   150
pectora, sunt animi et rebus spectata iuventus."

   Dixerat Aeneas.   ille os oculosque loquentis
iamdudum et totum lustrabat lumine corpus.
tum sic pauca refert : " ut te, fortissime Teucrum,
accipio agnoscoque libens ! ut verba parentis   155
et vocem Anchisae magni voltumque recordor !
nam memini Hesionae visentem regna sororis
Laomedontiaden Priamum, Salamina petentem,
protinus Arcadiae gelidos invisere finis.
tum mihi prima genas vestibat flore iuventas,   160
mirabarque duces Teucros, mirabar et ipsum
Laomedontiaden, sed cunctis altior ibat
Anchises.   mihi mens iuvenali ardebat amore
compellare virum et dextrae coniungere dextram ;
accessi et cupidus Phenei sub moenia duxi.   165
ille mihi insignem pharetram Lyciasque sagittas
discedens chlamydemque auro dedit intertextam,
frenaque bina, meus quae nunc habet aurea Pallas.

¹³⁹ fundit P^1.   ¹⁴⁰ creditis $P\gamma^1$.
¹⁴⁷ afore $P^1\gamma^2$, *Servius*: adfore $M^2P^2\gamma^1$: atfore M^1: fore R.
¹⁶⁷ intertexto P^1R, *known to Servius.*

AENEID BOOK VIII

of mightiest Atlas, who on his shoulders sustains the heavenly spheres. Your sire is Mercury, whom fair Maia conceived and bore on Cyllene's cold peak; but Maia, if we have any trust in tales we have heard, is child of Atlas, the same Atlas who uplifts the starry heavens; so the lineage of the twain branches from one blood. Relying on this, no embassy did I plan, no crafty overtures to thee; myself I have brought, —myself and my own life—and am come a suppliant to thy doors. The same Daunian race pursues us, as thee, in cruel war; if they drive us forth, they deem that naught will stay them from laying all Hesperia utterly beneath their yoke, and from holding the seas that wash her above and below.[1] Take and return friendship; we have hearts valiant in war, high souls and manhood tried in action."

[152] Aeneas ceased. As he spake, Evander had long scanned his face, and eyes, and all his form; then thus briefly replies: "Bravest of the Teucrians, how gladly do I receive and recognize thee! How I recall thy father's words, and the voice and features of great Anchises! For I remember how Priam, Laomedon's son, when on his way to Salamis he came to see the realm of his sister Hesione, passed on to visit Arcadia's cold borders. In those days early youth clothed my cheeks with bloom, and I wondered at the chiefs of Troy, wondered at their prince, Laomedon's son; but towering above all moved Anchises. My heart burned with youthful ardour to accost him and clasp hand in hand; I drew near, and led him eagerly to Pheneus' city. Departing, he gave me a glorious quiver with Lycian shafts, a scarf inwoven with gold, and a pair of golden bits that now my Pallas possesses. There-

[1] The Adriatic and Tuscan seas.

VIRGIL

ergo et quam petitis, iuncta est mihi foedere dextra,
et, lux cum primum terris se crastina reddet, 170
auxilio laetos dimittam opibusque iuvabo.
interea sacra haec, quando huc venistis amici,
annua, quae differre nefas, celebrate faventes
nobiscum et iam nunc sociorum adsuescite mensis."

Haec ubi dicta, dapes iubet et sublata reponi 175
pocula gramineoque viros locat ipse sedili
praecipuumque toro et villosi pelle leonis
accipit Aenean solioque invitat acerno.
tum lecti iuvenes certatim araeque sacerdos
viscera tosta ferunt taurorum, onerantque canistris 180
dona laboratae Cereris, Bacchumque ministrant.
vescitur Aeneas simul et Troiana iuventus
perpetui tergo bovis et lustralibus extis.

Postquam exempta fames et amor compressus edendi,
rex Euandrus ait: "non haec sollemnia nobis, 185
has ex more dapes, hanc tanti numinis aram
vana superstitio veterumque ignara deorum
imposuit: saevis, hospes Troiane, periclis
servati facimus meritosque novamus honores.
iam primum saxis suspensam hanc aspice rupem, 190
disiectae procul ut moles desertaque montis
stat domus et scopuli ingentem traxere ruinam.
hic spelunca fuit, vasto summota recessu,
semihominis Caci facies quam dira tenebat,
solis inaccessam radiis; semperque recenti 195
caede tepebat humus, foribusque adfixa superbis
ora virum tristi pendebant pallida tabo.

¹⁸⁰ canistri *R.* ¹⁹⁰ pridem *R.*
¹⁹¹ deiectae *R.* ¹⁹⁴ tegebat *M¹PRγ.*

AENEID BOOK VIII

fore, the hand ye seek lo! I join with you in league, and when first to-morrow's dawn revisits earth, I will send you hence cheered by an escort, and will aid you with our stores. Meanwhile, since ye are come hither as friends, this yearly festival, which we may not defer, graciously solemnize with us, and even now become familiar with your comrades' board."

175 This said, he orders the repast and cups, already removed, to be replaced, and with his own hand ranges the guests on the grassy seat, and chief in honour he welcomes Aeneas to the cushion of a shaggy lion's hide, and invites him to a maple throne. Then chosen youths, and the priest of the altar, in emulous haste bring roast flesh of bulls, pile on baskets the gifts of Ceres, fashioned well, and serve the wine of Bacchus. Aeneas and, with him, the warriors of Troy feast on the long chine of an ox and the sacrificial meat.

184 When hunger was banished and the desire of food stayed, King Evander spoke: "These solemn rites, this wonted feast, this altar of a mighty Presence,—'tis no idle superstition, knowing not the gods of old, that has laid them on us. As saved from cruel perils, O Trojan guest, do we pay the rites, and repeat the worship due. Now first look at this rocky overhanging cliff, how the masses are scattered afar, how the mountain-dwelling stands desolate, and the crags have toppled down in mighty ruin! Here was once a cave, receding to unfathomed depth, never visited by the sun's rays, where dwelt the awful shape of half-human Cacus; and ever the ground reeked with fresh blood, and, nailed to its proud doors, faces of men hung pallid in ghastly

VIRGIL

huic monstro Volcanus erat pater : illius atros
ore vomens ignis magna se mole ferebat.
attulit et nobis aliquando optantibus aetas   200
auxilium adventumque dei. nam maximus ultor,
tergemini nece Geryonae spoliisque superbus,
Alcides aderat taurosque hac victor agebat
ingentis, vallemque boves amnemque tenebant.
at furiis Caci mens effera, ne quid inausum   205
aut intractatum scelerisve dolive fuisset,
quattuor a stabulis praestanti corpore tauros
avertit, totidem forma superante iuvencas.
atque hos, ne qua forent pedibus vestigia rectis,
cauda in speluncam tractos versisque viarum   210
indiciis raptos saxo occultabat opaco.
quaerenti nulla ad speluncam signa ferebant.
interea, cum iam stabulis saturata moveret
Amphitryoniades armenta abitumque pararet,
discessu mugire boves atque omne querellis   215
impleri nemus et colles clamore relinqui.
reddidit una boum vocem vastoque sub antro
mugiit et Caci spem custodita fefellit.
hic vero Alcidae furiis exarserat atro
felle dolor : rapit arma manu nodisque gravatum   220
robur, et aërii cursu petit ardua montis.
tum primum nostri Cacum videre timentem
turbatumque oculis : fugit ilicet ocior Euro
speluncamque petit ; pedibus timor addidit alas.

Ut sese inclusit ruptisque immane catenis   225
deiecit saxum, ferro quod et arte paterna
pendebat, fultosque emuniit obice postis,
ecce furens animis aderat Tirynthius omnemque

---

²⁰² Geryoni *R :* Geryonis *M (late).*
²⁰⁵ furis *M¹γ², Servius.*   ²⁰⁶ intemptatum *M².*
²¹² quaerentes *Rγ².*   ²¹⁴ parabat *M¹.*
²¹⁶ relinquit *P¹.*   ²²¹ et aerii] aetherii *M¹γ.*
²²³ oculi *some minor MSS., known to Servius :* oculos *γ¹.*

74

AENEID BOOK VIII

decay. This monster's sire was Vulcan; his were the black fires he belched forth, as he moved in mighty bulk. For us, too, time at last brought to our desire a god's advent and aid. For there came the mightest of avengers, even Alcides, glorying in the slaughter and spoils of triple Geryon, and this way drove his huge bulls in triumph, and his oxen filled vale and riverside. But Cacus, his wits wild with frenzy, that naught of crime or craft might prove to be left undared or unessayed, drove from their stalls four bulls of surpassing form, and as many heifers of peerless beauty. And these, that there might be no tracks pointing forward, he dragged by the tail into his cavern, and, with the signs of their course thus turned backwards, he hid them in the rocky darkness: whoso sought them could find no marks leading to the cave. Meanwhile, when Amphitryon's son was now moving the well-fed herds from their stalls, and making ready to set out, the oxen at parting lowed; all the grove they fill with their plaint, and with clamour quit the hills. One heifer returned the cry, lowed from the drear cavern's depths, and from her prison baffled the hopes of Cacus. Hereupon the wrath of Alcides furiously blazed forth with black gall; seizing in hand his weapons and heavily knotted club, he seeks with speed the crest of the soaring mount. Then first our folk saw Cacus afraid and with trouble in his eyes; in a twinkling he flees swifter than the East wind and seeks his cavern; fear lends wings to his feet.

[225] Soon as he shut himself in, and, bursting the chains, dropped the giant rock suspended in iron by his father's craft, which with its barrier blocked the firm-stayed entrance, lo! the Tirynthian came in a

VIRGIL

accessum lustrans huc ora ferebat et illuc,
dentibus infrendens.   ter totum fervidus ira   230
lustrat Aventini montem, ter saxea temptat
limina nequiquam, ter fessus valle resedit.
stabat acuta silex, praecisis undique saxis
speluncae dorso insurgens, altissima visu,
dirarum nidis domus opportuna volucrum.   235
hanc, ut prona iugo laevum incumbebat ad amnem,
dexter in adversum nitens concussit et imis
avolsam solvit radicibus; inde repente
impulit, impulsu quo maximus intonat aether,
dissultant ripae refluitque exterritus amnis.   240
at specus et Caci detecta apparuit ingens
regia et umbrosae penitus patuere cavernae,
non secus ac si qua penitus vi terra dehiscens
infernas reseret sedes et regna recludat
pallida, dis invisa, superque immane barathrum   245
cernatur, trepident immisso lumine Manes.
ergo insperata deprensum luce repente
inclusumque cavo saxo atque insueta rudentem
desuper Alcides telis premit, omniaque arma
advocat et ramis vastisque molaribus instat.   250
ille autem, neque enim fuga iam super ulla pericli,
faucibus ingentem fumum, mirabile dictu,
evomit involvitque domum caligine caeca,
prospectum eripiens oculis, glomeratque sub antro
fumiferam noctem commixtis igne tenebris.   255
non tulit Alcides animis, seque ipse per ignem
praecipiti iecit saltu, qua plurimus undam
fumus agit nebulaque ingens specus aestuat atra.
hic Cacum in tenebris incendia vana vomentem

<small>
238 advolsam M^1.   239 insonat R.
244 reserit M^1: reserat $M^2PR\gamma$.
246 trepidantque R.   247 in luce M^2R.
251 pericli est $P\gamma$.   257 iniecit $P\gamma$.
</small>

frenzy of wrath, and, scanning every approach, turned his face this way and that, gnashing his teeth. Thrice, hot with rage, he traverses the whole Aventine Mount; thrice he essays the stony portals in vain; thrice he sinks down wearied in the valley. There stood a pointed rock of flint, cut sheer away all around, rising above the cavern's ridge, and exceeding high to view, fit home for the nestlings of foul birds. This, as it leaned sloping with its ridge to the river on the left, he shook, straining against it from the right, and, wrenching it from its lowest roots, tore it loose; then of a sudden thrust it forth: with that thrust the mighty heaven thunders, the banks leap apart, and the affrighted river recoils. But the den of Cacus and his huge palace stood revealed, and, deep below, the darkling cave lay open: even as though beneath some force, the earth, gaping open deep below, should unlock the infernal abodes and disclose the pallid realms abhorred of the gods, and from above the vast abyss be descried, and the ghosts tremble at the inrushing light. On him, then, caught of a sudden by unlooked for day, pent in the hollow rock and bellowing uncouth roars, Alcides hurls missiles from above, calling all weapons to his aid, and rains upon him boughs and giant millstones. He, the while, for now no other escape from peril was left, belches from his throat dense smoke, wondrous to tell! and veils the dwelling in blinding gloom, blotting all view from the eyes, and rolling up in the cave's depth smoke-laden night, its blackness mingled with flame. In his fury Alcides brooked not this: headlong he dashed through the flame, where the smoke rolls its wave thickest, and through the mighty cave the mist surges black. Here as Cacus in the darkness vomits vain fires, he seizes him

VIRGIL

corripit in nodum complexus, et angit inhaerens 260
elisos oculos et siccum sanguine guttur.
panditur extemplo foribus domus atra revolsis
abstractaeque boves abiurataeque rapinae
caelo ostenduntur, pedibusque informe cadaver
protrahitur. nequeunt expleri corda tuendo 265
terribilis oculos, voltum villosaque saetis
pectora semiferi atque exstinctos faucibus ignis.
ex illo celebratus honos laetique minores
servavere diem, primusque Potitius auctor
et domus Herculei custos Pinaria sacri. 270
hanc aram luco statuit, quae Maxima semper
dicetur nobis et erit quae maxima semper.
quare agite, o iuvenes, tantarum in munere laudum
cingite fronde comas et pocula porgite dextris
communemque vocate deum et date vina volentes."
dixerat, Herculea bicolor cum populus umbra 276
velavitque comas foliisque innexa pependit,
et sacer implevit dextram scyphus. ocius omnes
in mensam laeti libant divosque precantur.

Devexo interea propior fit Vesper Olympo, 280
iamque sacerdotes primusque Potitius ibant,
pellibus in morem cincti, flammasque ferebant.
instaurant epulas et mensae grata secundae
dona ferunt cumulantque oneratis lancibus aras.
tum Salii ad cantus incensa altaria circum 285
populeis adsunt evincti tempora ramis,
hic iuvenum chorus, ille senum, qui carmine laudes
Herculeas et facta ferunt: ut prima novercae
monstra manu geminosque premens eliserit anguis,

[261] elidens *known to Servius*. [262] alta P^1.

AENEID BOOK VIII

in knot-like embrace, and, close entwined, throttles him till the eyes burst forth and the throat is drained of blood. Straightway the doors are torn off, and the dark den laid bare; the stolen oxen and forsworn plunder are shown to heaven, and the shapeless carcase is dragged forth by the feet. Men cannot sate their hearts with gazing on the terrible eyes, the face, and shaggy bristling chest of the brutish creature, and the quenched fires of his throat. From that time has this service been solemnized, and joyous posterity has kept the day—Potitius foremost, founder of the rite, and the Pinarian house, custodian of the worship of Hercules. He himself set in the grove this altar, which shall ever by us be called Mightiest, and mightiest shall it ever be. Come then, warriors, and, in honour of deeds so glorious, wreath your hair with leaves, and stretch forth the cup in your hands; call on our common god, and of good will pour ye the wine." He ceased; and thereon the twy-coloured poplar veiled his hair with the shade dear to Hercules, hanging down with festoon of leaves, and the sacred goblet charged his hand. Speedily all pour glad libation on the board, and offer prayer to the gods.

280 Meanwhile, evening draws nearer down heaven's slope, and now the priests went forth, Potitius at their head, girt with skins after their fashion, and bearing torches. They renew the banquet and bring the welcome offerings of a second repast, and heap the altars with laden platters. Then the Salii come to sing round the kindled altars, their brows bound with poplar boughs—one band of youths, the other of old men—and these in song extol the glories and deeds of Hercules: how first he strangled in his grip the twin serpents, the monsters of his step-

VIRGIL

ut bello egregias idem disiecerit urbes, 290
Troiamque Oechaliamque, ut duros mille labores
rege sub Eurystheo fatis Iunonis iniquae
pertulerit. " tu nubigenas, invicte, bimembris,
Hylaeumque Pholumque, manu, tu Cresia mactas
prodigia et vastum Nemea sub rupe leonem. 295
te Stygii tremuere lacus, te ianitor Orci
ossa super recubans antro semesa cruento;
nec te ullae facies, non terruit ipse Typhoeus
arduus arma tenens, non te rationis egentem
Lernaeus turba capitum circumstetit anguis. 300
salve, vera Iovis proles, decus addite divis,
et nos et tua dexter adi pede sacra secundo."
talia carminibus celebrant; super omnia Caci
speluncam adiciunt spirantemque ignibus ipsum.
consonat omne nemus strepitu collesque resultant. 305

Exim se cuncti divinis rebus ad urbem
perfectis referunt.   ibat rex obsitus aevo,
et comitem Aenean iuxta natumque tenebat
ingrediens varioque viam sermone levabat.
miratur facilisque oculos fert omnia circum 310
Aeneas, capiturque locis et singula laetus
exquiritque auditque virum monumenta priorum.
tum rex Euandrus, Romanae conditor arcis:
" haec nemora indigenae Fauni Nymphaeque tenebant
gensque virum truncis et duro robore nata, 315
quis neque mos neque cultus erat, nec iungere tauros

[291] Oechaliam eduros M^1.
[295] Nemaea M: Nemea $P^2R\gamma$: Nemeae P^1, *Servius*.
[306] exin Rb^2c.

---

[1] Juno, who in jealousy sent two snakes to kill Hercules in his cradle, and to whose craftiness it was due that Hercules had to serve Eurystheus for twelve years.

80

AENEID BOOK VIII

mother[1]; how likewise in war he dashed down peerless cities, Troy and Oechalia; how under King Eurystheus he bore a thousand grievous toils by the doom of cruel Juno. "Thou, unconquered one, thou with thy hand art slayer of the cloud-born creatures of double shape, Hylaeus and Pholus, the monsters of Crete, and the huge lion beneath Nemea's rock. Before thee the Stygian lakes trembled; before thee, the warder of Hell, as he lay on half-gnawn bones in his bloody cave; no shape daunted thee, no, not Typhoeus' self, towering aloft in arms; wit failed thee not when Lerna's snake encompassed thee with its swarm of heads. Hail, true seed of Jove, to the gods an added glory! graciously with favouring foot visit us and thy rites!" Such are their hymns of praise; and they crown all with the tale of Cacus' cavern, and the fire-breathing monster's self. All the woodland rings with the clamour, and the hills re-echo.

[306] Then, the sacred rites discharged, all return to the city. There walked the king, beset with years, and as he moved along kept Aeneas and his son at his side as companions, relieving the way with varied talk. Aeneas marvels as he turns his ready eyes all around, is charmed with the scene, and joyfully seeks and learns, one by one, the records of the men of yore. Then King Evander, founder of Rome's citadel: "In these woodlands the native Fauns and Nymphs once dwelt, and a race of men sprung from trunks of trees and hardy oak,[2] who had no rule nor art of life, and knew not how to

---

[2] *cf.* Homer, *Odyssey*, XIX. 163, where Penelope says to the disguised Odysseus: "Tell me of thine own stock, whence thou art, for thou art not sprung of oak or rock, as told in olden tales."

81

VIRGIL

aut componere opes norant aut parcere parto,
sed rami atque asper victu venatus alebat.
primus ab aetherio venit Saturnus Olympo,
arma Iovis fugiens et regnis exsul ademptis.   320
is genus indocile ac dispersum montibus altis
composuit legesque dedit, Latiumque vocari
maluit, his quoniam latuisset tutus in oris.
aurea quae perhibent illo sub rege fuere
saecula: sic placida populos in pace regebat,   325
deterior donec paulatim ac decolor aetas
et belli rabies et amor successit habendi.
tum manus Ausonia et gentes venere Sicanae,
saepius et nomen posuit Saturnia tellus;
tum reges asperque immani corpore Thybris,   330
a quo post Itali fluvium cognomine Thybrim
diximus; amisit verum vetus Albula nomen.
me pulsum patria pelagique extrema sequentem
Fortuna omnipotens et ineluctabile fatum
his posuere locis, matrisque egere tremenda   335
Carmentis Nymphae monita et deus auctor Apollo."

Vix ea dicta, dehinc progressus monstrat et aram
et Carmentalem Romani nomine portam
quam memorant, Nymphae priscum Carmentis
  honorem,
vatis fatidicae, cecinit quae prima futuros   340
Aeneadas magnos et nobile Pallanteum.
hinc lucum ingentem, quem Romulus acer Asylum
rettulit, et gelida monstrat sub rupe Lupercal,
Parrhasio dictum Panos de more Lycaei.
nec non et sacri monstrat nemus Argileti   345

³¹⁷ parto] rapto M^1.   ³²⁴ aureaque P^1. fuerunt $P\gamma$.
³³⁸ Romano R.   ³⁴¹ nomine R: nobine $P\gamma^1$.

---

[1] Servius says: *Varro autem Latium dici putat, quod latet Italia inter praecipitia Alpium et Apennini.* Mommsen

82

AENEID BOOK VIII

yoke the ox or to lay up stores, or to husband their gains; but tree-branches nurtured them and the huntsman's savage fare. First from heavenly Olympus came Saturn, fleeing from the weapons of Jove and exiled from his lost realm. He gathered together the unruly race, scattered over mountain heights, and gave them laws, and chose that the land be called Latium, since in these borders he had found a safe hiding-place.[1] Under his reign were the golden ages men tell of: in such perfect peace he ruled the nations; till little by little there crept in a race of worse sort and duller hue, the frenzy of war, and the passion for gain. Then came the Ausonian host and the Sicanian tribes, and ofttimes the land of Saturn laid aside her name.[2] Then kings arose, and fierce Thybris with giant bulk, from whose name we of Italy have since called our river Tiber; her true name ancient Albula has lost. Myself, from fatherland an outcast and seeking the ends of the sea, almighty Fortune and inevitable Fate planted on this soil; and the dread warnings of my mother, the nymph Carmentis, and Apollo's divine warrant, drove me hither."

[337] Scarce had he finished, when, advancing, he points out the altar and the Carmental Gate, as the Romans call it, tribute of old to the Nymph Carmentis, soothtelling prophetess, who first foretold the greatness of Aeneas' sons, and the glory of Pallanteum. Next he shows him a vast grove, where valiant Romulus restored an Asylum, and, beneath a chill rock, the Lupercal, bearing after Arcadian wont the name of Lycaean Pan. He shows withal the wood of holy Argiletum, and calls the place to

---

regards *Latium* as "the plain," in contrast with "the mountains," and connected with πλατύς, "broad," and *latus*, "side." [2] *cf.* Ausonia, Hesperia, Oenotria, Italia.

VIRGIL

testaturque locum et letum docet hospitis Argi.
hinc ad Tarpeiam sedem et Capitolia ducit,
aurea nunc, olim silvestribus horrida dumis.
iam tum religio pavidos terrebat agrestis
dira loci, iam tum silvam saxumque tremebant.   350
"hoc nemus, hunc," inquit, "frondoso vertice collem,
quis deus incertum est, habitat deus; Arcades ipsum
credunt se vidisse Iovem, cum saepe nigrantem
aegida concuteret dextra nimbosque cieret.
haec duo praeterea disiectis oppida muris,   355
reliquias veterumque vides monumenta virorum.
hanc Ianus pater, hanc Saturnus condidit arcem;
Ianiculum huic, illi fuerat Saturnia nomen."
   Talibus inter se dictis ad tecta subibant
pauperis Euandri, passimque armenta videbant   360
Romanoque Foro et lautis mugire Carinis.
ut ventum ad sedes, "haec," inquit, "limina victor
Alcides subiit, haec illum regia cepit.
aude, hospes, contemnere opes et te quoque dignum
finge deo, rebusque veni non asper egenis."   365
dixit et angusti subter fastigia tecti
ingentem Aenean duxit stratisque locavit
effultum foliis et pelle Libystidis ursae.
nox ruit et fuscis tellurem amplectitur alis.
   At Venus haud animo nequiquam exterrita mater,
Laurentumque minis et duro mota tumultu,   371
Volcanum adloquitur, thalamoque haec coniugis aureo
incipit et dictis divinum adspirat amorem:
"dum bello Argolici vastabant Pergama reges

³⁵⁰ tenebant M^1.   ³⁵⁷ arcem] urbem M^2R.
³⁶¹ latis M^1: cavernis R.   ³⁶⁵ deos P^1.

---

[1] The Argiletum probably gets its name from *argilla*, "white clay."

AENEID BOOK VIII

witness, and tells of the death of Argus his guest.[1] Hence he leads him to the Tarpeian house, and the Capitol—golden now, once bristling with woodland thickets. Even then the dread sanctity of the region awed the trembling rustics; even then they shuddered at the forest and the rock. "This grove," he cries, "this hill with its leafy crown,—though we know not what god it is—is yet a god's home: my Arcadians believe they have looked on Jove himself, while oft his right hand shook the darkening aegis and summoned the storm-clouds. Moreover, in these two towns, with walls o'erthrown, thou seest the relics and memorials of men of old. This fort father Janus built, that Saturn; Janiculum was this called, that Saturnia."[2]

359 So talking, each with each, they drew nigh the house of the poor Evander, and saw cattle all about, lowing in the Roman Forum and the brilliant Carinae. When they reached his dwelling: "These portals," he cries, "victorious Alcides stooped to enter; this mansion welcomed him. Dare, my guest, to scorn riches; fashion thyself also to be worthy of deity, and come not disdainful of our poverty." He said, and beneath the roof of his lowly dwelling led great Aeneas, and laid him on a couch of strewn leaves and the skin of a Libyan bear. Night rushes down, and clasps the earth with dusky wings.

370 But Venus, her mother's heart dismayed by no idle fear, moved by the threats and stern uprising of the Laurentes, addresses Vulcan, and in her golden nuptial chamber thus begins, breathing into her words divine love; "While Argive kings were

[2] cf. Cato: *Saturnia olim, ubi nunc Capitolium.* The fort of Janus was the Janiculum, on the right bank of the Tiber.

VIRGIL

debita casurasque inimicis ignibus arces, 375
non ullum auxilium miseris, non arma rogavi
artis opisque tuae, nec te, carissime coniunx,
incassumve tuos volui exercere labores,
quamvis et Priami deberem plurima natis,
et durum Aeneae flevissem saepe laborem. 380
nunc Iovis imperiis Rutulorum constitit oris:
ergo eadem supplex venio et sanctum mihi numen
arma rogo, genetrix nato. te filia Nerei,
te potuit lacrimis Tithonia flectere coniunx.
aspice, qui coeant populi, quae moenia clausis 385
ferrum acuant portis in me excidiumque meorum."

Dixerat et niveis hinc atque hinc diva lacertis
cunctantem amplexu molli fovet. ille repente
accepit solitam flammam, notusque medullas
intravit calor et labefacta per ossa cucurrit, 390
non secus atque olim, tonitru cum rupta corusco
ignea rima micans percurrit lumine nimbos.
sensit laeta dolis et formae conscia coniunx.
tum pater aeterno fatur devinctus amore:
"quid causas petis ex alto? fiducia cessit 395
quo tibi, diva, mei? similis si cura fuisset,
tum quoque fas nobis Teucros armare fuisset;
nec pater omnipotens Troiam nec fata vetabant
stare decemque alios Priamum superesse per annos.
et nunc, si bellare paras atque haec tibi mens est, 400
quidquid in arte mea possum promittere curae,

[378] -ve] -que M^1. incassum vetitos volui *Garrod (Classical Review*, xxxiii (1919), 105).
[382] nomen γ: numen *P*. [390] calefacta *R*.
[391] non] haut *M*. [394] devictus $P^2\gamma^1$.

AENEID BOOK VIII

ravaging in war Troy's doomed towers, and her ramparts fated to fall by hostile flames, no aid for the sufferers did I ask, no weapons of thine art and power; no, dearest consort, I would not task thee or thy toils for naught, heavy as was my debt to Priam's sons, and many the tears I shed for Aeneas' sore distress. Now, by Jove's commands, he has set foot in the Rutulian borders; therefore, I, who ne'er asked before, come a suppliant, and ask arms of the deity I revere, a mother for her son. Thee the daughter of Nereus, thee the spouse of Tithonus, could sway with tears.[1] Lo! what nations are mustering, what cities with closed gates whet the sword against me and the lives of my people!"

[387] The goddess ceased, and, as he falters, throws her snowy arms round about him and fondles him in soft embrace. At once he caught the wonted flame; the familiar warmth passed into his marrow and ran through his melting frame: even as when at times, bursting amid the thunder's peal, a sparkling streak of fire courses through the storm-clouds with dazzling light. His consort knew it, rejoicing in her wiles, and conscious of her beauty. Then spoke her lord, enchained by immortal love: "Why seekest so far for pleas? Whither, goddess, has fled thy faith in me? Had like care been thine, in those days too it had been right for me to arm the Trojans; nor was the almighty Father nor Fate unwilling that Troy stand or Priam live for ten years more. And now, if war is thy purpose, and this is thy intent, whatever care I can promise in my craft, whatever can be achieved

---

[1] Thetis, the daughter of Nereus, asked Hephaestus (Vulcan) to make armour for her son Achilles (*Iliad*, XVIII. 428 ff.). Aurora, wife of Tithonus, asked Vulcan to give armour to her son Memnon (*cf.* l. 489).

VIRGIL

quod fieri ferro liquidove potest electro,
quantum ignes animaeque valent, absiste precando
viribus indubitare tuis." ea verba locutus
optatos dedit amplexus placidumque petivit 405
coniugis infusus gremio per membra soporem.

Inde ubi prima quies medio iam noctis abactae
curriculo expulerat somnum, cum femina primum,
cui tolerare colo vitam tenuique Minerva
impositum, cinerem et sopitos suscitat ignis, 410
noctem addens operi, famulasque ad lumina longo
exercet penso, castum ut servare cubile
coniugis et possit parvos educere natos:
haud secus Ignipotens nec tempore segnior illo
mollibus e stratis opera ad fabrilia surgit. 415

Insula Sicanium iuxta latus Aeoliamque
erigitur Liparen, fumantibus ardua saxis,
quam subter specus et Cyclopum exesa caminis
antra Aetnaea tonant, validique incudibus ictus
auditi referunt gemitus, striduntque cavernis 420
stricturae Chalybum et fornacibus ignis anhelat,
Volcani domus et Volcania nomine tellus.
hoc tunc Ignipotens caelo descendit ab alto.

Ferrum exercebant vasto Cyclopes in antro,
Brontesque Steropesque et nudus membra Pyracmon. 425
his informatum manibus iam parte polita
fulmen erat, toto genitor quae plurima caelo
deicit in terras, pars imperfecta manebat.
tris imbris torti radios, tris nubis aquosae
addiderant, rutili tris ignis et alitis Austri. 430
fulgores nunc terrificos sonitumque metumque
miscebant operi flammisque sequacibus iras.

---

[406] infusum P^1R^1, *known to Servius as the reading of Probus.*
[412] exercens *M.*   [420] gemitum *R.*
[423] huc $P\gamma^1$.   tum $P\gamma^1$.

AENEID BOOK VIII

with iron or molten electrum, whatever fire and air may avail—cease with entreaty to mistrust thy powers!" Thus speaking, he gave the desired embrace, and, sinking on the bosom of his spouse, wooed calm slumber in every limb.

[407] Then, so soon as repose had banished sleep, in the mid career of now waning night, what time a housewife, whose task it is to eke out life with her distaff and Minerva's humble toil, awakes the embers and slumbering fire, adding night to her day's work, and keeps her handmaids toiling by lamplight at the long task, that she may preserve chaste her husband's bed, and rear her little sons: even so, and not more slothful at that hour, the Lord of Fire rises from his soft couch to the work of his smithy.

[416] Hard by the Sicanian coast and Aeolian Lipare rises an island, steep with smoking rocks. Beneath it thunders a cave, and the vaults of Aetna, scooped out by Cyclopean forges; strong strokes are heard echoing groans from the anvils, masses of Chalyb steel hiss in the caverns, and the fire pants in the furnace—the home of Vulcan and the land Vulcan's by name. Hither in that hour the Lord of Fire came down from high heaven.

[424] In the vast cave the Cyclopes were forging iron—Brontes and Steropes and Pyracmon with bared limbs. They had a thunderbolt, which their hands had shaped, such as full many the Father hurls down from all heaven upon earth, part already polished, while part remained unfinished. Three rays of twisted hail had they added to it, three of watery cloud, three of ruddy flame and the winged southern wind; now they were blending with the work frightful flashes, sound, and fear, and wrath with pursuing

VIRGIL

parte alia Marti currumque rotasque volucris
instabant, quibus ille viros, quibus excitat urbes,
aegidaque horriferam, turbatae Palladis arma, 435
certatim squamis serpentum auroque polibant,
conexosque anguis ipsamque in pectore divae
Gorgona, desecto vertentem lumina collo.
"tollite cuncta," inquit, "coeptosque auferte labores,
Aetnaei Cyclopes, et huc advertite mentem: 440
arma acri facienda viro. nunc viribus usus,
nunc manibus rapidis, omni nunc arte magistra.
praecipitate moras." nec plura effatus; at illi
ocius incubuere omnes pariterque laborem
sortiti. fluit aes rivis aurique metallum 445
volnificusque chalybs vasta fornace liquescit.
ingentem clipeum informant, unum omnia contra
tela Latinorum, septenosque orbibus orbis
impediunt. alii ventosis follibus auras
accipiunt redduntque, alii stridentia tingunt 450
aera lacu. gemit impositis incudibus antrum.
illi inter sese multa vi bracchia tollunt
in numerum versantque tenaci forcipe massam.

Haec pater Aeoliis properat dum Lemnius oris,
Euandrum ex humili tecto lux suscitat alma 455
et matutini volucrum sub culmine cantus.
consurgit senior tunicaque inducitur artus
et Tyrrhena pedum circumdat vincula plantis;
tum lateri atque umeris Tegeaeum subligat ensem,
demissa ab laeva pantherae terga retorquens. 460
nec non et gemini custodes limine ab alto

[439] deiecto *R*.   [443] at] et *P*[1].

---

[1] *cf. Georgics*, IV. 171-175.

AENEID BOOK VIII

flames. Elsewhere they were hurrying on for Mars a chariot and flying wheels, wherewith he stirs up men and cities; and eagerly with golden scales of serpents were burnishing the awful aegis, armour of wrathful Pallas, the interwoven snakes, and the Gorgon's self on the breast of the goddess, with neck severed and eyes revolving. "Away with all!" he cries; "take hence your tasks begun, Cyclopes of Aetna, and hither turn your thoughts! Arms for a brave warrior must ye make. Now is need of strength, now of swift hands, now of all your masterful skill. Fling off delay!" No more he said; but they with speed all bent to the toil, allotting the labour equally. Brass and golden ore flow in streams, and wounding steel is molten in the vast furnace. A giant shield they shape, to confront alone all the weapons of the Latins, and weld it sevenfold, circle on circle. Some with panting bellows make the blasts come and go, others dip the hissing brass in the lake, while the cavern groans under the anvils laid upon it. They with mighty force, now one, now another, raise their arms in measured cadence, and turn the metal with gripping tongs.[1]

454 While on the Aeolian shores the lord of Lemnos speeds on this work, the kindly light and the morning songs of birds beneath the eaves roused Evander from his humble home. The old man rises, clothes his limbs in a tunic, and wraps his feet in Tyrrhenian sandals. Then to his side and shoulders he buckles his Tegean sword, twisting back the panther's hide that drooped from the left.[2] Moreover, two guardian

[1] The hide is probably brought round to the right side, so as not to be in the way of the sword-hilt, which is on the left. Others take it to mean "flinging back (over the shoulder) a hide, so that it hung down over the left."

91

VIRGIL

praecedunt gressumque canes comitantur erilem.
hospitis Aeneae sedem et secreta petebat
sermonum memor et promissi muneris heros:
nec minus Aeneas se matutinus agebat: 465
filius huic Pallas, illi comes ibat Achates.
congressi iungunt dextras mediisque residunt
aedibus et licito tandem sermone fruuntur.
rex prior haec:

" Maxime Teucrorum ductor, quo sospite numquam
res equidem Troiae victas aut regna fatebor, 471
nobis ad belli auxilium pro nomine tanto
exiguae vires: hinc Tusco claudimur amni,
hinc Rutulus premit et murum circumsonat armis.
sed tibi ego ingentis populos opulentaque regnis 475
iungere castra paro, quam fors inopina salutem
ostentat. fatis huc te poscentibus adfers.
haud procul hinc saxo incolitur fundata vetusto
urbis Agyllinae sedes, ubi Lydia quondam
gens, bello praeclara, iugis insedit Etruscis. 480
hanc multos florentem annos rex deinde superbo
imperio et saevis tenuit Mezentius armis.
quid memorem infandas caedes, quid facta tyranni
effera? di capiti ipsius generique reservent!
mortua quin etiam iungebat corpora vivis, 485
componens manibusque manus atque oribus ora,
tormenti genus, et sanie taboque fluentis
complexu in misero longa sic morte necabat.
at fessi tandem cives infanda furentem
armati circumsistunt ipsumque domumque, 490

[462] procedunt P^1.   [472] numine P^1.
[474] circumtonat M^2.
[477] adfer *known to Servius*.

AENEID BOOK VIII

dogs go before from the lofty threshold, and attend their master's steps. To the lodging and seclusion of his guest, Aeneas, the hero, made his way, mindful of his words and the service promised. Nor less early was Aeneas astir. With the one walked his son Pallas; with the other, Achates. As they meet, they clasp hands, sit them down in the midst[1] of the dwellings, and at last enjoy free converse. The king thus begins:

470 "Mightiest captain of the Teucrians,—for, while thou livest, never will I own the power or realm of Troy vanquished—our strength to aid in war is scant for such a name.[2] On this side we are hemmed in by the Tuscan river; on that the Rutulian presses hard, and thunders in arms about our wall. Yet I purpose to link with thee mighty peoples and a camp rich in kingdoms,[3]—the salvation that unforeseen chance reveals. 'Tis at the call of Fate thou comest hither. Not far hence, builded of ancient stone, lies the peopled city of Agylla, where of old the war-famed Lydian race settled on the Etruscan heights. For many years it prospered, till King Mezentius ruled it with arrogant sway and cruel arms. Why recount the despot's heinous murders? Why his savage deeds? God keep the like for himself and for his breed! Nay, he would even link dead bodies with the living, fitting hand to hand and face to face (grim torture!) and, in the oozy slime and poison of that dread embrace, thus slay them by a lingering death. But at last, outworn, his citizens in arms besiege the monstrous madman, himself and

---

[1] The conference takes place in the open air.
[2] It is Evander's name and fame that brought Aeneas hither.
[3] A reference to the twelve states of Etruria governed by their *Lucumones*.

93

VIRGIL

obtruncant socios, ignem ad fastigia iactant.
ille inter caedem Rutulorum elapsus in agros
confugere et Turni defendier hospitis armis.
ergo omnis furiis surrexit Etruria iustis,
regem ad supplicium praesenti Marte reposcunt.   495
his ego te, Aenea, ductorem milibus addam.
toto namque fremunt condensae litore puppes,
signaque ferre iubent; retinet longaevus haruspex
fata canens: 'o Maeoniae delecta iuventus,
flos veterum virtusque virum, quos iustus in hostem
fert dolor et merita accendit Mezentius ira,   501
nulli fas Italo tantam subiungere gentem:
externos optate duces.'   tum Etrusca resedit
hoc acies campo, monitis exterrita divum.
ipse oratores ad me regnique coronam   505
cum sceptro misit mandatque insignia Tarchon,
succedam castris Tyrrhenaque regna capessam.
sed mihi tarda gelu saeclisque effeta senectus
invidet imperium seraeque ad fortia vires.
natum exhortarer, ni mixtus matre Sabella   510
hinc partem patriae traheret.   tu, cuius et annis
et generi fata indulgent, quem numina poscunt,
ingredere, o Teucrum atque Italum fortissime ductor.
hunc tibi praeterea, spes et solacia nostri,
Pallanta adiungam; sub te tolerare magistro   515
militiam et grave Martis opus, tua cernere facta
adsuescat, primis et te miretur ab annis.
Arcadas huic equites bis centum, robora pubis
lecta, dabo, totidemque suo tibi nomine Pallas."

Vix ea fatus erat, defixique ora tenebant   520
Aeneas Anchisiades et fidus Achates

₄₉₂ caedes M^2: cedes P.
₅₁₂ fatum $P^1R\gamma^1$.   indulges P^1: indulgeet R.
₅₁₉ suo sibi $P^2\gamma^1$: tuo sibi M^1.   nomine Mc, Servius: munere $PR\gamma b$.

AENEID BOOK VIII

his palace, cut down his followers, and hurl fire on his roof. He, amid the carnage, flees for refuge to Rutulian soil, and finds shelter among the weapons of Turnus his friend. So all Etruria has risen in righteous fury; with instant war they demand the king for punishment. Of these thousands, Aeneas, I will make thee chief; for their ships throng all the shore clamouring, and they bid the standards advance, but the aged soothsayer restrains them with prophecy of fate: 'O chosen warriors of Maeonia, flower and chivalry of an olden race,—ye, whom just resentment launches against the foe, and Mezentius inflames with righteous wrath, no man of Italy may sway a race so proud: choose ye stranger leaders!' At that the Etruscan lines settled down on yonder plain, awed by Heaven's warning; Tarchon himself has sent me envoys with the royal crown and sceptre, and offers the ensigns of power, bidding me join the camp and mount the Tyrrhene throne. But the frost of sluggish eld, outworn with years, and strength too sere for deeds of valour, begrudge me the command. My son would I urge thereto, were it not that, of mingled blood by Sabine mother, he drew from her a share in his fatherland. Thou, to whose years and race Fate is kind, whom Heaven calls, take up thy task, most valiant leader of Trojans and Italians both. Nay more, I will join with thee Pallas here, our hope and comfort; under thy guidance let him learn to endure warfare and the stern work of battle; let him behold thy deeds, and revere thee from his early years. To him will I give two hundred Arcadian horse, choice flower of our manhood, and in his own name Pallas will give thee as many more."

⁵²⁰ Scarce had he ended; and Aeneas son of Anchises and faithful Achates, holding their eyes

VIRGIL

multaque dura suo tristi cum corde putabant,
ni signum caelo Cytherea dedisset aperto.
namque improviso vibratus ab aethere fulgor
cum sonitu venit et ruere omnia visa repente   525
Tyrrhenusque tubae mugire per aethera clangor.
suspiciunt: iterum atque iterum fragor increpat ingens;
arma inter nubem caeli in regione serena
per sudum rutilare vident et pulsa tonare.
obstipuere animis alii, sed Troius heros   530
adgnovit sonitum et divae promissa parentis.
tum memorat, "ne vero, hospes, ne quaere profecto,
quem casum portenta ferant: ego poscor Olympo;
hoc signum cecinit missuram diva creatrix,
si bellum ingrueret, Volcaniaque arma per auras   535
laturam auxilio.
heu quantae miseris caedes Laurentibus instant!
quas poenas mihi, Turne, dabis! quam multa sub undas
scuta virum galeasque et fortia corpora volves,
Thybri pater! poscant acies et foedera rumpant."   540

Haec ubi dicta dedit, solio se tollit ab alto
et primum Herculeis sopitas ignibus aras
excitat hesternumque Larem parvosque Penates
laetus adit; mactant lectas de more bidentis
Euandrus pariter, pariter Troiana iuventus.   545
post hinc ad navis graditur sociosque revisit:
quorum de numero, qui sese in bella sequantur,
praestantis virtute legit; pars cetera prona
fertur aqua segnisque secundo defluit amni,
nuntia ventura Ascanio rerumque patrisque.   550

⁵²⁷ intonat *Servius*.   ⁵²⁸ in *omitted* M¹.   ⁵²⁹ sonare PRγ¹.

AENEID BOOK VIII

downcast, would long have mused on many a peril in their own sad hearts, had not Cythera's queen granted a sign from the cloudless sky. For unforeseen, comes quivering from heaven a flash with thunder, and all seemed in a moment to reel, while the Tyrrhenian trumpet-blast pealed through the sky. They glance up; again and yet again crashed the mighty roar. In the serene expanse of heaven they see arms, amid the clouds, gleaming red in the clear air, and clashing in thunder. The rest stood aghast; but the Trojan hero knew the sound and the promise of his goddess mother. Then he cries: "Ask not, my friend, ask not, I pray, what fortune the portents bode; 'tis I who am summoned of Heaven. This sign the goddess who bore me foretold she would send, if war was at hand, and to my succour would bring through the air arms wrought by Vulcan. Alas, what carnage awaits the hapless Laurentines! What a price, Turnus, shalt thou pay me! How many shields and helms and bodies of the brave, shalt thou, O father Tiber, sweep beneath thy waves! Let them call for battle and break their covenants!"

541 These words said, he rose from his lofty throne, and first quickens the slumbering altars with fire to Hercules, and gladly draws nigh to the Lar of yesterday [1] and the lowly household gods. Alike Evander and alike the warriors of Troy, offer up ewes duly chosen. Next he fares to the ships and revisits his men, of whose number he chooses the foremost in valour to attend him to war; the rest glide down the stream and idly float with the favouring current, to bear news to Ascanius of his father and his fortunes.

[1] We are to assume that, on the day of his arrival, Aeneas had offered sacrifice to the Lar, or tutelary spirit, of the dwelling whose hospitality he enjoyed.

VIRGIL

dantur equi Teucris Tyrrhena petentibus arva;
ducunt exortem Aeneae, quem fulva leonis
pellis obit totum, praefulgens unguibus aureis.

Fama volat parvam subito volgata per urbem,
ocius ire equites Tyrrheni ad litora regis. 555
vota metu duplicant matres, propiusque periclo
it timor et maior Martis iam apparet imago.
tum pater Euandrus dextram complexus euntis
haeret, inexpletus lacrimans, ac talia fatur:
"o mihi praeteritos referat si Iuppiter annos, 560
qualis eram, cum primam aciem Praeneste sub ipsa
stravi scutorumque incendi victor acervos
et regem hac Erulum dextra sub Tartara misi,
nascenti cui tris animas Feronia mater
(horrendum dictu) dederat, terna arma movenda 565
(ter leto sternendus erat; cui tum tamen omnis
abstulit haec animas dextra et totidem exuit armis):
non ego nunc dulci amplexu divellerer usquam,
nate, tuo, neque finitimo Mezentius umquam
huic capiti insultans tot ferro saeva dedisset 570
funera, tam multis viduasset civibus urbem.
at vos, o superi, et divum tu maxime rector
Iuppiter, Arcadii, quaeso, miserescite regis
et patrias audite preces: si numina vestra
incolumem Pallanta mihi, si fata reservant, 575
si visurus eum vivo et venturus in unum,
vitam oro; patior quemvis durare laborem.
sin aliquem infandum casum, Fortuna, minaris,
nunc, nunc o liceat crudelem abrumpere vitam,
dum curae ambiguae, dum spes incerta futuri, 580

---

⁵⁵⁵ Tyrrhena *Pγ¹*. limina *Pγ¹*. ⁵⁵⁶ proprius *PR*.
⁵⁵⁹ inexpletum *P¹, preferred by Servius*. lacrimis *M, known to Servius*. ⁵⁶⁶ tunc *MPRγc*: tum *b*.
⁵⁶⁹ finitimos *P¹*. usquam *PRγ¹*. ⁵⁷¹ munera *P¹*.
⁵⁷⁶ vivum *R*. ⁵⁷⁷ patiar *P²γ*. ⁵⁷⁹ nunc o nunc *R*.

AENEID BOOK VIII

Horses are given to the Teucrians who seek the Tyrrhene fields; for Aeneas they lead forth a chosen steed, all caparisoned in a tawny lion's skin, glittering with claws of gold.

⁵⁵⁴ Suddenly, spreading through the little town, flies a rumour, that horsemen are speeding to the shores of the Tyrrhene king. In alarm mothers redouble their vows; more close on peril treads fear, and the image of the War-god now looms larger. Then Evander, clasping the hand of his departing son, clings to him insatiate in tears and thus speaks: "O if Jupiter would bring me back the years that are sped, and make me what I was when under Praeneste's very walls I struck down the foremost ranks, burned the up-piled shields, victorious, and with this right hand sent down to Tartarus King Erulus, whom at his birth his mother Feronia had given (awful to tell!) three lives with threefold armour to wear—thrice had he to be laid low in death; yet on that day this hand bereft him of all his lives and as often stripped him of his armour—then never should I now be torn, my son, from thy sweet embrace. Never on this his neighbour's head would Mezentius have heaped scorn, dealt with the sword so many cruel deaths, nor widowed the city of so many of her sons! But ye, O powers above, and thou, O Jupiter, mighty ruler of the gods, pity, I pray, the Arcadian king, and hear a father's prayer. If your will, if destiny keep my Pallas safe, if I live still to see him, still to meet him, for life I pray; any toil soever have I patience to endure. But if, O Fortune, thou threatenest some dread mischance, now, oh, now may I break the thread of cruel life, —while fears are doubtful, while hope reads not the

99

VIRGIL

dum te, care puer, mea sera et sola voluptas,
complexu teneo, gravior neu nuntius auris
volneret." haec genitor digressu dicta supremo
fundebat; famuli conlapsum in tecta ferebant.

Iamque adeo exierat portis equitatus apertis,   585
Aeneas inter primos et fidus Achates,
inde alii Troiae proceres, ipse agmine Pallas
in medio, chlamyde et pictis conspectus in armis,
qualis ubi Oceani perfusus Lucifer unda,
quem Venus ante alios astrorum diligit ignis,   590
extulit os sacrum caelo tenebrasque resolvit.
stant pavidae in muris matres oculisque sequuntur
pulveream nubem et fulgentis aere catervas.
olli per dumos, qua proxima meta viarum,
armati tendunt; it clamor, et agmine facto   595
quadrupedante putrem sonitu quatit ungula campum.

Est ingens gelidum lucus prope Caeritis amnem,
religione patrum late sacer; undique colles
inclusere cavi et nigra nemus abiete cingunt.
Silvano fama est veteres sacrasse Pelasgos,   600
arvorum pecorisque deo, lucumque diemque,
qui primi finis aliquando habuere Latinos.
haud procul hinc Tarcho et Tyrrheni tuta tenebant
castra locis, celsoque omnis de colle videri
iam poterat legio et latis tendebat in arvis.   605
huc pater Aeneas et bello lecta iuventus
succedunt, fessique et equos et corpora curant.

At Venus aetherios inter dea candida nimbos
dona ferens aderat; natumque in valle reducta
ut procul egelido secretum flumine vidit,   610

[581] sola et sera *MR*.   [582] complexus M^2R.   ne $P^2\gamma^1$.
[583] dicta] maesta M^1.   [610] et gelido $M^2PR\gamma$.

AENEID BOOK VIII

future, while thou, beloved boy, my late and lone delight, art held in my embrace; and may no heavier tidings wound mine ear!" These words the father poured forth at their last parting; his servants bore him swooning within the palace.

585 And now the horsemen had issued from the open gates, Aeneas at their head with loyal Achates, then other princes of Troy; Pallas himself at the column's centre, conspicuous in scarf and blazoned armour—even as the Morning Star, whom Venus loves above all the stellar fires, when, bathed in Ocean's wave, he uplifts in heaven his sacred head and melts the darkness. On the walls mothers stand trembling, and follow with their eyes the dusty cloud and the squadrons gleaming with brass. They through the brushwood, where the journey's goal is nearest, fare in their armour; a shout mounts up, they form in column, and with galloping tramp the horse-hoof shakes the crumbling plain.

597 Near Caere's cold stream there stands a vast grove, widely revered with ancestral awe; on all sides curving hills enclose it, and girdle the woodland with dark fir-trees. Rumour tells that the old Pelasgians who first, in time gone by, held the Latin borders, dedicated both grove and festal day to Silvanus, god of fields and flock. Not far from thence Tarchon and the Tyrrhenians camped in a sheltered spot, and now from a high hill all the host could be seen, their tents pitched in the wide fields. Hither come father Aeneas and the warriors chosen for battle, and refresh their steeds and wearied frames.

608 But Venus, lovely goddess, drew nigh, bearing her gifts amid the clouds of heaven; and when afar she saw her son apart in a secluded vale by the cool

VIRGIL

talibus adfata est dictis seque obtulit ultro:
" en perfecta mei promissa coniugis arte
munera, ne mox aut Laurentis, nate, superbos,
aut acrem dubites in proelia poscere Turnum."
dixit et amplexus nati Cytherea petivit, 615
arma sub adversa posuit radiantia quercu.
ille, deae donis et tanto laetus honore,
expleri nequit atque oculos per singula volvit,
miraturque interque manus et bracchia versat
terribilem cristis galeam flammasque vomentem, 620
fatiferumque ensem, loricam ex aere rigentem,
sanguineam, ingentem, qualis cum caerula nubes
solis inardescit radiis longeque refulget;
tum levis ocreas electro auroque recocto,
hastamque et clipei non enarrabile textum. 625
 Illic res Italas Romanorumque triumphos
haud vatum ignarus venturique inscius aevi
fecerat Ignipotens, illic genus omne futurae
stirpis ab Ascanio pugnataque in ordine bella.
fecerat et viridi fetam Mavortis in antro 630
procubuisse lupam, geminos huic ubera circum
ludere pendentis pueros et lambere matrem
impavidos, illam tereti cervice reflexa
mulcere alternos et corpora fingere lingua.
nec procul hinc Romam et raptas sine more Sabinas 635
consessu caveae, magnis Circensibus actis,
addiderat, subitoque novum consurgere bellum
Romulidis Tatioque seni Curibusque severis.
post idem inter se posito certamine reges
armati Iovis ante aram paterasque tenentes 640
stabant et caesa iungebant foedera porca.
haud procul inde citae Mettum in diversa quadrigae

---

⁶²⁰ minantem $P\gamma^1$.   ⁶²⁸ omnipotens M.
⁶³³ reflexam M^1.   ⁶⁴⁰ aras R.   pateram M.

AENEID BOOK VIII

stream, she thus addressed him, of free will presenting herself to view; "Lo! the presents perfected by my lord's promised skill! so that thou mayest not shrink, my child, from challenging anon the haughty Laurentines or brave Turnus to battle." Cytherea spake, and sought her son's embrace, and set up the arms all radiant under an oak before him. He, rejoicing in the divine gift and in honour thus signal, cannot be sated, as he rolls his eyes from piece to piece, admiring and turning over in his hands and arms the helmet, terrific with plumes and spouting flames, the death-dealing sword, the stiff brazen corslet, blood-red and huge,—even as when a dark-blue cloud kindles with the sun's rays and gleams afar; then the smooth greaves of electrum and refined gold, the spear, and the shield's ineffable fabric.

[626] There the story of Italy and the triumphs of Rome had the Lord of Fire fashioned, not unversed in prophecy, or unknowing of the age to come; there, every generation of the stock to spring from Ascanius, and the wars they fought one by one. He had fashioned, too, the mother-wolf outstretched in the green cave of Mars; around her teats the twin boys hung playing, and mouthed their dam without fear; she, with shapely neck bent back, fondled them by turns, and moulded their limbs with her tongue. Not far from this he had set Rome and the Sabines, lawlessly carried off, what time the great Circus-games were held, from the theatre's seated throng; then the sudden uprising of a fresh war between the sons of Romulus and aged Tatius and his stern Cures. Next, the self-same kings, their strife laid at rest, stood armed before Jove's altar, cup in hand, and each with each made covenant o'er sacrifice of swine. Not far thence, four-horse cars, driven apart, had torn Mettus

VIRGIL

distulerant (at tu dictis, Albane, maneres!)
raptabatque viri mendacis viscera Tullus
per silvam, et sparsi rorabant sanguine vepres.   645
nec non Tarquinium eiectum Porsenna iubebat
accipere ingentique urbem obsidione premebat;
Aeneadae in ferrum pro libertate ruebant.
illum indignanti similem similemque minanti
aspiceres, pontem auderet quia vellere Cocles   650
et fluvium vinclis innaret Cloelia ruptis.

In summo custos Tarpeiae Manlius arcis
stabat pro templo et Capitolia celsa tenebat,
Romuleoque recens horrebat regia culmo.
atque hic auratis volitans argenteus anser   655
porticibus Gallos in limine adesse canebat;
Galli per dumos aderant arcemque tenebant.
defensi tenebris et dono noctis opacae:
aurea caesaries ollis atque aurea vestis,
virgatis lucent sagulis, tum lactea colla   660
auro innectuntur, duo quisque Alpina coruscant
gaesa manu, scutis protecti corpora longis.
hic exsultantis Salios nudosque Lupercos
lanigerosque apices et lapsa ancilia caelo
extuderat, castae ducebant sacra per urbem   665
pilentis matres in mollibus. hinc procul addit
Tartareas etiam sedes, alta ostia Ditis,
et scelerum poenas, et te, Catilina, minaci
pendentem scopulo Furiarumque ora trementem;

⁶⁴³ dispulerant *M²*.   ⁶⁵⁷ Galli] olli *R*.
⁶⁶⁰ tunc *Pγ*.   ⁶⁶¹ coruscat *Pγ¹*.

---

¹ In the imperial city there was a "house of Romulus," with thatched roof, on both the Capitol and the Palatine.

104

AENEID BOOK VIII

asunder (but thou, O Alban, shouldst have stood by thy words!), and Tullus dragged through the woods the liar's limbs, and the brambles dripped with dew of blood. There, too, was Porsenna, bidding them admit the banished Tarquin, and hemming the city with mighty siege: the sons of Aeneas rushed on the sword for freedom's sake. Him thou mightest have seen like one in wrath, like one who threats, for that Cocles dared to tear down the bridge, and Cloelia broke her bonds and swam the river.

652 At the top, Manlius, warder of the Tarpeian fort, stood before the temple, and held the lofty Capitol; the palace was rough, fresh with the thatch of Romulus.[1] And here the silver goose,[2] fluttering through gilded colonnades, cried that the Gauls were on the threshold. The Gauls were near amid the thickets, laying hold of the fort, shielded by darkness, and the boon of shadowy night. Golden are their locks and golden their raiment; they glitter in striped cloaks, and their milk-white necks are entwined with gold; two Alpine pikes each brandishes in hand, and long shields guard their limbs. Here he had wrought the dancing Salii and naked Luperci, the crests bound with wool, and the shields that fell from heaven; and in cushioned cars chaste matrons moved through the city in solemn progress.[3] Away from these he adds also the abodes of Hell, the high gates of Dis, the penalties of sin, and thee, Catiline, hanging on a frowning cliff, and trembling at the

[2] In 390 B.C., when the Gauls attacked the Capitol, they were driven back by Manlius, who had been roused from sleep by cackling geese.

[3] Roman matrons were allowed to ride at sacred processions in *pilenta*, because of their self-sacrifice after the capture of Veii, 395 B.C.

VIRGIL

secretosque pios, his dantem iura Catonem.   670
haec inter tumidi late maris ibat imago,
aurea, sed fluctu spumabat caerula cano,
et circum argento clari delphines in orbem
aequora verrebant caudis aestumque secabant.
in medio classis aeratas, Actia bella,   675
cernere erat, totumque instructo Marte videres
fervere Leucaten auroque effulgere fluctus.
hinc Augustus agens Italos in proelia Caesar
cum patribus populoque, Penatibus et magnis dis,
stans celsa in puppi, geminas cui tempora flammas   680
laeta vomunt patriumque aperitur vertice sidus.
parte alia ventis et dis Agrippa secundis
arduus agmen agens; cui, belli insigne superbum,
tempora navali fulgent rostrata corona.
hinc ope barbarica variisque Antonius armis,   685
victor ab Aurorae populis et litore rubro,
Aegyptum viresque Orientis et ultima secum
Bactra vehit, sequiturque (nefas) Aegyptia coniunx.
una omnes ruere ac totum spumare reductis
convolsum remis rostrisque tridentibus aequor.   690
alta petunt; pelago credas innare revolsas
Cycladas aut montis concurrere montibus altos:
tanta mole viri turritis puppibus instant.
stuppea flamma manu telisque volatile ferrum

⁶⁷² spumabant *minor MSS*.   ⁶⁸⁰ stat *R*. cui] huic *P²γ*.
⁶⁸⁶ Aurorae] Europae *R*.   ⁶⁹² altis *known to Servius*.
⁶⁹⁴ telique *R*.

---

[1] cf. *Aen*. III. 12, with note.
[2] See note on *Eclogues*, IX. 47.
[3] The *corona navalis*, a crown adorned with ships' beaks, was a very special distinction that was won by Agrippa.

AENEID BOOK VIII

faces of the Furies; far apart, the good, and Cato giving them laws. Amidst these scenes flowed wide the likeness of the swelling sea, all gold, but the blue water foamed with white billows, and round about dolphins, shining in silver, swept the seas with their tails in circles, and cleft the tide. In the centre could be seen brazen ships with Actium's battle; one might see all Leucate aglow with War's array, and the waves ablaze with gold. Here Augustus Caesar, leading Italians to strife, with peers and people, and the great gods of the Penates,[1] stands on the lofty stern; his joyous brows pour forth a double flame, and on his head dawns his father's star.[2] Elsewhere Agrippa with favouring winds and gods, high-towering, leads his column; his brows gleam with the beaks of the naval crown,[3] proud device of war. Here Antonius with barbaric might and varied arms, victor from the nations of the dawn and from the ruddy sea,[4] brings with him Egypt and the strength of the East and utmost Bactra; and there follows him (O shame!) his Egyptian wife. All rush on at once, and the whole sea foams, uptorn by the sweeping oars, and triple-pointed beaks. To the deep they speed; thou wouldst deem the Cyclades, uprooted, were floating on the main, or that mountains high clashed with mountains: in such mighty ships the seamen assail the towered sterns.[5] Flaming tow and shafts of winged steel are showered from their hands;

---

[4] This is the *mare Erythraeum*, or Indian Ocean, not the Red Sea, as we know it.

[5] Conington takes *mole* in the sense of *molimine*, "with giant effort." Benoist refers *tanta mole* to the huge ships of Antony, while the *turritae puppes* are the ships of Octavius, which Agrippa, as Servius tells us, armed with towers. This seems the most plausible solution of a much debated passage.

107

VIRGIL

spargitur, arva nova Neptunia caede rubescunt.   695
regina in mediis patrio vocat agmina sistro,
necdum etiam geminos a tergo respicit anguis.
omnigenumque deum monstra et latrator Anubis
contra Neptunum et Venerem contraque Minervam
tela tenent. saevit medio in certamine Mavors   700
caelatus ferro, tristesque ex aethere Dirae,
et scissa gaudens vadit Discordia palla,
quam cum sanguineo sequitur Bellona flagello.
Actius haec cernens arcum intendebat Apollo
desuper: omnis eo terrore Aegyptus et Indi,   705
omnis Arabs, omnes vertebant terga Sabaei.
ipsa videbatur ventis regina vocatis
vela dare et laxos iam iamque immittere funis.
illam inter caedes pallentem morte futura
fecerat Ignipotens undis et Iapyge ferri,   710
contra autem magno maerentem corpore Nilum
pandentemque sinus et tota veste vocantem
caeruleum in gremium latebrosaque flumina victos.
at Caesar, triplici invectus Romana triumpho
moenia, dis Italis votum immortale sacrabat,   715
maxima ter centum totam delubra per urbem.
laetitia ludisque viae plausuque fremebant;
omnibus in templis matrum chorus, omnibus arae;
ante aras terram caesi stravere iuvenci.
ipse, sedens niveo candentis limine Phoebi,   720
dona recognoscit populorum aptatque superbis
postibus; incedunt victae longo ordine gentes,

---

⁶⁹⁸ nigenumque *M*¹, hence Niligenumque *Lachmann, and* amnigenumque *Hoffmann*.   ⁷⁰⁰ tenens *Pγ*¹.
⁷⁰¹ divae *M*²*R*.   ⁷⁰⁴ tendebat *Pγ*.
⁷¹⁹ iuvencis *M*¹*γ*¹.   ⁷²² gentes] matres *R*.

---

¹ The twin snakes are a symbol of death. *cf. Aen.* II. 203, VII. 450, VIII. 289.

AENEID BOOK VIII

Neptune's fields redden with strange slaughter. In the midst the queen calls upon her hosts with their native cymbal, nor as yet casts back a glance at the twin snakes behind.[1] Monstrous gods of every form and barking Anubis wield weapons against Neptune and Venus and against Minerva. In the midst of the fray storms Mavors, embossed in steel, with the fell Furies from on high; and in rent robe Discord strides exultant, while Bellona follows her with bloody scourge. Actian Apollo saw the sight, and from above was bending his bow; at that terror all Egypt and India, all Arabians, all Sabaeans, turned to flee. The queen herself was seen to woo the winds, spread sail, and now, even now, fling loose the slackened sheets. Her, amid the carnage, the Lord of Fire had fashioned pale at the coming of death, borne on by waves and the wind of Iapyx; while over against her was the mourning Nile, of mighty frame, opening wide his folds and with all his raiment welcoming the vanquished to his azure lap and sheltering streams.[2] But Caesar, entering the walls of Rome in triple triumph,[3] was dedicating to Italy's gods his immortal votive gift—three hundred mighty fanes throughout the city. The streets rang with gladness and games and shouting; in all the temples was a band of matrons, in all were altars, and before the altars slain steers strewed the ground. Himself, seated at the snowy threshold of shining Phoebus, reviews the gifts of nations and hangs them on the proud portals. The conquered peoples move in long

[2] The Nile-god "would be represented with a water-coloured robe, the bosom of which he would throw open" (Conington).

[3] In August, 29 B.C., Augustus celebrated a triple triumph for victories in Dalmatia, at Actium, and at Alexandria.

109

VIRGIL

quam variae linguis, habitu tam vestis et armis.
hic Nomadum genus et discinctos Mulciber Afros,
hic Lelegas Carasque sagittiferosque Gelonos   725
finxerat; Euphrates ibat iam mollior undis,
extremique hominum Morini, Rhenusque bicornis,
indomitique Dahae, et pontem indignatus Araxes.
  Talia per clipeum Volcani, dona parentis,
miratur rerumque ignarus imagine gaudet,   730
attollens umero famamque et fata nepotum.

₇₂₄ hinc *P*γ.   ₇₂₅ hinc Pγ.
₇₂₆ tinxerat *R*.   ₇₃₁ fata] facta *c, Servius.*

AENEID BOOK VIII

array, as diverse in fashion of dress and arms as in tongues. Here Mulciber had portrayed the Nomad race and the ungirt Africans, here the Leleges and Carians and quivered Gelonians. Euphrates moved now with humbler waves, and the Morini were there, furthest of mankind and the Rhine of double horn,[1] the untamed Dahae, and Araxes chafing at his bridge.[2]

⁷²⁹ Such sights he admires on the shield of Vulcan, his mother's gift, and, though he knows not the deeds, he rejoices in their portraiture, uplifting on his shoulder the fame and fortunes of his children's children.

---

[1] *cf.* 77 above, and see note 2 on *Georg.* IV. 372. Here there may be a reference to the two mouths, the Rhine and the Waal.

[2] A bridge over the Araxes, built by Alexander the Great, but later swept away by a flood, was replaced by Augustus.

LIBER IX

ATQUE ea diversa penitus dum parte geruntur,   MPR
Irim de caelo misit Saturnia Iuno
audacem ad Turnum.   luco tum forte parentis
Pilumni Turnus sacrata valle sedebat.
ad quem sic roseo Thaumantias ore locuta est: 5
"Turne, quod optanti divum promittere nemo
auderet, volvenda dies en attulit ultro.
Aeneas urbe et sociis et classe relicta
sceptra Palatini sedemque petit Euandri.
nec satis: extremas Corythi penetravit ad urbes   10
Lydorumque manum collectos armat agrestis.
quid dubitas? nunc tempus equos, nunc poscere currus.
rumpe moras omnis et turbata arripe castra."
dixit et in caelum paribus se sustulit alis
ingentemque fuga secuit sub nubibus arcum.   15
adgnovit iuvenis duplicisque ad sidera palmas
sustulit ac tali fugientem est voce secutus:
"Iri, decus caeli, quis te mihi nubibus actam
detulit in terras? unde haec tam clara repente
tempestas? medium video discedere caelum   20
palantisque polo stellas. sequor omina tanta,

¹¹ manus $P\gamma^1$. et collectos γ^1.   ¹⁷ et MR.   ²¹ sequar M.

---

[1] Corythus had founded Cortona, the principal Etruscan city.

BOOK IX

AND while in the far distance such deeds befell, Saturnian Juno sent Iris from heaven to gallant Turnus, who as it chanced was then seated within a hallowed vale, in the grove of his sire Pilumnus. To him, with roseate lips, thus spake the child of Thaumas:

⁶ "Turnus, that which no god had dared to promise to thy prayers, lo, the circling hour has brought unasked! Aeneas, leaving town, comrades, and fleet, seeks the Palatine realm, and Evander's dwelling. Nor does that suffice; he has won his way to Corythus' utmost cities,[1] and is mustering in armed bands the Lydian country-folk. Why hesitate? Now, now is the hour to call for steed and car; break off delay, and seize the bewildered camp!" She spake, and on poised wings rose into the sky, cleaving in flight her mighty bow beneath the clouds.[2] The youth knew her, and, raising his two upturned hands to heaven, with such words pursued her flight: "Iris, glory of the sky, who has brought thee down to me, wafted upon the clouds to earth? Whence this sudden brightness of the air? I see the heavens part asunder, and the stars that roam in the firmament.[3] I follow the mighty omen, whoso thou art

[2] *cf. Aen.* v. 657-8.
[3] The mist veiling the heavens is rent asunder, revealing the stars beyond.

113

VIRGIL

quisquis in arma vocas." et sic effatus ad undam
processit summoque hausit de gurgite lymphas,
multa deos orans, oneravitque aethera votis.
Iamque omnis campis exercitus ibat apertis, 25
dives equum, dives pictaï vestis et auri
(Messapus primas acies, postrema coercent
Tyrrhidae iuvenes, medio dux agmine Turnus), 28
ceu septem surgens sedatis amnibus altus 30
per tacitum Ganges aut pingui flumine Nilus
cum refluit campis et iam se condidit alveo.
hic subitam nigro glomerari pulvere nubem FMPR
prospiciunt Teucri ac tenebras insurgere campis.
primus ab adversa conclamat mole Caicus: 35
"quis globus, o cives, caligine volvitur atra?
ferte citi ferrum, date tela, ascendite muros,
hostis adest, heia!" ingenti clamore per omnis
condunt se Teucri portas et moenia complent.
namque ita discedens praeceperat optimus armis 40
Aeneas, si qua interea fortuna fuisset,
neu struere auderent aciem neu credere campo;
castra modo et tutos servarent aggere muros.
ergo etsi conferre manum pudor iraque monstrat,
obiciunt portas tamen et praecepta facessunt, 45
armatique cavis exspectant turribus hostem.
Turnus, ut ante volans tardum praecesserat agmen,
viginti lectis equitum comitatus, et urbi
improvisus adest: maculis quem Thracius albis
portat equus cristaque tegit galea aurea rubra. 50
"ecquis erit, mecum, iuvenes, qui primus in hostem?
en"—ait et iaculum attorquens emittit in auras,

²² et *omitted* P². ²⁵ omnis] adeo M¹².
²⁹ vertitur arma tenens et toto vertice supra est. *This verse, given by inferior MSS., is taken from* VII. 784.
³³ magno Pγ¹. ³⁷ scandite M¹: et scandite FR.
⁴² acies R. ⁴⁴ furor *Nonius.* monstrant F.
⁵² intorquens M.

114

AENEID BOOK IX

that callest to arms!" And with these words he went onward to the river, and took up water from the brimming flood, calling oft on the gods and burdening heaven with vows.

²⁵ And now all the army was advancing on the open plain, rich in horses, rich in broidered robes and gold —Messapus marshalling the van, the sons of Tyrrhus the rear, and Turnus their captain in the centre of the line:—even as Ganges, rising high in silence with his seven peaceful streams, or Nile, when his rich flood ebbs from the fields, and at length he is sunk into his channel. Here the Teucrians descry a sudden cloud gathering in black dust, and darkness rising on the plains. First cries Caïcus from the rampart's front: "What mass, my countrymen, rolls onward in murky gloom? Quick with the sword! Serve weapons, climb the walls! The enemy is upon us, ho!" With mighty clamour the Teucrians seek shelter through all the gates and man the ramparts. For so at his departure, Aeneas, best of warriors, had charged; were aught to chance meanwhile, they should not dare to array their line or trust the field; let them but guard camp and walls, secure behind their mound. Therefore, though shame and wrath prompt to conflict, yet they bar the gates and do his bidding, awaiting the foe under arms and within covert of the towers. Turnus, as he had flown forward in advance of his tardy column, with a following of twenty chosen horse comes upon the city unobserved: a Thracian steed, spotted with white, bears the prince, and a golden helm with crimson crest guards his head. "Gallants, is there one, who with me will be first against the foe to—lo!" he cries, and whirling a javelin sends it skyward—the pre-

VIRGIL

principium pugnae, et campo sese arduus infert.
clamorem excipiunt socii fremituque sequuntur
horrisono; Teucrum mirantur inertia corda, 55
non aequo dare se campo, non obvia ferre
arma viros, sed castra fovere. huc turbidus atque huc
lustrat equo muros aditumque per avia quaerit
ac veluti pleno lupus insidiatus ovili
cum fremit ad caulas, ventos perpessus et imbris, 60
nocte super media; tuti sub matribus agni
balatum exercent; ille asper et improbus ira
saevit in absentis; collecta fatigat edendi
ex longo rabies et siccae sanguine fauces:
haud aliter Rutulo muros et castra tuenti 65
ignescunt irae, duris dolor ossibus ardet.
qua temptet ratione aditus, et quae via clausos
excutiat Teucros vallo atque effundat in aequum?
classem, quae lateri castrorum adiuncta latebat, MPR
aggeribus saeptam circum et fluvialibus undis, 70
invadit sociosque incendia poscit ovantis
atque manum pinu flagranti fervidus implet.
tum vero incumbunt (urget praesentia Turni)
atque omnis facibus pubes accingitur atris.
diripuere focos; piceum fert fumida lumen 75
taeda et commixtam Volcanus ad astra favillam.

Quis deus, o Musae, tam saeva incendia Teucris
avertit? tantos ratibus quis depulit ignis?
dicite. prisca fides facto, sed fama perennis.
tempore quo primum Phrygia formabat in Ida 80
Aeneas classem et pelagi petere alta parabat,
ipsa deum fertur genetrix Berecyntia magnum

[53] campis *R*. [54] clamore *FR*γ[2], *known to Servius*.
[66] durus *P*γ[1]. *After* ardet *Conington and most earlier editors place a comma*.
[67] qua via *FMP*[2]γ, *Servius:* quae via *P*[1]*R, known to Servius*.
[68] aequor *P*[1]*F*[2].   [77] qui *P*γ[1].
[79] sed] sit *R*.   [82] genetrix fertur *R*.

116

AENEID BOOK IX

lude of battle—and advances proudly o'er the plain. His comrades take up the shout, and follow with dreadful din; they marvel at the Teucrians' craven hearts, crying: "They trust not themselves to a fair field, they face not the foe in arms, but they hug the camp." Hither and thither he rides wildly round the walls, seeking entrance where way is none. And as when a wolf, lying in wait about a crowded fold, roars beside the pens at midnight, enduring winds and rains; safe beneath their mothers the lambs keep bleating; he, fierce and reckless in his wrath, rages against the prey beyond his reach, tormented by the long-gathering fury of famine, and by his dry, bloodless jaws:—even so, as he scans wall and camp, the Rutulian's wrath is aflame; resentment is hot within his iron bones. By what device shall he essay entrance? By what path hurl the prisoned Teucrians from their rampart, and pour them on the plain? Hard by the camp's side lay the fleet, fenced about with mounds and the flowing river; this he assails, calling for fire to his exulting comrades, and with hot haste fills his hand with a blazing pine. Then indeed they fall to, spurred on by Turnus' presence, and all the band armed them with murky torches. Lo! they have stripped the hearths; smoking brands fling a pitchy glare, and the Fire-god wafts to heaven the sooty cloud.

[77] What god, ye Muses, turned such fierce flames from the Teucrians? Who drove away from the ships such vast fires? Tell me; faith in the tale is old, but its fame is everlasting. In the days when on Phrygian Ida, Aeneas was first fashioning his fleet and preparing to sail the deep seas, the very Mother of gods, 'tis said, the Berecyntian queen, thus spake to

VIRGIL

vocibus his adfata Iovem: "da, nate, petenti,
quod tua cara parens domito te poscit Olympo.
pinea silva mihi, multos dilecta per annos,　　　　　85
lucus in arce fuit summa, quo sacra ferebant,
nigranti picea trabibusque obscurus acernis:
has ego Dardanio iuveni, cum classis egeret,
laeta dedi; nunc sollicitam timor anxius angit.
solve metus atque hoc precibus sine posse parentem, 90
ne cursu quassatae ullo neu turbine venti
vincantur; prosit nostris in montibus ortas."

　Filius huic contra, torquet qui sidera mundi:
"o genetrix, quo fata vocas? aut quid petis istis?
mortaline manu factae immortale carinae　　　　　95
fas habeant? certusque incerta pericula lustret
Aeneas? cui tanta deo permissa potestas?
immo ubi defunctae finem portusque tenebunt
Ausonios olim, quaecumque evaserit undis
Dardaniumque ducem Laurentia vexerit arva,　　100
mortalem eripiam formam magnique iubebo
aequoris esse deas, qualis Nereia Doto
et Galatea secant spumantem pectore pontum."
dixerat, idque ratum Stygii per flumina fratris,
per pice torrentis atraque voragine ripas　　　　105
adnuit et totum nutu tremefecit Olympum.

　Ergo aderat promissa dies et tempora Parcae
debita complerant, cum Turni iniuria Matrem
admonuit ratibus sacris depellere taedas.
hic primum nova lux oculis offulsit et ingens　　110

　　　[90] parentum M^1.　　[91] neu MR.　　[103] et]aut R.
　　　[110] effulsit P.

118

AENEID BOOK IX

mighty Jove: "Grant, O son, to my prayer, what thy dear mother asks of thee, now lord of Olympus.[1] A grove I had upon the mountain's crest, whither men brought me offerings,—a pine-forest beloved for many years, dim with dusky firs and trunks of maple. These, when he lacked a fleet, I gave gladly to the Dardan youth; now anxious fear tortures my troubled breast. Relieve my terrors, and let a mother's prayer avail thus much, that they be overcome neither by stress of voyage nor by blast of wind. Be it a boon to them that they grew upon our hills."

[93] To her replied her son, who sways the starry world: "O mother, whither dost thou summon fate? Or what seekest thou for these of thine? Should hulls framed by mortal hand have immortal rights? And should Aeneas in surety traverse unsure perils? To what god is such power allowed? Nay, when, their service done, they one day gain an Ausonian haven, from all that have escaped the waves, and borne the Dardan chief to the fields of Laurentum, will I take away their mortal shape, and bid them be goddesses of the great sea, like unto Doto, Nereus' child, and Galatea, who cleave with their breasts the foaming deep." He said; and by the waters of his Stygian brother, by the banks that seethe with pitch in black swirling abyss, he nodded assent, and with the nod made all Olympus tremble.

[107] So the promised day was come, and the Destinies had fulfilled their appointed times, when Turnus' outrage warned the Mother to ward off the brands from her sacred ships. Then first there flashed upon the eyes a strange light, and from the

---

[1] He therefore has power to grant her petition. Servius says that Cybele appeals to her son's gratitude, because when Cronos wished to devour him, she had saved his life.

VIRGIL

visus ab Aurora caelum transcurrere nimbus
Idaeique chori; tum vox horrenda per auras
excidit et Troum Rutulorumque agmina complet:
"ne trepidate meas, Teucri, defendere navis,
neve armate manus: maria ante exurere Turno 115
quam sacras dabitur pinus. vos ite solutae,
ite deae pelagi; genetrix iubet." et sua quaeque
continuo puppes abrumpunt vincula ripis   FMPR
delphinumque modo demersis aequora rostris
ima petunt. hinc virgineae, mirabile monstrum, 120
reddunt se totidem facies pontoque feruntur. 122

    Obstipuere animi Rutulis, conterritus ipse
turbatis Messapus equis, cunctatur et amnis
rauca sonans revocatque pedem Tiberinus ab alto. 125
at non audaci Turno fiducia cessit;
ultro animos tollit dictis atque increpat ultro:
"Troianos haec monstra petunt, his Iuppiter ipse
auxilium solitum eripuit, non tela neque ignes
exspectant Rutulos. ergo maria invia Teucris 130
nec spes ulla fugae: rerum pars altera adempta est,
terra autem in nostris manibus; tot milia gentes
arma ferunt Italae. nil me fatalia terrent,
si qua Phryges prae se iactant, responsa deorum:
sat fatis Venerique datum est, tetigere quod arva 135
fertilis Ausoniae Troes. sunt et mea contra
fata mihi, ferro sceleratam exscindere gentem,
coniuge praerepta, nec solos tangit Atridas

   [120] monstrum] dictu R.
   [121] quot prius aeratae steterant ad litora prorae. *This verse, given only by inferior MSS., is taken from* x. 223.
   [123] animis Rutuli $FR\gamma^2$.   [124] turbatus P^1R.
   [130] exspectans M^1.   [132] gentis MR.
   [135] est *omitted by* M.

---

   [1] By *Idaei chori* the poet means the attendants upon Cybele; *cf. Aen.* III. 111.

AENEID BOOK IX

Dawn a vast cloud was seen to speed athwart the sky, with Ida's choirs in its train;[1] thereon through the air fell an awful voice, filling the Trojan and Rutulian ranks: "Trouble not, ye Teucrians, to defend my ships, nor take weapons into your hands. Turnus shall have leave to burn up the seas sooner than my sacred pines. Go ye free; go, goddesses of ocean; the Mother bids it." And at once each ship rends her cable from the bank, and like dolphins they dip their beaks and dive to the water's depths; then as maiden forms—O wondrous portent!—they emerge in like number and bear out to sea.

[123] Amazed were the hearts of the Rutulians; Messapus himself was terror-stricken, his steeds affrighted; and the hoarsely murmuring stream is stayed, as Tiberinus turns back his footsteps from the deep. But fearless Turnus lost not heart; nay, he raises their courage with his words—nay, he chides them: "'Tis the Trojans these portents assail; Jupiter himself has bereft them of their wonted succour; they await not Rutulian sword and fire.[2] Thus the seas are pathless for the Teucrians, and hope of flight there is none. One half the world is lost to them, but the earth is in our hands: in such thousands are the nations of Italy under arms. Naught do I dread all the fateful oracles of heaven whereof these Phrygians boast: to Fate and Venus all claims are paid, in that the Trojans have touched our rich Ausonia's fields. I too have my fate to meet theirs—to cut down with the sword a guilty race that has robbed me of my bride! Not the sons of Atreus

---

[2] Their "wonted succour" must be the means of flight, *i.e.* the ships, which the gods have taken away, thus forestalling the Rutuli, who would otherwise have destroyed them with fire and sword.

VIRGIL

iste dolor solisque licet capere arma Mycenis.
'sed periisse semel satis est': peccare fuisset   140
ante satis, penitus modo non genus omne perosos
femineum: quibus haec medii fiducia valli
fossarumque morae, leti discrimina parva,
dant animos.   at non viderunt moenia Troiae
Neptuni fabricata manu considere in ignis?   145
sed vos, o lecti, ferro quis scindere vallum
apparat et mecum invadit trepidantia castra?
non armis mihi Volcani, non mille carinis
est opus in Teucros.   addant se protinus omnes
Etrusci socios.   tenebras et inertia furta   150
Palladii, caesis summae custodibus arcis,
ne timeant, nec equi caeca condemur in alvo:
luce palam certum est igni circumdare muros.
haud sibi cum Danais rem faxo et pube Pelasga
esse ferant, decimum quos distulit Hector in annum.
nunc adeo, melior quoniam pars acta diei,   156
quod superest, laeti bene gestis corpora rebus
procurate, viri, et pugnam sperate parari."

Interea vigilum excubiis obsidere portas
cura datur Messapo et moenia cingere flammis.   160
bis septem Rutuli, muros qui milite servent,
delecti; ast illos centeni quemque sequuntur
purpurei cristis iuvenes auroque corusci.

¹⁴⁰ sed] si γ^2.
¹⁴¹ non modo R: modo nec *some old MSS.* of Pierius: modo nunc *Venice edition of* 1472.   perosos $F^2M^2\gamma^1$: perosum γ^2.
¹⁴³ discrimine $F^1M\gamma$.   parvo $F^2MP^2R\gamma$: parvas P^1.
¹⁴⁶ quis] qui *MSS.*
¹⁵¹ *Found in all good MSS., but generally rejected.* cf. II. 166.   summae] late F^1R.   ¹⁵⁵ ferant] putent $MR\gamma^2$.
¹⁵⁶ diei est M^2R.   ¹⁶⁰ flamma FR.
¹⁶¹ Rutulo M^1.   ¹⁶² secuti R.

AENEID BOOK IX

alone are touched by that pang, nor has Mycenae alone the right to take up arms. 'But to have perished once is enough!' Nay, to have sinned once had been enough, so that henceforth they should loathe utterly well-nigh all womankind—these men to whom this trust in a sundering rampart, these delaying dykes—slight barriers against death—afford courage![1] Yet have they not seen Troy's battlements, the work of Neptune's hand, sink in flames? But ye, my chosen, who of you makes ready, at the sword's point, to hew down the rampart and rush with me on their bewildered camp? I need not the arms of Vulcan nor a thousand ships, to meet the Trojans. Let all Etruria join them forthwith in alliance. Darkness and cowardly theft of their Palladium,[2] with slaughter of guards on the citadel-height, let them not fear; nor shall we lurk in a horse's dusky womb! In broad day, in the sight of all, I mean to gird their walls with fire. I will make them nowise think they have to do with Danaans and Pelasgic chivalry, whom Hector kept at bay till the tenth year. Now, since the fairer part of the day is spent, for what remains, gallants, joyfully refresh yourselves after your good service, and be assured that we are preparing for the fray."

[159] Meanwhile charge is given to Messapus to blockade the gates with posted sentries, and to encircle the battlements with fires. Twice seven Rutulians are chosen to guard the walls with soldiers, but on each attend an hundred men, purple-plumed

---

[1] The argument is this: one would have expected them to be haters of women, rather than commit a second offence like that of abducting Helen, especially as they are cowards who refuse to face a fight.

[2] *cf. Aen.* II 166.

VIRGIL

discurrunt variantque vices fusique per herbam
indulgent vino et vertunt crateras aënos. MPR
conlucent ignes, noctem custodia ducit 166
insomnem ludo.

Haec super e vallo prospectant Troes et armis
alta tenent, nec non trepidi formidine portas
explorant pontisque et propugnacula iungunt, 170
tela gerunt.   instat Mnestheus acerque Serestus,
quos pater Aeneas, si quando adversa vocarent,
rectores iuvenum et rerum dedit esse magistros.
omnis per muros legio, sortita periclum,
excubat exercetque vices, quod cuique tuendum est.

Nisus erat portae custos, acerrimus armis, 176
Hyrtacides, comitem Aeneae quem miserat Ida
venatrix, iaculo celerem levibusque sagittis,
et iuxta comes Euryalus, quo pulchrior alter
non fuit Aeneadum Troiana neque induit arma, 180
ora puer prima signans intonsa iuventa.
his amor unus erat pariterque in bella ruebant;
tum quoque communi portam statione tenebant.
Nisus ait: "dine hunc ardorem mentibus addunt,
Euryale, an sua cuique deus fit dira cupido? 185
aut pugnam aut aliquid iamdudum invadere magnum
mens agitat mihi, nec placida contenta quiete est.
cernis, quae Rutulos habeat fiducia rerum.
lumina rara micant, somno vinoque soluti
procubuere, silent late loca.   percipe porro, 190
quid dubitem et quae nunc animo sententia surgat.
Aenean acciri omnes, populusque patresque,

---

[171] instant *MR*.   [173] iuveni *known to Servius.*
[189] sepulti *Servius.*

AENEID BOOK IX

and sparkling with gold. To and fro they rush, and take their turns, or stretched along the grass, drink their fill of wine and upturn bowls of bronze. The fires burn bright, and the warders spend the sleepless night in games.

168 On this scene the Trojans look forth from the rampart above, as in arms they hold the summit; in trembling haste they test the gates and link bridges[1] and battlements, sword in hand. Mnestheus and valiant Serestus urge on the work, whom father Aeneas, should misfortune ever call, left as leaders of the warriors and rulers of the state. Along the walls the whole host, dividing the peril, keeps watch, and serves in turns, where each should mount guard.

176 Nisus was guardian of the gate, most valiant of warriors, son of Hyrtacus, whom Ida the huntress had sent in Aeneas' train with fleet javelin and light arrows. At his side was Euryalus—none fairer among the Aeneadae, or of all who donned the Trojan arms—a boy who showed on his unshaven cheek the first bloom of youth. A common love was theirs; side by side they would charge in the fray; now too they together were mounting sentry at the gate. Nisus cries: "Do the gods, Euryalus, put this fire in our hearts, or does his own wild longing become to each man a god? Long has my heart been astir to dare battle or some great deed, and peaceful quiet contents it not. Thou seest what faith in their fortunes possesses the Rutulians. Few are their gleaming lights; relaxed with wine and slumber, they lie prone; far and wide reigns silence. Learn then what I ponder, and what purpose now rises in my mind. People and senate—all cry that Aeneas

[1] The bridges or gangways connect towers standing outside the walls with the battlements.

VIRGIL

exposcunt mittique viros, qui certa reportent.
si tibi quae posco promittunt (nam mihi facti
fama sat est), tumulo videor reperire sub illo   195
posse viam ad muros et moenia Pallantea."
obstipuit magno laudum percussus amore
Euryalus; simul his ardentem adfatur amicum:
"mene igitur socium summis adiungere rebus,
Nise, fugis? solum te in tanta pericula mittam?   200
non ita me genitor, bellis adsuetus Opheltes,
Argolicum terrorem inter Troiaeque labores
sublatum erudiit, nec tecum talia gessi,
magnanimum Aenean et fata extrema secutus:
est hic, est animus lucis contemptor et istum   205
qui vita bene credat emi, quo tendis, honorem."
 Nisus ad haec: "equidem de te nil tale verebar, FMPR
nec fas, non: ita me referat tibi magnus ovantem
Iuppiter aut quicumque oculis haec aspicit aequis.
sed si quis, quae multa vides discrimine tali,   210
si quis in adversum rapiat casusve deusve,
te superesse velim; tua vita dignior aetas.
sit qui me raptum pugna pretiove redemptum
mandet humo, solita aut si qua id Fortuna vetabit,
absenti ferat inferias decoretque sepulchro.   215
neu matri miserae tanti sim causa doloris,
quae te sola, puer, multis e matribus ausa
persequitur, magni nec moenia curat Acestae."
ille autem, "causas nequiquam nectis inanis,
nec mea iam mutata loco sententia cedit.   220
acceleremus," ait. vigiles simul excitat: illi
succedunt servantque vices; statione relicta
ipse comes Niso graditur regemque requirunt.

₂₀₇ ad haec] ait *P*². ₂₀₉ aspicis *P*.
₂₁₄ humo: *FM*² *punctuate after* humo, *P*² *and Priscian after* solita; *Servius knows both readings.*

should be summoned, and men be sent to take him sure tidings. If they promise the boon I ask for thee —for to me the glory of the deed is enough— methinks beneath yonder mound I may find a path to the walls and fortress of Pallanteum." Dazed was Euryalus, smitten with mighty love of praise, and thus at once speaks to his fiery friend: "Dost thou shrink then, Nisus, from linking me with thee in this high emprise? Shall I send thee alone into such great perils? Not thus did my sire, the old warrior Opheltes, train me as his child amid Argive terrors and the travails of Troy, nor thus at thy side have I played my part, following high-souled Aeneas and his utmost fate. Here, here is a soul that scorns the light, and counts that fame, whereto thou strivest, cheaply bought with life."

207 To this Nisus: "Of thee, surely, I had no such fear, nay, nay, 'twere a sin—so may great Jupiter, or whoso looks on this deed with favouring eyes, bring me back to thee in triumph! But if—as oft thou seest in like hazards—if some god or chance sweep me to disaster, I would that thou survive; thy youth is worthier of life. Let there be one to commit me to earth, rescued from battle or ransomed at a price; or if, as oft befalls, some chance deny this, to render rites to the absent and the honour of a tomb.[1] Nor let me, my child, be the cause of such grief to thy poor mother, who, alone of many mothers, has dared to follow thee to the end, nor heeds great Acestes' city."[2] But he: "Vainly dost thou weave idle pleas, nor does my purpose now change or give way. Hasten we!" he said, and therewith rouses the guards. They come up, and take their turn; he, quitting his post, walks by Nisus' side as they seek the prince.

[1] *i.e.* a cenotaph. [2] *cf. Aen.* v. 715 and 750.

VIRGIL

Cetera per terras omnis animalia somno
laxabant curas et corda oblita laborum: 225
ductores Teucrum primi, delecta iuventus,
consilium summis regni de rebus habebant,
quid facerent quisve Aeneae iam nuntius esset.
stant longis adnixi hastis et scuta tenentes
castrorum et campi medio. tum Nisus et una 230
Euryalus confestim alacres admittier orant;
rem magnam, pretiumque morae fore. primus Iulus
accepit trepidos ac Nisum dicere iussit.
tum sic Hyrtacides: "audite o mentibus aequis,
Aeneadae, neve haec nostris spectentur ab annis, MPR
quae ferimus. Rutuli somno vinoque soluti 236
conticuere; locum insidiis conspeximus ipsi,
qui patet in bivio portae, quae proxima ponto;
interrupti ignes, aterque ad sidera fumus
erigitur; si fortuna permittitis uti, 240
quaesitum Aenean et moenia Pallantea,
mox hic cum spoliis, ingenti caede peracta,
adfore cernetis. nec nos via fallet euntis:
vidimus obscuris primam sub vallibus urbem
venatu adsiduo et totum cognovimus amnem." 245

Hic annis gravis atque animi maturus Aletes:
"di patrii, quorum semper sub numine Troia est,
non tamen omnino Teucros delere paratis,
cum talis animos iuvenum et tam certa tulistis
pectora." sic memorans umeros dextrasque tenebat
amborum et voltum lacrimis atque ora rigabat. 251

---

[237] conticuere] procubuere $P\gamma^1$: *cf. Aen.* IX. 190.
[241] et] ad *c. This verse, in some MSS. known to Servius, appeared after* 243; *so Mackail.*
[243] fallit *PR*.   [244] moenibus $P^2\gamma^1$.   [246] animis *R*.

AENEID BOOK IX

²²⁴ All creatures else throughout all lands were soothing their cares in sleep, and their hearts were forgetful of sorrows: but the chief Teucrian captains, flower of their chivalry, held council on the nation's weal, what they should do, or who now should be messenger to Aeneas. They stand, leaning on their long spears and grasping their shields, in the midst of camp and plain.¹ Then Nisus and Euryalus together eagerly crave speedy audience; the matter, say they, is weighty and will requite the pause. Iülus was first to welcome the impatient pair, and to bid Nisus speak. Then thus the son of Hyrtacus: "Listen, ye men of Aeneas, with kindly minds, nor let this our offer be judged by our years. Relaxed with wine and slumber, the Rutulians lie silent; our own eyes have marked the ground for stratagem, where it opens in the forked way by the gate nearest the sea. The line of fires is broken, and black smoke rises to the sky. If ye permit us to use the chance, and seek Aeneas and the walls of Pallanteum, soon shall ye see us here again, laden with spoils after mighty slaughter has been wrought. Nor will the way deceive us as we go. Down the dim valleys in our frequent hunting we have seen the outskirts of the town and have come to know all the river."

²⁴⁶ Then Aletes, stricken in years and sage in council: "Gods of our fathers, whose presence watches ever over Troy, not utterly, despite all, do ye purpose to blot out the Trojan race, seeing that ye have brought us such spirit in our youths and such unwavering souls." So saying, he caught both by shoulder and hand, while tears rained down his

¹ *i.e.* in the middle of the open space which the Romans left in the centre of a camp.

VIRGIL

"quae vobis, quae digna, viri, pro laudibus istis
praemia posse rear solvi? pulcherrima primum
di moresque dabunt vestri; tum cetera reddet
actutum pius Aeneas atque integer aevi 255
Ascanius, meriti tanti non immemor umquam."
"immo ego vos, cui sola salus genitore reducto,"
excipit Ascanius, " per magnos, Nise, Penates
Assaracique Larem et canae penetralia Vestae
obtestor: quaecumque mihi fortuna fidesque est, 260
in vestris pono gremiis: revocate parentem,
reddite conspectum; nihil illo triste recepto.
bina dabo argento perfecta atque aspera signis
pocula, devicta genitor quae cepit Arisba,
et tripodas geminos, auri duo magna talenta, 265
cratera antiquum, quem dat Sidonia Dido.
si vero capere Italiam sceptrisque potiri
contigerit victori et praedae dicere sortem,
vidisti quo Turnus equo, quibus ibat in armis
aureus; ipsum illum, clipeum cristasque rubentis 270
excipiam sorti, iam nunc tua praemia, Nise.
praeterea bis sex genitor lectissima matrum
corpora captivosque dabit suaque omnibus arma,
insuper his campi quod rex habet ipse Latinus.
te vero, mea quem spatiis propioribus aetas 275
insequitur, venerande puer, iam pectore toto
accipio et comitem casus complector in omnis.
nulla meis sine te quaeretur gloria rebus;
seu pacem seu bella geram, tibi maxima rerum
verborumque fides."   contra quem talia fatur 280
Euryalus: "me nulla dies tam fortibus ausis
dissimilem arguerit: tantum fortuna secunda

---

[263] dicere (*with erasure above* i) *M* : dicere *P* : ducere *Rγ²*.
[274] his] is *M* : campis *R*. quos *M¹P²γ*.
[282] *Servius punctuated after* tantum. *So Ribbeck.*

AENEID BOOK IX

cheeks and face. "What, sirs, what guerdon shall I deem worthy to be paid you for deeds so glorious? The first and fairest heaven and your own hearts shall give; then the rest shall the good Aeneas straightway repay, and the youthful Ascanius, forgetful never of service so noble." "Nay," breaks in Ascanius, "I, whose sole safety lies in my sire's return, I adjure you both, O Nisus, by the great gods of the house, by the Lar of Assaracus, and by hoary Vesta's shrine —all my fortune, all my trust, I lay upon your knees; recall my father, give him back to sight; with him recovered all grief vanishes. A pair of goblets will I give, wrought in silver and rough with chasing, that he took when Arisba was vanquished; and two tripods, two great talents of gold, and an ancient bowl that Dido of Sidon gave. But if it be our lot to take Italy, to wield a victor's sceptre and to assign the spoil, thou hast seen the horse and the armour wherewith Turnus rode, all in gold—that same horse, the shield and the crimson plumes will I set apart from the lot, thy reward, O Nisus, even now. Moreover my father will give twice six matrons of choicest beauty, and men captives, each with his armour, and, therewith too, whate'er domain King Latinus himself holds.[1] But thee, oh youth revered, whom my age follows at nearer distance, at once I take all to my heart, and embrace as my comrade in every chance. No glory shall be sought for my own lot without thee; be peace or be war on hand, in thee shall be my chiefest trust in deed and in word."

280 To him thus spoke Euryalus in reply: "Never shall time prove me unmeet for such bold emprise, so but Fortune prove kind, not cruel. But

---

[1] *i.e.* the land now held by the king, the royal domain, is to go to Nisus.

VIRGIL

haud adversa cadat.   sed te super omnia dona
unum oro: genetrix Priami de gente vetusta
est mihi, quam miseram tenuit non Ilia tellus   285
mecum excedentem, non moenia regis Acestae.
hanc ego nunc ignaram huius quodcumque pericli est
inque salutatam linquo; nox et tua testis
dextera, quod nequeam lacrimas perferre parentis.
at tu, oro, solare inopem et succurre relictae.   290
hanc sine me spem ferre tui : audentior ibo
in casus omnis."   percussa mente dedere
Dardanidae lacrimas, ante omnis pulcher Iulus,
atque animum patriae strinxit pietatis imago.
tum sic effatur :   295
"sponde digna tuis ingentibus omnia coeptis.
namque erit ista mihi genetrix nomenque Creusae
solum defuerit, nec partum gratia talem
parva manet.   casus factum quicumque sequentur,
per caput hoc iuro, per quod pater ante solebat :   300
quae tibi polliceor reduci rebusque secundis,
haec eadem matrique tuae generique manebunt."
sic ait inlacrimans; umero simul exuit ensem
auratum, mira quem fecerat arte Lycaon
Gnosius atque habilem vagina aptarat eburna.   305
dat Niso Mnestheus pellem horrentisque leonis
exuvias, galeam fidus permutat Aletes.
protinus armati incedunt; quos omnis euntis
primorum manus ad portas, iuvenumque senumque,
prosequitur votis.   nec non et pulcher Iulus,   310
ante annos animumque gerens curamque virilem,
multa patri mandata dabat portanda : sed aurae
omnia discerpunt et nubibus inrita donant.

   Egressi superant fossas noctisque per umbram
castra inimica petunt, multis tamen ante futuri   315

₂₈₃ haud] aut $M^2\gamma^2a^2bc$, *Servius*. ₂₈₇ est *omitted by* M^1PR.
  ₂₉₂ dederunt $PR\gamma$.   ₂₉₆ spondeo a^1c.   ₂₉₉ sequetur P.

AENEID BOOK IX

from thee, above all thy gifts, this one thing I ask. A mother I have, of Priam's ancient line, whom neither the Ilian land nor King Acestes' city could keep, poor soul, from faring forth with me. Her now I leave without knowledge of this peril, be it what it may, and without word of farewell, because —night and thy right hand be witness—I could not bear a mother's tears. But do thou, I pray, comfort the helpless, and relieve the desolate. Let me take with me this hope in thee; more boldly shall I meet all hazards."

292 Touched to the heart, the Dardanians shed tears —fair Iülus before them all, and the picture of filial love touched his soul. Then thus he spoke : " Be sure that all shall be worthy of thy mighty enterprise; for she shall be a mother to me, lacking but the name Creüsa; nor does slight honour await her who bore such a son. Whatever chance attend thy deed, I swear by this head whereby my father was wont to swear, what I promise to thee on thy prosperous return shall abide the same for thy mother and thy house." So he speaks weeping; and therewithal strips from his shoulder the gilded sword, fashioned with wondrous art by Lycaon of Gnosus and fitted for use with ivory sheath. To Nisus Mnestheus gives a skin, spoil of a shaggy lion: faithful Aletes exchanges his helmet. At once they advance in arms and as they go all the company of princes, young and old, escort them to the gate with vows. Likewise fair Iülus, with a man's mind and a spirit beyond his years gave many a charge to carry to his father. But the breezes scatter all and give them fruitless to the clouds!

314 Issuing, they cross the trenches, and through the shadow of night seek that fatal camp—yet des-

133

VIRGIL

exitio.   passim somno vinoque per herbam
corpora fusa vident, arrectos litore currus,
inter lora rotasque viros, simul arma iacere,
vina simul.   prior Hyrtacides sic ore locutus:
" Euryale, audendum dextra; nunc ipsa vocat res.   320
hac iter est.   tu, ne qua manus se attollere nobis
a tergo possit, custodi et consule longe;
haec ego vasta dabo et lato te limite ducam."
sic memorat vocemque premit; simul ense superbum
Rhamnetem adgreditur, qui forte tapetibus altis   325
exstructus toto proflabat pectore somnum,
rex idem et regi Turno gratissimus augur;
sed non augurio potuit depellere pestem.
tris iuxta famulos temere inter tela iacentis
armigerumque Remi premit aurigamque sub ipsis   330
nactus equis ferroque secat pendentia colla;
tum caput ipsi aufert domino truncumque relinquit
sanguine singultantem; atro tepefacta cruore
terra torique madent.   nec non Lamyrumque
    Lamumque
et iuvenem Serranum, illa qui plurima nocte   335
luserat, insignis facie, multoque iacebat
membra deo victus; felix, si protinus illum
aequasset nocti ludum in lucemque tulisset.
impastus ceu plena leo per ovilia turbans
(suadet enim vesana fames) manditque trahitque   340
molle pecus mutumque metu, fremit ore cruento.
nec minor Euryali caedes; incensus et ipse
perfurit ac multam in medio sine nomine plebem,

        ³¹⁶ umbram *R*.   ³²⁹ tela] lora *R*.
        ³⁴¹ multumque *M¹P¹R*.

AENEID BOOK IX

tined first to be the doom of many. Everywhere they see bodies stretched along the grass in drunken sleep, chariots atilt on the shore, men lying amid wheels and harness, their arms and flagons all about. First the son of Hyrtacus thus began: "Euryalus, the hand must dare; now the occasion itself invites; here lies our way. Watch thou, that no arm be raised against us from behind, and keep wide outlook. Here will I deal destruction, and by a broad path show thee the way." So speaks he, then checks his voice, and at once drives his sword at haughty Rhamnes, who, haply pillowed on high coverlets, was drawing from all his breast the breath of sleep—a king himself, and King Turnus' best-beloved augur; but not by augury could he avert his doom. Three attendants he slew at his side, as they lay carelessly amid their arms, and Remus' armour-bearer, and the charioteer, catching him at the horses' feet. Their drooping necks he severs with the sword; then lops off the head of their lord himself, and leaves the trunk spurting blood; ground and couch reek with the warm black gore. Lamyrus, too, he slays, and Lamus, and youthful Serranus, of wondrous beauty, who had played long that night, and lay with limbs vanquished by the god's abundance;[1] happy he, had he played on, making that game one with the night, and pursuing it to the dawn! Even so, an unfed lion, rioting through full sheepfolds, for the madness of hunger constrains him, mangles and rends the feeble flock that are dumb with fear, and growls with blood-stained mouth. Nor less is the slaughter of Euryalus; he too, all aflame, storms madly, and falls on the vast and unnamed multitude before him,

[1] The god is Sleep; less probably, Bacchus. For the playing, *cf.* l. 167 above.

135

VIRGIL

Fadumque Herbesumque subit Rhoetumque Abarimque,
ignaros; Rhoetum vigilantem et cuncta videntem; 345
sed magnum metuens se post cratera tegebat:
pectore in adverso totum cui comminus ensem
condidit adsurgenti et multa morte recepit.
purpuream vomit ille animam et cum sanguine mixta
vina refert moriens; hic furto fervidus instat. 350
iamque ad Messapi socios tendebat; ibi ignem
deficere extremum et religatos rite videbat
carpere gramen equos: breviter cum talia Nisus
(sensit enim nimia caede atque cupidine ferri) MPRV
"absistamus," ait; "nam lux inimica propinquat. 355
poenarum exhaustum satis est, via facta per hostis."
multa virum solido argento perfecta relinquunt
armaque craterasque simul pulchrosque tapetas.
Euryalus phaleras Rhamnetis et aurea bullis
cingula, Tiburti Remulo ditissimus olim 360
quae mittit dona, hospitio cum iungeret absens,
Caedicus; ille suo moriens dat habere nepoti;
post mortem bello Rutuli pugnaque potiti:
haec rapit atque umeris nequiquam fortibus aptat.
tum galeam Messapi habilem cristisque decoram 365
induit. excedunt castris et tuta capessunt.

Interea praemissi equites ex urbe Latina,
cetera dum legio campis instructa moratur,
ibant et Turno regi responsa ferebant,
tercentum, scutati omnes, Volcente magistro. 370
iamque propinquabant castris muroque subibant,

---

³⁴⁹ purpureum *known to Servius, and to be construed with* ensem.   ³⁶⁴ aptant *V*.
³⁶⁹ regis *Servius. So Sabb. and Mackail.*   ³⁷¹ muros *Pγ*.

AENEID BOOK IX

Fadus and Herbesus, Rhoetus and Abaris—unconscious these; but Rhoetus was awake and saw it all, yet in his fear crouched behind a mighty bowl. Right in his breast, as he rose close by, the foe plunged his sword its full length, and drew it back steeped in death.[1] Rhoetus belches forth his red life, and dying casts up wine mixed with blood; the other hotly pursues his stealthy work. And now he drew near Messapus' followers. There he saw the last fires flickering, and horses, duly tethered, cropping the grass; when Nisus briefly speaks thus—for he saw his comrade swept away by reckless lust of carnage: "Let us away; for the unfriendly dawn is nigh. Vengeance is sated to the full; a path is cut through the foe." Many a soldier's arms, wrought in solid silver, they leave behind—and bowls therewith, and beautiful carpets. Euryalus takes the trappings of Rhamnes and his gold-studded sword-belt, gifts that of old wealthy Caedicus sent to Remulus of Tibur, when plighting friendship far away; he when dying gave them to his grandson for his own; after his death the Rutulians captured them in war and battle. These he tears away, and fits upon his valiant breast—all in vain. Then he dons Messapus' shapely helm, with its graceful plumes. They issue forth from the camp and make for safety.

367 Meanwhile horsemen, sent forward from the Latin city, while the rest of the force halts arrayed upon the plains, came bearing a reply to King Turnus—three hundred, all under shield, with Volcens as leader. And now they were nearing the camp and coming under the wall, when at a distance they

[1] Rendered by some "welcomed him with abundant death."

VIRGIL

cum procul hos laevo flectentis limite cernunt
et galea Euryalum sublustri noctis in umbra
prodidit immemorem radiisque adversa refulsit.
haud temere est visum: conclamat ab agmine
    Volcens   375
"state, viri. quae causa viae? quive estis in armis?
quove tenetis iter?" nihil illi tendere contra,
sed celerare fugam in silvas et fidere nocti.
obiciunt equites sese ad divortia nota
hinc atque hinc omnemque abitum custode coronant.
silva fuit late dumis atque ilice nigra   381
horrida, quam densi complebant undique sentes;
rara per occultos lucebat semita calles.
Euryalum tenebrae ramorum onerosaque praeda
impediunt fallitque timor regione viarum.   385
Nisus abit. iamque imprudens evaserat hostis
atque locos, qui post Albae de nomine dicti
Albani (tum rex stabula alta Latinus habebat),
ut stetit et frustra absentem respexit amicum:
"Euryale infelix, qua te regione reliqui?   390
quave sequar, rursus perplexum iter omne revolvens
fallacis silvae?" simul et vestigia retro
observata legit dumisque silentibus errat.
audit equos, audit strepitus et signa sequentum.
nec longum in medio tempus, cum clamor ad auris 395
pervenit ac videt Euryalum, quem iam manus omnis
fraude loci et noctis, subito turbante tumultu,
oppressum rapit et conantem plurima frustra.
quid faciat? qua vi iuvenem, quibus audeat armis
eripere? an sese medios moriturus in hostis   400
inferat et pulchram properet per volnera mortem?

---

³⁷⁵ aggere $P\gamma^1$.   ³⁷⁸ silvis $P\gamma$.
³⁸⁰ aditum $M^2P^2RV\gamma^1$.   ³⁸² complerant PRV.
³⁸³ ducebat M^2, *known to Servius*.   ³⁸⁷ lucos a^2c.
³⁹¹ resolves M^1.   ⁴⁰⁰ hostis] enses P, *known to Servius*.

AENEID BOOK IX

see the two turning away by a pathway to the left; and in the glimmering shadows of night his helm betrayed the thoughtless Euryalus, as it flashed back the light. Not unheeded was the sight. From his column shouts Volcens: "Halt, sirs! Wherefore on a journey? Who are ye in arms? Or whither are ye going?" They essay no response, but speed their flight to the wood and trust to night. On this side and that the horsemen bar the well-known crossways, and with sentinels girdle every outlet. The forest spread wide with shaggy thickets and dark ilex; dense briers filled it on every side; here and there glimmered the path through the hidden glades. Euryalus is hampered by the shadowy branches and the burden of his spoil, and fear misleads him in the line of the paths. Nisus gets clear; and now, in heedless course, he had escaped the foe to the place afterward styled Alban from Alba's name—at that time King Latinus had there his stately stalls—when he halted and looked back in vain for his lost friend. "Unhappy Euryalus, where have I left thee? Or where shall I follow, again unthreading all the tangled path of the treacherous wood?" Therewith he scans and retraces his footsteps, and wanders in the silent thickets. He hears the horses, hears the shouts and signals of pursuit. Nor was the interval long, when a cry reached his ears, and he sees Euryalus, whom, now betrayed by the ground and night and bewildered by the sudden turmoil, the whole band is dragging away overpowered and struggling violently in vain. What can he do? With what force, what arms dare he rescue the youth? Or shall he cast himself on his doom amid the foe, and win mid wounds a swift and glorious death?

VIRGIL

ocius adducto torquens hastile lacerto,
suspiciens altam Lunam sic voce precatur:
"tu, dea, tu praesens nostro succurre labori,
astrorum decus et nemorum Latonia custos.   405
si qua tuis umquam pro me pater Hyrtacus aris   MPR
dona tulit, si qua ipse meis venatibus auxi
suspendive tholo aut sacra ad fastigia fixi,
hunc sine me turbare globum et rege tela per auras."
dixerat et toto conixus corpore ferrum   410
conicit.   hasta volans noctis diverberat umbras
et venit aversi in tergum Sulmonis ibique
frangitur, ac fisso transit praecordia ligno.
volvitur ille vomens calidum de pectore flumen
frigidus et longis singultibus ilia pulsat.   415
diversi circumspiciunt.   hoc acrior idem
ecce aliud summa telum librabat ab aure.
dum trepidant, it hasta Tago per tempus utrumque,
stridens, traiectoque haesit tepefacta cerebro.
saevit atrox Volcens nec teli conspicit usquam 420
auctorem nec quo se ardens immittere possit.
"tu tamen interea calido mihi sanguine poenas
persolves amborum" inquit; simul ense recluso
ibat in Euryalum.   tum vero exterritus, amens,
conclamat Nisus, nec se celare tenebris   425
amplius aut tantum potuit perferre dolorem:
"me, me, adsum, qui feci, in me convertite ferrum,
o Rutuli! mea fraus omnis; nihil iste nec ausus
nec potuit; caelum hoc et conscia sidera testor;

---

[403] altam lunam et $MPV\gamma$: altam ad lunam et R: altam lunam (*without* et) *early editors*.   [412] adversi $MPR\gamma$.
[415] pulsant R.   [416] acrius $M^2P^2\gamma^1$.   [417] telum summa $P\gamma$.
[418] iit $P\gamma$.   [420] umquam M^1,

140

AENEID BOOK IX

Quickly he draws back his arm with poised spear, and looking up to the moon on high, thus prays: "Thou goddess, be thou present and aid our endeavour, O Latona's daughter, glory of the stars and guardian of the groves; if ever my father Hyrtacus brought any gifts for me to thy altars, if ever I have honoured[1] thee with any from my own hunting, have hung offerings in thy dome, or fastened them on thy holy roof,[2] grant me to confound yon troop, and guide my weapons through the air." He ended, and with all his straining body flung the steel. The flying spear whistles through the shadows of night, strikes the turned back of Sulmo, then snaps, and with the broken wood pierces the midriff. Spouting a warm torrent from his breast he rolls over chill in death, and long gasps heave his sides. This way and that they gaze round. All the fiercer, lo! he is poising another weapon from the ear-tip. While they hesitate, the spear goes whizzing through Tagus' either temple, and lodged warm in the cloven brain. Volcens storms with rage, yet nowhere espies the sender of the dart, nor where to vent his rage. "Yet thou, meanwhile, with thy hot blood, shalt pay me vengeance for both," he cried, and as he spake, rushed with drawn sword on Euryalus. Then indeed, frantic with terror, Nisus shrieks aloud; no longer could he hide himself in darkness or endure such agony: "On me—on me—here am I who did the deed—on me turn your steel, O Rutulians! Mine is all the guilt; he neither dared nor could have done aught; this heaven be witness and the all-seeing

[1] The word *auxi* has a special religious sense here, like *mactare*.
[2] By *fastigia* is meant the gable-roof of the exterior, over the entrance; the *tholus* is the domed interior.

141

VIRGIL

tantum infelicem nimium dilexit amicum." 430
talia dicta dabat, sed viribus ensis adactus
transabiit costas et candida pectora rumpit.
volvitur Euryalus leto, pulchrosque per artus
it cruor inque umeros cervix conlapsa recumbit:
purpureus veluti cum flos succisus aratro 435
languescit moriens, lassove papavera collo
demisere caput, pluvia cum forte gravantur.
at Nisus ruit in medios, solumque per omnis
Volcentem petit, in solo Volcente moratur.
quem circum glomerati hostes hinc comminus atque hinc 440
proturbant. instat non setius ac rotat ensem
fulmineum, donec Rutuli clamantis in ore
condidit adverso et moriens animam abstulit hosti.
tum super exanimum sese proiecit amicum
confossus placidaque ibi demum morte quievit. 445

Fortunati ambo! si quid mea carmina possunt,
nulla dies umquam memori vos eximet aevo,
dum domus Aeneae Capitoli immobile saxum
accolet imperiumque pater Romanus habebit.

Victores praeda Rutuli spoliisque potiti 450
Volcentem exanimum flentes in castra ferebant.
nec minor in castris luctus Rhamnete reperto
exsangui et primis una tot caede peremptis,
Serranoque Numaque. ingens concursus ad ipsa
corpora seminecisque viros tepidaque recentem 455
caede locum et plenos spumanti sanguine rivos.

⁴³² transadibit M^1: transadigit $M^2P\gamma$. pectora candida R. rupit R.   ⁴⁴³ hostis P^2.
⁴⁵⁵ tepidam M^1: tepidum $M^2PR\gamma^1$, *known to Servius.* tepida γ^2bc, *Servius.* recenti $P\gamma^1$, *known to Servius.*
⁴⁵⁶ pleno MP^2. spumantis MPR, *Servius.*

AENEID BOOK IX

stars! He but loved his hapless friend too well."
Thus was he pleading; but the sword, driven with
force, has passed through the ribs and rends the
snowy breast. Euryalus rolls over in death; athwart
his lovely limbs runs the blood, and his drooping
neck sinks on his shoulder: as when a purple flower,
severed by the plough, droops in death; or as poppies, with weary neck, bow the head, when weighted
by some chance shower. But Nisus rushes amidst
them, and sole among all seeks Volcens, to Volcens
alone gives heed. Round him the foe cluster, and
on every side seek to hurl him back. Onward none
the less he presses, whirling his lightning blade,
till he plunged it full in the face of the shrieking
Rutulian, and, dying, bereft his foe of life. Then,
pierced through and through, he flung himself above
his lifeless friend, and there at length, in the peace
of death, found rest.

446 Happy pair! If aught my verse avail, no
day shall ever blot you from the memory of time, so
long as the house of Aeneas shall dwell on the Capitol's unshaken rock, and the Father of Rome hold
sovereign sway![1]

450 The victorious Rutulians, masters of plunder
and spoils, with tears bore lifeless Volcens to the
camp. Nor in that camp was the wailing less,
when Rhamnes was found drained of life, and so many
chieftains slain in a single carnage, here Serranus,
and here Numa. A mighty throng rushes to the
dead and dying men, to the ground fresh with warm
slaughter and the full streams of foaming blood. In

---

[1] By the *domus Aeneae* is meant not merely the Julian
house, but the Roman people. The *pater Romanus* refers to
the imperial line.

VIRGIL

adgnoscunt spolia inter se galeamque nitentem
Messapi et multo phaleras sudore receptas.

    Et iam prima novo spargebat lumine terras
Tithoni croceum linquens Aurora cubile;   460
iam sole infuso, iam rebus luce retectis,
Turnus in arma viros, armis circumdatus ipse,
suscitat, aeratasque acies in proelia cogit
quisque suas variisque acuunt rumoribus iras.
quin ipsa arrectis (visu miserabile) in hastis   465
praefigunt capita et multo clamore sequuntur
Euryali et Nisi.

Aeneadae duri murorum in parte sinistra
opposuere aciem (nam dextera cingitur amni)
ingentisque tenent fossas et turribus altis   470
stant maesti; simul ora virum praefixa movebant,
nota nimis miseris atroque fluentia tabo.

    Interea pavidam volitans pinnata per urbem
nuntia Fama ruit matrisque adlabitur auris
Euryali. at subitus miserae calor ossa reliquit;   475
excussi manibus radii revolutaque pensa.
evolat infelix et femineo ululatu,
scissa comam, muros amens atque agmina cursu
prima petit, non illa virum, non illa pericli
telorumque memor; caelum dehinc questibus implet:
"hunc ego te, Euryale, aspicio? tune ille senectae 481
sera meae requies, potuisti linquere solam,
crudelis? nec te sub tanta pericula missum
adfari extremum miserae data copia matri?
heu! terra ignota canibus date praeda Latinis   485

    464 suos *MSS. (except M) and Servius, who makes it mean* comites.
    465 *omitted in P, but added at top of page by late hand.* mirabile M^1, *Servius (on* II. 558).
    469 dextra $M^1 R \gamma^1$.   471 videbant $P\gamma$.
    481 illa *R*.   484 extremis MP^1.
    485 data *most MSS.:* date *late MSS., read by Bentley and many editors.*

AENEID BOOK IX

mutual converse they note the spoils, Messapus' shining helmet, and the trappings won back with much sweat.

⁴⁵⁹ And now early Dawn, leaving the saffron bed of Tithonus, was sprinkling her fresh rays upon the earth;[1] now the sun streamed in, now day unveiled the world. Turnus, himself in armour clad, summons his men to arms, and each leader marshals to battle his mailed lines, and whets their anger with divers tales. Nay, on uplifted spears, O piteous sight! they affix and follow with loud clamour the heads, the very heads, of Euryalus and of Nisus. On the rampart's left side—for the right is girded by the river—the hardy sons of Aeneas have set their opposing line, hold the broad trenches, and on the high towers stand sorrowing, moved withal by those uplifted heads, that, alas! they know too well, now dripping with dark gore.

⁴⁷³ Meanwhile, winged Fame, flitting through the trembling town, speeds with the news and steals to the ears of Euryalus' mother. Then at once warmth left her hapless frame: the shuttle is dashed from her hands, and the thread unwound. Forth flies the unhappy dame, and with a woman's shrieks and torn tresses, makes madly for the walls and the foremost ranks—heedless she of men, heedless of peril and of darts; then fills the sky with her plaints: "Is it thus, Euryalus, that I see thee? Thou that wert the late solace of my age, couldst thou leave me alone, cruel one? Nor, when sent on such perilous errand, might thy poor mother bid thee a last farewell? Alas! Thou liest in a strange land, given as prey to the dogs and fowls of Latium! Nor have I, thy

---

[1] Repeated from *Aen.* IV. 584-5.

VIRGIL

alitibusque iaces! nec te, tua funera, mater
produxi pressive oculos aut volnera lavi,
veste tegens, tibi quam noctes festina diesque
urgebam, et tela curas solabar anilis.
quo sequar? aut quae nunc artus avolsaque membra
et funus lacerum tellus habet? hoc mihi de te, 491
nate, refers? hoc sum terraque marique secuta?
figite me, si qua est pietas, in me omnia tela
conicite, o Rutuli, me primam absumite ferro;
aut tu, magne pater divum, miserere, tuoque 495
invisum hoc detrude caput sub Tartara telo,
quando aliter nequeo crudelem abrumpere vitam."
hoc fletu concussi animi, maestusque per omnis
it gemitus, torpent infractae ad proelia vires.
illam incendentem luctus Idaeus et Actor 500
Ilionei monitu et multum lacrimantis Iuli
corripiunt interque manus sub tecta reponunt.

At tuba terribilem sonitum procul aere canoro
increpuit; sequitur clamor caelumque remugit.
accelerant acta pariter testudine Volsci 505
et fossas implere parant ac vellere vallum.
quaerunt pars aditum et scalis ascendere muros,
qua rara est acies interlucetque corona
non tam spissa viris. telorum effundere contra FMPR
omne genus Teucri ac duris detrudere contis, 510
adsueti longo muros defendere bello.
saxa quoque infesto volvebant pondere, si qua
possent tectam aciem perrumpere, cum tamen omnis
ferre iuvat subter densa testudine casus.

---

⁴⁸⁶ funera *MSS., Servius, Nonius, Donatus, Macrobius:*
funere *conjectured by Bembo.*
⁴⁹⁴ primum *P¹.* ⁵⁰⁶ pellere *M²R.* vallo *M².*
⁵¹⁴ iuvat *F (in an erasure):* iubat *P²γ:* iubet *P¹:* lubat *M¹:*
libet *M²R.*

146

AENEID BOOK IX

mother, led thee—thy corpse[1]—forth to burial, or closed thine eyes, or bathed thy wounds, shrouding thee with the robe which, in haste, night and day, I toiled at for thy sake, beguiling with the loom the sorrows of age.[2] Whither shall I follow? or what land now holds thy mangled limbs and dismembered body? Is this all, my son, thou bringest back to me of thyself? Is it this I have followed by land and sea? Pierce me if ye have aught of feeling, on me hurl all your weapons, O Rutulians; destroy me first with your steel; or do thou, great Father of the gods, be pitiful, and with thy bolt hurl down to hell this hateful life, since in no wise else can I break life's cruel bonds!" At that wailing their spirits were shaken, and a groan of sorrow passed through all; their strength is numbed and crushed for battle; and as thus she kindles grief, Idaeus and Actor, bidden by Ilioneus and the sorely weeping Iülus, catch her up and bear her in their arms within.

503 But the trumpet with brazen song rang out afar its fearful call; a shout follows and the sky re-echoes. Forth the Volscians speed in even line, driving on their tortoise-shield, and intent to fill the moat and pluck down the palisade. Some seek entrance, and essay to scale the walls with ladders, where the line is thin, and light gleams through the less dense ring of men. In return, the Teucrians shower missiles of every sort, and thrust the foe down with strong poles, trained by long warfare to defend their walls. Stones too they rolled of deadly weight, if haply they might break through the sheltered ranks: but these, beneath their compact shield,

[1] In *tua funera* there is a pathetic correction of *te*.
[2] She had been making a rich robe as a gift for her son, but it could not even adorn his corpse.

VIRGIL

nec iam sufficiunt; nam qua globus imminet ingens,
immanem Teucri molem volvuntque ruuntque, 516
quae stravit Rutulos late armorumque resolvit
tegmina. nec curant caeco contendere Marte
amplius audaces Rutuli, sed pellere vallo
missilibus certant. 520
parte alia horrendus visu quassabat Etruscam
pinum et fumiferos infert Mezentius ignis;
at Messapus equum domitor, Neptunia proles,
rescindit vallum et scalas in moenia poscit.

Vos, o Calliope, precor, adspirate canenti, 525
quas ibi tum ferro strages, quae funera Turnus
ediderit, quem quisque virum demiserit Orco,
et mecum ingentis oras evolvite belli. 528
Turris erat vasto suspectu et pontibus altis, 530
opportuna loco, summis quam viribus omnes
expugnare Itali summaque evertere opum vi
certabant, Troes contra defendere saxis
perque cavas densi tela intorquere fenestras.
princeps ardentem coniecit lampada Turnus 535
et flammam adfixit lateri, quae plurima vento MPR
corripuit tabulas et postibus haesit adesis.
turbati trepidare intus frustraque malorum
velle fugam. dum se glomerant retroque residunt
in partem, quae peste caret, tum pondere turris 540
procubuit subito et caelum tonat omne fragore.
semineces ad terram, immani mole secuta,
confixique suis telis et pectora duro
transfossi ligno veniunt. vix unus Helenor
et Lycus elapsi: quorum primaevus Helenor, 545

⁵²⁴ in] ad $P\gamma^1$.
⁵²⁹ et meministis enim, divae, et memorare potestis (= VII.
645) *given by R, but omitted by most MSS.*
⁵³⁷ adesis $M^1P\gamma$: adhaesis M^2 : adhessis R.

148

AENEID BOOK IX

delight to brave all chances. Yet now they fail; for where a massed throng threatens, the Teucrians roll up and hurl down a mighty mass, that laid low the Rutulians far and wide and broke their coverlet of armour. Nor do the bold Rutulians care longer to contend in blind warfare, but strive with darts to clear the ramparts. Elsewhere, grim to behold, Mezentius was brandishing his Etruscan pine and hurls smoking brands; while Messapus, the seed of Neptune, tamer of horses, tears down the rampart and calls for ladders to mount the battlements.[1]

[525] Do thou, O Calliope, thou and thy sisters, I pray, inspire me while I sing, what slaughter, what deaths, Turnus dealt on that day, and whom each warrior sent down to doom; and unroll with me the mighty scroll of war.

[530] A tower loomed high above, with lofty gangways,[2] posted on vantage-ground, which all the Italians strove with utmost strength to storm, and with utmost force of skill to overthrow: the Trojans in turn made defence with stones, and hurled showers of darts through the open loopholes. First Turnus flung a blazing torch and made fast its fire in the side; this, fanned by the wind, seized the planks and lodged in the gateways it consumed. Within, troubled and terrified, men vainly seek escape from disaster. While they huddle close and fall back to the side free from ruin, lo! under the sudden weight the tower fell, and all the sky thunders with the crash. Half dead they come to the ground, the monstrous mass behind them, pierced by their own shafts, and their breasts impaled by the cruel splinters. Scarcely do Helenor and Lycus alone escape— Helenor in prime of youth, whom a Licymnian slave

[1] *cf. Aen.* VII. 691.   [2] See note on 170 above.

VIRGIL

Maeonio regi quem serva Licymnia furtim
sustulerat vetitisque ad Troiam miserat armis,
ense levis nudo parmaque inglorius alba.
isque ubi se Turni media inter milia vidit,
hinc acies atque hinc acies adstare Latinas,   550
ut fera, quae densa venantum saepta corona
contra tela furit seseque haud nescia morti
inicit et saltu supra venabula fertur,
haud aliter iuvenis medios moriturus in hostis
inruit et qua tela videt densissima tendit.   555
at pedibus longe melior Lycus inter et hostis
inter et arma fuga muros tenet altaque certat
prendere tecta manu sociumque attingere dextras.
quem Turnus pariter cursu teloque secutus
increpat his victor: "nostrasne evadere, demens,   560
sperasti te posse manus?" simul arripit ipsum
pendentem et magna muri cum parte revellit;
qualis ubi aut leporem aut candenti corpore cycnum
sustulit alta petens pedibus Iovis armiger uncis,
quaesitum aut matri multis balatibus agnum   565
Martius a stabulis rapuit lupus.   undique clamor
tollitur: invadunt et fossas aggere complent;
ardentis taedas alii ad fastigia iactant.
Ilioneus saxo atque ingenti fragmine montis
Lucetium portae subeuntem ignisque ferentem,   570
Emathiona Liger, Corynaeum sternit Asilas,
hic iaculo bonus, hic longe fallente sagitta,
Ortygium Caeneus, victorem Caenea Turnus,
Turnus Ityn Cloniumque, Dioxippum Promolumque
et Sagarim et summis stantem pro turribus Idan,   575

---

⁵⁵² ruit $P^2\gamma^1$.   ⁵⁵⁸ dextra R.

---

[1] He was too young to win distinction, and therefore had no device on his shield.

AENEID BOOK IX

had borne secretly to the Maeonian king, and had sent to Troy in forbidden arms, lightly accoutred with naked sword and white shield, as yet unfamed.[1] Soon as he saw himself in the midst of Turnus' thousands, the Latin lines standing on this side, and standing on that, like a wild beast that, hedged about by the hunters' serried ring, rages against their shafts, flings itself on the death foreseen, and with a bound springs upon the spears—even so the youth rushes to death amidst the foe, and where he sees the weapons thickest, makes his way. But Lycus, far swifter of foot, amid foes, amid arms, gains the walls and strives to clutch the coping, and reach the hands of his comrades. Him Turnus following alike with foot and spear, taunts thus in triumph: "Fool, didst thou hope to escape our hands?" Therewith he seizes him as he hangs, and tears him down with a mighty mass of wall: even as when the bearer of Jove's bolt, as he soars aloft, has swept away in his crooked talons some hare or snowy-bodied swan; or as when the wolf of Mars[2] has snatched from the fold a lamb that its mother seeks with much bleating. On all sides a shout goes up; on they press, and with heaps of earth fill up the trenches; some toss blazing brands on to the roofs. Ilioneus lays Lucetius low with a rock, huge fragment of a mountain, as, carrying fire, he nears the gate. Liger slays Emathion, Asilas Corynaeus; the one skilled with the javelin, the other with the arrow stealing from afar. Caeneus fells Ortygius; Turnus victorious Caeneus; Turnus Itys and Clonius, Dioxippus and Promolus, and Sagaris, and Idas, as he stood on the topmost towers; Capys slays Privernus.

[2] Because Romulus and Remus, the offspring of Mars, were suckled by a she-wolf.

VIRGIL

Privernum Capys. hunc primo levis hasta Themillae
strinxerat: ille manum proiecto tegmine demens
ad volnus tulit; ergo alis adlapsa sagitta
et laevo infixa est lateri manus abditaque intus
spiramenta animae letali volnere rupit.   580
stabat in egregiis Arcentis filius armis,
pictus acu chlamydem et ferrugine clarus Hibera,
insignis facie, genitor quem miserat Arcens,
eductum matris luco Symaethia circum
flumina, pinguis ubi et placabilis ara Palici: 585
stridentem fundam positis Mezentius hastis
ipse ter adducta circum caput egit habena
et media adversi liquefacto tempora plumbo
diffidit ac multa porrectum extendit harena.

Tum primum bello celerem intendisse sagittam   590
dicitur, ante feras solitus terrere fugacis,
Ascanius, fortemque manu fudisse Numanum,
cui Remulo cognomen erat, Turnique minorem
germanam nuper thalamo sociatus habebat.
is primam ante aciem digna atque indigna relatu   595
vociferans tumidusque novo praecordia regno
ibat et ingentem sese clamore ferebat:
"non pudet obsidione iterum valloque teneri,
bis capti Phryges, et morti praetendere muros?
en qui nostra sibi bello conubia poscunt!   600
quis deus Italiam, quae vos dementia adegit?
non hic Atridae nec fandi fictor Ulixes:
durum a stirpe genus natos ad flumina primum
deferimus saevoque gelu duramus et undis;
venatu invigilant pueri silvasque fatigant,   605
flectere ludus equos et spicula tendere cornu;

---

⁵⁷⁹ adfixa *Pγ, Servius.* lateri manus] alte lateri *Housman.*
⁵⁸⁴ matris γ, *Macrobius:* Martis *MPRb:* matis *c.*
⁵⁸⁶ hastis] armis *Rγ².*
⁵⁹⁹ morte *M¹:* Marti *some inferior MSS.*, accepted by Henry.
protendere *M¹.*   ⁶⁰⁴ saevo] duro *Pγ.*

AENEID BOOK IX

Him Themillas spear had first grazed lightly; he, madly casting down his shield, carried his hand to the wound. So the arrow winged its way, and pinning the hand to his left side, buried itself deep within, and tore with fatal wound the breathing-ways of life. The son of Arcens stood in glorious arms, his scarf embroidered with needlework, and bright with Iberian blue—of noble form, whom his father Arcens had sent, a youth reared in his mother's grove about the streams of Symaethus, where stands Palicus' altar, gift-laden and gracious. But, dropping his spears, Mezentius with tight-drawn thong thrice whirled about his head the whizzing sling, with molten bullet cleft in twain the temples of his opposing foe, and stretched him at full length in the deep sand.

590 Then first, 'tis said, Ascanius aimed his swift shaft in war, till now wont to affright the fleeing quarry, and with his hand laid low brave Numanus, Remulus by surname, who but lately had won as bride Turnus' younger sister. He stalked before the foremost line, shouting words meet and unmeet to utter, his heart puffed up with new-won royalty, and strode forward in huge bulk, crying:

598 "Are ye not shamed, twice captured Phrygians, again to be cooped within beleaguered ramparts, and with walls to ward off death? Lo! these are they who by the sword claim our brides for theirs! What god, what madness, has driven you to Italy? Here are no sons of Atreus, no fable-forging Ulysses! A race of hardy stock, we first bring our new-born sons to the river, and harden them with the water's cruel cold; as boys they keep vigil for the chase, and tire the forests; their sport is to rein the steed and level

153

VIRGIL

at patiens operum parvoque adsueta iuventus
aut rastris terram domat aut quatit oppida bello;
omne aevum ferro teritur versaque iuvencum
terga fatigamus hasta, nec tarda senectus   610
debilitat viris animi mutatque vigorem:
canitiem galea premimus, semperque recentis
comportare iuvat praedas et vivere rapto.
vobis picta croco et fulgenti murice vestis,
desidiae cordi, iuvat indulgere choreis,   615
et tunicae manicas et habent redimicula mitrae.
o vere Phrygiae, neque enim Phryges, ite per alta
Dindyma, ubi adsuetis biforem dat tibia cantum;
tympana vos buxusque vocat Berecyntia matris
Idaeae: sinite arma viris et cedite ferro."   620

  Talia iactantem dictis ac dira canentem
non tulit Ascanius, nervoque obversus equino
contendit telum diversaque bracchia ducens
constitit, ante Iovem supplex per vota precatus:
"Iuppiter omnipotens, audacibus adnue coeptis.   625
ipse tibi ad tua templa feram sollemnia dona
et statuam ante aras aurata fronte iuvencum,
candentem pariterque caput cum matre ferentem,
iam cornu petat et pedibus qui spargat harenam."
audiit et caeli genitor de parte serena   630
intonuit laevum, sonat una fatifer arcus.
effugit horrendum stridens adducta sagitta
perque caput Remuli venit et cava tempora ferro
traicit. "i, verbis virtutem inlude superbis!

₆₁₀ tarda] sera *Servius.*   ₆₂₃ intendit *Pγ.*   ₆₃₁ letifer *Pγ.*
₆₃₂ et fugit *PRγ²*.   adducta] adlapsa *Pγ.*
₆₃₄ transigit *P¹*: transadigit *R:* transiit *P²*. i *omitted M¹Rγ².*

---

¹ The Oriental *mitra* was like a bonnet, fastened with
ribbons. The ordinary tunic had no sleeves. *cf. Aen.* IV.
216.

AENEID BOOK IX

shafts from the bow; but, patient of toil, and inured to want, our youth tames earth with the hoe or shakes cities in battle. All our life is worn with iron's use; with spear reversed we goad our bullocks' flanks, and sluggish age weakens not our hearts' strength nor changes our vigour. On white hairs we press the helm: and we ever delight to drive in fresh booty and live on plunder. But ye are clothed in embroidered saffron and gleaming purple; sloth is your joy, your delight is to indulge the dance; your tunics have sleeves and your turbans ribbons.[1] O ye Phrygian women, indeed!—for Phrygian men are ye not—go ye over the heights of Dindymus, where to accustomed ears the pipe utters music from double mouths! The timbrels call you, and the Berecynthian boxwood of the mother of Ida:[2] leave arms to men, and quit the sword."

[621] As thus he vaunts with words of ominous strain, Ascanius brooked it not, but facing him, levelled his shaft from the horse-hair string, and drawing his arms wide apart paused, first invoking Jove thus with suppliant vows: "Jupiter almighty, give assent to my bold emprise! My own hand shall bring thee yearly gifts in thy temple, and set before thine altar a bullock with gilded brow, snowy white, carrying his head high as his mother, that already can butt with horn and can spurn with hoof the sand." The Father heard, and from a clear space of sky thundered on the left; that instant rang the fatal bow. With awful whirr speeds forth the tight-drawn shaft, passes through the head of Remulus, and cleaves with its steel the hollow temples. "Go, mock valour with

[2] The pipe, timbrels, and boxwood flute were characteristics of the worship of Cybele, which came from Phrygia. *cf. Aen.* III. 111.

VIRGIL

bis capti Phryges haec Rutulis responsa remittunt."
hoc tantum Ascanius: Teucri clamore sequuntur   636
laetitiaque fremunt animosque ad sidera tollunt.

  Aetheria tum forte plaga crinitus Apollo
desuper Ausonias acies urbemque videbat,
nube sedens, atque his victorem adfatur Iulum: 640
"macte nova virtute, puer: sic itur ad astra,
dis genite et geniture deos. iure omnia bella
gente sub Assaraci fato ventura resident;
nec te Troia capit." simul haec effatus ab alto
aethere se mittit, spirantis dimovet auras   645
Ascaniumque petit. formam tum vertitur oris
antiquum in Buten. hic Dardanio Anchisae
armiger ante fuit fidusque ad limina custos;
tum comitem Ascanio pater addidit. ibat Apollo
omnia longaevo similis, vocemque coloremque   650
et crinis albos et saeva sonoribus arma,
atque his ardentem dictis adfatur Iulum:
"sit satis, Aenide, telis impune Numanum
oppetiisse tuis: primam hanc tibi magnus Apollo
concedit laudem et paribus non invidet armis: 655
cetera parce, puer, bello." sic orsus Apollo
mortalis medio aspectus sermone reliquit
et procul in tenuem ex oculis evanuit auram.
adgnovere deum proceres divinaque tela
Dardanidae pharetramque fuga sensere sonantem.   660
ergo avidum pugnae dictis et numine Phoebi
Ascanium prohibent, ipsi in certamina rursus

<small>   645 misit $P\gamma^1$.   646 forma *PR*. *So Rib. and Sabb.*
    651 albos] flavos *R*.   657 aspectu *MPR*.
    661 et] ac *PR*.</small>

AENEID BOOK IX

haughty words! This answer the twice captured Phrygians send back to the Rutulians." Thus only spoke Ascanius. The Teucrians second him with cheers, shout for joy, and lift their hearts to heaven.

[638] Then it chanced that in the realm of sky long-haired Apollo, cloud-enthroned, was looking down on the Ausonian lines and town, and thus he addresses triumphant Iülus: "A blessing, child, on thy young valour! So man scales the stars, O son of gods and sire of gods to be![1] Rightly shall all wars, that fate may bring, sink beneath the house of Assaracus to rest; nor can Troy contain thee." So saying, he darts from high heaven, parts the breathing gales, and seeks Ascanius. Then he changes the fashion of his features to those of aged Butes, who aforetime was armour-bearer to Dardan Anchises, and trusty watcher at his gate; thereafter the child's father made him henchman to Ascanius. On strode Apollo, in every wise like the old man, in voice and hue, in white locks and savage-sounding arms, and speaks these words to fiery Iülus: "Be it enough, son of Aeneas, that beneath thy shafts Numanus has fallen unavenged; this maiden glory great Apollo vouchsafes thee, nor grudges the weapons that match his own; for the rest, my child, refrain from war." Thus Apollo began, but while yet speaking, left the sight of men and far away from their eyes vanished into thin air. The Dardan princes knew the god, and his heavenly arms, and heard his quiver rattle as he flew. Therefore, at the behest and will of Phoebus, they check Ascanius, eager though he was for the

[1] The "gods to be" are the future Caesars, descended from Aeneas and Ascanius, who are of "the house of Assaracus." There is a reference in 642f. to the closing of the temple of Janus by Augustus in 29 B.C.

VIRGIL

succedunt animasque in aperta pericula mittunt.
it clamor totis per propugnacula muris,
intendunt acris arcus ammentaque torquent.   665
sternitur omne solum telis, tum scuta cavaeque
dant sonitum flictu galeae, pugna aspera surgit:
quantus ab occasu veniens pluvialibus Haedis
verberat imber humum, quam multa grandine nimbi
in vada praecipitant, cum Iuppiter horridus Austris 670
torquet aquosam hiemem et caelo cava nubila rumpit.
   Pandarus et Bitias, Idaeo Alcanore creti,
quos Iovis eduxit luco silvestris Iaera,
abietibus iuvenes patriis et montibus aequos,
portam, quae ducis imperio commissa, recludunt,   675
freti armis, ultroque invitant moenibus hostem.
ipsi intus dextra ac laeva pro turribus adstant,
armati ferro et cristis capita alta corusci:
quales aëriae liquentia flumina circum,
sive Padi ripis, Athesim seu propter amoenum,   680
consurgunt geminae quercus intonsaque caelo
attollunt capita et sublimi vertice nutant.
inrumpunt aditus Rutuli ut videre patentis.
continuo Quercens et pulcher Aquiculus armis
et praeceps animi Tmarus et Mavortius Haemon   685
agminibus totis aut versi terga dedere
aut ipso portae posuere in limine vitam.
tum magis increscunt animis discordibus irae
et iam collecti Troes glomerantur eodem
et conferre manum et procurrere longius audent.   690
   Ductori Turno, diversa in parte furenti

---

⁶⁶⁷ atflictu *M*: adflictu *R*: fluctu γ¹: flictu *P Servius*.
⁶⁷⁴ patriis iuvenes *P*γ.   ⁶⁷⁶ armis] animis *Bentley*.
⁶⁷⁸ coruscant *M*.   ⁶⁷⁹ Liquetia γ²b²c, *Servius*.
⁶⁸⁵ Marus *M*.   ⁶⁸⁶ aut versi] aversi *P¹*γ¹.
⁶⁸⁹ eodem] in unum *R*.
⁶⁹⁰ manum] gradum *Nonius*.   procedere *Nonius*.

158

AENEID BOOK IX

fray, themselves fare to the fight again, and fling their lives into gaping perils. The shout runs from tower to tower, all along the walls; they bend their eager bows and whirl their thongs.[1] All the ground is strewn with spears; shields and hollow helms ring as they clash; the fight swells fierce; mighty as the storm that, coming from the west, beneath the rainy Kid-stars lashes the ground; thick as the hail that storm-clouds shower on the deep, when Jupiter, grim with southern gales, whirls the watery tempest, and bursts the hollow clouds in heaven.

672 Pandarus and Bitias, sprung from Alcanor of Ida, whom the wood-nymph Iaera bore in the grove of Jupiter—youths tall as their native pines and hills—fling open the gate entrusted to them by their captain's charge, and relying on their arms, freely invite the foe to enter the walls. Themselves within, to right and left, stand before the towers, sheathed in iron, with waving plumes upon their lofty heads: even as high in air beside the flowing streams, whether on Padus' banks or by pleasant Athesis, twin oaks soar aloft, raising to heaven their unshorn heads and nodding their lofty crowns. In rush the Rutulians when they see the entrance clear. Straightway Quercens and Aquicolus, beautiful in arms, and Tmarus, reckless at heart, and Haemon, seed of Mars, with all their columns are routed and turn to flight, or in the very gateway lay down their life. At this, wrath waxes fiercer in their battling souls, and now the Trojans rally and swarm to the spot, and venture to close hand to hand and make longer sallies.

691 To Turnus the chief, as far away he storms and

[1] The thong, fastened to the middle of the shaft, gave impetus to the throw.

VIRGIL

turbantique viros, perfertur nuntius, hostem
fervere caede nova et portas praebere patentis.
deserit inceptum atque immani concitus ira
Dardaniam ruit ad portam fratresque superbos.   695
et primum Antiphaten (is enim se primus agebat),
Thebana de matre nothum Sarpedonis alti,
coniecto sternit iaculo; volat Itala cornus
aëra per tenerum stomachoque infixa sub altum
pectus abit, reddit specus atri volneris undam   700
spumantem et fixo ferrum in pulmone tepescit.
tum Meropem atque Erymanta manu, tum ster-
   nit Aphidnum;
tum Bitian ardentem oculis animisque frementem,
non iaculo, neque enim iaculo vitam ille dedisset,
sed magnum stridens contorta phalarica venit,   705
fulminis acta modo, quam nec duo taurea terga
nec duplici squama lorica fidelis et auro
sustinuit: conlapsa ruunt immania membra,
dat tellus gemitum et clipeum super intonat ingens.
talis in Euboico Baiarum litore quondam   710
saxea pila cadit, magnis quam molibus ante
constructam ponto iaciunt, sic illa ruinam
prona trahit penitusque vadis inlisa recumbit;
miscent se maria et nigrae attolluntur harenae;
tum sonitu Prochyta alta tremit durumque cubile 715
Inarime Iovis imperiis imposta Typhoeo.

  Hic Mars armipotens animum virisque Latinis
addidit et stimulos acris sub pectore vertit
immisitque Fugam Teucris atrumque Timorem.
undique conveniunt, quoniam data copia pugnae, 720

       710 qualis *Pγ*.   **719** Furorem *P¹*.

AENEID BOOK IX

confounds his foe, comes news that the enemy, flushed with fresh slaughter, flings wide his gates. He quits the work in hand, and stirred with giant fury, rushes to the Dardan gate and the haughty brethren. And first Antiphates, for first came he, the bastard son of tall Sarpedon by a Theban mother, he slays with cast of javelin. Through the yielding air flies the Italian cornel-shaft, and lodging in the gullet, runs deep into the breast; the wound's dark chasm gives back a foaming tide, and the steel grows warm in the pierced lung. Then Meropes and Erymas, then Aphidnus his hand lays low; then Bitias falls, fire in his eyes and rage in his heart, yet not under a javelin—for not to a javelin had he given his life—but with a mighty hiss a whirled pike sped, driven like a thunderbolt. This not two bulls' hides nor the trusty corslet with double scales of gold could withstand. The giant limbs totter and fall; earth groans, and the huge shield thunders over him. So on the Euboic shore of Baiae falls at times a rocky mass, which, builded first of mighty blocks, men cast into the sea:[1] so as it falls, it trails havoc, and crashing into the waters finds rest in the depths; the seas are in turmoil and the black sands mount upward; then at the sound lofty Prochyta trembles, and Inarime's rugged bed, laid by Jove's command above Typhoeus.

717 Hereupon Mars, the mighty in war, lent fresh strength and valour to the Latins, and in their hearts plied his eager goads, and let slip Flight and dark Terror among the Teucrians. From all sides gather the Latins, since scope for fight is given, and the god

[1] A reference to the building of massive piers running out into the sea, whether as a breakwater or as the foundation of a projecting villa.

161

VIRGIL

bellatorque animo deus incidit.
Pandarus, ut fuso germanum corpore cernit,
et quo sit fortuna loco, qui casus agat res,
portam vi magna converso cardine torquet,
obnixus latis umeris, multosque suorum   725
moenibus exclusos duro in certamine linquit;
ast alios secum includit recipitque ruentis,
demens, qui Rutulum in medio non agmine regem
viderit inrumpentem ultroque incluserit urbi,
immanem veluti pecora inter inertia tigrim.   730
continuo nova lux oculis effulsit et arma
horrendum sonuere; tremunt in vertice cristae
sanguineae clipeoque micantia fulmina mittit.
adgnoscunt faciem invisam atque immania membra
turbati subito Aeneadae.   tum Pandarus ingens 735
emicat et mortis fraternae fervidus ira
effatur: "non haec dotalis regia Amatae,
nec muris cohibet patriis media Ardea Turnum:
castra inimica vides; nulla hinc exire potestas."
olli subridens sedato pectore Turnus: 740
"incipe, si qua animo virtus, et consere dextram:
hic etiam inventum Priamo narrabis Achillem."
dixerat. ille rudem nodis et cortice crudo
intorquet summis adnixus viribus hastam:
excepere aurae: volnus Saturnia Iuno   745
detorsit veniens portaeque infigitur hasta.
"at non hoc telum, mea quod vi dextera versat,
effugies; neque enim is teli nec volneris auctor."
sic ait et sublatum alte consurgit in ensem
et mediam ferro gemina inter tempora frontem   750
dividit impubesque immani volnere malas.

⁷²¹ animos *M*¹.   ⁷²² cernit] vidit *P*γ.
⁷²³ quis *PR*γ¹.   ⁷²⁴ multa *PR*γ.   ⁷³¹ offulsit *R*.
⁷³³ clipei *P*γ¹.   mittunt *PR*γ¹.   ⁷⁴¹ animi *R*.
⁷⁴⁷ versat] librat *P*γ.   ⁷⁴⁸ is] es *P*γ.

162

AENEID BOOK IX

of battle seizes on their souls. Pandarus, when he sees his brother's fallen form, sees how fortune stands, and what chance sways the day, with mighty effort pushes with his broad shoulders and swings the gate round on its hinge, leaving many a comrade shut outside the walls in the cruel fray; but others he encloses with himself, welcoming them as on they rush. Madman! not to have seen the Rutulian prince bursting in amid the throng, and wantonly to have shut him within the town, like a monstrous tiger among the helpless herds. Straightway a new light flashed from Turnus' eyes and his armour rang terribly; the blood-red plumes quiver on his crest, and lightnings shoot gleaming from his shield. In sudden dismay the sons of Aeneas recognize that hateful form and those giant limbs. Then huge Pandarus springs forward, and, blazing with wrath for his brother's death, cries: "This is not Amata's bridal palace, nor is it midmost Ardea, holding Turnus within his native walls. A foeman's camp thou seest; no chance is there to escape hence." To him Turnus, smiling with untroubled mood: "Begin, if thy heart has aught of courage, and close with me: that here too an Achilles has been found shalt thou bear word to Priam." He ended; the other, striving with all his might, hurls his spear, rough with knots and unpeeled bark. The winds received it; Saturnian Juno turned aside the coming blow, and the spear lodges in the gate. "But not from this weapon, that my right arm wields amain, shalt thou escape; for not such is he who brings weapon and wound." So saying, he rises high upon his uplifted sword; the steel cleaves the brow in twain full between the temples, and with ghastly wound severs the beardless cheeks.

VIRGIL

fit sonus, ingenti concussa est pondere tellus;
conlapsos artus atque arma cruenta cerebro
sternit humi moriens atque illi partibus aequis
huc caput atque illuc umero ex utroque pependit.   755
   Diffugiunt versi trepida formidine Troes,
et si continuo victorem ea cura subisset,
rumpere claustra manu sociosque immittere portis,
ultimus ille dies bello gentique fuisset.
sed furor ardentem caedisque insana cupido   760
egit in adversos.
principio Phalerim et succiso poplite Gygen
excipit: hinc raptas fugientibus ingerit hastas
in tergum; Iuno viris animumque ministrat.
addit Halym comitem et confixa Phegea parma,   765
ignaros deinde in muris Martemque cientis
Alcandrumque Haliumque Noëmonaque Pryta-
   nimque.
Lyncea tendentem contra sociosque vocantem
vibranti gladio conixus ab aggere dexter
occupat, huic uno deiectum comminus ictu   770
cum galea longe iacuit caput, inde ferarum
vastatorem Amycum, quo non felicior alter
ungere tela manu ferrumque armare veneno,
et Clytium Aeoliden et amicum Crethea Musis,
Crethea Musarum comitem, cui carmina semper   775
et citharae cordi numerosque intendere nervis;
semper equos atque arma virum pugnasque canebat.
   Tandem ductores audita caede suorum
conveniunt Teucri, Mnestheus acerque Serestus,
palantisque vident socios hostemque receptum.   780
et Mnestheus: "quo deinde fugam, quo ten-
   ditis?" inquit.

<small>⁷⁶⁴ tergum $M\gamma$: tergus P^1R.   ⁷⁶⁵ confixum $M^2P^2\gamma^1$.
⁷⁶⁹ dextra M^1.   ⁷⁷⁰ desectum γ^1.
⁷⁷³ unguere (*initial* u *in rasura*) P: tingere *Bentley*:
tinguere *Sabb.*   ⁷⁸¹ fuga P^1.</small>

164

AENEID BOOK IX

There is a crash, earth is shaken by the vast weight; dying, he stretches on the ground his fainting limbs and brain-bespattered armour, while, lo! in equal halves his head dangles this way and that from either shoulder.

⁷⁵⁶ The Trojans turn and scatter in hasty terror; and, if forthwith the victor had taken thought to burst the bars perforce and let in his comrades at the gates, that day had been the last for the war and the nation. But rage and the mad lust of slaughter drove him in fury on the foe in front. First he catches Phaleris, and Gyges, whom he hamstrings; then, seizing their spears, he hurls them on the backs of the flying crowd; Juno lends strength and courage. Halys he sends to join them and Phegeus, his shield transfixed; then, as, all unwitting, on the walls they rouse the fray, Alcander and Halius, Noemon and Prytanis. As Lynceus moves to meet him and calls on his comrades he, from the rampart on the right, with sweep of flashing sword, smites him; severed by a single close-dealt blow, his head with helmet capped lay far away. Next fell Amycus, scourge of beasts, whom none excelled in skill of hand to anoint the dart and arm the steel with venom; and Clytius, son of Aeolus, and Cretheus, delight of the Muses—Cretheus, the Muses' comrade, whose joy was ever in song and lyre and in stringing of notes upon the chords; ever he sang of steeds and weapons, of men and battles.

⁷⁷⁸ At last, hearing of the slaughter of their men, the Teucrian captains, Mnestheus and gallant Serestus, come up, and see their comrades scattered and the foe within the gates. And Mnestheus: "Whither then, whither, do ye bend your flight? What other

VIRGIL

"quos alios muros, quae iam ultra moenia habetis?
unus homo et vestris, o cives, undique saeptus
aggeribus tantas strages impune per urbem
ediderit? iuvenum primos tot miserit Orco?   785
non infelicis patriae veterumque deorum
et magni Aeneae, segnes, miseretque pudetque?"

Talibus accensi firmantur et agmine denso
consistunt. Turnus paulatim excedere pugna
et fluvium petere ac partem, quae cingitur unda. 790
acrius hoc Teucri clamore incumbere magno
et glomerare manum, ceu saevum turba leonem
cum telis premit infensis: at territus ille,
asper, acerba tuens, retro redit et neque terga
ira dare aut virtus patitur, nec tendere contra 795
ille quidem hoc cupiens potis est per tela virosque.
haud aliter retro dubius vestigia Turnus
improperata refert et mens exaestuat ira.
quin etiam bis tum medios invaserat hostis,
bis confusa fuga per muros agmina vertit: 800
sed manus e castris propere coit omnis in unum,
nec contra viris audet Saturnia Iuno
sufficere: aëriam caelo nam Iuppiter Irim
demisit, germanae haud mollia iussa ferentem,
ni Turnus cedat Teucrorum moenibus altis.   805
ergo nec clipeo iuvenis subsistere tantum
nec dextra valet: iniectis sic undique telis
obruitur. strepit adsiduo cava tempora circum
tinnitu galea et saxis solida aera fatiscunt,
discussaeque iubae capiti, nec sufficit umbo   810

⁷⁸² quaeve ultra $P\gamma^1$. ⁷⁸⁶ nonne M^2.
⁷⁸⁹ pugnae PR. ⁷⁹³ at] ac MR.

AENEID BOOK IX

walls, what other battlements have ye now beyond? Shall one man, my countrymen, and he compassed on every side by your ramparts, unscathed deal such carnage throughout the city? Shall he send down to death so many of our noblest youths? Dastards! have ye no pity, no shame, for your hapless country, for your ancient gods, for great Aeneas?"

788 Kindled by such words, they take heart and halt in dense array. Step by step Turnus withdraws from the fight, making for the river and the part encircled by the stream. All the more fearlessly the Teucrians press on him with loud shouts and mass their ranks — as when a crowd with levelled spears beset a savage lion: but he, affrighted, yet fierce and glaring angrily, gives ground, and neither wrath nor courage lets him turn his back, nor yet, fain though he be, can he make his way through hunters and through spears. Even thus Turnus in doubt retraces his unhurried steps, his heart seething with rage. Nay, even then twice had he attacked the foe, twice he drove them in flying rout along the walls: but the whole host hastily gathers in a body from the camp, nor durst Saturnian Juno grant him strength to oppose them, for Jupiter sent Iris down through the sky from Heaven, charged with no gentle behests for his sister,[1] should Turnus leave not the Teucrians' lofty ramparts. Therefore, neither with shield nor sword-arm can the soldier hold his own; with such a hail of darts is he overwhelmed on all sides. Round his hollow temples the helmet echoes with ceaseless clash; the solid brass gapes beneath the rain of stones; the horsehair crest is rent from the head, and the shield's boss withstands not the

---

[1] *i.e.* Juno, who is *et soror et coniunx* (*Aen.* I. 47).

VIRGIL

ictibus; ingeminant hastis et Troes et ipse
fulmineus Mnestheus.   tum toto corpore sudor
liquitur et piceum (nec respirare potestas)
flumen agit, fessos quatit aeger anhelitus artus.
tum demum praeceps saltu sese omnibus armis   815
in fluvium dedit.   ille suo cum gurgite flavo
accepit venientem ac mollibus extulit undis
et laetum sociis abluta caede remisit.

⁸¹⁴ aeger] acer *known to Servius*.   ⁸¹⁶ flavo] vasto *P*γ¹.

AENEID BOOK IX

blows: the Trojans and Mnestheus himself, with lightning force, launch a storm of spears. Then o'er all his body flows the sweat and runs in pitchy stream, nor has he breathing space; and a sickly panting shakes his wearied limbs. Then at length, with headlong leap, he plunges in full armour into the river. Tiber with his yellow flood received him as he came, uplifted him on buoyant waters, and, washing away the carnage, returned the joyous hero to his comrades.

LIBER X

Panditur interea domus omnipotentis Olympi MPRV
conciliumque vocat divum pater atque hominum rex
sideream in sedem, terras unde arduus omnis
castraque Dardanidum aspectat populosque Latinos.
considunt tectis bipatentibus, incipit ipse: 5
" caelicolae magni, quianam sententia vobis
versa retro tantumque animis certatis iniquis?
abnueram bello Italiam concurrere Teucris.
quae contra vetitum discordia? quis metus aut hos
aut hos arma sequi ferrumque lacessere suasit? 10
adveniet iustum pugnae, ne arcessite, tempus,
cum fera Karthago Romanis arcibus olim
exitium magnum atque Alpis immittet apertas:
tum certare odiis, tum res rapuisse licebit.
nunc sinite et placitum laeti componite foedus." 15
  Iuppiter haec paucis, at non Venus aurea contra
pauca refert:
"o pater, o hominum rerumque aeterna potestas
(namque aliud quid sit, quod iam implorare queamus?)
cernis, ut insultent Rutuli, Turnusque feratur 20
per medios insignis equis tumidusque secundo
Marte ruat? non clausa tegunt iam moenia Teucros:

    ⁴ spectat $P^2\gamma$.   ¹¹ adveniat γ.   ¹⁵ laeti placidum M.
  ²⁰ feratur ... tumidusque *omitted* M^1.   ²² claustra M^1.

---

[1] The palace of Olympus has doors at the east and west ends. Through the former comes the sun at dawn; through the latter it returns at night.

170

BOOK X

Meanwhile there is thrown open the palace of omnipotent Olympus, and the Sire of gods and King of men calls a council to his starry dwelling, whence, high-throned, he surveys all lands, the Dardan camp, and the Latin peoples. Within the double-doored hall [1] they take their seats, and the king begins:

[6] "Mighty sons of Heaven, wherefore is your judgment reversed, and why strive ye with hearts so discordant? I had forbidden Italy to clash in war with Troy. What feud is this, in face of my command? What terror has bidden these or those to rush to arms and provoke the sword? There shall come—hasten it not—a lawful time for battle, when fierce Carthage shall one day let loose upon the heights of Rome mighty destruction, and open upon her the Alps.[2] Then shall it be lawful to vie in hate, then to ravage; now let be and cheerfully assent to the covenant I ordain."

[16] Thus Jupiter in brief; but not briefly golden Venus makes reply:

"O Father, O eternal sovereignty of men and things—for what else can there be which we may yet entreat?—seest thou how insolent are the Rutulians, and how Turnus fares elate through the midst upon his chariot, and rushes in swollen pride along the tide of war? No longer do barred walls shelter the

[2] A reference to Hannibal's invasion of Italy in 218 B.C.

VIRGIL

quin intra portas atque ipsis proelia miscent
aggeribus moerorum et inundant sanguine fossas.
Aeneas ignarus abest.   numquamne levari   25
obsidione sines? muris iterum imminet hostis
nascentis Troiae nec non exercitus alter,   MPR
atque iterum in Teucros Aetolis surgit ab Arpis
Tydides.   equidem credo, mea volnera restant
et tua progenies mortalia demoror arma.   30
si sine pace tua atque invito numine Troes
Italiam petiere, luant peccata neque illos
iuveris auxilio : sin tot responsa secuti,
quae Superi Manesque dabant, cur nunc tua quisquam
vertere iussa potest aut cur nova condere fata?   35
quid repetam exustas Erycino in litore classis,
quid tempestatum regem ventosque furentis
Aeolia excitos aut actam nubibus Irim?
nunc etiam Manis (haec intemptata manebat
sors rerum) movet et superis immissa repente   40
Allecto, medias Italum bacchata per urbes.
nil super imperio moveor; speravimus ista,
dum fortuna fuit; vincant quos vincere mavis.
si nulla est regio, Teucris quam det tua coniunx
dura, per eversae, genitor, fumantia Troiae   45
excidia obtestor, liceat dimittere ab armis
incolumem Ascanium, liceat superesse nepotem.
Aeneas sane ignotis iactetur in undis
et, quamcumque viam dederit Fortuna, sequatur:
hunc tegere et dirae valeam subducere pugnae.   50
est Amathus, est celsa mihi Paphus atque Cythera

²⁴ fossae *MR*.   ²⁸ surget *Mγ*.   ³⁵ iura potes *R*.
⁴⁸ sane] procul *R*.   undis] oris $P^2\gamma^1$.   ⁴⁹ quacumque *P*.
⁵⁰ durae *R*.   ⁵¹ atque alta Cythera $P^2R\gamma^1$.

AENEID BOOK X

Teucrians; nay, within the gates and even on their rampart heights they join battle, and flood the trenches with gore. Aeneas, unwitting, is far away. Wilt thou never suffer the leaguer to be raised? Once more a foe threatens the walls of infant Troy, yea, a second host; and once more against the Trojans rises from his Aetolian Arpi a son of Tydeus. Truly, methinks, my wounds are yet to come, and I, thy offspring, delay a mortal spear.[1] If without thy leave and despite thy deity, the Trojans have sought Italy, let them expiate their sin, nor aid thou them with succour. But if they have but followed all the oracles, given by gods above and gods below, why is any one now able to overthrow thy bidding or why to build the fates anew? Why should I recall the fleet burned on the strand of Eryx?[2] Why the king of storms, and his raging gales roused from Aeolia,[3] or Iris wafted from the clouds? Now she even stirs the shades—this quarter of the world was yet untried—and Allecto, launched of a sudden on the upper world, raves through the midst of Italian towns. I reck naught of empire; that was my hope, while Fortune stood; let them win whom thou wouldst have win. If there is no country for thy relentless consort to bestow upon the Teucrians, by the smoking ruins of desolate Troy, I beseech thee, O Father, let me dismiss Ascanius from arms unscathed—let my grandson still live! Aeneas, indeed, may well be tossed on unknown waters, and follow Fortune, what path soever she point out: this child let me avail to shield and withdraw from the dreadful fray. Amathus is mine, mine high Paphus and Cythera, and Idalia's

---

[1] Diomede, son of Tydeus, wounded Venus when she rescued Aeneas. See Homer, *Iliad*, v. 336.
[2] *cf. Aen.* v. 604 *sq.* [3] *cf. Aen.* I. 50 *sq.*

VIRGIL

Idaliaeque domus: positis inglorius armis
exigat hic aevum. magna dicione iubeto MPRV
Karthago premat Ausoniam: nihil urbibus inde
obstabit Tyriis.   quid pestem evadere belli 55
iuvit et Argolicos medium fugisse per ignis,
totque maris vastaeque exhausta pericula terrae,
dum Latium Teucri recidivaque Pergama quaerunt?
non satius, cineres patriae insedisse supremos
atque solum, quo Troia fuit? Xanthum et Simoenta 60
redde, oro, miseris iterumque revolvere casus
da, pater, Iliacos Teucris."   tum regia Iuno
acta furore gravi: "quid me alta silentia cogis
rumpere et obductum verbis volgare dolorem?
Aenean hominum quisquam divumque subegit 65
bella sequi aut hostem regi se inferre Latino?
Italiam petiit fatis auctoribus: esto;
Cassandrae impulsus furiis: num linquere castra
hortati sumus aut vitam committere ventis?
num puero summam belli, num credere muros, 70
Tyrrhenamque fidem aut gentis agitare quietas?
quis deus in fraudem, quae dura potentia nostra
egit? ubi hic Iuno demissave nubibus Iris?
indignum est Italos Troiam circumdare flammis
nascentem et patria Turnum consistere terra, 75
cui Pilumnus avus, cui diva Venilia mater:
quid face Troianos atra vim ferre Latinis,
arva aliena iugo premere atque avertere praedas?
quid soceros legere et gremiis abducere pactas, MPR
pacem orare manu, praefigere puppibus arma? 80

⁵³ exiget *V*.   ⁵⁹ patriae cineres *P*₂
⁷¹ -que] -ve *RV*.   ⁷² nostri *M*¹. *read by Lejay.*

174

AENEID BOOK X

shrine: here, laying arms aside, let him live out his inglorious days! Bid Carthage in mighty sway crush Ausonia; from her shall come no hindrance to Tyrian towns. What has it availed to escape the plague of war, to have fled through the midst of Argive fires, to have exhausted all the perils of sea and desolate lands, while his Teucrians seek Latium and a new-born Troy? Were it not better to have settled on the last ashes of their country, and the soil where once was Troy? Restore, I pray, Xanthus and Simois to a hapless people, and let the Teucrians retrace once more the woes of Ilium!"

[62] Then royal Juno, spurred by fierce frenzy: "Why forcest thou me to break my deep silence and publish to the world my hidden sorrow? Did any man or god constrain Aeneas to seek war and advance as a foe upon King Latinus? 'He sought Italy at the call of Fate.' So be it—driven on by Cassandra's raving! Did I urge him to quit the camp, or entrust his life to the winds? To commit the issue of war, the charge of battlements, to a child? To tamper with Tyrrhene faith or stir up peaceful folk? What god, what pitiless power of mine drove him to his harm? Where in this is Juno, or Iris sent down from the clouds? Ay, 'tis shameful that Italians should gird thy infant Troy with flames, and that Turnus set foot on his native soil—Turnus, whose grandsire is Pilumnus, whose mother divine Venilia! But what that the Trojans with smoking brands assail the Latins, that they set their yoke upon the fields of others, and drive off the spoil? What that they choose whose daughters they shall wed, and drag from her lover's breast the plighted bride?[1] That they proffer peace with the hand but array their

[1] The reference is to Aeneas, suing for the hand of Lavinia.

VIRGIL

tu potes Aenean manibus subducere Graium
proque viro nebulam et ventos obtendere inanis,
et potes in totidem classem convertere nymphas:
nos aliquid Rutulos contra iuvisse nefandum est?
Aeneas ignarus abest: ignarus et absit.   85
est Paphus Idaliumque tibi, sunt alta Cythera:
quid gravidam bellis urbem et corda aspera temptas?
nosne tibi fluxas Phrygiae res vertere fundo
conamur? nos? an miseros qui Troas Achivis
obiecit? quae causa fuit, consurgere in arma   90
Europamque Asiamque et foedera solvere furto?
me duce Dardanius Spartam expugnavit adulter
aut ego tela dedi fovive cupidine bella?
tum decuit metuisse tuis: nunc sera querellis
haud iustis adsurgis et inrita iurgia iactas."   95

Talibus orabat Iuno, cunctique fremebant
caelicolae adsensu vario, ceu flamina prima
cum deprensa fremunt silvis et caeca volutant
murmura, venturos nautis prodentia ventos.
tum pater omnipotens, rerum cui prima potestas, 100
infit (eo dicente deum domus alta silescit
et tremefacta solo tellus, silet arduus aether,
tum Zephyri posuere, premit placida aequora pontus):
"accipite ergo animis atque haec mea figite dicta.
quandoquidem Ausonios coniungi foedere Teucris 105
haud licitum nec vestra capit discordia finem:
quae cuique est fortuna hodie, quam quisque
    secat spem,

₈₃ classes *M*. ₉₆ Iuno] dictis *P : cf. Aen.* VI. 124.
₁₀₀ prima] summa $M^2P\gamma^1$. ₁₀₅ Ausoniis $P^2\gamma^1$. Teucros $P\gamma^1$.
₁₀₆ licitum est *R, Servius.*

176

AENEID BOOK X

ships with armour? Thou hast power to steal Aeneas from Grecian hands, and in place of a man to offer them mist and void air, and thou hast power to turn their fleet into as many nymphs:[1] but that we in turn have given some aid to the Rutuli, is that monstrous? 'Aeneas unwitting is far away'; unwitting and far away let him be! 'Paphus is thine, Idalium, and high Cythera': why meddle with savage hearts, and a city teeming with war? Is it I that essay to overthrow from the foundation Phrygia's tottering state? Is it I? Or is it he who flung the hapless Trojans in the Achaeans' path? What cause was there that Europe and Asia should uprise in arms and break bonds of peace by treachery? Was it I that led the Dardan adulterer to ravage Sparta? Was it I that gave him weapons or fostered war with lust? Then shouldst thou have feared for thine own; now too late thou risest with unjust complaints, and bandiest bickering words in vain."

[96] Thus pleaded Juno, and all the celestial company murmured assent in diverse wise: even as when rising blasts, caught in the forest, murmur, and roll their dull moanings, betraying to sailors the oncoming of the gale. Then the Father Almighty, prime potentate of the world, begins: as he speaks, the high house of the gods grows silent and earth trembles from her base; silent is high heaven; then the Zephyrs are hushed; Ocean stills his waters into rest.

[104] "Take therefore to heart and fix there these words of mine. Since it may not be that Ausonians and Teucrians join alliance, and your disunion admits no end, whate'er the fortune of each to-day, whate'er the hope each pursues, be he Trojan or be he

[1] *cf. Aen.* IX. 80 *sq.*

VIRGIL

Tros Rutulusve fuat, nullo discrimine habebo,
seu fatis Italum castra obsidione tenentur
sive errore malo Troiae monitisque sinistris.   110
nec Rutulos solvo. sua cuique exorsa laborem
fortunamque ferent. rex Iuppiter omnibus idem;
fata viam invenient." Stygii per flumina fratris,
per pice torrentis atraque voragine ripas
adnuit et totum nutu tremefecit Olympum.   115
hic finis fandi. solio tum Iuppiter aureo
surgit, caelicolae medium quem ad limina ducunt.

Interea Rutuli portis circum omnibus instant
sternere caede viros et moenia cingere flammis.
at legio Aeneadum vallis obsessa tenetur,   120
nec spes ulla fugae. miseri stant turribus altis
nequiquam et rara muros cinxere corona.
Asius Imbrasides Hicetaoniusque Thymoetes
Assaracique duo et senior cum Castore Thymbris
prima acies; hos germani Sarpedonis ambo,   125
et Clarus et Thaemon, Lycia comitantur ab alta.
fert ingens toto conixus corpore saxum,
haud partem exiguam montis, Lyrnesius Acmon,
nec Clytio genitore minor nec fratre Menestheo.
hi iaculis, illi certant defendere saxis   130
molirique ignem nervoque aptare sagittas.
ipse inter medios, Veneris iustissima cura,
Dardanius caput, ecce, puer detectus honestum,
qualis gemma micat, fulvum quae dividit aurum,
aut collo decus aut capiti, vel quale per artem   135
inclusum buxo aut Oricia terebintho
lucet ebur; fusos cervix cui lactea crinis

¹⁰⁸ Rutulusve γ.   ¹¹⁰ monitisve Pγ¹.   ¹¹¹ quisque M¹.
¹²⁶ alta] Ida Pγ¹.   ¹³⁷ cervix fusos Pγ.

AENEID BOOK X

Rutulian, no distinction shall I make, whether it be Italy's fate that holds the camp in leaguer, or Troy's baneful error and misleading prophecies. Nor do I free the Rutulians.[1] Each one's own course shall bring him weal or woe. Jupiter is king over all alike; the fates shall find their way." By the waters of his Stygian brother, by the banks that seethe with pitch and black swirling waters, he nodded assent, and with the nod made all Olympus tremble. So passed the parley. Then from his golden throne rose Jupiter, and the celestial company gather round and escort him to the threshold.

[118] Meanwhile, about every gate the Rutulians press on, to slaughter the foe with the sword, and to gird the ramparts with flame. But the host of the Aeneadae is held pent within the palisades, and hope of escape is none. Forlorn and helpless they stand on the high towers, and girdle the walls with scanty ring. Asius, son of Imbrasus, and Thymoetes, son of Hicetaon, and the two Assaraci, and Castor, and old Thymbris are the foremost rank; at their side are Sarpedon's two brothers, Clarus and Thaemon, come from lofty Lycia. One, straining his whole frame, uplifts a giant rock, no scant fragment of a mount, even Acmon of Lyrnesus, huge as his father Clytius, or his brother Mnestheus. Some with darts and some with stones, they strive to ward off the foe, and hurl fire and fit arrows to the string. In their midst, lo! the Dardan boy himself, Venus' most rightful care, his comely head uncovered, glitters like a jewel inset in yellow gold to adorn or neck or head, or as ivory gleams, skilfully inlaid in boxwood or Orician terebinth; his milk-white neck

[1] *i.e.* from obligations. Jupiter's decree is to bind them as well as the Trojans.

179

VIRGIL

accipit et molli subnectit circulus auro.
te quoque magnanimae viderunt, Ismare, gentes,
volnera derigere et calamos armare veneno, 140
Maeonia generose domo, ubi pinguia culta
exercentque viri Pactolusque inrigat auro.
adfuit et Mnestheus, quem pulsi pristina Turni
aggere **moerorum** sublimem gloria tollit,
et Capys: hinc nomen Campanae ducitur urbi. 145

Illi inter sese duri certamina belli
contulerant: media Aeneas freta nocte secabat.
namque ut ab Euandro castris ingressus Etruscis
regem adit et regi memorat nomenque genusque,
quidve petat quidve ipse ferat, Mezentius arma 150
quae sibi conciliet, violentaque pectora Turni
edocet, humanis quae sit fiducia rebus
admonet immiscetque preces: haud fit mora, Tarchon
iungit opes foedusque ferit; tum libera fati
classem conscendit iussis gens Lydia divum, 155
externo commissa duci. Aeneia puppis
prima tenet, rostro Phrygios subiuncta leones;
imminet Ida super, profugis gratissima Teucris.
hic magnus sedet Aeneas secumque volutat
eventus belli varios, Pallasque sinistro 160
adfixus lateri iam quaerit sidera, opacae
noctis iter, iam quae passus terraque marique.

Pandite nunc Helicona, deae, cantusque movete,

[138] subnectens *PR.*   [140] dirigere $M\gamma^2$.   [154] fatis *Servius.*
[162] iter] idem M^1.   [163] monete $P\gamma^1$.

---

[1] *cf. Aen.* VIII. 503. Now that they have a foreign leader, fate will not oppose them.

AENEID BOOK X

receives his streaming locks, clasped in circlet of pliant gold. Thee, too, Ismarus, thy high-souled clansmen saw aiming wounds and arming shafts with venom, thou noble scion of a Lydian house, where men till rich fields and Pactolus waters them with gold. There too was Mnestheus, whom yesterday's triumph of thrusting Turnus from the rampart heights exalts to the stars; and Capys, from whom comes the name of the Campanian city.

146 Thus they had clashed in stubborn warfare's conflict: and Aeneas at midnight was cleaving the seas. For soon as, leaving Evander and entering the Tuscan camp, he meets the king, and to the king announces his name and his race, the aid he seeks, and the aid he himself offers; informs him of the forces Mezentius is gathering to his side, and the violence of Turnus' spirit; then warns him, what faith may be put in things human, and with pleas mingles entreaties—without delay Tarchon joins forces and strikes a treaty; then, freed from Fate,[1] the Lydian people embark under heaven's ordinance, entrusting themselves to a foreign leader. Aeneas' ship leads the van with Phrygian lions beneath her beak, above them, towering Ida, sight most welcome to Trojan exiles.[2] There sits great Aeneas, pondering the changing issues of war; and Pallas, clinging close to his left side, asks him now of the stars, their guide through darksome night, and now of his trials by land and sea.

163 Now fling wide Helicon, ye goddesses, and wake your song—what host comes the while with

---

[2] The ship's figure-head is a representation of Mount Ida (doubtless the mountain-god), while below it are the lions of Cybele. (*cf.* IX. 80 *sq.*)

VIRGIL

quae manus interea Tuscis comitetur ab oris
Aenean armetque rates pelagoque vehatur.   165
   Massicus aerata princeps secat aequora Tigri,
sub quo mille manus iuvenum, qui moenia Clusi
quique urbem liquere Cosas, quis tela sagittae
gorytique leves umeris et letifer arcus.
una torvus Abas: huic totum insignibus armis   170
agmen et aurato fulgebat Apolline puppis.
sescentos illi dederat Populonia mater
expertos belli iuvenes, ast Ilva trecentos
insula, inexhaustis Chalybum generosa metallis.
tertius ille hominum divumque interpres Asilas,   175
cui pecudum fibrae, caeli cui sidera parent
et linguae volucrum et praesagi fulminis ignes,
mille rapit densos acie atque horrentibus hastis.
hos parere iubent Alpheae ab origine Pisae,
urbs Etrusca solo. sequitur pulcherrimus Astyr,   180
Astyr equo fidens et versicoloribus armis.
ter centum adiciunt (mens omnibus una sequendi),
qui Caerete domo, qui sunt Minionis in arvis,   MPRV
et Pyrgi veteres intempestaeque Graviscae.
   Non ego te, Ligurum ductor fortissime bello,   185
transierim, Cinyre, et paucis comitate Cupavo,
cuius olorinae surgunt de vertice pinnae
(crimen, Amor, vestrum) formaeque insigne paternae.
namque ferunt luctu Cycnum Phaëthontis amati,
populeas inter frondes umbramque sororum   190
dum canit et maestum musa solatur amorem,

¹⁶⁸ Cosam P^1. ¹⁷⁸ hastis] armis $P\gamma^1$.
¹⁷⁹ Alphea $M\gamma^2$, *Priscian*.
¹⁸⁶ Cinire $V\gamma^2 b^1 c^2$: Cinyrae M: cinera P: cumarre R:
cinere $\gamma^1 c^1$.

---

[1] The Chalybes were famous workers of iron; *cf. Aen.*
VIII. 420.
[2] *i.e.* to thee, Love, and thy mother, Venus. Cycnus,
father of Cupavo, loved Phaëthon, and was a witness of this

182

AENEID BOOK X

Aeneas from the Tuscan shores, arming the ships and riding o'er the sea.

166 At their head Massicus cleaves the waters in the bronze-plated Tiger under him is a band of a thousand youths, who have left the walls of Clusium and the city of Cosae; their weapons arrows, light quivers on the shoulders, and deadly bows. With him is grim Abas, all his train in dazzling armour, his vessel gleaming with a gilded Apollo. To him Populonia had given six hundred of her sons, all skilled in war, but Ilva three hundred—an island rich in the Chalybes' inexhaustible mines.[1] Third comes Asilas, famous interpreter between gods and men, whom the victims' entrails obey, and the stars of heaven, the tongues of birds and prophetic lightning fires. A thousand men he hurries to war in serried array and bristling with spears. These Pisa bids obey him—city of Alphean birth, but set in Tuscan soil. Then follows Astyr, of wondrous beauty —Astyr, relying on his steed and many-coloured arms. Three hundred more—all of one soul in following—come from the men who have their home in Caere and in the plains of Minio, in ancient Pyrgi, and fever-stricken Graviscae.

185 Nor would I pass thee by, O Cinyras, bravest in war of Ligurian captains, or thee, Cupavo, with thy scanty train, from whose crest rise the swan-plumes—a reproach, O Love, to thee and thine [2]— even the badge of his father's form. For they tell that Cycnus, in grief for his loved Phaëthon, while he is singing and with music solacing his woeful love amid the shade of his sisters' leafy poplars, drew

youth's destruction by Jupiter. Being plunged into grief, he was transformed into a swan. The sisters of Phaëthon were at the same time changed into poplars.

VIRGIL

canentem molli pluma duxisse senectam,
linquentem terras et sidera voce sequentem.
filius, aequalis comitatus classe catervas,
ingentem remis Centaurum promovet: ille   195
instat aquae saxumque undis immane minatur
arduus, et longa sulcat maria alta carina.

Ille etiam patriis agmen ciet Ocnus ab oris,
fatidicae Mantus et Tusci filius amnis,
qui muros matrisque dedit tibi, Mantua, nomen, 200
Mantua, dives avis, sed non genus omnibus unum:
gens illi triplex, populi sub gente quaterni,
ipsa caput populis, Tusco de sanguine vires.
hinc quoque quingentos in se Mezentius armat,
quos patre Benaco velatus harundine glauca   205
Mincius infesta ducebat in aequora pinu.
it gravis Aulestes centenaque arbore fluctum
verberat adsurgens; spumant vada marmore verso.
hunc vehit immanis Triton et caerula concha   MPR
exterrens freta, cui laterum tenus hispida nanti 210
frons hominem praefert, in pristim desinit alvus;
spumea semifero sub pectore murmurat unda.
tot lecti proceres ter denis navibus ibant
subsidio Troiae et campos salis aere secabant.

Iamque dies caelo concesserat almaque curru   215
noctivago Phoebe medium pulsabat Olympum:
Aeneas (neque enim membris dat cura quietem)
ipse sedens clavumque regit velisque ministrat.

¹⁹⁴ aequali *M*¹.   ²⁰² illis *V*.   ²⁰⁷ fluctus *R*.

---

[1] In the territory of Mantua were three races, each master of four cities. Once head of a confederacy of twelve Tuscan

AENEID BOOK X

over his form the soft plumage of hoary eld, leaving earth and seeking the stars with his cry. His son, following on ship-board with a band of like age, drives with oars the mighty Centaur; over the water towers the monster, and threatens to hurl a monstrous rock into the waves from above, while with long keel he furrows the deep seas.

[198] Yonder, too, Ocnus summons a host from his native shores, son of prophetic Manto and the Tuscan river, who gave thee, O Mantua, ramparts and his mother's name—Mantua, rich in ancestry, yet not all of one stock: three races are there, and under each race four peoples:[1] herself the head of the peoples, her strength from Tuscan blood. Hence, too, Mezentius arms five hundred against himself,[2] whom Mincius, child of Benacus, crowned with gray sedge, leads over the seas in their hostile ships of pine. On comes Aulestes heavily, lashing the waves as he rises to the stroke of a hundred oars; the waters foam as the surface is uptorn. He sails in the huge Triton, whose shell affrights the blue billows: its shaggy front, as it floats, shows a man down to the waist, its belly ends in a fish; beneath the monster's breast the wave gurgles in foam. So many the chosen chiefs who sailed in thrice ten ships to the succour of Troy, and cut the briny plains with brazen beak.

[215] And now day had passed from the sky and gracious Phoebe was trampling mid-heaven with her night-roving steeds; Aeneas, for care allows no rest to his limbs, sat at his post, his own hand guiding the rudder and tending the sails. And lo! in mid

cities (*cf.* Livy, v. 33), Mantua in the time of Pliny was the only Tuscan city north of the Po.

[2] They had taken up arms against the tyrant.

VIRGIL

atque illi medio in spatio chorus, ecce, suarum
occurrit comitum: nymphae, quas alma Cybebe   220
numen habere maris nymphasque e navibus esse
iusserat, innabant pariter fluctusque secabant,
quot prius aeratae steterant ad litora prorae.
adgnoscunt longe regem lustrantque choreis.
quarum quae fandi doctissima Cymodocea   225
pone sequens dextra puppim tenet ipsaque dorso
eminet ac laeva tacitis subremigat undis.
tum sic ignarum adloquitur: "vigilasne, deum gens,
Aenea? vigila et velis immitte rudentis.
nos sumus, Idaeae sacro de vertice pinus,   230
nunc pelagi Nymphae, classis tua. perfidus ut nos
praecipites ferro Rutulus flammaque premebat,
rupimus invitae tua vincula teque per aequor
quaerimus. hanc Genetrix faciem miserata refecit
et dedit esse deas aevumque agitare sub undis.   235
at puer Ascanius muro fossisque tenetur   MPRV
tela inter media atque horrentis Marte Latinos.
iam loca iussa tenet forti permixtus Etrusco
Arcas eques; medias illis opponere turmas,
ne castris iungant, certa est sententia Turno.   240
surge age et Aurora socios veniente vocari
primus in arma iube et clipeum cape, quem dedit ipse
invictum Ignipotens atque oras ambiit auro.
crastina lux, mea si non inrita dicta putaris,
ingentis Rutulae spectabit caedis acervos."   245
dixerat, et dextra discedens impulit altam,
haud ignara modi, puppim: fugit illa per undas
ocior et iaculo et ventos aequante sagitta.

---

²²¹ nomen *P*γ¹.   ²²³ quot] quae *P*².   puppis *M*¹.
²³⁷ horrentis *MR:* orrentis γ¹*b:* ardentis *P*γ¹.
²³⁸ tenent *MV*.   ²⁴² ipse] igni *V*.
²⁴⁵ spectabis *MP*γ¹, *known to Servius.*

AENEID BOOK X

course a band of his own company meets him, for the nymphs whom gracious Cybele had bidden be deities of the sea, and turn from ships to nymphs, came swimming abreast and cleaving the billows, as many as the brazen prows that once lay moored to shore. They know their king from afar, and encircle him with dances. From among them, Cymodocea, who was most skilled in speech, following behind, grasps the stern with her right hand, and herself rises breast high above the wave, while with her left hand she oars her way upon the silent waters. Then thus she accosts the prince, all unaware: "Wakest thou, Aeneas, scion of gods? Wake and fling loose the sheets of thy sails. We—pines of Ida, from her sacred crest, now nymphs of the sea—are thy fleet! When the traitorous Rutulian was driving us headlong with fire and sword, reluctant we broke thy bonds, and are seeking thee over the main. This new shape the Great Mother gave us in pity, and granted us to be goddesses and spend our life beneath the waves. But thy boy Ascanius is hemmed in by wall and trench, in the midst of arms and of Latins, bristling with war. Already the Arcadian horse, joined with brave Etruscans, hold the appointed place; to bar their way with interposing squadrons, lest they approach the camp, is Turnus' fixed resolve. Up, then, and with the coming dawn first bid thy friends be called to arms, and take thou the shield which the Lord of Fire himself gave thee—the shield invincible, and rimmed about with gold. To-morrow's light, if thou deem not my words idle, shall look on mighty heaps of Rutulian carnage." She ended, and at parting, with her right hand she drove the tall ship on, well knowing how; on it speeds over the wave, fleeter than javelin and wind-swift arrow.

VIRGIL

inde aliae celerant cursus.   stupet inscius ipse
Tros Anchisiades, animos tamen omine tollit.   250
tum breviter supera aspectans convexa precatur:
"alma parens Idaea deum, cui Dindyma cordi
turrigeraeque urbes biiugique ad frena leones,
tu mihi nunc pugnae princeps, tu rite propinques
augurium Phrygibusque adsis pede, diva, secundo."
tantum effatus.   et interea revoluta ruebat   256
matura iam luce dies noctemque fugarat.

Principio sociis edicit, signa sequantur
atque animos aptent armis pugnaeque parent se.
iamque in conspectu Teucros habet et sua castra,   260
stans celsa in puppi, clipeum cum deinde sinistra
extulit ardentem.   clamorem ad sidera tollunt   MPR
Dardanidae e muris, spes addita suscitat iras,
tela manu iaciunt, quales sub nubibus atris
Strymoniae dant signa grues àtque aethera tranant 265
cum sonitu, fugiuntque Notos clamore secundo.
at Rutulo regi ducibusque ea mira videri
Ausoniis, donec versas ad litora puppis
respiciunt totumque adlabi classibus aequor.
ardet apex capiti cristisque a vertice flamma   270
funditur et vastos umbo vomit aureus ignis:
non secus ac liquida si quando nocte cometae
sanguinei lugubre rubent, aut Sirius ardor
ille, sitim morbosque ferens mortalibus aegris,
nascitur et laevo contristat lumine caelum.   275

₂₅₁ super $PV\gamma^1$: spectans M^1.   ₂₅₆ rubebat $P^2\gamma^1$: ruebant M^1.   ₂₇₀ a] ac $PR\gamma$.   ₂₇₁ aereus MR.

AENEID BOOK X

Then the rest quicken their speed. Marvelling, the Trojan son of Anchises is in amaze, yet cheers his soul with the omen. Then looking at the vault above, he briefly prays: "Gracious lady of Ida, mother of the gods, to whom Dindymus is dear, and tower-crowned cities, and lions coupled to thy rein, be thou now my leader in the fight, do thou duly prosper the omen, and attend thy Phrygians, O goddess, with favouring step!" Thus much he said; and meanwhile the returning day was rushing on with fulness of light, and had chased away the night.

[258] First he commands his comrades to follow his signals, attune their hearts to combat and fit themselves for the fray. And now, as he stands on the high stern, he had his Trojans and his camp in view, when at once he lifted high in his left hand his blazing shield. The Dardans from the walls raise a shout to the sky; fresh hope kindles wrath; they shower their darts amain—even as amid black clouds Strymonian cranes give signal, while clamorously they skim the air, and flee before the south winds with joyous cries.[1] But to the Rutulian king and the Ausonian captains these things seemed marvellous, till, looking back, they behold the shoreward-facing sterns, and the whole sea moving onward with the ships. On the hero's head blazes the helmet-peak, flame streams from the crest aloft, and the shield's golden boss spouts floods of fire—even as when in the clear night comets glow blood-red in baneful wise; or even as fiery Sirius, that bearer of drought and pestilence to feeble mortals, rises and saddens the sky with baleful light.

[1] They are returning, at the end of winter, to their home on the Strymon.

VIRGIL

Haud tamen audaci Turno fiducia cessit
litora praecipere et venientis pellere terra.   277
"quod votis optastis, adest, perfringere dextra. 279
in manibus Mars ipse viris. nunc coniugis esto   280
quisque suae tectique memor, nunc magna referto
facta, patrum laudes. ultro occurramus ad undam,
dum trepidi egressisque labant vestigia prima.
audentis Fortuna iuvat."
haec ait et secum versat, quos ducere contra   285
vel quibus obsessos possit concredere muros.
  Interea Aeneas socios de puppibus altis
pontibus exponit. multi servare recursus
languentis pelagi et brevibus se credere saltu,
per remos alii. speculatus litora Tarchon,   290
qua vada non spirant nec fracta remurmurat unda,
sed mare inoffensum crescenti adlabitur aestu,
advertit subito proras sociosque precatur :
"nunc, o lecta manus, validis incumbite remis;
tollite, ferte rates; inimicam findite rostris   295
hanc terram, sulcumque sibi premat ipsa carina.
frangere nec tali puppim statione recuso,
arrepta tellure semel." quae talia postquam
effatus Tarchon, socii consurgere tonsis
spumantisque rates arvis inferre Latinis,   300
donec rostra tenent siccum et sedere carinae
omnes innocuae. sed non puppis tua, Tarchon.
namque inflicta vadis dorso dum pendet iniquo,
anceps sustentata diu, fluctusque fatigat,
solvitur atque viros mediis exponit in undis;   305
fragmina remorum quos et fluitantia transtra
impediunt retrahitque pedes simul unda relabens.

<small>
²⁷⁸ (= IX. 127) *omitted by MPγ*.   ²⁸⁰ viri *R*.
²⁸¹ referte *Pγ¹*.   ²⁸³ egressi *Rγ, known to Servius*.
²⁹¹ sperat *PRγ, preferred by Servius*.
²⁹³ proram *M²*: prora *R*.   ²⁹⁷ puppes *PRγ²*.
³⁰³ vadi *P¹, Probus*.   ³⁰⁷ pedem *M²*.
</small>

190

AENEID BOOK X

²⁷⁶ Yet fearless Turnus lost not the firm hope, to seize the shore first, and drive the coming foe from land. "What in your prayers ye have craved, ye now may do—break through with the sword! The war-god's self is in brave men's hands![1] Now let each be mindful of his wife and home; now recall the great deeds, the glories of our sires! Let us on and meet them at the water's edge, while they are confused, and their feet falter, as first they land. Fortune aids the daring." So saying, he ponders with himself whom to lead to the attack, or to whom he may entrust the beleaguered walls.

²⁸⁷ Meanwhile Aeneas lands his crews from the tall ships by gangways. Many watch for the ebb of the spent sea, and boldly leap into the shallows; others use oars. Tarchon, marking the shore where the shallows heave not nor the broken billow roars, but the sea, unchecked, glides up with spreading flow, suddenly turns his prows thither and implores his men: "Now, O chosen band, bend to your stout oars! Uplift, drive on your barques; cleave with your beaks this hostile shore, and let the keel herself plough a furrow. In such resting-place I shrink not from shipwreck, so but once I win the land." When Tarchon has thus spoken, his comrades rise on to their oars, and drive their foaming ships upon the Latin fields, till the beaks gain the dry land and every hull comes to rest unscathed. But not thy ship, Tarchon; for while, dashing amid the shallows, she hangs upon an uneven ridge, long poised in doubtful balance, and wearies the waves, she breaks up and plunges her crew amid the billows. Broken oars and floating thwarts entangle them, while the ebbing wave sucks back their feet.

[1] Or, reading *viri*, "Comrades, Mars himself (= the battle itself) is in your hands!"

VIRGIL

Nec Turnum segnis retinet mora, sed rapit acer
totam aciem in Teucros et contra in litore sistit.
signa canunt. primus turmas invasit agrestis   310
Aeneas, omen pugnae, stravitque Latinos,
occiso Therone, virum qui maximus ultro
Aenean petit. huic gladio perque aerea suta,
per tunicam squalentem auro latus haurit apertum.
inde Lichan ferit, exsectum iam matre perempta   315
et tibi, Phoebe, sacrum, casus evadere ferri
quod licuit parvo. nec longe, Cissea durum
immanemque Gyan, sternentis agmina clava,
deiecit Leto: nihil illos Herculis arma
nec validae iuvere manus genitorque Melampus,   320
Alcidae comes usque gravis dum terra labores
praebuit. ecce Pharo, voces dum iactat inertis,
intorquens iaculum clamanti sistit in ore.
tu quoque, flaventem prima lanugine malas
dum sequeris Clytium infelix, nova gaudia, Cydon, 325
Dardania stratus dextra, securus amorum,
qui iuvenum tibi semper erant, miserande iaceres,
ni fratrum stipata cohors foret obvia, Phorci
progenies, septem numero, septenaque tela
coniciunt: partim galea clipeoque resultant   330
inrita, deflexit partim stringentia corpus
alma Venus. fidum Aeneas adfatur Achaten:
"suggere tela mihi: non ullum dextera frustra
torserit in Rutulos, steterunt quae in corpore Graium
Iliacis campis." tum magnam corripit hastam   335
et iacit: illa volans clipei transverberat aera
Maeonis et thoraca simul cum pectore rumpit.
huic frater subit Alcanor fratremque ruentem

₃₁₇ quo $P^2\gamma^1$: cui R, *known to Servius*.   ₃₂₁ cum M^1.
₃₂₂ Pharon M^2P^1, *Servius*.   ₃₂₃ clamantis $MP\gamma$.
₃₃₄ steterint M^1. quae] -que $M^2R\gamma$. *So Mackail.*

192

AENEID BOOK X

308 Nor does dull delay hold Turnus back, but swiftly he sweeps his whole army upon the Trojans, and plants it against them on the shore. The trumpets sound. First dashed Aeneas on the rustic ranks—fair omen for the fight—and laid low the Latins, slaying Theron, who in his might dared assail the hero Aeneas. Driven through the brazen joints and through tunic rough with gold, the sword drank from his pierced side. Next he strikes Lichas, who was cut from his dead mother's womb, and consecrated to thee, Phoebus, for that as a babe he was suffered to escape the peril of the steel. Hard by, he cast down to death sturdy Cisseus and giant Gyas, as they with clubs laid low the ranks: naught availed them the arms of Hercules, or their stout hands and Melampus their sire—even Alcides' comrade, while earth yielded him grievous travails. Lo! as Pharus flings forth idle words, he launches his javelin and plants it in his bawling mouth. Thou, too, hapless Cydon, while thou followest thy new delight, Clytius, whose cheeks are golden with early down—thou hadst fallen under the Dardan hand and lain, O piteous sight, forgetful of all thy youthful loves, had not thy brethren's serried band met the foe—children of Phorcus, seven in number, and seven the darts they throw. Some from helmet and shield glance idly; some, so that they but graze the body, kindly Venus turned aside. Thus Aeneas speaks to loyal Achates: "Bring me store of weapons; none shall my hand hurl at Rutulians in vain, of all that once on Ilium's plains were lodged in bodies of the Greeks." Then he seizes a great spear and hurls it; flying, it crashes through the brass of Maeon's shield, rending corslet and breast at once. To his aid runs up Alcanor, and with his right arm brother upholds

VIRGIL

sustentat dextra: traiecto missa lacerto
protinus hasta fugit servatque cruenta tenorem,   340
dexteraque ex umero nervis moribunda pependit.
tum Numitor iaculo fratris de corpore rapto
Aenean petiit; sed non et figere contra
est licitum, magnique femur perstrinxit Achatae.

Hic Curibus, fidens primaevo corpore, Clausus   345
advenit et rigida Dryopem ferit eminus hasta
sub mentum graviter pressa pariterque loquentis
vocem animamque rapit traiecto gutture: at ille
fronte ferit terram et crassum vomit ore cruorem.
tres quoque Threicios Boreae de gente suprema   350
et tris, quos Idas pater et patria Ismara mittit,
per varios sternit casus. accurrit Halaesus
Auruncaeque manus, subit et Neptunia proles,
insignis Messapus equis. expellere tendunt
nunc hi, nunc illi; certatur limine in ipso   355
Ausoniae. magno discordes aethere venti
proelia ceu tollunt animis et viribus aequis;
non ipsi inter se, non nubila, non mare cedit;
anceps pugna diu, stant obnixa omnia contra:
haud aliter Troianae acies aciesque Latinae   360
concurrunt, haeret pede pes densusque viro vir.

At parte ex alia, qua saxa rotantia late
impulerat torrens arbustaque diruta ripis,
Arcadas, insuetos acies inferre pedestris,
ut vidit Pallas Latio dare terga sequaci   365
(aspera quis natura loci dimittere quando
suasit equos), unum quod rebus restat egenis,
nunc prece, nunc dictis virtutem accendit amaris:
"quo fugitis, socii? per vos et fortia facta,

³⁴⁹ ferit] premit $P\gamma^1$.   ³⁵⁸ cedunt M^1.
³⁶³ intulerat $R\gamma$.
³⁶⁶ quos $P\gamma^1$. *Priscian interprets* quando *as* aliquando, *Servius as* siquidem.

194

AENEID BOOK X

falling brother; piercing the arm, the spear flies right onward, keeping its bloody course, and the dying arm hung by the sinews from the shoulder. Then Numitor, tearing the lance from his brother's body, aimed at Aeneas, yet could not also strike him full, but grazed the thigh of great Achates.

345 Now comes up Clausus from Cures, trusting in his youthful frame, and from a distance smites Dryops under the chin with his stiff shaft driven amain, and piercing his throat robs him, even as he speaks, of voice and life together; but Dryops smites the ground with his forehead, and from his mouth vomits thick gore. Three Thracians, too, of the exalted race of Boreas, and three, whom their father Idas and their native Ismarus sent forth, he lays low in divers wise. Halaesus runs to his side, and the Auruncan bands; the scion, too, of Neptune comes up, Messapus glorious with his steeds. Now these, now those, strain to thrust back the foe; on Ausonia's very threshold is the struggle. As in wide heaven warring winds rise to battle, matched in spirit and strength; they yield not to one another—not winds, not clouds, not sea; long is the battle doubtful; all things stand locked in struggle; even so clash the ranks of Troy and the ranks of Latium, foot fast with foot, and man massed with man.

362 But in another part, where a torrent had driven far and wide rolling boulders and bushes uptorn from the banks, soon as Pallas saw his Arcadians, unused to charge on foot, turn to flight before pursuing Latium—for the roughness of ground lured them for once to resign their steeds—then, as the one hope in such strait, now with entreaties, now with bitter words, he fires their valour: "Friends, whither flee ye? By your brave deeds I pray you, by your King

VIRGIL

per ducis Euandri nomen devictaque bella 370
spemque meam, patriae quae nunc subit aemula laudi,
fidite ne pedibus.　ferro rumpenda per hostis
est via.　qua globus ille virum densissimus urget,
hac vos et Pallanta ducem patria alta reposcit.
numina nulla premunt, mortali urgemur ab hoste 375
mortales; totidem nobis animaeque manusque.
ecce, maris magna claudit nos obice pontus,
deest iam terra fugae; pelagus Troiamne petemus?"
haec ait et medius densos prorumpit in hostis.

 Obvius huic primum, fatis adductus iniquis, 380
fit Lagus. hunc, magno vellit dum pondere saxum,
intorto figit telo, discrimina costis
per medium qua spina dabat, hastamque receptat
ossibus haerentem. quem non super occupat Hisbo,
ille quidem hoc sperans: nam Pallas ante ruentem, 385
dum furit, incautum crudeli morte sodalis
excipit atque ensem tumido in pulmone recondit.
hinc Sthenium petit et Rhoeti de gente vetusta
Anchemolum, thalamos ausum incestare novercae.
vos etiam, gemini, Rutulis cecidistis in arvis, 390
Daucia, Laride Thymberque, simillima proles,
indiscreta suis gratusque parentibus error;
at nunc dura dedit vobis discrimina Pallas:
nam tibi, Thymbre, caput Euandrius abstulit ensis,
te decisa suum, Laride, dextera quaerit 395
semianimesque micant digiti ferrumque retractant.

 Arcadas accensos monitu et praeclara tuentis
facta viri mixtus dolor et pudor armat in hostis.

[377] *Servius knows* magno, magna, *and* magni.
[378] petamus $M^2R\gamma^1$.　　[381] vellit magno $PR\gamma$.
[383] dedit R.　　[390] agris $P\gamma^1$.　　[398] pudor] furor R.

AENEID BOOK X

Evander's name, by the wars ye have won, by my hopes, now springing up to match my father's renown—trust not to flight. 'Tis the sword must hew a way through the foe. Where yonder mass of men presses thickest, there your noble country calls you back, with Pallas at your head. No gods press upon us; mortals, by mortal foes are we driven; we have as many lives, as many hands as they. Lo! ocean hems us in with mighty barrier of sea; even now earth fails our flight; shall we seek the main or Troy?" So speaking, he dashes on into the midst of the serried foe.

380 First Lagus meets him, drawn thither by unkind fate; him, while tearing at a stone of vast weight, he pierces with hurled javelin, where the spine midway between the ribs made a parting, and plucks back the spear from its lodging in the bones. Nor does Hisbo surprise him, falling on him from above, and hopeful though he be; for Pallas, as he rushes on, reckless and enraged o'er his comrade's cruel death, has welcome ready and buries his sword in his swollen[1] lung. Next he assails Sthenius, and Anchemolus of Rhoetus' ancient line, who dared defile his stepdame's bed. Ye too, twin brethren, fell on Rutulian plains, Larides and Thymber, sons of Daucus, most like in semblance, indistinguishable to kindred, and to their own parents a sweet perplexity. But a grim difference now has Pallas made between you. For thy head, Thymber, had Evander's sword swept off; while thy severed hand, Larides, seeks its master, and the dying fingers twitch and clutch again at the sword.

397 Fired by his chiding and beholding his glorious deeds, the Arcadians are armed by mingled wrath

[1] *i.e.* with rage.

197

VIRGIL

tum Pallas biiugis fugientem Rhoetea praeter
traicit. hoc spatium tantumque morae fuit Ilo.   400
Ilo namque procul validam derexerat hastam :
quam medius Rhoeteus intercipit, optime Teuthra,
te fugiens fratremque Tyren ; curruque volutus
caedit semianimis Rutulorum calcibus arva.
ac velut optato ventis aestate coortis   405
dispersa immittit silvis incendia pastor ;
correptis subito mediis extenditur una
horrida per latos acies Volcania campos ;
ille sedens victor flammas despectat ovantis :
non aliter socium virtus coit omnis in unum   410
teque iuvat, Palla. sed bellis acer Halaesus
tendit in adversos seque in sua colligit arma.
hic mactat Ladona Pheretaque Demodocumque,
Strymonio dextram fulgenti deripit ense
elatam in iugulum, saxo ferit ora Thoantis   415
ossaque dispersit cerebro permixta cruento.
fata canens silvis genitor celarat Halaesum :
ut senior leto canentia lumina solvit,
iniecere manum Parcae telisque sacrarunt
Euandri.   quem sic Pallas petit ante precatus :   420
"da nunc, Thybri pater, ferro, quod missile libro,
fortunam atque viam duri per pectus Halaesi.
haec arma exuviasque viri tua quercus habebit."
audiit illa deus ; dum texit Imaona Halaesus,
Arcadio infelix telo dat pectus inermum.   425

At non caede viri tanta perterrita Lausus,
pars ingens belli, sinit agmina : primus Abantem
oppositum interimit, pugnae nodumque moramque.

<small>401 direxerat $M^2P\gamma$.
417 cavens, *known to Servius.* celaret M^1.</small>

AENEID BOOK X

and shame to face the foe. Then Pallas pierces Rhoeteus, as he flies past in his car. Thus much respite, thus much delay Ilus gained; for at Ilus he had launched from afar his strong spear, and Rhoeteus intercepts it midway, fleeing from thee, noble Teuthras, and from Tyres thy brother. Rolling from the car in death, he spurns with his heels the Rutulian fields. And as in summer, when the winds he longed for have risen, some shepherd kindles fires here and there among the woods; on a sudden the mid-spaces catch, and Vulcan's bristling battle-line spreads o'er the broad fields unbroken; he, from his seat, gazes down victorious on the revelling flames: even so all thy comrades' chivalry rallies to one point in aid of thee, Pallas! But Halaesus, bold in war, advances to confront them, and gathers himself behind his shield. He slays Ladon, and Pheres, and Demodocus; with gleaming sword he lops off Strymonius' hand, raised against his throat; then smites Thoas in the face with a stone, and scattered the bones, mingled with blood and brains. His sire, prophetic of fate, had hidden Halaesus in the woods: when, with advance of age, he relaxed his glazing eyes in death, the Fates laid hand on him and devoted him to Evander's darts. Him Pallas assails, first praying thus: "Grant now, father Tiber, to the steel I poise and hurl, a prosperous way through stout Halaesus' breast; thy oak shall hold these arms and the hero's spoils." The god heard the prayer; while Halaesus shielded Imaon, the luckless man offers his defenceless breast to the Arcadian lance.

426 But Lausus, a mighty portion of the war, lets not his ranks be dismayed by the hero's vast carnage; first he cuts down Abas, who faces him, the battle's

VIRGIL

sternitur Arcadiae proles, sternuntur Etrusci,
et vos, o Grais imperdita corpora, Teucri. 430
agmina concurrunt ducibusque et viribus aequis.
extremi addensent acies nec turba moveri
tela manusque sinit. hinc Pallas instat et urget,
hinc contra Lausus, nec multum discrepat aetas,
egregii forma, sed quis Fortuna negarat 435
in patriam reditus. ipsos concurrere passus
haud tamen inter se magni regnator Olympi;
mox illos sua fata manent maiore sub hoste.

Interea soror alma monet succedere Lauso
Turnum, qui volucri curru medium secat agmen. 440
ut vidit socios: "tempus desistere pugnae;
solus ego in Pallanta feror, soli mihi Pallas
debetur; cuperem ipse parens spectator adesset."
haec ait, et socii cesserunt aequore iusso.
at Rutulum abscessu iuvenis tum, iussa superba 445
miratus, stupet in Turno corpusque per ingens
lumina volvit obitque truci procul omnia visu,
talibus et dictis it contra dicta tyranni:
"aut spoliis ego iam raptis laudabor opimis
aut leto insigni; sorti pater aequus utrique est. 450
tolle minas." fatus medium procedit in aequor.
frigidus Arcadibus coit in praecordia sanguis.
desiluit Turnus biiugis, pedes apparat ire
comminus; utque leo, specula cum vidit ab alta
stare procul campis meditantem in proelia taurum, 455
advolat: haud alia est Turni venientis imago.
hunc ubi contiguum missae fore credidit hastae,

⁴³² addensant *MP²R*γ.   ⁴⁴¹ pugna *R*.
⁴⁴⁶ miratur *R*γ¹.   ⁴⁵⁵ in *omitted by P*γ.

AENEID BOOK X

knot[1] and barrier. Then falls the youth of Arcadia, the Etruscans fall, and ye, O Trojans, whose bodies the Greeks wasted not. The armies close, matched in captains, as in might; the rearmost crowd upon the van, and the throng suffers not weapons or hands to move. Here Pallas presses and strains; there Lausus confronts him; the two nearly matched in years, and peerless in beauty, but to them fortune had denied return to their fatherland. Yet the king of great Olympus suffered them not to meet face to face; ere long each has his own fate awaiting him beneath a greater foe.

439 Meanwhile his gracious sister warns Turnus to go to Lausus' aid, and with his swift car he cleaves the ranks between. As he saw his comrades: "'Tis time," he cries, "to stand aside from battle; I alone encounter Pallas; to me alone is Pallas due; I would that his father himself were here to see!" He said, and at his bidding his comrades withdrew from the field. But when the Rutulians retired, then the youth, marvelling at the haughty behest, stands in amaze at Turnus, rolls his eyes over that giant frame, and with fierce glance scans all from afar, then with these words meets the monarch's words: "Soon shall I win praise either for kingly spoils or for a glorious death; my sire is equal to either lot: away with threats!" So saying, he advances into the midfield: cold gathers the blood at the hearts of the Arcadians. Down from his car leapt Turnus; on foot he makes ready to close with the other. And as when from some lofty outlook a lion has seen a bull stand afar on the plain, meditating battle, on he rushes; even such seemed the coming of Turnus. But Pallas, when he deemed his foe within range of a spear-cast, advanced

[1] The metaphor comes from a knot, difficult to untie.

201

VIRGIL

ire prior Pallas, si qua fors adiuvet ausum
viribus imparibus, magnumque ita ad aethera fatur:
"per patris hospitium et mensas, quas advena
    adisti, 460
te precor, Alcide, coeptis ingentibus adsis.   MR
cernat semineci sibi me rapere arma cruenta
victoremque ferant morientia lumina Turni."
audiit Alcides iuvenem magnumque sub imo
corde premit gemitum lacrimasque effundit inanis. 465
tum genitor natum dictis adfatur amicis:
"stat sua cuique dies, breve et inreparabile tempus
omnibus est vitae; sed famam extendere factis,
hoc virtutis opus. Troiae sub moenibus altis
tot gnati cecidere deum, quin occidit una 470
Sarpedon, mea progenies. etiam sua Turnum
fata vocant metasque dati pervenit ad aevi."
sic ait atque oculos Rutulorum reicit arvis.

At Pallas magnis emittit viribus hastam
vaginaque cava fulgentem deripit ensem. 475
illa volans, umeri surgunt qua tegmina summa,
incidit atque viam clipei molita per oras
tandem etiam magno strinxit de corpore Turni.

Hic Turnus ferro praefixum robur acuto
in Pallanta diu librans iacit atque ita fatur: 480
"aspice, num mage sit nostrum penetrabile telum."
dixerat; at clipeum, tot ferri terga, tot aeris,
quem pellis totiens obeat circumdata tauri,
vibranti cuspis medium transverberat ictu
loricaeque moras et pectus perforat ingens. 485

[475] diripit $M\gamma^2$.   [476] summa] prima R.   [477] est molita M^1.
[481] aspicesut (= aspicis ut?) M^1.   magi R.
[483] quem] cum M^2R, *Servius*.   [484] medium cuspis $R\gamma$.

AENEID BOOK X

the first, if haply chance would aid the venture of his ill-matched strength, and thus to great heaven he cries: "By my father's welcome, and the board whereto thou camest a stranger, I beseech thee, Alcides, aid my high emprise! May Turnus see me strip the bloody arms from his dying limbs, and may his glazing eyes endure a conqueror!" Alcides heard the youth, and deep in his heart stifled a heavy groan, and shed idle tears. Then with kindly words the Father bespeaks his son:[1] "Each has his day appointed; short and irretrievable is the span of life to all: but to lengthen fame by deeds—that is valour's task. Under Troy's high walls fell those many sons of gods; yea, with them fell mine own child Sarpedon.[2] For Turnus too his own fate calls, and he has reached the goal of his allotted years." So he speaks, and turns his eyes away from the Rutulian fields.

474 But Pallas hurls his spear with all his strength and plucks his flashing sword from its hollow scabbard. On flies the shaft and strikes where the top of the mail rises to guard the shoulder; then, forcing a way through the shield's rim, at last even grazed the mighty frame of Turnus.

479 At this, Turnus, long poising his oaken shaft, tipped with sharp steel, hurls it against Pallas, speaking thus: "See whether our weapon be not the more piercing!" He ended; but with quivering stroke the point tears through the centre of the shield, with all its plates of iron, all its plates of brass, all the bull-hide's overlaying folds; then pierces the corslet's barrier and the mighty breast. In vain he

---

[1] Hercules was son of Jupiter by Alcmene.
[2] *cf.* Homer, *Iliad*, XVI. 477 *sq.*

VIRGIL

ille rapit calidum frustra de volnere telum :
una eademque via sanguis animusque sequuntur.
corruit in volnus (sonitum super arma dedere)
et terram hostilem moriens petit ore cruento.
quem Turnus super adsistens: 490
" Arcades, haec," inquit, " memores mea dicta referte
Euandro: qualem meruit, Pallanta remitto.
quisquis honos tumuli, quidquid solamen humandi est,
largior: haud illi stabunt Aeneia parvo
hospitia." et laevo pressit pede talia fatus 495
exanimem, rapiens immania pondera baltei
impressumque nefas: una sub nocte iugali
caesa manus iuvenum foede thalamique cruenti,
quae Clonus Eurytides multo caelaverat auro;
quo nunc Turnus ovat spolio gaudetque potitus. 500
nescia mens hominum fati sortisque futurae
et servare modum, rebus sublata secundis!
Turno tempus erit, magno cum optaverit emptum
intactum Pallanta, et cum spolia ista diemque
oderit. at socii multo gemitu lacrimisque 505
impositum scuto referunt Pallanta frequentes.
o dolor atque decus magnum rediture parenti !
haec te prima dies bello dedit, haec eadem aufert,
cum tamen ingentis Rutulorum linquis acervos! MPR

Nec iam fama mali tanti, sed certior auctor 510
advolat Aeneae, tenui discrimine leti
esse suos, tempus versis succurrere Teucris.
proxima quaeque metit gladio latumque per agmen

⁴⁸⁶ pectore *R:* corpore γ¹.
⁴⁹⁰ sic ore profatur *added by R.*
⁵¹² versis tempus *P.*

---

[1] *i.e.* dead. Evander has earned or merited this affliction, by reason of his treason to Italy.

AENEID BOOK X

plucks the warm dart from the wound; by one and the same road follow blood and life. Prone he falls upon the wound, his armour clashes over him, and, dying, he smites the hostile earth with blood-stained mouth. Then standing over him, Turnus cries: "Arcadians, give heed, and bear these my words back to Evander: even as he has merited,[1] I send him back Pallas! Whatever honour a tomb gives, whatever solace a burial, I freely grant; yet his welcome of Aeneas shall cost him dear." So saying, with his left foot he trod upon the dead, tearing away the belt's huge weight and the story of the crime thereon engraved[2]—the youthful band foully slain on one nuptial night, and the chambers drenched with blood—which Clonus, son of Eurytus, had richly chased in gold. Now Turnus exults in the spoil, and glories in the winning. O mind of man, knowing not fate or coming doom or how to keep bounds when uplifted with favouring fortune! To Turnus shall come the hour when for a great price will he long to have bought an unscathed Pallas, and when he will abhor those spoils and that day. But with many moans and tears his friends throng round Pallas and bear him back laid upon his shield. O the great grief and yet great glory to thy father of that home-coming of thine! This day first gave thee to war, this also takes thee hence; yet vast are the piles thou leavest of Rutulian dead!

[510] And now not mere rumour of the bitter blow, but a surer messenger, flies to Aeneas—that his men are but a hair's-breadth removed from death, that 'tis time to succour the routed Teucrians. With the sword he mows down all the nearest ranks, and

[2] The story of the murder of the sons of Aegyptus by the daughters of Danaus.

205

VIRGIL

ardens limitem agit ferro, te, Turne, superbum
caede nova quaerens.   Pallas, Euander, in ipsis   515
omnia sunt oculis, mensae, quas advena primas
tunc adiit, dextraeque datae.   Sulmone creatos
quattuor hic iuvenes, totidem quos educat Ufens,
viventis rapit, inferias quos immolet umbris
captivoque rogi perfundat sanguine flammas.   520
inde Mago procul infensam contenderat hastam.
ille astu subit—at tremibunda supervolat hasta—
et genua amplectens effatur talia supplex:
" per patrios Manis et spes surgentis Iuli
te precor, hanc animam serves gnatoque patrique.   525
est domus alta, iacent penitus defossa talenta
caelati argenti, sunt auri pondera facti
infectique mihi.   non hic victoria Teucrum
vertitur aut anima una dabit discrimina tanta."
dixerat.   Aeneas contra cui talia reddit: 530
" argenti atque auri memoras quae multa talenta,
gnatis parce tuis.   belli commercia Turnus
sustulit ista prior iam tum Pallante perempto.
hoc patris Anchisae Manes, hoc sentit Iulus."
sic fatus galeam laeva tenet atque reflexa   535
cervice orantis capulo tenus applicat ensem.
nec procul Haemonides, Phoebi Triviaeque sacerdos,
infula cui sacra redimibat tempora vitta,
totus conlucens veste atque insignibus armis:
quem congressus agit campo, lapsumque superstans
immolat ingentique umbra tegit; arma Serestus   541
lecta refert umeris, tibi, rex Gradive, tropaeum.

Instaurant acies Volcani stirpe creatus
Caeculus et veniens Marsorum montibus Umbro.

⁵²¹ infestam $PR\gamma^1$: contenderet M^1.
⁵²² at $PRM^3\gamma^1$: in M^1: en M^2: ac $M(late)\gamma^2b$.
⁵²³ et] in M^1: en M^2: et M^3.   ⁵²⁴ surgentis] heredis $P^2\gamma^1$.
⁵³³ illa M.   ⁵³⁶ oranti P^1.
⁵³⁹ armis] albis *Probus, perhaps* P^1.   ⁵⁴³ instaurat M^1.

AENEID BOOK X

fiercely drives with the steel a broad path through the host, seeking thee, Turnus, still flushed with new-wrought slaughter. Pallas, Evander, all stands before his eyes—the board whereto he then came first, a stranger, and the right hands pledged. Then, four youths, sons of Sulmo, and as many reared by Ufens, he takes alive, to offer as victims to the dead and to sprinkle the funeral flame with captive blood. Next at Magus from afar he had aimed the hostile lance. Deftly he cowers—the lance flies quivering o'er him—and, clasping the hero's knees, he speaks thus in suppliance: "By the spirit of thy father, by thy hope in growing Iülus, I entreat thee, save this life for a son and for a sire. A stately house have I; buried deep within lie talents of chased silver, and mine are masses of gold, wrought and unwrought. Not on me turns the victory of Troy, nor will one life make difference so great." He spoke, and Aeneas thus replied: "Those many talents of silver and gold thou tellest of, spare for thy sons. Such trafficking in war Turnus first put away, even in the hour when Pallas was slain. Thus judges my father Anchises' spirit, thus Iülus." So speaking, he grasps the helmet with his left hand, and bending back the suppliant's neck, drives the sword up to the hilt. Hard by was Haemon's son, priest of Phoebus and Trivia, his temples wreathed in the fillet's sacred band, all glittering in his robe and in resplendent arms. Him he meets and drives over the plain; then, bestriding the fallen, slaughters him and wraps him in mighty darkness; his armour Serestus gathers and carries away on his shoulders, a trophy, King Gradivus, unto thee!

[543] Caeculus, born of Vulcan's race, and Umbro, who comes from the Marsian hills, repair the ranks.

VIRGIL

Dardanides contra furit. Anxuris ense sinistram 545
et totum clipei ferro deiecerat orbem
(dixerat ille aliquid magnum vimque adfore verbo
crediderat, caeloque animum fortasse ferebat
canitiemque sibi et longos promiserat annos): MPRV
Tarquitus exsultans contra fulgentibus armis, 550
silvicolae Fauno Dryope quem nympha crearat,
obvius ardenti sese obtulit. ille reducta
loricam clipeique ingens onus impedit hasta;
tum caput orantis nequiquam et multa parantis
dicere deturbat terrae truncumque tepentem 555
provolvens super haec inimico pectore fatur:
"istic nunc, metuende, iace. non te optima mater
condet humi patrioque onerabit membra sepulchro:
alitibus linquere feris aut gurgite mersum
unda feret piscesque impasti volnera lambent." 560
protinus Antaeum et Lucam, prima agmina Turni,
persequitur fortemque Numam fulvumque Camertem,
magnanimo Volcente satum, ditissimus agri
qui fuit Ausonidum et tacitis regnavit Amyclis.
Aegaeon qualis, centum cui bracchia dicunt 565
centenasque manus, quinquaginta oribus ignem
pectoribusque arsisse, Iovis cum fulmina contra
tot paribus streperet clipeis, tot stringeret ensis:
sic toto Aeneas desaevit in aequore victor,
ut semel intepuit mucro. quin ecce Niphaei 570
quadriiugis in equos adversaque pectora tendit.
atque illi longe gradientem et dira frementem
ut videre, metu versi retroque ruentes
effunduntque ducem rapiuntque ad litora currus.

⁵⁵⁸ humo M^2. patriove $PR\gamma$.   ⁵⁶⁵ cui] qui V^1.
⁵⁷² et] ac M^1.   ⁵⁷⁴ currum R.

208

AENEID BOOK X

Against them storms the Dardan. His sword had lopped off Anxur's left arm with all the circle of the shield—he had uttered some brave vaunt and thought his hand would match his word, and perchance lifted his soul heaven-high and promised himself hoary eld and length of years—when, in the pride of gleaming arms, Tarquitus, whom the Nymph Dryope had borne to silvan Faunus, crossed his fiery course. Drawing back his spear, he pins the corslet and the shield's huge burden together; then, as the youth vainly pleaded and is fain to say many a word, he dashes his head to the ground, and as he spurns the trunk, yet warm, above him speaks thus from pitiless heart: " Lie now there, thou terrible one! No loving mother shall lay thee in earth, nor load thy limbs with ancestral tomb. To birds of prey shalt thou be left; or, sunk beneath the flood, the wave shall bear thee on, and hungry fish shall suck thy wounds." Next he o'ertakes Antaeus and Lucas, foremost of Turnus' ranks, and brave Numa, and tawny Camers, son of noble Volcens, who was wealthiest in the land of the Ausonians, and reigned over silent Amyclae. Even as Aegaeon, who, men say, had a hundred arms and a hundred hands, and flashed fire from fifty mouths and breasts, what time against Jove's thunders he clanged with as many like shields, and bared as many swords;[1] so Aeneas o'er the whole plain gluts his victorious rage, when once his sword grew warm. Nay, see! he turns upon Niphaeus' four-horse car and his opposing front; and lo! when they mark his long strides and deadly rage, in terror they turn, and, rushing backward, fling forth their master and whirl the chariot to the shore.

---

[1] *i.e.* fifty shields, all alike, and fifty swords.

VIRGIL

Interea biiugis infert se Lucagus albis
in medios fraterque Liger; sed frater habenis 576
flectit equos, strictum rotat acer Lucagus ensem.
haud tulit Aeneas tanto fervore furentis:
inruit adversaque ingens apparuit hasta.
cui Liger: 580
"non Diomedis equos nec currum cernis Achilli
aut Phrygiae campos: nunc belli finis et aevi
his dabitur terris."   vesano talia late
dicta volant Ligeri.   sed non et Troius heros
dicta parat contra, iaculum nam torquet in hostem. 585
Lucagus ut pronus pendens in verbera telo
admonuit biiugos, proiecto dum pede laevo
aptat se pugnae, subit oras hasta per imas
fulgentis clipei, tum laevum perforat inguen;
excussus curru moribundus volvitur arvis. 590
quem pius Aeneas dictis adfatur amaris:
"Lucage, nulla tuos currus fuga segnis equorum
prodidit aut vanae vertere ex hostibus umbrae;
ipse rotis saliens iuga deseris."   haec ita fatus
arripuit biiugos; frater tendebat inertis 595
infelix palmas, curru delapsus eodem:
"per te, per qui te talem genuere parentes,
vir Troiane, sine hanc animam et miserere precantis."
pluribus oranti Aeneas: "haud talia dudum
dicta dabas.   morere et fratrem ne desere frater." 600
tum latebras animae pectus mucrone recludit.
talia per campos edebat funera ductor
Dardanius, torrentis aquae vel turbinis atri
more furens. tandem erumpunt et castra relinquunt
Ascanius puer et nequiquam obsessa iuventus. 605

[575] bigis $P\gamma^1$.   [585] hostis P^1R : hostes $P^2\gamma$.
[587] traiecto M.   [588] aptet $P\gamma^1$.
[594] deserit P^1 [595] inermis $P^1\gamma^2$.

AENEID BOOK X

⁵⁷⁵ Meanwhile, with their two white steeds, there dash into the midst Lucagus and Liger his brother; but the brother guides the steeds with the reins, while Lucagus fiercely whirls his drawn sword. Their furious onset Aeneas could not brook, but rushed upon them, and towered gigantic with opposing spear. To him Liger: "Not Diomede's horses dost thou see, nor Achilles' car, nor Phrygia's plains; this hour shall upon this soil end thy warfare and thy life." Such words fly abroad from mad Liger's lips. But not in words the Trojan hero shapes reply, for he hurls his javelin against the foe. Then, as Lucagus, bending forward to the stroke, urged on his steeds with the sword, even when, with left foot advanced, he gets ready for the fray, there comes the spear through the lowest rim of his gleaming shield, then pierces the left groin; tumbling from the car, he rolls in death upon the plain, while good Aeneas bespeaks him with bitter words: "Lucagus, no coward flight of thy steeds has betrayed thy car; no vain shadow of a foe has turned them back; thyself, leaping from the wheels, forsakest thy beasts." So saying, he seized the steeds; down-gliding from the self-same car, the brother piteously outstretched his helpless hands: "By thyself, by the parents who gave life to such a son, O hero of Troy, spare this life, and have pity on my prayer!" Longer had been his plea, but Aeneas: "Not such erewhile were thy words. Die, and let not brother forsake brother!" —then with the sword he cleft open the bosom, wherein is life's lurking-place. Such were the deaths the Dardan chieftain wrought o'er the plains, raging like torrent-brook or black tempest. At last the boy Ascanius and the vainly beleaguered warriors burst forth and leave the camp.

211

VIRGIL

Iunonem interea compellat Iuppiter ultro:
"o germana mihi atque eadem gratissima coniunx,
ut rebare, Venus (nec te sententia fallit)
Troianas sustentat opes, non vivida bello
dextra viris animusque ferox patiensque pericli." 610
cui Iuno submissa · "quid, o pulcherrime coniunx,
sollicitas aegram et tua tristia iussa timentem?
si mihi, quae quondam fuerat quamque esse decebat,
vis in amore foret, non hoc mihi namque negares,
omnipotens, quin et pugnae subducere Turnum 615
et Dauno possem incolumem servare parenti.
nunc pereat Teucrisque pio det sanguine poenas.
ille tamen nostra deducit origine nomen,
Pilumnusque illi quartus pater, et tua larga
saepe manu multisque oneravit limina donis." 620

Cui rex aetherii breviter sic fatur Olympi:
"si mora praesentis leti tempusque caduco
oratur iuveni meque hoc ita ponere sentis,
tolle fuga Turnum atque instantibus eripe fatis.
hactenus indulsisse vacat. sin altior istis 625
sub precibus venia ulla latet totumque moveri
mutarive putas bellum, spes pascis inanis."

Et Iuno adlacrimans: "quid, si, quae voce gravaris,
mente dares atque haec Turno rata vita maneret?
nunc manet insontem gravis exitus, aut ego veri 630
vana feror. quod ut o potius formidine falsa
ludar et in melius tua, qui potes, orsa reflectas!"

Haec ubi dicta dedit, caelo se protinus alto
misit agens hiemem nimbo succincta per auras,

⁶¹² iussa] dicta *PR*γ.   ⁶¹⁷ pio] suo *known to Servius.*
⁶¹⁸ deducet *P*γ¹.   ⁶²¹ fatus *M²R.*   ⁶²⁹ data *R.*

212

AENEID BOOK X

⁶⁰⁶ Meanwhile Jupiter opens speech with Juno: "O sister and dearest wife in one, 'tis Venus, as thou didst deem—nor errs thy judgment—that upholds the Trojan power, not their own right hands, quick for war, and their proud souls, patient of peril." To him Juno meekly: "Why, my fairest lord, vexest thou a sick heart, that fears thy stern commands? Had my love the force that once it had, and still should have, this boon surely thou wouldst not deny me, even the power to withdraw Turnus from the fray, and preserve him in safety for his father Daunus. But now let him perish and with innocent blood make atonement to the Trojans! Yet from our lineage he derives his name, for Pilumnus was his sire four generations gone; and oft has he heaped thy threshold with many a gift from a lavish hand."

⁶²¹ To her the king of heavenly Olympus thus briefly spake: "If thy prayer be for a respite from present death, and a reprieve for the doomed youth—if thou understandest that such is my will, take Turnus away in flight, and snatch him from impending fate. Thus far is there room for indulgence. But if thought of deeper favour lurks beneath thy prayers, and thou deemest that the war's whole course may be moved or altered, thou nursest an idle hope."

⁶²⁸ And Juno weeping: "What if thy heart should grant what thy tongue begrudges, and this life I crave should remain assured to Turnus? Now a heavy doom awaits him for no guilt, or I wander blind to truth. Yet, O that rather I were mocked by lying fears, and that thou, who canst, wouldst bend thy purposes to a better end!"

⁶³³ These words said, straightway she through the air darted from high heaven, driving her storm-chariot cloud-engirdled; and sought the army of

VIRGIL

Iliacamque aciem et Laurentia castra petivit.   635
tum dea nube cava tenuem sine viribus umbram
in faciem Aeneae (visu mirabile monstrum)
Dardaniis ornat telis, clipeumque iubasque
divini adsimulat capitis, dat inania verba,
dat sine mente sonum gressusque effingit euntis;   640
morte obita qualis fama est volitare figuras
aut quae sopitos deludunt somnia sensus.
at primas laeta ante acies exsultat imago
inritatque virum telis et voce lacessit.
instat cui Turnus stridentemque eminus hastam   645
conicit; illa dato vertit vestigia tergo.
tum vero Aenean aversum ut cedere Turnus
credidit atque animo spem turbidus hausit inanem:
"quo fugis, Aenea? thalamos ne desere pactos;
hac dabitur dextra tellus quaesita per undas."   650
talia vociferans sequitur strictumque coruscat
mucronem, nec ferre videt sua gaudia ventos.

Forte ratis celsi coniuncta crepidine saxi
expositis stabat scalis et ponte parato,
qua rex Clusinis advectus Osinius oris.   655
huc sese trepida Aeneae fugientis imago
conicit in latebras, nec Turnus segnior instat
exsuperatque moras et pontis transilit altos.
vix proram attigerat: rumpit Saturnia funem
avolsamque rapit revoluta per aequora navem.   660
illum autem Aeneas absentem in proelia poscit;
obvia multa virum demittit corpora morti,
tum levis haud ultra latebras iam quaerit imago,

⁶³⁹ verba *in rasura*, *P*: membra γ².
⁶⁴⁰ gressum *M*.   ⁶⁵⁹ rupit *R*γ².
⁶⁶⁰⁻⁶⁶⁵ *Ribbeck, following two Paris MSS., accepts the following order:* 660, 663, 664, 661, 662, 665. *Mackail puts* 665 *between* 662 *and* 663.

⁶⁶¹ ille *PR*γ. Aenean *P¹R* (ille autem Aenean *known to Servius*).

214

AENEID BOOK X

Ilium and the camp of Laurentum. Then the goddess out of hollow mist fashions a thin, strengthless phantom in the likeness of Aeneas, a monstrous marvel to behold, decks it with Dardan weapons, and counterfeits the shield and plumes on his godlike head, gives it unreal words, gives a voice without thought, and mimicks his gait as he moves; —even like shapes that flit, 'tis said, when death is past, or like dreams that mock the slumbering senses. But exultant, the phantom stalks before the foremost ranks, with weapons provokes the foe, and with cries defies him. On it rushes Turnus, and from afar hurls a hissing spear; the phantom wheels round in flight. Then indeed, when Turnus deemed that Aeneas had turned and yielded, and with bewildered soul drank in the empty hope: "Whither," he cries, "dost flee, Aeneas? Forsake not thy plighted bridal chamber; this hand shall give thee the land thou hast sought overseas." With such clamour he follows, and brandishes his naked blade, nor sees that the winds bear away his triumph!

653 It chanced that, moored to the ledge of a lofty rock, with ladders let down and gangway ready, stood the ship, wherein king Osinius sailed from the coasts of Clusium. Hither the hurrying phantom of flying Aeneas flings himself to shelter; nor with less speed Turnus follows, surmounts all hindrances, and springs across the lofty bridge. Scarce had he touched the prow when Saturn's daughter snaps the cable and sweeps the sundered ship over the ebbing waters. But meantime Aeneas is challenging his vanished foe to battle, and sends down to death many bodies of warriors who cross his path. Then the airy phantom seeks shelter no longer, but soaring

VIRGIL

sed sublime volans nubi se immiscuit atrae.
cum Turnum medio interea fert aequore turbo. 665
respicit ignarus rerum ingratusque salutis
et duplicis cum voce manus ad sidera tendit:
"omnipotens genitor, tanton me crimine dignum
duxisti et talis voluisti expendere poenas?
quo feror? unde abii? quae me fuga quemve reducit?
Laurentisne iterum muros aut castra videbo? 671
quid manus illa virum, qui me meaque arma secuti?
quosne (nefas) omnis infanda in morte reliqui
et nunc palantis video gemitumque cadentum
accipio? quid ago? aut quae iam satis ima dehiscat 675
terra mihi? vos o potius miserescite, venti;
in rupes, in saxa (volens vos Turnus adoro)
ferte ratem saevisque vadis immittite syrtis,
quo neque me Rutuli nec conscia fama sequatur."
haec memorans animo nunc huc, nunc fluctuat illuc,
an sese mucrone ob tantum dedecus amens 681
induat et crudum per costas exigat ensem,
fluctibus an iaciat mediis et litora nando
curva petat Teucrumque iterum se reddat in arma.
ter conatus utramque viam, ter maxima Iuno 685
continuit iuvenemque animi miserata repressit.
labitur alta secans fluctuque aestuque secundo
et patris antiquam Dauni defertur ad urbem.

At Iovis interea monitis Mezentius ardens
succedit pugnae Teucrosque invadit ovantis. 690
concurrunt Tyrrhenae acies atque omnibus uni,

⁶⁶⁵ interea medio *Rb*.   ⁶⁶⁸ tanto *Pγ*.
⁶⁷⁰ abeo *P¹*. quemve] quo *M¹*: quove *M²*: quemve *M (late, in margin)*.
⁶⁷³ quosque *M¹R*: quosve *M²Pγ*: quosne *b, Asper (cited by Servius)*.
⁶⁷⁴ pallentis *M¹*.   ⁶⁷⁵ aut] et *M¹*.   ⁶⁸¹ mucroni *P¹R*.

216

AENEID BOOK X

aloft blends with a dark cloud, while meantime the gale is whirling Turnus o'er mid ocean. Unknowing of the truth and unthankful for escape, he looks back and raises his voice and clasped hands to heaven: "Almighty Father! hast thou deemed me worthy of reproach so great, and is it thy will that I pay such penalty? Whither am I bound? Whence am I come? What flight bears me home, or in what guise? Shall I look again on the camp or walls of Laurentium? What of that warrior band who followed me and my standard? Whom, one and all—Oh! the shame!—I have left in the jaws of a cruel death, and now I see them scattered and hear their groans as they fall. What shall I do? What earth could now gape deep enough for me? Nay, rather, O ye winds, be pitiful! On rock, on reef drive the ship—from my heart I, Turnus, implore you—and cast it on some sandbank's ruthless shoal, where neither Rutuli nor Rumour that knows my shame may follow!" So saying, he wavers in spirit this way and that, whether for disgrace so foul he should madly fling himself on his sword and drive the cruel steel through his ribs, or plunge amid the waves, and seek by swimming to gain the winding shore, and once more cast himself against the Trojan arms. Thrice he essayed either way; thrice mighty Juno stayed his hand and held him back in pity of heart. On he glides, cleaving the deep, with wave and tide to speed him, and is borne home to his father Daunus' ancient city.[1]

689 But meanwhile at Jove's behest fiery Mezentius takes up the battle and assails the triumphant Teucrians. The Tyrrhene ranks rush together, and press

---

[1] Ardea in Latium.

217

VIRGIL

uni odiisque viro telisque frequentibus instant.
ille velut rupes, vastum quae prodit in aequor,
obvia ventorum furiis expostaque ponto,
vim cunctam atque minas perfert caelique marisque,
ipsa immota manens, prolem Dolichaonis Hebrum   696
sternit humi, cum quo Latagum Palmumque fugacem,
sed Latagum saxo atque ingenti fragmine montis
occupat os faciemque adversam, poplite Palmum
succiso volvi segnem sinit, armaque Lauso   700
donat habere umeris et vertice figere cristas.
nec non Euanthen Phrygium Paridisque Mimanta
aequalem comitemque, una quem nocte Theano
in lucem genitori Amyco dedit et face praegnas
Cisseis regina Parin : Paris urbe paterna   705
occubat, ignarum Laurens habet ora Mimanta.
ac velut ille canum morsu de montibus altis
actus aper, multos Vesulus quem pinifer annos
defendit multosque palus Laurentia, silva
pastus harundinea, postquam inter retia ventum est,
substitit infremuitque ferox et inhorruit armos,   711
nec cuiquam irasci propiusve accedere virtus,
sed iaculis tutisque procul clamoribus instant,
haud aliter, iustae quibus est Mezentius irae,
non ulli est animus stricto concurrere ferro ;   715
missilibus longe et vasto clamore lacessunt.
ille autem impavidus partis cunctatur in omnis,
dentibus infrendens, et tergo decutit hastas.

Venerat antiquis Corythi de finibus Acron,
Graius homo, infectos linquens profugus hymenaeos :

705 Paris] creat $M^2 P R \gamma$: crepat M^1: Paris *conjectured by Bentley*: regina creat: Paris *Ellis*.
706 occupat $M^1 R$.   709 -que] -ve P.
712 -ve] -qve $P\gamma$.
717-718 *placed after* 713 *by Scaliger: so Ribbeck, Hirtzel, Janell, Mackail.*

218

AENEID BOOK X

on him alone with all their hatred, on him alone with all their ceaseless darts. Even as a cliff that juts into the vast deep, exposed to the raving winds and braving the main, that endures all the stress, all the menace of sky and sea, itself fixed unshaken—so he lays low on earth Hebrus, son of Dolichaon, and with him Latagus and Palmus, swift of foot; but Latagus he smites of a sudden full in the mouth and face with a huge fragment of mountain-rock, while Palmus he hamstrings, and leaves him slowly writhing; his armour he gives Lausus to wear upon his shoulders, and his plumes to fix upon his crest. Evanthes too, the Phrygian, and Mimas, comrade of Paris and his peer in age, whom Theano bore to his sire Amycus the self-same night that Cisseus' royal daughter, pregnant with a firebrand,[1] gave birth to Paris: Paris sleeps in the city of his fathers; Mimas, unknown rests on the Laurentine shore. And lo! even as the boar, driven by sharp-toothed hounds from mountain-heights, whom pine-crowned Vesulus has sheltered for many years, or for many years the Laurentine marsh, pasturing him on thick-growing reeds, when once he is come amid the toils, halts, snorts savagely, and bristles up his shoulders, and none have courage to rage or come near him, but all at safe distance assail him with darts and shouts—even so, of all that had righteous hatred of Mezentius, none had heart to meet him with drawn sword; from afar they provoke him with missiles and far-echoing shouts. But he, undaunted, halts, turning on every side with gnashing teeth, and shakes the javelins from his shield.

⁷¹⁹ There had come from the ancient bounds of Corythus Acron, a Greek, leaving in exile nuptials

[1] See VII. 319, 320, with note.

219

VIRGIL

hunc ubi miscentem longe media agmina vidit, 721
purpureum pinnis et pactae coniugis ostro,
impastus stabula alta leo ceu saepe peragrans,
(suadet enim vesana fames) si forte fugacem
conspexit capream aut surgentem in cornua cervum,
gaudet, hians immane, comasque arrexit et haeret 726
visceribus super incumbens, lavit improba taeter
ora cruor:
sic ruit in densos alacer Mezentius hostis.
sternitur infelix Acron et calcibus atram 730
tundit humum exspirans infractaque tela cruentat.
atque idem fugientem haud est dignatus Oroden MPRV
sternere nec iacta caecum dare cuspide volnus;
obvius adversoque occurrit seque viro vir
contulit, haud furto melior sed fortibus armis. 735
tum super abiectum posito pede nixus et hasta:
"pars belli haud temnenda, viri, iacet altus Orodes."
conclamant socii laetum paeana secuti.
ille autem exspirans: "non me, quicumque es, inulto,
victor, nec longum laetabere; te quoque fata 740
prospectant paria atque eadem mox arva tenebis."
ad quae subridens mixta Mezentius ira:
"nunc morere. ast de me divum pater atque
    hominum rex
viderit." hoc dicens eduxit corpore telum.
olli dura quies oculos et ferreus urget 745
somnus, in aeternam clauduntur lumina noctem.

  Caedicus Alcathoum obtruncat, Sacrator Hydaspen,
Partheniumque Rapo et praedurum viribus Orsen,
Messapus Cloniumque Lycaoniumque Ericeten,
illum infrenis equi lapsu tellure iacentem, 750

---

⁷²⁷ accumbens *PR*.
⁷³⁷ viris *b²c, known to Servius*. altus] actus *M*. ⁷⁴¹ arma *M*.
⁷⁴² atquae *VP²γ*: atquaec *P¹*: atque *M¹a*: atquem *M²a²c*:
ad quem *Rb*.
220

AENEID BOOK X

unfulfilled. When Mezentius saw him afar, dealing havoc amid the ranks, gay in crimson plumes and the purple of his plighted bride, even as often an unfed lion, ranging the deep coverts, for maddening hunger prompts him, if haply he has spied a timorous roe or stately-antlered stag, exults with mouth terribly agape, uprears his mane, and clings crouching over the flesh, his cruel lips bathed in foul gore—so Mezentius springs lightly upon the massed foemen. Down goes hapless Acron, hammers the black ground with his heels as he breathes his last, and dyes with blood the broken spear. And the same arm deigned not to lay low Orodes as he fled, nor to deal with cast of spear a wound unseen; full face to face he ran to meet him and opposed him as man against man, prevailing not by stealth but by strength of arms. Then, planting his foot on the fallen foe and straining at his spear, "Ho men!" he cries, "low lies great Orodes—no mean portion of the war!" His comrades join their shouts, taking up the joyous cry of triumph. But he, breathing his last: "Not unavenged shall I be, O victor, whoe'er thou art, nor long shalt thou exult; for thee too a like doom keeps watch, and in these same fields thou soon shalt lie." To this Mezentius, smiling amid his wrath: "Now die; but let the sire of gods and king of men see to me!" So saying, he drew the weapon from the hero's body; stern repose and iron slumber press upon his eyes, and their orbs close in everlasting night.

[747] Caedicus slaughters Alcathous, Sacrator Hydaspes, Rapo Parthenius, and Orses of wondrous strength; Messapus slays Clonius and Ericetes, Lycaon's son—the one, as he lay on the ground, fallen from his unbridled steed, the other as he came

VIRGIL

hunc peditem. pedes et Lycius processerat Agis;
quem tamen haud expers Valerus virtutis avitae
deicit; at Thronium Salius, Saliumque Nealces
insignis iaculo et longe fallente sagitta.

Iam gravis aequabat luctus et mutua Mavors 755
funera; caedebant pariter pariterque ruebant
victores victique, neque his fuga nota neque illis.
di Iovis in tectis iram miserantur inanem MPR
amborum et tantos mortalibus esse labores:
hinc Venus, hinc contra spectat Saturnia Iuno; 760
pallida Tisiphone media inter milia saevit.
at vero ingentem quatiens Mezentius hastam
turbidus ingreditur campo. quam magnus Orion,
cum pedes incedit medii per maxima Nerei
stagna viam scindens, umero supereminet undas, 765
aut summis referens annosam montibus ornum,
ingrediturque solo et caput inter nubila condit:
talis se vastis infert Mezentius armis.

Huic contra Aeneas, speculatus in agmine longo,
obvius ire parat. manet imperterritus ille, 770
hostem magnanimum opperiens, et mole sua stat;
atque oculis spatium emensus, quantum satis hastae:
"dextra mihi deus et telum, quod missile libro,
nunc adsint! voveo praedonis corpore raptis
indutum spoliis ipsum te, Lause, tropaeum 775
Aeneae." dixit stridentemque eminus hastam
iecit; at illa volans clipeo est excussa proculque
egregium Antoren latus inter et ilia figit,

---

[751] peditem pedes. et *so punctuated* M^2P^2. *The other punctuation* peditem. pedes et *is a conjecture of Peerlkamp's.*
[754] insignis M^1a^2: insidiis M^2PRVb.
[756] cedebant $P^1R\gamma$, *known to Servius*: cedebat P^2.
[763] campum M.
[769] huc P^1: hunc MP^2. *On* longo, *see Appendix*.
[777] inicit γ. at *omitted by* $M^1\gamma$.

AENEID BOOK X

on foot. On foot had Lycian Agis also advanced; yet him Valerus, lacking naught of ancestral prowess, struck down; Thronius falls by Salius, and Salius by Nealces, famed for the javelin and the arrow that steals from afar.

755 Now the heavy hand of Mars was dealing out equal woe and mutual death. Alike they slew and alike they fell—victors and vanquished, and neither these nor those knew flight. The gods in Jove's halls pity the vain wrath of either host, and grieve that mortals should endure such toils. Here Venus looks on, there over against her Saturnian Juno: pale Tisiphone rages amid the thousands of men. But now Mezentius, shaking his mighty spear, advances like a whirlwind on the plain. Great as Orion, when cleaving a path he stalks on foot through the vast pools of mid-ocean, towers with his shoulder above the waves, or, as he carries off an aged ash from mountain-heights, walks the ground with head hidden in the clouds: such Mezentius strode in his giant armour.

769 On the other side Aeneas espying him in the long battle-line, moves to meet him. Undaunted he abides, awaiting his noble foe, and steadfast in his bulk; then, with eye measuring the distance that might suffice his spear: "May this right hand, my deity, and the hurtling dart I poise, now aid me! I vow thee, Lausus, thy very self, clad in spoils stripped from the robber's corpse, as my trophy of Aeneas."[1] He spoke, and threw from far his whistling spear; on it flies, glanced from the shield, and hard by pierces noble Antores betwixt side and

---

[1] Instead of the usual trunk of wood, hung with the arms of the vanquished foe, the living Lausus, clothed in the armour of Aeneas, is to be his trophy.

VIRGIL

Herculis Antoren comitem, qui missus ab Argis
haeserat Euandro atque Itala consederat urbe.   780
sternitur infelix alieno volnere caelumque
aspicit et dulcis moriens reminiscitur Argos.
tum pius Aeneas hastam iacit; illa per orbem
aere cavum triplici, per linea terga tribusque
transiit intextum tauris opus imaque sedit   785
inguine; sed viris haud pertulit. ocius ensem
Aeneas, viso Tyrrheni sanguine laetus,
eripit a femine et trepidanti fervidus instat.
ingemuit cari graviter genitoris amore,
ut vidit, Lausus, lacrimaeque per ora volutae.   790
  Hic mortis durae casum tuaque optima facta,
si qua fidem tanto est operi latura vetustas,
non equidem nec te, iuvenis memorande, silebo.
  Ille pedem referens et inutilis inque ligatus
cedebat clipeoque inimicum hastile trahebat.   795
proripuit iuvenis seseque immiscuit armis
iamque adsurgentis dextra plagamque ferentis
Aeneae subiit mucronem ipsumque morando
sustinuit; socii magno clamore sequuntur,
dum genitor nati parma protectus abiret,   800
telaque coniciunt proturbantque eminus hostem
missilibus. furit Aeneas tectusque tenet se.
ac velut, effusa si quando grandine nimbi
praecipitant, omnis campis diffugit arator,
omnis et agricola, et tuta latet arce viator,   805
aut amnis ripis aut alti fornice saxi,
dum pluit in terris, ut possint sole reducto
exercere diem: sic obrutus undique telis

---

⁷⁸⁵ transiet *M*¹.
⁷⁹¹ optime *M*²*R*, *known to Servius.*
⁷⁹⁶ prorupit *PR*.   ⁷⁹⁷ dextrae *P*², *Servius.*
⁷⁹⁸ subigit *M*¹.   ⁸⁰⁵ arte *most MSS. and Servius. See Appendix.*   ⁸⁰⁷ possit *M*¹*R*¹.

224

AENEID BOOK X

flank—Antores, comrade of Hercules, who, sent from Argos, had cloven to Evander, and settled in an Italian town. He falls, alas! by a wound meant for another, and gazes on the sky, and dying, dreams of his sweet Argos. Then good Aeneas casts a spear; through the hollow shield of threefold brass, through the linen folds, and inwoven work of triple bullhides, it sped, and sank low in the groin, yet carried not home its strength. Quickly Aeneas, gladdened by the sight of the Tuscan's blood, snatches his sword from the thigh and presses hotly on his bewildered foe. Deeply Lausus groaned for love of his dear sire, when he saw the sight, and tears rolled down his face.

⁷⁹¹ And here death's cruel gloom and thy most glorious deeds—if so be that ancient days may win credence for such prowess—I in sooth will not leave unsung, nay, nor thyself, O youth, so worthy to be sung!

⁷⁹⁴ The father, disabled and encumbered, was now giving ground with retreating steps, trailing from his buckler his foeman's lance. Forth dashed the youth and plunged into the fray; and even as Aeneas' hand rose to deal the blow, he caught up the hero's point and stayed him by this check. His comrades follow with loud cries, until the father, guarded by his son's shield, might withdraw; and showering their javelins beat back the foe with missiles from afar. Aeneas, infuriate, keeps himself under shelter. And as when at times storm-clouds pour down in showers of hail, every ploughman, every husbandman flees the fields, and the wayfarer cowers in safe stronghold, be it river's bank or vault of lofty rock, while the rain falls upon the lands, that so, when the sun returns, they may pursue the day's task:

VIRGIL

Aeneas nubem belli, dum detonet omnis,
sustinet et Lausum increpitat Lausoque minatur: 810
"quo moriture ruis maioraque viribus audes?
fallit te incautum pietas tua."   nec minus ille
exsultat demens, saevae iamque altius irae
Dardanio surgunt ductori, extremaque Lauso
Parcae fila legunt: validum namque exigit ensem 815
per medium Aeneas iuvenem totumque recondit.
transiit et parmam mucro, levia arma minacis,
et tunicam, molli mater quam neverat auro,
implevitque sinum sanguis; tum vita per auras
concessit maesta ad Manis corpusque reliquit. 820
at vero ut voltum vidit morientis et ora,
ora modis Anchisiades pallentia miris,
ingemuit miserans graviter dextramque tetendit
et mentem patriae strinxit pietatis imago.
"quid tibi nunc, miserande puer, pro laudibus istis, 825
quid pius Aeneas tanta dabit indole dignum?
arma, quibus laetatus, habe tua, teque parentum
manibus et cineri, si qua est ea cura, remitto.
hoc tamen infelix miseram solabere mortem:
Aeneae magni dextra cadis." increpat ultro 830
cunctantis socios et terra sublevat ipsum,
sanguine turpantem comptos de morte capillos.

Interea genitor Tiberini ad fluminis undam
volnera siccabat lymphis corpusque levabat
arboris adclinis trunco.   procul aerea ramis 835
dependet galea et prato gravia arma quiescunt.

₈₁₂ fallet te *P* : fallite *R* : fallete γ^1.   ₈₁₅ fila] lina $P\gamma^3$.
₈₁₇ transit *R*.   media arma minaci *R*.   ₈₁₉ sinus $M^1\gamma^2$.
₈₂₄ strinxit *M* : subiit *P* : subit *R*.
₈₃₄ levabat *γbc* : lavabat *MPR*.

226

AENEID BOOK X

even thus, o'erwhelmed by javelins on all sides, Aeneas endures the war-cloud until all its thunder is spent, chiding Lausus the while, and threatening Lausus: "Whither rushest thou to thy death, with daring beyond thy strength? Thy love betrays thee into rashness." Yet none the less the youth riots madly; now fierce wrath rises higher in the Dardan leader's heart, and the Fates gather up Lausus' last threads; for Aeneas drives the sword sheer through the youth's body, and buries it within to the hilt. The point pierced the targe—frail arms for one so threatening—and the tunic his mother had woven him of pliant gold; blood filled his breast, then through the air the life fled sorrowing to the Shades, and left the body. But when Anchises' son saw the look on that dying face—that face so pale in wondrous wise—heavily he groaned in pity, and stretched forth his hand, as the likeness of his own filial love rose before his soul. "What now, unhappy boy, shall good Aeneas give thee for these thy glories? What guerdon worthy of such a heart? Keep for thine own the arms wherein thou didst delight; and if such a care may touch thee, thyself I give back to the spirits and ashes of thy sires. Yet, hapless one! this shall solace thee for thy sad death: 'tis by the hand of great Aeneas thou dost fall." Nay, he chides the laggard comrades and uplifts their chief from the earth, where he befouled with blood his seemly ordered locks.

833 Meanwhile by the wave of the Tiber river, the father staunched his wounds with water, and rested his reclining frame against a tree's trunk. Hard by, his brazen helmet hangs from the boughs, and his heavy arms lie in peace on the meadow. Chosen

VIRGIL

stant lecti circum iuvenes: ipse aeger, anhelans
colla fovet, fusus propexam in pectore barbam;
multa super Lauso rogitat multumque remittit,
qui revocent maestique ferant mandata parentis. 840
at Lausum socii exanimem super arma ferebant
flentes, ingentem atque ingenti volnere victum.
adgnovit longe gemitum praesaga mali mens;
canitiem multo deformat pulvere et ambas
ad caelum tendit palmas et corpore inhaeret. 845
" tantane me tenuit vivendi, nate, voluptas,
ut pro me hostili paterer succedere dextrae,
quem genui? tuane haec genitor per volnera servor,
morte tua vivens? heu, nunc misero mihi demum
exsilium infelix, nunc alte volnus adactum! 850
idem ego, nate, tuum maculavi crimine nomen,
pulsus ob invidiam solio sceptrisque paternis.
debueram patriae poenas odiisque meorum:
omnis per mortis animam sontem ipse dedissem.
nunc vivo neque adhuc homines lucemque relinquo.
sed linquam." simul hoc dicens attollit in aegrum 856
se femur et, quamquam vis alto volnere tardat,
haud deiectus equum duci iubet. hoc decus illi,
hoc solamen erat, bellis hoc victor abibat
omnibus. adloquitur maerentem et talibus infit: 860
" Rhoebe, diu, res si qua diu mortalibus ulla est,
viximus. aut hodie victor spolia illa cruenta
et caput Aeneae referes Lausique dolorum
ultor eris mecum, aut aperit si nulla viam vis,
occumbes pariter: neque enim, fortissime, credo, 865
iussa aliena pati et dominos dignabere Teucros."

⁸³⁸ corpore *P*γ.
⁸³⁹ multum] multom *P*¹: multos γ²*bc*².
⁸⁴⁴ multo] immundo *M*².
⁸⁵⁰ exilium γ¹*a*¹, *Servius:* exitium *MPR*.
⁸⁵⁷ quamquam vis] quamvis *P*². tardet *M*²*P*²γ¹*bc*.
⁸⁶² cruenti *P*¹, *known to Servius*.   ⁸⁶³ dolorem *P*γ¹.

228

AENEID BOOK X

men stand round; he himself, sick and panting, eased his neck, while over his chest streams his flowing beard. Many a time he asks for Lausus, and many a time he sends messengers to recall him, and convey the charge of his grieving sire. But Lausus his weeping comrades were bearing lifeless on his armour—a mighty one and laid low by a mighty wound. The ill-boding heart knew their wail afar. His hoary hair he defiles with a shower of dust, spreads both hands to heaven, and clasps his arms about the corpse: "My son! and did such joy of life possess me, that in my stead I suffered thee to meet the foeman's sword—thee, whom I begat? Am I, thy father, saved by these wounds of thine, and living by thy death? Ah me! now at last is come to me, alas! the bitterness of exile; now is my wound driven deep! Yea, and I, my son, stained thy name with guilt—I, driven in loathing from the throne and sceptre of my fathers. Long have I owed my punishment to my country and my people's hate; by any form of death should I myself have yielded up my guilty life. Now I live on, and leave not yet daylight and mankind; but leave I will." And with the word he raises himself on his stricken thigh, and though his force flags by reason of the deep wound, yet, undismayed, he bids his horse be brought. This was his pride, this his solace; on this he passed victorious from every battle. He addresses the grieving beast and accosts it thus: "Rhoebus, long have we lived, if to mortal beings aught be long. To-day thou shalt either bear off in victory yonder bloody spoils with the head of Aeneas, and avenge with me the sufferings of Lausus, or, if no force opens a way, thou shalt die with me; for thou, gallant steed, wilt not deign, methinks, to brook a stranger's bidding

VIRGIL

dixit et exceptus tergo consueta locavit
membra manusque ambas iaculis oneravit acutis,
aere caput fulgens cristaque hirsutus equina.
sic cursum in medios rapidus dedit. aestuat ingens 870
uno in corde pudor mixtoque insania luctu.

Atque hic Aenean magna ter voce vocavit. 873
Aeneas adgnovit enim laetusque precatur:
"sic pater ille deum faciat, sic altus Apollo! 875
incipias conferre manum."
tantum effatus, et infesta subit obvius hasta.
ille autem: "quid me erepto, saevissime, nato
terres? haec via sola fuit, qua perdere posses.
nec mortem horremus nec divum parcimus ulli. 880
desine: nam venio moriturus et haec tibi porto
dona prius." dixit telumque intorsit in hostem.
inde aliud super atque aliud figitque volatque
ingenti gyro, sed sustinet aureus umbo.
ter circum adstantem laevos equitavit in orbis, 885
tela manu iaciens, ter secum Troius heros
immanem aerato circumfert tegmine silvam.
inde ubi tot traxisse moras, tot spicula taedet
vellere et urgetur pugna congressus iniqua,
multa movens animo iam tandem erumpit et inter 890
bellatoris equi cava tempora conicit hastam.
tollit se arrectum quadrupes et calcibus auras
verberat effusumque equitem super ipse secutus
implicat eiectoque incumbit cernuus armo.
clamore incendunt caelum Troesque Latinique. 895
advolat Aeneas vaginaque eripit ensem

[872] = XII. 668, *omitted by* $MPR\gamma^1 a^1 b$.
[883] fugitque $M^1 P^1 c^1$.   [884] aereus MP.
[887] agmine γ^2.   [894] cernulus $P^2 R \gamma^1$.

230

AENEID BOOK X

and a Trojan lord!" He spoke, and, mounting the beast, settled his limbs as was his wont, and charged either hand with sharp javelins, his head glittering with brass and bristling with horse-hair plume. Thus he swiftly dashed into the midst. In that single heart surges a vast tide of shame and madness mingled with grief.

[873] And now thrice in loud tones he called Aeneas. Yea, and Aeneas knew the call, and offers joyful prayer: "So may the great father of the gods grant it, so Apollo on high! Mayest thou begin the combat!" So much said, he moves on to meet him with levelled spear. But he: "Why seek to affright me, fierce foe, now my son is taken? This was the one way whereby thou couldst destroy me. We shrink not from death, nor heed we any of the gods. Cease; for I come to die, first bringing thee these gifts." He spoke, and hurled a javelin at his foe; then plants another and yet another, wheeling in wide circle; but the boss of gold withstands all. Thrice round his watchful foe he rode, turning to the left and launching darts from his hand; thrice the Trojan hero bears round with him the vast forest of spears upon his brazen shield. Then, weary of prolonging so many delays, of plucking out so many darts, and hard pressed in the unequal fray, at last with much pondering in heart, he springs forth and hurls his lance full between the war-horse's hollow temples. The steed rears up, lashes the air with its feet, then throws the rider and itself coming down above, entangles him; then falls over him in headlong plunge, and with shoulder out of joint. With their cries Trojans and Latins set heaven aflame. Up flies Aeneas, plucks his sword from the scabbard, and

VIRGIL

et super haec: "ubi nunc Mezentius acer et illa
effera vis animi?" contra Tyrrhenus, ut auras
suspiciens hausit caelum mentemque recepit:
"hostis amare, quid increpitas mortemque minaris?
nullum in caede nefas, nec sic ad proelia veni,   901
nec tecum meus haec pepigit mihi foedera Lausus.
unum hoc per si qua est victis venia hostibus oro:
corpus humo patiare tegi. scio acerba meorum
circumstare odia: hunc, oro, defende furorem   905
et me consortem nati concede sepulchro."
haec loquitur iuguloque haud inscius accipit ensem
undantique animam diffundit in arma cruore.

⁸⁹⁸ ut] et $M^2P^2R^1\gamma^1$.
⁹⁰⁸ anima P^1. defundit $R\gamma^1$. cruorem MP^1.

AENEID BOOK X

thus above him cries: "Where now is bold Mezentius, and that wild fierceness of soul?" To him the Tuscan, as with eyes upturned to the air he drank in the heaven and regained his sense: "Bitter foe, why thy taunts and threats of death? No sin is there in slaying me; not on such terms came I to battle, nor is such the pact my Lausus pledged between me and thee. This alone I ask, by whatsoever grace a vanquished foe may claim: suffer my body to be laid in earth. I know that my people's fierce hatred besets me. Guard me, I pray, from their fury, and grant me fellowship with my son within the tomb." So speaks he, and, unfaltering, welcomes the sword to his throat, and pours forth his life over his armour in streams of blood.

LIBER XI

Oceanum interea surgens Aurora reliquit: MPR
Aeneas, quamquam et sociis dare tempus humandis
praecipitant curae turbataque funere mens est,
vota deum primo victor solvebat Eoo.
ingentem quercum decisis undique ramis 5
constituit tumulo fulgentiaque induit arma,
Mezenti ducis exuvias, tibi, magne, tropaeum,
bellipotens; aptat rorantis sanguine cristas
telaque trunca viri, et bis sex thoraca petitum
perfossumque locis, clipeumque ex aere sinistrae 10
subligat atque ensem collo suspendit eburnum.
tum socios (namque omnis eum stipata tegebat
turba ducum) sic incipiens hortatur ovantis:

"Maxima res effecta, viri; timor omnis abesto,
quod superest; haec sunt spolia et de rege superbo 15
primitiae manibusque meis Mezentius hic est.
nunc iter ad regem nobis murosque Latinos.
arma parate animis et spe praesumite bellum,
ne qua mora ignaros, ubi primum vellere signa
adnuerint superi pubemque educere castris, 20

[18] *Servius notes that* animis *may be taken with either the words preceding or those following.* M²*punctuates after* animis.

[1] Aeneas has two duties to perform, to bury the dead and to pay his vow. The latter he attends to first, according to

234

BOOK XI

MEANWHILE dawn rose and left the ocean. Aeneas, though his sorrows urge to give time for his comrades' burial, and death has bewildered his soul, yet as the Day-star rose, began to pay the gods his vows of victory.[1] A mighty oak, its branches lopped all about, he plants on a mound, and arrays in the gleaming arms stripped from Mezentius the chief, a trophy to thee, thou Lord of War.[2] Thereto he fastens the crests dripping with blood, the soldier's broken darts, and the breastplate smitten and pierced twice six times; to the left hand he binds the brazen shield, and from the neck hangs the ivory sword. Then his triumphant comrades—for the whole band of chieftains thronged close about him—he thus begins to exhort:

[14] "Mighty deeds have we wrought, my men; for what remains, away with all fear! These are the spoils and firstfruits of a haughty king; and here is Mezentius, as fashioned by my hands. Now lies our march to Latium's king and walls. Prepare your weapons with courage and with your hopes anticipate the war; so that, soon as the gods above grant us to pluck hence our standards, and from the camp to lead

Roman ritual; his inclination would have led him to bury his comrades first.

[2] In the trophy here described, the tree-trunk doubtless represents the body of the vanquished foe.

235

VIRGIL

impediat segnisve metu sententia tardet.
interea socios inhumataque corpora terrae
mandemus, qui solus honos Acheronte sub imo est.
ite," ait, "egregias animas, quae sanguine nobis
hanc patriam peperere suo, decorate supremis 25
muneribus maestamque Euandri primus ad urbem
mittatur Pallas, quem non virtutis egentem
abstulit atra dies et funere mersit acerbo."

Sic ait inlacrimans recipitque ad limina gressum,
corpus ubi exanimi positum Pallantis Acoetes 30
servabat senior, qui Parrhasio Euandro
armiger ante fuit, sed non felicibus aeque
tum comes auspiciis caro datus ibat alumno.
circum omnis famulumque manus Troianaque turba
et maestum Iliades crinem de more solutae. 35
ut vero Aeneas foribus sese intulit altis,
ingentem gemitum tunsis ad sidera tollunt
pectoribus maestoque immugit regia luctu.
ipse caput nivei fultum Pallantis et ora
ut vidit levique patens in pectore volnus 40
cuspidis Ausoniae, lacrimis ita fatur obortis:
"tene," inquit, "miserande puer, cum laeta veniret,
invidit Fortuna mihi, ne regna videres
nostra neque ad sedes victor veherere paternas?
non haec Euandro de te promissa parenti 45
discedens dederam, cum me complexus euntem
mitteret in magnum imperium metuensque moneret
acris esse viros, cum dura proelia gente.
et nunc ille quidem spe multum captus inani
fors et vota facit cumulatque altaria donis; 50

²¹ -ve *M¹R*: -que *M²Pγ*. ²³ est *omitted in PR*.
²⁴ qui *Macrobius*. ²⁵ = VI. 429. ³⁰ exanime *M*, -is *R*.

236

AENEID BOOK XI

forth the host, no delay may impede us unawares or faltering purpose retard us through fear. Meanwhile let us commit to earth the unburied bodies of our comrades—sole honour theirs in nether Acheron. Go," he said, " grace with the last rites those noble souls, who with their blood have won for us this our country; and first let Pallas be sent to Evander's mourning city, he whom, lacking naught of valour, the black day swept off and plunged in bitter death."

[29] So he speaks weeping, and retraces his steps to the threshold, where Pallas' lifeless body was laid, watched by old Acoetes, who erstwhile was armour-bearer to Parrhasian Evander, but now with less happy auspices went as appointed guardian to his loved foster-child. Around stood all the attendant train and Trojan throng, with the Ilian women, their hair unloosed for mourning in wonted wise. But when Aeneas entered the lofty portal, they smote their breasts and raised a mighty wail to the stars, and the royal dwelling rang with their sorrowful lamentation. He, when he saw the pillowed head and face of Pallas, snowy-white, and, on his smooth breast, the gaping wound from Ausonian spear, thus speaks, amid upwelling tears: "Was it thou, unhappy boy, that Fortune grudged me in her happy hour, that thou mightest not look upon my realm, nor ride triumphant to thy father's home? Not such the parting promise touching thee I gave thy sire Evander, when he embraced me as I went, and sent me forth to win great empire, yet warned me in fear that valiant were the men and hardy the race we confronted. And now he, much beguiled by idle hope, perchance is offering vows and heaping the

VIRGIL

nos iuvenem exanimum et nil iam caelestibus ullis
debentem vano maesti comitamur honore.
infelix, nati funus crudele videbis!
hi nostri reditus exspectatique triumphi?
haec mea magna fides? at non, Euandre, pudendis 55
volneribus pulsum aspicies, nec sospite dirum
optabis nato funus pater.   ei mihi, quantum
praesidium Ausonia et quantum tu perdis, Iule!"

Haec ubi deflevit, tolli miserabile corpus
imperat, et toto lectos ex agmine mittit 60
mille viros, qui supremum comitentur honorem
intersintque patris lacrimis, solacia luctus
exigua ingentis, misero sed debita patri.
haud segnes alii cratis et molle feretrum
arbuteis texunt virgis et vimine querno 65
exstructosque toros obtentu frondis inumbrant.
hic iuvenem agresti sublimem stramine ponunt,
qualem virgineo demessum pollice florem
seu mollis violae seu languentis hyacinthi,
cui neque fulgor adhuc nec dum sua forma recessit; 70
non iam mater alit tellus virisque ministrat.
tum geminas vestis auroque ostroque rigentis
extulit Aeneas, quas illi laeta laborum
ipsa suis quondam manibus Sidonia Dido
fecerat et tenui telas discreverat auro. 75
harum unam iuveni supremum maestus honorem
induit arsurasque comas obnubit amictu,
multaque praeterea Laurentis praemia pugnae
aggerat et longo praedam iubet ordine duci;

⁵⁴ exoptati *R*.   ⁶⁹ ordine *PR*.   ⁷⁵ = IV. 264.

AENEID BOOK XI

altars high with gifts; we, in sorrow, attend with bootless rites the lifeless son, who no more owes aught to any gods of heaven. Unhappy! thou wilt behold the bitter funeral of thy son! Is this our return, our awaited triumph? Is this my sure pledge? Yet shall not thine eyes, Evander, look on one routed with shameful wounds nor shalt thou, his father, pray for a death accursed, because thy son is saved.[1] Ah me! how great a protection is lost to thee, Ausonia, how great to thee, Iülus!"

[59] His lamentation ended, he bids them raise the piteous corpse, and sends a thousand men chosen from his whole host to attend the last rite and share the father's tears—scant solace for grief so vast, but due to a father's sorrow. Others in haste plait the wicker-frame of a soft bier with arbute shoots and oaken twigs, and shroud the high-piled couch with leafy canopy. Here they lay the youth aloft on his rustic bed, like to a flower culled by maiden's finger, be it of tender violet or drooping hyacinth, whose sheen and native grace not yet have faded, but no more does its mother earth give strength and nurture. Then Aeneas brought forth two robes, stiff with gold and purple, which Sidonian Dido, delighting in the toil, had once herself with her own hands wrought for him, interweaving the web with threads of gold. Of these he sadly drapes one round the youth as a last honour, and in its covering veils those locks the fire shall claim; withal heaps up many a prize from the Laurentine fray,[2] and bids the spoils be borne in

---

[1] The son's dishonour would make an otherwise dreaded death welcome to the father. Some think that it is the son's death for which the father is supposed to pray.

[2] The Latian forces led by Turnus included the Laurentes, whose capital was Lavinium.

VIRGIL

addit equos et tela, quibus spoliaverat hostem. 80
vinxerat et post terga manus, quos mitteret umbris
inferias, caeso sparsurus sanguine flammas,
indutosque iubet truncos hostilibus armis
ipsos ferre duces inimicaque nomina figi.
ducitur infelix aevo confectus Acoetes, 85
pectora nunc foedans pugnis, nunc unguibus ora,
sternitur et toto proiectus corpore terrae.
ducunt et Rutulo perfusos sanguine currus.
post bellator equus positis insignibus Aethon
it lacrimans guttisque umectat grandibus ora. 90
hastam alii galeamque ferunt; nam cetera Turnus
victor habet. tum maesta phalanx Teucrique sequuntur
Tyrrhenique omnes et versis Arcades armis.
postquam omnis longe comitum praecesserat ordo,
substitit Aeneas gemituque haec addidit alto: 95
"nos alias hinc ad lacrimas eadem horrida belli
fata vocant: salve aeternum mihi, maxime Palla,
aeternumque vale." nec plura effatus ad altos
tendebat muros gressumque in castra ferebat.

Iamque oratores aderant ex urbe Latina, 100
velati ramis oleae veniamque rogantes:
corpora, per campos ferro quae fusa iacebant,
redderet ac tumulo sineret succedere terrae;
nullum cum victis certamen et aethere cassis;
parceret hospitibus quondam socerisque vocatis. 105
quos bonus Aeneas haud aspernanda precantis

---

[82] sparsuros a^2bc. flammam $R\gamma$.
[93] omnes] duces R, *Servius*. [94] processerat γ^2.
[95] edidit M^2R. [101] precantes R, *Servius*.

AENEID BOOK XI

long train; then adds the steeds and arms of which he had stripped the foe. The victims' hands he had bound behind their backs, even to send them as offerings to the Shades, sprinkling the flames with the blood of the slain. He bids the chiefs themselves bear tree-trunks clad in hostile arms, with foemen's names affixed. Hapless Acoetes, outworn with years, is led along, marring now his breast with clenched fists, now his face with nails, and anon he flings his whole frame prone upon the earth. Cars likewise they lead, bespattered with Rutulian blood. Behind, the war-steed Aethon, his trappings laid aside, goes weeping, and big drops wet his face.[1] Others carry the spear and helmet: for all else Turnus, as victor, holds. Then follows a mournful host—the Teucrians, and all the Tuscans and the Arcadians with arms reversed. When all the retinue of his comrades had advanced far ahead, Aeneas halted, and with deep sigh spake this word more: "Me the same grim destiny of war summons hence to other tears: hail thou for evermore, noblest Pallas, and for evermore farewell!" And without further words he turned to the lofty walls and bent his steps towards the camp.

100 And now came envoys from the Latin city, o'ershaded with olive boughs and craving grace; the bodies that lay strewn by the sword o'er the plain they prayed him to restore and suffer to rest beneath an earthen mound. No war, they plead, is waged with vanquished men, bereft of air of heaven; let him spare men once called hosts, and fathers of their brides![2] To them good Aeneas courteously grants

[1] *cf. Iliad*, XVII. 426 ff., where the horses of Achilles weep.
[2] Latinus had promised his daughter to Aeneas, and perhaps similar alliances were arranged.

VIRGIL

prosequitur venia et verbis haec insuper addit:
"quaenam vos tanto fortuna indigna, Latini,
implicuit bello, qui nos fugiatis amicos?
pacem me exanimis et Martis sorte peremptis   110
oratis? equidem et vivis concedere vellem.
nec veni, nisi fata locum sedemque dedissent,
nec bellum cum gente gero: rex nostra reliquit
hospitia et Turni potius se credidit armis.
aequius huic Turnum fuerat se opponere morti.   115
si bellum finire manu, si pellere Teucros
apparat, his mecum decuit concurrere telis;
vixet, cui vitam deus aut sua dextra dedisset.
nunc ite et miseris supponite civibus ignem."
dixerat Aeneas. illi obstipuere silentes   120
conversique oculos inter se atque ora tenebant.

Tum senior semperque odiis et crimine Drances
infensus iuveni Turno sic ore vicissim
orsa refert: "o fama ingens, ingentior armis,
vir Troiane, quibus caelo te laudibus aequem?   125
iustitiaene prius mirer belline laborum?
nos vero haec patriam grati referemus ad urbem
et te, si qua viam dederit Fortuna, Latino
iungemus regi. quaerat sibi foedera Turnus.
quin et fatalis murorum attollere moles   130
saxaque subvectare umeris Troiana iuvabit."
dixerat haec, unoque omnes eadem ore fremebant.
bis senos pepigere dies et pace sequestra
per silvas Teucri mixtique impune Latini
erravere iugis. ferro sonat alta bipenni   135
fraxinus, evertunt actas ad sidera pinos,

---

[118] sua] cui *P*.
[126] iustitiane *MR*, *both readings known to Priscian and Servius.* laborem *Rγ²*.
[131] subiectare *P¹*.   [134] silvam *M*.

AENEID BOOK XI

the prayer he could not spurn, and adds these words besides: "What spiteful chance, ye Latins, has entangled you in so terrible a war, that ye fly from us your friends? Do ye ask me peace for the dead slain by the lot of battle? Gladly would I grant it to the living too. Nor had I come, had not fate assigned me here a place and home, nor wage I war with your people: it is your king who forsook our alliance and preferred to trust himself to Turnus' sword. Fairer it had been for Turnus to face this death. If he seeks to end the war by the strong hand, if he seeks to drive out the Trojans, with me he should have contended with these weapons: that one of us should have lived, to whom heaven or his own right hand had granted life. Now go, and kindle the fire beneath your hapless countrymen." Aeneas ceased: they stood dumb in silence, and kept their eyes and faces turned on one another.

[122] Then aged Drances, ever the foe of youthful Turnus in hate and calumny, thus speaks in reply: "O great in glory, greater in arms, thou hero of Troy, how with my praises may I extol thee to the sky? Am I to marvel first at thy justice or at thy toils in war? We indeed will gratefully bear these words back to our native city, and, if fortune grant a way, will unite thee with Latinus our king. Let Turnus seek alliances for himself! Nay, it will be our delight to rear those massive walls thy destiny ordains, and on our shoulders to bear the stones of Troy." He ceased, and all with one voice murmured assent. For twice six days they made truce, and, with peace interposing, Teucrians and Latins o'er the forest heights roamed scatheless together. The lofty ash rings under the two-edged axe; they lay low

243

VIRGIL

robora nec cuneis et olentem scindere cedrum
nec plaustris cessant vectare gementibus ornos.
    Et iam Fama volans, tanti praenuntia luctus,
Euandrum Euandrique domos et moenia replet,   140
quae modo victorem Latio Pallanta ferebat.
Arcades ad portas ruere et de more vetusto
funereas rapuere faces; lucet via longo
ordine flammarum et late discriminat agros.
contra turba Phrygum veniens plangentia iungit   145
agmina. quae postquam matres succedere tectis
viderunt, maestam incendunt clamoribus urbem.
at non Euandrum potis est vis ulla tenere,
sed venit in medios. feretro Pallante reposto
procubuit super atque haeret lacrimansque gemensque,   150
et via vix tandem voci laxata dolore est:
"non haec, o Palla, dederas promissa parenti,
cautius ut saevo velles te credere Marti.
haud ignarus eram, quantum nova gloria in armis
et praedulce decus primo certamine posset.   155
primitiae iuvenis miserae bellique propinqui
dura rudimenta et nulli exaudita deorum
vota precesque meae! tuque, o sanctissima coniunx,
felix morte tua neque in hunc servata dolorem!
contra ego vivendo vici mea fata, superstes   160
restarem ut genitor. Troum socia arma secutum
obruerent Rutuli telis! animam ipse dedissem
atque haec pompa domum me, non Pallanta referret!
nec vos arguerim, Teucri, nec foedera nec quas

    ¹⁴⁰ conplet *M²*.   ¹⁴⁵ iungunt *M*.
    ¹⁴⁹ Pallanta *M²*.
    ¹⁵¹ vocis *P²γ·* voces *M¹*: voci *M²P¹R*.
    ¹⁵² *Some place a period after* parenti: petenti *known to Servius.*
    ¹⁶⁴ arguerem *R*.

AENEID BOOK XI

star-towering pines, and ceaselessly their wedges cleave oak and fragrant cedar, and groaning wains convey the mountain-ash.

[139] And now winged Fame, harbinger of that heavy grief, fills Evander's ears, Evander's house and city—Fame, that but now proclaimed Pallas victorious in Latium. The Arcadians streamed to the gates, and after their ancient wont, seized funeral torches; the road gleams with the long line of flame, and parts the fields afar.[1] The Phrygian band, moving to meet them, joins the wailing throng. Soon as the matrons saw them draw near their homes, their shrieks set the mourning city ablaze. But no force can withhold Evander; he rushes into the midst, and, when the bier is set down, casts himself upon Pallas, and clings to him weeping and moaning, and scarce from sorrow at the last does his speech find open way: "Not such, O Pallas, was the promise thou hadst given thy sire, that thou wouldst seek more warily to entrust thyself to cruel Mars! Well knew I how strong was the fresh glory of arms and the oversweet pride of battle's first day! O bitter firstfruits of thy youth! O cruel schooling in close-neighbouring war! O vows, O prayers of mine, to which no god gave ear! And thou, my blessed spouse,[2] happy in thy death, and spared not for this grief! But I, living on, have overcome my destiny, only to linger thus—thy father! Would I had followed Troy's allied arms, to be overwhelmed by Rutulian darts! Would I had given my own life, and this funeral-pomp were bringing me—not Pallas—home! Yet I would not blame you, ye Trojans, nor our covenant, nor the

[1] The line of light, stretching across the fields at night, divides them like a roadway.
[2] Like *sancte parens*, *Aen.* v. 80.

245

VIRGIL

iunximus hospitio dextras: sors ista senectae 165
debita erat nostrae.   quod si immatura manebat
mors gnatum, caesis Volscorum milibus ante
ducentem in Latium Teucros cecidisse iuvabit.
quin ego non alio digner te funere, Palla,
quam pius Aeneas et quam magni Phryges et quam 170
Tyrrhenique duces, Tyrrhenum exercitus omnis.
magna tropaea ferunt, quos dat tua dextera Leto;
tu quoque nunc stares immanis truncus in armis,
esset par aetas et idem si robur ab annis,
Turne.   sed infelix Teucros quid demoror armis ? 175
vadite et haec memores regi mandata referte:
quod vitam moror invisam, Pallante perempto,
dextera causa tua est, Turnum gnatoque patrique
quam debere vides.   meritis vacat hic tibi solus
fortunaeque locus.   non vitae gaudia quaero 180
(nec fas), sed gnato Manis perferre sub imos."

   Aurora interea miseris mortalibus almam
extulerat lucem, referens opera atque labores:
iam pater Aeneas, iam curvo in litore Tarchon
constituere pyras.   huc corpora quisque suorum 185
more tulere patrum, subiectisque ignibus atris
conditur in tenebras altum caligine caelum.
ter circum accensos cincti fulgentibus armis
decurrere rogos, ter maestum funeris ignem
lustravere in equis ululatusque ore dedere. 190
spargitur et tellus lacrimis, sparguntur et arma.
it caelo clamorque virum clangorque tubarum.
hic alii spolia occisis derepta Latinis
coniciunt igni, galeas ensisque decoros

<small>168 iuvaret *M :* iuvare *R*.   172 ferant *Rγ¹*.
176 audite *R*.   188 cuncti *R*.</small>

246

AENEID BOOK XI

hands we clasped in friendship: this lot was due to my gray hairs. But if untimely death awaited my son, it shall be my joy that, after slaying his Volscian thousands, he fell leading the Trojans into Latium! Nay, Pallas, I myself could deem thee worthy of no other death than good Aeneas does, than the mighty Phrygians, than the Tyrrhene captains, and all the Tyrrhenian host. Great are the trophies they bring, to whom thy hand deals death;[1] thou, too, Turnus, wouldst now be standing, a monstrous trunk arrayed in arms, had thine age and strength of years been as his! But why do I, unhappy, stay the Teucrians from conflict? Go, and forget not to bear this message to your king: that I drag on a life hateful now that Pallas is slain, the cause is thy right hand, which thou seest owes Turnus to son and to sire. That sole field is left thee for thy merits and thy fortune. I ask not for joy in life—that cannot be— but to bear tidings to my son in the shades below."

[182] Meanwhile Dawn had uplifted her kindly light for weary men, recalling them to task and toil. Now father Aeneas, now Tarchon, had set up pyres on the winding shore. Hither, after the fashion of their fathers, they each brought the bodies of their kin, and as the murky fires are lit beneath, high heaven is veiled in the gloom of darkness. Thrice, girt in glittering armour, they ran their course round the blazing piles; thrice circled on their steeds the mournful funeral-fire, and uttered the voice of wailing. Tears stream on earth, and stream on armour; cries of men and blare of clarions mount to heaven. And now some fling on the fire Latin spoils stripped from the slain, helmets and goodly swords, bridles

[1] The slain warriors themselves are said to bring the trophies Pallas can display.

VIRGIL

frenaque ferventisque rotas, pars munera nota, 195
ipsorum clipeos et non felicia tela.
multa boum circa mactantur corpora Morti,
saetigerosque sues raptasque ex omnibus agris
in flammam iugulant pecudes. tum litore toto
ardentis spectant socios semustaque servant 200
busta, neque avelli possunt, nox umida donec
invertit caelum stellis ardentibus aptum.

  Nec minus et miseri diversa in parte Latini
innumeras struxere pyras, et corpora partim
multa virum terrae infodiunt avectaque partim 205
finitimos tollunt in agros urbique remittunt;
cetera confusaeque ingentem caedis acervum
nec numero nec honore cremant; tunc undique vasti
certatim crebris conlucent ignibus agri.
tertia lux gelidam caelo dimoverat umbram: 210
maerentes altum cinerem et confusa ruebant
ossa focis tepidoque onerabant aggere terrae.
iam vero in tectis, praedivitis urbe Latini,
praecipuus fragor et longi pars maxima luctus.
hic matres miseraeque nurus, hic cara sororum 215
pectora maerentum puerique parentibus orbi
dirum exsecrantur bellum Turnique hymenaeos;
ipsum armis ipsumque iubent decernere ferro,
qui regnum Italiae et primos sibi poscat honores.
ingravat haec saevus Drances solumque vocari 220
testatur, solum posci in certamina Turnum.
multa simul contra variis sententia dictis
pro Turno, et magnum reginae nomen obumbrat,
multa virum meritis sustentat fama tropaeis.

₂₀₂ fulgentibus *R.*
₂₀₇ stragis *R.*
₂₁₄ longe *bc, approved by Servius.*
₂₂₀ haec] et *Pγ¹.*
₂₂₄ virum] simul *M¹.*

AENEID BOOK XI

and glowing wheels; others, offerings familiar to the dead—their own shields and luckless weapons. Around, many a stout ox is sacrificed to Death; bristly swine and cattle harried from all the country are slaughtered over the flames. Then, over all the shore, they watch their comrades burning, and keep guard above the charred pyres, nor can tear themselves away till dewy night rolls round the heaven, inset with gleaming stars.[1]

203 Nor less, elsewhere, the hapless Latins built pyres innumerable. Of their many slain, some they bury in the earth, some they raise and carry to the neighbouring fields or send home to the city; the rest, a mighty mass of indistinguishable slaughter, they burn unreckoned and unhonoured: then on all sides, emulous with close-clustering fires, flare the broad fields. The third morn had withdrawn chill shade from heaven; mournfully they stirred from the pyres the bones mingled with deep ashes, and heaped above them a warm mound of earth. But within the walls, in the city of rich Latinus, is the chief uproar and the long wail's largest portion. Here mothers and their sons' unhappy brides, here the loving hearts of sorrowing sisters, and boys bereft of sires, call curses on the fell war and on Turnus' nuptials: "He, he himself," they cry, "should decide the issue by arms and the sword, he who claims for himself the realm of Italy and foremost honours." Fierce Drances weights the scale, and bears witness that Turnus alone is called, alone is summoned to battle. Over against them, the while, many an opinion in varied phrase speaks for Turnus, the shadow of the queen's great name is his shelter, and many a tale with well-won trophies upholds the hero.

[1] *cf. Aen.* II. 250 and IV. 482 (= VI. 797).

VIRGIL

Hos inter motus, medio in flagrante tumultu, 225
ecce super maesti magna Diomedis ab urbe
legati responsa ferunt : nihil omnibus actum
tantorum impensis operum, nil dona neque aurum
nec magnas valuisse preces, alia arma Latinis
quaerenda, aut pacem Troiano ab rege petendum. 230
deficit ingenti luctu rex ipse Latinus.
fatalem Aenean manifesto numine ferri
admonet ira deum tumulique ante ora recentes.
ergo concilium magnum primosque suorum
imperio accitos alta intra limina cogit. 235
olli convenere ruuntque ad regia plenis
tecta viis.   sedet in mediis et maximus aevo
et primus sceptris haud laeta fronte Latinus.
atque hic legatos Aetola ex urbe remissos,
quae referant, fari iubet et responsa reposcit 240
ordine cuncta suo.   tum facta silentia linguis,
et Venulus dicto parens ita farier infit:

"Vidimus, o cives, Diomede Argivaque castra
atque iter emensi casus superavimus omnis,
contigimusque manum, qua concidit Ilia tellus. 245
ille urbem Argyripam patriae cognomine gentis
victor Gargani condebat Iapygis agris.
postquam introgressi et coram data copia fandi,
munera praeferimus, nomen patriamque docemus,
qui bellum intulerint, quae causa attraxerit Arpos. 250
auditis ille haec placido sic reddidit ore :

"'O fortunatae gentes, Saturnia regna,
antiqui Ausonii, quae vos fortuna quietos
sollicitat suadetque ignota lacessere bella?

---

[230] petendam $M^1P R\gamma$: petendum *Servius*.
[236] fluuntque $P^2 R\gamma$.
[243] Diomede $a^2 b^2 c$: Diomeden $MPR\gamma$: Diomedem *inferior MSS*.
[247] arvis b^2, *Servius*.   [251] edidit M^2.

250

AENEID BOOK XI

²²⁵ Amid this stir, at the fiery turmoil's height, lo! to crown all, from Diomede's great city the envoys bring a gloomy answer: naught has been gained at cost of so much toil; naught have gifts of gold or strong prayers availed; Latium must seek other arms or sue for peace to the Trojan king. Beneath his weight of grief even king Latinus sinks. That Aeneas is called of fate, guided by heaven's clear will, is the warning given by angry gods and the fresh graves before his eyes. Therefore his high council, the foremost of his people, he summons by royal command and convenes within his lofty portals. They assembled, streaming to the king's palace through the crowded streets. In their midst, eldest in years and first in regal state, with little joy upon his brow, sits Latinus, and now bids the envoys, returned from the Aetolian city, tell what tidings they bring back, and demands full answers, each in order. Then on all tongues fell silence, and, obedient to his word, Venulus thus begins:

²⁴³ "We have seen, O citizens, Diomede and his Argive camp; we have achieved our journey, overcome all perils, and grasped the hand whereby the land of Ilium fell. He was founding his city of Argyripa, named after his father's race, in the conquered fields of Iapygian Garganus. Soon as we entered, and liberty was given to speak before his face, we proffer our gifts, and declare our name and country, who are its invaders, and what cause has led us to Arpi. He heard and thus replied with unruffled mien:

²⁵² "'O happy peoples of Saturn's realm, sons of old Ausonia, what chance vexes your calm and lures you to provoke warfare unknown? All we who with

VIRGIL

quicumque Iliacos ferro violavimus agros   255
(mitto ea, quae muris bellando exhausta sub altis,
quos Simois premat ille viros), infanda per orbem
supplicia et scelerum poenas expendimus omnes,
vel Priamo miseranda manus: scit triste Minervae
sidus et Euboicae cautes ultorque Caphereus.   260
militia ex illa diversum ad litus abacti
Atrides Protei Menelaus adusque columnas
exsulat, Aetnaeos vidit Cyclopas Ulixes.
regna Neoptolemi referam versosque penates
Idomenei? Libycone habitantis litore Locros?   265
ipse Mycenaeus magnorum ductor Achivum
coniugis infandae prima intra limina dextra
oppetiit, devictam Asiam subsedit adulter.
invidisse deos, patriis ut redditus aris
coniugium optatum et pulchram Calydona viderem!
nunc etiam horribili visu portenta sequuntur,   271
et socii amissi petierunt aethera pinnis
fluminibusque vagantur aves (heu dira meorum
supplicia!) et scopulos lacrimosis vocibus implent.
haec adeo ex illo mihi iam speranda fuerunt   275
tempore, cum ferro caelestia corpora demens
adpetii et Veneris violavi volnere dextram.
ne vero, ne me ad talis impellite pugnas.

²⁶¹ adacti *M²*.
²⁶⁴, ²⁶⁵ *placed after 268 by Ribbeck, Benoist, and others.*
²⁶⁷ inter *Pγ¹, Macrobius*.
²⁶⁸ devicta Asia *γ²b²c, preferred by Servius.* possedit *M²Rγ², Macrobius.*
²⁷² amissis *P¹*: admissis *known to Servius.*
²⁷⁵ adeo] eadem *Pγ¹*.

---

[1] As the Greeks were returning from Troy, Pallas Minerva sent a storm upon them, and Nauplius, king of Euboea, hung

AENEID BOOK XI

steel profaned the fields of Troy—I speak not of the sorrows we suffered in war beneath her lofty walls, of the heroes whom yonder Simois o'erwhelms—we, the wide world over, have paid all manner of penalties for guilt in nameless tortures, a band that even Priam might pity: witness Minerva's baleful star, the Euboic cliffs, and avenging Caphereus.[1] From that warfare driven to diverse shores, Menelaus, son of Atreus, is in exile far as the pillars of Proteus; and Ulysses has looked on the Cyclopes of Aetna. Shall I tell of the realm of Neoptolemus and the home of Idomeneus o'erthrown! or of the Locrians who dwell on Libya's shore? Even the Mycenaean, the mighty Achaeans' chief, scarce within the threshold, fell by his wicked wife's hand; behind vanquished Asia lurked a paramour![2] Ah! that heaven hath begrudged me return to my country's altars, and sight of the wife I long for, and lovely Calydon! Even now, portents of dreadful view pursue me; my lost comrades have winged their way to the sky or haunt the streams as birds—alas! the dire punishment of my people!—and fill the cliffs with their tearful cries.[3] Such, even such, was the fate I had to look for from that hour when with the steel I madly assailed celestial limbs, and profaned the hand of Venus with a wound.[4] Nay, nay, urge me not to

out false lights, so that the fleet was wrecked on the promontory of Caphereus.

[2] Aegisthus, paramour of Clytemnestra, aided her in the murder of the returning Agamemnon. Thus for the victor came "first the triumph, then the assassin's stroke."

[3] Some of the companions of Diomede were changed into sea-birds, which haunted the Diomede Islands off the Apulian promontory of Garganus.

[4] How Diomede wounded Aphrodite is told in *Iliad*, v. 318 ff.

253

VIRGIL

nec mihi cum Teucris ullum post eruta bellum
Pergama, nec veterum memini laetorve malorum. 280
munera, quae patriis ad me portatis ab oris,
vertite ad Aenean.   stetimus tela aspera contra
contulimusque manus: experto credite, quantus
in clipeum adsurgat, quo turbine torqueat hastam.
si duo praeterea talis Idaea tulisset 285
terra viros, ultro Inachias venisset ad urbes
Dardanus et versis lugeret Graecia fatis.
quidquid apud durae cessatum est moenia Troiae,
Hectoris Aeneaeque manu victoria Graium
haesit et in decimum vestigia rettulit annum. 290
ambo animis, ambo insignes praestantibus armis;
hic pietate prior.   coeant in foedera dextrae,
qua datur; ast armis concurrant arma cavete.'
et responsa simul quae sint, rex optime, regis
audisti et quae sit magno sententia bello." 295

Vix ea legati, variusque per ora cucurrit
Ausonidum turbata fremor: ceu saxa morantur
cum rapidos amnis, fit clauso gurgite murmur
vicinaeque fremunt ripae crepitantibus undis.
ut primum placati animi et trepida ora quierunt, 300
praefatus divos solio rex infit ab alto:

"Ante equidem summa de re statuisse, Latini,
et vellem et fuerat melius, non tempore tali
cogere concilium, cum muros adsidet hostis.
bellum importunum, cives, cum gente deorum 305
invictisque viris gerimus, quos nulla fatigant

[279] diruta bellum est *R*.   [281] portastis *bc, Servius*.
[285] certatum *M²*.   [304] obsidet *Mbc²*.

AENEID BOOK XI

such battles! Neither have I any war with Teucer's race since Troy's towers fell, nor have I joyful remembrance of the ills of old. The gifts that ye bring me from your country's bounds take rather to Aeneas. We have faced his fierce weapons, and fought him hand to hand: trust one who proved it, how huge he looms above his shield, with what whirlwind he hurls his spear! Had Ida's land borne two others like to him, the Trojans had even stormed the towns of Inachus,[1] and Greece would be mourning, with doom reversed. In all our tarrying before the walls of stubborn Troy, it was by the hand of Hector and Aeneas that the Greeks' victory was halted and withdrew its advent till the tenth year. Both were renowned for courage, both eminent in arms; Aeneas was first in piety. Join hand to hand in treaty, as best ye may; but beware your swords clash not with his!' Thou hast heard, noble King, what the King replies, and what he counsels on this mighty war."

[296] Scarce thus the envoys, when a various murmur ran along the troubled lips of Ausonia's sons: even as, when rocks delay a rushing river, there rises a roar from the pent-up flood, and the neighbouring banks echo to the plashing waters. Soon as minds were calmed and restless tongues were hushed, the king, first calling on heaven, from his high throne begins:

[302] "That ere now, O Latins, we had determined on our country's weal, I both could wish, and it had been better; not to convene a council at such an hour, when the foe is seated at our walls. A war unblest, O my countrymen, we are waging with a race divine, with men unconquered; no battles weary

[1] Inachus was the first king of Argos, and Argos indicates Greek cities in general.

VIRGIL

proelia, nec victi possunt absistere ferro.
spem si quam adscitis Aetolum habuistis in armis,
ponite. spes sibi quisque; sed haec quam an-
    gusta, videtis.
cetera qua rerum iaceant perculsa ruina,   310
ante oculos interque manus sunt omnia vestras.
nec quemquam incuso: potuit quae plurima virtus
esse, fuit; toto certatum est corpore regni.
nunc adeo, quae sit dubiae sententia menti,
expediam et paucis (animos adhibete) docebo.   315
est antiquus ager Tusco mihi proximus amni,
longus in occasum, finis super usque Sicanos;
Aurunci Rutulique serunt et vomere duros
exercent collis atque horum asperrima pascunt.
haec omnis regio et celsi plaga pinea montis   320
cedat amicitiae Teucrorum, et foederis aequas
dicamus leges sociosque in regna vocemus;
considant, si tantus amor, et moenia condant.
sin alios finis aliamque capessere gentem
est animus possuntque solo decedere nostro,   325
bis denas Italo texamus robore navis;
seu pluris complere valent, iacet omnis ad undam
materies; ipsi numerumque modumque carinis
praecipiant, nos aera, manus, navalia demus.
praeterea, qui dicta ferant et foedera firment,   330
centum oratores prima de gente Latinos
ire placet pacisque manu praetendere ramos,
munera portantis aurique eborisque talenta
et sellam regni trabeamque insignia nostri.
consulite in medium et rebus succurrite fessis."   335
  Tum Drances idem infensus, quem gloria Turni
obliqua invidia stimulisque agitabat amaris,
largus opum et lingua melior, sed frigida bello

³¹⁵ et *omitted* $P^2\gamma$.   ³²⁴ -que] -ve $P\gamma$.
³³⁵ fessis] vestris $P\gamma^1$.   ³³⁸ linguae P^1, *Servius*.

AENEID BOOK XI

them and even in defeat they cannot let go the sword. If ye had any hope in alliance with Aetolian arms, resign it. Each is his own hope; but how slender this is, ye see. All else, with what wide ruin it lies smitten, is before your eyes and within your grasp. Nor blame I any; what valour's utmost could do is done; with our realm's whole strength have we striven. Now mark: the judgment of my wavering mind I will unfold, and, if ye pay heed, will instruct you in brief. There is an ancient domain of mine bordering the Tuscan river, stretching far westward, even beyond Sicanian bounds. Auruncans and Rutulians sow the seed, work the stubborn hills with the share, and graze their roughest slopes. Let all this tract, with a pine-clad belt of mountain height, pass to the Trojans in friendship; let us name just terms of treaty, and invite them to share our realm. Let them settle, if so strong be their desire, and build their city. But if they have a mind to lay hold of other bounds, and another nation, and are free to quit our soil, let us build twice ten ships of Italian oak; or if they can man more, all the timber lies at the water's edge; themselves shall prescribe the number and fashion of their vessels; we will give brass, labour, and docks. Further, to bear our word and seal the pact, I would have a hundred envoys go forth, Latins of noblest birth, proffering in their hands boughs of peace, and carrying gifts—talent-weights of gold and ivory, and the chair and robe, ensigns of our royalty. Give counsel for the commonweal, and uphold our weary fortunes!"

[336] Then Drances, hostile as before, whom the renown of Turnus goaded with the bitter stings of furtive envy, lavish of wealth and valiant of tongue, though his hand was cold for battle, in counsel

VIRGIL

dextera, consiliis habitus non futtilis auctor,
seditione potens (genus huic materna superbum 340
nobilitas dabat, incertum de patre ferebat;)
surgit et his onerat dictis atque aggerat iras:
"Rem nulli obscuram nostrae nec vocis egentem
consulis, o bone rex: cuncti se scire fatentur,
quid fortuna ferat populi, sed dicere mussant. 345
det libertatem fandi flatusque remittat,
cuius ob auspicium infaustum moresque sinistros
(dicam equidem, licet arma mihi mortemque minetur)
lumina tot cecidisse ducum totamque videmus
consedisse urbem luctu, dum Troia temptat 350
castra, fugae fidens, et caelum territat armis.
unum etiam donis istis, quae plurima mitti
Dardanidis dicique iubes, unum, optime regum,
adicias, nec te ullius violentia vincat,
quin natam egregio genero dignisque hymenaeis 355
des pater, et pacem hanc aeterno foedere iungas.
quod si tantus habet mentes et pectora terror,
ipsum obtestemur veniamque oremus ab ipso,
cedat, ius proprium regi patriaeque remittat.
quid miseros totiens in aperta pericula civis 360
proicis, o Latio caput horum et causa malorum?
nulla salus bello; pacem te poscimus omnes,
Turne, simul pacis solum inviolabile pignus.
primus ego, invisum quem tu tibi fingis (et esse
nil moror), en supplex venio. miserere tuorum! 365
pone animos et pulsus abi! sat funera fusi

³⁴¹ ferebant P^1R.   ³⁴⁵ petat $M^1\gamma^2$.
³⁵⁶ iungas] firmes M^2R, *Servius*.
³⁶⁶ funere $P^2\gamma^1$.   fuso $P\gamma^1$: fusis M.

AENEID BOOK XI

deemed no mean adviser, in faction strong (his mother's high birth ennobled his lineage; from his sire obscure rank he drew), rises and with these words loads and heaps high their wrath:

343 "A subject dark to no one and needing no voice of ours, O gracious king, is that whereon thou takest our counsel! All confess they know what course the public fortune prompts, but they shrink from speech. Let him grant liberty of speech and abate his blustering pride, through whose disastrous auspices and perverse ways (yea I will speak, though with arms and death he threaten me) we see so many glorious leaders have fallen and the whole city is sunk in mourning, while he, confident in flight, assails the Trojan camp and affrights heaven with his arms. One more add to those many gifts thou bidst us send and promise to the sons of Dardanus—one more, most gracious king—and let no man's violence prevail to stay thee from giving thy daughter, as a father may, to a peerless son in worthy nuptials, and making this bond of peace in eternal covenant. But if such terror possess our minds and hearts, let us entreat the prince himself and implore him, even him, of his grace, to yield and give up his own rights [1] to king and country. Why fling thy hapless fellow-citizens so oft into gaping perils, O spring and source to Latium of these her woes? No safety is there in war; for peace we pray thee, Turnus, one and all, and, along with peace, for its one inviolable pledge. I first, I whom thou feignest to be thy foe —but that I waive—lo, I come in suppliance! Pity thine own folk; doff thy pride; and, beaten, give way! Routed, we have seen enough of death and

[1] Called "his own rights" in irony. Latinus, of course, had the right to dispose of his daughter's hand.

259

VIRGIL

vidimus, ingentis et desolavimus agros.
aut si fama movet, si tantum pectore robur
concipis aut si adeo dotalis regia cordi est,
aude atque adversum fidens fer pectus in hostem. 370
scilicet ut Turno contingat regia coniunx,
nos animae viles, inhumata infletaque turba,
sternamur campis? etiam tu, si qua tibi vis,
si patrii quid Martis habes, illum aspice contra,
qui vocat." 375

Talibus exarsit dictis violentia Turni;
dat gemitum rumpitque has imo pectore voces:
"larga quidem, Drance, semper tibi copia fandi
tum cum bella manus poscunt, patribusque vocatis
primus ades. sed non replenda est curia verbis, 380
quae tuto tibi magna volant, dum distinet hostem
agger moerorum nec inundant sanguine fossae.
proinde tona eloquio (solitum tibi) meque timoris
argue tu, Drance, quando tot stragis acervos
Teucrorum tua dextra dedit passimque tropaeis 385
insignis agros. possit quid vivida virtus,
experiare licet: nec longe scilicet hostes
quaerendi nobis; circumstant undique muros.
imus in adversos? quid cessas? an tibi Mavors
ventosa in lingua pedibusque fugacibus istis 390
semper erit?
pulsus ego? aut quisquam merito, foedissime, pulsum
arguet, Iliaco tumidum qui crescere Thybrim
sanguine et Euandri totam cum stirpe videbit
procubuisse domum atque exutos Arcadas armis? 395
haud ita me experti Bitias et Pandarus ingens

[367] designavimus $P\gamma^1$. [369] aut] et PR.
[378] semper Drance $PR\gamma$, *Servius*. [381] detinet M.
[382] aggere $MPR\gamma^1 c$. nec] et $P\gamma^1$.
[391] M^1 *adds* nequiquam armis terrebimus hostem.
[393] arguit M^1.

AENEID BOOK XI

have made wide lands desolate. Or, if glory stir thee, if in thy heart thou nursest such strength, or if the dower of a palace be to thee so dear—be bold, and fearlessly advance thy breast to meet the foe. What! that Turnus may be blessed with a royal bride, are we, forsooth, we worthless lives, a crowd unburied and unwept, to be strewn upon the plains? Do thou also, if any might be thine, if thou hast aught of the War-god of thy sires, look him in the face who challenges!"

[376] At these words out blazed the fury of Turnus: he heaves a groan, and from his bosom's depth breaks forth with this cry: "Plenteous indeed, Drances, ever is thy stream of speech in the hour when battle calls for hands; and when the senate is summoned, thou art first to appear! But we need not to fill the council-house with words—those big words that fly securely from thy lips, while rampart-walls keep off the foe, and the trenches swim not yet with blood. Go, thunder on in eloquence—thy wonted way—and do thou, Drances, charge me with fear, since thy hand hath reared such slaughter-heaps of Teucrians, and everywhere thou adornest the fields with trophies. What living valour may achieve, 'tis in thy power to make trial; nor in sooth are our foes far to seek; on every side they beset our walls. Shall we move to meet them? Why lingerest? Will thy prowess lodge for ever in that windy tongue, and in those flying feet? I *beaten*? Or shall any one, foul liar, justly brand me beaten, that shall see swollen Tiber rise high with Ilian blood, and all Evander's house and line laid prostrate, and his Arcadians stripped of arms? Not such did Bitias and giant Pandarus prove me, nor those thousand men whom

VIRGIL

et quos mille die victor sub Tartara misi,
inclusus muris hostilique aggere saeptus.
'nulla salus bello.'   capiti cane talia, demens,
Dardanio rebusque tuis.   proinde omnia magno   400
ne cessa turbare metu atque extollere viris
gentis bis victae, contra premere arma Latini.
nunc et Myrmidonum proceres Phrygia arma tremescunt,
nunc et Tydides et Larisaeus Achilles,
amnis et Hadriacas retro fugit Aufidus undas.   405
vel cum se pavidum contra mea iurgia fingit,
artificis scelus, et formidine crimen acerbat.
numquam animam talem dextra hac (absiste moveri)
amittes: habitet tecum et sit pectore in isto.
nunc ad te et tua magna, pater, consulta revertor.   410
si nullam nostris ultra spem ponis in armis,
si tam deserti sumus et semel agmine verso
funditus occidimus neque habet Fortuna regressum,
oremus pacem et dextras tendamus inertis.
quamquam o si solitae quicquam virtutis adesset!   415
ille mihi ante alios fortunatusque laborum
egregiusque animi, qui, ne quid tale videret,
procubuit moriens et humum semel ore momordit.
sin et opes nobis et adhuc intacta iuventus
auxilioque urbes Italae populique supersunt,   420
sin et Troianis cum multo gloria venit
sanguine (sunt illis sua funera, parque per omnis
tempestas)—cur indecores in limine primo
deficimus? cur ante tubam tremor occupat artus?
multa dies variique labor mutabilis aevi   425
rettulit in melius, multos alterna revisens

 404 *Rejected by some editors; cf.* II. 197.   410 magne *M*.
412 simul *P*γ.   418 semul *P*: simul *M*¹*R*.   422 suntque *R*.
425 variusque *M*²*P*²γ¹, *Macrobius, Nonius.*
426 multosque *M*²

262

AENEID BOOK XI

in one day my conquering arm sent down to hell, cooped though I was within their walls and girt by foemen's ramparts. *No safety in war!* Chant such bodings, fool, for the Dardan's head and thine own lot! Go on; cease not to confound all with thy great alarms, extol the might of a twice-conquered people, and in turn decry the arms of Latinus. Now the Myrmidon princes tremble before Phrygian arms, now Tydeus' son and Achilles of Larissa, and Aufidus' stream recoils from the Adriatic wave. Or listen when he feigns himself affrighted at my chiding—the knavish villain—and sharpens calumny with terror! Never shalt thou lose such life as thine—be not troubled—by this right hand: let it dwell with thee, and abide in thy craven breast! Now, sire, I return to thee and this weighty debate of thine. If thou restest no further hope in our arms, if so forlorn are we, and in one repulse of our lines have fallen on utter ruin, nor can Fortune retrace her steps, let us pray for peace and stretch forth helpless hands! Yet, oh, if we had aught of our wonted valour! Blest beyond others in his toil, and peerless in soul would I hold the man, who, to shun such a sight, has fallen in death and once for all has bitten the dust. But if we still have means, a manhood still unharmed, cities and nations of Italy still supporting us; but if even the Trojans have won glory at much bloodshed's cost (they too have their deaths, and the storm swept over all alike)—why faint we ignobly upon the threshold's edge? Why, ere the trumpet sounds, does trembling seize our limbs? Many an ill has time repaired, and the shifting toil of changing years; many a man has Fortune, fitful visitant,

VIRGIL

lusit et in solido rursus Fortuna locavit.
non erit auxilio nobis Aetolus et Arpi:
at Messapus erit felixque Tolumnius et quos
tot populi misere duces, nec parva sequetur   430
gloria delectos Latio et Laurentibus agris.
est et Volscorum egregia de gente Camilla,
agmen agens equitum et florentis aere catervas.
quod si me solum Teucri in certamina poscunt
idque placet tantumque bonis communibus obsto, 435
non adeo has exosa manus Victoria fugit,
ut tanta quicquam pro spe temptare recusem.
ibo animis contra, vel magnum praestet Achillem
factaque Volcani manibus paria induat arma
ille licet.   vobis animam hanc soceroque Latino 440
Turnus ego, haud ulli veterum virtute secundus,
devovi.   'solum Aeneas vocat.'   et vocet oro,
nec Drances potius, sive est haec ira deorum,
morte luat, sive est virtus et gloria, tollat."

Illi haec inter se dubiis de rebus agebant   445
certantes: castra Aeneas aciemque movebat.
nuntius ingenti per regia tecta tumultu
ecce ruit magnisque urbem terroribus implet:
instructos acie Tiberino a flumine Teucros
Tyrrhenamque manum totis descendere campis.   450
extemplo turbati animi concussaque volgi
pectora et arrectae stimulis haud mollibus irae.
arma manu trepidi poscunt, fremit arma iuventus,
flent maesti mussantque patres. hic undique clamor
dissensu vario magnus se tollit ad auras,   455
haud secus atque alto in luco cum forte catervae
consedere avium, piscosove amne Padusae

⁴³² *cf.* VII. 803 f.   ⁴⁴⁰ Latini *M*¹   ⁴⁵⁵ ad] in *PR*γ.

AENEID BOOK XI

mocked, then once more set up upon firm ground. No aid to us will be the Aetolian and his Arpi: yet Messapus will be, and Tolumnius the fortunate, and all the leaders sent by many a nation; nor will scant fame attend the flower of Latium and the Laurentine land. We have Camilla too, of the glorious Volscian race, leading her troop of horse and squadrons gay with brass. But if I alone am called by the Teucrians to combat, and such is your will, and I thus thwart the common good, Victory has not shrunk from these my hands with such loathing, that for hope so high I should decline to venture aught. I will face him boldly, even though he outmatch great Achilles and don like armour, wrought by Vulcan's hands. To you and my bride's sire, Latinus, have I, Turnus, second in valour to none of my fathers, devoted this life. *Aeneas calls on him alone.* So let him call, I pray! nor let Drances in my stead, if heaven's wrath be here, appease it by his death; nor, if here be prowess and glory, let him win the palm!"

445 Thus, in mutual strife, were they debating doubtful issues: Aeneas the while moved from camp to field. Lo, amid wild uproar, a messenger rushes through the royal halls and fills the city with great alarms: in battle-array, he cries, the Teucrians and the Tyrrhene force are sweeping down from the Tiber river over all the plain. Straightway the minds of the people are confounded, their bosoms shaken, and their passions roused by no gentle spur. With wildly waving hands they call for arms; "arms!" the young men shout; the weeping fathers moan and mutter. And now, from every side, there rises to heaven a loud din with varied discord: even as when flocks of birds haply settle in some tall grove, or

VIRGIL

dant sonitum rauci per stagna loquacia cycni.
"immo," ait, "o cives," arrepto tempore Turnus,
"cogite concilium et pacem laudate sedentes; 460
illi armis in regna ruunt." nec plura locutus
corripuit sese et tectis citus extulit altis.
"tu, Voluse, armari Volscorum edice maniplis,
duc," ait, " et Rutulos. equitem, Messapus, in armis,
et cum fratre Coras, latis diffundite campis. 465
pars aditus urbis firmet turrisque capessat;
cetera, qua iusso, mecum manus inferat arma."
   Ilicet in muros tota discurritur urbe.
concilium ipse pater et magna incepta Latinus
deserit ac tristi turbatus tempore differt, 470
multaque se incusat, qui non acceperit ultro
Dardanium Aenean generumque adsciverit urbi.
praefodiunt alii portas aut saxa sudesque
subvectant. bello dat signum rauca cruentum
bucina. tum muros varia cinxere corona 475
matronae puerique; vocat labor ultimus omnis.
nec non ad templum summasque ad Palladis arces
subvehitur magna matrum regina caterva,
dona ferens, iuxtaque comes Lavinia virgo,
causa mali tanti, oculos deiecta decoros. 480
succedunt matres et templum ture vaporant
et maestas alto fundunt de limine voces:
"armipotens, praeses belli, Tritonia virgo,
frange manu telum Phrygii praedonis, et ipsum
pronum sterne solo portisque effunde sub altis." 485
cingitur ipse furens certatim in proelia Turnus.
iamque adeo rutilum thoraca indutus aënis

₄₆₃ maniplos $P\gamma^1$. ₄₆₄ equites $P^2R\gamma$.
₄₆₆ firment M^1R. capessant R.
₄₆₉ consilium M^1. ₄₇₁ quod $P^2\gamma$.
₄₈₀ mali tantis M^1b^1: malis tantis Rb^2c^1.
₄₈₃ praesens $M^2P^2\gamma^1$, *Macrobius*.
₄₈₇ Rutulum $MP\gamma$.

266

AENEID BOOK XI

when, by Padusa's fish-filled stream, hoarse-throated swans scream among the clamorous pools. "Nay; citizens," cries Turnus, seizing the moment, "convene a council, and sit praising peace; yonder they rush upon the realm in arms." No more he spake, but up he sprang, and sped swiftly forth from the high halls. "Thou, Volusus," he cries, "bid the Volscian squadrons arm, and lead out the Rutulians! Thou, Messapus, and thou, Coras, with thy brother, spread the horsemen under arms over the broad plains. Let some guard the city gates and man the towers; let the rest charge with me, where I shall command."

468 At once from all the city there is a rush to the walls. Lord Latinus himself, dismayed by the disastrous hour, quits the council and postpones his high designs, oft chiding himself that he gave not ready welcome to Dardan Aeneas, nor, for his city's sake, adopted him as son. Others dig trenches before the gates or shoulder stones and stakes. The hoarse clarion gives bloody signal for battle. Then lo! a motley ring of matrons and boys girdle the walls; the final struggle summons all. Moreover the queen, with a great throng of mothers, rides [1] up to the temple of Pallas and her towered heights, bearing gifts, and at her side the maid Lavinia, source of all that woe, her beauteous eyes downcast. Ascending, the matrons fill the temple with smoke of incense and from the high threshold pour sad lamentations: "O mighty in arms, mistress in war, Tritonian maid, break with thine hand the spear of the Phrygian pirate, hurl him prone to earth and stretch him prostrate beneath our lofty gates." As for Turnus, he, with emulous fury, girds himself for the fray. And now he has donned his flashing breastplate and

[1] Even as the Roman matrons rode in *pilenta* in their sacred processions (*cf. Aen.* VIII. 665).

VIRGIL

horrebat squamis surasque incluserat auro,
tempora nudus adhuc, laterique accinxerat ensem,
fulgebatque alta decurrens aureus arce   490
exsultatque animis et spe iam praecipit hostem:
qualis ubi abruptis fugit praesepia vinclis
tandem liber equus campoque potitus aperto
aut ille in pastus armentaque tendit equarum
aut adsuetus aquae perfundi flumine noto   495
emicat, arrectisque fremit cervicibus alte
luxurians, luduntque iubae per colla, per armos.

  Obvia cui Volscorum acie comitante Camilla
occurrit portisque ab equo regina sub ipsis
desiluit, quam tota cohors imitata relictis   500
ad terram defluxit equis; tum talia fatur:
"Turne, sui merito si qua est fiducia forti,
audeo et Aeneadum promitto occurrere turmae
solaque Tyrrhenos equites ire obvia contra.
me sine prima manu temptare pericula belli,   505
tu pedes ad muros subsiste et moenia serva."
Turnus ad haec, oculos horrenda in virgine fixus:
"o decus Italiae virgo, quas dicere gratis
quasve referre parem? sed nunc, est omnia quando
iste animus supra, mecum partire laborem.   510
Aeneas, ut fama fidem missique reportant
exploratores, equitum levia improbus arma
praemisit, quaterent campos; ipse ardua montis
per deserta iugo superans adventat ad urbem.
furta paro belli convexo in tramite silvae, 515
ut bivias armato obsidam milite fauces.
tu Tyrrhenum equitem conlatis excipe signis;
tecum acer Messapus erit turmaeque Latinae
Tiburtique manus; ducis et tu concipe curam."

        ⁵⁰⁷ horrenda virgine *M*¹: fixis *M*¹: fixos γ.
        ⁵¹⁰ superat *M*¹.

AENEID BOOK XI

bristles with brazen scales; his legs he had sheathed in gold, his temples are yet bare, and his sword he had buckled to his side. Glittering in gold, he runs down from the fortress height; he exults in courage, and in hope even now seizes the foe—even as, when a horse, bursting his tether, has fled the stalls, free at last, and lord of the open plain, either, mark you! he makes for the pastures and herds of mares, or, wont to bathe in the well-known river, he darts forth, and neighs, with head out-stretched high in wanton joy, while his mane plays over neck and over shoulder.

498 To meet him sped Camilla, attended by the Volscian array, and hard by the gates the queen leaped from her horse; at whose example all her troop quitted their steeds and glided to earth. Then thus she speaks: "Turnus, if the brave may justly place aught of trust in themselves, I dare and promise to face Aeneas' cavalry, and singly ride to meet the Tyrrhene horse. Suffer this hand to essay war's first perils; do thou on foot stay by the walls and guard the town." To this Turnus, with eyes fixed upon the dread maid: "O maiden, glory of Italy, what thanks shall I try to utter or repay? But now, since thy spirit soars above all, share thou with me the toil. Aeneas—so rumour tells, and scouts sent forth report the tidings true—has insolently thrown forward his light-armed horse, to sweep the plains; himself, o'erpassing the ridge, marches by the mountain's lonely steeps upon the town. Snares of war I lay in an over-arched pathway 'mid the wood, to block with armed troops the gorge's double jaws. Do thou in battle array await the Tyrrhene horse; with thee shall be the valiant Messapus, the Latin squadrons, and Tiburtus' troop: take thou too a

VIRGIL

sic ait et paribus Messapum in proelia dictis 520
hortatur sociosque duces et pergit in hostem.
    Est curvo anfractu valles, accommoda fraudi
armorumque dolis, quam densis frondibus atrum
urget utrimque latus, tenuis quo semita ducit
angustaeque ferunt fauces aditusque maligni. 525
hanc super in speculis summoque in vertice montis
planities ignota iacet tutique receptus,
seu dextra laevaque velis occurrere pugnae,
sive instare iugis et grandia volvere saxa.
huc iuvenis nota fertur regione viarum 530
arripuitque locum et silvis insedit iniquis.
    Velocem interea superis in sedibus Opim,
unam ex virginibus sociis sacraque caterva,
compellabat et has tristis Latonia voces
ore dabat: "graditur bellum ad crudele Camilla, 535
o virgo, et nostris nequiquam cingitur armis,
cara mihi ante alias. neque enim novus iste Dianae
venit amor subitaque animum dulcedine movit.
pulsus ob invidiam regno virisque superbas
Priverno antiqua Metabus cum excederet urbe, 540
infantem fugiens media inter proelia belli
sustulit exilio comitem matrisque vocavit
nomine Casmillae, mutata parte, Camillam.
ipse sinu prae se portans iuga longa petebat
solorum nemorum; tela undique saeva premebant 545
et circumfuso volitabant milite Volsci.
ecce fugae medio summis Amasenus abundans
spumabat ripis; tantus se nubibus imber
ruperat. ille, innare parans, infantis amore

    [526] in speculis] in *omitted R:* e $P\gamma^1$.
    [527] recessus M^2R, *known to Servius.*
    [533] sacris socia *R.*
    [534] conpellat *R.* tristi *R.*

AENEID BOOK XI

captain's charge." This said, with like words he heartens Messapus and the allied captains to battle, and moves against the foe.

⁵²² There lies a vale with sweeping curve, fit site for stratagems and wiles of war, hemmed in on either side by a wall black with dense leafage. Hither leads a narrow path, with straitened gorge and jealous approach. Above it, amid the watch-towers of the mountain-top, lies a hidden plain and a safe shelter, whether one would charge from right or left, or take stand upon the ridge and roll down giant stones. Hither the warrior repairs by a familiar line of road, and, seizing his ground, sat him down within the perilous woods.[1]

⁵³² Meanwhile, in Heaven's halls Latona's daughter addressed fleet Opis, one of her maiden sisterhood and sacred band, and opened her lips to these words of sorrow: "Camilla goes forth to the cruel war, O maiden, and vainly girds on our arms, dear as she is to me beyond others. For no new love is this that has come to Diana nor sudden the spell wherewith it has stirred her heart. When, driven from his realm through hatred of his tyrant might, Metabus was leaving Privernum's ancient city, as he fled amid the press of battle-strife, he took with him his infant child to share his exile, and called her, after her mother Casmilla's name, but slightly changed, Camilla. The father, carrying her before him on his breast, sought the long ridges of lonely woodland: on every side pressed fierce weapons, and with wide-spread soldiery hovered the Volscians. Lo! athwart his flight, Amasenus was foaming in flood above his highest banks, so fierce a rain had burst from the clouds. Fain to swim the stream, he is checked by

[1] *i.e.* involving peril for Aeneas.

271

VIRGIL

tardatur caroque oneri timet.   omnia secum   550
versanti subito vix haec sententia sedit:
telum immane manu valida quod forte gerebat
bellator, solidum nodis et robore cocto,
huic natam, libro et silvestri subere clausam,
implicat atque habilem mediae circumligat hastae; 555
quam dextra ingenti librans ita ad aethera fatur:
'alma, tibi hanc, nemorum cultrix, Latonia virgo,
ipse pater famulam voveo; tua prima per auras
tela tenens supplex hostem fugit.   accipe, testor,
diva tuam, quae nunc dubiis committitur auris.' 560
dixit et adducto contortum hastile lacerto
immittit: sonuere undae, rapidum super amnem
infelix fugit in iaculo stridente Camilla.
at Metabus, magna propius iam urgente caterva,
dat sese fluvio, atque hastam cum virgine victor 565
gramineo, donum Triviae, de caespite vellit.
non illum tectis ullae, non moenibus urbes
accepere, neque ipse manus feritate dedisset:
pastorum et solis exegit montibus aevum.
hic natam in dumis interque horrentia lustra   570
armentalis equae mammis et lacte ferino
nutribat, teneris immulgens ubera labris.
utque pedum primis infans vestigia plantis
institerat, iaculo palmas armavit acuto
spiculaque ex umero parvae suspendit et arcum. 575
pro crinali auro, pro longae tegmine pallae
tigridis exuviae per dorsum a vertice pendent.
tela manu iam tum tenera puerilia torsit
et fundam tereti circum caput egit habena
Strymoniamque gruem aut album deiecit olorem. 580

[552] ferebat M^2.
[554] huc R^1.
[570] hinc P^1.
[574] armavit] onerant b, *Servius*.

272

AENEID BOOK XI

love for his babe, and he fears for his precious burden. Of a sudden, as he inly pondered every course, he settled on this reluctant resolve: the huge spear, which the warrior haply bore in his stout hand, hard-knotted and of seasoned oak—to this he fastens his child, encased in bark of wild cork-wood, and bound her featly round the centre of the shaft; then poising it in his giant hand, thus cries to the heavens: 'Gracious one, dweller in the woodland, Latonian maid, this child I vow to thy service, I her father; thine are the first weapons she holds, as through the air, thy suppliant, she flees the foe. Accept, O goddess, I implore, for thine own, her whom now I commit to the uncertain breeze.' He said, and, drawing back his arm, launches the spinning shaft: loud roared the waters, over the rushing river flees hapless Camilla upon the whizzing steel. But Metabus, now that a great band pressed closer upon him, plunges into the flood, and in triumph plucks from the grassy turf his offering to Trivia, the spear and the maid. Him no cities received to their homes or walls, nor in his wild mood would he himself have yielded thereto: amid shepherds and on the lone mountains he passed his days. Here amid brakes and beasts' rugged lairs he nursed his child on milk at the breast of a wild mare from the herd, squeezing the teats into her tender lips. And soon as her baby feet had planted her earliest steps, he armed her hands with a pointed lance, and hung quiver and bow from her little shoulder. In place of gold to clasp her hair, in place of long trailing robe, there hang from her head adown the back a tiger's spoils. Even then with tender hand she hurled her childish darts, swung round her head the smooth-thonged sling, and struck down Strymonian

VIRGIL

multae illam frustra Tyrrhena per oppida matres
optavere nurum; sola contenta Diana
aeternum telorum et virginitatis amorem
intemerata colit. vellem haud correpta fuisset
militia tali, conata lacessere Teucros: 585
cara mihi comitumque foret nunc una mearum.
verum age, quandoquidem fatis urgetur acerbis,
labere, nympha, polo finisque invise Latinos,
tristis ubi infausto committitur omine pugna.
haec cape et ultricem pharetra deprome sagittam: 590
hac, quicumque sacrum violarit volnere corpus,
Tros Italusve, mihi pariter det sanguine poenas.
post ego nube cava miserandae corpus et arma
inspoliata feram tumulo patriaeque reponam."
dixit: at illa levis caeli delapsa per auras 595
insonuit, nigro circumdata turbine corpus.

At manus interea muris Troiana propinquat
Etruscique duces equitumque exercitus omnis,
compositi numero in turmas. fremit aequore toto
insultans sonipes et pressis pugnat habenis 600
huc conversus et huc; tum late ferreus hastis
horret ager campique armis sublimibus ardent.
nec non Messapus contra celeresque Latini
et cum fratre Coras et virginis ala Camillae
adversi campo apparent hastasque reductis 605
protendunt longe dextris et spicula vibrant,
adventusque virum fremitusque ardescit equorum.

---

[592] -ve *c, Servius:* -que *MPRγb (in the last over an erasure).*
[595] demissa *PRγc:* dimissa *b.*
[601] obversus *Rγ²*.   [602] armis] hastis *Pγ¹*.
[605] reductas *M¹*.   [606] praetendunt *M¹*.

274

AENEID BOOK XI

crane or snowy swan. Many a mother in Tyrrhene towers longed for her as daughter in vain; content with Diana alone, she cherishes unsullied a lifelong love for her weapons and her maidenhood. I would that she had not been swept away in warfare such as this, nor essayed to brave the Teucrians: so were she still my darling and a sister of my train. But come, seeing that untimely doom weighs upon her, glide from heaven, O nymph, and seek the Latin borders, where under evil omen they join in the gloomy fray. Take these,[1] and draw from my quiver an avenging shaft: by it let the foe, whoe'er he be, Trojan or Italian, that with wound shall profane her sacred limbs, pay me forfeit in like manner with his blood. Then in the hollow of a cloud I will bear body and armour of the hapless maid unspoiled to the tomb, and lay them away in her own land." She spoke; but Opis sped down with whirring sound through heaven's light air, her form enshrouded in black whirlwind.

597 But meanwhile the Trojan band draws near the walls, with the Etruscan chiefs and all their mounted array, marshalled by number into squadrons. The war-steed prances neighing o'er all the plain, and, fighting the tight-drawn rein, swerves hither and thither: far and wide the field bristles with the steel of spears, and the plains are ablaze with uplifted arms. Likewise, over against them, Messapus, and the fleet Latins, and Coras with his brother, and maid Camilla's troop, come into view, confronting them on the plain; with hands back-drawn afar, they thrust the lance and brandish the javelin; the marching of men and neighing of steeds grows fiery-

---

[1] *i.e.* her bow and arrows.

275

VIRGIL

iamque intra iactum teli progressus uterque
substiterat : subito erumpunt clamore furentisque
exhortantur equos, fundunt simul undique tela   610
crebra nivis ritu, caelumque obtexitur umbra.
continuo adversis Tyrrhenus et acer Aconteus
conixi incurrunt hastis primique ruinam
dant sonitu ingenti perfractaque quadrupedantum
pectora pectoribus rumpunt : excussus Aconteus 615
fulminis in morem aut tormento ponderis acti
praecipitat longe et vitam dispergit in auras.

Extemplo turbatae acies, versique Latini
reiciunt parmas et equos ad moenia vertunt :
Troes agunt, princeps turmas inducit Asilas.   620
iamque propinquabant portis, rursusque Latini
clamorem tollunt et mollia colla reflectunt ;
hi fugiunt penitusque datis referuntur habenis :
qualis ubi alterno procurrens gurgite pontus
nunc ruit ad terram scopulosque superiacit unda 625
spumeus extremamque sinu perfundit harenam,
nunc rapidus retro atque aestu revoluta resorbens
saxa fugit litusque vado labente relinquit :
bis Tusci Rutulos egere ad moenia versos,
bis reiecti armis respectant terga tegentes.   630
tertia sed postquam congressi in proelia totas
implicuere inter se acies legitque virum vir,
tum vero et gemitus morientum et sanguine in alto
armaque corporaque et permixti caede virorum
semianimes volvuntur equi ; pugna aspera surgit. 635
Orsilochus Remuli, quando ipsum horrebat adire,
hastam intorsit equo ferrumque sub aure reliquit.

[609] constiterant M^1.   [612] adversi $MP^2R\gamma$.
[613] ruina P^2 *and two* codices Moretani *cited by Ribbeck.*
[614] sonitum $MP\gamma^1$. ingentem $P\gamma^1$ (*M has* ruinam dant sonitum ingenti).   [624] procumbens R.   [625] terras M. suberigit R: superlicit P. *Hence Sabb adopts* superiicit. undam γ, *Servius.*

276

AENEID BOOK XI

fierce. And now in its advance each host had halted within spear-cast of each; with sudden shout they dash forth, and spur on their furious steeds; at once from all sides they shower darts as thick as snow-flakes, and the sky is veiled in shade. Forthwith Tyrrhenus and fierce Aconteus charge with spears amain, and are first to go down with mighty crash, breaking and shattering their chargers, breast against breast. Aconteus, flung off like thunderbolt or mass driven forth from an engine, is hurled headlong afar, and scatters his life into the air.

[618] Straightway the lines waver, and the Latins, routed, cast their shields behind them, and turn their horses cityward. The Trojans give chase; Asilas in the van leads the squadrons. And now they were drawing nigh the gates, when again the Latins raise their shout, and wheel about their chargers' supple necks; the others flee, and retreat afar with loosened rein: as when ocean, advancing with alternate flood, now rushes shoreward, dashes o'er the cliffs in a wave of foam, and drenches the utmost sands with its swelling curve; now flees in fast retreat and in its surge sucks back revolving stones, leaving the strand with gliding shoal. Twice the Tuscans drove the routed Rutulians to the city; twice, repulsed, they glance backwards, as they sling behind them their protecting shields. But when, clashing in the third encounter, the whole lines stood interlocked, and man marked man, then in truth rose groans of the dying, and deep in blood welter arms and bodies and horses, wounded unto death, and mingled with slaughtered riders: fierce swells the fight. Orsilochus hurled a lance at Remulus' steed— for its lord he shrank to meet—and left the steel

VIRGIL

quo sonipes ictu furit arduus altaque iactat
volneris impatiens arrecto pectore crura.
volvitur ille excussus humi. Catillus Iollan   640
ingentemque animis, ingentem corpore et armis,
deicit Herminium, nudo cui vertice fulva
caesaries nudique umeri; nec volnera terrent;
tantus in arma patet. latos huic hasta per armos
acta tremit duplicatque virum transfixa dolore.   MR
funditur ater ubique cruor; dant funera ferro   646
certantes pulchramque petunt per volnera mortem.

At medias inter caedes exsultat Amazon,
unum exserta latus pugnae, pharetrata Camilla,
et nunc lenta manu spargens hastilia denset,   650
nunc validam dextra rapit indefessa bipennem;
aureus ex umero sonat arcus et arma Dianae.
illa etiam, si quando in tergum pulsa recessit,
spicula converso fugientia dirigit arcu.
at circum lectae comites, Larinaque virgo   655
Tullaque et aeratam quatiens Tarpeia securim,
Italides, quas ipsa decus sibi dia Camilla
delegit pacisque bonas bellique ministras:
quales Threiciae cum flumina Thermodontis
pulsant et pictis bellantur Amazones armis,   660
seu circum Hippolyten seu cum se Martia curru
Penthesilea refert, magnoque ululante tumultu
feminea exsultant lunatis agmina peltis.

Quem telo primum, quem postremum, aspera virgo,
deicis? aut quot humi morientia corpora fundis? 665
Euneum Clytio primum patre, cuius apertum

<small>⁶³⁸ ferit M^1R. ⁶⁴⁴ tantum R. ⁶⁵⁰ densat $M^1R\gamma$.
⁶⁵³ in tergum si quando b, *Ribbeck*. ⁶⁵⁷ dia $M^2\gamma^1 b$,
Servius: diva $M^1\gamma^2c^1$: dura R. ⁶⁵⁸ bonae $R\gamma^2$.</small>

AENEID BOOK XI

beneath its ear. At this blow the charger rears furious, and, brooking not the wound, with chest uplifted flings his legs on high; hurled forth, Remulus rolls on earth. Catillus strikes down Iollas, and Herminius, giant in courage, giant in body and arms; on his bare head stream his yellow locks, and bare are his shoulders; for him wounds have no terrors; so vast a frame faces the steel. Through his broad shoulders the driven spear comes quivering, and, piercing through, bends him double with anguish. Everywhere the dark blood streams; they deal carnage, clashing with the sword, and seek amid wounds a glorious death.

648 But in the heart of the slaughter, like an Amazon, one breast bared for the fray, and quiver-girt, rages Camilla; and now tough javelins she showers thick from her hand, now a stout battle-axe she snatches with unwearied grasp; the golden bow, armour of Diana, clangs from her shoulders. And even if, back pressed, she withdraws, she turns her bow and aims darts in her flight. But round her are her chosen comrades, maiden Larina and Tulla, and Tarpeia, shaking an axe of bronze, daughters of Italy, whom godlike Camilla herself chose to be her pride, good handmaids both in peace and war. Such are the Amazons of Thrace, when they tramp over Thermodon's streams and war in blazoned armour, whether round Hippolyte, or when Penthesilea, child of Mars, returns in her chariot, and, amid loud tumultuous cries, the woman-host exult with crescent shields.

664 Whom first, whom last, fierce maid, does thy dart strike down? How many a frame dost thou stretch dying on earth? First Euneus, son of Clytius, whose unguarded breast, as he faces her, she

279

VIRGIL

adversi longa transverberat abiete pectus.
sanguinis ille vomens rivos cadit atque cruentam
mandit humum moriensque suo se in volnere versat.
tum Lirim Pagasumque super : quorum alter habenas
suffosso revolutus equo dum colligit, alter   671
dum subit ac dextram labenti tendit inermem,
praecipites pariterque ruunt. his addit Amastrum
Hippotaden, sequiturque incumbens eminus hasta
Tereaque Harpalycumque et Demophoonta
    Chromimque ;   675
quotque emissa manu contorsit spicula virgo,
tot Phrygii cecidere viri.   procul Ornytus armis
ignotis et equo venator Iapyge fertur,
cui pellis latos umeros erepta iuvenco
pugnatori operit, caput ingens oris hiatus   680
et malae texere lupi cum dentibus albis,
agrestisque manus armat sparus ; ipse catervis
vertitur in mediis et toto vertice supra est.
hunc illa exceptum (neque enim labor agmine verso)
traicit et super haec inimico pectore fatur :   685
" silvis te, Tyrrhene, feras agitare putasti ?
advenit qui vestra dies muliebribus armis
verba redarguerit. nomen tamen haud leve patrum
manibus hoc referes, telo cecidisse Camillae."

  Protinus Orsilochum et Buten, duo maxima
    Teucrum   690
corpora : sed Buten aversum cuspide fixit   MPR
loricam galeamque inter, qua colla sedentis
lucent et laevo dependet parma lacerto ;
Orsilochum fugiens magnumque agitata per orbem
eludit gyro interior sequiturque sequentem ;   695
tum validam perque arma viro perque ossa securim,
altior exsurgens, oranti et multa precanti

---

⁶⁷¹ suffuso $M^2R\gamma$, *preferred by Servius.*   ⁶⁷² inertem γ.
⁶⁸⁸ redargueret $MR(?)\gamma$: redarguerit *Priscian.*

280

AENEID BOOK XI

pierces through with her long pine-shaft. Spouting streams of blood, he falls, bites the gory dust, and, dying, writhes upon his wound. Then Liris she fells, and Pagasus above him: while one, thrown from his stabbed horse, gathers up the reins, and the other, coming up, stretches an unharmed hand to stay his fall, headlong they fall together. To these she adds Amastrus, son of Hippotas; and, bending to the task, she follows from far with her spear Tereus, and Harpalycus, and Demophoon, and, Chromis; and as many darts as she sent spinning from her hand, so many Phrygians fell. At a distance rides the hunter Ornytus in strange armour on an Iapygian steed: a hide stripped from a steer swathes the warrior's broad shoulders, his head is shielded by a wolf's huge gaping mouth and white-fanged jaws, and his hand is armed with rustic pike; himself he moves in the midmost ranks, a full head above all. Him she caught—for easy it was amid the rout— and pierced, then above him thus cries with pitiless heart: "Tuscan, didst thou think thou wert chasing beasts in the forests? The day is come that with woman's weapons shall refute the vaunts of thee and thine. Yet no slight renown is this thou shalt carry to thy father's shades—to have fallen by the spear of Camilla!"

690 Next she slays Orsilochus and Butes, two Teucrians of mightiest frame. Butes she pierced with spear-point in the back, 'twixt corslet and helm, where the rider's neck gleams, and the shield hangs from the left arm; Orsilochus she flees, and, chased in a wide circle, foils him, wheels into an inner ring and pursues the pursuer; then rising higher, she drives her strong axe again and again through armour and through bone, albeit he implores and prays oft

VIRGIL

congeminat; volnus calido rigat ora cerebro.
incidit huic subitoque aspectu territus haesit
Appenninicolae bellator filius Auni, 700
haud Ligurum extremus, dum fallere fata sinebant.
isque ubi se nullo iam cursu evadere pugnae
posse neque instantem reginam avertere cernit,
consilio versare dolos ingressus et astu
incipit haec: "quid tam egregium, si femina forti 705
fidis equo? dimitte fugam et te comminus aequo
mecum crede solo pugnaeque accinge pedestri:
iam nosces, ventosa ferat cui gloria fraudem."
dixit, at illa furens acrique accensa dolore
tradit equum comiti paribusque resistit in armis, 710
ense pedes nudo puraque interrita parma.
at iuvenis, vicisse dolo ratus, avolat ipse
(haud mora) conversisque fugax aufertur habenis
quadrupedemque citum ferrata calce fatigat.
"vane Ligus frustraque animis elate superbis, 715
nequiquam patrias temptasti lubricus artis,
nec fraus te incolumem fallaci perferet Auno."
haec fatur virgo, et pernicibus ignea plantis
transit equum cursu frenisque adversa prehensis
congreditur poenasque inimico ex sanguine sumit: 720
quam facile accipiter saxo sacer ales ab alto
consequitur pinnis sublimem in nube columbam
comprensamque tenet pedibusque eviscerat uncis;
tum cruor et volsae labuntur ab aethere plumae.

At non haec nullis hominum sator atque deorum
observans oculis summo sedet altus Olympo. 726

[705] laudem *M²P* (l *in an erasure*).

AENEID BOOK XI

for mercy; the wound spatters the face with warm brain. Now fell in her way, and paused in terror at the sudden vision, the warrior son of Aunus, dweller upon the Apennine, not the meanest in Liguria, while Fate allowed him to deceive.[1] He, when he sees that by no fleetness can he escape combat or turn the queen from her onset, essaying to ply guile with policy and craft, thus begins: "What great glory is it, if thou, though a woman, trustest in thy strong steed? Away with flight; dare to meet me hand to hand on equal ground, and gird thee to fight afoot; soon shalt thou know to whom vainglory brings bane." He spake, but she, furious and burning with the bitter smart, passes her horse to a comrade and confronts him in equal arms, afoot and unafraid, with naked sword and shield unblazoned. But the youth, deeming he had won by guile, himself darts away, pausing not, and turning his bridle rushes off in flight, goading his charger to speed with iron spur. "Foolish Ligurian, vainly puffed up in pride of heart, for naught hast thou tried thy slippery native tricks, nor shall cunning take thee home unscathed to lying Aunus!" So cries the maiden, and, with fleet foot, swift as lightning, crosses the horse's path, and, seizing the reins, meets him face to face and takes vengeance from his hated blood: lightly as a falcon, bird of augury,[2] darting from a lofty rock, o'ertakes on her wings a dove in a cloud aloft, then holds her in his clutch and with crooked claws tears out her heart, while blood and rent plumage flutter from the sky.

725 But not with unseeing eyes the Sire of gods and men sits throned on high Olympus, viewing the

[1] The Ligurians were notorious liars, and so long as he lived he was conspicuous among them. [2] As sacred to Apollo.

VIRGIL

Tyrrhenum genitor Tarchonem in proelia saeva
suscitat et stimulis haud mollibus incutit iras.
ergo inter caedes cedentiaque agmina Tarchon
fertur equo variisque instigat vocibus alas, 730
nomine quemque vocans, reficitque in proelia pulsos.
" quis metus, o numquam dolituri, o semper inertes
Tyrrheni, quae tanta animis ignavia venit?
femina palantis agit atque haec agmina vertit?
quo ferrum quidve haec gerimus tela inrita dextris?
at non in Venerem segnes nocturnaque bella 736
aut ubi curva choros indixit tibia Bacchi. MR
exspectate dapes et plenae pocula mensae
(hic amor, hoc studium), dum sacra secundus haruspex
nuntiet ac lucos vocet hostia pinguis in altos." 740
haec effatus equum in medios, moriturus et ipse,
concitat et Venulo adversum se turbidus infert
dereptumque ab equo dextra complectitur hostem
et gremium ante suum multa vi concitus aufert.
tollitur in caelum clamor cunctique Latini 745
convertere oculos. volat igneus aequore Tarchon,
arma virumque ferens; tum summa ipsius ab hasta
defringit ferrum et partis rimatur apertas,
qua volnus letale ferat; contra ille repugnans
sustinet a iugulo dextram et vim viribus exit. 750
utque volans alte raptum cum fulva draconem
fert aquila implicuitque pedes atque unguibus haesit;
saucius at serpens sinuosa volumina versat
arrectisque horret squamis et sibilat ore,
arduus insurgens; illa haud minus urget obunco 755

⁷²⁸ incitat $M^1P\gamma b$ (M^2, *with a point above* n, *indicates error*):
inicit Rc: incutit *Heinsius*.
⁷³⁸ exspectare *inferior MSS*. ⁷⁴³ offert $R\gamma$.

AENEID BOOK XI

scene. He rouses Tyrrhenian Tarchon to the fierce fray, and pricks him to wrath by no gentle spur. So, amid the slaughter and wavering columns, Tarchon rides, and goads his squadrons with diverse cries, calling each man by name, and rallying the routed to the fight. "What fear, ye Tuscans, never to be stung by shame, sluggards always, what utter cowardice has fallen on your hearts? Does a woman drive you in disorder and rout these ranks? To what end bear we the sword? or why these idle weapons in our hands? But not laggard are ye for love and nightly frays, or when the curved flute proclaims the Bacchic dance. Look to the feasts and the cups on the loaded board (this your passion, this your delight!) till the favouring seer announce the sacrifice, and the fat victim call you to the deep groves!" So saying, he spurs his horse into the midst, ready himself also to die, and charges like whirlwind full upon Venulus; then tearing the foe from his steed, grips him with his right hand, clasps him to his breast, and spurring with might and main, carries him off. A shout uprises to heaven, as all the Latins turned their eyes upon the sight. Like lightning flies Tarchon along the plain, the arms and the man before him; then from the head of his foe's spear breaks off the steel, and searches for an unguarded place, where he may deal a deadly wound; the other, struggling against him, keeps the hand from off his throat and baffles force with force. And, as when a tawny eagle, soaring on high, carries a serpent she has caught, her feet entwined and her claws clinging tight, but the wounded snake writhes its sinuous coils, and rears its bristling scales, and hisses with its mouth, towering aloft; she no less with crooked beak assails her

VIRGIL

luctantem rostro, simul aethera verberat alis:
haud aliter praedam Tiburtum ex agmine Tarchon   M
portat ovans. ducis exemplum eventumque secuti
Maeonidae incurrunt. tum fatis debitus Arruns
velocem iaculo et multa prior arte Camillam   760
circuit et, quae sit fortuna facillima, temptat.
qua se cumque furens medio tulit agmine virgo,
hac Arruns subit et tacitus vestigia lustrat;
qua victrix redit illa pedemque ex hoste reportat,
hac iuvenis furtim celeris detorquet habenas.   765
hos aditus iamque hos aditus omnemque pererrat
undique circuitum et certam quatit improbus hastam.

Forte sacer Cybelo Chloreus olimque sacerdos
insignis longe Phrygiis fulgebat in armis
spumantemque agitabat equum, quem pellis aënis   770
in plumam squamis auro conserta tegebat.
ipse peregrina ferrugine clarus et ostro
spicula torquebat Lycio Gortynia cornu;
aureus ex umeris erat arcus et aurea vati
cassida; tum croceam chlamydemque sinusque
   crepantis   775
carbaseos fulvo in nodum collegerat auro,
pictus acu tunicas et barbara tegmina crurum.
hunc virgo, sive ut templis praefigeret arma
Troia, captivo sive ut se ferret in auro,
venatrix unum ex omni certamine pugnae   780
caeca sequebatur totumque incauta per agmen
femineo praedae et spoliorum ardebat amore,

---

⁷⁶⁸ Cybelo *Mbc, Servius:* Cybele γ: Cybelae *Macrobius.*
⁷⁷⁴ umero γ. erat] sonat γa²c.

AENEID BOOK XI

struggling victim, while her wings flap the air: even so from the Tiburtian line Tarchon carries off his prey in triumph. Following their chief's example and success, Maeonia's sons make onslaught. Then Arruns, due to his fate, circles round fleet Camilla with javelin and deep cunning—in this surpassing her [1]—and tries what chance may be easiest. Wherever the infuriate maid dashed amid the ranks, there Arruns creeps up and silently tracks her footsteps; where she returns victorious and retires from the foe, there the youth stealthily turns his swift reins. This approach he essays, and now that, and traverses the whole circuit round about, the unerring spear quivering in his relentless hand.

768 It chanced that Chloreus, sacred to Cybelus,[2] and once a priest, glittered resplendent afar in Phrygian armour, and spurred his foaming charger, whose covering was a skin, plumed with brazen scales and clasped with gold. Himself ablaze in the deep hue of foreign purple, he launched Gortynian shafts from Lycian bow: golden was that bow upon his shoulders, and golden was the seer's helmet; his saffron scarf and its rustling linen folds were gathered into a knot by yellow gold; embroidered with the needle were his tunic and barbaric hose. Him, whether in hope to fasten on temple-gate Trojan arms, or to flaunt herself in golden spoil, the maiden, singling out from all the battle fray, blindly pursued in huntress fashion, and recklessly raged through all the ranks with a woman's passion for booty and for

---

[1] Others take *prior* as meaning "before he strikes," or, like φθάσας, "anticipating her."
[2] As Servius says, Cybelus the mountain is here put for the deity worshipped upon it. Editors commonly read "Cybelae," but the authority for this is weak.

287

VIRGIL

telum ex insidiis cum tandem tempore capto MP
concitat et superos Arruns sic voce precatur:
"summe deum, sancti custos Soractis Apollo, 785
quem primi colimus, cui pineus ardor acervo
pascitur et medium freti pietate per ignem
cultores multa premimus vestigia pruna,
da, pater, hoc nostris aboleri dedecus armis,
omnipotens.   non exuvias pulsaeve tropaeum 790
virginis aut spolia ulla peto : mihi cetera laudem
facta ferent; haec dira meo dum volnere pestis
pulsa cadat, patrias remeabo inglorius urbes." MPR
  Audiit et voti Phoebus succedere partem
mente dedit, partem volucris dispersit in auras: 795
sterneret ut subita turbatam morte Camillam,
adnuit oranti; reducem ut patria alta videret,
non dedit, inque Notos vocem vertere procellae.
ergo ubi missa manu sonitum dedit hasta per auras,
convertere animos acris oculosque tulere 800
cuncti ad reginam Volsci.   nihil ipsa nec aurae
nec sonitus memor aut venientis ab aethere teli,
hasta sub exsertam donec perlata papillam
haesit, virgineumque alte bibit acta cruorem.
concurrunt trepidae comites dominamque ruentem
suscipiunt.   fugit ante omnis exterritus Arruns, 806
laetitia mixtoque metu, nec iam amplius hastae
credere nec telis occurrere virginis audet.
ac velut ille, prius quam tela inimica sequantur,

⁷⁸⁶ primis *P.*   ⁷⁹⁴ votis *Macrobius.*
⁷⁹⁹ ubi] ut *M²PR.*   ⁸⁰¹ auras *bc²,* *Servius.*

AENEID BOOK XI

spoil: when at length, seizing the chance, Arruns from ambush summons his lance, and thus prays aloud to Heaven:

⁷⁸⁵ "Apollo, most high of gods, guardian of holy Soracte, whose chief worshippers are we, for whom is fed the blaze of the pine-wood heap, while we thy votaries, passing in strength of faith amid the fire, plant our steps on the deep embers[1]—grant that this shame be effaced by our arms, O Father Almighty! I seek no plunder, no trophy of the maid's defeat, nor any spoils; other feats shall bring me fame; so but this dread scourge fall stricken beneath my blow, inglorious I will return to the cities of my sires."

⁷⁹⁴ Phoebus heard, and in his heart vouchsafed that half his prayer should prosper; half he scattered to the flying breezes. To o'erthrow and strike down Camilla in sudden death, he yielded to his prayer; that his noble country should see his return he granted not, and the blasts bore his accents to the southern gales. Therefore, when the spear, sped from his hand, whizzed through the air, all the Volscians turned their eager eyes and minds upon the queen. She herself, neither of air, nor of sound, nor of weapon coming from the sky recked aught, till the spear, borne home, beneath the bare breast found lodging, and, driven deep, drank her maiden blood. In alarm, her comrades hurry around her, and catch their falling queen. Startled above all, Arruns flees in mingled joy and fear, and no more dares he to trust his lance, or to meet the maiden's weapons. And lo! even as the wolf, when he has slain a shepherd or a great steer, ere hostile darts can pursue

---

[1] In the ancient rites on Mount Soracte, the worshippers walked three times through a pine-fire, carrying offerings to the god. *Cf.* Pliny, *Nat. Hist.* VII. 2, 19.

VIRGIL

continuo in montis sese avius abdidit altos   810
occiso pastore lupus magnove iuvenco,
conscius audacis facti, caudamque remulcens
subiecit pavitantem utero silvasque petivit:
haud secus ex oculis se turbidus abstulit Arruns
contentusque fuga mediis se immiscuit armis.   815
illa manu moriens telum trahit, ossa sed inter
ferreus ad costas alto stat volnere mucro.
labitur exsanguis, labuntur frigida leto
lumina, purpureus quondam color ora reliquit.
tum sic exspirans Accam, ex aequalibus unam,   820
adloquitur, fida ante alias quae sola Camillae,
quicum partiri curas, atque haec ita fatur:
" hactenus, Acca soror, potui; nunc volnus acerbum
conficit et tenebris nigrescunt omnia circum.
effuge et haec Turno mandata novissima perfer: 825
succedat pugnae Troianosque arceat urbe.
iamque vale." simul his dictis linquebat habenas,
ad terram non sponte fluens. tum frigida toto
paulatim exsolvit se corpore lentaque colla
et captum Leto posuit caput, arma relinquens,   830
vitaque cum gemitu fugit indignata sub umbras.
tum vero immensus surgens ferit aurea clamor
sidera: deiecta crudescit pugna Camilla;
incurrunt densi simul omnis copia Teucrum
Tyrrhenique duces Euandrique Arcades alae.   835

   At Triviae custos iamdudum in montibus Opis
alta sedet summis spectatque interrita pugnas;
utque procul medio iuvenum in clamore furentum

---

⁸¹⁹ relinquit *c*.
⁸²¹ fidaın *M²Pγ¹* : fida *M¹Rc*, Servius.
⁸²² quacum *P²γ²c*.   ⁸²⁶ urbi *P¹R*.
⁸³⁰ relinquens *M* (*late*), *P²γ* : reliquens *P¹* : relinquit *M¹*
reliquit *R* : relinquont Probus, *according to D. Servius.*
&c Sabb.   ⁸³⁵ Tyrrhenumque *M*.
⁸³⁸ iuenem *P¹* : -um *P²* : iuvenum *γ²*. furentem *Mγ²*

290

AENEID BOOK XI

him, straightway plunges by pathless ways among the high mountains, conscious of a reckless deed, and slackening his tail claps it quivering beneath his belly, and seeks the woods: even so does Arruns, in confusion, steal away from sight, and, bent on flight, plunges amidst the armed throng. She, with dying hand, tugs at the dart; but between the bones the iron point stands fast beside the ribs within the deep wound. Bloodless she sinks; her eyes sink, chill with death; the once radiant hue has left her face. Then, as her breath fails, she thus accosts Acca, a maiden of equal years and true to Camilla beyond all else, sole sharer of her cares, and thus she speaks: "Thus far, sister Acca, has my strength availed; now the bitter wound o'erpowers me, and all around grows dim and dark. Haste away, and bear to Turnus this my latest charge, to take my place in the battle, and ward the Trojans from the town. And now farewell!" With these words she dropped the reins, gliding helplessly to earth. Then, growing chill, she slowly freed herself from all the body's bonds, drooped her nerveless neck and the head which Death had seized, letting fall her weapons: and with a moan life passed indignant to the Shades below. Then indeed a boundless uproar rose, striking the golden stars: Camilla fallen, the fight waxes fiercer; on they rush in crowds together, all the Teucrian host, the Tyrrhene chiefs, and Evander's Arcadian squadrons.

836 But Opis, Trivia's sentinel, has long been seated high on the mountain top, and, undismayed, watches the combat. And when far off, amid the din of

VIRGIL

prospexit tristi mulcatam morte Camillam,
ingemuitque deditque has imo pectore voces: 840
"heu nimium, virgo, nimium crudele luisti
supplicium, Teucros conata lacessere bello!
nec tibi desertae in dumis coluisse Dianam
profuit aut nostras umero gessisse sagittas.
non tamen indecorem tua te regina reliquit 845
extrema iam in morte, neque hoc sine nomine letum
per gentis erit aut famam patieris inultae.
nam quicumque tuum violavit volnere corpus,
morte luet merita." fuit ingens monte sub alto
regis Dercenni terreno ex aggere bustum 850
antiqui Laurentis opacaque ilice tectum;
hic dea se primum rapido pulcherrima nisu
sistit et Arruntem tumulo speculatur ab alto.
ut vidit laetantem animis ac vana tumentem,
"cur," inquit, "diversus abis? huc derige gressum, 855
huc periture veni, capias ut digna Camillae
praemia. tune etiam telis moriere Dianae?"
dixit et aurata volucrem Threissa sagittam   FMPR
deprompsit pharetra cornuque infensa tetendit
et duxit longe, donec curvata coirent 860
inter se capita et manibus iam tangeret aequis,
laeva aciem ferri, dextra nervoque papillam.
extemplo teli stridorem aurasque sonantis
audiit una Arruns haesitque in corpore ferrum.
illum exspirantem socii atque extrema gementem 865
obliti ignoto camporum in pulvere linquunt;
Opis ad aetherium pinnis aufertur Olympum.

  Prima fugit domina amissa levis ala Camillae,
turbati fugiunt Rutuli, fugit acer Atinas,

⁸³⁹ multatam c^1.
⁸⁴⁴ sagittas M: pharetras $PR\gamma$.
⁸⁴⁵ relinquet $P\gamma b^1 c$: relinquit b^2. ⁸⁴⁹ dea] ea M^1.
⁸⁵⁴ laetantem animis M^1: fulgentem armis $M^2 P R \gamma$.
⁸⁵⁶ Camilla R.

292

AENEID BOOK XI

raging warriors, she espied Camilla done piteously to death, she sighed and from her heart's depth uttered these words: "Alas! too cruel, too cruel, O maiden, the forfeit thou hast paid for essaying to brave the Teucrians in battle! Naught has it availed thee, all lonely mid the wilds, to have served Diana, or to have carried our shafts upon thy shoulder. Yet thy queen has not left thee unhonoured even in death's last hour; nor shall this thy doom be without renown among the nations, nor shalt thou bear the reproach of one unavenged; for whoso hath with wound profaned thy limbs shall pay the debt of death." Under the mountain height stood a mound of earth, the mighty tomb of Dercennus, Laurentine king of old, screened by shadowy ilex; here first the beauteous goddess, with swift spring, plants her feet, and from the barrow's height espies Arruns. When she saw him exulting in spirit and swelling with pride: "Why," she cries, "strayest so far? Hither turn thy steps, hither come to thy death and for Camilla receive due guerdon! Shalt thou, even thou, die by Diana's darts?" So spake the Thracian nymph, and from gilded quiver plucked a winged shaft, stretched the bow with full intent, and drew it far, till the curving ends should meet together and, with levelled hands, she should touch the steel's point with her left, her breast with her right and with the bow-string. Straightway, at the selfsame moment, Arruns heard the whistling dart and whirring air, and the steel was lodged in his breast. Him, gasping and moaning his last, his forgetful comrades leave on the unknown dust of the plain; Opis wings her way to heavenly Olympus.

[868] First flees, their mistress lost, Camilla's light squadron; in rout flee the Rutulians, flees valiant

293

VIRGIL

disiectique duces desolataque manipli 870
tuta petunt et equis aversi ad moenia tendunt.
nec quisquam instantis Teucros letumque ferentis
sustentare valet telis aut sistere contra,
sed laxos referunt umeris languentibus arcus
quadrupedumque putrem cursu quatit ungula
    campum. 875
volvitur ad muros caligine turbidus atra
pulvis et e speculis percussae pectora matres
femineum clamorem ad caeli sidera tollunt.
qui cursu portas primi inrupere patentis,
hos inimica super mixto premit agmine turba, 880
nec miseram effugiunt mortem, sed limine in ipso,
moenibus in patriis atque intra tuta domorum
confixi exspirant animas. pars claudere portas,
nec sociis aperire viam nec moenibus audent
accipere orantis, oriturque miserrima caedes 885
defendentum armis aditus inque arma ruentum.
exclusi ante oculos lacrimantumque ora parentum
pars in praecipitis fossas urgente ruina
volvitur, immissis pars caeca et concita frenis
arietat in portas et duros obice postis. 890
ipsae de muris summo certamine matres
(monstrat amor verus patriae), ut videre Camillam,
tela manu trepidae iaciunt ac robore duro
stipitibus ferrum sudibusque imitantur obustis
praecipites, primaeque mori pro moenibus ardent. 895

    Interea Turnum in silvis saevissimus implet MPR
nuntius et iuveni ingentem fert Acca tumultum:
deletas Volscorum acies, cecidisse Camillam,
ingruere infensos hostis et Marte secundo

---

[870] defecti M^1.   [871] equos $P\gamma$.
[875] quadripedo F^1R: quadripedem F^2.
[877] e *omitted* F^1M^1b.   [882] inter $FP\gamma$, *Macrobius*.
[895] audent $M^2\gamma^2bc$, *Servius*.

AENEID BOOK XI

Atinas; scattered captains, and troops left leaderless make for shelter, and, wheeling their horses, gallop to the walls. Nor can any with arms check the onset of death-dealing Trojans, nor stand against it, but their unstrung bows they cast on fainting shoulders, and in their galloping course the horse-hoof shakes the crumbling plain. On rolls to the walls a cloud of dust, black and murky, and from the watch-towers mothers, beating their breasts, uplift to the stars of heaven their womanish cries. Upon such as first broke at full speed through the open gates, there presses hard a throng of foes, mingling with their ranks, nor escape they a piteous death, but on the very threshold, their native walls about them, and within the shelter of their homes, they are thrust through, and gasp away their lives. Some close the gates, and dare not open a way to their friends, nor receive them in the town, implore as they may; and slaughter most pitiful ensues, these guarding the entry sword in hand, and those rushing upon the sword. Shut out before the eyes and gaze of weeping parents, some, driven by the rout, roll headlong into the trenches; some, charging blindly with loosened rein, batter at the gates and stoutly-barred doors. The very mothers from the walls, in keenest rivalry (true love of country points the way), when they marked Camilla, flung weapons with trembling hands, and hastily do the work of the steel with stout oak-poles and seared stakes, and foremost are fain to die out upon their walls.

⁸⁹⁶ Meanwhile among the forests the woeful tidings fill Turnus' ears, and Acca brings the warrior her tale of mighty turmoil: the Volscian ranks destroyed, Camilla fallen, the foe fiercely advancing and sweep-

VIRGIL

omnia corripuisse, metum iam ad moenia ferri. 900
ille furens (et saeva Iovis sic numina poscunt)
deserit obsessos collis, nemora aspera linquit.
vix e conspectu exierat campumque tenebat,
cum pater Aeneas, saltus ingressus apertos,
exsuperatque iugum silvaque evadit opaca. 905
sic ambo ad muros rapidi totoque feruntur
agmine nec longis inter se passibus absunt;
ac simul Aeneas fumantis pulvere campos
prospexit longe Laurentiaque agmina vidit,
et saevum Aenean adgnovit Turnus in armis 910
adventumque pedum flatusque audivit equorum.
continuoque ineant pugnas et proelia temptent,
ni roseus fessos iam gurgite Phoebus Hibero
tinguat equos noctemque die labente reducat.
considunt castris ante urbem et moenia vallant. 915

⁹⁰¹ poscunt] pellunt *R*. ⁹⁰³ campos *M*¹.
⁹¹⁰ adgnovit] conspexit *P*γ. ⁹¹¹ adventus *M*. flatum *R*.
⁹¹² ineunt *M*¹*b*. temptant γ*c*.

AENEID BOOK XI

ing the field in triumphant warfare, the panic now passing to the town. He, raging—and Jove's stern will so demands—quits the hills' ambush, and leaves the rough woodland. Scarce had he passed from view and gained the plain, when father Aeneas, entering the unguarded pass, scales the ridge, and issues from the shady wood. So both march toward the walls, swiftly and in full force, nor far distant from each other: and at the same moment Aeneas descried afar the plain smoking with dust, and saw the Laurentine hosts, and Turnus was aware of fell Aeneas in arms, and heard the coming of feet and the snorting of steeds. And straightway would they enter the fray and essay conflict, but ruddy Phoebus now laves his weary team in the Iberian flood, and, as day ebbs, brings back the night. Before the city they encamp and strengthen the ramparts.

LIBER XII

Turnus ut infractos adverso Marte Latinos MPR
defecisse videt, sua nunc promissa reposci,
se signari oculis, ultro implacabilis ardet
attollitque animos.   Poenorum qualis in arvis,
saucius ille gravi venantum volnere pectus,   5
tum demum movet arma leo, gaudetque comantis
excutiens cervice toros fixumque latronis
impavidus frangit telum et fremit ore cruento:
haud secus accenso gliscit violentia Turno.
tum sic adfatur regem atque ita turbidus infit: 10
"nulla mora in Turno; nihil est, quod dicta retractent
ignavi Aeneadae, nec quae pepigere recusent:
congredior.   fer sacra, pater, et concipe foedus.
aut hac Dardanium dextra sub Tartara mittam,
desertorem Asiae, (sedeant spectentque Latini)   15
et solus ferro crimen commune refellam,
aut habeat victos, cedat Lavinia coniunx."
  Olli sedato respondit corde Latinus:
"o praestans animi iuvenis, quantum ipse feroci
virtute exsuperas, tanto me impensius aequum est   20
consulere atque omnis metuentem expendere casus.
sunt tibi regna patris Dauni, sunt oppida capta

[16] crimen ferro *Rc.*

BOOK XII

When Turnus sees the Latins crushed and faint of heart through war's reverse, his own pledge now claimed, and himself the mark of every eye, forthwith he blazes with wrath unappeasable and raises high his spirit. As in Punic fields a lion, when wounded, lo! with grievous stroke of huntsmen in the breast, then only wakes to war, joyously tosses from his neck his shaggy main, and snaps, undaunted, the robber's implanted dart, roaring with blood-stained mouth: even so in Turnus' kindling soul the fury swells. Then thus he accosts the king, and with these wild words begins:

11 "With Turnus lies no delay! no need is there for the coward sons of Aeneas to recall their words or to renounce their pact! I go to meet him. Bring the holy rites, sire, and frame the covenant. Either with this arm will I hurl to hell the Dardan, the Asian runaway—let the Latins sit and see it— and with my single sword refute the nation's shame;[1] or let him be lord of the vanquished, let Lavinia pass to him as bride!"

18 To him Latinus with unruffled soul replied: "O youth of matchless spirit, the more in proud valour thou dost excel, all the more heedfully is it meet that I ponder and with fear weigh every chance. Thou hast thy father Daunus' realms, hast

[1] All are under the slur of cowardice.

VIRGIL

multa manu, nec non aurumque animusque Latino est.
sunt aliae innuptae Latio et Laurentibus arvis,
nec genus indecores. sine me haec haud mollia fatu 25
sublatis aperire dolis, simul hoc animo hauri:
me natam nulli veterum sociare procorum
fas erat, idque omnes divique hominesque canebant.
victus amore tui, cognato sanguine victus,
coniugis et maestae lacrimis, vincla omnia rupi: 30
promissam eripui genero, arma impia sumpsi.
ex illo qui me casus, quae, Turne, sequantur
bella vides, quantos primus patiare labores.
bis magna victi pugna vix urbe tuemur
spes Italas; recalent nostro Thybrina fluenta 35
sanguine adhuc campique ingentes ossibus albent.
quo referor totiens? quae mentem insania mutat?
si Turno exstincto socios sum adscire paratus,
cur non incolumi potius certamina tollo?
quid consanguinei Rutuli, quid cetera dicet 40
Italia, ad mortem si te (Fors dicta refutet!)
prodiderim, natam et conubia nostra petentem?
respice res bello varias; miserere parentis
longaevi, quem nunc maestum patria Ardea longe
dividit." haudquaquam dictis violentia Turni 45
flectitur; exsuperat magis aegrescitque medendo.
ut primum fari potuit, sic institit ore: MR
"quam pro me curam geris, hanc precor, optime,
    pro me

---
²⁴ arvis *M, Servius:* agris *PRγbc.*
⁴⁶ ardescitque tuendo (*on margin* aegrescit) *M.*
⁴⁷ incipit *Mγ²*, *Donatus.*

AENEID BOOK XII

many a town thy hand has taken; Latinus, too, has gold and good will. Other unwed maids there are in Latium and Laurentum's fields, and of no ignoble birth. Suffer me to utter this hard saying, stripped of all disguise, and withal drink this into thy soul: for me to ally my child to any of her old-time wooers, was forbidden, and this all gods and men foretold.[1] Overborne by love of thee, overborne by kindred blood[2] and tears of my sorrowing queen, I broke all fetters, snatched the betrothed from her promised husband, and drew the unholy sword. From that day, Turnus, thou seest what perils, what wars pursue me, what heavy burdens thou above all dost bear. Twice vanquished in mighty battle, we scarce guard within our walls the hopes of Italy; Tiber's streams are still warm with our blood, the boundless plains still white with our bones. Why drift I back so often?[3] What madness turns my purpose? If, with Turnus dead, I am ready to link them to me as allies, why not rather end the strife while he still lives? What will thy Rutulian kinsmen say, what the rest of Italy, if—Fortune refute the word!—I should betray thee to death, while thou wooest our daughter in marriage? Think on war's changes and chances; pity thine aged father, whom now his native Ardea parts far away from us in sorrow!"

[45] In no wise do his words bend the fury of Turnus; still higher it mounts, more inflamed with the healing. Soon as he could speak he thus began: "The care thou hast on my behalf, most gracious lord, on my

[1] *cf.* VII. 95 above.
[2] Amata, wife of Latinus, was sister to Venilia, mother of Turnus.
[3] *i.e.* from what must be his inevitable decision.

301

VIRGIL

deponas letumque sinas pro laude pacisci.
et nos tela, pater, ferrumque haud debile dextra 50
spargimus, et nostro sequitur de volnere sanguis.
longe illi dea mater erit, quae nube fugacem
feminea tegat et vanis sese occulat umbris."
  At regina, nova pugnae conterrita sorte,
flebat et ardentem generum moritura tenebat: 55
"Turne, per has ego te lacrimas, per si quis Amatae
tangit honos animum (spes tu nunc una, senectae
tu requies miserae, decus imperiumque Latini
te penes, in te omnis domus inclinata recumbit),
unum oro: desiste manum committere Teucris. 60
qui te cumque manent isto certamine casus,
et me, Turne, manent: simul haec invisa relinquam
lumina nec generum Aenean captiva videbo."
accepit vocem lacrimis Lavinia matris
flagrantis perfusa genas, cui plurimus ignem 65
subiecit rubor et calefacta per ora cucurrit.
Indum sanguineo veluti violaverit ostro
si quis ebur, aut mixta rubent ubi lilia multa
alba rosa: talis virgo dabat ore colores.
illum turbat amor, figitque in virgine voltus. 70
ardet in arma magis paucisque adfatur Amatam:
"ne, quaeso, ne me lacrimis neve omine tanto
prosequere in duri certamina Martis euntem,
o mater; neque enim Turno mora libera mortis.
nuntius haec, Idmon, Phrygio mea dicta tyranno 75
haud placitura refer: cum primum crastina caelo
puniceis invecta rotis Aurora rubebit,

---

[1] *cf.* v. 230, uitamque volunt pro laude pacisci.
[2] In the *Iliad* (at v. 311 ff.) Aeneas is rescued by Aphrodite who spreads before him a fold of her garment. Else-
302

AENEID BOOK XII

behalf, I pray, resign, and suffer me to barter death for fame.[1] I too, sire, can scatter darts and no weakling steel from this right hand, and from our strokes too flows blood. Far from him will be his goddess-mother to shelter the runaway, woman-like, with a cloud, and to conceal herself in empty shadows."[2]

[54] But the queen, dismayed by the new terms of conflict, wept, and clung to her fiery son, ready to die: "Turnus, by these my tears, by aught of reverence for Amata that yet may touch thy heart—thou art now our only hope, thou the comfort of my sad old age; in thine hands are the honour and sovereignty of Latinus, on thee rests all our sinking house—one boon I beg: forbear to fight the Trojans. What perils soever await thee in that combat of thine, await me also, Turnus; with thee I will quit this hateful light, nor in captivity see Aeneas as my son." Lavinia heard her mother's words, her burning cheeks steeped in tears, while a deep blush kindled its fire, and mantled o'er her glowing face. As when one stains Indian ivory with crimson dye, or as when white lilies blush with many a blended rose—such hues her maiden features showed. Him love throws into turmoil, and he fastens his looks upon the maid; then, fired yet more for the fray, briefly he addresses Amata:

[72] "Nay, I beseech thee, not with tears, not with such omen, as I pass to stern war's conflicts, do thou send me forth, O my mother; nor truly has Turnus freedom to delay his death. Idmon, be my herald and bear this my message to the Phrygian king—message he will not welcome: soon as to-morrow's Dawn, riding in crimson car,

where, however, Apollo and Poseidon rescue him in a cloud (*Iliad*, v. 344; xx. 321 ff.; *cf.* III. 380).

303

VIRGIL

non Teucros agat in Rutulos; Teucrum arma
    quiescant
et Rutuli; nostro dirimamus sanguine bellum;
illo quaeratur coniunx Lavinia campo." 80
  Haec ubi dicta dedit rapidusque in tecta recessit,
poscit equos gaudetque tuens ante ora frementis,
Pilumno quos ipsa decus dedit Orithyia,
qui candore nives anteirent, cursibus auras.
circumstant properi aurigae manibusque lacessunt 85
pectora plausa cavis et colla comantia pectunt.
ipse dehinc auro squalentem alboque orichalco
circumdat loricam umeris, simul aptat habendo
ensemque clipeumque et rubrae cornua cristae,
ensem, quem Dauno ignipotens deus ipse parenti 90
fecerat et Stygia candentem tinxerat unda.
exim, quae mediis ingenti adnixa columnae
aedibus adstabat, validam vi corripit hastam,   MPR
Actoris Aurunci spolium, quassatque trementem
vociferans: "nunc, o numquam frustrata vocatus 95
hasta meos, nunc tempus adest; te maximus Actor,
te Turni nunc dextra gerit.   da sternere corpus
loricamque manu valida lacerare revolsam
semiviri Phrygis et foedare in pulvere crinis
vibratos calido ferro murraque madentis." 100
his agitur furiis, totoque ardentis ab ore
scintillae absistunt, oculis micat acribus ignis;
mugitus veluti cum prima in proelia taurus
terrificos ciet atque irasci in cornua temptat,
arboris obnixus trunco, ventosque lacessit 105
ictibus aut sparsa ad pugnam proludit harena.

        [79] Rutulum b^2c^2.   [85] propere $R\gamma^1$.
        [92] columna γb^1.   [100] cadentis $P\gamma^1$.
        [102] exsistunt R.   [103] primam M^1: primum R.
        [104] atque] aut M^2PRb^1.

AENEID BOOK XII

reddens in the sky, let him not lead Teucrians against Rutulians—let Teucrian arms and Rutulians have rest—with our own blood let us settle the war; on that field be Lavinia wooed and won!"

81 These words said, with haste withdrawing home, he calls for his steeds, and joys to see them neighing before his face—the steeds that Orithyia's self gave as a glory to Pilumnus, for that they excelled the snows in whiteness, the gales in speed. The eager charioteers stand round, patting with hollow palms their sounding chests, and combing their flowing manes. Next he binds upon his shoulders a corslet stiff with gold and pale mountain-bronze; withal, he fits for wear sword and shield and the horns of his ruddy crest [1]; the sword the divine Lord of Fire had himself wrought for his father Daunus and dipped, all glowing, in the Stygian wave. Then, his mighty spear, which stood leaning upon a giant column amid the hall, he seizes with strong hand, spoil of Auruncan Actor, and shakes it quivering, while he cries aloud: "Now, O spear, that never failed my call, now the hour is come! Thee mighty Actor once bore; thee now the hand of Turnus wields. Grant me to lay low the body, with strong hand to tear and rend away the corslet of this Phrygian eunuch, and to defile in dust his locks, crisped with heated iron and bedrenched in myrrh!" Such is the frenzy driving him: from all his face shoot fiery sparks; his eager eyes flash flame—even as a bull, ere the battle begins, awakes a fearful bellowing, and, essaying to throw wrath into his horns, charges a tree's trunk; he lashes the winds with his blows, and paws the sand in prelude for the fray.[2]

[1] The crest rested upon two projecting sockets made of horn.   [2] *cf. Georgics*, III. 232-234.

VIRGIL

Nec minus interea maternis saevus in armis
Aeneas acuit Martem et se suscitat ira,
oblato gaudens componi foedere bellum.
tum socios maestique metum solatur Iuli, 110
fata docens, regique iubet responsa Latino
certa referre viros et pacis dicere leges.

Postera vix summos spargebat lumine montis
orta dies, cum primum alto se gurgite tollunt
Solis equi lucemque elatis naribus efflant: 115
campum ad certamen magnae sub moenibus urbis
dimensi Rutulique viri Teucrique parabant
in medioque focos et dis communibus aras
gramineas. alii fontemque ignemque ferebant,
velati limo et verbena tempora vincti. 120
procedit legio Ausonidum pilataque plenis
agmina se fundunt portis. hinc Troius omnis
Tyrrhenusque ruit variis exercitus armis,
haud secus instructi ferro, quam si aspera Martis
pugna vocet; nec non mediis in milibus ipsi 125
ductores auro volitant ostroque superbi,
et genus Assaraci Mnestheus et fortis Asilas
et Messapus equum domitor, Neptunia proles.
utque dato signo spatia in sua quisque recessit,
defigunt tellure hastas et scuta reclinant. 130
tum studio effusae matres et volgus inermum
invalidique senes turris et tecta domorum
obsedere, alii portis sublimibus adstant.

At Iuno e summo, qui nunc Albanus habetur

---

¹¹³ summo *M*.   ¹¹⁷ demensi *M*γ¹.
¹²⁰ lino *MSS.* (*except two in Paris*), *Servius:* limo *given by Servius as the reading attributed to Virgil by Caper and Hyginus.*

¹²⁴ [ferro] bello *M*.   ¹²⁶ decori *PR*γ.
¹²⁸ *cf.* VII. 691; IX. 523; X. 353.   ¹³⁰ telluri *R*.
¹³² et] ac *PR*γ.   ¹³³ instant *R*.

306

AENEID BOOK XII

¹⁰⁷ Nor less, meantime, Aeneas, fierce in the arms his mother gave,[1] whets his valour and stirs his heart with wrath, rejoicing that the war is settled by the compact offered. Then he comforts his comrades, and sad Iülus' fear, teaching them of fate, and bids bear firm answer to King Latinus and declare the terms of peace.

¹¹³ Scarce was the morrow's dawn sprinkling the mountain-tops with light, what time the Sun's steeds first rise from the deep flood, and breathe light from uplifted nostrils, when Rutulians and Teucrians marched out and made ready the lists for the combat under the great city's walls, and in the midst hearths and grassy altars to their common deities. Others were bringing fountain-water and fire, draped in aprons[2] and their brows bound with vervain. Forth moved the Ausonian host, and troops, close-banded, pour from the crowded gates. On this side streams forth all the Trojan and Tyrrhene host in diverse armament, accoutred in steel, even as though the harsh battle-strife called them. Nor less, amid their thousands, the captains dart to and fro, brilliant in gold and purple, Mnestheus of the line of Assaracus, and brave Asilas, and Messapus, tamer of horses, seed of Neptune. Soon as, on given signal, each has retired to his own ground, they plant their spears in earth, and rest their shields against them. Then, eagerly streaming forth, mothers and the unarmed throng, and feeble old men, have beset towers and house-tops; others stand upon the lofty gates.

¹³⁴ But Juno, from the hill-summit now called

[1] Made by Vulcan at the request of Venus; *cf. Aen.* VIII. 608 ff.

[2] The *limus* was an apron worn by priests, so called because it had a transverse stripe of purple.

VIRGIL

(tum neque nomen erat neque honos aut gloria monti),
prospiciens tumulo campum aspectabat et ambas 136
Laurentum Troumque acies urbemque Latini.
extemplo Turni sic est adfata sororem,
diva deam, stagnis quae fluminibusque sonoris
praesidet; hunc illi rex aetheris altus honorem 140
Iuppiter erepta pro virginitate sacravit:
"nympha, decus fluviorum, animo gratissima nostro,
scis ut te cunctis unam, quaecumque Latinae
magnanimi Iovis ingratum ascendere cubile,
praetulerim caelique libens in parte locarim: 145
disce tuum, ne me incuses, Iuturna, dolorem.
qua visa est Fortuna pati Parcaeque sinebant
cedere res Latio, Turnum et tua moenia texi:
nunc iuvenem imparibus video concurrere fatis,
Parcarumque dies et vis inimica propinquat. 150
non pugnam aspicere hanc oculis, non foedera possum.
tu pro germano si quid praesentius audes,
perge; decet. forsan miseros meliora sequentur."

Vix ea, cum lacrimas oculis Iuturna profudit
terquequaterque manu pectus percussit honestum. 155
"non lacrimis hoc tempus," ait Saturnia Iuno:
"accelera et fratrem, si quis modus, eripe morti;
aut tu bella cie conceptumque excute foedus.
auctor ego audendi." sic exhortata reliquit
incertam et tristi turbatam volnere mentis. 160

Interea reges, ingenti mole Latinus
quadriiugo vehitur curru, cui tempora circum
aurati bis sex radii fulgentia cingunt,

---

¹⁴² carissima *PR*γ. ¹⁴³ Latinis *P*² (is *in rasura*) γ¹.
¹⁵¹ in foedere *M*¹.
*⁶¹ rex ingenti de mole *M*¹. ¹⁶² quadrigo *P*γ¹.

AENEID BOOK XII

Alban—at that time the mount had neither name nor fame nor honour—looking forth, gazed upon the plain, upon the double lines of Laurentum and Troy, and upon the city of Latinus. Straightway thus, goddess to goddess, she spake to Turnus' sister, mistress of the meres and sounding rivers: such dignity Jupiter, heaven's high lord, hallowed to her in return for theft of maidenhood: "O nymph, glory of rivers, to my heart most dear, thou knowest how, above all Latin maids that have mounted to high-souled Jove's thankless bed, thee alone I have preferred, and to thee have gladly given a place in heaven: learn, Juturna, the grief that will be thine, so that me thou mayest not blame. Where Fortune seemed to permit, and the Fates suffered Latium's state to prosper, I shielded Turnus and thy city. Now I see the prince confront unequal destiny; and the day of doom and the enemy's stroke draw nigh. Upon this battle, this treaty, mine eyes cannot look: do thou, if thou darest aught of more present help for thy brother's sake, go on; it is thy part. Perchance on the unhappy happier days shall wait."

154 Scarcely thus she spake, when Juturna's eyes streamed with tears, and thrice, yea four times, her hand smote her comely breast. "No time is this for tears," cries Saturnian Juno; "hasten, and if any means there be, snatch thy brother from death; or do thou waken battle, and dash from their hands the treaty they have framed. 'Tis I who bid thee dare." Thus having counselled, she left her doubtful and distracted in soul under the cruel wound.

161 Meanwhile the kings ride forth, Latinus in mighty pomp drawn in four-horse car, twelve golden rays circling his gleaming brows, emblem of his

VIRGIL

Solis avi specimen; bigis it Turnus in albis,
bina manu lato crispans hastilia ferro.   165
hinc pater Aeneas, Romanae stirpis origo,
sidereo flagrans clipeo et caelestibus armis,
et iuxta Ascanius, magnae spes altera Romae,
procedunt castris, puraque in veste sacerdos
saetigeri fetum suis intonsamque bidentem   170
attulit admovitque pecus flagrantibus aris.
illi ad surgentem conversi lumina solem
dant fruges manibus salsas et tempora ferro
summa notant pecudum paterisque altaria libant.
tum pius Aeneas stricto sic ense precatur: 175
" esto nunc Sol testis et haec mihi Terra precanti,
quam propter tantos potui perferre labores,
et pater omnipotens et tu Saturnia coniunx,
iam melior, iam, diva, precor; tuque inclute Mavors,
cuncta tuo qui bella, pater, sub numine torques; 180
Fontisque Fluviosque voco, quaeque aetheris alti
religio et quae caeruleo sunt numina ponto:
cesserit Ausonio si fors victoria Turno,
convenit Euandri victos discedere ad urbem,
cedet Iulus agris, nec post arma ulla rebelles 185
Aeneadae referent ferrove haec regna lacessent.
sin nostrum adnuerit nobis Victoria Martem
(ut potius reor et potius di numine firment),
non ego nec Teucris Italos parere iubebo
nec mihi regna peto: paribus se legibus ambae 190
invictae gentes aeterna in foedera mittant.

[176] praecanti M^1: precanti $M^2\gamma^2$, *Servius:* vocanti $PR\gamma^1$.
[178] coniunx] Iuno M^1a^2c, *Servius* (cf. 156).
[184] decedere M^1.   [188] propius di R.   numina P (a *in rasura*) $R\gamma$.

310

AENEID BOOK XII

ancestral Sun;[1] while Turnus comes behind a snow-white pair, his hand brandishing two spears with broad heads of steel. On this side father Aeneas, source of the Roman stock, ablaze with starry shield and celestial arms, and, close by, Ascanius, second hope of mighty Rome, issue from the camp; while in spotless raiment a priest has brought the young of a bristly boar and an unshorn sheep of two years old, and set the beasts beside the blazing altars. The heroes, turning their eyes to the rising sun, sprinkle salted meal from their hands, mark the foreheads of the victims with the knife,[2] and from goblets pour libations on the altars. Then good Aeneas, drawing his sword, thus makes prayer:

176 "Now be the Sun witness to my call, and this Earth, for whose sake I have been able to endure such travails, and the Father Almighty, and thou his consort, Saturnia—now kindlier, now at last, I pray, O goddess: and thou, famed Mavors, thou the sire that wieldest all warfare under thy sway; and on Founts and Floods I call, on all the majesty of high heaven and powers that tenant the blue seas: if haply victory fall to Turnus the Ausonian, 'tis agreed that the vanquished withdraw to Evander's city. Iülus shall quit the soil; nor ever in after-time shall the sons of Aeneas return for renewed war, or attack this realm with the sword. But if Victory grant that the battle be ours—as I rather deem, and so rather may the gods confirm it with their power!—I will not bid the Italians be subject to Teucrians, nor do I seek the realm for mine; under equal terms let both nations, unconquered, enter upon an everlasting compact.

---

[1] Latinus was descended from the Sun through Circe, mother of Faunus.

[2] *i.e.* by cutting off a lock of hair to be burnt.

VIRGIL

sacra deosque dabo; socer arma Latinus habeto,
imperium sollemne socer; mihi moenia Teucri
constituent urbique dabit Lavinia nomen."

Sic prior Aeneas; sequitur sic deinde Latinus, 195
suspiciens caelum, tenditque ad sidera dextram:
"haec eadem, Aenea, terram, mare, sidera iuro,
Latonaeque genus duplex Ianumque bifrontem
vimque deum infernam et duri sacraria Ditis;
audiat haec genitor, qui foedera fulmine sancit. 200
tango aras, medios ignis et numina testor:
nulla dies pacem hanc Italis nec foedera rumpet,
quo res cumque cadent, nec me vis ulla volentem
avertet, non, si tellurem effundat in undas,
diluvio miscens, caelumque in Tartara solvat; 205
ut sceptrum hoc" (dextra sceptrum nam forte gerebat)
"numquam fronde levi fundet virgulta nec umbras,
cum semel in silvis imo de stirpe recisum
matre caret posuitque comas et bracchia ferro;
olim arbos, nunc artificis manus aere decoro 210
inclusit patribusque dedit gestare Latinis."
talibus inter se firmabant foedera dictis
prospectu in medio procerum. tum rite sacratas
in flammam iugulant pecudes et viscera vivis
eripiunt cumulantque oneratis lancibus aras. 215

At vero Rutulis impar ea pugna videri
iamdudum et vario misceri pectora motu;
tum magis, ut propius cernunt non viribus aequis.

²⁰² rumpit P^1: rumpat $P^2\gamma$.
²¹³ prospectu M: conspectu *other MSS.* in *omitted* M^1P^1.

---

[1] *cf.* the oath of Achilles in Homer, *Iliad*, I. 234 ff.

AENEID BOOK XII

Gods and their rites I will give; let Latinus, as my sire, keep the sword; as my sire, keep his wonted command For me, the Teucrians shall raise walls, and Lavinia give the city her name."

195 Thus first Aeneas, and after him Latinus thus follows, uplifting eyes to heaven, and outstretching his right hand to the stars: " By these same Powers I swear, Aeneas, by Earth, Sea, Stars, Latona's twofold offspring, and two-faced Janus, and the might of gods below, and the shrines of cruel Dis: may the great Sire hear my words, who sanctions treaties with his thunderbolt! I touch the altars, I adjure these fires and gods that stand between us: no time shall break this peace and truce for Italy, howsoever things shall issue; nor shall any force turn aside my will, not though, commingling all in deluge, it should plunge land into water, and dissolve Heaven into Hell: even as this sceptre"[1] (for haply in his hand he bore his sceptre) "shall never burgeon with light leafage into branch or shade, now that once hewn in the forest from the nether stem, it is reft of its mother, and beneath the steel has shed its leaves and twigs; once a tree, now the craftsman's hand has cased it in seemly bronze and given it to sires of Latium to bear." With such words they sealed faith between them, amid the gazing lords; then over the flame duly slay the hallowed beasts, and tear out the live entrails, and pile the altars with laden chargers.

216 But to the Rutulians long had the battle seemed unequal, and their hearts, swayed to and fro, had long been in turmoil; and now the more, the more closely they scan its ill-matched strength.[2] Turnus

With *cernunt* one may supply either *pugnam* or *eos* (the combatants). Some regard *non viribus aequis* as an interpolation or a stop-gap; Ribbeck thinks the passage is incomplete.

VIRGIL

adiuvat incessu tacito progressus et aram
suppliciter venerans demisso lumine Turnus   220
tabentesque genae et iuvenali in corpore pallor.
quem simul ac Iuturna soror crebrescere vidit
sermonem et volgi variare labantia corda,
in medias acies, formam adsimulata Camerti
(cui genus a proavis ingens clarumque paternae   225
nomen erat virtutis et ipse acerrimus armis),
in medias dat sese acies, haud nescia rerum,
rumoresque serit varios ac talia fatur:
"non pudet, o Rutuli, pro cunctis talibus unam
obiectare animam? numerone an viribus aequi   230
non sumus? en, omnes et Troes et Arcades hi sunt,
fatalesque manus, infensa Etruria Turno.
vix hostem, alterni si congrediamur, habemus.
ille quidem ad superos, quorum se devovet aris,
succedet fama vivusque per ora feretur;   235
nos patria amissa dominis parere superbis
cogemur, qui nunc lenti consedimus arvis."

Talibus incensa est iuvenum sententia dictis
iam magis atque magis serpitque per agmina murmur;
ipsi Laurentes mutati ipsique Latini.   240
qui sibi iam requiem pugnae rebusque salutem
sperabant, nunc arma volunt foedusque precantur
infectum et Turni sortem miserantur iniquam.
his aliud maius Iuturna adiungit et alto
dat signum caelo, quo non praesentius ullum   245
turbavit mentes Italas monstroque fefellit.
namque volans rubra fulvus Iovis ales in aethra
litoreas agitabat avis turbamque sonantem

₂₂₁ tabentes a^2c, *Donatus on* 219: pubentes *most MSS*.
₂₃₀ an] ac P^2. aequis $P\gamma$. ₂₃₂ fatalisque $P^1\gamma c$, *Servius*
₂₃₇ lentis γ^1. armis $M^1\gamma^1$ (lentis . . . armis *Bentley*).
₂₃₉ iam] tum $P\gamma$. ₂₄₅ praestantius R.
₂₄₇ fulvus rubra M^1. Iovis] acer P (*cf.* sacer ales, XI. 721)

314

AENEID BOOK XII

swells the unrest by advancing with noiseless tread and humbly adoring the altar with downcast eye— swells it by his wasted cheeks and by the pallor of his youthful frame. Soon as Juturna his sister saw these whispers spread, and the hearts of the throng wavering in doubt, into the midmost ranks, in feigned semblance of Camers—noble his ancestral house, glorious the renown of his father's worth, himself most valiant in arms—into the midmost ranks she plunges, knowing well her task, scatters diverse rumours, and thus cries: "Are ye not ashamed, Rutulians, for all a host like ours to set at hazard one single life? In numbers, or in might, are we not their match? All of them, mark you, are here Trojans and Arcadians, and the fate-led bands of Etruria, hostile to Turnus: should but every other man of us join battle, scarce find we, each of us, a foe. He, indeed, shall mount on fame to the gods, to whose altars he vows his life, and shall move living on the lips of men:[1] we, our country lost, shall bow perforce to haughty masters—we, who to-day sit listless upon the fields!"

238 With such words the warriors' resolve is kindled yet more and more, and a murmur creeps from rank to rank. Even the Laurentines, even the Latins are changed; and they who of late hoped for rest from the fray, and safety for their fortunes, now long for arms, pray the covenant may be undone, and pity Turnus' unjust fate. To these Juturna adds another and mightier impulse, and in high heaven shows a sign, than which none was more potent to confound Italian minds and cheat them with its miracle. For, flying through the ruddy sky, Jove's golden bird was chasing the fowls of the shore and the clamorous

[1] *cf. Georgics*, III: 9.

315

VIRGIL

agminis aligeri, subito cum lapsus ad undas
cycnum excellentem pedibus rapit improbus uncis. 250
arrexere animos Itali cunctaeque volucres
convertunt clamore fugam (mirabile visu)
aetheraque obscurant pinnis hostemque per auras
facta nube premunt, donec vi victus et ipso
pondere defecit praedamque ex unguibus ales 255
proiecit fluvio, penitusque in nubila fugit.

Tum vero augurium Rutuli clamore salutant
expediuntque manus, primusque Tolumnius augur
"hoc erat, hoc, votis," inquit, "quod saepe petivi.
accipio, adgnoscoque deos; me, me duce ferrum 260
corripite, o miseri, quos improbus advena bello
territat, invalidas ut aves, et litora vestra
vi populat. petet ille fugam penitusque profundo
vela dabit. vos unanimi densate catervas
et regem vobis pugna defendite raptum." 265

Dixit et adversos telum contorsit in hostis
procurrens; sonitum dat stridula cornus et auras
certa secat. simul hoc, simul ingens clamor, et omnes
turbati cunei calefactaque corda tumultu.
hasta volans, ut forte novem pulcherrima fratrum 270
corpora constiterant contra, quos fida crearat
una tot Arcadio coniunx Tyrrhena Gylippo,
horum unum ad medium, teritur qua sutilis alvo
balteus et laterum iuncturas fibula mordet,
egregium forma iuvenem et fulgentibus armis, 275
transadigit costas fulvaque effundit harena.

[261] miseri] Rutuli $\gamma^2 bc$.   [264] densete *R, Servius*.
[273] mediam M^1.   alveo P^1: auro M.
[275] *cf.* VI. 861.

---

[1] To indicate their wish to fight, according to Servius, this being a *consensio militaris.* Conington renders "make their hands ready to fight." (So also Benoist.)

AENEID BOOK XII

rout of their winged troop, when, swooping suddenly to the water, shameless he snatches up in his crooked talons a stately swan. All alert become the Italians, when lo! one and all, wondrous to behold, the birds wheel clamorously their flight, and, darkening the sky with wings, in serried cloud drive their foe through the air, till, overborne by the onset and the sheer weight, the bird gave way, dropped the booty from his talons into the stream, and sped far within the clouds.

[257] Then in truth the Rutulians hail the omen with a cheer and spread out their hands.[1] And first of all Tolumnius the augur cries: "This it was, this, that my vows have often sought! I accept it, I acknowledge the gods. With me, me at your head, snatch up the sword, O hapless people, whom, like frail birds, a shameless alien affrights with war, and rudely ravages your coasts. He too will take to flight, and spread sail far across the deep. Do ye with one accord close up your ranks, and defend in battle the king thus snatched from you!"

[266] He spoke, and, darting forward, hurled his spear full against the foe; the whistling cornel-shaft sings, and splits the air, unerring. With the deed, at once uprises a mighty shout, the crowds are all confusion, and their hearts heated with turmoil. On flies the spear, where, as it chanced, nine brethren of goodly stature stood in its path—the many borne of one faithful Tuscan wife to Arcadian Gylippus. One of these near the waist, where the stitched belt chafes the belly, and the buckle bites the linked sides [2]— a youth of comely form and gleaming armour—it pierces clean through the ribs and stretches on the

[2] *i.e.* the ends of the belt. Others refer the expression to the edges of the ribs.

VIRGIL

at fratres, animosa phalanx accensaque luctu,
pars gladios stringunt manibus, pars missile ferrum
corripiunt caecique ruunt.   quos agmina contra
procurrunt Laurentum; hinc densi rursus inundant
Troes Agyllinique et pictis Arcades armis :   281
sic omnis amor unus habet decernere ferro.
diripuere aras, it toto turbida caelo
tempestas telorum ac ferreus ingruit imber,
craterasque focosque ferunt.   fugit ipse Latinus 285
pulsatos referens infecto foedere divos.
infrenant alii currus aut corpora saltu
subiciunt in equos et strictis ensibus adsunt.

Messapus regem regisque insigne gerentem
Tyrrhenum Aulesten, avidus confundere foedus, 290
adverso proterret equo : ruit ille recedens
et miser oppositis a tergo involvitur aris
in caput inque umeros.   at fervidus advolat hasta
Messapus teloque orantem multa trabali
desuper altus equo graviter ferit atque ita fatur: 295
"hoc habet, haec melior magnis data victima divis."
concurrunt Itali spoliantque calentia membra.
obvius ambustum torrem Corynaeus ab ara
corripit et venienti Ebyso plagamque ferenti
occupat os flammis : olli ingens barba reluxit   300
nidoremque ambusta dedit.   super ipse secutus
caesariem laeva turbati corripit hostis
impressoque genu nitens terrae applicat ipsum;

<small>**283** it] et $P^1\gamma^1$: id M^1.   **287** aut] et M.
288 adstant M^2.</small>

AENEID BOOK XII

yellow sand. But of his brethren—a gallant band, and fired by grief—part draw their swords, part seize the missile steel, and rush blindly on. Against them charge the Laurentine columns; from their side again pour thickly in Trojans and Agyllines and Arcadians with blazoned arms. Thus all are ruled by one passion, to let the sword decide. Lo! they have stripped the altars; through the whole sky flies a thickening storm of javelins and the iron rain falls fast: bowls and hearth-fires are carried off. Latinus himself takes flight, bearing back his defeated gods, the covenant now void; the others rein their cars or vault upon their steeds and with drawn swords are on the scene.

289 Messapus, eager to rend the truce asunder, with charging steed scares off Tuscan Aulestes, a king[1] and wearing a king's device. Backward he rushes, and whirled, poor man, upon the altars behind, is thrown on head and on shoulders. But Messapus flashes forth like fire, spear in hand, and, aloft on his horse, smites heavily down upon him with massive shaft, though sorely he pleads; then cries thus: "He has it;[2] here is a nobler victim given to the mighty gods!" The Italians crowd around and strip his warm limbs. Standing in the path, Corynaeus snatches up a charred brand from the altar, and as Ebysus comes up and aims a blow, dashes flames in his face: his mighty beard blazed up, and sent forth a smell of fire. Then himself pursuing the stroke, he clutches in his left hand the locks of his bewildered foe, and with thrust of his bended knee bears his body to earth, and there

[1] He was an Etruscan *Lucumo* or *Lars*.
[2] *i.e.* he has his death-blow: an expression used by spectators when a gladiator was struck.

319

VIRGIL

sic rigido latus ense ferit. Podalirius Alsum,
pastorem primaque acie per tela ruentem, 305
ense sequens nudo superimminet: ille securi
adversi frontem mediam mentumque reducta
disicit et sparso late rigat arma cruore.
olli dura quies oculos et ferreus urget
somnus, in aeternam clauduntur lumina noctem. 310

At pius Aeneas dextram tendebat inermem
nudato capite atque suos clamore vocabat:
"quo ruitis? quaeve ista repens discordia surgit?
o cohibete iras! ictum iam foedus et omnes
compositae leges; mihi ius concurrere soli; 315
me sinite atque auferte metus; ego foedera faxo
firma manu; Turnum debent haec iam mihi sacra."
has inter voces, media inter talia verba,
ecce viro stridens alis adlapsa sagitta est,
incertum qua pulsa manu, quo turbine adacta, 320
quis tantam Rutulis laudem, casusne deusne,
attulerit: pressa est insignis gloria facti
nec sese Aeneae iactavit volnere quisquam.

Turnus ut Aenean cedentem ex agmine vidit
turbatosque duces, subita spe fervidus ardet; 325
poscit equos atque arma simul saltuque superbus
emicat in currum et manibus molitur habenas.
multa virum volitans dat fortia corpora Leto,
semineces volvit multos aut agmina curru
proterit aut raptas fugientibus ingerit hastas. 330
qualis apud gelidi cum flumina concitus Hebri
sanguineus Mavors clipeo intonat atque furentis
bella movens immittit equos; illi aequore aperto
ante Notos Zephyrumque volant, gemit ultima pulsu

³⁰⁴ feret $M^1\gamma^2$. pedit P.   ³¹⁰ conduntur P.
³¹¹ inertem M^1.   ³¹³ quaeve] quove R.
³²¹ -ve . . . -ve M.   ³³⁰ aut] et R.
³³² increpat $P\gamma$, *Servius*. furentis] furenti R: prementi M^1.

320

AENEID BOOK XII

smites his side with unyielding sword. Podalirius, pursuing with naked steel, overhangs the shepherd Alsus, as in foremost line he rushes amid the darts; but Alsus, swinging back his axe, severs full in front his enemy's brow and chin, and drenches his armour with widely spattered gore. Stern repose and iron slumber press upon his eyes, and their orbs close in everlasting night.

311 But good Aeneas, with head bared, was stretching forth his unarmed hand, and calling loudly to his men: "Whither do ye rush? What means this sudden outburst of strife? O curb your rage! Truce is already stricken, and all its terms fixed; mine alone is the right to do battle. Give me way and banish fears; this hand shall prove the treaty true; already these rites make Turnus mine!" Amid these cries, amid such words, lo! against him a whizzing arrow winged its way, launched by what hand, sped whirling by whom, none knows, nor who—chance or god—brought Rutulians such honour: hidden is the fame of that high deed, and no one vaunted him of the wounding of Aeneas.

324 Soon as Turnus saw Aeneas withdrawing from the ranks, and his captains in confusion, he glows with the fire of sudden hope, calls for horses, calls for arms, with a bound leaps proudly into his chariot, and firmly grasps the reins. In his swift course many a brave man's body he gives to death; many a man he tumbles half-slain, or crushes whole ranks beneath his car, or, seizing spear after spear, showers them upon the fugitives. Even as when, at full speed, by the streams of icy Hebrus blood-stained Mavors thunders with his shield, and, rousing war, gives rein to his frenzied steeds; they o'er the open plain outstrip the South wind and the West; utmost

VIRGIL

Thraca pedum circumque atrae Formidinis ora 335
Iraeque Insidiaeque, dei comitatus, aguntur:
talis equos alacer media inter proelia Turnus
fumantis sudore quatit, miserabile caesis
hostibus insultans: spargit rapida ungula rores
sanguineos mixtaque cruor calcatur harena. 340
iamque Neci Sthenelumque dedit Thamyrumque
    Pholumque,
hunc congressus et hunc, illum eminus; eminus
    ambo
Imbrasidas, Glaucum atque Laden, quos Imbra-
    sus ipse
nutrierat Lycia paribusque ornaverat armis,
vel conferre manum vel equo praevertere ventos. 345
  Parte alia media Eumedes in proelia fertur,
antiqui proles bello praeclara Dolonis,
nomine avum referens, animo manibusque parentem,
qui quondam, castra ut Danaum speculator adiret,
ausus Pelidae pretium sibi poscere currus: 350
illum Tydides alio pro talibus ausis
adfecit pretio, nec equis adspirat Achillis.
hunc procul ut campo Turnus prospexit aperto,
ante levi iaculo longum per inane secutus,
sistit equos biiugis et curru desilit atque 355
semianimi lapsoque supervenit, et pede collo
impresso dextrae mucronem extorquet et alto
fulgentem tinguit iugulo atque haec insuper addit:
"en agros et quam bello, Troiane, petisti,
Hesperiam metire iacens: haec praemia, qui me 360
ferro ausi temptare, ferunt, sic moenia condunt."

³⁵⁶ elabsoque. *P*¹, *Servius.*   ³⁵⁷ expresso *M*¹.   dextra *R*γ¹

AENEID BOOK XII

Thrace moans with the beat of their hoofs, and around him speed black Terror's forms, and Anger, and Ambush, attendants on the god: with like eagerness amid the fray Turnus goads his sweat-smoking horses, trampling on the foes, piteously slain; the galloping hoof splashes bloody dews, and spurns the gore and mingled sand. And now he has given Sthenelus to death, and Thamyrus, and Pholus, these in close encounter, the first from afar; from afar the sons of Imbrasus, Glaucus and Lades, whom Imbrasus himself had nurtured in Lycia and equipped with like arms, either to fight hand to hand or on horseback to outstrip the winds.

346 Elsewhere Eumedes rides to the midmost fray, war-famed scion of ancient Dolon, in name renewing his grandsire, in heart and hand his sire, who of old, for going in espial to the Danaan camp, dared to ask as his wage the car of Peleus' son; but for such daring far other wage did the son of Tydeus pay him, and no more sets he his hopes upon Achilles' steeds.[1] Him Turnus descries afar on the open plain, and, first following him with light javelin through the long space between them, then stays his twin-yoked steeds, and leaps from his car; now descends on the fallen, dying man, and, planting his foot on his neck, wrests the sword from his hand, dyes the glittering blade deep in his throat, and adds these words withal: "Lo! Trojan, lie there, and measure out the fields and that Hesperia thou didst seek in war: such meed is theirs, who dare to tempt me with the sword; so stablish they their walls!" Then with

[1] The story of Dolon, who for the promised reward of Achilles' chariot and horses undertook to explore by night the Grecian camp, but was put to death by Diomede, the son of Tydeus, is told in Homer, *Iliad*, x. 314 ff.

VIRGIL

huic comitem Asbyten coniecta cuspide mittit
Chloreaque Sybarimque Daretaque Thersilochumque
et sternacis equi lapsum cervice Thymoeten.
ac velut Edoni Boreae cum spiritus alto   365
insonat Aegaeo sequiturque ad litora fluctus;
qua venti incubuere, fugam dant nubila caelo:
sic Turno, quacumque viam secat, agmina cedunt
conversaeque ruunt acies; fert impetus ipsum
et cristam adverso curru quatit aura volantem.   370
non tulit instantem Phegeus animisque frementem:
obiecit sese ad currum et spumantia frenis
ora citatorum dextra detorsit equorum.
dum trahitur pendetque iugis, hunc lata retectum
lancea consequitur rumpitque infixa bilicem·   375
loricam et summum degustat volnere corpus.
ille tamen clipeo obiecto conversus in hostem
ibat et auxilium ducto mucrone petebat,
cum rota praecipitem et procursu concitus axis
impulit effunditque solo, Turnusque secutus   380
imam inter galeam summi thoracis et oras
abstulit ense caput truncumque reliquit harenae.

   Atque ea dum campis victor dat funera Turnus,
interea Aenean Mnestheus et fidus Achates
Ascaniusque comes castris statuere cruentum,   385
alternos longa nitentem cuspide gressus.
saevit et infracta luctatur harundine telum
eripere auxilioque viam, quae proxima, poscit;
ense secent lato volnus telique latebras
rescindant penitus, seseque in bella remittant. 390
iamque aderat Phoebo ante alios dilectus Iapyx

[380] effudit *Rγ*.   [382] harena *Rγ*.
[385] comes] puer *R*.   [389] latebram *PR*.

AENEID BOOK XII

cast of spear he sends Asbytes to bear him company, and Chloreus and Sybaris, Dares and Thersilochus, and Thymoetes, flung from the neck of his restive horse. And as when the blast of the Edonian North-wind roars on the deep Aegean, and drives the billows shoreward; where the winds swoop, the clouds scud through the sky: so, wherever Turnus cleaves a path, the ranks give way, and lines turn and run; his own speed bears him on, and the breeze, as his chariot meets it, tosses his flying plume. Phegeus brooked not his onset and fiery rage; before the chariot he flung himself, and with his right hand wrenched aside the jaws of the furious steeds, foaming on the bits. While he is dragged along clinging to the yoke, the broad spear-head reaches his unguarded side, rends the two-plated corslet where it lodged, and with its wound just grazes the surface of the flesh. Yet he, with shield before him, turned and was making for his foe, seeking succour from his drawn sword, when the wheel and axle, whirling onward, struck him headlong and flung him to the ground, and Turnus, following, with sweep of blade between the helmet's lowest rim and the breastplate's upper edge, smote off his head, and left the trunk upon the sand.

383 And while Turnus thus victoriously deals havoc over the plains, Mnestheus meantime and loyal Achates, and Ascanius by their side, set down Aeneas in the camp, all bleeding and staying every other step upon his long spear. Raging, he struggles to pluck out the head of the broken shaft, and calls for the nearest road to relief, bidding them with broad sword cut the wound, tear open to the bottom the weapon's lair, and send him back to battle. And now drew near Iapyx, Iasus' son, dearest beyond

325

VIRGIL

Iasides, acri quondam cui captus amore
ipse suas artes, sua munera, laetus Apollo
augurium citharamque dabat celerisque sagittas.
ille ut depositi proferret fata parentis, 395
scire potestates herbarum usumque medendi
maluit et mutas agitare inglorius artis.
stabat acerba fremens, ingentem nixus in hastam,
Aeneas, magno iuvenum et maerentis Iuli
concursu, lacrimis immobilis. ille retorto 400
Paeonium in morem senior succinctus amictu
multa manu medica Phoebique potentibus herbis
nequiquam trepidat, nequiquam spicula dextra
sollicitat prensatque tenaci forcipe ferrum.
nulla viam Fortuna regit, nihil auctor Apollo 405
subvenit, et saevus campis magis ac magis horror
crebrescit propiusque malum est. iam pulvere caelum
stare vident, subeunt equites et spicula castris
densa cadunt mediis. it tristis ad aethera clamor
bellantum iuvenum et duro sub Marte cadentum. 410

Hic Venus, indigno nati concussa dolore,
dictamnum genetrix Cretaea carpit ab Ida,
puberibus caulem foliis et flore comantem
purpureo; non illa feris incognita capris
gramina, cum tergo volucres haesere sagittae. 415
hoc Venus, obscuro faciem circumdata nimbo,
detulit, hoc fusum labris splendentibus amnem
inficit, occulte medicans, spargitque salubris

---

[394] dabat *PR*, "vera lectio" (*Servius*): dedit *M*: dedi γ[1].
[397] multas *P*[1]*c*[1].   [398] fixus *M*[1].
[400] reporto *R*.   [401] Paeonidum *M*: Paeonum *P*.
[404] pressat *R*.   [408] subeuntque *R*.
[417] pendentibus *R*: plendentibus *P*[1].

---

[1] *i.e.* unlike music and prophecy, wherein the voice is used. But the idea of obscurity is also included, for the profession of medicine does not lead to great fame.

326

AENEID BOOK XII

others to Phoebus, to whom once gladly did Apollo's self, with love's sting smitten, offer his own arts, his own powers—his augury, his lyre and swift arrows. He, to defer the fate of a sire sick unto death, chose rather to know the virtues of herbs and the practice of healing, and to ply, inglorious, the silent arts.[1]
Bitterly chafing, Aeneas stood propped on his mighty spear, amid a great concourse of warriors along with sorrowing Iülus, himself unmoved by their tears. The aged leech, with robe rolled back, and girt in Paeonian fashion, with healing hand and Phoebus' potent herbs makes much ado—in vain; in vain with his hand pulls at the dart, and with gripping tongs tugs at the steel. No Fortune guides his path, in no wise does Apollo's counsel aid: and more and more the fierce alarm swells o'er the plains, and nigher draws disaster. Now they see the sky upborne on columns of dust; on come the horsemen, and shafts fall thick amidst the camp. Heavenward mounts the dismal cry of men that fight and men that fall beneath the stern War-god's hand.

[411] Hereupon Venus, smitten by her son's cruel pain, with a mother's care plucks from Cretan Ida a dittany[2] stalk, clothed with downy leaves and purple flower; not unknown is that herb to wild goats, when winged arrows have lodged in their flank. This Venus bore down, her face veiled in dim mist; this she steeps with secret healing in the river-water poured into bright-brimming ewer, and

---

[2] The dittany (*dictamnus*) takes its name from Mt. Dicte in Crete, where, according to Aristotle, Cicero and others, wild goats found a cure for their wounds in the eating of the herb.

VIRGIL

ambrosiae sucos et odoriferam panaceam.
fovit ea volnus lympha longaevus Iapyx 420
ignorans, subitoque omnis de corpore fugit
quippe dolor, omnis stetit imo volnere sanguis.
iamque secuta manum nullo cogente sagitta
excidit, atque novae rediere in pristina vires.
"arma citi properate viro! quid statis?" Iapyx 425
conclamat primusque animos accendit in hostem.
"non haec humanis opibus, non arte magistra
proveniunt, neque te, Aenea, mea dextera servat:
maior agit deus atque opera ad maiora remittit."
ille avidus pugnae suras incluserat auro 430
hinc atque hinc oditque moras hastamque coruscat.
postquam habilis lateri clipeus loricaque tergo est,
Ascanium fusis circum complectitur armis
summaque per galeam delibans oscula fatur :
"disce, puer, virtutem ex me verumque laborem, 435
fortunam ex aliis.   nunc te mea dextera bello
defensum dabit et magna inter praemia ducet:
tu facito, mox cum matura adoleverit aetas,
sis memor et te animo repetentem exempla tuorum
et pater Aeneas et avunculus excitet Hector." 440

  Haec ubi dicta dedit, portis sese extulit ingens,
telum immane manu quatiens; simul agmine denso
Antheusque Mnestheusque ruunt omnisque relictis
turba fluit castris.   tum caeco pulvere campus
miscetur pulsuque pedum tremit excita tellus. 445
vidit ab adverso venientis aggere Turnus,
videre Ausonii, gelidusque per ima cucurrit

^{421–425} *omitted* γ¹.   ⁴²² in volnere *P²Rγ²*.
⁴²³ manu *M¹P²γ²*: manus *P¹γ¹*.
⁴²⁸ te *omitted M¹*. Aenean *M¹*.   ⁴⁴⁰ *cf*. III. 343.   ⁴⁴⁴ ruit *P*.

AENEID BOOK XII

sprinkles ambrosia's healthful juices and fragrant panacea.[1] With that water aged Iapyx laved the wound, unwitting; and suddenly, of a truth, all pain fled from the body, all blood was staunched deep in the wound. And now, following his hand, without constraint, the arrow fell out, and newborn strength returned, as of yore. "Quick! bring him arms! Why stand ye?" loudly cries Iapyx, foremost to fire their spirit against the foe. "Not by mortal aid comes this, not by masterful art, nor doth hand of mine save thee, Aeneas; a mightier one—a god—works here, and sends thee back to mightier deeds." He, eager for the fray, had sheathed his legs in gold, on right and left, and, scorning delay, is brandishing his spear. Soon as the shield is fitted to his side, and the corslet to his back, he clasps Ascanius in armed embrace, and, lightly kissing his lips through the helm, he cries: "Learn valour from me, my son, and true toil; fortune from others. To-day my hand shall shield thee in war and lead thee where are great rewards: see thou, when soon thy years have grown to ripeness, that thou be mindful thereof, and, as thou recallest the pattern of thy kin, let thy sire Aeneas, and thy uncle Hector stir thy soul!"

441 These words uttered, forth from the gates he passed in his might, his hand brandishing a massive spear: with him rush Antheus and Mnestheus in serried column, and all the throng streams from the forsaken camp. Then the plain is a turmoil of blinding dust, and the startled earth trembles under the tramp of feet. From the facing rampart Turnus saw them coming; the Ausonians saw, and a cold

[1] Ambrosia, food of immortals, and panacea, the "cure for all," are two mythical plants.

329

VIRGIL

ossa tremor; prima ante omnis Iuturna Latinos
audiit adgnovitque sonum et tremefacta refugit.
ille volat campoque atrum rapit agmen aperto.   450
qualis ubi ad terras abrupto sidere nimbus
it mare per medium; miseris, heu, praescia longe
horrescunt corda agricolis; dabit ille ruinas
arboribus stragemque satis, ruet omnia late;
ante volant sonitumque ferunt ad litora venti: 455
talis in adversos ductor Rhoeteius hostis   MPRV
agmen agit, densi cuneis se quisque coacti
adglomerant. ferit ense gravem Thymbraeus Osirim,
Arcetium Mnestheus, Epulonem obtruncat Achates,
Ufentemque Gyas; cadit ipse Tolumnius augur,   460
primus in adversos telum qui torserat hostis.
tollitur in caelum clamor versique vicissim
pulverulenta fuga Rutuli dant terga per agros.
ipse neque aversos dignatur sternere morti
nec pede congressos nec equo nec tela ferentis   465
insequitur; solum densa in caligine Turnum
vestigat lustrans, solum in certamina poscit.

Hoc concussa metu mentem Iuturna virago
aurigam Turni media inter lora Metiscum
excutit et longe lapsum temone relinquit;   470
ipsa subit manibusque undantis flectit habenas,
cuncta gerens, vocemque et corpus et arma Metisci.
nigra velut magnas domini cum divitis aedes
pervolat et pinnis alta atria lustrat hirundo,
pabula parva legens nidisque loquacibus escas,   475

⁴⁴⁹ adgnoscit *P*.   ⁴⁵⁴ ruit *M*.   ⁴⁵⁵ volans *MP²γ¹*.
⁴⁵⁷ coacti *M²*.   ⁴⁶⁴ adversos *MPγ*.
⁴⁶⁵ congressus *P*. aequo *M* (*late*) *PR*: eque *M¹*: aeque *M²*.
⁴⁷⁰ reliquit *M¹ PRγ*.

330

AENEID BOOK XII

shudder ran through their inmost marrow: first before all the Latins Juturna heard and knew the sound, and in terror fled away. Aeneas wings his way, and sweeps his dark column over the open plain. As when a tempest bursts, and a storm-cloud moves towards land through mid-ocean, the hearts of hapless husbandmen, alas! know it from far and shudder—downfall will it bring to trees and havoc to crops, it will o'erthrow all far and wide—before it fly the winds, and waft their voices shoreward: even so the Rhoeteian[1] chief full against the foe brings up his band; densely they gather, each and all, to his side in close-packed columns. Thymbraeus smites mighty Osiris with the sword, Mnestheus slays Arcetius, Achates Epulo, Gyas Ufens; falls too even the augur Tolumnius, who first had hurled his spear full against the foe. A shout rises to heaven, and in turn the routed Rutulians mid clouds of dust turn their backs in flight across the fields. Himself he deigns not to lay low the fugitives in death nor assails he such as meet him on foot or on horse or wield their darts: Turnus alone he, with searching glance, tracks out through the thick gloom, alone summons to battle.

468 Stricken in heart with such fear, Juturna, the warrior-maid, flings forth Metiscus, Turnus' charioteer, from amid his reins, and leaves him afar, fallen from the pole; herself takes his place, and guides with her hands the flowing thongs, assuming all that Metiscus had,—his voice, form, arms. As when a black swallow flits through a rich lord's ample mansion and wings her way through stately halls, gleaning for her chirping nestlings tiny crumbs

---

[1] *i.e.* Trojan.

VIRGIL

et nunc porticibus vacuis, nunc umida circum
stagna sonat: similis medios Iuturna per hostis
fertur equis rapidoque volans obit omnia curru,
iamque hic germanum iamque hic ostentat ovantem,
nec conferre manum patitur, volat avia longe.   480
haud minus Aeneas tortos legit obvius orbis
vestigatque virum et disiecta per agmina magna
voce vocat. quotiens oculos coniecit in hostem
alipedumque fugam cursu temptavit equorum,
aversos totiens currus Iuturna retorsit.   485
heu, quid agat? vario nequiquam fluctuat aestu
diversaeque vocant animum in contraria curae.
huic Messapus, uti laeva duo forte gerebat
lenta, levis cursu, praefixa hastilia ferro,
horum unum certo contorquens derigit ictu.   490
substitit Aeneas et se collegit in arma,
poplite subsidens; apicem tamen incita summum
hasta tulit summasque excussit vertice cristas.
tum vero adsurgunt irae, insidiisque subactus,
diversos ubi sentit equos currumque referri,   495
multa Iovem et laesi testatus foederis aras
iam tandem invadit medios et Marte secundo
terribilis saevam nullo discrimine caedem
suscitat irarumque omnis effundit habenas.

Quis mihi nunc tot acerba deus, quis carmine caedes
diversas obitumque ducum, quos aequore toto   501
inque vicem nunc Turnus agit, nunc Troius heros,
expediat? tanton placuit concurrere motu,
Iuppiter, aeterna gentis in pace futuras?
Aeneas Rutulum Sucronem (ea prima ruentis   505

⁴⁷⁹ ostendit M^1. ⁴⁸¹ totos V.
⁴⁸⁵ adversos M (*late*) $P\gamma c$.
⁴⁹⁵ sentit M : sensit *most MSS*.
⁴⁹⁶ testatur PR. ⁵⁰⁵ furentis V.

332

AENEID BOOK XII

and scraps of food, and twitters now in the empty courts, now about the watery pools: even so Juturna is borne by the steeds through the enemy's midst, and winging her way in swift chariot scours all the field. And now here, and now there, she displays her triumphant brother, yet suffers him not to close in fight, but flits far away. None the less Aeneas threads the winding maze to meet him, and tracks his steps, and amid the scattered ranks with loud cry calls him. Oft as he cast eyes on his foe and strove by running to match the flight of the winged steeds, so oft Juturna turned and wheeled her car. Ah, what to do? Vainly he tosses on a shifting tide, and conflicting cares call his mind this way and that. Against him Messapus, who haply in left hand bore two tough shafts tipped with steel, lightly advancing, levels one and whirls it with unerring stroke. Aeneas halted, and gathered himself behind his shield, sinking upon his knee; yet the swift spear bore off his helmet-peak, and dashed from his head the topmost plumes. Then indeed his wrath swells, and o'erborne by the treachery, when he sees that the steeds and chariot of his foe are withdrawn afar, having oft appealed to Jove and the altars of the broken treaty, now at last he plunges into the midst, and adown the tide of war terribly awakes grim indiscriminate carnage, flinging loose all the reins of passion.

500 What god can now unfold for me so many horrors, who in song can tell such diverse deaths, and the fall of captains, whom now Turnus, now the Trojan hero, drives in turn o'er all the plain? Was it thy will, O Jupiter, that in so vast a shock should clash nations that thereafter would dwell in everlasting peace? Aeneas, meeting Rutulian Sucro,—that

333

VIRGIL

pugna loco statuit Teucros), haud multa morantem,
excipit in latus et, qua fata celerrima, crudum
transadigit costas et cratis pectoris ensem.   MPR
Turnus equo deiectum Amycum fratremque Diorem,
congressus pedes, hunc venientem cuspide longa,   510
hunc mucrone ferit curruque abscisa duorum
suspendit capita et rorantia sanguine portat.
ille Talon Tanaimque neci fortemque Cethegum,
tris uno congressu, et maestum mittit Oniten,
nomen Echionium matrisque genus Peridiae;   515
hic fratres Lycia missos et Apollinis agris
et iuvenem exosum nequiquam bella Menoeten,
Arcada, piscosae cui circum flumina Lernae
ars fuerat pauperque domus nec nota potentum
limina conductaque pater tellure serebat.   520
ac velut immissi diversis partibus ignes
arentem in silvam et virgulta sonantia lauro,
aut ubi decursu rapido de montibus altis
dant sonitum spumosi amnes et in aequora currunt
quisque suum populatus iter: non segnius ambo   525
Aeneas Turnusque ruunt per proelia; nunc, nunc
fluctuat ira intus, rumpuntur nescia vinci
pectora, nunc totis in volnera viribus itur.

Murranum hic, atavos et avorum antiqua sonantem
nomina per regesque actum genus omne Latinos,   530
praecipitem scopulo atque ingentis turbine saxi
excutit effunditque solo: hunc lora et iuga subter
provolvere rotae, crebro super ungula pulsu

---

⁵⁰⁶ morantis *V*.   ⁵¹¹ abscissa *MR*.
⁵¹⁵ nomine *M*, *known to Servius:* nomine chionium *Rγ*.
⁵²⁰ limina *M*: munera *most MSS. and Servius.* sedebat *M*¹.
⁵²² **ardentem *M*¹: aerentem *P*.**   ⁵³² **excutit] excipit *M*.**

334

AENEID BOOK XII

combat first brought the Trojan onset to a stand—with brief delay smites him upon the flank, and, where death comes speediest, drives the cruel steel through the ribs that fence the chest. Turnus dismounts Amycus and his brother Diores, and, assailing them on foot, strikes the one with long spear as he advances, the other with his sword; then, hanging from his car the severed heads of the twain, he bears them off dripping with blood. Aeneas sends to death Talos and Tanais and brave Cethegus, three at one onslaught, and sad Onites, of Echionian name,[1] whose mother was Peridia; Turnus the brothers sent from Lycia and Apollo's fields,[2] and Menoetes of Arcadia, who in youth loathed warfare in vain: round fish-haunted Lerna's streams had been his craft and humble home, nor knew he the portals of the great, but his father sowed on hired soil. And like fires launched from opposing sides upon a dry forest and thickets of crackling laurel, or as when in swift descent from mountain-heights foaming rivers roar and race seaward, each leaving its own path waste: with no less fury the twain, Aeneas and Turnus, sweep through the battle; now, now wrath surges within them; bursting are their hearts, knowing not to yield; now, with main strength, they rush upon wounds.

529 Murranus, as he vaunts of grandsires, and grandsires' sires of ancient name, and a whole line traced through Latin kings, headlong with a stone and mighty whirling rock Aeneas dashes down and tumbles on the ground; under reins and yoke the wheels rolled him along, and o'er him, trampling him

[1] *i.e.* of Theban name or stock. Echion was the mythical founder of Thebes.
[2] *cf. Aen.* x. 126. Lycia was a favourite haunt of Apollo.

VIRGIL

incita nec domini memorum proculcat equorum.
ille ruenti Hyllo animisque immane frementi   535
occurrit telumque aurata ad tempora torquet:
olli per galeam fixo stetit hasta cerebro.
dextera nec tua te, Graium fortissime Cretheu,
eripuit Turno, nec di texere Cupencum,
Aenea veniente, sui; dedit obvia ferro   540
pectora nec misero clipei mora profuit aerei.
te quoque Laurentes viderunt, Aeole, campi
oppetere et late terram consternere tergo:
occidis, Argivae quem non potuere phalanges
sternere nec Priami regnorum eversor Achilles;   545
hic tibi mortis erant metae, domus alta sub Ida,
Lyrnesi domus alta, solo Laurente sepulchrum.
totae adeo conversae acies omnesque Latini,
omnes Dardanidae, Mnestheus acerque Serestus
et Messapus equum domitor et fortis Asilas   550
Tuscorumque phalanx Euandrique Arcades alae,
pro se quisque viri summa nituntur opum vi;
nec mora nec requies, vasto certamine tendunt.

Hic mentem Aeneae genetrix pulcherrima misit,
iret ut ad muros urbique adverteret agmen   555
ocius et subita turbaret clade Latinos.
ille ut vestigans diversa per agmina Turnum
huc atque huc acies circumtulit, aspicit urbem
immunem tanti belli atque impune quietam.
continuo pugnae accendit maioris imago;   560
Mnesthea Sergestumque vocat fortemque Serestum

[541] aerei *Aldine edition* (1501): aeris *MSS.   So Mackail.*
[559] quietem *Rγ¹*.

AENEID BOOK XII

down with many a beat, rush the hoofs of the steeds that remember not their lord. The other, as Hyllus rushes on with boundless fury at heart, meets him and whirls a dart at his gold-bound brow: piercing the helm, the spear stood fast in his brain. Nor did thy right hand, Cretheus, thou bravest of the Greeks, save thee from Turnus, nor did his gods shield their Cupencus when Aeneas came:[1] he put his breast in the weapon's path, and the brazen buckler's stay, alas! availed him not. Thee too, Aeolus, the Laurentine plains saw sink, and spread thy frame abroad o'er the earth: thou fallest, whom the Argive battalions could not lay low, nor Achilles, destroyer of Priam's realms. Here was thy bourne of death; beneath Ida was thy stately home,—thy stately home at Lyrnesus, in Laurentine soil thy sepulchre. Yea, the whole lines, turning to the fray—all the Latins and all the Greeks, Mnestheus and valiant Serestus; Messapus, tamer of horses, and brave Asilas; the Tuscan battalion and Evander's Arcadian squadrons—each doing his all, strain with utmost force of strength; no stint, no stay; in measureless conflict they struggle.

554 Hereupon his beauteous mother inspired Aeneas with the thought to advance on the walls, fling his column on the town, and confound the Latins with sudden disaster. While he, tracking Turnus here and there throughout the host, swept his glance this way and that, he views the city free from that fierce warfare, peaceful and unharmed. Straightway a vision of greater battle fires his heart; he calls his captains, Mnestheus and Sergestus, and brave

[1] According to Servius, *Cupencus* in the Sabine language means a priest, corresponding to *Flamen* and *Pontifex* in Latin. Hence *di sui*.

VIRGIL

ductores tumulumque capit, quo cetera Teucrum
concurrit legio, nec scuta aut spicula densi
deponunt.   celso medius stans aggere fatur:
"ne qua meis esto dictis mora; Iuppiter hac stat;   565
neu quis ob inceptum subitum mihi segnior ito.
urbem hodie, causam belli, regna ipsa Latini,
ni frenum accipere et victi parere fatentur,
eruam et aequa solo fumantia culmina ponam.
scilicet exspectem, libeat dum proelia Turno   570
nostra pati rursusque velit concurrere victus?
hoc caput, o cives, haec belli summa nefandi.
ferte faces propere foedusque reposcite flammis."
dixerat, atque animis pariter certantibus omnes
dant cuneum densaque ad muros mole feruntur.   575
scalae improviso subitusque apparuit ignis.
discurrunt alii ad portas primosque trucidant,
ferrum alii torquent et obumbrant aethera telis.
ipse inter primos dextram sub moenia tendit
Aeneas magnaque incusat voce Latinum   580
testaturque deos, iterum se ad proelia cogi,
bis iam Italos hostis, haec altera foedera rumpi.
exoritur trepidos inter discordia civis:
urbem alii reserare iubent et pandere portas
Dardanidis ipsumque trahunt in moenia regem;   585
arma ferunt alii et pergunt defendere muros:
inclusas ut cum latebroso in pumice pastor
vestigavit apes fumoque implevit amaro,
illae intus trepidae rerum per cerea castra
discurrunt magnisque acuunt stridoribus iras;   590

⁵⁶⁶ fatetur *M*¹.   ⁵⁷⁵ ferentur *P*¹.
⁵⁸² haec iam altera *M*².   ⁵⁸⁷ ut cum] veluti *M*.

AENEID BOOK XII

Serestus, and plants himself on a mound, where the rest of the Teucrian host throng thickly around, yet drop not shield nor spear. Standing in their midst on the mounded height he cries: "Let naught delay my command; God is on our side; nor let any, I pray, be slower to advance because the venture is so sudden. Yon city, the cause of war, the very seat of Latinus' realm, unless they consent to receive our yoke, and to submit as vanquished, this very day will I o'erthrow, and lay its smoking roofs level with the ground. Am I, forsooth, to wait till it be Turnus' humour to bide battle with me, and till, once beaten, he choose to meet me a second time? This, fellow-citizens, is the head, this the sum, of the accursed war. Bring brands with speed, and in fire reclaim the treaty." He ceased,—and lo! with hearts alike emulous, all form a wedge and advance in serried mass to the walls. In a moment ladders and sudden flames are seen. Some rush to the several gates and cut down the foremost guards; others hurl their steel and veil the sky with javelins. Himself in the van, Aeneas uplifts his hand to the walls, loudly reproaches Latinus, and calls the gods to witness that again he is forced into battle, that twice the Italians become his foes, and that this treaty is the second broken. Strife uprises among the startled citizens: some bid unbar the town and throw wide the gates to the Dardans, and would drag the king himself to the ramparts; others bring arms, and haste to defend the walls. As when some shepherd has tracked bees to their lair in rocky covert, and filled it with stinging smoke; they within, startled for their safety, scurry to and fro through the waxen fortress, and with loud buzzings

VIRGIL

volvitur ater odor tectis, tum murmure caeco
intus saxa sonant, vacuas it fumus ad auras.
  Accidit haec fessis etiam fortuna Latinis,
quae totam luctu concussit funditus urbem.
regina ut tectis venientem prospicit hostem,   595
incessi muros, ignis ad tecta volare,
nusquam acies contra Rutulas, nulla agmina Turni,
infelix pugnae iuvenem in certamine credit
exstinctum et, subito mentem turbata dolore,
se causam clamat crimenque caputque malorum,   600
multaque per maestum demens effata furorem,
purpureos moritura manu discindit amictus
et nodum informis leti trabe nectit ab alta.
quam cladem miserae postquam accepere Latinae,
filia prima manu floros Lavinia crinis   605
et roseas laniata genas, tum cetera circum
turba furit; resonant latae plangoribus aedes.
hinc totam infelix volgatur fama per urbem.
demittunt mentes, it scissa veste Latinus,
coniugis attonitus fatis urbisque ruina,   610
canitiem immundo perfusam pulvere turpans.
  Interea extremo bellator in aequore Turnus   614
palantis sequitur paucos iam segnior atque   615
iam minus atque minus successu laetus equorum.
**attulit hunc illi caecis terroribus aura
commixtum clamorem arrectasque impulit auris**
confusae sonus urbis et inlaetabile murmur.
"ei mihi! quid tanto turbantur moenia luctu?   620
quisve ruit tantus diversa clamor ab urbe?"

---

⁵⁹⁶ incedi *M¹*: incendi *γ*: incensi *R*.
⁶⁰⁵ floros *Probus, Servius*: flavos *MSS*.
⁶⁰⁷ latae *M¹Rc*: late *M²Pγb*.
⁶¹², ⁶¹³ multaque se incusat, qui non acceperit ante | Dardanium Aenean generumque adsciverit ultro *omitted MPRγb*; *taken from* xi. 471, 472.

340

AENEID BOOK XII

whet their rage; the black reek rolls through their dwelling, the rocks within hum with hidden murmur, and smoke issues to the empty air.

⁵⁹³ This further fate befell the labouring Latins, and shook the whole city to her base with grief. When from her palace the queen sees the foe approach, the walls assailed, flames mounting to the roofs, yet nowhere Rutulian ranks, no troops of Turnus to meet them, alas! she thinks her warrior slain in combat, and, her mind distraught by sudden anguish, cries out that she is the guilty source and spring of sorrows, and uttering many a wild word in the frenzy of grief, resolved to die, rends her purple robes, and from a lofty beam fastens the noose of a hideous death. Soon as the unhappy Latin women learned this disaster, first her daughter Lavinia, her hand tearing her flowery tresses and roseate cheeks, then all the throng around her, madly rave; the wide halls ring with lamentations. Thence the woeful rumour spreads throughout the town. Hearts sink; with rent raiment goes Latinus dazed at his wife's doom and his city's downfall, defiling his hoary hairs with showers of unclean dust.

⁶¹⁴ Meanwhile Turnus, battling on the plain's far edge, is pursuing scanty stragglers, slacker now and less and less exultant in the triumph of his steeds. To him the breeze bore that cry blended with terrors unknown, and on his straining ears smote the sound and joyless murmur of the town in turmoil. "Ah me! what is this great sorrow that shakes the walls? What is this cry speeding from the distant

VIRGIL

sic ait adductisque amens subsistit habenis.
atque huic, in faciem soror ut conversa Metisci
aurigae currumque et equos et lora regebat,
talibus occurrit dictis: "hac, Turne, sequamur   625
Troiugenas, qua prima viam victoria pandit:
sunt alii, qui tecta manu defendere possint.
ingruit Aeneas Italis et proelia miscet:
et nos saeva manu mittamus funera Teucris.
nec numero inferior, pugnae nec honore recedes."   630
Turnus ad haec:
"o soror, et dudum adgnovi, cum prima per artem
foedera turbasti teque haec in bella dedisti,
et nunc nequiquam fallis dea. sed quis Olympo
demissam tantos voluit te ferre labores?   635
an fratris miseri letum ut crudele videres?
nam quid ago? aut quae iam spondet Fortuna salutem?
vidi oculos ante ipse meos me voce vocantem
Murranum, quo non superat mihi carior alter,
oppetere ingentem atque ingenti volnere victum.   640
occidit infelix ne nostrum dedecus Ufens
aspiceret; Teucri potiuntur corpore et armis.
exscindine domos (id rebus defuit unum),
perpetiar, dextra nec Drancis dicta refellam?   644
terga dabo et Turnum fugientem haec terra videbit?
usque adeone mori miserum est? vos o mihi, Manes,
este boni, quoniam superis adversa voluntas.
sancta ad vos anima atque istius inscia culpae
descendam, magnorum haud umquam indignus
   avorum."

Vix ea fatus erat, medios volat ecce per hostis   650
vectus equo spumante Saces, adversa sagitta   MP

₆₂₄ gerebat $P\gamma^1$.   ₆₂₇ possunt P.
₆₃₅ perferre R.   ₆₃₉ superat] fuerat M^1.
₆₄₁ nostrum ne P.   ₆₄₇ aversa PR.

342

AENEID BOOK XII

town?" So he speaks, and in frenzy draws in the reins and halts. Thereon his sister, as, changed to the form of his charioteer Metiscus, she guided car and steeds and reins, meets him with these words: "This way, Turnus, pursue we the sons of Troy, where victory first opens a path; others there are whose hands can guard their homes. Aeneas falls upon the Italians with turmoil of battle; let our hand too deal fierce havoc among his Teucrians! Neither in tale of dead, nor in fame of war, shalt thou come off the worse." To this Turnus: "Sister, both long since I knew thee, when first thou didst craftily mar the pact and fling thyself into this war, and now thou vainly hidest thy deity. But who willed that thou be sent down from Olympus to bear such sore toils? Was it that thou mightest see thy hapless brother's cruel death? For what may I do? Or what chance can now assure me safety? Before my very eyes, as loudly he called upon me, have I seen Murranus fall,—no other dearer than he is left me—a mighty soul and laid low by a mighty wound. Fallen is luckless Ufens, that so he might not view our shame: the Teucrians hold his corpse and armour. The razing of their homes—the one thing lacking to my lot—shall I endure it, nor with my sword refute Drances' taunts? Shall I turn my back, and shall this land see Turnus in flight? Is death all so sad? Be kind to me, ye Shades, since the gods above have turned their faces from me. A stainless soul, and ignorant of that reproach, I will descend to you, never unworthy of my mighty sires of old!"

650 Scarce had he spoken, when lo! borne on foaming steed through the foemen's midst speeds Saces, wounded full in face by an arrow, and, rush-

VIRGIL

saucius ora, ruitque implorans nomine Turnum:
"Turne, in te suprema salus; miserere tuorum.
fulminat Aeneas armis summasque minatur
deiecturum arces Italum excidioque daturum,　　655
iamque faces ad tecta volant.　in te ora Latini,
in te oculos referunt; mussat rex ipse Latinus,
quos generos vocet aut quae sese ad foedera flectat.
praeterea regina, tui fidissima, dextra
occidit ipsa sua lucemque exterrita fugit.　　660
soli pro portis Messapus et acer Atinas
sustentant acies.　circum hos utrimque phalanges
stant densae strictisque seges mucronibus horret
ferrea: tu currum deserto in gramine versas."
obstipuit varia confusus imagine rerum　　665
Turnus et obtutu tacito stetit; aestuat ingens
uno in corde pudor mixtoque insania luctu
et furiis agitatus amor et conscia virtus.　　MPV
ut primum discussae umbrae et lux reddita menti,
ardentis oculorum orbis ad moenia torsit　　670
turbidus eque rotis magnam respexit ad urbem.

Ecce autem flammis inter tabulata volutus
ad caelum undabat vertex turrimque tenebat,
turrim, compactis trabibus quam eduxerat ipse
subdideratque rotas pontisque instraverat altos.　　675
"iam iam fata, soror, superant: absiste morari;
quo deus et quo dura vocat Fortuna, sequamur.
stat conferre manum Aeneae, stat, quidquid acerbi est,
morte pati; neque me indecorem, germana, videbis
amplius.　hunc, oro, sine me furere ante furorem."　　680

[662] aciem *P*.　　[666] *cf.* x. 870 *f.*　　[677] qua dura *P*.

AENEID BOOK XII

ing on, calls for aid by name on Turnus: "Turnus, in thee lies our last hope; pity thy people! Aeneas thunders in arms, and threatens to overthrow Italy's highest towers and give them to destruction: even now brands are flying to the roofs. To thee the Latins turn their looks, to thee their eyes; King Latinus himself mutters in doubt, whom to call his sons, or towards what alliance to incline. Moreover the queen, all whose trust was in thee, has fallen by her own hand, and fled in terror from the light. Alone before the gates Messapus and valiant Atinas sustain our lines. Around these on either side stand serried squadrons, and a harvest of steel bristles with drawn swords; yet thou wheelest thy car o'er the deserted sward." Aghast and bewildered by the changeful picture of disaster, Turnus stood mutely gazing; within that single heart surges mighty shame, and madness mingled with grief, and love stung by fury, and the consciousness of worth. Soon as the shadows scattered and light dawned afresh on his mind, his blazing eyeballs he turned wrathfully upon the walls and from his car looked back upon the spacious city.

672 But lo! from storey to storey a rolling spire of flame was eddying heavenward, and fastening upon a tower—a tower that he himself had reared of jointed beams and set on wheels and slung with lofty gangways.[1] "Now, my sister, now Fate triumphs; cease to hinder; where God and cruel Fortune call, let us follow! Resolved am I to meet Aeneas, resolved to bear in death all its bitterness; nor longer, sister mine, shalt thou behold me shamed. With this madness suffer me ere the end, I pray, to be a mad-

---

[1] *cf.* the account at IX. 530 ff. These defensive towers were provided with wheels, and with gangways, which could be lowered to the walls.

VIRGIL

dixit et e curru saltum dedit ocius arvis
perque hostis, per tela ruit maestamque sororem
deserit ac rapido cursu media agmina rumpit.
ac veluti montis saxum de vertice praeceps
cum ruit, avolsum vento, seu turbidus imber   685
proluit aut annis solvit sublapsa vetustas;
fertur in abruptum magno mons improbus actu
exsultatque solo, silvas, armenta virosque   MPRV
involvens secum: disiecta per agmina Turnus
sic urbis ruit ad muros, ubi plurima fuso   690
sanguine terra madet striduntque hastilibus aurae,
significatque manu et magno simul incipit ore:
" parcite iam, Rutuli, et vos tela inhibete, Latini:
quaecumque est fortuna, mea est; me verius unum
pro vobis foedus luere et decernere ferro."   695
discessere omnes medii spatiumque dedere.

At pater Aeneas audito nomine Turni
deserit et muros et summas deserit arces
praecipitatque moras omnis, opera omnia rumpit,
laetitia exsultans, horrendumque intonat armis;   700
quantus Athos aut quantus Eryx aut ipse coruscis
cum fremit ilicibus quantus gaudetque nivali
vertice se attollens pater Appenninus ad auras.
iam vero et Rutuli certatim et Troes et omnes
convertere oculos Itali, quique alta tenebant   705
moenia quique imos pulsabant ariete muros,
armaque deposuere umeris. stupet ipse Latinus
ingentis, genitos diversis partibus orbis,
inter se coiisse viros et cernere ferro.
atque illi, ut vacuo patuerunt aequore campi,   710
procursu rapido, coniectis eminus hastis,

---

[701] Athon *b¹c*, *Servius*.
[709] et *omitted c.* cernere *P¹, Seneca* (Ep. 58. 3), *Servius:*
discernere *b, known to Priscian:* decernere *most MSS., known to Servius.*

346

AENEID BOOK XII

man." He said, and leapt quickly from his car to the field, and rushing through foes and through spears, leaves his sorrowing sister, and burst in rapid course amid their columns. And as when a rock from mountain-top rushes headlong, torn away by the blast—whether the whirling storm has washed it free, or time stealing on with lapse of years has loosened it; down the steep with mighty rush sweeps the reckless mass, and bounds over the earth, rolling with it trees, herds, and men: so amid the scattered ranks Turnus rushes to the city-walls, where the ground is deepest drenched with spilled blood, and the air is shrill with spears; then beckons with his hand and thus begins aloud: "Forbear now, Rutulians, and ye Latins, stay your darts. Whatever fortune is here is mine; 'tis better that I alone in your stead atone for the covenant, and decide the issue with the sword." All drew apart from the midst and gave him room.

697 But father Aeneas, hearing Turnus' name, forsakes the walls, forsakes the lofty fortress, flings aside all delay, breaks off all tasks, and, exultant with joy, thunders terribly on his arms: vast as Athos, vast as Eryx or vast as Father Apennine himself, when he roars with his quivering oaks, and joyously lifts heavenward his snowy head. Now indeed, all turned emulous eyes,—Rutulians, and Trojans, and Italians, both they who held the lofty ramparts, and they whose ram battered the walls below—and doffed the armour from their shoulders. Latinus himself is amazed that these mighty men, born in far distant climes, are met together and make decision with the sword. And they, soon as the lists were clear on the open plain, dash swiftly forward, first

VIRGIL

invadunt Martem clipeis atque aere sonoro.
dat gemitum tellus; tum crebros ensibus ictus
congeminant; fors et virtus miscentur in unum.
ac velut ingenti Sila summove Taburno 715
cum duo conversis inimica in proelia tauri
frontibus incurrunt; pavidi cessere magistri;
stat pecus omne metu mutum mussantque iuvencae,
quis nemori imperitet, quem tota armenta sequantur; MPR
illi inter sese multa vi volnera miscent 720
cornuaque obnixi infigunt et sanguine largo
colla armosque lavant; gemitu nemus omne remugit:
non aliter Tros Aeneas et Daunius heros
concurrunt clipeis; ingens fragor aethera complet.
Iuppiter ipse duas aequato examine lances 725
sustinet et fata imponit diversa duorum,
quem damnet labor et quo vergat pondere letum.

Emicat hic, impune putans, et corpore toto
alte sublatum consurgit Turnus in ensem
et ferit: exclamant Troes trepidique Latini, 730
arrectaeque amborum acies: at perfidus ensis
frangitur in medioque ardentem deserit ictu,
ni fuga subsidio subeat. fugit ocior Euro,
ut capulum ignotum dextramque aspexit inermem.
fama est praecipitem, cum prima in proelia iunctos 735
conscendebat equos, patrio mucrone relicto,
dum trepidat, ferrum aurigae rapuisse Metisci:
idque diu, dum terga dabant palantia Teucri,
sufficit; postquam arma dei ad Volcania ventum est,
mortalis mucro, glacies ceu futtilis, ictu 740

---

[713] crebris $M^1\gamma^1$.   [714] miscetur V.
[715] silva $R\gamma^1$, known to Servius.
[719] pecori γ^2.   [720] proelia γ^1.
[727] et] aut b, Nonius, Servius.
[732] ictum M^1R.   [735] primum $PR\gamma$. ad $P\gamma^1$.

348

AENEID BOOK XII

hurling their spears from far, and rush on the fray with shields and clanging brass. Earth groans; then with the sword they shower blow on blow, chance and valour blending in one. And as in mighty Sila or on Taburnus' height, when two bulls charge, brow to brow, in mortal battle, back in terror fall the keepers, the whole herd stands mute with dread, and the heifers dumbly ponder who shall be lord of the forest, whom all the herds shall follow; they with mighty force deal mutual wounds, gore with butting horns, and bathe neck and shoulders in streaming blood; all the woodland re-echoes with the bellowing: even so Trojan Aeneas and the Daunian hero clash shield on shield; the mighty crash fills the sky. Jupiter himself upholds two scales in even balance, and lays therein the diverse destinies of both, whom the strife dooms, and with whose weight death sinks down.[1]

728 Now forth springs Turnus, deeming it safe, rises full height on his uplifted sword, and strikes. The Trojans and expectant Latins cry aloud; both hosts are on tiptoe with excitement. But the traitorous sword snaps, and in mid stroke fails its fiery lord, did not flight come to his succour. Swifter than the East wind he flies, soon as he marks an unknown hilt in his defenceless hand. Fame tells that in his headlong haste, when first mounting behind his yoked steeds for battle, he left his father's blade behind and in his haste snatched up the steel of Metiscus his charioteer; and for long that served, while the straggling Teucrians turned their backs: but when it met the god-wrought armour of Vulcan, the mortal blade, like brittle ice,

[1] For this weighing of the fates, see Homer, *Iliad*, XXII. 209 ff. The sinking scale means death.

VIRGIL

dissiluit; fulva resplendent fragmina harena.
ergo amens diversa fuga petit aequora Turnus
et nunc huc, inde huc incertos implicat orbis;
undique enim densa Teucri inclusere corona
atque hinc vasta palus, hinc ardua moenia cingunt. 745
　Nec minus Aeneas, quamquam tardata sagitta
interdum genua impediunt cursumque recusant,
insequitur trepidique pedem pede fervidus urget;
inclusum veluti si quando flumine nactus
cervum aut puniceae saeptum formidine pinnae 750
venator cursu canis et latratibus instat;
ille autem, insidiis et ripa territus alta,
mille fugit refugitque vias; at vividus Umber
haeret hians, iam iamque tenet similisque tenenti
increpuit malis morsuque elusus inani est. 755
tum vero exoritur clamor, ripaeque lacusque
responsant circa et caelum tonat omne tumultu.
ille simul fugiens Rutulos simul increpat omnis,
nomine quemque vocans, notumque efflagitat
　　ensem.　　　　　　　　　　　　　　　　MP
Aeneas mortem contra praesensque minatur 760
exitium, si quisquam adeat, terretque trementis,
excisurum urbem minitans, et saucius instat.
quinque orbis explent cursu totidemque retexunt
huc illuc; neque enim levia aut ludicra petuntur
praemia, sed Turni de vita et sanguine certant. 765
　Forte sacer Fauno foliis oleaster amaris
hic steterat, nautis olim venerabile lignum,
servati ex undis ubi figere dona solebant
Laurenti divo et votas suspendere vestis;
sed stirpem Teucri nullo discrimine sacrum 770

₇₄₁ resplendet fragmen *M²R*.
₇₄₄ densa Teucri *PR, Servius:* Teucri densa *M.*
₇₄₆ tardante *M²c².*　　₇₅₃ ac *M¹b¹*.
₇₅₄ tenens *Rc*.

350

AENEID BOOK XII

flew asunder at the stroke; the fragments glitter on the yellow sand. So Turnus madly flees here and there over the plain, and now this way and now that entwines wavering circles; for on all hands the Teucrians enclosed him in crowded ring, and here a waste fen, there steep ramparts engirdle him.

⁷⁴⁶ Nor less, though at times his knees, retarded by the arrow-wound, impede him and deny their speed, does Aeneas pursue, and hotly press, foot to foot, upon his panting foe: as when a hunter hound has caught a stag, pent in by a stream, or hedged about by the terror of crimson feathers, and, running and barking, presses him close; the stag, in terror of the snares and lofty bank, flees to and fro in a thousand ways, but the keen Umbrian clings close with jaws agape, and now, now grips, or, as though he gripped, snaps his jaws, and baffled, bites on naught. Then indeed uprises the din; banks and pools around make answer, and all heaven thunders with the tumult. Turnus, even as he flees, even then upbraids all the Rutulians, calling each by name, and clamouring for the sword he knew. Aeneas in turn threatens death and instant doom, should one draw nigh, and affrights his trembling foes with threats to raze the town, and though wounded presses on. Five circles they cover at full speed, and unweave as many this way and that; for no slight or sportive prize they seek, but for Turnus life and blood they strive.

⁷⁶⁶ Haply here had stood a bitter-leaved wild olive, sacred to Faunus, a tree revered of old by mariners, whereon, when saved from the waves, they were wont to fasten their gifts to the god of Laurentum and hang up their votive raiment; but the Teucrians, heeding naught, had shorn the sacred

351

VIRGIL

sustulerant, puro ut possent concurrere campo.
hic hasta Aeneae stabat, huc impetus illam
detulerat, fixam et lenta radice tenebat.
incubuit voluitque manu convellere ferrum
Dardanides, teloque sequi quem prendere cursu   775
non poterat.   tum vero amens formidine Turnus
"Faune, precor, miserere," inquit, "tuque optima ferrum
Terra tene, colui vestros si semper honores,
quos contra Aeneadae bello fecere profanos."
dixit opemque dei non cassa in vota vocavit.   780
namque diu luctans lentoque in stirpe moratus
viribus haud ullis valuit discludere morsus
roboris Aeneas.   dum nititur acer et instat,
rursus in aurigae faciem mutata Metisci
procurrit fratrique ensem dea Daunia reddit.   785
quod Venus audaci nymphae indignata licere
accessit telumque alta ab radice revellit.
olli sublimes, armis animisque refecti,
hic gladio fidens, hic acer et arduus hasta,
adsistunt contra certamina Martis anheli.   790

Iunonem interea rex omnipotentis Olympi
adloquitur, fulva pugnas de nube tuentem:
"quae iam finis erit, coniunx? quid denique restat?
indigetem Aenean scis ipsa et scire fateris
deberi caelo fatisque ad sidera tolli.   795
quid struis? aut qua spe gelidis in nubibus haeres?

₇₇₃ et *omitted* M^2b^1. ab radice M^2P.   ₇₇₉ ferro γ^2.
₇₈₂ discurrere $M^1\gamma^2$: convellere a^1c.
₇₈₄ conversa M^2P.   ₇₈₈ animumque P^1.
₇₉₀ certamine *b, known to Servius.*

AENEID BOOK XII

stem, that in clear lists they might contend. Here stood the spear of Aeneas; hither its force had borne it, and was holding it fast in the tough root. The Dardan stooped, fain to pluck away the steel perforce, and pursue with javelin him he could not catch by speed of foot. Then indeed Turnus, frantic with terror, cried: "Faunus, have pity, I pray, and thou, most gracious Earth, hold fast the steel, if ever I have reverenced your worship, which, in other wise, Aeneas' sons have defiled by war." He spoke, and to no fruitless vow did he invoke the aid of heaven. For long though he wrestled and lingered o'er the stubborn stem, by no strength availed Aeneas to unlock the oaken bite. While fiercely he tugs and strains, the Daunian goddess,[1] changing once again into the form of charioteer Metiscus, runs forward and restores the sword to her brother. But Venus, wroth that such license is granted the bold nymph, drew nigh, and plucked the weapon from the deep root. At full height, in arms and heart renewed—one trusting to his sword, one fiercely towering with his spear—breathless[2] both, they stand facing the War-god's strife.

[791] Meanwhile the king of almighty Olympus accosts Juno, as from a golden cloud she gazes on the fray: "What now shall be the end, O wife? What remains at the last? Thyself knowest, and dost confess to know it, that Aeneas, as Hero of the land, is claimed of heaven, and the Fates exalt him to the stars. What plannest thou? Or in what hope lingerest thou in the chill clouds? Was it

---

[1] Juturna.
[2] Benoist takes *anheli* with *Martis*, the strife "of breathless Mars," but for this bold expression no parallel can be cited.

353

VIRGIL

mortalin decuit violari volnere divum?
aut ensem (quid enim sine te Iuturna valeret?)
ereptum reddi Turno et vim crescere victis?
desine iam tandem precibusque inflectere nostris,   800
ne te tantus edit tacitam dolor et mihi curae
saepe tuo dulci tristes ex ore recursent.
ventum ad supremum est.   terris agitare vel undis
Troianos potuisti, infandum accendere bellum,
deformare domum et luctu miscere hymenaeos: 805
ulterius temptare veto."   sic Iuppiter orsus;
sic dea submisso contra Saturnia voltu:

"Ista quidem quia nota mihi tua, magne, voluntas,
Iuppiter, et Turnum et terras invita reliqui:
nec tu me aeria solam nunc sede videres   810
digna indigna pati, sed flammis cincta sub ipsam
starem aciem traheremque inimica in proelia Teucros.
Iuturnam misero (fateor) succurrere fratri
suasi et pro vita maiora audere probavi,
non ut tela tamen, non ut contenderet arcum;   815
adiuro Stygii caput implacabile fontis,
una superstitio superis quae reddita divis.
et nunc cedo equidem pugnasque exosa relinquo.
illud te, nulla fati quod lege tenetur,
pro Latio obtestor, pro maiestate tuorum: 820
cum iam conubiis pacem felicibus, esto,
component, cum iam leges et foedera iungent,
ne vetus indigenas nomen mutare Latinos
neu Troas fieri iubeas Teucrosque vocari

⁸⁰¹ ni P^1: nec bc.   edit $P^1\gamma^1$, *Diomedes, Servius:* edat $MP^2\gamma^2bc$.   ⁸⁰² recusent M^1c^1.   ⁸⁰⁹ relinquo P^2.
⁸¹¹ ipsam M: ipsa P.   ⁸¹² acie P.
⁸²⁴ Teucrosve $P\gamma$.

AENEID BOOK XII

well that by mortal's wound a god should be profaned? or that the lost sword—for without thee what could Juturna avail?—should be restored to Turnus, and the vanquished gain fresh force? Cease now, I pray, and bend to our entreaties, that such great grief may not consume thee in silence, nor to me may bitter cares so oft return from thy sweet lips. The end is reached. To chase the Trojans over land or wave, to kindle monstrous war, to mar a happy home and blend bridals with woe—this power hast thou had; farther to attempt I forbid!" Thus Jupiter began: thus, with downcast look, the goddess, child of Saturn, replied:

808 "Even because I knew, great Jove, that such was thy pleasure, have I, though loth, left Turnus and the earth; else wouldst thou not see me now, alone on my airy throne, enduring fair and foul; but girt in flame would I take my stand close to the very ranks, and drag the Teucrians into deadly fray. As for Juturna, I counselled her, I own, to succour her hapless brother, and for his life's sake sanctioned still greater deeds of daring, yet not to level the arrow, not to bend the bow: I swear by the inexorable fountain-head of Styx, sole name of dread ordained for gods above. And now I yield, yea, yield, and quit the strife in loathing. This boon, banned by no law of fate, for Latium's sake, for thine own kin's greatness,[1] I entreat from thee: when anon with happy bridal rites—so be it!—they plight peace, when anon they join in laws and treaties, command not the native Latins to change their ancient name, nor to become Trojans and be

---

[1] Saturn, father of Jupiter, had once reigned in Latium, and from him Latinus was descended. *cf. Aen.* VII. 45-49.

VIRGIL

aut vocem mutare viros aut vertere vestem.   825
sit Latium, sint Albani per saecula reges,
sit Romana potens Itala virtute propago;
occidit, occideritque sinas cum nomine Troia."

Olli subridens hominum rerumque repertor:
"es germana Iovis Saturnique altera proles: 830
irarum tantos volvis sub pectore fluctus.
verum age et inceptum frustra submitte furorem:
do quod vis, et me victusque volensque remitto.
sermonem Ausonii patrium moresque tenebunt,
utque est, nomen erit; commixti corpore tantum   835
subsident Teucri.   morem ritusque sacrorum
adiciam faciamque omnis uno ore Latinos.
hinc genus Ausonio mixtum quod sanguine surget,
supra homines, supra ire deos pietate videbis
nec gens ulla tuos aeque celebrabit honores."   840
adnuit his Iuno et mentem laetata retorsit;
interea excedit caelo nubemque relinquit.

His actis aliud genitor secum ipse volutat
Iuturnamque parat fratris dimittere ab armis.
dicuntur geminae pestes cognomine Dirae,   845
quas et Tartaream Nox intempesta Megaeram
uno eodemque tulit partu, paribusque revinxit
serpentum spiris ventosasque addidit alas.
hae Iovis ad solium saevique in limine regis
apparent acuuntque metum mortalibus aegris,   850
si quando letum horrificum morbosque deum rex
molitur, meritas aut bello territat urbes.
harum unam celerem demisit ab aethere summo
Iuppiter inque omen Iuturnae occurrere iussit:
illa volat celerique ad terram turbine fertur.   855

⁸²⁵ vestes *P*γ.   ⁸³⁵ tanto *R.*

AENEID BOOK XII

called Teucrians, nor to change their tongue and alter their attire: let Latium be, let Alban kings endure through ages, let be a Roman stock, strong in Italian valour: fallen is Troy, and fallen let her be, together with her name!"

829 Smiling on her, the creator of men and things replied: "True sister of Jove art thou, and Saturn's other child, such waves of wrath surge deep within thy breast! But come, allay the rage thus vainly stirred: I grant thy wish, and yield me, conquered and content. Ausonia's sons shall keep their fathers' speech and ways, and as it is, so shall be their name: the Teucrians shall but sink down, merged in the mass. Their sacred laws and rites will I add and make all to be Latins of one tongue. Hence shall arise a race, blended with Ausonian blood, which thou shalt see o'erpass men, o'erpass gods in godliness, nor shall any nation with equal zeal celebrate thy worship." Juno assented thereto, and joyfully changed her purpose; meanwhile she passes from heaven, and quits the cloud.

843 This done, the Father revolves another purpose in his heart, and prepares to withdraw Juturna from her brother's side. Men tell of twin fiends, the Dread Ones named, whom with hellish Megaera untimely Night bore in one and the same birth, wreathing them alike with snaky coils and clothing them with wings of wind. These attend by the throne of Jove, and on the threshold of the grim monarch, and whet the fears of feeble mortals, whene'er heaven's king deals diseases and awful death, or affrights guilty towns with war. One of these Jove sent swiftly down from high heaven, and bade her meet Juturna as a sign. She wings her way, and darts to earth in swift whirlwind. Even

VIRGIL

non secus ac nervo per nubem impulsa sagitta,
armatam saevi Parthus quam felle veneni,
Parthus sive Cydon, telum immedicabile, torsit,
stridens et celeris incognita transilit umbras:
talis se sata Nocte tulit terrasque petivit. 860
postquam acies videt Iliacas atque agmina Turni,
alitis in parvae subitam collecta figuram,
quae quondam in bustis aut culminibus desertis
nocte sedens serum canit importuna per umbras;
hanc versa in faciem Turni se pestis ob ora 865
fertque refertque sonans clipeumque everberat alis.
illi membra novus solvit formidine torpor,
arrectaeque horrore comae et vox faucibus haesit.

At, procul ut Dirae stridorem adgnovit et alas,
infelix crinis scindit Iuturna solutos, 870
unguibus ora soror foedans et pectora pugnis:
"quid nunc te tua, Turne, potest germana iuvare?
aut quid iam durae superat mihi? qua tibi lucem
arte morer? talin possum me opponere monstro?
iam iam linquo acies. ne me terrete timentem, 875
obscenae volucres: alarum verbera nosco
letalemque sonum, nec fallunt iussa superba
magnanimi Iovis. haec pro virginitate reponit?
quo vitam dedit aeternam? cur mortis adempta est
condicio? possem tantos finire dolores 880
nunc certe, et misero fratri comes ire per umbras!
immortalis ego? aut quicquam mihi dulce meorum
te sine, frater, erit? o quae satis ima dehiscat

<small>
862 subito Pγ¹.　conversa M : coniecta Pγ¹.
865 ob] inob M¹ : in M² : ad Pγ.
870 scindit crinis R.　　　874 possim R.
883 quam Pγ¹.　ima] iam P¹ : alta c.　dehiscet P¹.
</small>

358

AENEID BOOK XII

as an arrow, shot from string through a cloud, which, armed with gall of fell poison, a Parthian— a Parthian or a Cydonian—has launched, a shaft beyond all cure; whizzing, it leaps through the swift shadows, known of none: so sped the child of Night, and sought the earth. Soon as she sees the Ilian ranks and Turnus' troops, suddenly shrinking to the shape of that small bird which oft, perched at night on tombs or deserted roofs, chants her late, ill-omened lay amid the shadows, so changed in form before the face of Turnus the fiend flits screaming to and fro, and wildly beats his buckler with her wings. A strange numbness unknits his limbs with dread; his hair stood up in terror and the voice clave to his throat.

[869] But when from afar Juturna knew the Dread One's whizzing wings, she rends, hapless one, her loosened tresses, marring, in sisterly grief, her face with nails and her breast with clenched hands: "What now, my Turnus, can thy sister avail thee? Or what more awaits me, that have endured so much? With what art may I prolong thy day? Can I face such a portent? Now, now I quit the field. Affright not my fluttering soul, ye ill-boding birds! I know your beating wings, and their dreadful sound, nor fail I to mark the haughty mandates of high-hearted Jove. Is this his requital for my maidenhood? Wherefore gave he me life eternal? Why of the law of death am I bereaved? Now surely could I end such anguish, and pass at my poor brother's side amid the shadows! I immortal! Nay, will aught of mine be sweet to me without thee, my brother? O what deepest earth can gape enough

VIRGIL

terra mihi Manisque deam demittat ad imos?"
tantum effata caput glauco contexit amictu, 885
multa gemens, et se fluvio dea condidit alto.
　Aeneas instat contra telumque coruscat
ingens arboreum et saevo sic pectore fatur:
"quae nunc deinde mora est? aut quid iam, Turne, retractas?
non cursu, saevis certandum est comminus armis. 890
verte omnis tete in facies et contrahe, quidquid
sive animis sive arte vales; opta ardua pinnis
astra sequi clausumque cava te condere terra."
ille caput quassans "non me tua fervida terrent
dicta, ferox: di me terrent et Iuppiter hostis." 895
nec plura effatus saxum circumspicit ingens,
saxum antiquum, ingens, campo quod forte iacebat,
limes agro positus, litem ut discerneret arvis;
vix illud lecti bis sex cervice subirent,
qualia nunc hominum producit corpora tellus: 900
ille manu raptum trepida torquebat in hostem,
altior insurgens et cursu concitus heros.
sed neque currentem se nec cognoscit euntem
tollentemve manus saxumve immane moventem;
genua labant, gelidus concrevit frigore sanguis. 905
tum lapis ipse viri, vacuum per inane volutus,
nec spatium evasit totum neque pertulit ictum.
ac velut in somnis, oculos ubi languida pressit
nocte quies, nequiquam avidos extendere cursus
velle videmur et in mediis conatibus aegri 910
succidimus; non lingua valet, non corpore notae
sufficiunt vires, nec vox aut verba sequuntur:
sic Turno, quacumque viam virtute petivit,

⁸⁸⁴ demittit *P*¹.
⁸⁹³ clausumque *MRγ*: clausumve *P*.
⁸⁹⁹ illum *Mb*.
⁹⁰⁴ tollentemque *Mγ*¹. *So Sabb.* manu *Pγ*². saxumque *γc*.
⁹¹³ quamcumque *P*¹.

360

AENEID BOOK XII

for me, and send me down, a goddess, to the nethermost shades?" So saying, she veiled her head in mantle of grey and with many a moan the goddess plunged into the deep river.

⁸⁸⁷ Aeneas presses on against the foe, brandishing his massy, tree-like spear, and, in wrathful spirit, thus cries: "What more delay is there now? or why, Turnus, dost thou yet draw back? Not with swift foot, but hand to hand in fierce arms, must we contend. Change thyself into all shapes, yea, muster all thy powers of courage or of skill; wing thy flight, if thou wilt, to the stars aloft, or hide thee within earth's hollow prison!" The other, shaking his head: "Thy fiery words, proud one, daunt me not; 'tis the gods daunt me, and the enmity of Jove." No more he speaks, then glancing round, espies a giant stone, a giant stone and ancient, which haply lay upon the plain, set for a landmark, to ward dispute from the fields. This scarce twice six chosen men could uplift upon their shoulders, men of such frames as earth now begets: but the hero, with hurried grasp, seized and hurled it at his foe, rising to his height and at swiftest speed. But he knows not himself as he runs, nor as he moves, as he raises his hands, or throws the mighty stone; his knees totter, his blood is frozen cold. Yea, the hero's stone itself, whirled through the empty void, traversed not all the space, nor carried home its blow. And as in dreams of night, when languorous sleep has weighed down our eyes, we seem to strive vainly to press on our eager course, and in mid effort sink helpless: our tongue lacks power, our wonted strength fails our limbs, nor voice nor words ensue: so to Turnus, howsoe'er by valour he sought to win his

VIRGIL

successum dea dira negat.   tum pectore sensus
vertuntur varii; Rutulos aspectat et urbem   915
cunctaturque metu telumque instare tremescit,
nec quo se eripiat, nec qua vi tendat in hostem,
nec currus usquam videt aurigamve sororem.

Cunctanti telum Aeneas fatale coruscat,
sortitus fortunam oculis, et corpore toto   920
eminus intorquet.   murali concita numquam
tormento sic saxa fremunt, nec fulmine tanti
dissultant crepitus.   volat atri turbinis instar
exitium dirum hasta ferens orasque recludit
loricae et clipei extremos septemplicis orbis.   925
per medium stridens transit femur.   incidit ictus
ingens ad terram duplicato poplite Turnus.
consurgunt gemitu Rutuli totusque remugit
mons circum et vocem late nemora alta remittunt.
ille humilis supplexque oculos dextramque pre-
   cantem   930
protendens "equidem merui, nec deprecor," inquit:
"utere sorte tua.   miseri te si qua parentis
tangere cura potest, oro (fuit et tibi talis
Anchises genitor), Dauni miserere senectae
et me, seu corpus spoliatum lumine mavis,   935
redde meis.   vicisti et victum tendere palmas
Ausonii videre; tua est Lavinia coniunx:
ulterius ne tende odiis."   stetit acer in armis
Aeneas, volvens oculos, dextramque repressit; MP
et iam iamque magis cunctantem flectere sermo   940
coeperat, infelix umero cum apparuit alto
balteus et notis fulserunt cingula bullis

⁹¹⁶ letumque *P*.   ⁹¹⁸ -ve] -que *Rγ*.
⁹²² tanto *P*.   ⁹³⁰ supplex oculos *PRγ²*.

AENEID BOOK XII

way, the dread goddess denies fulfilment. Then through his soul shifting fancies whirl; he gazes on his Rutulians and the town, he falters in fear, and trembles at the threatening lance; neither sees he whither he may escape, nor with what force bear against the foe; nor anywhere is his car, nor his sister, the charioteer.

⁹¹⁹ As he wavers, Aeneas brandishes the fateful spear, seeking with his eyes the happy chance, then hurls it from far with all his strength. Never stone shot from engine of siege roars so loud, never crash so great bursts from thunderbolt. Like black whirlwind on flies the spear, bearing fell destruction, and pierces the corslet's rim and the sevenfold shield's utmost circle: whizzing it passes right through the thigh. Under the blow, with knee beneath him bent down to earth, huge Turnus sank. Up spring with a groan the Rutulians all; the whole hill re-echoes round about, and far and near the wooded steeps send back the sound. He, in lowly suppliance, uplifting eyes and pleading hands: "Yea, I have earned it," he cries, "and I ask not mercy; use thou thy chance. If any thought of a parent's grief can touch thee, I pray thee—in Anchises thou, too, hadst such a father—pity Daunus' old age, and give back me, or, if so thou please, my lifeless body, to my kin. Victor thou art; and as vanquished, have the Ausonians seen me stretch forth my hands: Lavinia is thine for wife; press not thy hatred further."

⁹³⁸ Fierce in his arms, Aeneas stood with rolling eyes, and stayed his hand; and now more and more, as he paused, these words began to sway him, when lo! high on the shoulder was seen the luckless baldric, and there flashed the belt with its well-

VIRGIL

Pallantis pueri, victum quem volnere Turnus
straverat atque umeris inimicum insigne gerebat.
ille, oculis postquam saevi monumenta doloris   945
exuviasque hausit, furiis accensus et ira
terribilis: "tune hinc spoliis indute meorum
eripiare mihi? Pallas te hoc volnere, Pallas
immolat et poenam scelerato ex sanguine sumit,"
hoc dicens ferrum adverso sub pectore condit   950
fervidus.   ast illi solvuntur frigore membra
vitaque cum gemitu fugit indignata sub umbras.

₉₆₈ *cf.* XI. 831.

AENEID BOOK XII

known studs—belt of young Pallas, whom Turnus had smitten and stretched vanquished on earth, and now wore on his shoulders his foeman's fatal badge.[1] The other, soon as his eyes drank in the trophy, that memorial of cruel grief, fired with fury and terrible in his wrath: "Art thou, thou clad in my loved one's spoils, to be snatched hence from my hands? 'Tis Pallas, Pallas who with this stroke sacrifices thee, and takes atonement of thy guilty blood!" So saying, full in his breast he buries the sword with fiery zeal. But the other's limbs grew slack and chill, and with a moan life passed indignant to the Shades below.

[1] *cf. Aen.* x. 496 ff. There seems to be a double meaning in *inimicum*.

THE MINOR POEMS

THE MINOR POEMS

THE poems of the Virgilian Appendix are found in none of the great Virgilian Codices, and the text of numerous passages is therefore very uncertain. For an account of the MSS. of these poems, one must consult Ribbeck's *Virgil*, vol. iv. (Leipzig, 1868); Ellis, *Appendix Vergiliana* (Oxford, 1907); and Vollmer, *Poetae Latini Minores*, vol. i. (Leipzig, 1910). Only the more noteworthy variants are here given.

Among the many other important works bearing on these poems are the following: Heyne-Lemaire's *Virgil*, vol. v. (Paris, 1820); Forbiger's *Virgil*, vol. iii. (Leipzig, 1875); Benoist's *Virgil*, vol. ii. (Paris, 1880); Ellis, "On some Disputed Passages of the *Ciris*," and "Further Notes on the *Ciris* and other Poems of the *Appendix Vergiliana*," in *American Journal of Philology*, viii. (1887); Rothstein, "De Diris et Lydia Carminibus," in *Rheinisches Museum*, xxiii. (1888); Leo's *Culex* (Berlin, 1891); Vollmer, "Coniectanea," in *Rheinisches Museum*, lv. (1900); Curcio, *Poeti Latini Minori*, vol. ii. (Catania, 1905); Linforth, "Notes on the Pseudo-Virgilian *Ciris*," in *American Journal of Philology*, xxvii. (1906); Sudhaus, "Die Klage der *Ciris*," in *Rheinisches Museum*, lx. (1906); Housman, "The Apparatus Criticus of the *Culex*," in *Transactions of the Cambridge Philological Society*, vol. vi., part i. (1908);

THE MINOR POEMS

Keppler, *Ueber Copa* (Leipzig, 1908); Plésent, *Le Culex* (Paris, 1910); Skutsch, *Aus Vergils Frühzeit* (Leipzig, 1901, '06); Birt, *Jugendverse und Heimatpoesie Vergils* (Leipzig, 1910); Phillimore, "The Text of the *Culex*," in *Classical Philology*, vol. v. (1910). Professor Phillimore is one of three English scholars who have upheld the genuineness of the *Culex* as an early work of Virgil, the other two being S. Elizabeth Jackson (*Classical Quarterly*, 1911, pp. 163 ff.) and W. Warde Fowler (*Classical Review*, 1914, pp. 119 ff.). See also D. L. Drew's *Culex* (Oxford, 1925).

Impressed by the apparent force of the external evidence, J. W. Mackail is inclined to think that the *Culex* may have been written by Virgil as an exercise, and thus set aside before the poet had "put the vitalising Virgilianising touches to it," which the *Moretum*, for example, exhibits. As to the *Ciris*, he agrees with Skutsch that this was wholly or mainly the work of Gallus, not of Virgil, while the *Dirae* and *Lydia* were composed by a third poet of the Virgilian circle. He finds nothing Virgilian in the *Copa* or the *Catalepton*, though the three Catullan *Priapea* possess "no small measure of grace and charm." (J. W. Mackail, "Virgil and Virgilianism," in his *Lectures on Poetry*, London, 1911.) See also Appendix, pp. 523 ff.

CULEX*

Lusimus, Octavi, gracili modulante Thalia
atque ut araneoli tenuem formavimus orsum.
lusimus: haec propter Culicis sint carmina dicta,
omnis ut historiae per ludum consonet ordo
notitiae. doctrina, vaces licet: invidus absit.   5
quisquis erit culpare iocos Musamque paratus,
pondere vel Culicis levior famaque feretur.
posterius graviore sono tibi Musa loquetur
nostra, dabunt cum securos mihi tempora fructus,
ut tibi digna tuo poliantur carmina sensu.   10

³ dicta *V*: docta Ω.   ⁴ ut *It.*: et.
⁵ notitiaeque ducum voces Ω, *Leo, Vollmer*: ductum *Vat.*
1586 : notitiae, doctumque voces *Ellis*. *The readings and
interpretation adopted are Phillimore's, but must be regarded
as merely an approximation to the original verse, which
cannot be recovered.*
⁷ feratur *Scaliger*.   ¹⁰ digna tuo *Bembo*: dignato Ω.

---

* The principal MSS. containing the *Culex*, as given by Vollmer, are the following:—

S = fragmentum Stabulense, Paris, 17177, of the 10th century.

F = Fiechtianus, or Mellicensis (designated as *M* by Ellis), of the 10th century.

C = Cantabrigiensis, Kk. v. 34, of the 10th century.

V = Vaticanus 2759, of the 13th century.

Γ = Corsinianus 43 F 5, of the 14th century.

L = a group of MSS. of the so-called *ludus iuvenalis* of Virgil, designated as *W, B, E, A, T*, from the 9th to the 11th century.

570

CULEX

We have trifled, O Octavius,[1] while a slender Muse marked the measure, and lo! like tiny spiders, have fashioned our thin-spun task. We have trifled: to this end let our Gnat's song be sung, that in sportive mood throughout its course our argument may harmonize with epic story. A truce to thee, O Art; let Envy begone! Whoso is ready to blame our jests and Muse, shall be deemed lighter than even our Gnat in weight and name. Hereafter shall our Muse speak to thee in deeper tones, when the seasons yield me their fruits in peace, that so thou mayest find her verses polished, and worthy of thy taste.

---

[1] The later Augustus, who is still a *puer* (vv. 26, 37) when thus addressed. The young Octavius assumed the *toga virilis* in his fifteenth year, in 48 B.C., before which event this dedication, if genuine, must have been written. Inasmuch, however, as the poem, in our opinion, is certainly non-Virgilian, we must assume that the writer is simulating Virgilian authorship.

Exc. = selections, in certain MSS. of the 12th to 14th centuries, found in an anthology of the 11th century.

As a group, the above-named MSS. are designated as Ω.

To these Ellis adds some MSS., *e.g.* b = Mus. Brit. Add. 16562, written in 1400, and Vat(icanus) 1586, of the 14th or 15th century. Occasional references must be made to late MSS. which were emended by Italian scholars of the Renaissance. As a group, these are designated as *It*. The most notable among them is the Helmstadiensis 332, of the 15th century, designated as *H*.

VIRGIL

Latonae magnique Iovis decus, aurea proles,
Phoebus erit nostri princeps et carminis auctor
et recinente lyra fautor, sive educat illum
Arna Chimaereo Xanthi perfusa liquore,
seu decus Asteriae seu qua Parnasia rupes   15
hinc atque hinc patula praepandit cornua fronte,
Castaliaeque sonans liquido pede labitur unda.
quare, Pierii laticis decus, ite, sorores
Naides, et celebrate deum ludente chorea.
et tu, sancta Pales, ad quam ventura recurrunt   20
agrestum bona fetura—sit cura tenentis
aerios nemorum cultus silvasque virentis :
te cultrice vagus saltus feror inter et antra.

Et tu, cui meritis oritur fiducia chartis,
Octavi venerande, meis adlabere coeptis,   25
sancte puer : tibi namque canit non pagina bellum
triste Iovis ponitque . . . .
Phlegra, Giganteo sparsa est quae sanguine tellus,
nec Centaureos Lapithas compellit in ensis,
urit Erichthonias Oriens non ignibus arces ;   30
non perfossus Athos nec magno vincula ponto
iacta meo quaerent iam sera volumine famam,
non Hellespontus pedibus pulsatus equorum,
Graecia cum timuit venientis undique Persas :

[19] plaudente *Bembo, Ellis.*
[20] ventura] tutela *Phillimore.* recurrit Ω.
[21] agrestum bona secura *FCL* : ag. bona sis : tecum *Phillimore.*   [24] chartis] tantis *Phillimore.*
[27] <acies quibus horruit olim> *conjectured by Bücheler.*

---

[1] *i.e.* Delos.
[2] Far below the real summit of Parnassus, the rocky cliffs that tower above Delphi present two peaks, between which, in a deep chasm, flows the Castalian stream.   [3] The Muses.

CULEX

¹¹ The glory of Latona and mighty Jove, their golden offspring, even Phoebus, shall be the fount and source of our song, and he with resounding harp shall inspire, whether Arna nurture him—Arna, steeped in the Chimaera's stream of Xanthus—or the glory of Asteria,¹ or that land where Parnassus' ridge, with broad brow, spreads his horns this way and that, and Castalia's singing waves glide in their watery course.² Wherefore, come, ye sister Naiads,³ glory of the Pierian spring, and throng about the god in sportive dance. Thou too, holy Pales, to whom, as they appear, the blessings of husbandmen return with increase, be thine the care of him who keeps the lofty forest-homes and woodlands green; whilst thou dost tend them, freely I roam among the glades and caves.

²⁴ Thou also, O Octavius revered,⁴ who by the writings thou hast earned winnest confidence, graciously attend my venture, O holy youth! For thee, indeed, my page sings not Jove's gloomy war,⁵ nor plants the lines wherewith Phlegra once bristled, the land that was sprinkled with the Giants' blood, nor drives the Lapiths upon the Centaurs' swords; the East burns not the Erichthonian towers⁶ with flames: 'tis not the piercing of Athos, not the casting of fetters upon the mighty deep, not the Hellespont, smitten with horses' hooves, what time Greece feared the Persians, as they streamed from every side, that at this late hour shall, through my book, seek fame:

⁴ The epithets *venerande* and *sanctus* are suggested by the youth and innocence of the boy, "who wore the same toga as priests and magistrates" (Professor Warde Fowler).

⁵ The battle between Jupiter and the Giants, fought in Phlegra.

⁶ *i.e.* Athens, burnt by the Persians, of which Erichthonius was one of the early kings; *cf. Georgics*, III. 113.

VIRGIL

mollia sed tenui pede currere carmina, versu   35
viribus apta suis Phoebo duce ludere gaudet.
hoc tibi, sancte puer: memorabilis et tibi certet
gloria perpetuum lucens, mansura per aevum,
et tibi sede pia maneat locus, et tibi sospes
debita felicis memoretur vita per annos,   40
grata bonis lucens.   sed nos ad coepta feramur.
    Igneus aetherias iam Sol penetrarat in arces,
candidaque aurato quatiebat lumina curru,
crinibus et roseis tenebras Aurora fugarat:
propulit e stabulis ad pabula laeta capellas   45
pastor et excelsi montis iuga summa petivit,
lurida qua patulos velabant gramina collis.
iam silvis dumisque vagae, iam vallibus abdunt
corpora, iamque omni celeres e parte vagantes
tondebant tenero viridantia gramina morsu.   50
scrupea desertis errabant ad cava ripis
pendula proiectis carpuntur et arbuta ramis
densaque virgultis avide labrusca petuntur;
haec suspensa rapit carpente cacumina morsu
vel salicis lentae vel quae nova nascitur alnus,   55
haec teneras fruticum sentis rimatur, at illa
imminet in rivi, praestantis imaginis, undam.
    O bona pastoris (si quis non pauperis usum
mente prius docta fastidiat et probet illis
somnia luxuriae spretis), incognita curis,   60
quae lacerant avidas inimico pectore mentes!

---

³⁶ apta] acta *Ellis, after a Paris MS.*, 8207.
⁴⁰ numeretur *Sillig.*
⁴² penetrabat, *Leo, Vollmer.*   ⁴⁵ laeta] nota *Thilo.*
⁴⁷ rorida *Haupt:* florida *Jacobs, Ellis.*
⁵⁰ tenerae ... myrtus *Phillimore.*
⁵¹ desertas (-is) herebant Ω.   ripis *Ellis:* rupes *or* rupis Ω.
⁵⁷ prostantis imaginis umbram *Ellis.*
⁶⁰ somnia *Haupt, Ellis:* otia *Phillimore:* omnia Ω.   spretis
V: pretiis.   ⁶¹ inim. p.] nimia cuppedine *Ellis.*

CULEX

but 'tis her joy that her gentle songs run with slender foot, and sport, under Phoebus' guidance, as befits her strength. This she sings for thee, holy youth; for thee also may ennobling fame be zealous, shining for all time, and abiding throughout the ages; for thee also may a place be stablished in the blest abode, and as thy due may there be recorded a life preserved through happy years, shining for the joy of the good! But let me pass to my emprise.

[42] The fiery sun had now made his way unto heaven's heights,[1] and from gilded car was scattering his gleaming rays, and Dawn with roseate locks had routed darkness, when a shepherd drove forth his goats from their folds to the joyous pastures, and sought a lofty mountain's highest ridges, where pale grasses clothed the spreading slopes. As they roam, they hide themselves now in the woods and thickets, now in the vales, and now, wandering swiftly to and fro, they cropped the rich grasses with nibbling bite. Leaving the banks, they strayed toward rocky hollows, the o'erhanging arbute trees are shorn of their outstretching branches and the wild vines' thick shoots are greedily assailed. One, poised aloft, snatches with eager bite the tips, it may be of the pliant willow, or of fresh growing alder; this gropes amid the thickets' tender briars, while that hangs over the water of the stream, its wondrous mirror.

[58] O the blessings of the shepherd[2]—if one would not, with mind already schooled, disdain the poor man's ways, and in scorn of them give approval to dreams of wealth—blessings those cares know not, that rend greedy hearts within

---

[1] *i.e.* from the lower world. The time is early morn, not midday.

[2] *cf. Georgics*, II. 458 ff.

VIRGIL

si non Assyrio fuerint bis lauta colore
Attalicis opibus data vellera, si nitor auri
sub laqueare domus animum non tangit avarum
picturaeque decus, lapidum nec fulgor in ulla 65
cognitus utilitate manet, nec pocula gratum
Alconis referunt Boethique toreuma nec Indi
conchea baca maris pretio est: at pectore puro
saepe super tenero prosternit gramine corpus,
florida cum tellus, gemmantis picta per herbas 70
vere notat dulci distincta coloribus arva;
atque illum, calamo laetum recinente palustri
otiaque invidia degentem et fraude remota
pollentemque sibi, viridi iam palmite lucens
Tmolia pampineo subter coma velat amictu. 75
illi sunt gratae rorantes lacte capellae
et nemus et fecunda Pales et vallibus intus
semper opaca novis manantia fontibus antra.

Quis magis optato queat esse beatior aevo,
quam qui mente procul pura sensuque probando 80
non avidas agnovit opes nec tristia bella
nec funesta timet validae certamina classis
nec, spoliis dum sancta deum fulgentibus ornet
templa vel evectus finem transcendat habendi,
adversum saevis ultro caput hostibus offert? 85
illi falce deus colitur, non arte politus,
ille colit lucos, illi Panchaia tura
floribus agrestes herbae variantibus addunt;

[62] fuerint] feriunt *Phillimore:* fervent *Ellis.*
[64] tangit *W:* angit *Exc. Ellis:* anget *Bücheler.*
[66] gratum] Graium *Heinsius.*
[67] referent *CV*Γ.   Boethi] Rhoeci *Lachmann.*
[71] dulci *Exc. H:* dulcis Ω: dubiis *V*².
[88] addunt Γ, *Ellis:* adsunt Ω.

CULEX

warring breasts! What though fleeces, twice dipped in Assyrian dye, be not bought for wealth of Attalus, though gleam of gold beneath the fretted ceiling of a house, and brilliancy of painting, move not a greedy soul, though flashing gems be never deemed to have aught of worth, though goblets of Alcon and reliefs of Boëthus bring no joy,[1] and the Indian Ocean's pearls be of no esteem; yet, with heart free from guile, upon the soft sward he oft outstretches his frame, while blossoming earth, painted with jewelled grasses, in sweet spring marks the fields, picked out with varied hues; and lo! as he delights in the mere's resounding reeds, and takes his ease apart from envy and deceit, and is strong in his own strength, the leafage of Tmolus and the sheen of green boughs enwraps him beneath a cloak of vines. His are pleasing goats that drip their milky dew, his the woodland and fruitful Pales, and, deep within the vales, shaded grottoes ever trickling with fresh springs.

[79] Who in a happier age could be more blest than he who, dwelling afar, with pure soul and feelings well tested knows not the greed of wealth, and fears not grim wars or the fatal conflicts of a mighty fleet, nor yet, if so he may but adorn the gods' holy temples with gleaming spoils, or high uplifted may surpass the limits of wealth, wilfully risks his life, confronting savage foes? He reverences a god shaped by pruning-knife, not by artist's skill; he reverences the groves; for him the grasses of the field, mottled with flowers, yield Panchaean incense;[2]

---

[1] An Alcon is mentioned in *E.* v. 11. Like Boëthus, who is referred to by Pliny (*N.H.* XXXIII. 12, 55), he was probably a sculptor or engraver in metals.

[2] *cf. Georgics*, II. 139.

VIRGIL

illi dulcis adest requies et pura voluptas,
libera, simplicibus curis; huc imminet, omnis   90
derigit huc sensus, haec cura est subdita cordi,
quolibet ut requie victu contentus abundet,
iucundoque liget languentia corpora somno.
o pecudes, o Panes et o gratissima Tempe
fontis Hamadryadum, quarum non divite cultu   95
aemulus Ascraeo pastor sibi quisque poetae
securam placido traducit pectore vitam!

Talibus in studiis baculo dum nixus apricas
pastor agit curas et dum non arte canora
compacta solitum modulatur harundine carmen,   100
tendit inevectus radios Hyperionis ardor,
lucidaque aetherio ponit discrimina mundo,
qua iacit Oceanum flammas in utrumque rapacis.
et iam compellente vagae pastore capellae
ima susurrantis repetebant ad vada lymphae,   105
quae subter viridem residebant caerula muscum.
iam medias operum partis evectus erat Sol,
cum densas pastor pecudes cogebat in umbras.
ut procul aspexit luco residere virenti,
Delia diva, tuo, quo quondam victa furore   110
venit Nyctelium fugiens Cadmeis Agaue,
infandas scelerata manus e caede cruenta—
quae gelidis bacchata iugis requievit in antro,
posterius poenam nati de morte datura.
hic etiam viridi ludentes Panes in herba   115

---

⁹² ut requiem victus *CL*.
⁹³ liget *V*: licet Ω: levet *Exc*.   ⁹⁵ frondis *Heinsius*.
⁹⁶ pastori quisque *V*, *Ellis*. poetae *H*: poeta Ω.
¹⁰⁰ solitum *It*: solidum Ω.
¹¹⁴ datura *Aldine* 1534; futuram *CL*: futurum Γ*V*.

378

CULEX

his are sweet repose and unsullied pleasure, free, with simple cares. This is his goal, toward this he directs every sense; this is the thought lurking within his heart, that, content with any fare, he may be rich in repose, and in pleasant sleep may enchain his weary frame. O flocks, O Pans, O vales of Hamadryads, delightful in your springs, in whose humble worship the shepherds, vying each for himself with the bard of Ascra,[1] spend with tranquil hearts a care-free life.

[98] Amid such joys, while leaning on his staff the shepherd cons his sunny themes, and while, with no artful melody, on his joined reeds he attunes the wonted lay, burning Hyperion, mounting aloft, extends his rays, and, parting midway heaven's vault, there plants his light where into either Ocean he flings his ravenous flames. And now, driven by the shepherd, the straying goats were wending back to the pools of whispering water, which settled dark beneath the verdant moss. Now had the Sun ridden o'er the mid portion of his course, when the shepherd began to gather his flocks within the thick shade. Then[2] from a distance he saw them settle in thy green grove, O Delian goddess, whither once, smitten with madness, came Cadmus' daughter, Agave, flying from Nyctelius,[3] her cursed hands defiled with blood of slaughter—Agave, who once had revelled on the cold heights, then rested in the cave, doomed at later day for her son's death to pay penance. Here, too, Pans sporting upon the green

[1] Hesiod; *cf. Eclogues*, VI. 70; *Georgics*, II. 176.
[2] The Latin sentence has no grammatical conclusion; "then" is a substitute for "when."
[3] *i.e.* Bacchus. On recovering her senses, Agave conceived a horror of Bacchus, the god whose rites she was celebrating when she slew Pentheus.

VIRGIL

et Satyri Dryadesque chorus egere puellae
Naiadum coetu: tantum non Orpheus Hebrum
restantem tenuit ripis silvasque canendo,
quantum te, pernix, remorantur, diva, chorea
multa tuo laetae fundentes gaudia voltu,   120
ipsa loci natura domum, resonante susurro,
quis dabat et dulci fessas refovebat in umbra.

Nam primum prona surgebant valle patentes
aeriae platanus, inter quas impia lotos,
impia, quae socios Ithaci maerentis abegit,   125
hospita dum nimia tenuit dulcedine captos.
at quibus insigni curru proiectus equorum
ambustus Phaethon luctu mutaverat artus,
Heliades, teneris implexae bracchia truncis,
candida fundebant tentis velamina ramis.   130
posterius, cui Demophoon aeterna reliquit
perfidiam lamentanti mala: perfide multis,
perfide, Demophoon, et nunc dicende puellis!
quam comitabantur, fatalia carmina, quercus,
quercus ante datae Cereris quam semina vitae: 135
illas Triptolemi mutavit sulcus aristis.
hic magnum Argoae navi decus edita pinus
proceros decorat silvas hirsuta per artus,
ac petit aeriis contingere montibus astra.

[116] chorus (χορούς) Γ′L.
[119] pernigre morantem Ω: pernice morantur Ellis.
[124] platanus Γ: platani VWAT.
[129] implexae Heinsius: amplexae Ω.
[132] lamentanti Weber, Ellis: lamentandi MSS. perfide V²: perfida Ω.
[133] dicende Leo: deflende Scaliger: defende.
[137] addita VΓ, Vollmer.
[139] ac petit Heinsius, Ellis: appetit Ω. motibus Scaliger.

380

CULEX

grass, and Satyrs, and Dryad maids with the Naiad
throng, once trod their dances. Not so much did
Orpheus with his song stay Hebrus, lingering within
his banks, or stay the woods, as much as with their
dance they keep thee tarrying, O fleet goddess,
gladly shedding many joys upon thy countenance—
even they, to whom, of its very nature, the place
with its echoing whisper gave a home, refreshing
their weary forms in its sweet shade.

[123] For first, in the sloping vale, there arose spreading planes, towering high, and among them the
wicked lotus—wicked for that she seduced the comrades of the sorrowing Ithacan, while she welcomed
and held them captive with undue charm.[1] Then
they, whose limbs Phaëthon, hurled forth in flames
from the resplendent car of the Sun's steeds, had
through grief transformed,—the Heliads,[2] their arms
entwining the slender stems—from outstretched
branches lavished their white veiling. Next came
she,[3] to whom, lamenting his perfidy, Demophoon
left unending grief—ah! Demophoon, "perfidious"
called of many, even still worthy to be called of
maidens "perfidious"! Oaks attended her, chanters
of the fates[4]—oaks once given for man's sustenance
before the grains of Ceres: these oaks the furrow of
Triptolemus exchanged for ears of corn.[5] Here the
great glory of the Argoan ship,[6] the lofty pine,
shaggy in her stately limbs, adorns the woods, and
on the skyey mountains is fain to reach the stars.

---

[1] cf. Homer, *Odyssey*, IX. 83 ff.

[2] i.e. Phaëthon's sisters, who were turned into poplars.

[3] Phyllis, who at death was changed into an almond-tree.
She died of grief, supposing that Demophoon had deserted her.

[4] Referring to the oracle at Dodona; cf. *Georgics*, I. 8 and
147 ff.

[5] cf. *Georgics*, I. 19.   [6] cf. *Eclogues*, IV. 34 and 38.

VIRGIL

ilicis et nigrae species et fleta cupressus 140
umbrosaeque manent fagus hederaeque ligantes
bracchia, fraternos plangat ne populus ictus,
ipsaeque escendunt ad summa cacumina lentae
pinguntque aureolos viridi pallore corymbos;
quis aderat veteris myrtus non nescia fati. 145
at volucres patulis residentes dulcia ramis
carmina per varios edunt resonantia cantus.
his suberat gelidis manans e fontibus unda,
quae levibus placidum rivis sonat acta liquorem;
et quaqua geminas avium vox obstrepit auris, 150
hac querulae referunt voces, quis nantia limo
corpora lympha fovet; sonitus alit aeris echo,
argutis et cuncta fremunt ardore cicadis.
at circa passim fessae cubuere capellae
excelsis subter dumis, quos leniter adflans 155
aura susurrantis poscit confundere venti.

Pastor, ut ad fontem densa requievit in umbra,
mitem concepit proiectus membra soporem,
anxius insidiis nullis, sed lentus in herbis
securo pressos somno mandaverat artus. 160
stratus humi dulcem capiebat corde quietem,
ni Fors incertos iussisset ducere casus.
nam solitum volvens ad tempus tractibus isdem
immanis vario maculatus corpore serpens,
mersus ut in limo magno subsideret aestu, 165
obvia vibranti carpens, gravis aere, lingua,
squamosos late torquebat motibus orbis:

¹⁴⁰ et fleta *Ellis*: et leta Ω.   ¹⁴¹ monent *Sillig*.
¹⁴³ escendunt *Heyne*: accedunt Γ: excedunt *VCL*.
¹⁴⁹ liquorum *Haupt, Leo*.   ¹⁵⁰ quaqua *Barth*: quamquam.
¹⁵⁵ subter *Heyne*: super: supra Γ.
¹⁶⁵ subsideret *Bembo*: sub sideris: *Ellis thinks a verse has been lost.*
¹⁶⁷ montibus *VΓL*.

CULEX

Still stand the shapely black ilex, the cypress of grief, shadowy beeches, and ivies binding the poplar's arms, lest, for her brother's sake,[1] she smite herself with blows: themselves, fast clinging, mount to the very tops, and paint their golden clusters with pale green. Hard by these was the myrtle, not unknowing of her fate of old.[2] The birds, the while, settling on the spreading branches, sing songs resounding in varied melodies. Beneath was water trickling from cold springs, which, wending in fine rills, murmurs in its peaceful current; and where'er voice of birds strikes upon twin ears, there in querulous tone respond the frogs, whose bodies, afloat in the mire, are nurtured by its moisture. The echoing air swells the sounds, and amid the heat all nature is humming with the shrill cicadas. Here and there, round about, lay the weary goats beneath the lofty thickets, which a breath of whispering wind, gently blowing thither, essays to disturb.

[157] Soon as by the spring amid the deep shade the shepherd sought repose with limbs outstretched, he fell upon a gentle sleep; troubled by no treachery, but lying at ease upon the grass, he had consigned his o'erpowered frame to care-free slumber. Prone upon the ground, he was enjoying to the full sweet restfulness—had not Fortune bade him draw uncertain lots!

[163] For, gliding along at his wonted time in the self-same course, a monstrous serpent, speckled and mottled in body, with intent to plunge in the mire and seek shelter from the exceeding heat,—noisome of breath, and snatching with darting tongue at all in his way—in far-circling movements was twisting

---

[1] *i.e.* for Phaëthon's sake.
[2] Myrsine, priestess of Venus, was changed into a myrtle.

383

VIRGIL

tollebant irae venientis ad omnia visus.
iam magis atque magis corpus revolubile volvens
attollit nitidis pectus fulgoribus, effert   170
sublimi cervice caput, cui crista superne
edita, purpureo lucens maculatur amictu,
aspectuque micant flammarum lumina torvo.
metabat sese circum loca, cum videt ingens
adversum recubare ducem gregis. acrior instat   175
lumina diffundens intendere et obvia torvus
saepius arripiens infringere, quod sua quisquam
ad vada venisset. naturae comparat arma:
ardet mente, furit stridoribus, insonat ore,
flexibus eversis torquentur corporis orbes,   180
manant sanguineae per tractus undique guttae,
spiritus erumpit fauces. cui cuncta parantur,
parvulus hunc prior umoris conterret alumnus,
et mortem vitare monet per acumina. namque
qua diducta genas pandebant lumina, gemmans   185
hac senioris erat naturae pupula telo
icta levi, cum prosiluit furibundus et illum
obtritum Morti misit, cui dissitus omnis
spiritus excessit sensus. tum torva tenentem
lumina respexit serpentem comminus; inde   190
impiger, exanimis, vix compos mente refugit,
et validum dextra detraxit ab arbore truncum.
qui casus sociarit opem numenve deorum,
prodere sit dubium, valuit sed vincere talis
horrida squamosi volventia membra draconis,   195

¹⁶⁸ irae *Leo:* herbae *Ribbeck:* acies *Vollmer:* aurae Ω.
¹⁷⁰ effert *Friesemann, Ellis:* ecfert *Ribbeck:* ecce *Leo:* et se Ω.   ¹⁷⁴ ingens] amens *Phillimore.*
¹⁷⁶ torvo Ω: torua Γ.   ¹⁷⁸ computat Γ, *Ellis.*
¹⁷⁹ insonat Γ: intonat.   ¹⁸⁰ torquetur *VCL.*
¹⁸² parantur *Housman:* paranti.
¹⁸⁵ gemmans *Schrader:* gemmas Γ: gemmis Ω.
¹⁸⁶ natura Γ: mature *Bothe, Ellis.*   ¹⁹¹ exanimus.

CULEX

his scaly coils : as on he came, he upraised his eyes in anger to survey the whole scene. Now, rolling more and more his writhing body, he uplifts his breast with gleaming flashes; on his towering neck he rears his head, and his crest rises aloft; his purple coat shines and sparkles, and his blazing eye gleams with savage look. He was surveying the ground round about, when, lying in his way, the monster espied the guardian of the flock. More fiercely he rolls his eyes and presses on in his course, and more often does he seize and crush what lies in his path, infuriate that any man had come to his waters. Nature's weapons he makes ready : he rages in mind, he hisses in wrath; his mouth resounds; his body's coils writhe in upheaving curves; all along his course trickle drops of blood; his breathing bursts his jaws.

[182] Him, against whom all is preparing, a tiny nursling of the damp affrights in time, and warns by its sting to avoid death. For where the eyes were parted and opened their lids, there the old man's jewelled orb was smitten by the light dart Nature had furnished. Thereat, full of rage, he leaped forth, and crushed and slew the Gnat, whose breath, all dispersed, quitted his senses. Then, near at hand, as it fixed its fierce eyes upon him, he espied the serpent; and thereon with speed, dismayed and wellnigh reft of wit, he fled aback, and with his hand tore from a tree a sturdy bough. What chance gave him aid, or what spirit divine, it were hard to tell, but such as he was, he availed to worst the scaly serpent's dreadful writhing limbs, and as it

VIRGIL

atque reluctantis crebris foedeque petentis
ictibus ossa ferit, cingunt qua tempora cristae.
et quod erat tardus somni languore remoti
nec senis aspiciens timor obcaecaverat artus,
hoc minus implicuit dira formidine mentem.   200
quem postquam vidit caesum languescere, sedit.

Iam quatit et biiugis oriens Erebois equos Nox
et piger aurata procedit Vesper ab Oeta,
cum grege compulso pastor, duplicantibus umbris,
vadit et in fessos requiem dare comparat artus.   205
cuius ut intravit levior per corpora somnus
languidaque effuso requierunt membra sopore,
effigies ad eum Culicis devenit et illi
tristis ab eventu cecinit convicia mortis.
"quis," inquit, "meritis ad quae delatus acerbas   210
cogor adire vices? tua dum mihi carior ipsa
vita fuit vita, rapior per inania ventis.
tu lentus refoves iucunda membra quiete,
ereptus taetris e cladibus; at mea Manes
viscera Lethaeas cogunt transnare per undas;   215
praeda Charonis agor, vidi et flagrantia taedis
limina: conlucent infernis omnia templis.
obvia Tisiphone, serpentibus undique compta,
et flammas et saeva quatit mihi verbera.   pone
Cerberus, et diris flagrant latratibus ora,   220
anguibus hinc atque hinc horrent cui colla reflexis,
sanguineique micant ardorem luminis orbes.

---

198 remoti *Vollmer:* remoto.
199 nec senis *Hertzberg:* nescius Ω: nec prius *Sillig.*
200 implevit *V¹.*
210 quis inquit *Heyne:* quid inquit Γ: inquit quid.
212 ventis] Averni *Heinsius.*
216 vidi et Γ: vides (vidi) ut.
217 limina *AT:* lumina.   220 et] en *Ribbeck, Vollmer.*
221 horrent *H:* arent Ω.   222 sanguineaque.

CULEX

struggles and assails in hideous wise, he with frequent strokes smites its bones, where the crest fringes its temples; and in that he was dulled with the drowsiness of the sleep he had shaken off, and fear at sight of his foe had not yet benumbed his aged limbs, he did not so much confuse his mind with direful terror; but, soon as he saw the monster languish in death, he sat him down.

202 Now Night, arising, was urging on her steeds in the two-horse car of Erebus,[1] and slow Vesper was advancing from golden Oeta,[2] when the shepherd, his flock folded, wended his way in the thickening shadows, and prepared to give rest to his weary frame. Soon as gentle sleep passed o'er his body, and his listless limbs, steeped in slumber, sank to rest, there descended upon him the spectre of the Gnat, and sang him reproachful strains by reason of his sad death: "What deserts are mine?" he cries, "and to what ills am I wafted, who am called to face a bitter requital? While thy life was dearer to me than life itself, I am swept by the winds through empty space. Thou, at thine ease, in sweet repose refreshest thy limbs, thou that wast snatched from a hideous death; but my remains the Shades compel to pass o'er Lethe's waters; as Charon's spoil am I driven, and thresholds aflame with brands have I beheld: in those regions below all is ablaze. Tisiphone, her locks wreathed on every side with serpents, besets the way and brandishes before me fires and cruel scourges; behind her is Cerberus, his mouths inflamed with fearful barking, his necks bristling with twisted snakes this way and that, and his eyes flashing the fire of a blood-red light. Alas!

---

[1] Night is sister and wife of Erebus.
[2] *cf. Eclogues*, VIII. 30.

VIRGIL

heu, quid ab officio digressa est gratia, cum te
restitui superis leti iam limine ab ipso?
praemia sunt pietatis ubi, pietatis honores? 225
in vanas abiere vices, et rure recessit
Iustitiae prior illa fides.   instantia vidi
alterius, sine respectu mea fata relinquens
ad parilis agor eventus: fit poena merenti.
poena sit exitium; modo sit tum grata voluntas, 230
exsistat par officium.   feror avia carpens,
avia Cimmerios inter distantia lucos;
quam circa tristes densentur in omnia poenae!
nam vinctus sedet immanis serpentibus Otos,
devinctum maestus procul aspiciens Ephialten, 235
conati quondam cum sint rescindere mundum;
et Tityos, Latona, tuae memor anxius irae
(implacabilis ira nimis) iacet alitis esca.
terreor, a, tantis insistere, terreor, umbris,
ad Stygias revocatus aquas! vix ultimus amni 240
exstat, nectareas divum qui prodidit escas,
gutturis arenti revolutus in omnia sensu.
quid saxum procul adverso qui monte revolvit,
contempsisse dolor quem numina vincit acerbans?
otia quaerentem frustra sinite; ite puellae, 245
ite, quibus taedas accendit tristis Erinys:

---

²²⁶ iure *B*Γ.   ²²⁷ Iustitia et *Schrader*.
²²⁸ relinques? *Phillimore*.
²³³ agmina *Jacobs:* ostia *Ellis*.
²³⁶ rescindere *V:* inscendere Ω.
²³⁷ tuas ... iras Ω (*except V*).
²⁴⁰ ad ... aquas *commonly taken with what follows*.
²⁴⁴ acerbans *V:* acerbas *SL:* -am Γ.
²⁴⁵ sinite, ite *Leo:* siblite: sub lite Γ: sub lite? quid illae *Phillimore*.   ²⁴⁶ accendi *Ellis*.

CULEX

why failed my kindness to win the service due, when even from Death's very threshold, I restored thee to the living? Where is the guerdon of kindness, where kindness' due return? Gone to an empty requital, and that old-time faith in Justice has passed from out the land.[1] I saw the fate which threatened another; mine own I left without regard, and now am driven to a doom like unto his: punishment falls to the deserving. Let the punishment be death; only let there be a grateful heart, let an equal service be rendered!

[231] "I take my way o'er pathless regions—pathless regions far away amid Cimmerian groves, and about me throng the woeful penalties for all misdeeds. For, fast bound with serpents, monstrous Otus sits, mournfully gazing at Ephialtes, enchained hard by, for that once they essayed to tear down heaven[2]; and Tityus in distress, mindful, O Latona, of thy wrath (too insatiate thy wrath!) is lying there, meat for winged fowl.[3] I fear, ah! I fear me to press nigh such mighty shades,—I, called back to the Stygian waters. With head scarce rising above the stream, stands he who betrayed the nectar-feasts of the gods,[4] turning in all directions with fever-stricken throat. What of him, who rolls a stone up the mount afar, whom embittering pain convicts of having scorned the gods?[5] Let me be,—me, vainly seeking repose; go, ye maidens,[6] go ye, for whom gloomy Erinys[7] kindled the torches: in guise of Hymen Erinys spake the

---

[1] cf. Georgics, II. 473 f. [2] cf. Aen. VI. 582.
[3] cf. Aen. VI. 595. [4] Tantalus.
[5] i.e. Sisyphus; cf. Georgics, III. 39.
[6] The Danaids; cf. Aen. X. 497.
[7] cf. Aen. II. 337.

VIRGIL

sicut Hymen praefata dedit conubia Mortis.
atque alias alio densas super agmine turmas:
impietate fera vecordem Colchida matrem,
anxia sollicitis meditantem volnera natis; 250
iam Pandionias miseranda prole puellas,
quarum vox Ityn edit Ityn, quo Bistonius rex
orbus epops maeret volucris evectus in auras.
at discordantes Cadmeo semine fratres
iam truculenta ferunt infestaque lumina corpus 255
alter in alterius, iamque aversatur uterque,
impia germani manat quod sanguine dextra.
eheu, mutandus numquam labor! auferor ultra
in diversa magis, distantia nomina cerno,
Elysiam tranandus agor delatus ad undam. 260
obvia Persephone comites heroidas urget
adversas praeferre faces. Alcestis ab omni
inviolata vacat cura, quod saeva mariti
in Chalcodoniis Admeti fata morata est.
ecce, Ithaci coniunx semper decus, Icariotis, 265
femineum concepta decus, manet et procul illa
turba ferox iuvenum, telis confixa, procorum.
quid, misera Eurydice, tanto maerore recesti
poenaque respectus et nunc manet Orpheos in te?
audax ille quidem, qui mitem Cerberon umquam 270
credidit aut ulli Ditis placabile numen

²⁴⁸ *Vollmer recognizes an anacoluthon; Leo thinks a verse has fallen out.* densant *Ellis.* supero *Haupt.*
²⁵¹ Pandionia *Housman.* miserandas Ω, *Housman.*
²⁵⁹ numina *CBE.* ²⁶⁰ Elysium tranamus *Ellis.*
²⁶⁴ fata *Bembo:* tura *Ribbeck:* iura *Unger:* causa *Ellis:* cura Ω.
²⁶⁶ decus manet, et *Ellis.*

CULEX

boding words, and brought a marriage fraught with death. Ay, and other ranks there are, thronging line upon line: the Colchian mother,[1] frenzied with wicked savagery, musing on distressful wounds for her affrighted children; anon, the sisters of Pandion's piteous stock,[2] whose voice cries *Itys, Itys,* as, bereft of him, the Bistonian king[3] mourns in his hoopoe shape, wafted to the winged breezes. Yea, and the quarrelling brothers of Cadmus' line[4] cast fierce, unfriendly glances upon each other's person, and now each recoils, for his unholy hand drips with a brother's blood. Alas! this anguish that shall never change!

258 "On to far different sights am I hurried; famous spirits I descry afar; across Elysium's waters I must swim, and thither I am borne. In my path, Persephone urges the heroine throng[5] to raise before them their confronting torches. Alcestis, unscathed, is free from all care, for that she stayed the cruel fate of her husband Admetus among the Chalcodonians. Lo! the Ithacan's wife,[6] ever his glory, daughter of Icarius, deemed the glory of womankind; and, hard by, waits that arrogant throng of youthful suitors, pierced with arrows. Why, poor Eurydice, hast thou withdrawn in such sorrow? And why even now waits upon thee punishment for that backward look of Orpheus? Bold indeed was he, who thought that Cerberus was ever mild, or that the godhead of Dis could be appeased of any, and who,

[1] Medea; *cf. Eclogues,* VIII. 47 ff.
[2] Philomela and Procne; *cf. Eclogues,* VI. 78.
[3] Tereus, father of Itys.
[4] Eteocles and Polynices.
[5] A band of women, such as encountered Odysseus in the lower world; *cf.* Homer, *Odyssey,* XI. 225 ff.
[6] Penelope.

VIRGIL.

nec timuit Phlegethonta, furens, ardentibus undis
nec maesta obtenta Ditis ferrugine regna
defossasque domos ac Tartara nocte cruenta
obsita nec faciles Ditis sine iudice sedes,   275
iudice, qui vitae post mortem vindicat acta.
sed Fortuna valens audacem fecerat ante:
iam rapidi steterant amnes et turba ferarum
blanda voce sequax regionem insederat Orphei,
iamque imam viridi radicem moverat alte   280
quercus humo . . . . . . silvaeque sonorae
sponte sua cantus rapiebant cortice avara.
labentis biiugis etiam per sidera Lunae
pressit equos, et tu cupientis, menstrua virgo,
auditura lyram, tenuisti nocte relicta.   285
haec eadem potuit, Ditis, te vincere, coniunx,
Eurydicenque ultro ducendam reddere: non fas,
non erat invictae divae exorabile mortis.
illa quidem, nimium Manis experta severos,
praeceptum signabat iter, nec rettulit intus   290
lumina nec divae corrupit munera lingua;
sed tu crudelis, crudelis tu magis, Orpheu,
oscula cara petens rupisti iussa deorum.
dignus amor venia; gratum, si Tartara nossent,
peccatum: meminisse grave est. vos sede piorum, 295
vos manet heroum contra manus.   hic et uterque
Aeacides: Peleus namque et Telamonia virtus

272 furentem *Bembo, Ellis.*
274 defossasque VB^2: nec fossasque Ω, *Vollmer.*
275 Dictaeo *Scaliger.*
281 steterant amnes (*from* 278) *has supplanted the original.*
283 luna *CBE.*
284 cupientis *Leo:* currentis (-es).
294 venia est *Exc.*   Tartara] numina Γ.

CULEX

in his frenzy, feared not Phlegethon nor his blazing waters, nor the mournful realms of Dis, o'erlaid with gloom, the dwellings of Tartarus, buried deep, and beset with cruel night, nor the abodes of Dis, easy of entry were there not a judge [1]—a judge, who after death passes sentence on the deeds of life. But Fortune, potent in the past, had made him bold. Ere then, swift rivers had stood still; the throng of wild beasts, following by reason of his alluring voice, had pressed close upon Orpheus; and ere then, from the green ground, the oak had moved its deepest root aloft, and of their own free will the whistling woods were snatching his songs with greedy bark. Even in their gliding course amid the stars he checked Luna's twin-yoked steeds, and at their desire, thou thyself, O maiden of the month, eager to hear the lyre, didst hold them back, deserting the night. This same lyre availed to conquer thee, O bride of Dis, and make thee of thine own will restore Eurydice, to be led away. No right over unvanquished death had the goddess, no right that would yield to prayer. Eurydice indeed, who ere this had found the Shades too stern, was marking out the path prescribed, and turned not her eyes to gaze within, nor annulled the goddess' gifts by speech. But thou cruel one, thou more cruel, Orpheus, seeking her dear kisses, didst break the commandments of the gods ! Worthy of pardon was thy love; pleasing thy sin, did Hell but know: yet grievous is the remembrance.[2]

295 " For you, O heroines, over against you in the house of the righteous, there waits a band of heroes. Here are the two sons of Aeacus: for Peleus and

[1] *cf. Aen.* VI. 431.
[2] This seems to refer back to 268 above; Eurydice remembers with sorrow.

393

VIRGIL

per secura patris laetantur numina, quorum
conubis Venus et Virtus iniunxit honorem:
hunc rapuit serva: ast illum Nereis amavit. 300
assidet hac iuvenis; sociat te gloria sortis,
alter, in excessum, referens a navibus ignis
Argolicis Phrygios torva feritate repulsos.

"O quis non referat talis divortia belli,
quae Troiae videre viri viderque Grai, 305
Teucria cum magno manaret sanguine tellus,
et Simois Xanthique liquor, Sigeaque praeter
litora, cum Troas saevi ducis Hectoris ira
truderet in classis inimica mente Pelasgas
volnera tela neces ignis inferre paratos? 310
ipsa vagis namque Ida potens feritatis, et ipsa
Ida faces altrix cupidis praebebat alumnis,
omnis ut in cineres Rhoetei litoris ora
classibus ambustis flamma lacrimante daretur.
hinc erat oppositus contra Telamonius heros 315
obiectoque dabat clipeo certamina, et illinc
Hector erat, Troiae summum decus, acer uterque;
fluminibus veluti fragor <est, cum vere vagantur>

---

³⁰⁰ hanc *Vollmer.* rapuit ferit ast serva *Bembo:* rapuit Periboea *Schrader:* rapit Hesiona, ast *Heinsius, Ellis.*
³⁰¹ huic *Ellis.* sociat de Ω: sociate *V.*
³⁰² alter] acer *Bembo.* inexcis(s)um *B*Γ: inexcelsum *V.*
³⁰³ torva *Bembo:* turba. feritate] ferit arte Γ: trepidante *Ellis.*
³⁰⁷ propter *Heinsius, Ellis.*
³⁰⁹ truderet *Baehrens:* vi daret *Leo:* videre (vidi).
³¹¹ ipsa vagis] ipsa iugis *Bembo:* ipsas vagit Γ: ipsa sudis *Ellis.* potens] parens *Ellis.*
³¹⁸⁻³²⁰ *given according to Vollmer's conjectural restoration.*

CULEX

valiant Telamon rejoice, care-free through their sire's divinity [1]—they upon whose nuptials Venus and Valour bestowed glory: captivated was the one by his bondmaid; [2] the other was loved of a Nereid.[3] Here, at their side, is seated a youth; [4] with him the fame of thy lot, O second youth, allies thee unto death, for thou tellest of the Phrygian fires thrust back from the Greek ships with wild and savage valour.

304 " O who could not tell of the partings in such a war, which the heroes of Troy and the heroes of Greece beheld, what time the Teucrian soil streamed with plenteous blood, and Simois and the flowing Xanthus; and what time, along the Sigean shores, Hector, stern and angry captain, drove the Trojans with hostile intent against the Pelasgian ships, ready to assail with wounds and weapons, with death and flames? For, as they roamed abroad, Ida herself, queen of savage life, Ida herself, their nursing mother, furnished brands to her sons at their desire, that so the whole Rhoetean shore might be given over to ashes, as with the tear-dropping flame of pine the ships were consumed. On one side, arrayed against the foe, was the hero sprung of Telamon, offering combat from under his covering shield; and on the other was Hector, Troy's chief glory, both eager for the fray. Even as on rivers is heard a roar, when in spring-time they descend from

---

[1] Peleus and Telamon live among the blest, because their father Aeacus received the gift of immortality.

[2] Hesione, daughter of Laomedon, whom Hercules, on conquering Troy, gave as captive to Telamon, by whom she became mother of Ajax.

[3] Thetis, who married Peleus, was the mother of Achilles.

[4] Achilles; the second youth is Ajax.

VIRGIL

<mont>ibus in se<getes, sic alter proicit ignes> 318A
tegminibus telisque super, <quis hostibus arma>
eriperet reditus, alter Volcania ferro   320
volnera protectus depellere navibus instat.

" Hos erat Aeacides voltu laetatus honores,
Dardaniaeque alter fuso quod sanguine campis
Hectoreo victor lustravit corpore Troiam.
rursus acerba fremunt, Paris hunc quod letat, et huius
firma dolis Ithaci virtus quod concidit icta.   326
huic gerit aversos proles Laertia voltus,
et iam Strymonii Rhesi victorque Dolonis,
Pallade iam laetatur ovans, rursusque tremescit:
iam Ciconas iamque horret atrox Laestrygonas ipse.
illum Scylla rapax, canibus succincta Molossis,   331
Aetnaeusque Cyclops, illum Zanclaea Charybdis
pallentesque lacus et squalida Tartara terrent.

" Hic et Tantaleae generamen prolis Atrides
assidet, Argivum lumen, quo flamma regente   335
Doris Erichthonias prostravit funditus arces.
reddidit, heu, Graius poenas tibi, Troia, ruenti,
Hellespontiacis obiturus reddidit undis.
illa vices hominum testata est copia quondam,
ne quisquam propriae Fortunae munere dives   340
iret inevectus caelum super: omne propinquo
frangitur invidiae telo decus.   ibat in altum

[322] hos *Haupt:* hoc Ω: hic *V.*   honore *Scaliger.*
[326] firma *Leo:* alta *Scaliger:* arma.
[330] lestrigone (*last word lost*) Ω: -es ipse *V:* -as ipse *Ribbeck.*   limen *Ellis:* litus *Vollmer.*
[332] Zanclea *V:* metuenda Ω: et verida Γ.
[337] Troia ruenti *Bembo:* troia furenti *VSL:* troias venti Γ.

CULEX

the mountains upon the corn-fields: so from above
the one hurls fires upon shields and darts, that
thereby he may rob the foe of weapons of return;
the other, guarding himself with his sword, presses
on to ward off from the ships the assaults of Vulcan.

³²² "At these glories the son of Aeacus was glad
of countenance, and likewise the other, for that,
when the Dardan fields were drenched with blood,
he victoriously compassed Troy with the body of
Hector. Again, they chafe bitterly, for that Paris
slew the one, and the other's sturdy valour fell
stricken by the Ithacan's wiles. From him the seed
of Laertes[1] keeps his countenance averted; and now,
as victor over Strymonian Rhesus and over Dolon,
and now, as triumphant over Pallas, rejoices, then
again trembles: he, the dreaded one, shudders, now
at the Cicones, and now at the Laestrygonians. Him
ravenous Scylla, girt with her Molossian hounds, and
the Cyclops of Aetna affright; him Zanclaean Charybdis, and the dim lakes and foul Tartarus.

³³⁴ "Here too beside him sits the son of Atreus,
offspring of the race of Tantalus, the light of Greece,
beneath whose rule Doric flame utterly laid low
the Erichthonian citadels.[2] The Greeks, alas! paid
penance to thee, O Troy, for thy fall—paid it, when
doomed to death in the Hellespont's waves.[3] That
force bore witness in its time to human vicissitudes,
lest anyone, enriched by his own Fortune's bounty,
should mount exalted above the heavens: all glory
is shattered by Envy's nigh-awaiting dart.[4] The

[1] Ulysses.
[2] *i.e.* Troy, Erichthonius being son of Dardanus. Yet at 30, above, the same expression is used of Athens.
[3] Used for the whole Aegean. The Greeks were shipwrecked off Euboea.
[4] "Envy" here is retribution or Nemesis.

VIRGIL

vis Argea petens patriam, ditataque praeda
arcis Erichthoniae ; comes huic erat aura secunda
per placidum cursu pelagus ; Nereis ad undas 345
signa dabat, sparsim flexis super acta carinis :
cum seu caelesti fato seu sideris ortu
undique mutatur caeli nitor, omnia ventis,
omnia turbinibus sunt anxia.   iam maris unda
sideribus certat consurgere, iamque superne 350
corripere et soles et sidera cuncta minatur
ac ruere in terras caeli fragor. hic modo laetans
copia nunc miseris circumdatur anxia fatis,
immoriturque super fluctus et saxa Capherei,
Euboicas aut per cautis Aegaeaque late 355
litora, cum Phrygiae passim vaga praeda peremptae
omnis in aequoreo fluitat iam naufraga fluctu.

"Hic alii resident pariles virtutis honore
heroes, mediisque siti sunt sedibus, omnes,
omnes Roma decus magni quos suspicit orbis. 360
hic Fabii Deciique, hic est et Horatia virtus,
hic et fama vetus, numquam moritura, Camilli,
Curtius et, mediis quem quondam sedibus urbis
devotum telis consumpsit gurges in unda,
Mucius et, prudens ardorem corpore passus, 365
cui cessit Lydi timefacta potentia regis.
hic Curius clarae socius virtutis et ille

₃₄₅ ab unda *Paldam :* ab undis *Housman.*
₃₄₆ sparsim flexis *Ellis :* passim flexis *Housman :* parsim flexis Γ : pars inflexis Ω, *commonly read.*
₃₅₂ laetans *Ellis :* l(a)etum : letam Γ : laeta *commonly read.*
₃₅₆ peremptae *H, Bembo :* -ta.   ₃₅₇ naufraga (-ge) luctu Γ*V.*
₃₅₈ resident *Ellis :* sident *or* sidunt.
₃₆₀ suspicit *Heinsius :* suscipit.
₃₆₃ mediis Γ*V :* medius *SFCL.*
₃₆₄ telis *Ellis :* livens *Housman :* pallens *Leo :* bellis Ω.

398

CULEX

Argive power was passing seaward, seeking its homeland, and fattened with spoils from the Erichthonian citadel. A favourable breeze attended it in peaceful course upon the deep; a Nereid was giving signals towards the main, riding, now here and now there, above the curved keels: when lo! either by fate of heaven, or through some rising star, on all sides the sky's brightness changes; all is troubled by blasts, all by whirlwinds. Now the sea's waves strive to mount to the stars, and now aloft the crashing sky threatens to seize all, both suns and stars, and dash them to earth. Here the host—but lately joyous, now afflicted—is beset by unhappy fates, and perishes upon the floods and rocks of Caphereus, or along the Euboean cliffs and broad Aegean shores, while all the prey from plundered Phrygia, drifting far and near, tossed in wreckage upon the ocean waves.

358 "Here abide others like unto them in valorous repute, all heroes, settled in the midst of these abodes, all whom Rome esteems as the glory of the mighty world. Here are the Fabii and the Decii, and here the brave Horatius; here Camillus, whose olden fame shall never die; and Curtius, whom once in the midst of the city's homes, willing victim of javelins, the flood swallowed up in its waters;[1] and wise Mucius, who in his flesh endured the flames, and to whom the might of the Lydian king yielded in fear.[2] Here is Curius, allied to glorious valour,

---

[1] A reference to the Lacus Curtius in the Roman Forum, into which a youth named Curtius rode on his horse at full speed, then disappeared.

[2] C. Mucius, when threatened with torture and death by Porsenna (called Lydian because he was Etruscan), thrust his right hand into the altar-flames and held it there until it was consumed.

VIRGIL

Flaminius, devota dedit qui corpora flammae,
(iure igitur tales sedes, pietatis honores),
Scipiadaeque duces, quorum devota triumphis 370
moenia Romanis Libycae Karthaginis horrent.
 "Illi laude sua vigeant: ego Ditis opacos
cogor adire lacus, viduos, a, lumine Phoebi,
et vastum Phlegethonta pati, quo, maxime Minos,
conscelerata pia discernis vincula sede. 375
ergo iam causam mortis, iam dicere vitae
verberibus saevae cogunt sub iudice Poenae,
cum mihi tu sis causa mali, nec conscius adsis;
sed tolerabilibus curis haec immemor audis
et tamen ut vades, dimittes omnia ventis. 380
digredior numquam rediturus: tu cole fontem
et viridis nemorum silvas et pascua laetus;
et mea diffusas rapiantur dicta per auras."
dixit et extrema tristis cum voce recessit.
 Hunc ubi sollicitum dimisit inertia vitae, 385
interius graviter regementem, nec tulit ultra
sensibus infusum Culicis de morte dolorem,
quantumcumque sibi vires tribuere seniles
(quis tamen infestum pugnans devicerat hostem),
rivum propter aquae viridi sub fronde latentem 390
conformare locum capit impiger. hunc et in orbem

368 Flam(m)inius *has perhaps supplanted* Caecilius, *read by Loensis.*
371 romanis $V\Gamma$: rapidis *SFCL:* vepretis *Haupt:* sub lappis *Ellis.*
374 maxime *Nodell:* maxima.   375 discernit.
376 ergo quam ... iam Ω: iam ... iam *Heyne:* quom ... tum *Ellis.*
379 tolerabilius cures. *Ellis.* audis? *Ellis.*
380 et tamen ut vadis Ω: et mane ut vades *Usener:* ut tamen audieris *Ellis:* et temere, ut vades, dimittes somnia ventis *Busche.*
381 fontem Γ: fontes (is).
383 *Scaliger placed after* 380. et Ω: at *Heyne.*

CULEX

and great Flaminius,[1] who gave his body a victim to the flame (justly then hath he such an abode, piety's reward) and those Scipio chiefs, doomed by whose Roman triumphs the walls of Libyan Carthage are become a desolation.

372 "Let them live in their renown: but I am forced to pass to those shadowy pools of Dis, that are, alas! bereft of the light of Phoebus, and to suffer waste Phlegethon, whereby, O mighty Minos, thou partest the prison-house of the wicked from the abode of the righteous! So before the judge the cruel Fiends with scourges force me to plead my cause, now of death, and now of life,[2] though thou art cause of my ill, and aidest not with thy witness, but with lightly borne cares hearest these my words, unmindful, and despite of all, when thou goest thy way, thou wilt dismiss all to the winds. I pass hence, never to return; do thou, rejoicing, haunt the spring, and green forest-groves, and pastures; and for my words, let them be swept aside by the random breezes!" He spake, and with the last accents sadly went his way.

385 Now when life's langour quitted that anxious shepherd, from whose breast heavy sighs resounded, and when no more could he brook the sorrow for the Gnat's death that flooded his senses, then in so far as his aged strength suffered him—wherewith, none the less, he had fought and vanquished his fierce foe— hard by the running stream that lurked beneath green leafage, he busily begins to fashion a place, marking

---

[1] If the reading is correct, this is some person unknown. If "Caecilius" should be read, the reference would be to Caecilius Metellus, who once rescued the Palladium from the burning temple of Vesta, and thereby lost his eyes.

[2] The issue is one of eternal weal or woe.

401

VIRGIL

destinat ac ferri capulum repetivit in usum,
gramineam viridi ut foderet de caespite terram.
iam memor inceptum peragens sibi cura laborem
congestum cumulavit opus, atque aggere multo 395
telluris tumulus formatum crevit in orbem.
quem circum lapidem levi de marmore formans
conserit; assiduae curae memor. hic et acanthos
et rosa purpureum crescent pudibunda ruborem
et violae omne genus; hic est et Spartica myrtus 400
atque hyacinthos et hic Cilici crocus editus arvo,
laurus item Phoebi surgens decus; hic rhododaphne
liliaque et roris non avia cura marini
herbaque turis opes priscis imitata Sabina
chrysanthusque hederaeque nitor pallente corymbo,
et bocchus Libyae regis memor. hic amarantus 406
bumastusque virens et semper florida tinus.
non illinc Narcissus abest, cui gloria formae
igne Cupidineo proprios exarsit in artus;
et quoscumque novant vernantia tempora flores, 410
his tumulus super inseritur. tum fronte locatur
elogium, tacita format quod littera voce:
"parve Culex, pecudum custos tibi tale merenti
funeris officium vitae pro munere reddit."

³⁹⁹ rubicunda *FCL*: rubibunda *B*.   ruborem Γ*V*: terrorem *L*: tenorem *Plésent*.
⁴⁰⁰ parthica *V*: pastica Γ
⁴⁰² decus surgens Ω: decus ut sua pagina *V*: urgens *Vollmer*: ingens *Housman*.   ⁴⁰⁴ Sabinas *V*.
⁴⁰⁷ pinus Ω: tinus *Salmasius*.   ⁴⁰⁸ cui] qui *Leo*.
⁴¹¹ hic Γ.   ⁴¹² firmat *V*Γ*C*: firma *L*.

CULEX

it in circular form, and oft turning to service his iron spade, to dig up grassy sods from the green turf. And now his mindful care, pursuing the toil begun, heaped up a towering work, and with broad rampart the earthy mound grew into the circle he had traced. Round about this, mindful of constant care, he sets stones, fashioned from polished marble.

[398] Here are to grow acanthus and the blushing rose with crimson bloom, and violets of every kind. Here are Spartan myrtle and hyacinth, and here saffron, sprung from Cilician fields, and soaring laurel, the glory of Phoebus. Here are oleander, and lilies, and rosemary, tended in familiar haunts, and the Sabine plant,[1] which for men of old feigned rich frankincense; and marigold, and glistening ivy, with pale clusters, and bocchus, mindful of Libya's king.[2] Here are amaranth, blooming bumastus,[3] and ever-flowering laurestine. Yonder fails not the Narcissus, whose noble beauty kindled with Love's flame for his own[4] limbs; and what flowers soever the spring seasons renew, with these the mound is strewn above. Then upon its face is placed an epitaph, which letters thus fashion with silent voice: "Little Gnat, to thee, so well deserving, the guardian of the flocks pays this service of death in return for the boon of life."

---

[1] The savin, *juniperus sabina*.

[2] This unknown plant was named from Bocchus, a king of Mauretania, probably the father-in-law of Jugurtha, though perhaps a later king of the same name.

[3] *cf. Georgics*, II. 102, and for *tinus*, or laurestine, *Ib.* IV. 112, and 141.

[4] The youth Narcissus, falling in love with his own image, as reflected in a fountain, pined away and was changed into the flower that bears his name.

CIRIS *

Etsi me, vario iactatum laudis amore
irritaque expertum fallacis praemia volgi,
Cecropius suavis exspirans hortulus auras
florentis viridi sophiae complectitur umbra,
ut mens curet eo dignum sibi quaerere carmen   5
longe aliud studium atque alios accincta labores
(altius ad magni suspexit sidera mundi
et placitum paucis ausa est ascendere collem):
non tamen absistam coeptum detexere munus,
in quo iure meas utinam requiescere Musas   10
et leviter blandum liceat deponere amorem.

Quod si mirificum genus o Mes<sala . . .>
(mirificum sed enim, modo sit tibi velle libido),
si me iam summa Sapientia pangeret arce,

¹ vario] vano *Heinsius.*   ³ auras] herbas A^1.
⁵ ut mens *Bücheler:* tum mea(ea) *or* tu mea. curet *Leo:* quiret *Bücheler:* nec mens quivit *Némethy.*
⁷ suspexit *Schrader:* suspendit: suspensi *L.*
¹⁰ iure] rite *Schrader:* nure *Heinsius.*
¹¹ amorem *It.:* morem.
¹² *Thus Vollmer, but the passage is corrupt, the close of the verse being lost, and perhaps another verse as well.* Mes<sala parentum> *Leo:* genus omnes *MSS.*
¹³ sed enim] Valeri *Némethy.*

---

* The MSS. cited are B = Bruxellensis 10675-6 of the 12th century, containing however only ll. 454-541; *Exc.* (for which see introductory note to the *Culex*); and Z, designating a lost codex, which was the parent of the following:

CIRIS

Tossed though I am, this way and that, by love of renown, and knowing full well that the fickle throng's rewards are vain; though the Attic garden,[1] breathing forth sweet fragrance, enwraps me in fine-flowering Wisdom's verdant shade, so that my mind is fain to go in quest of a song worthy thereof, prepared though she is for far different tasks and far different toils—she has looked aloft to the stars of the mighty firmament, and has dared to climb the hill[2] that has found favour with few—yet I will not cease to fulfil the task I have begun, wherein I pray that my Muses may find their due repose, and lightly lay aside that seductive love.

[12] But if, O Messalla, thou <bearest with> a task so wondrous in kind—wondrous indeed, if only thy fancy favour it—if Wisdom, exalted partner of those four heirs of olden days,[3] now planted me on her

---

[1] Referring to the garden in Athens, where Epicurus used to teach.
[2] The hill of wisdom, or philosophy.
[3] The four philosophers—Plato, Aristotle, Zeno, and Epicurus.

H = Helmstadiensis 332, of the 15th century; L = Vaticanus 3255, written by Pomponius Laetus; A = Arundelianus 133 and R = Rehdigeranus 125, both of the 15th century. Ellis also cites U = Urbinas 353 of the Vatican Library, a late 15th century MS. To the articles cited on p. 368 should be added Ellis, " New Suggestions on the *Ciris*," in *American Journal of Philology*, xv. (1894). See Appendix, p. 527.

VIRGIL

quattuor antiquis heredibus edita consors, 15
unde hominum errores longe lateque per orbem
despicere atque humilis possem contemnere curas;
non ego te talem venerarer munere tali,
non equidem, quamvis interdum ludere nobis
et gracilem molli libeat pede claudere versum; 20
sed magno intexens, si fas est dicere, peplo,
qualis Erechtheis olim portatur Athenis,
debita cum castae solvuntur vota Minervae
tardaque confecto redeunt quinquennia lustro,
cum levis alterno Zephyrus concrebruit Euro 25
et prono gravidum provexit pondere currum.
felix illa dies, felix et dicitur annus,
felices, qui talem annum videre diemque.
ergo Palladiae texuntur in ordine pugnae,
magna Giganteis ornantur pepla tropaeis, 30
horrida sanguineo pinguntur proelia cocco.
additur aurata deiectus cuspide Typhon,
qui prius, Ossaeis conscendens aethera saxis,
Emathio celsum duplicabat vertice Olympum.

    Tale deae velum sollemni tempore portant; 35
tali te vellem, iuvenum doctissime, ritu
purpureos inter soles et candida lunae
sidera, caeruleis orbem pulsantia bigis,

---

[15] edita *Baehrens:* est data.   [17] possim: possum $H^1 L$.
[22] quale H^2.   [25] concrebuit HA.
[26] currum *Barth:* cursum.   [27] ille HL.
[31] sanguinea p. p. Gorgo *Baehrens*.
[33] conscendens *Kreunen:* consternens.
[34] duplicarat *Baehrens*.   [36] velim AR.

---

[1] The poem with which the writer would like to honour his patron is compared to the *peplos*, richly embroidered

406

CIRIS

topmost citadel, whence, o'er the world far and wide, I could look down upon the errors of men, and despise their lowly cares, thee I should not be honouring, great as thou art, with gift so slight—no verily, albeit at times we may be pleased to trifle, and to round a slender verse with smooth-running feet; but I should weave a story into an ample robe,[1] if thus to speak be lawful, such as is borne in Erechthean Athens, what time due vows are paid to chaste Minerva, and the fifth-year feast slowly returns at the lustre's close, when the gentle Westwind waxes strong against his rival of the East, and bears onward the car, heavy with its o'erhanging weight. Happy that day is called, happy that year, and happy are they who have looked upon such a year and such a day! Thus in due order are inwoven the battles of Pallas: the great robes are adorned with the trophies of Giants, and grim combats are depicted in blood-red scarlet. There is added he, who was hurled down by the golden spear —Typhon, who aforetime, when mounting into heaven on the rocks of Ossa, essayed to double the height of Olympus by piling thereon the Emathian mount.[2]

[35] Such is the goddess' sail, borne at the solemn season, and on such wise, most learned youth, would I fain enweave thee, amid roseate suns, and the moon's white star, that makes heaven throb with her

---

[1] with figures (*cf.* 29 *seq.*) which was offered to Athena at the great Panathenaic festival. This was solemnized every five years in the month of Hecatombaeon, the first month of the Attic year. The *peplos*, outstretched like a sail, was carried to the temple on a ship (here called *currus*) which was drawn through the streets of Athens on rollers.

[2] Pelion, a mountain of Thessaly, which Emathia here represents; *cf. Georgics*, I. 281 ff.

VIRGIL

naturae rerum magnis intexere chartis;
aeternum ut sophiae coniunctum carmine nomen 40
nostra tuum senibus loqueretur pagina saeclis.

Sed quoniam ad tantas nunc primum nascimur artes,
nunc primum teneros firmamus robore nervos,
haec tamen interea, quae possumus, in quibus aevi
prima rudimenta et iuvenes exegimus annos, 45
accipe dona meo multum vigilata labore
promissa atque diu iam tandem <reddita vota>
impia prodigiis ut quondam exterrita amoris
Scylla novos avium sublimis in aere coetus
viderit et tenui conscendens aethera pinna 50
caeruleis sua tecta supervolitaverit alis,
hanc pro purpureo poenam scelerata capillo,
pro patris solvens excisa et funditus urbe.

Complures illam et magni, Messalla, poetae
(nam verum fateamur: amat Polyhymnia verum) 55
longe alia perhibent mutatam membra figura
Scyllaeum monstro saxum infestasse voraci;
illam esse, aerumnis quam saepe legamus Ulixi,
candida succinctam latrantibus inguina monstris,
Dulichias vexasse rates et gurgite in alto 60
deprensos nautas canibus lacerasse marinis.
sed neque Maeoniae patiuntur credere chartae
nec malus istorum dubiis erroribus auctor.
namque alias alii volgo finxere puellas,

[40] alterno *Heinsius*. ut *omitted*.
[47] reddita vota *conjectured by Leo. In LA² the verse runs*.
et promissa tuis non magna exordia rebus.
[48] amoris *Scaliger:* miris *Heinsius:* mollis *Ellis:* amplis.
[53] pro(h) *Sillig, Vollmer.* patria *Haupt.*
[57] *So Haupt.* monstra saxosum infectata vocavi *A :* vocari *HL*.

408

CIRIS

celestial chariot,[1] into a great poem on Nature, so that unto late ages our page might speak thy name, linked in song with Wisdom's theme.

[42] But seeing that now for the first time our infant efforts are turned to such high arts,[2] since now first we are making strong our youthful sinews, this theme, nevertheless—'tis all we can offer—whereon we have spent life's earliest schooling, and the years of our youth—do thou meanwhile accept, a gift wrought by me with many a toilsome vigil, a vow long promised and now at last fulfilled. 'Tis the story of how, once upon a time, unfilial Scylla, frenzied by love's portents, saw in the sky aloft strange gatherings of birds, and, mounting the heaven on slender pinion, hovered on azure wings above her home, paying this penalty, accursed one, for the crimson lock, and for the utter uprooting of her father's city.

[54] Many great poets tell us, Messalla (for let us confess the truth: 'tis truth Polyhymnia loves) that she, with limbs changed to far different form, haunted the rock of Scylla with her voracious bulk. She it is, they say, of whom we read in the toils of Ulysses, how that, with howling monsters girt about her white waist, she often harried the Ithacan barques and in the swirling depths tore asunder with her sea-dogs the sailors she had clutched.[3] But neither do Homer's pages[4] suffer us to credit this tale nor does he who is the pernicious source[5] of those poets' sundry mistakes. For various writers have commonly feigned various maidens as the

---

[1] *cf. Aen.* x. 216.   [2] Viz. Epicurean philosophy.
[3] *cf. Eclogues,* VI. 74 ff.   [4] *i.e.* in *Odyssey,* XII.
[5] Who this is, is unknown. So Curcio. Benoist follows Sillig in rendering "the cause of the perilous wanderings of those mariners" (Ulysses and his crew), *i.e.* Neptune.

409

VIRGIL

quae Colophoniaco Scyllae dicantur Homero. 65
ipse Crataein ait matrem; sed sive Crataeis,
sive illam monstro generavit Echidna biformi,
sive est neutra parens atque hoc in carmine toto
inguinis est vitium et Veneris descripta libido;
sive etiam iactis speciem mutata venenis 70
infelix virgo (quid enim commiserat illa?
ipse pater timidam saeva complexus harena
coniugium castae violaverat Amphitrites) 73
horribilis circum vidit se sistere formas, 80
heu quotiens mirata novos expalluit artus, 81
ipsa suos quotiens heu pertimuit latratus! 82
at tamen exegit longo post tempore poenas, 74
ut cum cura suae vaheretur coniugis alto, 75
ipsa trucem multo misceret sanguine pontum;
seu vero, ut perhibent, forma cum vinceret omnis
et cupidos quaestu passim popularet amantes,
piscibus et canibusque malis vallata repente est 79
ausa quod est mulier numen fraudare deorum 83
et dictam Veneri voto intervertere poenam,
quam mala multiplici iuvenum consaepta caterva 85
dixerat atque animo meretrix iactata ferarum,
infamem tali merito rumore fuisse,
docta Palaepaphiae testatur voce Pachynus.

⁶⁵ dicuntur *A R*.
⁶⁶ ait *Heyne*: ei *Sillig*. Crataeis] erithei: Hecateis *Ellis*.
⁶⁷ generavit Echidna *Housman*: genuit gravena.
⁷⁰ iactis] exactis *L A*².
⁷² saeva] sola *Ruardi*: sicca *Haupt*.
⁷³⁻⁸³ *transpositions due to Reitzenstein*.
⁷⁵ suae] tuae: sui *Loensis*. Vollmer conjectures ut cum curvatae.
⁷⁹ et] heu *Schwabe*: en *Leo*: haec *Ellis*. Leo arranges thus: 78, 83, 84, 79, 80.
⁸⁴ voto intervertere *Sillig*: votorum vertere.
⁸⁵ consaepta *Sillig*: quod saepta.
⁸⁶ vixit eratque *Haupt*.
⁸⁷ merito rumore *Loensis*: meritorum more.
⁸⁸ Palaephatia ... papyrus *Aldine edition* 1517.

CIRIS

Scyllas named by Colophon's Homer. He himself says [1] that Crataeis was her mother; but whether Crataeis or Echidna bare that twy-formed monster; or whether neither was her mother, and throughout the poem she but portrays the sin of lustfulness and love's incontinence,[2] or whether, transformed through scattered poisons, the luckless maiden (luckless, I say, for of what wrong had she been guilty? Father Neptune himself had embraced the frightened maid on the lonely strand, and broken his conjugal vow to chaste Amphitrite) beheld awful shapes plant themselves about her: —how often, alas! did she marvel and grow pale at her strange limbs! how often, alas! did she turn in terror from her own baying! but still long afterwards she exacted penalty, for when the delight of his consort was riding upon the deep, she herself confounded the savage sea with much blood [3]—or whether, as 'tis said, seeing that she excelled all women in beauty, and in avarice made wanton havoc of her eager lovers, she of a sudden became fenced about with fell fishes and dogs, for that she, a woman, dared to defraud the powers divine, and to withhold from Venus the vow-appointed price, even the payment which a base harlot, encompassed by a thronging crowd of youths, and stirred with a wild and savage spirit, had imposed upon her lovers— that by this report she was with reason defamed, Pachynus has learned and so bears witness, speaking by the lips of Venus, queen of Old Paphos [4]:—what-

---

[1] *Odyssey*, XII. 125.
[2] The assumption being that the description of Scylla is allegorical.
[3] This probably refers to the transformation of Scylla. The *cura* is Neptune, husband of Amphitrite.
[4] There seems to have been an inscription about Scylla in the temple of Venus at Pachynus.

VIRGIL

quidquid et ut quisque est tali de clade locutus,
somnia sunt: potius liceat notescere Cirin 90
atque unam ex multis Scyllam non esse puellis.

Quare quae cantus meditanti mittere caecos
magna mihi cupido tribuistis praemia, divae
Pierides, quarum castos altaria postis
munere saepe meo inficiunt, foribusque hyacinthi 95
deponunt flores aut suave rubens narcissus
aut crocus alterna coniungens lilia caltha
sparsaque liminibus floret rosa, nunc age, divae,
praecipue nostro nunc aspirate labori
atque novum aeterno praetexite honore volumen. 100

Sunt Pandioniis vicinae sedibus urbes
Actaeos inter colles et candida Thesei
purpureis late ridentia litora conchis,
quarum non ulli fama concedere digna
stat Megara, Alcathoi quondam munita labore, 105
Alcathoi Phoebique: deus namque adfuit illi;
unde etiam citharae voces imitatus acutas
saepe lapis recrepat Cyllenia murmura pulsus
et veterem sonitu Phoebi testatur amorem.
hanc urbem, ante alios qui tum florebat in armis, 110
fecerat infestam populator remige Minos,
hospitio quod se Nisi Polyidos avito

---

⁹⁰ somnia sunt *Heinsius:* omnia sunt iam Nisi *Leo.*
⁹² caecos] certos *L.*
⁹⁴ aluaria "hives" *Unger:* alabastria *Bergk:* calparia *Haupt:* aliparia *Winton.*   ⁹⁵ floribusque *AR.*
¹⁰⁵ Alcathoi *Ribbeck:* Aethei: Argei *Heinsius.* munita *Aldine* 1517: mutata.
¹⁰⁶ decus.   ¹⁰⁷ imitantur *HLA.*
¹⁰⁸ munera *HA.*   ¹⁰⁹ honorem *HL.*
¹¹⁰ tunc *AR.*

CIRIS

soever and howsoever each has spoken of such disastrous state, 'tis all dreams: rather let the Ciris become known, and not a Scylla who was but one of many maidens.[1]

[92] Therefore, ye divine Muses, who, when I essayed to put forth my abstruse songs, granted me the high rewards I craved—ye, whose pure columns not seldom are stained by the altar-offerings that I bring; at whose temple-doors the hyacinths yield their bloom, or the sweet blushing narcissus, or the crocus and lilies, blended with alternate marigolds, and on whose threshold are scattered blooming roses—now come, ye goddesses, now breathe a special grace upon this toil, and crown this fresh scroll with glory immortal!

[101] Near to the home of Pandion[2] lie cities between the Attic hills and Theseus' gleaming shores, smiling from afar with their roseate shells;[3] and, worthy to yield to none of these in repute, stands Megara, whose walls were reared by the toil of Alcathous— by the toil of Alcathous and Phoebus, for him the god aided; whence too the stones, imitating the lyre's shrill notes, often, when smitten, re-echo Cyllene's murmurs,[4] and in their sound attest the ancient love of Phoebus. This city the prince who in those days was eminent above others in arms, even Minos, had ravaged and laid waste with his fleet, because Polyidos,[5] fleeing from the Carpathian

---

[1] The subject, then, is to be that Scylla who was transformed into the sea-fowl, called Ciris.   [2] Athens.

[3] This is the Megarid, which abounds in white marble, interspersed with shells. Here Theseus founded the Isthmian games.

[4] *i.e.* the music of the lyre. Mercury, its inventor, was born on Cyllene; *cf. Aen.* VIII. 139.

[5] The priest who was said to have once restored Glaucus, son of Minos, to life.

VIRGIL

Carpathium fugiens et flumina Caeratea
texerat.   hunc bello repetens Gortynius heros
Attica Cretaea sternebat rura sagitta.   115
sed neque tum cives neque tum rex ipse veretur
infesto ad muros volitantis agmine turmas
icere et indomitas virtute retundere mentes,
responsum quoniam satis est meminisse deorum.
nam capite a summo regis (mirabile dictu)   120
candida caesaries (florebant tempora lauro),
et roseus medio surgebat vertice crinis:
cuius quam servata diu natura fuisset,
tam patriam incolumem Nisi regnumque futurum
concordes stabili firmarant numine Parcae.   125
ergo omnis cano residebat cura capillo,
aurea sollemni comptum quem fibula ritu
crobylus et tereti nectebant dente cicadae.

Nec vero haec urbis custodia vana fuisset
(nec fuerat), ni Scylla novo correpta furore,   130
Scylla, patris miseri patriaeque inventa sepulchrum,
o nimium cupidis Minon inhiasset ocellis.
sed malus ille puer, quem nec sua flectere mater
iratum potuit, quem nec pater atque avus idem
Iuppiter (ille etiam Poenos domitare leones   135
et validas docuit viris mansuescere tigris,

₁₁₆ tum—tum *Haupt:* tunc—tunc.
₁₁₈ icere *Ellis:* dicere *HA¹R:* ducere *A²L:* deicere *Vollmer:* reicere *Heinsius.*   ₁₂₆ cano : caro *Aldine* 1517.
₁₂₈ crobylus et *Loensis:* corpsel(la)e *or* corselle : Cecropiae et *Scaliger:* morsilis et *Ellis.*
₁₂₉ urbis *Heinsius:* vobis.   ₁₃₀ ruerat *Ribbeck.*
₁₃₂ Minon *Bücheler:* Minoa *Lachmann:* si non.
₁₃₆ rabidas *Heyne.*

CIRIS

sea and the streams of Caeratus, had taken shelter in the ancestral home of Nisus. Seeking to win him back in war, the Gortynian hero [1] was strewing the Attic land with Cretan arrows. But neither in that hour do the citizens, nor in that hour does the king himself, fear to strike down the troops that flock in hostile band to the walls, or valorously to blunt the spirit of the unconquered foe, since it is enough to remember the answer of the gods. For surmounting the king's head (wondrous to tell) uprose white hair (the temples were decked with laurel), and midway on its crown was a roseate lock. As long as this preserved its nature, so long had the Fates, voicing in unison their fixed will,[2] given assurance that Nisus' country and kingdom would be secure. Thus all their care was centred in that hoary hair, which, adorned in wonted fashion, a golden buckle and close roll bound with a cicada's shapely clasp.[3]

[129] Nor truly would this defence of the city have been vain (nor had it been) were it not that Scylla, swept away by fresh madness—Scylla, who proved to be the ruin of her hapless father and her fatherland—gaped[4] and gazed upon Minos, ah! with too passionate eyes. But that mischievous boy, whom, when angered, neither his mother could sway, nor he, who was at once father and father's father, even Jupiter[5] (he even quelled Punic lions, and taught the stout strength of tigers to soften; he even taught gods

[1] cf. *Eclogues*, VI. 60.   [2] cf. *Eclogues*, IV. 47.
[3] Thucydides (I. 6) tells us that the old Athenians used to wear the hair on the top of the head in a knot, and secured with a pin shaped like a cicada.
[4] cf. Lucr. I. 36, and Munro *ad locum*.
[5] Venus, daughter of Jupiter, was by Jupiter mother of Cupid.

VIRGIL

ille etiam divos, homines—sed dicere magnum est),
idem tum tristis acuebat parvulus iras
Iunonis magnae, cuius (periuria divae
olim, sed meminere diu) periura puella   140
non ulli licitam violaverat inscia sedem,
dum sacris operata deae lascivit et extra
procedit longe matrum comitumque catervam,
suspensam gaudens in corpore ludere vestem
et tumidos agitante sinus Aquilone relaxans.   145
necdum etiam castos gustaverat ignis honores,
necdum sollemni lympha perfusa sacerdos
pallentis foliis caput exornarat olivae,
cum lapsa e manibus fugit pila, cumque relapsa est,
procurrit virgo.   quod uti ne prodita ludo   150
auratam gracili solvisses corpore pallam!
omnia quae retinere gradum cursusque morari
possent, o tecum vellem tu semper haberes!
non umquam violata manu sacraria divae
iurando, infelix, nequiquam iure piasses.   155
etsi quis nocuisse tibi periuria credat?
causa pia est: timuit fratri te ostendere Iuno.
at levis ille deus, cui semper ad ulciscendum
quaeritur ex omni verborum iniuria dictu,
aurea fulgenti depromens tela pharetra   160

[139] *Most editors make the parenthesis begin with* cuius. *As here,* Ellis.
[140] *So* Ellis.   olim di *Ribbeck:* olim se (si).
[141] nonnulli.   licitam *Unger:* lictam *L:* liceat *HAR*.
[143] caterva.
[149] cumque] quoque *Unger.* relapsa est *Heinsius:* relaps(a)e *or* relaxe *MSS.*
[151] auratam *Jacobs:* aurea iam (*sc.* pila): aureolam *Housman.* solvisses *Barth:* solvisset.
[154] non numquam *A.* manus *HAR*.
[155] iure *Barth:* iura.
[158] ad ulciscendum *Aldine edition* 1517: adolescendum (-ntum).   [159] dictu *H:* dicto *LAR*.

CIRIS

and men—but too large is the theme!), that same tiny boy at this time whetted the stern wrath of mighty Juno, whose home, forbidden to all, the perjured maid (perjuries goddesses remember from of old, yet remember long!) had unwittingly profaned;[1] for, as she was engaging in the goddess' rites, she indulged in a frolic, and went far beyond the band of matrons and her companions, rejoicing in the ungirdled robe that plays about her body, and throwing loose its swelling folds, as the North wind tosses it about. Not yet had the fire tasted the holy offerings; not yet had the priestess bathed in the wonted water and adorned her head with pale olive-leaves, when the ball slipped away from her hands, and as it rebounds the maiden runs forward. Would that thou hadst not been beguiled by play, and hadst not loosened the golden robe on thy slender body! O would that thou hadst ever with thee all thy apparel, which might have kept back thy steps and stayed thy course! Never would thy hand have profaned the sanctuary of the goddess, nor wouldst thou, unhappy one, with an oath have made vain expiation![2] And yet who would suppose that perjury had been thy bane? There is a righteous plea: Juno feared to show thee to her brother.[3] But that fickle god (by whom whatever falsehood lurks in any spoken word is ever sought for punishment), drawing golden shafts from his gleaming

---

[1] The story of the perjury is obscure. As to the parenthesis, "the inveteracy of the habit might be supposed to prevent its long continuance in any particular case" (ELLIS).

[2] Scylla must have sworn that she had not perjured herself.

[3] Juno's wrath, which could easily be aroused because of the amorous Jupiter, was feared by Scylla, who therefore swore falsely that she had not exposed her limbs in the temple of the goddess.

VIRGIL

(heu nimium terret, nimium Tirynthia visu),
virginis in tenera defixerat omnia mente.

Quae simul ac venis hausit sitientibus ignem
et validum penitus concepit in ossa furorem,
saeva velut gelidis Edonum Bistonis oris   165
ictave barbarico Cybeles antistita buxo,
infelix virgo tota bacchatur in urbe,
non storace Idaeo fragrantis picta capillos,
coccina non teneris pedibus Sicyonia servans,
non niveo retinens bacata monilia collo.   170
multum illi incerto trepidant vestigia cursu:
saepe redit patrios ascendere perdita muros,
aeriasque facit causam se visere turris;
saepe etiam tristis volvens in nocte querellas
sedibus ex altis tecti speculatur amorem   175
castraque prospectat crebris lucentia flammis.
nulla colum novit, carum non respicit aurum,
non arguta sonant tenui psalteria chorda,
non Libyco molles plauduntur pectine telae.
nullus in ore rubor: ubi enim rubor, obstat amori. 180
atque ubi nulla malis reperit solacia tantis
tabidulamque videt labi per viscera mortem,
quo vocat ire dolor, subigunt quo tendere fata,
fertur et horribili praeceps impellitur oestro,
ut patris, a demens, crinem de vertice sectum   185
furtim atque argute detonsum mitteret hosti.
namque haec condicio miserae proponitur una,

---

[161] *So Vollmer. The verse is probably corrupt.*
[165] gelidis *Constantius of Fano:* gelidi *Z.*
[168] flagrantis. tincta *Schrader:* uncta *Heinsius.*
[169] coccina *Baehrens:* cognita. Sicyonia *Constantius of Fano:* sic omnia *Z.*
[175] tecti *Heyne:* c(a)eli: ex aulae celsis *Haupt.*
[185] a(h) demum A^1: ademptum *L.* sectum H^2: serum H^1A^1R (*retained by Vollmer*): caesum *Ellis.*
[186] argute *Vollmer:* arguto. desponsum *Némethy.*

418

CIRIS

quiver (ah! too much terror does the Tirynthian[1] awake at sight of them!), had lodged them all in the maiden's gentle heart.

[163] Soon as she drank the fire into her thirsty veins, and caught deep within her marrow the potent frenzy, even as a fierce Thracian woman in the chill lands of the Edonians, or as a priestess of Cybele, inspired by barbaric box-wood flute, the luckless maid raves through the city. No balsam of Ida adorns her fragrant locks, no scarlet shoes of Sicyon protect her tender feet, no collar of pearls keeps she upon her snowy neck. Ever do her feet hurry to and fro in uncertain course; oft she returns, forlorn one, to climb her father's walls, and makes the plea that she is visiting the lofty towers; oft too at night, when pondering bitter complaints, from her high palace-home she watches for her love, and gazes forth to the camp, ablaze with frequent fires. Naught she knows of the distaff, she cares not for precious gold, the tuneful harp rings not with its slender strings, the loom's soft threads are smitten not with the Libyan comb.[2] No blush is on her cheeks; for in a blush love finds a bar. And when for ills so great she finds no comfort, and sees slow-wasting death steal o'er her frame, she fares whither anguish summons her, whither the fates compel her to hasten, and by awful frenzy is she driven headlong, so that, severing it with stealth and cunning from her father's head, she —mad girl—might send the shorn lock to the foe. For to the unhappy girl are offered these terms

---

[1] *i.e.* Juno, called Tirynthian from Tiryns in Argolis; *cf. Aen.* III. 547.

[2] Probably of ivory, for elephants were numerous in Libya.

VIRGIL

sive illa ignorans (quis non bonus omnia malit
credere, quam tanti sceleris damnare puellam?),
heu tamen infelix : quid enim imprudentia prodest?

Nise pater, cui direpta crudeliter urbe   191
vix erit una super sedes in turribus altis,
fessus ubi exstructo possis considere nido,
tu quoque avis metuere : dabit tibi filia poenas.
gaudete, o celeres, subnixae nubibus altis,   195
quae mare, quae viridis silvas lucosque sonantis
incolitis, gaudete, vagae blandaeque volucres,
vosque adeo, humanos mutatae corporis artus,
vos o crudeli fatorum lege, puellae
Dauliades, gaudete : venit carissima vobis,   200
cognatos augens reges numerumque suorum,
Ciris et ipse pater. vos, o pulcherrima quondam
corpora, caeruleas praevertite in aethera nubes,
qua novus ad superum sedes haliaeetos et qua
candida concessos ascendet Ciris honores.   205

Iamque adeo dulci devinctus lumina somno
Nisus erat, vigilumque procul custodia primis
excubias foribus studio iactabat inani,
cum furtim tacito descendens Scylla cubili
auribus arrectis nocturna silentia temptat   210

---

[187] *There is probably a lacuna after this verse. So Vollmer.*
[189] tanti sceleris *edition of* 1501 : tanto scelere.
[190] prudentia *AR.*
[194] metuere *G. Hermann :* moriere.
[197] blandaeque] laudate *HA¹R :* vagi laris ante *Ellis.*
[198] humani.
[199] crudeli *Aldine edition* 1517 : crudeles.
[201] sororum *Barth.*   [206] devictus *LAR.*
[208] servabat *Némethy.*   [210] erectis (us) *or* arreptis.

CIRIS

alone [1]—or perchance in ignorance she did the deed (what good man would not believe anything rather than convict the maid of such a crime?), yet alas! unblest was she: for what doth folly avail?

[191] O Nisus, father, who, when thy city has been cruelly despoiled, shalt have scarcely one home left in lofty turrets, where in weariness thou canst settle in thy high-built nest, thou too as a bird shalt be feared; thy daughter shall pay thee thy due.[2] Rejoice, ye swift creatures, that rest upon the lofty clouds, ye that dwell upon the sea, that dwell in green woods and echoing groves, rejoice, ye sweet birds that widely roam; yea, and ye too whose human limbs are changed by cruel law of the fates, ye Daulian maids,[3] rejoice; there comes one beloved by you, swelling the ranks of her royal kindred,[4] even Ciris and her father himself. Do ye, O forms once most fair, outstrip the clouds of heaven, and fly to the skies, where the new sea-eagle will climb to the homes of the gods, and the fair Ciris to the honours granted her.[5]

[206] And now, even now, the eyes of Nisus were fast bound in sweet sleep, and at the entrance doors hard by, with vain zeal the sentries on guard were keeping watch, when Scylla, stealthily descending from her silent couch, with straining ears essays the silence

---

[1] Minos would not return Scylla's love unless she betrayed her father in the manner described.

[2] Scylla, transformed into a sea-hawk, will be pursued by Nisus, transformed into a sea-eagle; cf. *Georgics*, I. 405.

[3] Philomela and Procne, who had also been changed into birds. Procne had married Tereus, king of Daulis.

[4] Philomela and Procne were daughters of the elder Pandion, king of Athens, while Nisus was son of the younger Pandion.

[5] Scylla's transformation is not regarded as a punishment.

VIRGIL

et pressis tenuem singultibus aera captat.
tum suspensa levans digitis vestigia primis
egreditur ferroque manus armata bidenti
evolat; at demptae subita in formidine vires
caeruleas sua furta prius testantur ad umbras.   215
nam qua se ad patrium tendebat semita limen,
vestibulo in thalami paulum remoratur et alte
suspicit ad celsi nictantia sidera mundi,
non accepta piis promittens munera divis.

Quam simul Ogygii Phoenicis filia Carme   220
surgere sensit anus (sonitum nam fecerat illi
marmoreo aeratus stridens in limine cardo),
corripit extemplo fessam languore puellam
et simul "o nobis sacrum caput," inquit, "alumna,
non tibi nequiquam viridis per viscera pallor   225
aegrotas tenui suffundit sanguine venas,
nec levis hoc faceres (neque enim pote) cura subegit,
aut fallor: quod ut o potius, Rhamnusia, fallar!
nam qua te causa nec dulcis pocula Bacchi
nec gravidos Cereris dicam contingere fetus?   230
qua causa ad patrium solam vigilare cubile,
tempore quo fessas mortalia pectora curas,
quo rapidos etiam requiescunt flumina cursus?
dic age nunc miserae saltem, quod saepe petenti
iurabas nihil esse mihi, cur maesta parentis   235

[214] devolat *Leo*. *A full stop is commonly placed at the end of the verse.*
[215] testatur *LAR*.   [216] lumen H^1L^1.
[217] remoratus. alte *Herzberg:* alti.
[218] celsi *Scaliger:* c(a)eli : adclinis *Leo.* nictantia *Scaliger:* mutantia H^1R: nutantia H^2AL.
[225] nequiquam *Ribbeck:* ne(nec)quicquam.
[226] egroto *H.* suffudit *L.*   [227] faceret *ARU*.
[228] aut] haud A^2L. quod ut o] *Schrader:* quod te A^2L: quod ita H^2. fallar *Juntine edition:* fallor *Z*.
[235] cur] cum *LAR:* tum H^1.

of night, and checking her sobs, catches at the fine
air. Then, poising her feet on tip-toe, she passes without and fares forth, her hand armed with two-edged
shears; but failure of strength in her sudden terror
first bears witness of her misdeeds to the shades of
heaven. For where the path led to her father's
threshold, she lingers a moment at the chamber-
entrance, and glances up at high heaven's flickering
stars, promising gifts that win no acceptance with
the righteous gods.

[220] Soon as aged Carme,[1] daughter of Ogygian
Phoenix, took note of her rising (for she had heard
the creaking of the bronze hinge[2] on the marble
threshold), straightway she seizes the faint and
weary maid, and therewith cries: "O precious
foster-child, whom we revere, 'tis not without
reason that throughout thy frame a sallow paleness
pours its thin blood through thy feverish veins, nor
has light trouble forced thee—nay, it could not—to
this deed, or else I am deceived: and O Rhamnusian
maid,[3] rather may I be deceived! For why else shall
I say thou touchest neither the cups of sweet Bacchus
nor the teeming fruits of Ceres? Why watchest thou
alone by thy father's bed in that hour, when the
hearts of men rest from weary cares, when even
rivers stay their swift course? Come, tell now at
least thy poor nurse that which, oft as I have
besought thee, thou hast sworn means naught—

[1] Carme, daughter of Phoenix, was loved by Jupiter.
Their daughter, Britomartis, being wooed by Minos, fled
into the sea. Rescued by Diana, she was worshipped in
Crete under the name Dictyna.

[2] cf. *Aen.* I. 449. The term *cardo* applies to the pivot and
socket upon which the door swings.

[3] Nemesis, who was worshipped especially at Rhamnus, in
Attica.

VIRGIL

formosos circum virgo remorere capillos?
ei mihi, ne furor ille tuos invaserit artus,
ille Arabae Myrrhae quondam qui cepit ocellos,
ut scelere infando (quod nec sinat Adrastea)
laedere utrumque uno studeas errore parentem! 240
quod si alio quovis animi iactaris amore
(nam te iactari, non est Amathusia nostri
tam rudis, ut nullo possim cognoscere signo),
si concessus amor noto te macerat igne,
per tibi Dictynae praesentia numina iuro, 245
prima deum mihi quae dulcem te donat alumnam,
omnia me potius digna atque indigna laborum
milia visuram, quam te tam tristibus istis
sordibus et senio patiar tabescere tali."

Haec loquitur, mollique ut se velavit amictu, 250
frigidulam iniecta circumdat veste puellam,
quae prius in tenui steterat succincta crocota.
dulcia deinde genis rorantibus oscula figens
persequitur miserae causas exquirere tabis,
nec tamen ante ullas patitur sibi reddere voces, 255
marmoreum tremebunda pedem quam rettulit intra.
illa autem "quid sic me," inquit, "nutricula, torques?
quid tantum properas nostros novisse furores?
non ego consueto mortalibus uror amore
nec mihi notorum deflectunt lumina voltus 260

---

²³⁶ remorere *Paris edition* 1501: morerere *H²LAR (adopted by Ellis, who takes it of rapturous longing)*: morere *H¹*.

²³⁹ sinit.   ²⁴¹ animi *Haupt*: animis *HA¹R*: animo *A²L*.
²⁴² nam] nec *AR*.
²⁴⁶ prima deum quae dulce mihi te donat.
²⁴⁷ laborum] laturam *A²L*.
²⁴⁹ senio *Ribbeck*: scoria *A²L*: morbo *R*: scora (=scoria) *Ellis*: sanie *Sudhaus*.
²⁵⁰ velarat *Heyne*.   ²⁵² crocota *Scaliger*: corona.
²⁵⁴ persequitur *edition* 1507: prosequitur *LAR*: persequimur *H*.   ²⁵⁶ intro *Ribbeck*.
²⁵⁷ sic *Leo*. quid enim me *Ellis*: quid (nunc) me.

CIRIS

why, unhappy maid, thou lingerest near thy father's beauteous locks? Ah me! may it not be that that madness has assailed thy limbs, which once took captive the eyes of Arabian Myrrha,[1] so that in monstrous sin (which Adrastea forbid!) thou shouldst be fain by one folly to wrong both parents! But if by some other passionate love thou art swayed (for that thou art, not so strange to me is the Amathusian,[2] that I cannot learn this by some sign), if a lawful flame wastes thee with familiar flame, I swear to thee by the divine presence of Dictyna,[3] who, first of the gods in my eyes, granted me a sweet foster-child in thee, that sooner shall I face all toils, thousands meet and unmeet, than suffer thee to pine away in such sad wretchedness and in such affliction."

250 Thus she cries, and, clad as she was in soft raiment, she casts her garb about the shivering maid, who before had stood, high-girt, in light saffron robe. Then, imprinting sweet kisses on her tear-bedewed cheeks, she earnestly seeks the causes of her wasting misery, yet suffers her not to make aught of reply, until, all trembling, she has withdrawn her marble-cold[4] feet within. Then cries the maid: "Why, dear nurse, dost thou thus torture me? Why so eager to know my madness? 'Tis no love common to mortals that inflames me; 'tis not the faces of friends that draw toward them my

---

[1] The story of Myrrha or Smyrna, who was guilty of incest with her father Cinyras and was afterwards transformed into the Arabian myrrh-tree, is told in Ovid, *Metam.* x. 298 ff.   [2] Venus.   [3] See note on 220, above.
[4] *cf. Georgics*, IV. 523.

VIRGIL

nec genitor cordi est: ultro namque odimus omnis.
nil amat hic animus, nutrix, quod oportet amari,
in quo falsa tamen lateat pietatis imago,
sed media ex acie mediisque ex hostibus. heu heu,
quid dicam quove aegra malum hoc exordiar ore? 265
dicam equidem, quoniam tu me non dicere, nutrix,
non sinis: extremum hoc munus morientis habeto.
ille, vides, nostris qui moenibus adsidet hostis,
quem pater ipse deum sceptri donavit honore,
cui Parcae tribuere nec ullo volnere laedi 270
(dicendum est, frustra circumvehor omnia verbis),
ille mea, ille idem oppugnat praecordia Minos.
quod per te divum crebros testamur amores
perque tuum memori sanctum mihi pectus alumnae,
ut me, si servare potes, nec perdere malis; 275
sin autem optatae spes est incisa salutis,
ne mihi, quam merui, invideas, nutricula, mortem.
nam nisi te nobis malus, o malus, optima Carme,
ante in conspectum, casusve deusve tulisset,
aut ferro hoc" (aperit ferrum quod veste latebat) 280
"purpureum patris dempsissem vertice crinem,
aut mihi praesenti peperissem volnere letum."

Vix haec ediderat, cum clade exterrita tristi
intonsos multo deturpat pulvere crinis
et graviter questu Carme complorat anili: 285
"o mihi nunc iterum crudelis reddite Minos,
o iterum nostrae Minos inimice senectae,

---

[265] aegra *Baehrens:* ausa *Sillig:* agam *HAR:* ipsa *L.*
[266] tu me non *Baehrens:* tu nunc non H^2: quid non tibi *L.*
[273] te per *HL.* obtestor HA^2L: testatur A^1.
[274] memoris. sanctum *Sillig:* auctum: haustum A^2L.
[275] servare potes *Ascensius:* versa repetes: versare potes A^2L. nec] ne *Aldine edition* 1517.
[277] ne *Aldine* 1517: nec.
[279] in *Drakenborch:* hunc *LAR:* hinc *H. Linforth* reads ante hoc confectum. [284] incomptos *Heinsius.*

CIRIS

eyes, 'tis not my father who is thus loved: nay more, I hate them all! This soul of mine, O nurse, loves naught that should be loved, naught wherein there lurks, albeit vain, some ghost of natural regard, but loves from midst the ranks of war, from midst our foes. Alas! Alas! What can I say? With what speech can I, sad one, launch forth upon this woe? Yet surely I will speak, since thou, O nurse, dost not permit me to be silent: this take thou as my last dying gift. Yonder foe, who, thou seest, is seated before our walls, to whom the Sire himself of the gods has given the glory of sceptre, and to whom the Fates have granted that he suffer from no wound (I must speak; vainly with my words do I travel round the whole story), 'tis he, 'tis he, that same Minos, that doth besiege my heart. O, I entreat thee by the many loves of the gods, and by thy heart, revered by me, thy mindful foster-child, do thou rather save me, if thou canst, and not destroy me. But if hope of the salvation I crave be cut off, grudge me not, dear nurse, the death I have deserved. For, good Carme, had not a perverse, yea, a perverse chance or god, brought thee first before my eyes, then either with this steel" (she reveals the steel, hidden in her robe)[1] "I should have taken from my father's head his crimson lock, or with single stroke before his eyes have won me death."

[283] Scarce had she uttered these words, when, affrighted by the fell disaster, Carme defiles her unshorn locks with a shower of dust, and in aged accents makes grievous lamentation: "O Minos, who now a second time[2] hast visited upon me thy cruelty! O Minos, in my old age a second time mine enemy! how

[1] *cf. Aen.* VI. 406.
[2] See note on 220, above.

VIRGIL

semper ut aut olim natae te propter eundem
aut Amor insanae luctum portavit alumnae!
tene ego tam longe capta atque avecta nequivi,   290
tam grave servitium, tam duros passa labores,
effugere, o bis iam exitium crudele meorum?
iam iam nec nobis aequo senioribus ullum
vivere uti cupiam vivit genus. ut quid ego amens
te erepta, o Britomarti, mei spes una sepulchri,   295
te, Britomarti, diem potui producere vitae?
atque utinam celeri nec tantum grata Dianae
venatus esses virgo sectata virorum,
Gnosia nec Partho contendens spicula cornu
Dictaeas ageres ad gramina nota capellas!   300
numquam tam obnixe fugiens Minois amores
praeceps aerii specula de montis abisses,
unde alii fugisse ferunt et numen Aphaeae
virginis adsignant; alii, quo notior esses,
Dictynam dixere tuo de nomine lunam.   305
sint haec vera velim; mihi certe, nata, peristi.
numquam ego te summo volitantem in vertice montis
Hyrcanos inter comites agmenque ferarum
conspiciam, nec te redeuntem amplexa tenebo.

²⁸⁸ ut *inserted by Schrader.*
²⁹² o bis iam *Housman:* obsistam.
²⁹³ aequo *Haupt:* ea que (quae): aevi *Heinsius:* heu quae *Vollmer.*
²⁹⁴ vivere uti cupiam *Sillig:* vivendi copiam *HAR:* vivendi causa est *Vollmer.*   ²⁹⁵ sepulchri] salutis *A¹R.*
²⁹⁹ nec Partho *Haupt:* neu Partho *Aldine edition* 1517: na(e)upharto.   ³⁰⁰ puellas *A¹R.*
³⁰² montis abisses *Scaliger:* montibus isses.
³⁰³ *One verse or more may have dropped out after* 302. *So Skutsch and Vollmer.*   ³⁰⁶ sunt *R.*
³⁰⁷ montis *wanting in HA¹R.*

428

CIRIS

truly through thee, and thee alone, has Love ever
brought grief, either to my child in other days, or
now to my distraught fosterling! Have I, who was
taken captive and carried off to this distant land,[1]
who have suffered such grievous servitude and harsh
travails, have I failed to escape thee, O thou who art
already for the second time the cruel destruction of
my loved ones? Now, now, even for me, who am
older than is meet, there lives no child, so that I
may long to live. Why have I, frenzied one, when
thou, Britomartis, thou, Britomartis, the sole hope of
my tomb, wert torn from me—why have I been able
to prolong my day of life? And would that thou,
maiden so dear to fleet Diana, hadst neither pursued,
a maiden, the hunt that belongs to men, nor, aiming
Gnosian shafts from Parthian bow, hadst driven the
Dictaean goats to their familiar meadows! Never
with such resolve to flee from Minos' passion wouldst
thou have sped headlong from the towering mountain-crag,[2] whence some relate that thou didst flee,
and assign thee the godhead of the virgin Aphaea;
but others, that so thy fame might be greater,[3] have
called the moon Dictyna after thy name. May this,
I pray, be true; for me at least, my child, thou art
no more. Never shall I see thee flitting on the
mountain's highest peak amid the Hyrcanian hounds,
thy comrades, and the wild beast throng, nor on thy
return shall I hold thee in my embrace.

[1] *i.e.* from Crete to Megara.
[2] *cf. Eclogues*, VIII. 59.
[3] The poet implies that the name Dictyna, by which
Diana, the Moon-goddess, was also known (*cf.* Tibullus, I.
iv. 25; Ovid, *Metamorphoses*, II. 441, etc.), had been given to
Britomartis herself. Pausanias (II. xxx. 3) tells us that
Britomartis was known as Dictyna in Crete, and as Aphaea
in Aegina.

VIRGIL

"Verum haec tum nobis gravia atque indigna fuere
tum, mea alumna, tui cum spes integra maneret, 311
et vox ista meas nondum violaverat auris.
tene etiam Fortuna mihi crudelis ademit,
tene, o sola meae vivendi causa senectae?
saepe tuo dulci nequiquam capta sopore, 315
cum premeret natura, mori me velle negavi,
ut tibi Corycio glomerarem flammea luto.
quo nunc me, infelix, aut quae me fata reservant?
an nescis, qua lege patris de vertice summo
edita candentis praetexat purpura canos, 320
quae tenuis patrio praes sit suspensa capillo?
si nescis, aliquam possum sperare salutem,
inscia quandoquidem scelus es conata nefandum:
sin est, quod metuo, per te, mea alumna, tuumque
expertum multis miserae mihi rebus amorem, 325
perdere saeva precor per numina Ilithyiae,
ne tantum facinus tam nulla mente sequaris.
non ego te incepto (fieri quod non pote) conor
flectere, Amor, neque est cum dis contendere nostrum!
sed patris incolumi potius denubere regno 330
atque aliquos tamen esse velis tibi, alumna, Penates.
hoc unum exitio docta atque experta monebo.
quod si non alia poteris ratione parentem
flectere (sed poteris; quid enim non unica possis?),
tum potius tandem ista, pio cum iure licebit, 335

³¹⁰ tunc *A R*: cum *L*.   ³¹¹ tum] tu.   ³¹² et] nec *H A*¹*R*.
³¹⁴ o *omitted H A R*.   ³¹⁸ numina servant *L*.
³²¹ praes sit *Ellis*: pressit (pręsit): spes sit *edition of* 1507 (*with* tenui).
³²⁴ per te mea *Gronovius*: per me tu (tua, *or* mea).
³²⁶ per te sacra *Scaliger*: parcere saeva *Vollmer*. numina *Heyne*: flumina.
³²⁷ nec *A R* (*Vollmer*).   tantum *Baehrens*: tantum *B*.
³²⁹ amore *edition of* 1534.   ³³² exilio *Baehrens*.
³³⁵ tum *Haupt*: tunc (tu).   tandem ista *Baehrens*: tamen ipsa *L A R*.

430

CIRIS

310 "But all this burden and this shame was mine, when hope of thee, my foster-child, still remained unshattered, and that tale of thine had not yet profaned my ears. Has cruel fortune taken thee also from me, thee, who alone art for my old age a cause of living? Ofttimes, vainly charmed by thy sweet slumber, though nature weighed heavy upon me, I was loth, I said, to die, for I would fain weave for thee a marriage-veil of Corycian yellow. To what end, unhappy one, or by what fate am I now held back? Or knowest thou not by what law the crimson, arising from the crown of thy father's head, fringes his shining hoary hair, the crimson that hangs as a slender surety [1] from thy father's lock? If thou knowest not, I may hope for some salvation, since all unknowing thou hast essayed a crime unspeakable. But if it is as I fear, then by thyself, my child, and by thy love, of which I, unhappy one! have had many a proof, and by the power of Ilithyia [2] so cruel to destroy, do not, I pray, with intent so foolish, pursue this great wickedness. I do not essay, O Love, to turn thee from thy purpose —that can not be—nor is it for me to contend with gods [3]; but may it be thy wish, my child, to wed when thy father's kingdom is safe, and at least to have for thyself some home! This one counsel I will give, I who am taught and schooled by disaster. But if in no other way thou canst sway thy sire (but this thou canst: for what couldst thou, an only child, not do?) then rather I pray (pious right shalt thou

---

[1] *i.e.* of the state, whose safety depended on the lock.
[2] According to *Odyssey*, XIX. 188, this goddess had a cave near Amnisus, in Crete.
[3] This is an apostrophe, addressed to Love, the deity.

VIRGIL

cum facti causam tempusque doloris habebis,
tum potius conata tua atque incepta referto;
meque deosque tibi comites, mea alumna, futuros
polliceor: nihil est, quod texitur ordine, longum."

His ubi sollicitos animi relevaverat aestus   340
vocibus et blanda pectus spe luserat aegrum,
paulatim tremebunda genis obducere vestem
virginis et placidam tenebris captare quietem,
inverso bibulum restinguens lumen olivo,
incipit ad crebrosque insani pectoris ictus   345
ferre manum, adsiduis mulcens praecordia palmis.
noctem illam sic maesta super marcentis alumnae
frigidulos cubito subnixa pependit ocellos.

Postera lux ubi laeta diem mortalibus almum
et gelida venientem ignem quatiebat ab Oeta,   350
quem pavidae alternis fugitant optantque puellae
(Hesperium vitant, optant ardescere Eoum),
praeceptis paret virgo nutricis et omnis
undique conquirit nubendi sedula causas.
temptantur patriae submissis vocibus aures,   355
laudanturque bonae pacis bona; multus inepto
virginis insolitae sermo novus errat in ore.
nunc tremere instantis belli certamina dicit
communemque timere deum; nunc regis amicis,
iamque ipsi verita est: orbum flet maesta parentem, 360

---

³³⁹ texuit *or* texat: texas *edition* 1517.
³⁴⁰ his *Aldine* 1517: hic *HAR*: hoc *L*.
³⁴¹ luserat *Aldine* 1534: viserat *HA²*: iusserat *A¹R*: clauserat *L*.
³⁴⁴ restringens.   ³⁴⁵ -que *added by Bothe*.
³⁴⁷ marcentis *Heinsius*: morientis.
³⁴⁹ *Vollmer holds that a verse has fallen out after this.*
³⁵⁰ venientem ignem *Haupt*: venienti mihi (mane).
³⁵⁶ inepte *Leo*.
³⁶⁰ iamque *Haupt*: namque. *Vollmer gives* namque ipsi verita est *in parentheses.*

432

CIRIS

have, for thou shalt have a plea for action and occasion for resentment)—then rather renew these thy attempts and essays. The gods and I—I promise thee, my child—will wait upon thee; no task proves long, which step by step is wrought."

340 When with these words she had lightened passion's troubled tide, and with soothing hope had beguiled her love-sick heart, little by little with trembling hands she essays to draw a veil over the maiden's cheeks, and with darkness to woo reposeful calm, uptilting the lamp of oil and quenching the thirsty light[1]; then lays her hand upon her mad heart's frequent throbs, soothing her bosom with constant fondling. Thus all that night, sad soul, she hung poised on elbow over the tear-chilled eyes of her drooping foster-child.

349 Soon as the morrow's dawn was joyously bringing kindly day to mortals, and on chill Oeta was scattering the rays of those advancing fires, which timorous maidens now flee and now crave (the star of Hesperus they shun, they long for Eos to blaze),[2] the girl obeys the bidding of her nurse, and here and there earnestly seeks all manner of pleas for wedlock. In soft accents she assails her father's ears, and praises the blessings of gentle peace; much strange speech flits from the foolish lips of the untutored maid: she trembles, she says, at the impending battle-strife, and fears the common god of war; now for the king's friends and now for himself is she afraid: sadly she bewails her bereaved

[1] The light was extinguished by tilting up the lamp and allowing the oil to cover the burning wick.
[2] *cf.* Catullus, LXII. 35.

VIRGIL

cum Iove communis qui non dat habere nepotes;
nunc etiam conficta dolo mendacia turpi
invenit et divum terret formidine civis;
nunc alia ex aliis (nec desunt) omina quaerit.
quin etiam castos ausa est corrumpere vates,   365
ut, cum caesa pio cecidisset victima ferro,
esset qui generum Minoa auctoribus extis
iungere et ancipitis suaderet tollere pugnas.

At nutrix, patula componens sulpura testa,
narcissum casiamque herbas contundit olentis   370
terque novena ligans triplici diversa colore
fila, "ter in gremium mecum," inquit, "despue, virgo,
despue ter, virgo: numero deus impare gaudet."
inde Iovi magno geminans Stygialia sacra,
sacra nec Idaeis anubus nec cognita Grais,   375
pergit, Amyclaeo spargens altaria thallo,
regis Iolciacis animum defigere votis.

Verum ubi nulla movet stabilem fallacia Nisum,
nec possunt homines nec possunt flectere divi,
(tanta est in parvo fiducia crine cavendi),   380
rursus ad inceptum sociam se iungit alumnae,
purpureumque parat rursus tondere capillum,
tam longo quod iam captat succurrere amori,
non minus illa tamen, revehi quod moenia Cressa
gaudeat: et cineri patria est iucunda sepulto.   385

Ergo iterum capiti Scylla est inimica paterno.

---

[361] qui non dat habere *Ellis:* qui quondam (quim, quin) habuere.   [362] confecta.   [364] omnia *R*.
[366] ut *Aldine edition* 1517: et.   [370] incendit *HA*.
[371] ligans *Ribbeck:* ligant (ligat).
[374] inde (hinc) magno geminat (generata) Iovi: geminans *Bothe*. Stygialia *Scaliger:* frigidula.
[375] Aeaeis *Heinsius*.   [381] adiungit *HL*.
[383] tam *Heyne:* cum longe (longo).
[384] revehi *A²:* rauci *A¹R:* Rhauci *Ellis and Unger*. Cressa *Schrader:* crescat (crescant).
[386] iterum *Heinsius:* metu: manu *Ellis*. capiti *H²:* capitis.

434

CIRIS

father, who suffers her not to give him grandchildren whom he would share with Jove.[1] Now, too, she conceives falsehoods feigned in base deceit, and affrights her fellow-citizens with the terrors of the gods; now for various omens, from this one and from that, she makes quest, nor fails to find them. Nay more, she dared to bribe holy seers, so that, when a victim fell, slain by sacred steel, one should prompt the king to join Minos to himself as son, and to put an end to the doubtful conflict.

369 But the nurse, mixing sulphur in a broad bowl, bruises therewith narcissus and cassia, savoury herbs, and thrice tying thrice nine threads, marked with three different hues, she cries: "Spit thrice into thy bosom, as I do, maiden; spit thrice, maiden: in an uneven number heaven delights."[2] Then, oft paying to mighty Jove the Stygian rites,[3] rites unknown to soothsayers, Trojan or Greek, she, sprinkling the altars with Amyclaean branch,[4] essays to bewitch the king's mind with Thessalian enchantments.

378 But when now no device moves steadfast Nisus, and neither men nor gods can sway him (such confidence in warding off peril places he in his little lock) again she allies herself with her foster-child's design, and again makes ready to shear the crimson hair, for now she is eager to relieve a passion so protracted,— yet not less so because of her joy in returning to the towns of Crete; our motherland is sweet, if only for our buried ashes.

386 Therefore once more Scylla assails her father's

---

[1] If she wedded Minos, Nisus and Jupiter would both be grandfathers to her children.
[2] cf. *Eclogues*, VIII. 73 ff.   [3] cf. *Aen*, IV. 638.
[4] Probably an olive-bough; cf. *Aen*. VI. 230.

VIRGIL

tum coma Sidonio florens deciditur ostro,
tum capitur Megara et divum responsa probantur,
tum suspensa novo ritu de navibus altis
per mare caeruleum trahitur Niseia virgo.   390
complures illam nymphae mirantur in undis,
miratur pater Oceanus et candida Tethys
et cupidas secum rapiens Galatea sorores,
illam etiam, iunctis magnum quae piscibus aequor
et glauco bipedum curru metitur equorum,   395
Leucothea parvusque dea cum matre Palaemon;
illam etiam, alternas sortiti vivere luces,
cara Iovis suboles, magnum Iovis incrementum,
Tyndaridae niveos mirantur virginis artus.
has adeo voces atque haec lamenta per auras   400
fluctibus in mediis questu volvebat inani,
ad caelum infelix ardentia lumina tendens,
lumina, nam teneras arcebant vincula palmas:

"Supprimite o paulum turbati flamina venti,
dum queror et divos (quamquam nil testibus illis   405
profeci) extrema moriens tamen adloquor hora.
vos ego, vos adeo, venti, testabor, et aurae,
vos, vos, humana si qui de gente venitis,
cernitis: illa ego sum cognato sanguine vobis,
Scylla (quod o salva liceat te dicere, Procne),   410
illa ego sum, Nisi pollentis filia quondam,

---

[387] tunc *AR* (*so in* 388, 389).   [389] navibus] manibus *H*[1].
[394] illa *H*[1]*LA*.   [397] illam *Heinsius:* illi.
[402] tendens] tollens *L*.
[408] vos humana *Leo, who also supposes that a verse preceding this is lost:* o numantina.   [409] cernitis? *Ellis.*

CIRIS

head. Then it is that his hair, rich in its Sidonian purple, is cut off; then that Megara is taken and the divine oracles are proved; then that, suspended in strange fashion from lofty ships, the maiden daughter of Nisus is dragged over the blue sea-waters. Many Nymphs marvel at her amid the waves[1]; father Neptune marvels, and shining Tethys, and Galatea, carrying off in her company her eager sisters. At her, too, marvels she who traverses the mighty main in her azure car, drawn by her team of fishes[2] and two-footed steeds, Leucothea, and little Palaemon with his goddess mother.[3] At her, too, marvel they who live by lot alternate days, the dear offspring of Jupiter, mighty seed of a Jupiter to be,[4] the Tyndaridae, who marvel at the maiden's snowy limbs. Yea, these cries and these laments she, in the midst of the waves, sent ringing through the air in her fruitless wailing, uplifting to heaven, hapless one, her blazing eyes—her eyes, for bonds confined her tender hands.[5]

404 "Stay, ye wild winds, O stay for a space your blasts while I make plaint, and, to the gods (albeit their witness has availed me naught) yet as I die, in my last hour, I raise my cry. You, ye winds and breezes, yea you, I will call to witness! Ye, if ye that meet me are of human stock,[6] ye discern me: I am Scylla, of blood akin to yours (of thy grace may I say this, O Procne!); I am she who once was daughter of mighty Nisus, she who was wooed in

---

[1] The passage is suggested by Catullus, LXIV. 14 ff.
[2] *i.e.* dolphins; *cf. Georgics*, IV. 388 ff.
[3] Ino, daughter of Cadmus.
[4] *cf. Eclogues*, IV. 49.   [5] *cf. Aen.* II. 405-6.
[6] She is addressing the birds, which have once been human beings.

VIRGIL

certatim ex omni petiit quam Graecia regno,
qua curvus terras amplectitur Hellespontus.
illa ego sum, Minos, sacrato foedere coniunx
dicta tibi: tamen haec, etsi non accipis, audis.   415
vinctane tam magni tranabo gurgitis undas?
vincta tot adsiduas pendebo ex ordine luces?
non equidem me alio possum contendere dignam
supplicio, quod sic patriam carosque penates
hostibus immitique addixi ignara tyranno.   420
verum istaec, Minos, illos scelerata putavi,
si nostra ante aliquis nudasset foedera casus,
facturos, quorum direptis moenibus urbis,
o ego crudelis, flamma delubra petivi;
te vero victore prius vel sidera cursus   425
mutatura suos, quam te mihi talia captae
facturum metui. iam iam scelus omnia vincit.
tene ego plus patrio dilexi perdita regno?
tene ego? nec mirum, voltu decepta puella
(ut vidi, ut perii! ut me malus abstulit error!)   430
non equidem ex isto speravi corpore posse
tale malum nasci; forma vel sidera fallas.

"Me non deliciis commovit regia dives,
dives curalio fragili et lacrimoso electro,
me non florentes aequali corpore nymphae,   435
non metus impendens potuit retinere deorum:
omnia vicit amor: quid enim non vinceret ille?

413 quam curvus e terris (e *omitted* R, terras A²). *Vollmer recognizes fragments of two verses.*
415 aspicis *Heinsius.*   416 victa R.
419 quod sic] quam quod L.   420 ingrata *Heinsius.*
421 istaec *Schrader:* est hec (hoc). verum est: haec *Vollmer.*   424 flammis A.
427 factorum (fatorum) HAR.
432 sidera HA¹: sidere. fallas *Haupt:* fallor (falle *or* fallat).   434 dives *added in Aldine edition* 1534.
436 impendens *Leo:* incendens (incensam).
437 vincit LAR.

438

CIRIS

rivalry by Greeks of every realm, wherever the winding Hellespont[1] embraces his lands. I am she, O Minos, whom by sacred compact thou didst call wife: this thou hearest, albeit thou payest no heed. Shall I in bonds float o'er the waves of so vast a sea? In bonds shall I be suspended for so many days, each following each? Yet that I am worthy of other punishment I may not plead, seeing that thus I surrendered my motherland and my dear home to foemen and to a tyrant—though I knew it not—thus pitiless. Yet shame so foul as this methought my countrymen might work me, should some mischance first disclose our alliance, and when their city walls were razed I, cruel one, alas! assailed their shrines with flames; but if thou wert victor, I deemed that the stars would change their courses ere thou shouldst do such deed to me, thy captive. Now, now 'tis wickedness that conquers all![2] Did I, forlorn one, love thee above my father's realm? Did I love thee? Yet 'tis not strange. A maiden, deceived by thy face—as I saw, how was I lost! how a fatal frenzy swept me away![3]—I did not deem that from that form of thine such guilt could spring. With thy beauty thou wouldst deceive even the stars!

433 "I was moved not by a palace rich in its delights —rich in frail coral and amber tears—was moved not by damsels of like youth and beauteous to behold; no fear of gods with its menace could hold me back: Love conquered all: for what could Love not conquer?

---

[1] The Hellespont is perhaps put for the whole Aegean; *cf. Culex*, 33.

[2] A variation on *omnia vincit Amor* (*Ecl.* x. 69). So Linforth. Others would render "thy crime surpasses all."

[3] = *Eclogues*, VIII. 41.

439

VIRGIL

non mihi iam pingui sudabunt tempora myrrha,
pronuba nec castos accendet pinus honores,
nec Libys Assyrio sternetur lectulus ostro.   440
magna queror: me ne illa quidem communis alumnam
omnibus iniecta tellus tumulabit harena.
mene inter matres ancillarisque maritas,
mene alias inter famularum munere fungi
coniugis atque tuae, quaecumque erit illa, beatae 445
non licuit gravidos penso devolvere fusos?
at belli saltem captivam lege necasses!   447
iam tandem casus hominum, iam respice, Minos¦ 454
sit satis hoc, tantum solam vidisse malorum,   455
vel fato fuerit nobis haec debita pestis,
vel casu incerto, merita vel denique culpa:
omnia nam potius quam te fecisse putabo."

Labitur interea revoluta ab litore classis,
magna repentino sinuantur lintea Coro,   460
flectitur in viridi remus sale, languida fessae
virginis in cursu moritur querimonia longo.
deserit angustis inclusum faucibus Isthmon,
Cypselidae magni florentia regna Corinthi;
praeterit abruptas Scironis protinus arces   465
infestumque suis dirae testudinis exit
spelaeum multoque cruentas hospite cautes.
iamque adeo tutum longe Piraeea cernit,
et notas, heu heu frustra, respectat Athenas.

⁴³⁹ odores *HL*.
⁴⁴¹ me ne *Heyne*: ne ut (nec et *or* ut): ne tu... tumulabis *Ellis*.
⁴⁴⁸⁻⁴⁵³ *the transposition of verses as indicated in the text is due to Sudhaus. So Vollmer.*
⁴⁵⁰ livescunt *Heinsius*: labescunt (labascunt).
⁴⁵¹ pristes *Barth*: pestes *or* pisces.
⁴⁵⁵ sola *HAR*: Scyllam *Haupt*.
⁴⁵⁷ incerto *Scaliger*: incepto.   ⁴⁵⁹ resoluta *Heinsius*.
⁴⁶⁴ et magni *Schrader*. Corinthum *Heyne*.
⁴⁶⁹ heu heu] secum heu.

CIRIS

No more shall my temples drip with rich myrrh, nor shall the bridal pine kindle its pure flames, nor shall the Libyan couch be strewn with Assyrian purple. Chiefly do I thus complain: even yonder earth, that is common to all, will not entomb me, her foster-child, with sprinkling of sand! Might not I, amid the mothers and married slave-women—might not I, amid other handmaids, have performed their task, and for thy happy wife, whoe'er she be, have unrolled the spindles, weighted with their coils? But O that at least, by law of war, thou hadst killed me, thy captive! Now, pray, now, O Minos, give heed to the chances of human-kind![1] Be it enough that I, and I alone, have looked upon thus much misery! Grant that this disaster has been due to me by fate, or has come by uncertain chance, or in fine by a guilt that deserves it: aught shall I believe rather than that thou hast been its author!"

[459] Meanwhile, set free from the shore, the fleet glides forth; the great sails swell with the sudden Northwest; the oar bends in the green salt water; the feeble wailing of the weary maid dies away in the long voyage. Behind her she leaves the Isthmus, shut in with its narrow throat, the rich realm at Corinth of the great son of Cypselus;[2] forthwith she passes Sciron's steep heights, and goes beyond the dread tortoise's cave, so fatal to her fellow-citizens, and the cliffs, stained with the blood of many a guest.[3] And now indeed she sees afar secure Piraeus, and looks back—alas! alas! in vain—upon

[1] She means that no human being has ever suffered like her.
[2] Periander.
[3] The robber Sciron used to throw his victims to a tortoise.

VIRGIL

iam procul e fluctu Salaminia suspicit arva 470
florentisque videt iam Cycladas; hinc Venus illi
Sunias, hinc statio contra patet Hermionea.
linquitur ante alias longe gratissima Delos
Nereidum matri et Neptuno Aegaeo.
prospicit incinctam spumanti litore Cythnon 475
marmoreamque Paron viridemque adlapsa Donysam
Aeginamque simul †salutiferamque Seriphum. 477
iam fesso tandem fugiunt de corpore vires, 448
et caput inflexa lentum cervice recumbit,
marmorea adductis livescunt bracchia nodis. 450
aequoreae pristes, inmania corpora ponti,
undique conveniunt et glauco in gurgite circum
verbere caudarum atque oris minitantur hiatu. 453
fertur et incertis iactatur ad omnia ventis, 478
(cumba velut magnas sequitur cum parvula classis
Afer et hiberno bacchatur in aequore turbo), 480
donec tale decus formae vexarier undis
non tulit ac miseros mutavit virginis artus
caeruleo pollens coniunx Neptunia regno.
sed tamen aeternum squamis vestire puellam,
infidosque inter teneram committere piscis 485
non statuit (nimium est avidum pecus Amphitrites):
aeriis potius sublimem sustulit alis,
esset ut in terris facti de nomine Ciris,
Ciris Amyclaeo formosior ansere Ledae.

⁴⁷⁷ sementiferam *A²L*. *The verse is faulty. Vollmer thinks two half lines are lost after* simul.
⁴⁸¹ vexarier *B*: vexavit *Z*. undis] aegros (aegram).
⁴⁸⁴ aeternum *Kreunen*: alternat *Leo*: alternans *Vollmer*: eternam (externam).   ⁴⁸⁹ Amyclaeae *Heinsius*.

442

CIRIS

famous Athens. Now at a distance, rising from the flood, the fields of Salamis she espies, lying apart from the waves, and now she sees the shining Cyclades: on this side the Venus of Sunium opens to her; on that, opposite, Hermione's town.[1] Then she leaves Delos, dearest beyond all to the mother of the Nereids and to Aegean Neptune;[2] she sees afar Cythnus, girt with foaming shore, and draws near to marble-white Paros and green Donysa, with Aegina and health-bringing Seriphus.[3] Now at length her strength flees from her weary frame, her head falls back heavy on her bended neck, her marble-white arms grow livid under the close-drawn knots. Monsters of the sea, giant forms of the deep, throng about her on all sides, and in the blue-grey waters threaten her with lashing tails and gaping mouths. Onward she moves, tossed to and fro by uncertain winds (even as a tiny skiff when it follows a great fleet, and an African hurricane riots upon the wintry sea) until Neptune's spouse,[4] queen of the azure realm, brooked it not that such a beauteous form should be harassed by the waves, and transformed the maiden's hapless limbs. But still she purposed not to clothe the gentle maid with scales for ever, or establish her amid treacherous fishes (all too greedy is Amphitrite's flock): rather she raised her aloft on airy wings, that she might live on earth as Ciris, named from the deed wrought[5]—Ciris, more beauteous than Leda's Amyclaean swan.

---

[1] The poet incorrectly substitutes Venus (Aphrodite) for Athena, who had a temple on Cape Sunium. Hermione was in the Argolid.   [2] cf. Aen. III. 74.

[3] An allusion, probably, to the story of Danae and Perseus, whose ark was washed upon the coast of Seriphus.

[4] Amphitrite.

[5] Ciris is from κείρειν, "cut" or "shear."

VIRGIL

Hic velut in niveo tenera est cum primitus ovo 490
effigies animantis et internodia membris
imperfecta novo fluitant concreta calore,
sic liquido Scyllae circumfusum aequore corpus
semiferi incertis etiam nunc partibus artus
undique mutabant atque undique mutabantur. 495
oris honos primum et multis optata labella
et patulae frontis species concrescere in unum
coepere et gracili mentum producere rostro;
tum qua se medium capitis discrimen agebat,
ecce repente, velut patrios imitatus honores, 500
puniceam concussit apex in vertice cristam;
at mollis varios intexens pluma colores
marmoreum volucri vestivit tegmine corpus
lentaque perpetuas fuderunt bracchia pinnas.
inde alias partes minioque infecta rubenti 505
crura nova macies obduxit squalida pelle
et pedibus teneris unguis adfixit acutos.
et tamen hoc demum miserae succurrere pacto
vix fuerat placida Neptuni coniuge dignum.
numquam illam post haec oculi videre suorum 510
purpureas flavo retinentem vertice vittas,
non thalamus Syrio fragrans accepit amomo,
nullae illam sedes: quid enim cum sedibus illi?
quae simul ut sese cano de gurgite velox
cum sonitu ad caelum stridentibus extulit alis 515
et multum late dispersit in aequora rorem,
infelix virgo nequiquam a morte recepta
incultum solis in rupibus exigit aevum,
rupibus et scopulis et litoribus desertis.

⁴⁹¹ animantur *BHL*.   ⁵⁰¹ purpuream A^2L.
⁵⁰³ mansurum A^2L.
⁵⁰⁶ novamque acies (-em). pellem (pellis).   ⁵⁰⁹ placide.
⁵¹² Syrio *Ascensius:* Tyrio. flagrans.
⁵¹³ cum *Heinsius:* iam.
⁵¹⁷ a *Aldine edition* 1534: *omitted in MSS.*

444

CIRIS

⁴⁹⁰ Hereon, as when at first in a snowy egg there is the soft outline of a living thing, and the limbs' imperfect junctures, as they grow together in unwonted heat, float about, yet incomplete; so with Scylla's body, encompassed by the waters of the deep, while the parts were even yet uncertain, the half-human joints were changing it throughout, and throughout were being changed. First, the lovely face and those lips yearned for by many, and the broad brow's charm, began to grow together and to prolong the chin with a slender beak. Then, where on the head the line appeared that parts the hair in equal portions, lo! of a sudden, as if copying her sire's glory, on her crown a tuft waved its crimson crest, while soft plumes, blending varied hues, clothed her marble-white body with vesture of wings, and the feeble arms put forth long feathers. Then other parts and the legs, coloured with blushing crimson, an unfamiliar leanness overlaid with rough skin, and to the tender feet fastened sharp nails. And yet to succour the hapless maiden in this manner only was scarce worthy of Neptune's gentle spouse. Never hereafter did the eyes of her kin behold her tying back her purple fillets upon her golden head; no chamber, fragrant with Syrian spice, no home welcomed her; what, indeed, had she to do with home? And soon as from the hoary tide with speed and uproar she arose to the sky on whirring wings, and far and wide has scattered a cloud of spray o'er the waters, the hapless maid, vainly recovered from death, lives her wild life among the lonely rocks—the rocks and cliffs and deserted shores.

VIRGIL

Nec tamen hoc ipsum poena sine: namque deum rex,
omnia qui imperio terrarum milia versat,   521
commotus talem ad superos volitare puellam,
cum pater exstinctus caeca sub nocte lateret,
illi pro pietate sua (nam saepe nitentum
sanguine taurorum supplex resperserat aras,   525
saepe deum largo decorarat munere sedes)
reddidit optatam mutato corpore vitam
fecitque in terris haliaeetos ales ut esset:
quippe aquilis semper gaudet deus ille coruscis.
huic vero miserae, quoniam damnata deorum   530
iudicio, fatique et coniugis, ante fuisset,
infesti apposuit odium crudele parentis.
namque ut in aetherio signorum munere praestans,
unum quem duplici stellatum sidere vidi,
Scorpios alternis clarum fugat Oriona;   535
sic inter sese tristis haliaeetos iras
et Ciris memori servant ad saecula fato.
quacumque illa levem fugiens secat aethera pinnis,
ecce inimicus, atrox, magno stridore per auras
insequitur Nisus; qua se fert Nisus ad auras, 540
illa levem fugiens raptim secat aethera pinnis.

[520] ipsum B^2: iterum B^1AR (*explained by Vollmer as referring to her sufferings after the metamorphosis*).
[522] superos] celum B^1.
[524] nitentum *edition of* 1507: videmus: vigentum *Ellis*.
[525] respexerat BH^1.   auras $BHLA$.
[526] longo decoravit AR.   sedem A^1.
[529] aquilis] aliis B^1: aliquis HA^1R.   coruscus.
[531] fatique *E. B. Greene*: patrisque *Heyne*: patriaeque *Sillig*: pactique (=*plighted*) *Ellis*: natique.
[533] lumine *Schrader*.
[534] stellatum *Juntine edition*: stellarum.
[535] fugat B: fugant.   [537] facto.
[538] aera AR.   [541] aera AR.

446

CIRIS

⁵²⁰ Yet even this not without penalty: for the king of the gods, who with his power sways all regions of the world, being grieved that a maid so wicked should be flitting to the world above, while under dark night's cover her father's light was quenched, unto him by reason of his piety (for oft with the blood of sleek bulls had he suppliantly besprinkled the altars, and oft with lavish gifts had he adorned the homes of the gods) granted under changed form the life he had craved, and suffered him to be on earth a winged sea-eagle, for in lightning-swift eagles that god ever delights. But upon that unhappy maid, since she had first been condemned by judgment of the gods, of fate and of her husband,[1] he laid an angry father's relentless hate. For even as, amid the grandeur of heaven's constellations, the glorious Scorpion, which alone I have seen bestarred with two-fold brilliance, puts to rout in alternate strife the gleaming Orion: so the sea-eagle and the Ciris, with ever remindful fate, maintain the fierceness of mutual wrath from age to age. Wherever she flees, cleaving the light air with her wings, lo! savage and ruthless, with loud whirr Nisus follows through the sky; where Nisus mounts skyward, she flees in haste, cleaving the light air with her wings.[2]

---

[1] Minos was the *coniunx* (to be) of Scylla.
[2] Lines 538–541 = *Georgics*, I. 406–9. In an interesting article in *Classical Quarterly*, XIX. (1925), 155 ff., Professor D'Arcy W. Thompson holds that the passage appeared first in the *Ciris*, because it is more appropriate there. See Appendix.

COPA*

Copa Surisca, caput Graeca redimita mitella,
  crispum sub crotalo docta movere latus,
ebria fumosa saltat lasciva taberna,
  ad cubitum raucos excutiens calamos:
"quid iuvat aestivo defessum pulvere abesse?   5
  quam potius bibulo decubuisse toro?
sunt topia et kalybae, cyathi, rosa, tibia, chordae,
  et triclia umbrosis frigida harundinibus.
en et Maenalio quae garrit dulce sub antro
  rustica pastoris fistula in ore sonat.   10
est et vappa, cado nuper defusa picato,
  et strepitans rauco murmure rivus aquae.
sunt et cum croceo violae de flore corollae
  sertaque purpurea lutea mixta rosa
et quae virgineo libata Achelois ab amne   15
  lilia vimineis attulit in calathis.
sunt et caseoli, quos iuncea fiscina siccat,
  sunt autumnali cerea pruna die
castaneaeque nuces et suave rubentia mala,
  est hic munda Ceres, est Amor, est Bromius.   20

  ³ fumosa *M*: famosa *SFL*.
  ⁷ kalybae (= καλύβαι) *Reichenbach*: *MSS.* have kalibes, calybes, chalybes, *or* calices.   ¹⁰ in ore *SFL*: more *M*.
  ¹³ et cum croceo *Leo*: etiam croceo.

* For the MSS. see the opening note on the *Dirae*.

448

COPA [1]

SYRISCA, the inn-keeper, her head bound with Greek kerchief, trained as she is to sway her tremulous limbs to the notes of her castanets, within her smoky tavern tipsily dances in wanton wise, shaking against her elbow her noisy reeds: [2] "What boots it to stay outside, when aweary with the summer's dust, rather than to recline on the thirsty couch of grass? [3] There are garden nooks and arbours, mixing-cups, roses, flutes, lyres, and cool bowers with shady canes. Lo! too, the pipe, which twitters sweetly within a Maenalian [4] grotto, sounds its rustic strain in a shepherd's mouth. There is fresh wine, too, just drawn from the pitched jar, and a water-brook running noisily with hoarse murmur; there are also chaplets of violet blossoms mixed with saffron, and yellow garlands blended with crimson roses; and lilies bedewed by a virgin stream, which a nymph [5] has brought in osier-baskets. There are little cheeses, too, dried in a basket of rushes; there are waxen plums of autumn's season, and chestnuts and sweetly blushing apples; there is Ceres' pure gift, with Love and Bacchus;

[1] This interesting little poem, written in elegiac couplets, was attributed to Virgil by the grammarian Charisius.
[2] The castanets were made of pieces of reed or wood.
[3] cf. "viridante toro . . . herbae" (*Aen.* V. 388).
[4] cf. *Georgics*, I. 17; *Eclogues*, VIII. 21.
[5] As *Achelous* is used for *aqua* in general (cf. *Georgics*, I. 9), so *Achelois* is used for a water-nymph or Naiad; cf. *Eclogues*, II. 45, 46.

VIRGIL

sunt et mora cruenta et lentis uva racemis,
　et pendet iunco caeruleus cucumis.
est tuguri custos, armatus falce saligna,
　sed non et vasto est inguine terribilis.
huc, Calybita, veni: lassus iam sudat asellus;　　25
　parce illi: Vestae delicium est asinus.
nunc cantu crebro rumpunt arbusta cicadae,
　nunc varia in gelida sede lacerta latet:
si sapis, aestivo recubans nunc prolue vitro,
　seu vis crystalli ferre novos calices.　　30
hic age pampinea fessus requiesce sub umbra,
　et gravidum roseo necte caput strophio,
formosum tenerae decerpens ora puellae.
　a pereat, cui sunt prisca supercilia!
quid cineri ingrato servas bene olentia serta?　　35
　anne coronato vis lapide ista tegi?"
" pone merum et talos. pereat, qui crastina curat!
　Mors aurem vellens 'vivite' ait, 'venio.'"

²⁵ huc *M:* huic *S.*
²⁶ Vestae *Voss:* vestrae.
²⁸ varia *M:* vero *S:* vere *L:* vepris *Ellis:* veprum *Haupt.*
²⁹ nunc] te *Paris* 8205.　　³¹ hic *S:* eia *or* hia.
³³ ore *S.*
³⁶ ista] ossa *Ilgen.* tegi] legi *Wernsdorff, who refers* ista *to* serta. "Wouldst have them culled at the crowning of thy tomb?" *Wilamowitz, retaining* tegi, *accepts Buecheler's view that* ista (= serta) *is an accusative with* coronato. "Wouldst thou be covered with a stone crowned therewith?" *This is possible, but highly improbable.*

³⁷ *Vollmer gives this verse only to the traveller, making v. 38 an epilogue. Other editors carry the inn-keeper's speech through to the end.*

450

COPA

there are blood-red mulberries with grapes in heavy clusters, and from its stalk hangs the blue-grey melon. There is the cot's guardian,[1] armed with sickle of willow, but not to be feared is he, for all his huge groin.

[25] "Come hither, priest of Cybele![2] Now thy wearied ass is sweating; spare him: the ass is Vesta's delight.[3] Now with constant song the cicadas rend the thickets;[4] now the spotted lizard lurks in her cool retreat: if thou art wise, lay thee down now and steep thyself in a bowl of summer-time,[5] or in fresh crystal cups, if thou wishest them brought. Come; rest here thy wearied frame beneath the shade of vines, and entwine thy heavy head in a garland of roses, sweetly snatching kisses from a tender maiden's lips. Ah! away with him that has the sternness of early days! Why keepest the fragrant wreaths for thankless ashes? Wouldst have those limbs covered with a crowned tombstone?"[6]

[37] "Set forth the wine and dice! Away with him who heeds the morrow! Death, plucking the ear, cries: 'Live; I come!'"

---

[1] Priapus.
[2] Used jocularly, the *galli* or priests of Cybele having a reputation as vagabonds or beggars.
[3] Because, according to the story, his braying warned Vesta of an assault by Priapus (*cf.* Ovid, *Fasti*, VI. 311 ff.).
[4] *cf. Georgics*, III. 328.   [5] *i.e.* one of unusual size.
[6] Garlands were laid on tombstones; *cf.* Propertius, III. xvi. 23. The *copa* asks the traveller to have the wreaths used for a feast, not for a funeral. He is supposed to yield to her allurements, and, citing an Epicurean maxim, to fling discretion to the winds.

MORETUM*

Iam nox hibernas bis quinque peregerat horas
excubitorque diem cantu praedixerat ales,
Simylus exigui cultor cum rusticus agri,
tristia venturae metuens ieiunia lucis,
membra levat vili sensim demissa grabato   5
sollicitaque manu tenebras explorat inertis
vestigatque focum, laesus quem denique sentit.
parvulus exusto remanebat stipite fumus
et cinis obductae celabat lumina prunae.
admovet his pronam submissa fronte lucernam   10
et producit acu stuppas umore carentes,
excitat et crebris languentem flatibus ignem.
tandem concepto, sed vix, fulgore recedit,
oppositaque manu lumen defendit ab aura
et reserat clausae quae pervidet ostia clavis.   15
fusus erat terra frumenti pauper acervus:
hinc sibi depromit, quantum mensura patebat,
quae bis in octonas excurrit pondere libras.
  Inde abit adsistitque molae parvaque tabella,
quam fixam paries illos servabat in usus,   20

⁷ sentit *H*: sensit.   ⁸ fumus] fomes *Scaliger*.
¹³ sed vix *Bücheler*: sed lux.   ¹⁵ clavi *H*.

---

* Besides *F*, *S*, *L*, for which see note at the opening of the *Culex*, Vollmer cites *P* = Paris 16236 of the 10th century; *D* = Paris 7930 of the 11th century; *R* = Vindob. 134

452

MORETUM[1]

Now had night completed ten of winter's hours, and with his crowing the sentinel cock had proclaimed day's advent, when Simylus, the rustic tiller of a meagre farm, fearful of stern hunger on the coming morn, slowly, from the cheap pallet whereon they were outstretched, uplifts his limbs, and with anxious hand feels his way through the lifeless night, and gropes for the hearth, which at last, not unscathed, he finds. From a burnt-out log still lingered a tiny stream of smoke, while ashes concealed the gleam of buried coals. Bending low his head, to these he applies his lamp aslant, draws out with a needle the dried-up wick, and with many a puff wakes up the sluggish fire. Rousing at last a gleam, though hard the task, he draws back, and with sheltering hand guards the light from the draught, while his key, peeping through, unlocks the closet-door. On the ground was outpoured a poor heap of corn: from this he helps himself to as much as the measure, which runs up to sixteen pounds in weight, would hold.

[19] And now, faring forth, he takes his place at the mill and on a tiny shelf, firmly fastened for such

[1] This idyll may be a rendering of a Greek poem by Parthenius. The subject had already been handled by Suevius early in the first century B.C.

---

of the 11th or 12th century; and *M* (embracing two Munich MSS., *m* and *n*, of the 11th or 12th century). Other MSS. are cited by Ellis.

VIRGIL

lumina fida locat.   geminos tum veste lacertos
liberat et cinctus villosae tegmine caprae
perverrit cauda silices gremiumque molarum.
advocat inde manus operi, partitus utrimque:
laeva ministerio, dextra est intenta labori.   25
haec rotat adsiduum gyris et concitat orbem
(tunsa Ceres silicum rapido decurrit ab ictu),
interdum fessae succedit laeva sorori
alternatque vices.   modo rustica carmina cantat
agrestique suum solatur voce laborem,   30
interdum clamat Scybalen.   erat unica custos,
Afra genus, tota patriam testante figura,
torta comam labroque tumens et fusca colore,
pectore lata, iacens mammis, compressior alvo,
cruribus exilis, spatiosa prodiga planta.   35
continuis rimis calcanea scissa rigebant.
hanc vocat atque arsura focis imponere ligna
imperat et flamma gelidos adolere liquores.

Postquam implevit opus iustum versatile finem,
transfert inde manu tusas in cribra farinas   40
et quatit, ac remanent summo purgamina dorso.
subsidit sincera foraminibusque liquatur
emundata Ceres.   levi tum protinus illam
componit tabula, tepidas super ingerit undas,
contrahit admixtos nunc fontes atque farinas,   45
transversat durata manu liquidoque coacto
interdum grumos spargit sale, iamque subactum

²² tegmine *S*: tergore.
²⁴ admovet. utrimque *It.*: utrique (utrumque *H*).
²⁶ haec] hinc *It.* adsiduis *H*.   ³³ calore.
³⁴ pectora.
³⁶ *given by H and a few other MSS. but commonly regarded as an interpolation.*
⁴⁰ transferat. inde] illa. tusas *Wolf:* fusas.
⁴¹ ac] h(a)ec: et.   ⁴² sincere.   ⁴³ emendata.
⁴⁵ fontes *FRM:* frondes *PDSL*.   ⁴⁷ gremio.

454

MORETUM

needs on the wall, he sets his trusty light. Then from his garment he frees his twin arms, and, girt in shaggy goat's hide, with tail-brush he carefully sweeps the stones and hollow of the mill. Next he summons his two hands to work, dividing them between the two-fold tasks: the left is bent on serving the grain, the right on plying the mill.[1] This, in constant round, turns and drives the wheel (the grain, bruised by the stones' swift blows, runs down); the left, at intervals, seconds her wearied sister, and takes her turn. Anon he sings rustic songs, and with rude strains solaces his toil; at times he shouts to Scybale. She was his only help, African in stock, her whole form proclaiming her country: her hair curly, her lips swollen and her hue dusky, her chest broad, her breast hanging low, her belly somewhat pinched, her legs thin, her feet broad and ample. Her rough shoes were torn with many a rent. Her he calls, and bids her place on the fire fuel to burn, and over the flame heat cold water.

[39] Soon as the revolving mill has filled up the measure due, his hand then transfers to a sieve the bruised meal and shakes it, and lo! the husks remain on the upper side. The corn, clean and pure, sinks down, filtering through the crevices. Then straightway on a smooth table he lays it out, pours o'er it warm water, packs together the now mingled moisture and meal, kneads it by hand till hardened and, the liquid subdued, from time to time sprinkles the heap with salt. And now he smooths off his vanquished

---

[1] In ancient mills, corn was ground by means of two stones, the lower of which, called *meta*, was shaped like a cone. The lower part of the upper stone fitted the *meta* like a cap. Poured into a receptacle above, the corn passed through a small hole above the *meta*, and was ground on the sides of the latter.

VIRGIL

levat opus palmisque suum dilatat in orbem
et notat impressis aequo discrimine quadris.
infert inde foco (Scybale mundaverat aptum 50
ante locum) testisque tegit, super aggerat ignis.
dumque suas peragit Volcanus Vestaque partes,
Simylus interea vacua non cessat in hora,
verum aliam sibi quaerit opem, neu sola palato
sit non grata Ceres, quas iungat comparat escas. 55
non illi suspensa focum carnaria iuxta,
durati sale terga suis truncique vacabant,
traiectus medium sparto sed caseus orbem
et vetus adstricti fascis pendebat anethi.
ergo aliam molitur opem sibi providus heros. 60

Hortus erat iunctus casulae, quem vimina pauca
et calamo rediviva levi munibat harundo,
exiguus spatio, variis sed fertilis herbis.
nil illi derat, quod pauperis exigit usus;
interdum locuples a paupere plura petebat. 65
nec sumptus erat ullius, sed regula curae:
si quando vacuum casula pluviaeve tenebant
festave lux, si forte labor cessabat aratri,
horti opus illud erat.   varias disponere plantas
norat et occultae committere semina terrae 70
vicinosque apte cura submittere rivos.
hic holus, hic late fundentes bracchia betae
fecundusque rumex malvaeque inulaeque virebant,
hic siser et nomen capiti debentia porra,
[hic etiam nocuum capiti gelidumque papaver,] 75
grataque nobilium requies lactuca ciborum,

⁵⁰ focos.   ⁵⁶ carnalia.
⁶⁰ heros] aeris *SL :* herbis *Ribbeck.*
⁶² redimita *H.*   ⁶⁵ plura] multa *It.*
⁶⁶ ullius (ullus *or* huius) opus Ω : *Mähly deleted* opus : illud opus *Ellis, Curcio.* recula *Ribbeck.*
⁷⁵ *This verse is lacking in the oldest MSS.*

MORETUM

work, with open palms broadens it into its rounded form, and marks it in four parts, stamped in equal divisions.[1] Then he puts it in the hearth (Scybale first had cleaned a fitting place), and covers it with tiles, heaping up the fire above. And while Vulcan and Vesta are playing their part, Simylus meanwhile in that idle hour is not slack, but seeks for himself another resource, and lest Ceres alone should not please the palate, he gathers dainties to add thereto. Near his hearth no larder hung from the ceiling; gammons and slices of bacon dried and salted were wanting, but old cheeses, their rounded surface pierced midway with rushes, were suspended in baskets of close-woven fennel. Therefore the prudent hero toils to provide himself with another resource.

[61] Adjoining the cottage was a garden, sheltered by a few osiers and reeds of slender stalk, ever springing up afresh: small in extent, but rich in various herbs. Naught did it lack that a poor man's need demands; at times the wealthy would turn to the poor man's stock for more. And naught did he spend thereon, but his daily toil was his guide: if ever rains or a holiday kept him idle in his cottage; if perchance the labouring plough was idle, that time fell to the garden. He knew how to set out various plants, to entrust seeds to the hidden soil, and about his plots to train some rills, conveniently near. Here throve cabbage, here beets, their arms far outspread, with rich sorrel, mallows, and elecampane; here skirret and leeks, that owe their name to the head,[2] and lettuce that brings pleasing

[1] cf. Aen. VII. 115.
[2] The *porrum capitatum* as contrasted with the *porrum sectile*, the latter being our cut-leek or chives.

VIRGIL

. . . . crescitque in acumina radix
et gravis in latum demissa cucurbita ventrem.
verum hic non domini (quis enim contractior illo ?),
sed populi proventus erat, nonisque diebus   80
venalis umero fascis portabat in urbem :
inde domum cervice levis, gravis aere redibat,
vix umquam urbani comitatus merce macelli.
caepa rubens sectique famem domat area porri,
quaeque trahunt acri voltus nasturtia morsu,   85
intibaque et Venerem revocans eruca morantem.
   Tunc quoque tale aliquid meditans intraverat hortum.
ac primum, leviter digitis tellure refossa,
quattuor educit cum spissis alia fibris ;
inde comas apii gracilis rutamque rigentem   90
vellit et exiguo coriandra trementia filo.
haec ubi collegit, laetum consedit ad ignem
et clara famulam poscit mortaria voce.
singula tum capitum nodoso cortice nudat
et summis spoliat coriis contemptaque passim   95
spargit humi atque abicit. servatum gramine bulbum
tinguit aqua lapidisque cavum dimittit in orbem.
his salis inspargit micas, sale durus adeso
caseus adicitur, dictas super ingerit herbas,
et laeva vestem saetosa sub inguina fulcit,   100
dextera pistillo primum fragrantia mollit
alia, tum pariter mixto terit omnia suco.
it manus in gyrum : paulatim singula vires

---

[77] *Inferior MSS. attempt to remedy the defective verse thus*
(e.g) : plurima crescit ibi surgitque in acumina radix.
[78] dimissa.   [80] profectus.
[81] humore : holerum.   [83] vacuus (-a) mercede.
[90] virentem, *H.*   [92] laetus *It.*
[96] adicit Ω. in germine *Schrader.*
[99] ingerit F^1H : inserit : interit *Ellis.*
[100] inguine S^1L.

458

MORETUM

relief to sumptuous banquets:[1] here sharp-pointed radish, and the heavy gourd, that swells into its broad belly. But this crop was not for the owner (for who more frugal than he?) but for the people; and every ninth day on his shoulders he would carry faggots to town for sale. Thence he would home return, light of neck, but heavy of pocket,[2] and seldom attended by the city-market's wares. His hunger red onion tames, and his plot of cut-leek, and nasturtium that with sharp taste pinches the face, and endive, and cole-wort that calls back a lagging love.

[87] At this hour, too, with some such plan in his thoughts had he entered the garden. At first, lightly digging up the ground with his fingers, he draws out four garlic bulbs with thick fibres, then plucks slender parsley-leaves and unbending rue, and coriander, trembling on its scanty stalk. These culled, he sat down by the pleasant fire, and loudly calls to the maid for a mortar. Then he strips the single heads of their rough membranes, and despoils them of the outermost skins, scattering about on the ground the parts thus slighted and casting them away. The bulb, saved with the leaves, he dips in water, and drops into the mortar's hollow circle. Thereon he sprinkles grains of salt, adds cheese hardened with consuming salt, and heaps on top the herbs we have named; and while his left hand gathers up the tunic about his shaggy flanks, his right first crushes with a pestle the fragrant garlic, then grinds all evenly in the juicy mixture. Round and round passes the hand: little by little the ele-

---

[1] Lettuce was eaten at the close of a feast, though from the time of Martial it appeared at the beginning; *cf.* Martial, XIII. xiv.   [2] *cf. Ecl.* I. 35.

VIRGIL

deperdunt proprias, color est e pluribus unus,
nec totus viridis, quia lactea frusta repugnant,   105
nec de lacte nitens, quia tot variatur ab herbis.
saepe viri naris acer iaculatur apertas
spiritus et simo damnat sua prandia voltu,
saepe manu summa lacrimantia lumina terget
immeritoque furens dicit convicia fumo.   110

Procedebat opus: non iam salebrosus, ut ante,
sed gravior lentos ibat pistillus in orbis.
ergo Palladii guttas instillat olivi
exiguique super vires infundit aceti
atque iterum commiscet opus mixtumque retractat. 115
tum demum digitis mortaria tota duobus
circuit inque globum distantia contrahit unum,
constet ut effecti species nomenque moreti.

Eruit interea Scybale quoque sedula panem,
quem laetus recipit manibus, pulsoque timore   120
iam famis inque diem securus Simylus illam,
ambit crura ocreis paribus, tectusque galero
sub iuga parentis cogit lorata iuvencos,
atque agit in segetes et terrae condit aratrum.

[105] frustra. [109] tergit D^1RM.
[111] non *SL*: nec. [112] lentus *PSL*. orbem *R It.*
[120] laetus] lotis *It.* [122] abit *P.*

MORETUM

ments lose their peculiar strength; the many colours blend into one, yet neither is this wholly green, for milk-white fragments still resist, nor is it a shining milky-white, for it is varied by so many herbs. Often the strong odour smites the man's open nostrils, and with wrinkled nose he condemns his breakfast fare, often drawing the back of his hand across his tearful eyes, and cursing in anger the innocent smoke.

111 The work goes on apace: no longer in uneven course, as before, but heavier in weight, the pestle moves on in slower circles. Therefore he lets fall upon it some drops of Minerva's oil, pouring o'er it strong vinegar in scanty stream, then once more stirs up the dish and handles the mixture afresh. And now at length he passes two fingers round all the mortar, and into one ball packs the sundry pieces, so that, in reality as in name, there is fashioned a perfect *moretum*.[1]

119 Meanwhile Scybale too, industrious maid, draws forth the bread, which he gladly welcomes to his hands; and now that fear of hunger is driven away, care-free for the day, Simylus dons his well-matched leggings and sheltering cap, forces his submissive bullocks under their leather-bound yokes, and drives them to the fields, there in the earth burying his plough.

[1] Thus is designated the rustic dish of herbs, which forms the subject of this curious sketch. Another reference to the *moretum* in Latin literature is in Ovid, *Fasti*, iv. 367, where we learn that the mixture was used at the feasts of Cybele. A prose description is given in Columella (XII. 57).

DIRAE

Battare, cycneas repetamus carmine voces:
divisas iterum sedes et rura canamus,
rura, quibus diras indiximus, impia vota.
ante lupos rapient haedi, vituli ante leones,
delphini fugient piscis, aquilae ante columbas, 5
et conversa retro rerum discordia gliscet—
multa prius fient quam non mea libera avena.
montibus et silvis dicam tua facta, Lycurge.

"Impia Trinacriae sterilescant gaudia vobis
nec fecunda, senis nostri felicia rura, 10
semina parturiant segetes, non pascua colles,
non arbusta novas fruges, non pampinus uvas,
ipsae non silvae frondes, non flumina montes."

Rursus et hoc iterum repetamus, Battare, carmen:

"Effetas Cereris sulcis condatis avenas, 15
pallida flavescant aestu sitientia prata,
immatura cadant ramis pendentia mala;

³ rura *H*: dura.   ⁴ rapiunt *M*: -ant *FL*.
⁷ avena *SFL*: sata (fata) *M*.   ⁸ fata *MF*.
¹⁰ nostris *M*.   ¹⁵ sulci *It*.

---

* The principal MSS. cited are *M* (see note at the opening of the *Moretum*) and *S*, *F*, *L* (see note at the opening of the *Culex*). For *Z* and *H* see note at the opening of the *Ciris*.

DIRAE[1]

O BATTARUS,[2] let us repeat the notes of the swan: again let us sing our divided homes and lands—those lands whereon we have pronounced our curses, unholy prayers. Sooner shall kids prey upon wolves, sooner calves upon lions; sooner shall dolphins flee before fishes, sooner eagles before doves, and a world-chaos, again returning, shall burst forth—yea, many things shall befall, sooner than my shepherd's reed shall be enslaved. To the mountains and woods will I tell thy deeds, Lycurgus.[3]

[9] "Unholy and unblest, may Trinacria's joys become barren for thee and thy fellows, and may the fruitful seeds in our old master's rich lands give birth to no corn-crops, the hills to no pastures, the trees to no fresh fruits, the vines to no grapes, the very woods to no leafage, the mountains to no streams!"

[14] Once more and yet again, O Battarus, let us repeat this strain:

"Outworn may the oats of Ceres be that ye bury in the furrows; pale and wan may the meadows become, parched with heat; unripened may the drooping apples fall from the boughs! Let leaves

[1] This imprecatory poem is evidently based on circumstances similar to those under which Virgil lost his farm. See vol. i. p. vii, and note in Appendix, p. 531.

[2] Nothing is known of Battarus. He was perhaps a neighbour, who, like the poet, was dispossessed of his farm.

[3] Lycurgus is one of the soldiers who have taken possession of the poet's land; *cf.* the plur. in ll. 9 and 10.

463

VIRGIL

desint et silvis frondes et fontibus umor,
nec desit nostris devotum carmen avenis.
haec Veneris vario florentia serta decore, 20
purpureo campos quae pingunt verna colore
(hinc aurae dulces, hinc suavis spiritus agri)
mutent pestiferos aestus et taetra venena;
dulcia non oculis, non auribus ulla ferantur."

Sic precor et nostris superent haec carmina votis: 25

"Lusibus et nostris multum cantata libellis
optima silvarum, formosis densa virectis,
tondebis viridis umbras: nec laeta comantis
iactabis mollis ramos inflantibus auris,
nec mihi saepe meum resonabit, Battare, carmen 30
militis impia cum succidet dextera ferro
formosaeque cadent umbrae, formosior illis
ipsa cades, veteris domini felicia ligna.
nequiquam! nostris potius devota libellis,
ignibus aetheriis flagrabis. Iuppiter (ipse 35
Iuppiter hanc aluit), cinis haec tibi fiat oportet.
Thraecis tum Boreae spirent immania vires,
Eurus agat mixtam fulva caligine nubem,
Africus immineat nimbis minitantibus imbrem,
cum tua cyaneo resplendens aethere silva 40
non iterum discet, crebro quae, Lydia, dixti.
vicinae flammae rapiant ex ordine vitis,

¹⁹ carmen] gramen *M.*
²¹ pingunt verna *Heinsius:* pingit avena.
²³ mittent *M.* ²⁶ lusibus *Putsch:* ludimus.
²⁸ tondebis *Gronovius:* tondemus (tundemus *or* tondentur)
³¹ succedet Ω: succaedet *Ellis.* ³² cadent *It.:* cadunt.
³³ ipse. regna *M.* ³⁵ flagrabis *It.:* flagrabit.
³⁶ tibi] a Iove *Maehly* (haec *omitted*).
⁴⁰ tu cyaneo resplendes *Vollmer.*
⁴¹ discet crebro quae etc. *Eskuché:* dicens Ω: dices *It.* crebro *M:* erebo *L:* nec ero "tua," Lydia, dici *Ellis:* quae *Eskuché:* tua dixti (dixi).

DIRAE

fail the woods, water fail the streams, but let the strain that curses fail not my reeds! May these flowery garlands of Venus, with their varied beauties, which in spring-time paint the fields with brilliant hues (hence, ye sweet breezes: hence, ye fragrant odours of the field!)—may they change to blasting heats and loathsome poisons; may nothing sweet to eyes, nothing sweet to ears be wafted!"

25 Thus I pray, and in our prayers may these strains abound!

"O thou best of woods, oft sung in our playful songs and verses, thou beauteous in thy wealth of green, thou shalt shear thy green shade: neither shalt thou boast of thy soft boughs' joyous leafage, as the breezes blow among them,[1] nor, O Battarus, shall it oft resound for me with my song. When with his axe the soldier's impious hand shall fell it, and the lovely shadows fall, thyself, more lovely than they, shalt fall, the old owner's happy timber. Yet all for naught! Rather, accursed by our verses, thou shalt burn with heaven's fires. O Jupiter ('twas Jupiter himself nurtured this wood), this must thou turn into ashes!

37 "Then let the strength of the Thracian North blow his mighty blasts; let the East drive a cloud with lurid darkness mixed; let the South-West menace with storm-clouds threatening rain, when thy woodland, gleaming in the dark-blue sky, shall not learn again what thou, O Lydia,[2] hast often uttered! Let neighbouring flames in order seize

[1] Ellis takes *auris* as dative: " toss to the gales that blow music into thy soft-swaying branches."
[2] Lydia is the poet's sweetheart.

VIRGIL

pascantur segetes, diffusis ignibus auras
transvolet, arboribus coniungat et ardor aristas.
pertica qua nostros metata est impia agellos,   45
qua nostri fines olim, cinis omnia fiat."

Sic precor et nostris superent haec carmina votis:

"Undae, quae vestris pulsatis litora lymphis,
litora, quae dulcis auras diffunditis agris,
accipite has voces: migret Neptunus in arva   50
fluctibus et spissa campos perfundat harena.
qua Volcanus agros pastus Iovis ignibus arsit,
barbara dicatur Libycae soror altera Syrtis."

Tristius hoc, memini, revocasti, Battare, carmen:

"Nigro multa mari dicunt portenta natare,   55
monstra repentinis terrentia saepe figuris,
cum subito emersere furenti corpora ponto:
haec agat infesto Neptunus caeca tridenti,
atrum convertens aestum maris undique ventis
et fuscum cinerem canis exhauriat undis.   60
dicantur mea rura ferum mare; nauta, caveto
rura, quibus diras indiximus, impia vota."

Si minus haec, Neptune, tuas infundimus auris,
Battare, fluminibus tu nostros trade dolores;
nam tibi sunt fontes, tibi semper flumina amica.   65
nil est quod perdam ulterius; merito omnia Ditis.

"Flectite currentis nymphas, vaga flumina, retro,
flectite et adversis rursum diffundite campis;

⁴³ auras *Heinsius:* aurae.   ⁴⁴ ardor *It.:* arbor.
⁴⁶ fiant *H*.
⁵² arsit *Ribbeck:* arcet: ardet *Scaliger*.
⁵⁴ revocasti *H :* revocasset Ω.
⁵⁷ ferenti *S*.   ⁵⁸ infesto *It.:* infesta.
⁶³ tuas *Heinsius:* tuis.   ⁶⁴ nostris *M*.
⁶⁵ flumina semper *S*.   ⁶⁶ em quod pergam ulteris *S*.

DIRAE

upon the vines, let the crops become their food, let the blaze in scattered fires wing its way athwart the breezes, and link the corn-ears with the trees! Where the unholy rod measured our fields, where once were our boundaries, let all become ashes!"

[47] Thus I pray, and in our prayers may these strains abound!

"O waves, that with your waters beat the shores; O shores, that o'er the fields scatter sweet breezes, give ear to these cries. Let Neptune with his waves pass to the tilth, and with thick sand cover the fields! Where Vulcan, feeding on the lands, has burned with heaven's fires, be it called a foreign sister of the Libyan sand, a second Syrtis!"

[54] This sadder strain, O Battarus, I remember thou didst recall:

"Many fearsome things, they say, swim in the black sea—monsters that oft-times terrify with forms unlooked for, when suddenly they have reared their bodies from out the raging deep. These hidden things may Neptune chase with threatening trident, on all sides upturning with the winds the murky sea-surge, and in his hoary waves swallowing the swarthy ashes![1] Let my lands be called the savage sea; beware, O sailor, of lands, whereon we have pronounced our curses, unholy prayers!"

[63] If this, O Neptune, we do not pour into thy ears, do thou, O Battarus, consign our sorrows to the streams; for to thee the springs, to thee the streams are ever friendly. No further ruin can I effect[2]; to Dis all belongs of right.

"Turn back your running waters, ye roving streams; turn back, and pour them again over the

---
[1] *i.e.* left by the fire described above.
[2] *i.e.* by my curses.

467

VIRGIL

incurrant amnes passim rimantibus undis
nec nostros servire sinant erronibus agros."   70

Dulcius hoc, memini, revocasti, Battare, carmen:

"Emanent subito sicca tellure paludes
et metat hic iuncos, spicas ubi legimus olim;
cogulet arguti grylli cava garrula rana."

Tristius hoc rursum dicit mea fistula carmen: 75

"Praecipitent altis fumantes montibus imbres,
et late teneant diffuso gurgite campos,
qui dominis infesta minantes stagna relinquant.
cum delapsa meos agros pervenerit unda,
piscetur nostris in finibus advena arator,   80
advena, civili qui semper crimine crevit."

O male devoti praetorum crimine agelli,
tuque inimica pii semper Discordia civis:
exsul ego indemnatus egens mea rura reliqui,
miles ut accipiat funesti praemia belli.   85
hinc ego de tumulo mea rura novissima visam,
hinc ibo in silvas; obstabunt iam mihi colles,
obstabunt montes, campos audire licebit:

"Dulcia rura valete, et Lydia dulcior illis,
et casti fontes et felix nomen agelli."   90

Tardius a miserae descendite monte capellae:
mollia non iterum carpetis pabula nota;
tuque resiste pater. en prima novissima nobis,
intueor campos: longum manet esse sine illis.

---

[70] servire B^1: exire ML.   [73] iungos spicos S.
[74] cogulet L: occultet S: occupet It.
[78] qui $It.$: quid dominus S.   relinquunt.
[79] cum delapsa meos *Reitzenstein*: unde (undae) ZMS: lapsa (elapsa) meos LM.
[80] pascetur S.   [81] crimina S.
[83] pii *Ellis*: tui.   [93] en $It.$: et: sit *Birt*.
[94] esses L.

DIRAE

opposing fields: let brooks from all sides rush in with deep-cleaving waters, nor let them suffer our lands to be enslaved to vagabonds!"

[71] This sweeter strain, O Battarus, I remember thou didst recall:

"Let marshes from parched ground suddenly spring forth, and, where once we gathered corn-ears, let this man reap rushes; let the croaking frog sour the chirping cricket's hollow lairs!"

[75] This sadder strain my pipe gives forth in turn:

"From high mountains let rains rush streaming down, and with outspread flood widely possess the plains; then with menace of evil to their lords let them leave stagnant pools! When the wave, gliding down, reaches my fields, then let the stranger ploughman fish within my bounds—the stranger, who has ever waxed rich through citizens condemned!"

[82] O ye fields accursed, ye that the praetors have condemned! and thou, O Discord, ever the foe of righteous citizens! I, a needy exile, though uncondemned, have left my fields, that a soldier may receive the wages of deadly war. From this mound will I look my last upon my lands; from this will I pass to the woods; soon will the hills, soon will the mountains impede my view, but the plains will be able to hear:

"Sweet lands, farewell! and thou, Lydia, farewell, sweeter than they, and ye, pure fountains, and ye fields of happy name!"

[91] Ah! more slowly come down from the hill, ye poor she-goats: never again shall ye browse on the soft pastures that ye know so well; and do thou, sire of the flock, stay behind! Lo, upon the plains, my first and last possession, I gaze: long must I be reft of them!

VIRGIL

"Rura valete iterum, tuque optima Lydia salve, 95
sive eris et si non, mecum morieris utrumque."

Extremum carmen revocemus, Battare, avena:

"Dulcia amara prius fient et mollia dura,
candida nigra oculi cernent et dextera laeva,
migrabunt casus aliena in corpora rerum, 100
quam tua de nostris emigret cura medullis.
quamvis ignis eris, quamvis aqua, semper amabo:
gaudia semper enim tua me meminisse licebit."

[98] fient *It.*: fiant.
[99] cernent *It.*: cernant *ML*.
[102] quamvis nix aderit *ub* (*Ellis*).

DIRAE

"Once more, ye fields, farewell, and fare thee well, good Lydia; whether thou wilt live, or not, in either case thou wilt die with me!"

⁹⁷ Our last strain, O Battarus, let us recall on the reed!

"Sweet shall become bitter, and soft hard; eyes shall see white as black, and right as left; atoms of things shall pass into bodies of other kinds, ere regard for thee pass from my heart.[1] Though fire, though water thou shalt be, ever will I love thee, for ever will it be permitted to think upon thy joys!"

---

[1] By *casus rerum* he means the dissolution of things; hence the atoms of a body, which, when reunited, form objects of a different kind. This is therefore a reference to the atomic theory of the Epicureans.

LYDIA*

Invideo vobis, agri formosaque prata,
hoc formosa magis, mea quod formosa puella
est vobis : tacite nostrum suspirat amorem.
vos nunc illa videt, vobis mea Lydia ludit,
vos nunc alloquitur, vos nunc arridet ocellis
et mea submissa meditatur carmina voce,
cantat et interea, mihi quae cantabat in aurem.

Invideo vobis, agri, discetis amare.
O fortunati nimium multumque beati,
in quibus illa pedis nivei vestigia ponet   10
aut roseis viridem digitis decerpserit uvam
(dulci namque tumet nondum vitecula Baccho)
aut inter varios, Veneris stipendia, flores
membra reclinarit teneramque illiserit herbam,
et secreta meos furtim narrabit amores.   15
gaudebunt silvae, gaudebunt mollia prata,
et gelidi fontes, aviumque silentia fient.
tardabunt rivi labentes (sistite lymphae),
dum mea iucundas exponat cura querelas.

² quod *SL :* quo *M.*
³ est vobis] in vobis *Heinsius :* ex vobis *Ellis.*
¹¹ digitis viridem *SL.*   ¹² dulci *H :* dulcia.
¹³ veneris *H :* venerem Ω. stipendia *SL :* spumantia *M :* dispendia *or* stipantia *It.*
¹⁴ declinarit.   ¹⁵ narrabis.
¹⁸ sistite *ub :* currite *commonly read :* lapsantes gurgite *Ellis.*

---

* The MSS. give the *Lydia* in sequence to the *Dirae* without separate title.   Jacobs first separated the two.

LYDIA[1]

I ENVY you, ye fields and lovely meads, for this more lovely that my lovely girl is yours: in silence she sighs for my love. You it is she now sees, with you my Lydia plays, to you she now makes speech, on you she now smiles with those dear eyes, and cons my songs with voice subdued, and sings the while those strains she was wont to sing into my ear.

[8] I envy you, ye fields; ye will learn to love. O fields, too happy, yea, much blest, in which she will set her snowy footsteps, or with rosy fingers, will pluck the green grape (for not yet swells the little vine with sweet juice), or amid varied flowers, tribute to Venus, she will lay down her limbs and crush the tender grass, and apart by herself will stealthily recount the tale of my love. The woods will rejoice, the soft meadows and cool springs will rejoice, and the birds will make a silence. The gliding brooks will pause (stay, ye waters!) till my heart sets forth its sweet complaints.

[1] This sentimental lament is independent of the *Dirae*, but came to be associated with that poem because the name "Lydia" is common to both compositions. See Appendix, p. 532.

VIRGIL

Invideo vobis, agri: mea gaudia habetis, 20
et vobis nunc est mea quae fuit ante voluptas.
at mihi tabescunt morientia membra dolore,
et calor infuso decedit frigore mortis,
quod mea non mecum domina est. non ulla puella
doctior in terris fuit aut formosior; ac si 25
fabula non vana est, tauro Iove digna vel auro
(Iuppiter avertas aurem) mea sola puella est.

Felix taure, pater magni gregis et decus, a te
vaccula non umquam secreta cubilia captans
frustra te patitur silvis mugire dolorem. 30
et pater haedorum felix semperque beate,
sive petis montis praeruptos, saxa pererrans,
sive tibi silvis nova pabula fastidire
sive libet campis: tecum tua laeta capella est.
et mas quacumque est, illi sua femina iuncta 35
interpellatos numquam ploravit amores.
cur non et nobis facilis, natura, fuisti?
cur ego crudelem patior tam saepe dolorem?

Sidera per viridem redeunt cum pallida mundum,
inque vicem Phoebi currens abit aureus orbis, 40
Luna, tuus tecum est: cur non est et mea mecum?
Luna, dolor nosti quid sit: miserere dolentis.
Phoebe, gerens nam laurus celebravit amorem;
et quae pompa deum, non silvis fama, locuta est?
(omnia vos estis) secum sua gaudia gestat 45

²² mihi *Aldine edition* 1517: male (mala): male *Lindsay*.
tabescunt *It.*: tabescant.   ²⁴ ulla *H*: illa.
²³ silvis *L*: silvas *S*: si vis *M*.
²⁵ quacumque *Ellis*: quocumque (quicunque *It.*).
²⁷ fuisti *Salmasius*: fuisset.
⁴⁰ Phoebo curras aeque *Lindsay*: currens abit *Eskuché*:
currens atque: coiens atque *Ellis*.   ⁴¹ tuus *b*: tui.
⁴³ nam *Ellis*: in te. Laurus *Lindsay*. celebravit *MFL*:
celebrabis *Scaliger*.   ⁴⁴ quae] qua est *Vollmer*. non *It.*:
nisi Ω.   ⁴⁵ scitis *Lindsay*.

474

LYDIA

[20] I envy you, ye fields; my joys ye possess, and now ye have her, who aforetime was my delight. But my dying limbs are wasting with grief, and warmth fails me, steeped in the chill of death, because my mistress is not with me. No girl on earth was more skilled or more lovely; and, if the tale be not false, then worthy of Jupiter as bull or as gold[1] (turn thine ear aside, O Jupiter!), is my girl alone.

[28] O happy bull, sire and pride of the mighty herd, never does the heifer, seeking stalls apart, suffer thee to low thy grief vainly to the woods. And thou, sire of the kids, happy and ever blest, whether thou, roaming o'er the rocks, seekest the steepy mountains or whether, in woods or on plains, it please thee to scorn fresh forage: with thee is thy happy mate. And wherever is a male, with him is ever joined his mate, and never has he bewailed an interrupted love. Why, O Nature, hast thou not with us too been kind? Why so oft do I suffer cruel grief?

[39] When through the green heavens the pale stars come back, and in turn the golden orb of Phoebus departs on his course, thy love,[2] O Moon, is with thee: why is not mine also with me? O Moon, thou knowest what grief is: pity one who grieves. For he who bears thee,[3] O Phoebus, celebrates love for the laurel; and what procession has told the story of a god, when fame has not told it in the woods? A god (ye gods are everywhere) carries his joys[4] with him,

---

[1] A reference to the myths of Europa and Danaë.

[2] Endymion, whom Luna visited on Mount Latmos.

[3] *i.e.* thy image in procession. Daphne, fleeing from the attention of Phoebus Apollo, was changed into a laurel.

[4] *e.g.* Apollo carries with him the laurel, and Pan his pipes.

VIRGIL

aut insparsa videt mundo: quae dicere longum est.
aurea quin etiam cum saecula volvebantur
condicio similisque foret mortalibus illis,
haec quoque praetereo: notum Minoidos astrum
quaeque virum virgo, sicut captiva, secuta est.   50
laedere, caelicolae, potuit vos nostra quid aetas,
condicio nobis vitae quo durior esset?

Ausus ego primus castos violare pudores,
sacratamque meae vittam temptare puellae,
immatura mea cogor nece solvere fata?   55
istius atque utinam facti mea culpa magistra
prima foret: letum vita mihi dulcius esset,
non mea, non ullo moreretur tempore fama,
dulcia cum Veneris furatus gaudia primum
dicerer, atque ex me dulcis foret orta voluptas.   60
nam mihi non tantum tribuerunt invida fata,
auctor ut occulti noster foret error amoris.

Iuppiter ante, sui semper mendacia factus,
cum Iunone, prius coniunx quam dictus uterque est,
gaudia libavit dulcem furatus amorem   65
et moechum tenera gavisa est laedere in herba
purpureos flores, quos insuper accumbebat,
Cypria, formoso supponens bracchia collo.
tum, credo, fuerat Mavors distentus in armis,
nam certe Volcanus opus faciebat, et ille   70
tristi turpabat malam ac fuligine barbam.

⁴⁸ foret] fuit *Ribbeck*.   ⁵³ egon *It*.
⁵⁴ vittam *Ascensius* 1507 : vitam.
⁵⁵ mea *Haupt*: me *or* meae.   fata *MFL* : facta *S*.
⁵⁶ facti *ML* : fati *F* : facta *S*.   ⁵⁸ ullo] nullo.
⁶¹ invidi fata *Heinsius* : impia vota.   ⁶³ sui] cui *Curcio*.
⁶⁶ moechum *Baehrens* : mecum (mea cum).
⁶⁷ occumbebat *F*.   ⁶⁸ Cypria] grandia *Lindsay*. bracchia
It. : gaudia Ω.   ⁷⁰ ille *Petry (Curcio)* : illi.
⁷¹ turpabatque mala *Lindsay* : malam ac *Vollmer* : mala
(*without* ac).

LYDIA

or sees them scattered through the world—to tell these would be a tedious task. Nay more, when the golden ages rolled their course, and mortals of those days were under like conditions—this also I pass over: well we know the star of Minos' daughter, and the maiden who, as captive, followed her lord.[1] Wherein, O denizens of heaven, could our age have injured you, that therefore life's conditions should be harder for us?

[53] Was I the first who dared to sully the chaste purity and assail the hallowed fillet[2] of his love, that by my death I am forced to pay the due of an untimely Fate? And O that my fault were the first prompter of that deed! Then were death sweeter to me than life. No, not mine the fame that at any time would die, for 'twould be said that I first had stolen Love's sweet joys, and from me had sprung that sweet pleasure. Nay, the envious fates have not granted me a boon so great, that our misdeed should be the beginning of secret love.

[63] Of yore Jupiter, who could at all times counterfeit false forms of himself, along with Juno, ere either was called a spouse, tasted the stolen joys of sweet love. The Cyprian, too, rejoiced that on the tender grass her lover[3] crushed the brilliant flowers whereon she lay, as she threw her arms about his lovely neck. At that time Mars, methinks, had been detained in warfare, for as to Vulcan, he too, surely, was busy at work, and with unsightly soot was defiling cheek and

---

[1] Ariadne, daughter of Minos, fled from Crete with Theseus, who abandoned her in Naxos. Dionysus, who found her there, raised her to the stars.
[2] *i.e.* the ribbon worn by free-born women, whether maidens or married.
[3] Adonis.

VIRGIL

non Aurora novos etiam ploravit amores,
atque rubens oculos roseo celavit amictu?
talia caelicolae. numquid minus aurea proles?
ergo quod deus atque heros, cur non minor aetas? 75

Infelix ego, non illo qui tempore natus,
quo facilis natura fuit. sors o mea laeva
nascendi, miserumque genus, quo sera libido est.
tantam Fata meae carnis fecere rapinam,
ut maneam, quod vix oculis cognoscere possis. 80

[73] rubeo. [74] proles *Vonck:* promo.
[78] quo] quoi *Naeke.*
[79] tantam fata meae *Heinsius:* tantum vita meae (tanta meae vitae): *Lindsay retains* vita. carnis *Baehrens:* cordis: cortis *Ellis.* rapinam] ruinam *Heinsius.*

LYDIA

beard. Has not Aurora, too, bewailed new loves,[1] and blushingly hidden her eyes in her roseate mantle? Thus have the denizens of heaven done: and the golden age, did it do less? Therefore what gods and heroes have done, why should not a later age do?

76 Unhappy I, who was not born in those days when Nature was kind! O my luckless birth-lot, and O the wretched race, in which desire is laggard! Such havoc have the Fates made of my life, that what remains of me your eyes could scarcely recognize.[2]

---

[1] Her old love was for Tithonus; her new one was for Orion, who was killed by Diana's arrows.

[2] "The *Lydia* is the most careful and finished of poems. We should admire it more if Virgil had never written the *Eclogues*" (W. M. Lindsay, *Classical Review*, XXXII. (1918), 62f.

PRIAPEA*

I

Vere rosa, autumno pomis, aestate frequentor
 spicis: una mihi est horrida pestis hiemps.
nam frigus metuo, et vereor ne ligneus ignem
 hic deus ignaris praebeat agricolis.

II

Ego haec, ego arte fabricata rustica,
ego arida, o viator, ecce populus
agellulum hunc, sinistra et ante quem vides,
erique villulam hortulumque pauperis
tuor malaque furis arceo manu.   5

Mihi corolla picta vere ponitur
mihi rubens arista sole fervido,
mihi virente dulcis uva pampino,
mihi coacta duro oliva frigore.

I. [1] autumno pomis *MSS.*: pomis autumno *Lachmann*.
[4] ignavis *Voss, accepted by Ribbeck, Buehrens, Vollmer*.
II. [2] o *It.*: omitted Ω.
[3] agellulum *u*: agellum Ω. sinistra et ante *Hand*: sinistre tante (stantem) *BZ*.   [5] tuor *It. Wagner*: tueor Ω.
[9] *So De Witt:* mihi glauca olivo (oliva) duro cocta frigo (frigore cocta) *MSS.*: mihique glauca (*or* duro) oliva cocta frigore *Wagner*: mihi caduca oliva, cocta frigore *Ellis*: mihi recocta glauca oliva frigore *Bücheler*. mihi gelata *Birt*.

* The principal MSS. cited are *B* and *Z*, for which see note at the opening of the *Ciris*. *Z* embraces *H*, *A*, and *R*.

PRIAPEA

I

IN spring I am covered with roses, in autumn with fruits, in summer with ears of corn: winter alone is to me a horrid plague. For the cold I dread, and am afraid that your god of wood may furnish fuel to heedless husbandmen.[1]

II [2]

Lo! 'tis I, O wayfarer, I, wrought with rustic skill, I, this dry poplar, that guard this little field thou seest in front and to the left, with the poor owner's cottage and small garden, and that shield them from the wicked hand of thieves.

[6] On me in spring is placed a garland gay; on me, in the scorching sun, the ruddy corn; on me the luscious grapes with tendrils green; on me the olive, when wrinkled by winter's cold.[3]

---

[1] The first three poems are *Priapea*, *i.e.* verses in honour of the god Priapus. The opening one, in elegiac couplets, is composed as if to be set up as an inscription on a wooden image of the god. In all three Priapus is himself the speaker (*hic deus*, like *hic homo = ego*).

[2] The verse of the original is the pure iambic trimeter.

[3] Olives were picked during a frost.

For other MSS. see Ellis. The title *Priapea* does not occur in the MSS., and in *Z* the title *Catalepton* is put at the head of the *Priapea*.

VIRGIL

Meis capella delicata pascuis 10
in urbem adulta lacte portat ubera,
meisque pinguis agnus ex ovilibus
gravem domum remittit aere dexteram,
teneraque matre mugiente vaccula
deum profundit ante templa sanguinem. 15

Proin, viator, hunc deum vereberis
manumque sursum habebis: hoc tibi expedit,
parata namque crux stat ecce mentula.
" velim pol," inquis. at pol ecce vilicus
venit, valente cui revolsa bracchio 20
fit ista mentula apta clava dexterae.

III

HUNC ego, o iuvenes, locum villulamque palustrem,
tectam vimine iunceo caricisque maniplis,
quercus arida rustica formitata securi,
nutrior; magis et magis fit beata quotannis.
huius nam domini colunt me deumque salutant 5
pauperis tuguri pater filiusque adulescens,
alter assidua colens diligentia, ut herbae,
aspera ut rubus a meo sit remota sacello,
alter parva manu ferens semper munera larga.
florido mihi ponitur picta vere corolla, 10
primitus tenera virens spica mollis arista,

II. ¹⁴ teneraque... vacula Ω: tenella *d'Orville:* tenerque
... buculus *Wagner.* ²¹ fuit *Z.*

III. ¹ o *added by Lachmann.*

³ formitata *BH:* formicata *M:* formidata *Med.:* formata
A R u: fomitata *I. Voss, and read by Vollmer:* fabricata
Ribbeck (after Schrader).

⁴ nutrior *BH* (*cf. Georg.* II. 425): nunc tuor *Scaliger:* en
tuor *Ribbeck.* fit *Baehrens:* ut Ω. magis ut magis sit *Ellis.*

⁵ me deumque *Aldine edition* 1517: mediumque Ω.

⁷ colens] cavens *L. Müller.*

PRIAPEA

¹⁰ From my pastures the dainty she-goat bears to town her udders swelled with milk; from my folds comes the fatted lamb to send home again the money-laden hand;[1] and the tender calf, amid her mother's lowing, pours forth her blood before the temples of the gods.

¹⁶ Therefore, O wayfarer, thou shalt fear this god, and hold thy hand high: this is worth thy while, for lo! there stands ready thy cross, the phallus.[2] "By Pollux! I'd like to,"[3] thou sayest. Nay, by Pollux, here comes the bailiff, whose stout arm, plucking away that phallus, finds in it a cudgel, well fitted to his right hand.

III[4]

O YOUTHS, this place and cottage in the marsh, thatched with osier shoots and handfuls of sedge, I support, I, a dried oak chipt into shape by farmer's axe; year by year, more and more rich it grows. For the owners of this poor hut, a father and youthful son, honour and greet me as a god; the one so honouring me with constant care that weeds and rough brambles are taken from my shrine; the other with lavish hand ever bringing humble gifts.

¹⁰ On me in flowery spring is placed a garland gay; on me the soft ear of corn, when first 'tis green on

---

[1] *cf. Eclogues*, I. 35, and IV. 21 f.
[2] The wayfarer can thus show that he is not stealing. Slaves guilty of theft could be crucified, but for the cross Priapus substitutes his own weapon, viz. the club projecting from his groin.
[3] *i.e.* to steal.
[4] The metre of the original is the so-called *Priapean*, a combination of the *Glyconic* and the *Pherecratean* (see any Latin Grammar).

483

VIRGIL

luteae violae mihi lacteumque papaver,
pallentesque cucurbitae et suave olentia mala,
uva pampinea rubens educata sub umbra.
sanguine haec etiam mihi—sed tacebitis—arma   15
barbatus linit hirculus cornipesque capella.
pro quis omnia honoribus nunc necesse Priapo est
praestare, et domini hortulum vineamque tueri.
quare hinc, o pueri, malas abstinete rapinas.
vicinus prope dives est neglegensque Priapus.   20
inde sumite: semita haec deinde vos feret ipsa.

[14] pampinea] *Garrod proposes* faginea *or* populea.
[15] sanguine haec ... arma *Voss:* sanguine hanc ... aram *Muretus:* sanguinea ... arma Ω.
[17] omnia Ω (omnibus *M*): munera *Riese:* munia *Maehly:* mutua *Baehrens.* nunc *Bücheler:* huic *Ribbeck:* hoc Ω: haec

PRIAPEA

the tender stalk, with yellow violets and milky poppy, pale melons and sweet-smelling apples, and blushing grape-clusters, reared beneath the vine-leaves' shade. These weapons, too, of mine—but you will be silent!—a little bearded goat and his horn-footed sister besmear with blood. For these offerings Priapus must now make full return, and guard the owner's vineyard and little garden.

[19] Therefore, away! boys, refrain from wicked plundering. Near by is a wealthy neighbour, and his Priapus is careless. Take from him; this path of itself will lead you from the place.

It. Priapo est *B:* Priape (est *omitted*) *Z. Garrod would read the line thus:* pro quis, quicquid honoris est, hoc necesse Priapo.
[20] Priapi *Heinsius.*   [21] semita *It.:* semitam Ω.

CATALEPTON*

I

De qua saepe tibi venit; sed, Tucca, videre
  non licet: occulitur limine clausa viri.
de qua saepe tibi, non venit adhuc mihi; namque
  si occulitur, longe est, tangere quod nequeas.
venerit, audivi. sed iam mihi nuntius iste   5
  quid prodest? illi dicite, cui rediit.

II

Corinthiorum amator iste verborum,
iste iste rhetor, namque quatenus totus

I. ¹ De qua] Delia *Scaliger.*   ³ de qua] Delia *Scaliger.*
⁶ dicite *MSS.:* dicito *Scaliger.* cui *Heyne:* qui *B:* qu(a)e
other *MSS.*
II. ² *Not included in the citation by Quintilian,* VIII. iii., 28,
and rejected by Ribbeck and Baehrens.

---

* See note at the opening of the *Priapea.* In *B* the title
Catalepton is nowhere given.
  On this title, see vol. i. p. vii. The metres of the *Cata-
lepton* are varied. The elegiac couplet prevails, being used
in I, III, IV, VII, VIII, IX, XI, XIIIa, XIV, and XV; but
the rest of the poems are composed in some form of iambic
measure. Thus the pure iambic trimeter is used in VI, X,
and XII, the choliambus (or scazon) in II and V, and the
iambic strophe (consisting of a trimeter coupled with a
dimeter) in XIII.

---

¹ This epigram has provoked much discussion. Before
Birt, commentators adopted Scaliger's conjecture *Delia* in
lines 1 and 3, and regarded the poem as a dialogue between
Tucca and the poet, who are rivals for the love of Delia.
But Birt revives the *de qua* of MSS., and explains the epi-
486

CATALEPTON

I[1]

She, of whom I have often told you, has come; but, Tucca, one may not see her. She's kept in hiding, barred within her husband's threshold. She, of whom I have often told you, has not yet come to me, for if she's kept in hiding, what one can't touch is far away. Suppose she has come; I have heard it. But now what good is that news to me? Tell it to him, for whom she has come back.

II[2]

It's Corinthian words the fellow adores, that sorry rhetorician! For, perfect Thucydides that he is, he

---

gram as a piece of conversation or fragment of a letter, all of it the utterance of the poet. The verb of saying is omitted in lines 1 and 3, as often in the epistolary style. The lady referred to is not named. In the last two lines the poet turns away from Tucca to address those who have brought him news of the lady's return. This, he implies, is a matter of perfect indifference to him. See Appendix, p. 533.

[2] This epigram is discussed by the translator in the *Transactions of the American Philological Association*, vol. xlvii., 1916, pp. 43 ff. The person assailed is T. Annius Cimber, a rhetorician who is said to have murdered his brother. In his rhetoric he was an Atticist, following Thucydides, who in his History has given so vivid a description of the Attic plague (II. 47-54). The writer uses *verba* in a double sense, "words" and "spells," and *Corinthiorum* implies "archaic" or "obsolete," involving an allusion to old bronzes as well as to Medea's poisons. In *Gallicum* there is an implied reference to the name *Cimber*, and *tau* suggests some peculiarity of pronunciation. Cimber, who wrote in Greek, evidently used the Ionic μίν and the tragic σφίν. As, then, for his pupils he mingled these uncouth sounds, so for his brother he concocted deadly spells.

VIRGIL

Thucydides, tyrannus Atticae febris:
tau Gallicum, min et sphin ut male illisit,
ita omnia ista verba miscuit fratri. 5

III

Aspice, quem valido subnixum Gloria regno
　altius et caeli sedibus extulerat:
terrarum hic bello magnum concusserat orbem,
　hic reges Asiae fregerat, hic populos;
hic grave servitium tibi iam, tibi, Roma, ferebat
　(cetera namque viri cuspide conciderant):
cum subito in medio rerum certamine praeceps
　corruit, e patria pulsus in exilium.
tale deae numen, tali mortalia nutu
　fallax momento temporis hora dedit. 10

IV

Quocumque ire ferunt variae nos tempora vitae,
　tangere quas terras quosque videre homines,
dispeream, si te fuerit mihi carior alter.
　alter enim quis te dulcior esse potest,

II. ³ tyrannus] bri(t)tan(n)us *MSS. of Quintilian*.
⁴ min et spin et *Baehrens:* enim et spin(e) et *MSS. of Quintilian:* mi et psin et *B:* min et psin et *H*. illi sit *R:* et "male illi sit" *Ellis*.
⁵ ita *or* ista *MSS.:* ita *MSS. of Quintilian*.
III. ⁵ tibi (*second*) *omitted B, hence* Romane (*Bücheler*).
⁹ nutu Ω: ritu *Haupt:* motu *Baehrens*.
¹⁰ dedit Ω: adedit *Sabbadini:* ferit *Baehrens:* premit *Ruhnken:* terit *Ellis*.
IV. ⁴ quis *u:* qui *other MSS*.

---

[1] It is generally supposed that the portrait upon which this poem is based was one of Alexander the Great. But line 8 makes this interpretation improbable, for though

488

is lord of the Attic fever; as his Gallic *tau*, his *min* and *sphin* he wickedly pounded up, so of all such word-spells he mixed a dose for his brother!

III[1]

BEHOLD one, whom, upborne on mighty sovereignty, Glory had highly exalted, even above the abodes of heaven! Earth's wide bounds had he shaken in war; Asia's kings, Asia's nations had he crushed;[2] now to thee, even to thee, O Rome (for all else had fallen before his spear), was he bringing grievous slavery, when lo! of a sudden, in the midst of his struggle for empire, headlong he fell, driven from fatherland into exile. Such is the goddess' will;[3] at such behest, in a moment of time, does the faithless hour deal out the doom of mortals.

IV[4]

WHITHERSOEVER the chances of our changing lives lead us to go, what lands soever to visit and what people to see, may I perish if any other shall be dearer to me than thou! For what other can be

---

Alexander died in Babylon and was buried in Egypt, no poet could have regarded him as *e patria pulsus in exilium*. Baehrens and Nettleship hold that the monarch in view was Phraates, king of Parthia, whom his subjects drove from his throne in 32 B.C. Pompey the Great and Mithridates have had their advocates, but all conditions may be satisfied by Marcus Antonius, who enjoyed with Cleopatra the homage of eastern peoples, and was a real menace to Italy and Rome. (So De Witt, in the *American Journal of Philology*, vol. xxxiii., 1912, pp. 321 ff.) See, however, Appendix, p. 533.

[2] *cf. Aen.* VIII. 685 ff.

[3] The goddess is Fortune or Nemesis.

[4] Addressed to the poet Octavius Musa, a friend of Horace as well as of Virgil. (*cf.* Horace, *Satires*, I. x. 82.)

VIRGIL

cui iuveni ante alios divi divumque sorores 5
 cuncta, neque indigno, Musa, dedere bona,
cuncta, quibus gaudet Phoebi chorus ipseque Phoebus?
 doctior o quis te, Musa, fuisse potest?
o quis te in terris loquitur iucundior uno?
 Clio tam certe candida non loquitur. 10
quare illud satis est, si te permittis amari;
 nam contra, ut sit amor mutuus, unde mihi?

V

ITE hinc, inanes, ite, rhetorum ampullae,
inflata rhoso non Achaico verba,
et vos, Selique Tarquitique Varroque,
scolasticorum natio madens pingui,
ite hinc, inane cymbalon iuventutis. 5
tuque, o mearum cura, Sexte, curarum
vale, Sabine; iam valete, formosi.
nos ad beatos vela mittimus portus,
magni petentes docta dicta Sironis,
vitamque ab omni vindicabimus cura. 10
ite hinc, Camenae, vos quoque ite iam sane,
dulces Camenae (nam fatebimur verum,
dulces fuistis); et tamen meas chartas
revisitote, sed pudenter et raro.

IV. ⁵ iuveni *B :* cum venit *Z.*
⁶ Musa *Aldine edition* 1517: multa Ω.
¹⁰ certe Ω: per te *Baehrens :* graece *Birt.*
V. ² rhoŗso *B :* roso *HMu :* rore *Aldine edition* 1517: et ore *Curcio :* rhythmo *Birt. The form* rhoso *is dubious, but probably represents* δρόσῳ, *as if* (d)hroso.' *See note in Ellis.*
⁵ inane *Heinsius :* inani *BHMu :* inanis *Aldine edition* 1517.
¹⁰ vindicabimus *Aldine editions :* vindicavimus *ZM :* vindicamus *B, Med.*
¹¹ ite iam sane *Haupt :* iam ite sane (lamite seve *or* sene) *BZM, Med.:* ite salvete *Ellis.* ¹² fatebitur *B.*

CATALEPTON

sweeter than thou, upon whom in thy youth, O Musa, beyond others—and not unworthily—the gods and sisters of the gods[1] have bestowed all blessings, all wherein the choir of Phoebus and Phoebus himself rejoice? O who can have been more skilled than thou, O Musa? O who in all the world speaks with more charm than thou—thou alone? Clio surely speaks not so clearly. Therefore 'tis enough if thou permittest thyself to be loved; for otherwise how may I cause that love to be returned?

V[2]

GET ye hence! away, ye empty paint-pots[3] of rhetoricians, ye words inflated, but not with Attic dew! And ye, Selius and Tarquitius and Varro, a tribe of pedants soaking in fat, get ye hence, ye empty cymbals of our youth! And thou, O Sextus Sabinus, my chiefest care, farewell! Now fare ye well, ye goodly youths!

[3] We are spreading our sails for blissful havens, in quest of great Siro's wise words, and from all care will redeem our life. Get ye hence, ye Muses! yea, away now even with you, ye sweet Muses! For the truth we must avow—ye have been sweet. And yet, come ye back to my pages, though with modesty and but seldom!

---

[1] *i.e.* gods and goddesses. Birt, however, regards the *divum sorores* as the Fates, the *Parcae*.

[2] Written, ostensibly, when Virgil was giving up his early rhetorical studies, and preparing to take up philosophy under Siro, the Epicurean. For details, see Nettleship in *Ancient Lives of Virgil*, p. 37.

[3] Horace also uses the word *ampullae* and the verb *ampullor* of bombastic language; *cf.* λήκυθος and ληκυθίζειν in Greek. The *ampullae* are properly "paint-pots" (see Wickham's note on Hor. *Epist.* I. iii. 14).

VIRGIL

VI

Socer, beate nec tibi nec alteri,
generque Noctuine, putidum caput,
tuoque nunc puella talis et tuo
stupore pressa rus abibit et mihi,
ut ille versus usquequaque pertinet: 5
"gener socerque, perdidistis omnia."

VII

Scilicet hoc sine fraude, Vari dulcissime, dicam:
dispeream, nisi me perdidit iste πόθος.
sin autem praecepta vetant me dicere, sane
non dicam, sed me perdidit iste puer.

VIII

Villula, quae Sironis eras, et pauper agelle,
verum illi domino tu quoque divitiae,
me tibi et hos una mecum, quos semper amavi,
si quid de patria tristius audiero,
commendo, in primisque patrem. tu nunc eris illi, 5
Mantua quod fuerat quodque Cremona prius.

VI. ³ tuone *Scaliger*: tuoque Ω.
⁴ abibit et *B*: habitet *ZM, Med.*: abibit? hei *Scaliger*.
⁶ *cf.* Catullus, xxix. 24, socer generque, p. o.
VII. ² πόθος *Spiro*: pothus (potus) Ω: putus *Scaliger*.
³ autem] artis *Heyne*.
VIII. ⁵ in primisque *Aldine edition* 1517: primisque Ω.

---

¹ To be taken as complementary to XII. In the latter epigram the father-in-law is called Atilius, a name which,

492

CATALEPTON

VI[1]

O FATHER-IN-LAW, whose riches benefit neither thyself nor thy neighbour, and thou, O son-in-law Noctuinus, thou addle-pate, now a girl so rare, assailed in thy drunken stupor, and in thine, will pass to the country,[2] and for me (how that verse everywhere applies!): "Son-in-law and father-in-law, ye have ruined all."[3]

VII

SURELY, my dearest Varius, in all honesty I'll say this: "Hang me, if that *amour* has not ruined me!" But if the rules forbid me so to speak,[4] of course I'll not say that, but—"that lad has ruined me!"

VIII[5]

O LITTLE villa, that once wast Siro's, and thou, poor tiny farm—yet to such an owner even thou wert wealth—to thee, if aught more sad I hear about our home-land, I entrust myself, and, along with me, those whom I have ever loved, my father first and foremost. Thou shalt now be to him what Mantua and what Cremona had been aforetime.

---

like Noctuinus, is probably fictitious. Professor De Witt's plausible theory is that Noctuinus is Antony, while the other is his uncle and father-in-law, C. Antonius (*American Journal of Philology*, vol. xxxiii., 1912, p. 319). See Appendix.

[2] The family is reduced to poverty through extravagance.

[3] In Catullus this verse applies to Caesar and Pompey.

[4] An intermixture of Greek words in Latin composition was not approved of by the best teachers.

[5] See the "Life of Virgil" in vol. i. pp. vii. and viii. The incidents referred to belong to the year 41 B.C.

VIRGIL

IX

Pauca mihi, niveo sed non incognita Phoebo,
  pauca mihi doctae dicite Pegasides.
victor adest, magni magnum decus ecce triumphi,
  victor, qua terrae quaque patent maria,
horrida barbaricae portans insignia pugnae,   5
  magnus ut Oenides utque superbus Eryx;
nec minus idcirco vestros expromere cantus
  maximus et sanctos dignus inire choros.
hoc itaque insuetis iactor magis, optime, curis,
  quid de te possim scribere quidve tibi.   10
namque (fatebor enim) quae maxima deterrendi
  debuit, hortandi maxima causa fuit.
pauca tua in nostras venerunt carmina chartas,
  carmina cum lingua, tum sale Cecropio,
carmina, quae Phrygium, saeclis accepta futuris,   15
  carmina, quae Pylium vincere digna senem.
molliter hic viridi patulae sub tegmine quercus
  Moeris pastores et Meliboeus erant,
dulcia iactantes alterno carmina versu,
  qualia Trinacriae doctus amat iuvenis.   20
certatim ornabant omnes heroida divi,
  certatim divae munere quoque suo.

³ victoria est *ZMu.*
¹⁵ Phrygium *Heinsius:* prciū *B*²*:* pilium *AR: whole line omitted B*¹*HM.*
²¹ divi *Dousa:* dive Ω.

---

[1] An encomium addressed to one of the Messallae, probably M. Valerius Messalla Corvinus (64 B.C.–8 A.D.), patron and friend of Tibullus, who triumphed over Aquitania in 27 B.C.

CATALEPTON

IX[1]

Some few thoughts, few but not unknown to shining Phoebus, impart to me, ye learned Muses!

[3] A conqueror comes—lo! the mighty glory of a mighty triumph—conqueror he, where'er lands and where'er seas are outspread, bearing grim tokens of barbaric strife, like unto Oeneus' mighty son,[2] or unto proud Eryx; nor less on that account most mighty in drawing forth your songs and worthy to enter your holy choirs. Therefore, noblest of men, the more am I fretted with unwonted cares, wondering what about thee or what for thee I have power to pen. For that which—yea, I will avow it—ought to have been chief reason for holding me back, has been chief reason for urging me along.

[13] Some few of thy songs have found place in my pages[3]—songs of Attic speech as well as Attic wit—songs that, welcomed by ages yet to be, are worthy to outlive the aged Phrygian,[4] worthy to outlive the aged man of Pylos.[5] Herein, under a spreading oak's green covert, were the shepherds Moeris and Meliboeus at their ease, throwing off in alternate verse sweet songs such as the learned youth[6] of Sicily loves. Emulously all the gods graced the heroine;[7] emulously the goddesses graced her with their several gifts.

---

[2] Meleager; or possibly Diomedes, son of Tydeus and grandson of Oeneus.

[3] The author of this poem has turned some Greek verses of Messalla's into Latin.   [4] Priam.

[5] Nestor, who in the Homeric narrative is living in the third generation of men.   [6] Theocritus.

[7] Probably Sulpicia, daughter of the orator Servius Sulpicius.

VIRGIL

felicem ante alias o te scriptore puellam
   altera non fama dixerit esse prior:
non illa, Hesperidum ni munere capta fuisset,   25
   quae volucrem cursu vicerat Hippomenen;
candida cycneo non edita Tyndaris ovo,
   non supero fulgens Cassiopea polo,
non defensa diu multum certamine equorum,
   optabant gravidae quam sibi quaeque manus,   30
saepe animam generi pro qua pater impius hausit,
   saepe rubro similis sanguine fluxit humus;
regia non Semele, non Inachis Acrisione,
   immiti expertae fulmine et imbre Iovem;
non cuius ob raptum pulsi liquere Penates   35
   Tarquinii patrios, filius atque pater,
illo quo primum dominatus Roma superbos
   mutavit placidis tempore consulibus.
multa neque immeritis donavit praemia alumnis,
   praemia Messallis maxima Publicolis.   40
nam quid ego immensi memorem studia ista laboris?
   horrida quid durae tempora militiae?
castra foro, te castra urbi praeponere, castra
   tam procul hoc gnato, tam procul hac patria?
immoderata pati iam frigora, iamque calores?   45
   sternere vel dura posse super silice?

[29] multum Ω: et multum *Sabbadini:* volucrum *Aldine edition* 1534: mulier *Ellis.*
[30] obtabant *B:* obstabant *Vollmer.* gravid(a)e Ω: Graiae *Aldine edition* 1534. quam *edition* 1473: quid *B:* quod *other MSS.* manus] nurum *Tollius.*
[32] similis Ω: Eleis *most editions:* pinguis *Baehrens:* sitiens *Birt.*
[34] in miti *B:* in(m)mitti *HM.* expertae *Scaliger:* expectat *B:* expectant *Z.*
[43] castra foro castra *B:* te *added by Bücheler:* foro solitos *Z:* foro rostris *Birt.*
[44] hoc ... hac] ac ... ac *MH:* haec ... haec *Ellis.*
[45] frigora *Aldine edition* 1517: sidera Ω.
[46] stertere *Aldine edition* 1534.

CATALEPTON

²³ O maiden happy beyond others with thee for her herald! None other may claim to excel her in fame: not she[1] who, had she not been tricked by the Hesperides' gift, had outrun in the race fleet Hippomenes; not the fair daughter of Tyndareus, born of the swan's egg;[2] not Cassiopea, gleaming in the heavens above; not she,[3] close-guarded long by the contest of steeds, whom each gift-laden hand craved for its own, for whom her wicked father oft drained the life of him who fain would be his son, and oft the ground, of like hue, flowed with red blood; not queenly Semele, not the Inachian daughter of Acrisius,[4] who knew Jove in the pitiless lightning and in the shower; not she,[5] for whose ravishing the Tarquins, son and sire, were driven forth, leaving their fathers' gods, what time Rome first changed proud tyranny for peaceful consuls.

³⁹ Many, and not unearned, are the rewards Rome has bestowed upon her sons, chiefest the rewards bestowed upon the Messallae Publicolae. For why should I recount thy tasks of toil immeasurable? Why the stern seasons of rugged warfare? How thou dost set the camp before the forum, the camp before the city—the camp that is so far away from this thy son, so far from this thy home? How thou endurest now extremest cold, and now extremest heat, and canst lay thyself down on even flinty rock? How oft,

---

[1] Atalanta.
[2] Helen.
[3] Hippodamia, daughter of Oenomaus.
[4] Danae, daughter of Acrisius of Argos, called *Inachis* because Inachus was the founder of Argos.
[5] Lucretia.

VIRGIL

saepe trucem adverso perlabi sidere pontum?
  saepe mare audendo vincere, saepe hiemem?
saepe etiam densos immittere corpus in hostes,
  communem belli non meminisse deum?   50
nunc celeres Afros, periurae milia gentis,
  aurea nunc rapidi flumina adire Tagi?
nunc aliam ex alia bellando quaerere gentem
  vincere et Oceani finibus ulterius?
non nostrum est tantas, non, inquam, attingere laudes,
  quin ausim hoc etiam dicere, vix hominum est. 56
ipsa haec, ipsa ferent rerum monumenta per orbem,
  ipsa sibi egregium facta decus parient.
nos ea, quae tecum finxerunt carmina divi
  Cynthius et Musae, Bacchus et Aglaie,   60
si laudem adspirare humilis, si adire Cyrenas,
  si patrio Graios carmine adire sales
possumus, optatis plus iam procedimus ipsis.
  hoc satis est; pingui nil mihi cum populo.

X

Sabinus ille, quem videtis, hospites,
ait fuisse mulio celerrimus

IX. ⁴⁷ perlabi *Aldine edition* 1517: perlabens Ω.
⁵⁰ non Ω: nec *Aldine edition* 1517. timuisse *A*.
⁶⁰ Musae *A*: Musa *BMH, retained by Birt*.
⁶¹ laude *Baehrens*. aspirarem *MH*. si (adire) *B*: sed *MHA*: et *Voss*.   ⁶² si *B*: sic *Zu, Med*.
X. ¹ Albinus *R*. quem] quidem *B*.
² multo Ω: mulio *Aldine edition* 1517.

---

¹ The home of Callimachus, the elegiac poet. Ellis takes *humilis* with *Cyrenas*, "Cyrene's unexalted style."
² This is a clever parody on the fourth poem of Catullus. Sabinus has been identified with the Sabinus of Cicero (*ad*

498

CATALEPTON

under unkindly stars, thou glidest o'er the savage deep? How oft in thy daring thou conquerest the sea, and oft the storm? And how oft thou flingest thyself upon the serried foe, heedless of the common god of war? How thou makest thy way, now to the nimble Africans, the swarms of a perjured race, now to the golden waters of swift Tagus? How in warfare thou seekest nation after nation, and conquerest even beyond Ocean's bounds?

[55] 'Tis not, not, I say, for us to attain to such glories; nay I should dare even this to say, 'tis scarce a task for mortal man. Even of themselves shall these exploits carry their records through the world; of themselves shall beget their own peerless renown. As for me, touching those songs which the gods have fashioned in concert with thee, even the Cynthian and the Muses, Bacchus and Aglaia, if, lowly as I am, I can breathe their praise, if I can approach Cyrene,[1] can approach the wit of Greece with a song of Rome, henceforth I advance even beyond my hopes. This is enough: naught have I to do with the stupid rabble.

X[2]

SABINUS yonder, whom you see, my friends, says he was once the fastest of muleteers, and never was

Fam. xv. 20) and with Ventidius Bassus of Aulus Gellius, xv. 4, who rose from humble life to the offices of praetor and consul. But it is most probable that the man referred to was a purely local celebrity, who, at the end of his active life, set up a votive offering to Castor and Pollux for having saved him from the perils of his calling. The offering took the form of a statuette or painting of himself, seated in a curule chair, the artist having perhaps taken as his model some dignified official of note, who had quite properly been so represented. (So Professor Elmer T. Merrill in *Classical Philology*, 1913.)

499

VIRGIL

neque ullius volantis impetum cisi
nequisse praeter ire, sive Mantuam
opus foret volare sive Brixiam.   5
et hoc negat Tryphonis aemuli domum
negare nobilem insulamve Caeruli,
ubi iste post Sabinus ante Quinctio
bidente dicit attodisse forfice
comata colla, ne Cytorio iugo   10
premente dura volnus ederet iuba.
Cremona frigida et lutosa Gallia,
tibi haec fuisse et esse cognitissima
ait Sabinus: ultima ex origine
tua stetisse dicit in voragine,   15
tua in palude deposisse sarcinas,
et inde tot per orbitosa milia
iugum tulisse, laeva sive dextera
strigare mula sive utrumque coeperat
. . . .   20
neque ulla vota semitalibus deis
sibi esse facta, praeter hoc novissimum,
paterna lora proximumque pectinem.
sed haec prius fuere: nunc eburnea
sedetque sede seque dedicat tibi,   25
gemelle Castor et gemelle Castoris.

³ ullius *Aldine edition* 1517: illius *B*.
⁶ et *Scaliger:* neque Ω.
⁷ -ne *A*.
⁹ dicet *AR*. forfice *Heyne:* forcipe *BH:* forpice *AR*.
¹⁰ ne quid orion *B:* ne quis torion *Z:* ne Cytorio *Maehly*.
¹⁵ dicit] ultima Ω.
¹⁶ deposisse *Scaliger:* de(o)posuisse Ω.
¹⁷ *After this line Birt inserts the following conjectural verse:*
iter parasse mulio, neque ipse non.

CATALEPTON

there any gig that raced along whose speed he was unable to pass, whether he had to race to Mantua or to Brixia. And this, says he, the noble house of his rival, Trypho, does not deny; nor the lodging-rooms of Caerulus, where he who afterwards was Sabinus, but ere that Quinctio, tells that with two-bladed shears he once clipped the hairy necks, lest, under the pressure of Cytorian yoke,[1] the harsh mane might cause some soreness.

[12] O cold Cremona and muddy Gaul, Sabinus says that this was and is well known to thee: he claims that from his earliest birthtime he stood in thy mire, in thy marsh laid by his packs, and thence over so many miles of rutty roads bore the yoke, whether the mule on left or on right or on both sides began to flag . . .; and that no vows to the gods of the by-ways were made by him save this at the last—his father's reins and the curry-comb close by.[2]

[24] But these things are past and gone; now he sits in his ivory chair and dedicates himself to thee, twin Castor, and to thee, Castor's twin-brother.

---

[1] *i.e.* box-wood yoke, because Cytorus, a mountain in Paphlagonia, abounded in box-wood trees.
[2] Or "next in value."

---

[19] mulas Ω: mula *edition* 1482. utrimque *Heinsius*.
[20] *Birt supplies:* pecus recalcitrare ferreo pede.
[22] sibi *Aldine edition* 1517: tibi Ω. propter *ZMuMed*.

501

VIRGIL

XI

Quis deus, Octavi, te nobis abstulit? an quae
  dicunt, a, nimio pocula ducta mero?
"vobiscum, si est culpa, bibi. sua quemque sequuntur
  fata: quid immeriti crimen habent cyathi?"
scripta quidem tua nos multum mirabimur et te 5
  raptum et Romanam flebimus historiam,
sed tu nullus eris. perversi dicite manes,
  hunc superesse patri quae fuit invidia?

XII

Superbe Noctuine, putidum caput,
datur tibi puella, quam petis, datur;
datur, superbe Noctuine, quam petis.
sed, o superbe Noctuine, non vides
duas habere filias Atilium, 5
duas, et hanc et alteram, tibi dari?
adeste nunc, adeste: ducit, ut decet,
superbus ecce Noctuinus hirneam.
Thalassio, Thalassio, Thalassio!

XI. ² dicunt a nimio *u:* dicunt animo (-mi) *BH:* dicuntur animo *AR, Med.:* dicunt Centaurum *Birt:* Centaurum nimio *Garrod.* ducta *Heinsius:* dura Ω.
  ³ culpabile *B.*   ⁴ facta *BMu.*
XII. ⁴ o *B:* omitted *Z.*
  ⁶ duas *Aldine edition* 1517: omitted Ω.
  ⁷ ducit *Z:* dicit *B (above the line).*
  ⁹ Thalassio *twice only* Ω : *thrice, Marius Victorinus.*

---

¹ Written in dialogue, and in the form of an epitaph, the subject of which is the Octavius Musa of *Catalepton* IV. above. Octavius, it would seem, has been "dead-drunk," and so is humorously treated as if he had died. He is a "son of Bacchus," and Bacchus (*i.e.* the wine) had died (was all

502

CATALEPTON

XI[1]

"WHAT god, Octavius, has snatched thee from us?
Or was it, as they say, the cups of o'er-strong wine
that thou, alas, didst quaff?"

"With you I drank, if that's a fault. His own
fate pursues each. Why should the guiltless cups be
blamed?"

"Thy writings, indeed, we shall much admire, and
that thou and thy Roman history are torn from us,
we shall much lament, but thou no more shalt be!"
Tell us, ye Spirits perverse: Why did ye grudge
that he should outlive his father?

XII[2]

PROUD Noctuinus, thou addle-pate, the girl thou
seekest is given thee, I say; the girl thou seekest,
proud Noctuinus, is given thee. But seest thou not,
thou proud Noctuinus, that Atilius has two daughters
—that two, both this and the other, are given thee?[3]
Come[4] ye now, come ye! Proud Noctuinus, see!
brings home, as is meet—a jug! Thalassio, Thalassio,
Thalassio![5]

consumed) before the son. (So F. de Marchi, in *Rivista di Filologia*, 1907, pp. 492 ff.)
Birt's attempt to introduce *Centaurum* in line 2 is due to an epigram of Callimachus (*Anth. Pal.* VII. 725), with a similar *motif*, and containing the words ἦ ῥα τὸ καὶ Κένταυρον; this may be right. The word would be governed by *abstulisse* understood: "was it those cups of strong wine, which they say overcame the Centaur?"

[2] A companion piece to VI. above. Noctuinus is drunk at his wedding.

[3] The second bride is the wine-jug.

[4] Addressed, probably, to the crowd in the street.

[5] With this salutation brides had been greeted ever since the days of Romulus.

VIRGIL

XIII

Iacere me, quod alta non possim, putas,
  ut ante, vectari freta
nec ferre durum frigus aut aestum pati
  neque arma victoris sequi?
valent, valent mihi ira et antiquus furor   5
  et lingua, qua adsim tibi
quid, impudice et improbande Caesari,   9
  seu furta dicantur tua   10
et prostitutae turpe contubernium   7
  sororis—o quid me incitas?
et helluato sera patrimonio   11
  in fratre parsimonia
vel acta puero cum viris convivia
  udaeque per somnum nates
et inscio repente clamatum insuper   15
  "Thalassio, Thalassio."
quid palluisti, femina? an ioci dolent?
  an facta cognoscis tua?
non me vocabis pulchra per Cotytia
  ad feriatos fascinos,   20
nec deinde te movere lumbos in stola
  prensis videbo altaribus
flavumque propter Thybrim olentis nauticum
  vocare, ubi adpulsae rates
stant in vadis caeno retentae sordido   25
  macraque luctantes aqua;
neque in culinam et uncta compitalia
  dapesque duces sordidas,

⁶ qua adsim (assim *B*) Ω: adsiem *Wagner*: sat sim *Scaliger*: adsignem *Bücheler*: mas sim *Ellis*. For the hiatus, *cf. Hor.* Epod. v. 100, xiii. 3.   ⁷,⁸ *placed after* 10 *Birt*.
²¹ stola *Bücheler*: latus *Baehrens*: caltula *Ribbeck*: ratulam *B*: rotulam *Z*.

504

CATALEPTON

XIII[1]

Dost think I am helpless, because I cannot, as heretofore, sail the deep seas, nor bear stern cold, nor endure summer heat, nor follow the victor's arms? Strong, strong are my wrath and old-time fury, and my tongue, wherewith I stand at thy side.

9 Why, thou shameless one, worthy of Caesar's ire! —whether thy secret crimes be told (thy prostituted sister's vile life within thy tent—O why dost thou spur me on?—and thy thrift in late hour at a brother's cost, when thy patrimony was squandered), or whether those banquets thou didst share in boyhood with men, thy body wet throughout the hours of sleep, and, over and above, the cry "Thalassio, Thalassio," raised on a sudden by one I know not: why, I ask, hast thou paled, O woman? Can mere jests pain thee? or dost recognize deeds that are thine own? Amid Cotytto's beauteous rites thou wilt not invite me to the long-disused symbols, nor, as thy hands grasp the altars, shall I see thee bestir thy loins beneath thy woman's robe, and, hard by the yellow Tiber, call to the boat-smelling throng, where the barques that have reached port stand in the shallows, fast in the filthy mire, and struggling with the scanty water; nor wilt thou lead me to the kitchen, to the greasy cross-roads' feast and its mean fare, with which and

[1] These iambics, written in the same couplet form as the first ten Epodes of Horace, are full of Archilochian venom, whether genuine or assumed. The poem is different from everything else that bears the name of Virgil, and Némethy assigns it definitely to Horace's authorship. De Witt, in the *American Journal of Philology*, vol. xxxiii., 1912, p. 320, gives some reasons for supposing Antony to be the object of attack.

505

VIRGIL

quibus repletus et salivosis aquis,
    obesam ad uxorem redis   30
et aestuantes dote solvis pantices,
    osusque lambis saviis.
nunc laede, nunc lacesse, si quicquam vales!
    et nomen adscribo tuum.
cinaede Luciene, liquerunt opes   35
    fameque genuini crepant.
videbo habentem praeter ignavos nihil
    fratres et iratum Iovem
scissumque ventrem et hirneosi patrui
    pedes inedia turgidos.   40

XIIIA

CALLIDA imago sub hac (caeli est iniuria) sede,
    antiquis, hospes, non minor ingeniis,
et quo Roma viro doctis certaret Athenis:
    ferrea sed nulli vincere fata datur.

XIV

Si mihi susceptum fuerit decurrere munus,
    o Paphon, o sedes quae colis Idalias,
Troius Aeneas Romana per oppida digno
    iam tandem ut tecum carmine vectus eat:

XIII. [29] et] ut Ω.
[31] dote *MHA* : nocte *Scaliger*: docte *B*.
[32] scelusque *Birt*.
[35] cinaede Luciene *Bücheler:* Cine delucci iâ te.
XIIIA. *In Z this epigram is found after* XIII. 16.
[1] Callide (Allide) mage : Callida *Birt* : imago *Bücheler and Birt*. sede *Birt*: saecli *MSS*. Pallida mole sub hac celavit membra Secundus *Riese:* Palladis arce sub hac Itali est

506

CATALEPTON

with slimy water thou satest thyself, then returnest to thy lumpish wife, untiest the boiling sausages her dowry provides, and then, hated though thou art, dost smother her with kisses.

³³ Now assail, now provoke me, if at all thou canst! Even thy name I add, thou wanton Lucienus! Now thy means have failed thee, and with hunger thy back teeth rattle! I shall yet see thee possessed of nothing but good-for-naught brothers and an angry Jove, thy stomach rent, and thy ruptured uncle's feet swollen with fasting.

XIIIA

A SCHOLAR's shade rests beneath this place[1]—a wrong done by heaven[2]—one not inferior to the great minds of old, and a man with whom Rome could challenge learned Athens: but to none is it given to vanquish iron Fate.

XIV[3]

IF it be my lot to finish the course I have begun, O thou[4] that dwellest in Paphos and in the Idalian groves, so that at length through Roman towns Trojan Aeneas may go his way, borne along with

---

[1] Nobody knows to whom this epitaph refers, and the first verse is largely conjectural.
[2] The gods are reproached for allowing the man to die; cf. *Culex*, 347.
[3] Written, apparently, after the poet had begun the *Aeneid*. See Appendix, p. 540.
[4] Venus.

---

inuria saecli *Ellis*: Palladi magna suae visa est iniuria sedis *Baehrens*.   XIV. ⁴ erat *Z*.

507

VIRGIL

non ego ture modo aut picta tua templa tabella 5
 ornabo et puris serta feram manibus—
corniger hos aries humilis et maxima taurus
 victima sacratos sparget honore focos,
marmoreusque tibi vel mille coloribus ales
 in morem picta stabit Amor pharetra. 10
adsis, o Cytherea: tuus te Caesar Olympo
 et Surrentini litoris ara vocat.

XV

VATE Syracosio qui dulcior Hesiodoque
 maior, Homereo non minor ore fuit,
illius haec quoque sunt divini elementa poetae
 et rudis in vario carmine Calliope.

XIV. ⁷ et] sed *Burmann*. maxima *B:* maximus *HM*.
 ⁸ sacrato *Heinsius*. spargit *BHM*.
 ⁹ vel] *Birt:* aut. vel mille col.] caput, ignicolorius *Ellis*.
 XV. *In the MSS. this follows upon* XIV. 12, *as if it were a portion of that poem.* ³ sint *HM*.

CATALEPTON

thee in worthy song: not with incense alone or with painted tablet will I adorn thy temple and with clean hands bring thee garlands, but the horned ram, a lowly offering, and the bull, noblest victim, with blood of sacrifice shall besprinkle the hallowed altars, and unto thee in marble, with his quiver painted, as is wont, in all its thousand hues, shall winged Love be set up. Come, O lady of Cythera! thine own Caesar and the altar of Sorrento's shore call thee from Olympus.

XV[1]

To that divine poet who was sweeter than the Syracusan bard,[2] greater than Hesiod, and not inferior to Homer in his speech—to him also belong these first efforts, even his untutored Muse in varied strain.

---

[1] An editorial epilogue, composed, according to Birt, by Varius, whose signature is to be found in the *vario* of the last line! Birt also infers that, as these couplets apply to the *Catalepton* only, they show that Virgil's literary executors repudiated the other minor poems attributed to him. See Appendix, p. 541.
[2] Theocritus.

APPENDIX

THE AENEID

Book VII

A VERY valuable book in connection with the second half of the *Aeneid* is *Virgile et les Origines d'Ostie*, by Jérôme Carcopino (Paris, 1919). It illustrates Virgil's familiarity with the topography and physical characteristics of ancient Latium, but the latest discussion of the problems involved is given by Rehm in *Das geographische Bild des alten Italien in Vergil's Aeneis*, Leipzig, 1932. Another serviceable work is *Vergil's Primitive Italy* by Catherine Saunders (Oxford University Press, 1930).

37. *Nunc age . . . Erato.* In the *Classical Review* (XLV, 1931, 216 ff.) F. A. Todd gives good reasons for supposing that Virgil here invokes Erato as Muse of Love. The epic is now to handle the story of Lavinia and the rival suitors, Turnus and Aeneas. So Apollonius invokes Erato at the opening of *Argonautica* III.

83 ff. In the elucidation of this and other passages, Carcopino (*op. cit.*, 338 ff.) has revived interest in the old work of Bonstetten, *Voyage sur la scène des six derniers livres de l'Enéide*, Genève, 1805.

The scene described here by Virgil is that of a forest of lofty trees, covering the slopes of a hill, at the base of which, amid the groves, is the oracle of Faunus, as well as a noisy spring, exhaling poisonous gases.

These conditions are fairly well satisfied at a

APPENDIX

point five kilometres north-east of Pratica (Lavinium), where, near the Via Ardeatina, is a small stagnant pond, called the Zolforata, which in wintertime becomes a group of five little lakes. Here milky water is constantly bubbling up, while sulphurous gases escape in such quantity and with such force as to make it dangerous for animals to enter the zone. At p. 342, Carcopino gives two photographs of La Zolforata.

150. The Numicius (or Numicus) is mentioned three times (150, 242, 797) in this book and always in close association with the Tiber. Its old identification with the Rio Torto between Lavinium and Ardea, which rested on Pliny the Elder (*Nat. Hist.* III, 56), must be given up, for Carcopino has shown conclusively that it must be the Canale dello Stagno, the ancient outlet of the *lacus Ostiensis*, or *palus Laurens*, only about three miles south of the Tiber mouth.

274. It is natural to suppose that *numero omni* is explained by *ter centum* (275), but Mackail renders the phrase " for all the train."

412. Alliteration is secured by (*magnum*) *manet* as compared with *tenet*, the phrase being balanced by *fortuna fuit*. Ardea has probably changed little since Virgil's day. Its walls, built in the fourth-third century B.C., are still impressive.

430. *in arma para.* Sabbadini inserts *iube* in his text, but in his note shows that it originated in the *iubet* of 432. The phrase *in arma* is harsh after *armari* and Peerlkamp conjectured *in arva*. But probably the passage is one of many that Virgil would have revised had he lived long enough.

543. *conversa:* Mackail adopts *convexa* as a nominative singular, meaning " gathering herself

APPENDIX

together," which is highly improbable. The ancient commentators who accepted *caeli convexa* regarded *per auras* as a synonym. Sabbadini makes meaning by substituting *ardua* for *auras*, " in heaven's steep vault." Cf. 562.

563. *Italiae medio*: Lejay has an interesting note (*Revue de Philologie*, XLI (1917), 565 ff.) on Virgil's use of some old legend, which made the spot here described " l'ombilic de l'Italie." It was in the territory of the Hirpini, a people of Samnium.

598. *omnisque in limine portus*. Servius and Donatus took *portus* as a nominative ("securitas omnis in promptu est"), and this interpretation, which makes good sense, we accept. On the other hand Heyne, who is followed by Conington and Mackail, took *portus* as a genitive, "altogether on the threshold of my harbour." In this case, *omnis* agrees either with the subject of *sum* understood or with that of *spolior*.

601 ff. For the remainder of this book one may profitably consult *Virgil's Gathering of the Clans*, by W. Warde Fowler (Blackwell, Oxford, 1918).

655 ff. As Lejay has observed (*Revue de Philologie*, XL (1916), 163 ff.), the hero Aventinus, a personage probably invented by Virgil, is so called because the Hercules legend is associated with the Aventine. He and his men, however, do not come from there, but are Sabines (665). The *veru* is also the weapon of the Volsci (*Georg*. II, 168), who spoke a Sabellian dialect. For the indefinite *gerunt* (664) Lejay compares *miscent* (*Georg*. II, 282).

674 ff. "Centaurs are the personification of avalanches, sweeping down the naked snow-clad slopes, forcing their path among the huge pine trees, and finally crushing through the underwood

APPENDIX

into the valley" (Mackail). See, too, the book referred to in the above note (601 ff.), pp. 54 ff., quoted in my *Love of Nature*, etc., pp. 223 f.

695 f. The verb *habent* seems to be used in two senses here, (1) "*form* the lines," and (2) "*hold* the heights." Mackail, however, thinks that *acies* is used, not in the military sense, but as rocky *edges*, or sharp cliffs. This is also the view of Slater. But see Van Buren in *Classical Review*, XXXIV (1920), 26 f.

698. *aequati numero*. The context seems to imply that this phrase refers to rhythmical measures. Servius, however, took it to mean "grouped in bands of equal number" and Mackail explains as "dressed or aligned by companies."

Book VIII

W. Warde Fowler in his *Aeneas at the Site of Rome* (Blackwell, Oxford, 1917) deals with this book, as also does D. L. Drew in Ch. I of his *The Allegory of the Aeneid* (Blackwell, Oxford, 1927).

1. *Laurenti ab arce*. Since it is doubtful whether there ever was a town Laurentum in addition to Lavinium, it seems best to take *Laurenti* here and in l. 38 as an ablative adjective. See Carcopino, *op. cit.*, pp. 198 ff., and Saunders, *op. cit.*, pp. 52 ff. Carcopino holds that Laurentum was merely the *civitas*, while Lavinium was its capital. The name Laurentum occurs in no inscriptions.

51. For Arcadian traditions connected with the site of Rome see Saunders, *ibid.*, pp. 39 ff.

65. Light is thrown upon the meaning of this verse, not only by ll. 74, 75 below, but also by *Georg.* IV, 368 ff.:

APPENDIX

et caput, unde altus primum se erumpit Enipeus
unde pater Tiberinus etc.

"That *caput*, that 'head' or reservoir of waters, makes its issue into the upper world as the source or sources of the Tiber; and these sources issue in a region of hill-fortresses, *celsae urbes* " (Mackail).

104. Evander's city was on the Palatine, between which and the river stood a temple of Hercules Victor with the *Ara Maxima* in front of it.

204. The "vale and riverside" would be the later *Forum Boarium*.

205. The original reading of M is *furis*, with *furiis* an early correction. It is probable that *furis* was a mere slip, like Sabbadini's *furs*. The form *fur* occurs in both the *Eclogues* and the *Georgics* (III, 407), but nowhere else in the *Aeneid*. It was probably regarded as unsuited to epic style.

275. *communemque deum.* Hercules is their common god, because Aeneas and Evander have formed an alliance. Servius gives several explanations (all improbable) of the term *communis*, one being that Hercules was both human and divine. A more plausible one is that the god is to be " a sharer of the feast." Thus Mackail.

337 ff. On this interesting passage, see Fowler's *Aeneas at the Site of Rome*, pp. 71 ff.

383. Not only Servius, but the correcting hands in M and P, punctuate after *rogo*, so that *genetrix nato* goes with the next sentence. Mackail follows suit, but the usual arrangement of the words seems far more natural.

421. Mackail takes *stricturae* to mean "the moulds of sand into which the molten metal is run,

APPENDIX

and in which it is squeezed together, *stringitur*, i.e. confined while it solidifies" (*Classical Review*, XXXII (1918), 106).

503. Mackail reminds us that in the Middle Ages the podestà in Italian republics had to be a foreigner.

526. *Tyrrhenus*. The Etruscan origin of the trumpet is often referred to in Greek literature. Moreover, we are here dealing with an Etruscan king and people.

532. *profecto*. Servius takes the word, like *vero*, as a *particula*, or adverb, but Mackail unexpectedly falls in with Ladewig's proposal to treat it as a participle. " to him who has embarked on this enterprise."

533. *ego poscor Olympo*. If the Daniel-Servius had not appended the note: *alii "Olympo" sequentibus iungunt*, it is probable that no modern editor would have punctuated after *poscor* instead of after *Olympo*. I see no reason for departing from the familiar reading.

569. *umquam*. Sabbadini rightly treats the *usquam* of PR as a careless repetition from the preceding verse.

654. Mackail follows Ribbeck in transposing this line to a place next after 641. This certainly gives a more consistent picture.

657. On *arcem tenebant* see note in Appendix on *Aen*. I, 400.

688. *nefas*. This word, which most editors, following Servius, regard as an exclamation, is taken by Mackail as a noun in apposition to *coniunx*, " the accursed one, his Egyptian wife."

APPENDIX

Book IX

47. *Turnus ut.* By accepting Schenkl's conjecture of *at* for *ut*, Mackail makes a simpler sentence, but the MSS. show no variant for *ut*.

146. *quis scindere* ... The MSS. give QVISCINDERE, for which see note in Appendix on *Aen.* VI, 601 ff. Editors who read *qui scindere* commonly take *qui* as interrogative, but Mackail tries to make it a relative, placing a comma after *castra* (147).

177 f. *Ida venatrix.* Mackail agrees with Conington in supposing that here *Ida* is not a mountain nymph, but the mountain itself, μήτηρ θηρῶν (*Il.*, XIV, 283).

268. *dicere sortem.* Sabbadini reads *deicere*, comparing *deiectam sortem*, *Aen.* V, 490.

314. Carcopino (*op. cit.*, 414) holds that the *fossae* here are the drainage canals which in Virgil's day led the water of the marshes to the sea.

412. *aversi.* The MSS. have *adversi*, which Mackail interprets as *opposite*. Sabbadini, retaining it, takes *tergum* as the shield, not the back, of Sulmo. With *tergum* as " back," we must surely read *aversi*.

464. *suas.* The reading *suos* has better authority, but can be adopted only on Mackail's theory that a verse has been lost between 463 and 464.

486. *tua funera.* The explanation of Servius that *funera* is a nominative singular, " one who conducts a funeral," is accepted by Mackail, but such a word occurs nowhere else. Sabbadini inserts *ad* before *tua funera*, " to thy funeral."

579. In view of the abrupt change of subject in this verse, Mackail adopts Housman's conjectural reading,

et laevo infixa est alte lateri, abditaque intus.

APPENDIX

But, as he himself says on l. 676 below, "we must not rewrite Virgil."

584. *matris*: the reading *Martis*, which has better MS. authority, is defended by Lejay (*Revue de Philologie*, XLI (1917), 189). The son of Arcens, however, came from Sicily, and nothing is known about a cult of Mars there.

679. Instead of *liquentia*, Servius read *Liquetia*, as the name of a river (probably the Livenza of to-day). Mackail assumes that *Liquentia* is the correct form of the proper name.

Book X

20 f. The omission in M of *feratur . . . tumidusque*, though regarded by Mackail as "a decided improvement," seems to have been quite accidental, the eye of the scribe having wandered from *Turnusque* to *tumidusque*.

139. *gentes*. The meaning of this word is doubtful. Though commonly taken of the Lydians who followed Ismarus, it may refer to the people in Italy against whom he fought. Thus Mackail, following La Cerda.

163 ff. On this catalogue of Trojan allies, see Saunders, *Vergil's Primitive Italy*, Ch. III, 64 ff.

176. *parent*. As *parere* (l. 179) naturally means "to obey," we see no reason for giving a different meaning to *parent*, which Servius interpreted as equivalent to *apparent*. The power of the augur is poetically, but justifiably, exaggerated.

186. As Mackail remarks, "the text of this line is desperate." Cinyrus is quite unknown, but in mythology there was a Cinyras, who was a king of Cyprus and was guilty of an incestuous passion

518

APPENDIX

for his daughter Myrrha, but this legend had nothing to do with that of Cycnus. Lejay, therefore, supposes (*Revue de Philologie*, XL (1916), 168 ff.) that *Cinyra et* was substituted by some scholiast for *Cycni* (son of Cycnus). In 188, *amor* is not personified. It is the love of Cycnus and Phaëthon, the symbol of which is worn by descendants of Cycnus, to whom that love is also a reproach.

266. W. Warde Fowler thinks that the birds, instead of migrating, are " simply changing their feeding-grounds on account of a local storm " (*Classical Review*, XXXII (1918), 65 f.).

539. *armis*. For *armis*, Ribbeck and Sabbadini adopt *albis*, as read by Probus. This would agree with both nouns, " in white attire and caparisons " (Mackail). The word *armis* in P conceals an earlier reading.

541. Is the *ingens umbra* the shadow cast by Aeneas or the shadow of death? Servius was in doubt. Surely Homer's expressions for death will help us to decide: cf. ἐρεβεννῇ νυκτὶ καλύψαι (*Il.* XIII, 425), τὸν δὲ σκότος ὄσσε κάλυψε (*ib.* XX, 393), νεφέλη δέ μιν ἀμφεκάλυψε κυανέη (*ib.* XX, 417).

769. *longo*. In R the final *o* is a correction of some earlier letter, and *m* (codex Minoraugiensis) has *longe*, which is read by Ribbeck and Sabbadini. The meaning " afar off " is very suitable here.

805. *tuta . . . arce*. Since *arce*, which according to Conington is " obviously the true reading," has little MS. authority, both Janell and Mackail adopt *tuta arte* in the sense of " a sheltering device." But *arte* should imply an artificial defence, not such as nature provides in the *ripae* and *saxum* of l. 806.

850. *exsilium*. Sabbadini records *exilium* as the

APPENDIX

original reading of P, but I can see no sign of an *l* corrected into *t*. The evidence of Servius, however, supported by the *Gudianus*, favours *exilium*, not *exitium*

Book XI

264 ff. In order that *referam* (264) may control the syntax of 269, Ribbeck placed 264, 265 after 268. This transposition Mackail regards as "an almost certain correction." But surely the stylistic effect of the exclamatory infinitive in 269 is worth keeping, and for such an infinitive without the usual *-ne*, see *Aen.* V, 615–16.

273. Both W. Warde Fowler and D'Arcy W. Thompson identify these birds of Diomede with shearwaters (*Classical Review*, XXXII (1918), 67 ff., 92 ff.).

317. On the *fines Sicani* see Carcopino, *op. cit.*, 458 ff. The *ager* here described extended from the mouth of the Tiber to the neighbourhood of Ardea, and included hill-country in which lived Auruncans, Rutulians, and Sicanians, already grouped together in *Aen.* VII, 795.

636 ff. Mackail regards 636–45 as an insertion, made possibly by Virgil's editors. But Varius and Tucca were not permitted to make additions, though they could reject matter. The MSS. give no indication of editorial revision at this point.

684. *agmine verso.* Mackail prefers to take these words with *traicit*, but surely it was the rout, rather than his lack of armour, that made it easy for Camilla to catch Ornytus.

760. *multa prior arte.* The meaning of *prior* would seem to be determined by its position between *multa* and *arte*.

APPENDIX

801. *aurae.* The form *auras*, which Servius read here and regarded as an archaic genitive, was probably taken by mistake from the ending of 799 above.

815. The phrase *contentus fuga*, lit. " strained in flight," is taken by some in the more prosaic sense of " satisfied with flight."

Book XII

" It is in my judgment the poet's most mature work." (W. Warde Fowler, in *The Death of Turnus*, Blackwell, Oxford, 1919, p. 1.) *The Death of Turnus* deals especially with Book XII.

52. " Longe," says Henry, means here " of no use." (Fowler, *ibid.*, p. 48.)

114 f. *cum primum*, etc. This beautiful picture of sun-rise, which reproduces a phrase coined by Ennius, *funduntque elatis naribus lucem*, reminds us of those marvellous heads of the horses of the Sun from the east pediment of the Parthenon, " flung up to catch the breath of morning."

120. *velati limo.* " The *limus* was an ancient sacrificial apron with a purple stripe (according to Servius), which probably indicates that the business of the wearer was to slay the victim." (Fowler, *op. cit.*, p. 53.)

161. *ingenti mole.* Servius explains as *pompa, ambitu.* This is probably correct, though Wagner refers the phrase to the *magnum corpus* of Latinus, and Mackail takes it with *curru* only.

221. *tabentesque genae.* The epithet *tabentes* is " certainly attractive and plausible " (Mackail), but *pubentes*, having MS. authority, is read by Janell, Sabbadini and Mackail. It is to be noticed,

521

APPENDIX

however, that the palaeographic difference between the two words is very slight, being confined to the first two letters, and, of these, P and T, written as capitals, sometimes resemble each other closely (Γ, T). Moreover, *tabentes* has the support of Donatus (on 219).

250. *cycnum excellentem*. Fowler (*op. cit.*, p. 72) takes the epithet to mean " rising in flight," but no parallel to such usage can be cited. That *excellere* once carried the transitive meaning *in altum extollere* is clear from the gloss in Festus cited by Fowler, but, as found in literature, the word is always used metaphorically, with the implication of an original and intransitive sense of " overtopping." The epithet, however, may very well imply here that the swan attacked was the " leader," as Fowler and Mackail take it.

285. Fowler and Mackail punctuate with a comma after *ferunt*. In that case they should place a comma after *divos* (286) as well.

465. Mackail's advocacy of *nec equo* instead of *aequo* is convincing. The phrase *pede aequo*, supposed to mean " in fair fight," is without parallel and quite dubious. The corrections in M point to an original *equo*, before which *nec* may easily have been lost.

474. The *hirundo* here is perhaps the swift rather than the swallow. Thus J. S. in *Classical Review*, XXXIII (1919), 68, and Fowler, *op. cit.*, 95.

520. *limina*. This gives an even better sense than *munera*, which means the " responsibilities " of the great. Cf. Horace, *Epod.* II, 8, *superba civium potentiorum limina*.

524. *in aequora*. It is impossible to tell whether this means " to the seas " or " to the plains."

APPENDIX

701 ff. *quantus Athos*, etc. For the comparison of Aeneas with mountains, see my *Love of Nature Among the Greeks and Romans*, pp. 33 and 220 ff.

The order of ascent is Eryx (2465 ft.), Athos (6350 ft.), and the Apennines. Several of the Apennine peaks outtop Athos, *e.g.*, Monte Cimone (7103 ft.), Monte Viglio (7075 ft.), Monte Terminillo (7260 ft.), Monte Vettore (8128 ft.), Monte Velino (8160 ft.), Monte Amaro (9170 ft.), and the Gran Sasso d'Italia (9560 ft.). Virgil is not necessarily thinking of the last named only, as Fowler and Mackail suppose. The Apennine range as a whole is eminent among mountains, as the Tiber is eminent among rivers, hence the term *pater* can be applied to both (cf. *pater Tiberinus*, *Georg.* IV. 369).

750. *puniceae formidine pinnae*. Cf. *Georg.* III. 372, and see note on that line.

790. Mackail places a comma after *contra*, and supposes that the sentence as a whole is unfinished.

THE MINOR POEMS

It is an accepted fact that the ancient *Life of Virgil* which has come down to us under the name of Donatus (fourth century) is essentially the work of Suetonius (second century). However, not all the material in the *Life* dates from Suetonius, and in an article on " Non-Suetonian Passages in the Life of Virgil formerly ascribed to Donatus " (*Transactions of the American Philological Association*, LVII (1926)), R. M. Geer has shown that " certain passages, two or three of which had been previously suspected," are " probably not from the hand of Suetonius, at least in their present form." Among these passages

APPENDIX

is the list of minor poems attributed to Virgil, running thus:

> "Deinde Catalepton et Priapea et Epigrammata et Diras, item Cirim et Culicem, cum esset annorum XVI, cuius materia talis est: pastor fatigatus aestu cum sub arbore condormisset et serpens ad eum proreperet, e palude culex provolavit atque inter duo tempora aculeum fixit pastori. At ille continuo culicem contrivit et serpentem interemit ac sepulchrum culici statuit et distichon fecit:
>
> > Parve culex pecudum custos tibi tale merenti funeris officium vitae pro munere reddit.
>
> Scripsit etiam de qua ambigitur Aetnam."

Geer discusses the style of the above passage and then concludes: "In view of all this it seems quite certain that the passage beginning *Deinde Catalepton* and ending with the quotation from the *Culex* must be an addition."

The statement made by Servius (fourth century) about the minor poems is this: "Scripsit etiam septem sive octo libros hos: Cirim Aetnam Culicem Priapeia Catalepton Epigrammata Copam Diras."

In America several prominent scholars have upheld the authenticity of the *Appendix* as a whole, and even Virgilian biography has been built up upon the quite uncertain foundation which it provides. Thus we have *Young Virgil's Poetry*, by E. K. Rand, in *Harvard Studies in Classical Philology*, XXX (1919), 103–85; *Vergil: A Biography*, by Tenney Frank (New York, 1922); and De Witt's *Virgil's Biographia Litteraria* (Toronto, 1923). A very fair presentation of "The Present Status of the Virgilian Appendix" is given

APPENDIX

by Henry M. Prescott in the special Vergil Number of the *Classical Journal*, XXVI (1930), 49–62.

In an article on "The Poems of the Appendix Vergiliana," published in the *Transactions of the American Philological Association*, LIII (1922), 5–34, the present writer examined the poems from the point of view of vocabulary, and arrived at the conclusion that there is a large non-Virgilian element in their diction, and that apart from the *Eclogues*, *Georgics*, and *Aeneid*, it is doubtful whether a single line of genuine Virgilian work has survived.

In a notable series of papers, Professor R. S. Radford presents a mass of detailed evidence in support of the view that most, if not all, of the poems of the *Appendix* are really the work of Ovid. These papers include the following: "The Juvenile Works of Ovid," in *Trans. Amer. Phil. Assoc.* LI (1920), 146–171; "The Priapea and the Vergilian Appendix," *ibid.*, LII (1921), 148–77; "The Language of the Pseudo-Vergilian Catalepton," *ibid.*, LIV (1923), 168–186; "Ovid's *Carmina Furtiva*," in the *Philological Quarterly*, VII (1928), 45–59; "The *Culex* and Ovid," in *Philologus*, LXXXVI (1930), 18–66. If we give due weight to the detailed evidence gathered so laboriously by Radford we must conclude that the *Appendix* as a whole is either the work of Ovid himself or of some poet or poets thoroughly steeped in Ovid. Certainly, the Ovidian colour of the *Appendix* as a whole is so strong that if Donatus and Servius had reported the poems to be Ovid's, nobody probably would have questioned the statement.

Within the limits allowed us, it is impossible to discuss this subject of authorship adequately, but it may be pointed out that few scholars have considered the following significant passage in the Donatus

525

APPENDIX

(Suetonius) Life of Virgil: *Quamvis igitur multa ψευδεπίγραφα, id est falsa inscriptione sub alieno nomine sint prolata ... tamen Bucolica liquido Vergilii esse minime dubitandum est, praesertim cum ipse poeta, tamquam hoc metuens, principium eius operis et in alio carmine suum esse testatus sit dicendo:*

"Carmina qui lusi pastorum audaxque iuventa,
Tityre, te patulae cecini sub tegmine fagi."
Georg. IV, 565 f.

It is clear that the ancient *Vita*, in its use of the term ψευδεπίγραφα, is referring to poems falsely attributed to Virgil, who in this striking passage placed the seal of his authorship upon both the *Georgics* and the *Bucolics*, but upon nothing else. From what his biographers themselves say, we infer that Virgil must have taken the greatest pains to suppress his immature and imperfect productions: "scripta sua sub ea condicione legavit ne quid ederent quod non a se editum esset." Even the *Aeneid* would never have survived except through an imperial decree: "edidit autem auctore Augusto Varius."

CULEX

French and Belgian scholars have little sympathy with the theory of Virgilian authorship of the *Culex*. Benoist, in his edition of the *Bucoliques et Géorgiques* (Paris, 1876), says (p. xc): " une étude attentive de la versification, de l'emploi des mots et des locutions, de la couleur poétique, de la construction des périodes, a prouvé suffisamment que Virgile n'avait aucune part à cette oeuvre. Il n'y a nulle transition possible d'un tel style à celui des *Bucoliques*. C'est

APPENDIX

un exercise de jeune homme qui s'essaye à la poésie en imitant Virgile et les poètes alexandrins."

Charles Plésent, in his two-volume study of the poem (Paris, 1910), gives abundant reasons for rejecting its authenticity, and Jean Hubaux, after noting that Plésent had found a large number of resemblances between the *Culex* and Ovid, and that Skutsch had established a connection between it and the *Remedium Amoris*, concludes that the *Culex* is *postérieur à Ovide* (*Les Thèmes Bucoliques dans la Poésie Latine*, Bruxelles, 1930). This conclusion is in harmony with that already reached some years before by Birt's disciple, Holtschmidt, in a praiseworthy dissertation, *De Culicis Carminis Sermone et de Tempore quo scriptum sit* (Marburg, 1913), viz. that the author was a contemporary of the Emperor Claudius.

The latest work on the subject is Radford's very scholarly article, " The *Culex* and Ovid," in *Philologus*, LXXXVI (1930), 18–66, which is really definitive, so far at least as in establishing the extraordinarily Ovidian character of the poem, in respect to vocabulary, phraseology, metrical features, mythology, and imaginative atmosphere. "There are in *Culex*," says Radford (p. 80), " fully 400 phrases, which are found also in Ovid, but *in no other poet* of the Golden Age (Lucretius to Ovid)."

The *Culex* is the work, not of Virgil, but either of Ovid or of some poet amazingly like Ovid.

CIRIS

A vast amount of controversial literature has been written upon the *Ciris*. Drachmann and Vollmer

APPENDIX

accept Virgilian authorship, but a host of competent scholars, including Sillig, Ganzemüller, Némethy, Klotz, and Birt, reject it. For a survey of this discussion see the Introduction to R. F. Thomason's article on " The *Ciris* and Ovid " in *Classical Philology*, XVIII (1923), 239–62, 334–44; XIX (1924), 147–56. In this article Thomason makes a detailed study of the language of the *Ciris*, and reaches conclusions which are in full accord with the views of Professor R. S. Radford respecting the Ovidian authorship of the whole Virgilian Appendix. Radford claims that the *Ciris*, which " had been begun long before and elaborated through many years of youth (ll. 44–47), was sent from Athens to Messalinus as a completed gift in 18 B.C." (" Ovid's *Carmina Furtiva*," p. 54).

1–11. The long opening sentence of the *Ciris* is characteristic. " One is impressed at once by the wide divergence between the sentence structure of the poem and that of the authenticated works of Virgil " (Crittenden, *The Sentence Structure of Virgil*, Ann Arbor, 1911, p. 63).

12. The dedication to a Messalla shows that the author of the poem belonged to the literary circle of Messalla, but nowhere in the ancient *Vitae* is such a claim made for Virgil. See, too, *Catalepton* IX.

13. *libido*: this word, nowhere found in Virgil, occurs 13 times in Ovid. Altogether, I have listed 131 words in the *Ciris* not to be found in Virgil, and Thomason has added 11 more. Many of these are very common in Ovid. Thus *ocellus* (132, 238, 348) occurs 20 times; *relevo* (340) and *tribuo* (93, 270), 19 times each; and *charta* (39, 62), 14 times. The non-Virgilian word *alumna* (*e.g.* 224) occurs 12 times in the *Ciris*.

59 ff. The dependence of this passage upon *Ecl.*

APPENDIX

VI, 74 ff. is discussed at length by K. Witte in *Hermes*, LVII (1922), 563 ff.

285. " This whole line is peculiarly Ovidian: for Ovid is the first poet to use *comploro*, and he alone has the phrase *questus aniles (Metam.* IX, 276)." Thomason, *op. cit.*, 237, note 2.

474. This line is the same as *Aeneid* III, 74, and the phrase *viridemque Donysam* (476) is found again in *Aeneid* III, 125. On the other hand, in place of *marmoreamque Paron* (476), found again in Ovid, *Metam.* VII, 465, we have *niveamque Paron* in *Aeneid* III. 126. The descriptive handling of the *Ciris* passage is more in Ovid's style than Virgil's.

541. In the paper referred to on p. 447, note 2, Professor Thompson claims the story of the *Ciris* as a fairy-tale, the κεῖρις not being a real bird, but representing the *luna senescens*, or " sickle-moon," which is " a fugitive in the morning twilight, with the sun following close behind."

COPA

The *Copa* appears in the list of minor Virgilian poems cited by Servius, but is absent from that given by Donatus. The external authority for Virgilian authorship is therefore weaker than usual.

In the *Classical Quarterly* (XVII, 1923, 73–81 and XIX, 1925, 37–42) D. L. Drew dwells upon a connection between the *Copa* and Theocritus, and tries to show that Propertius tacitly recognized Virgilian authorship.

A brief but very illuminating study of the *Copa* is made by Wilamowitz-Moellendorff in the last chapter of his *Hellenistische Dichtung* (Berlin, 1924, pp. 311–15).

APPENDIX

Wilamowitz shows that the poem echoes Propertius as well as Virgil and would date it shortly after 15 B.C. Indeed, he claims that the anonymous elegy " might better have found lodging in a Propertius collection," but at the time when these " intentional forgeries " appeared, " Virgil was the greater name."

This essay by Wilamowitz should not have been overlooked by Israel E. Drabkin, whose dissertation, *The Copa* (privately printed, 1930), is a laboured but ineffective advocacy of Virgilian authorship, for Professor Mackail's verdict still holds good. The *Copa* " is the work of a real poet: but the touch and handling are totally unlike Virgil's " (*Virgil and Virgilianism*, p. 49).

Jean Hubaux (*Les Thèmes Bucoliques*, etc., Bruxelles, 1930, p. 123) points out that the author of " this brilliant and original composition " must have read Horace as well as Virgil, " car il combine avec un rare bonheur les motifs bucoliques empruntés aux *Églogues* avec les scènes joyeuses de danses et de musique souvent décrites dans les *Odes*."

MORETUM

The *Moretum* is not included in the ancient lists of minor poems attributed to Virgil. Even Professor Rand, therefore, does not press the claim for Virgilian authorship. On the other hand, being " a work of finished and individual art " (Mackail), it is not unworthy of a great poet, though the realistic treatment of the theme differentiates the poem from the works of Virgil. Hubaux (*op. cit.*, 121) makes the interesting suggestion that the author took his cue from *Georg.* IV, 148, where Virgil, like a

APPENDIX

" grand seigneur des lettres," invites others to sing of gardens:

> praetereo atque aliis post me memoranda relinquo.

It is possible, too, that a *point d'appui* for the *Moretum* was provided by *Ecl.* II, 10, 11:

> Thestylis et rapido fessis messoribus aestu
> alia serpullumque herbas contundit olentis.

In a charming essay, *A Study of the Moretum* (Syracuse, N.Y. 1929), Florence L. Douglas makes the point that in his tenth book, *De Cultu Hortorum*, Columella shows familiarity with this poem. It does not follow, however, that he regarded Virgil as its author.

2. *excubitor*: this is the first of 69 non-Virgilian words in the *Moretum*.

DIRAE

The *Dirae* is listed among the minor poems of Virgil by both Donatus and Servius. Though an attempt has been made to father the work upon L. Varius, the friend of Virgil (P. J. Enk in *Mnemosyne*, Nova Series 47, 382–409), yet the view of Scaliger, who long ago attributed it to Valerius Cato, well known as a poet and critic of the Republican period, has won wide acceptance. Cato lost an inheritance in the confiscations under Sulla, wrote a work called *Indignatio*, and sang of his love for one Lydia. (See the remarks which follow upon the *Lydia*.) Hubaux believes that the *Dirae* preceded the first and ninth *Eclogues* of Virgil and to a certain extent inspired those poems (*op. cit.*, pp. 35–65).

APPENDIX

LYDIA

In the MSS. the *Lydia* is given in sequence to the *Dirae*, without special title, but in 1729 F. Jacobs discovered in one of the Vatican MSS. that verse 104 (= *Lydia*, 1) had the initial letter in red ink, indicating the beginning of a new poem, which is now generally recognized as the *Lydia*.

Lindsay holds this poem to be the *Lydia* of Valerius Cato (*Classical Review*, XXXII (1918), 62 ff.) and Prescott (*op. cit.*, p. 71) admits that Cato may be the author of both the *Dirae* and the *Lydia*, but both Rand (*op. cit.*, p. 182) and Frank (*op. cit.*, p. 131) take an untenable stand. They insist upon Virgilian authorship for the *Dirae*, but reject it for the *Lydia*. As a matter of fact the two poems are bound closely together, alike in MS. tradition as in subject-matter and sentiment. " Elles sont composées selon les mêmes conventions poétiques, écrites dans le même style et empreintes d'un même sentimentalisme, très personnel " (Hubaux, *op. cit.*, p. 46).

All the facts known about Valerius Cato are brought together by Professor R. P. Robinson in the *Transactions of the American Philological Association*, LIV (1923), 98-116.

PRIAPEA

Though the first three poems are concerned with Priapus, we are using the title *Priapea* merely for convenience of reference, inasmuch as in antiquity the three were included with the following poems in the *Catalepton* collection. Theodor Birt, in his edition of the *Catalepton* (Leipzig and Berlin, 1910), avoids the title *Priapea* altogether.

APPENDIX

It is highly probable that the title *Priapea*, in the list of minor works which Donatus and Servius attribute to Virgil, does not refer to these three poems at all, but to the large collection of eighty-one licentious poems under that name. In the majority of the MSS. containing the latter, they are ascribed to Virgil. (See R. F. Thomason, *The Priapea and Ovid*, pp. 3 ff.)

As to the group of three, Birt supposes that Virgil wrote them shortly before the *Eclogues*, and Tenney Frank finds a place for them between the *Eclogues* and the *Georgics*, but the presence of non-Virgilian words and grammatical usages leads us to look elsewhere for the authorship. The poems, however, betray Virgilian influence, and Galletier, finding that the third one and the *Copa* present bucolic variations on Virgilian themes, infers that they were composed by the same writer.

I

1. *rosa . . . frequentor.* Not before Suetonius do we find this verb used elsewhere with an ablative case (Galletier, *Epigrammata et Priapea*, p. 31).

II

10–11. "Un souvenir manifeste des vers 21–22 de la 4e *Églogue*" (*ibid.*, p. 25).

12–13. "Une véritable contamination de deux passages de la 1re *Églogue*," *i.e.* ll. 8 and 33–35 (*ibid.*, p. 25).

III

The writer of this poem had in view Virgil, *Ecl.* I, 48; II, 47; III, 89; VII, 12 and 34; as well as Tibullus I, x, 19 ff. (*ibid.*, p. 26).

6. *pauperis tuguri.* Cf. *Ecl.* I, 68 and *Copa* 23.

533

APPENDIX

CATALEPTON

Recent publications upon the *Catalepton* include Birt's *Erklärung des Catalepton* (Leipzig, 1910); Edouard Galletier's *Epigrammata et Priapea* (Paris, 1920); and two articles " à propos du *Catalepton*," in the *Revue de Philologie*, one by Jérôme Carcopino, Vol. XLVI (1922), 156–84; the other by E. Galletier, Vol. L (1926), 153–72. Birt believes in the substantial integrity of the *Catalepton* collection, and accepts Virgilian authorship except for the elegiacs on Messalla (IX) and the editorial epilogue (XV). His views are heartily supported by Rand, Tenney Frank and De Witt, who, however, see no reason for omitting the Messalla panegyric from the Virgilian list. On the other hand, Carcopino scoffs at the value of a verse collection made at the end of the first century A.D., the work, as he believes, of a literary forger writing " à la manière de Virgile." Galletier takes a middle stand. He holds that Carcopino has carried his scepticism too far, but he chides those credulous scholars who contribute to the discussion " nothing but their own personal impressions " (*op. cit.*, p. 154).

I

The fact that the first epigram involves Plotius Tucca and the last L. Varius, Virgil's literary exe-cutors, far from giving an assurance of genuineness to the collection, has but fanned the suspicions of many critics as to the authenticity of the poems. As Carcopino writes (*loc. cit.*, p. 179): " Qu'on examine de près les noms qui reviennent dans les *Epigrammes*, et la feinte sécurité qu'ils nous inspirent de prime

APPENDIX

abord ne tardera guère à se changer en une invincible méfiance."

II

This obscure epigram certainly passed as Virgil's at the time when Quintilian's *Institutio* was published, A.D. 92 or 93. Carcopino (*op. cit.*, p. 177) supposes that the forger of the collection used it as a kernel of reality about which to group his fictitious verses.

III

In view of all the evidence, it seems best to suppose that the subject of this poem is Alexander the Great. The world-conqueror had expressed a wish to be buried in Macedonia, and though Perdiccas tried to carry out this plan, it was never realized. As to l. 5, the interesting speculations of Livy, IX, 16–19, show that even in his day the fate of Rome, had it been attacked by Alexander, furnished a theme for rhetorical discussion. Galletier (*op. cit.*, 46) writes: " Cette pièce n'est que le développement en vers d'un lieu commun cher aux poètes et aux déclamateurs du premier siècle après Jésus-Christ sur l'incertitude des choses humaines et la fragilité de la gloire militaire." Both Galletier and Carcopino recognize in the epigram rhetorical characteristics of the style of Lucan and Seneca.

IV

This epigram, like I, VII, IX, and XI, is addressed to a prominent friend of the famous poet. But the writer " ne connaît pas la mesure dans l'éloge, accorde à son ami tous les dons des Muses et pousse l'humilité jusqu'à la platitude. Ce n'est pas sur ce

APPENDIX

ton ... que Virgile reconnaît les mérites ou la valeur de Mécène, de Gallus, de Pollion " (Galletier, *Epigrammata et Priapea*, 39).

V

"The poem is composed of two stanzas: one, his scornful valedictory to teachers of rhetoric (or possibly his fellow-students), and to the noxious pedantry of the schoolroom; the other, an announcement of a new programme " (Prescott, *op. cit.*, 49).

The value, as a record, of this interesting composition in limping iambics depends largely or wholly on the theory accepted as to the origin of the *Catalepton* collection as a whole. In the " romantic biographies " that have been written on Virgil the poem naturally plays a large part. See Tenney Frank, *op. cit.*, 20, 47; De Witt, *op. cit.*, 33, 36, etc. Galletier admits its Virgilian origin, and very aptly compares Lamartine's *Adieux à la Poésie*, in his *Méditations Poétiques :*

" Adieu donc, adieu, voici l'heure,
Lyre aux soupirs melodieux!

Peut-être à moi, lyre chérie,
Tu reviendras dans l'avenir! "

9. *dicta Sironis :* this need not denote Siro himself, but merely an Epicurean school. Cf. *Aetna*, 538;

dicta libelli, Heraclite, tui.

14. *pudenter:* the word is commonly taken as referring to licentious poetry, now forsworn, but Prescott thinks it more likely that the poet " is inviting the Muses to visit him rarely and not to stay too long."

APPENDIX

VI

De Witt's theory as to the identity of Noctuinus is rejected by Galletier: " Il serait bien étrange que les anciens n'eussent rien su de cette haine du poète pour le triumvir " (*Epigrammata et Priapea*, 44). Galletier himself thinks that *Catalepton* I, VI, and XII are linked together in " un petit roman d'amour," in which a rejected suitor pours scorn upon his successful rival and his kin.

VII

1. *Vari:* see note on *Catalepton* I above.
2. πόθος: A. W. Van Buren notes that Πόθος and Pothus occur as proper names, " chiefly as slaves and freedmen in the early imperial period and even somewhat earlier " (*Classical Review*, XXXVII (1922), 115–16).

VIII

In his able article on " The *Priapea* and the Vergilian Appendix " (*Transactions of the American Philological Association*, LII (1921), 148 ff.), Radford presents the view that this and other poems in the *Catalepton* are Virgilian " impersonations," similar in character to the " impersonations " of Tibullus (Tibullus IV, 13; II, 3 and 5). In both cases he supposes that Ovid was the actual author.

IX

This poem illustrates the difficulties encountered if we recognize the Virgilian authorship of the *Catalepton* collection.

Messalla's triumph was won in 27 B.C., so that if

APPENDIX

Virgil wrote this "prosy poem," as Prescott calls it, he did so "in the decade when he was composing the *Aeneid*." Yet both Rand and Prescott accept this quite untenable view. As for Tenney Frank, he advocates the still more extravagant theory that the occasion of the poem was Messalla's victory over Octavius in the first battle of Philippi, 42 B.C. Thus Virgil " trouve moyen d'être attaché à Octave et de louer en même temps l'ennemi qui l'a vaincu sur le champ de bataille " (Galletier in *Revue des Études Anciennes*, XXV (1923), 194 ff.).

Birt wisely rejects Virgilian authorship for the elegy. Ribbeck (*Appendix Vergiliana*, 12) identifies the author with the Lygdamus of the Tibullan collection. Némethy attributes the poem to Ovid (*De Ovidio Elegiae in Messallam Auctore*, Budapest, 1909), and Radford holds that, as it was written in 27 B.C., when Ovid was in his seventeenth year, it is that poet's earliest extant work (*Transactions of the American Philological Association*, LI (1920), 159).

2. *Pegasides*. This synonym for *Musae*, nowhere found in Virgil, occurs in Ovid, *Her.* XV, 27; *Trist.* III, 7, 15, etc. Similarly, the following proper nouns, frequently in evidence in Ovid, are absent from Virgil: Oenides, 6; Cassiopea, 28; Semele and Inachis, 33.

13. *chartas:* this un-Virgilian word occurs 14 times in Ovid. That the poem is "not Virgilian in style" does not trouble De Witt, who remarks: "Virgil himself did not consider it Virgilian and did not wish it to be included in his published works" (*op. cit.*, 54).

17. According to Frank, the resemblance between this verse and the opening line of the *Eclogues* implies that Virgil acknowledges Messalla's influence over

APPENDIX

him in pastoral poetry. Yet Messalla was six years younger than Virgil, and in 42 B.C. was only two-and-twenty years of age. See Galletier, *ibid.*, p. 176, note 1.

47–53. *À propos* of this passage, it has been remarked that " no Latin poem in a restricted space shows proportionately so many parallels to the *Ciris* as *Cat.* IX, which is likewise dedicated to a Messalla" (P. John, *Rheinisches Museum*, LXIII (1908), 100). John is convinced that *Cat.* III, *Cat.* IX, and the *Ciris* are by one and the same poet.

X

In the *Classical Review*, XV (1901), 217, Professor W. A. Heidel attributes the authorship of this parody poem to Furius Bibaculus of Cremona, the friend of Catullus.

XIII

It seems incredible that on the basis of such evidence as we possess, any Virgilian scholars should claim Virgilian authorship for this foul effusion, " une des pièces les plus ordurières qui soient dans la latinité," as Galletier characterises it (*ibid.*, p. 195). And yet, on the strength of this abusive epode, our " romantic biographers " make up a story of Virgil's military and sordid experiences, of which we hear absolutely nothing in the ancient *Vitae* themselves.

9. *Caesari.* Galletier supposes that the reference is to Augustus and his attempts to improve public morals, but Carcopino, with much more plausibility, finds evidence in the poem that the Caesar here mentioned is the Emperor Domitian (*op. cit.*, p. 168).

23. *Thybrim:* Carcopino claims that Virgil introduced the form *Thybris* (for *Tiberis*) into Latin verse.

APPENDIX

It occurs 17 times in the *Aeneid*, but never in either the *Georgics* or the *Eclogues*, and therefore its appearance in this epode, far from revealing the hand of Virgil, proves that these iambics were written at a much later time by one who did not hesitate to vulgarize a form consecrated to epic usage (*op. cit.*, 164; also *Virgile et les Origines d'Ostie*, Paris, 1919, 577 ff.).

40. *inedia turgidos:* neither of these closing words is found in Virgil, and in the 40 short verses of the poem there are as many as 24 un-Virgilian words. Némethy takes the lampoon to be an Horatian epode, while Jean Hubaux edits it as *Une Épode d'Ovide* (in *Serta Leodiensia*, Liége, 1930: Bibliothèque de la Faculté de Philosophie et Lettres de l'Université de Liége, Fascicule XLIV). Radford, of course, attributes all the *Catalepton* poems to Ovid. See " Ovid's *Carmina Furtiva* " in *Philological Quarterly*, VII (1928), 45-59.

XIIIa

Galletier thinks this interpolated epigram is " une pièce moderne, écrite pour un moderne par un humaniste " (*Epigrammata et Priapea*, 225).

XIV

See note in Appendix on *Catalepton* VIII. As Radford says: " the actual writer knows perfectly well that Virgil never finished " the *Aeneid* (*The Priapea and the Vergilian Appendix*, 163). Birt, to be sure, supposes that Virgil composed the lines at the time when Augustus, writing from Spain, was urging him to complete the *Aeneid*. Such scholars as Heyne, Buecheler, Schanz, Teuffel, and Leo have attributed

APPENDIX

the poem to some friend of Virgil's. That it is a forgery is proved convincingly by Galletier (*Epigrammata et Priapea*, 35 ff.).

5. *tabella*: this word occurs 44 times in Ovid, but nowhere in Virgil.

XV

Assuming Virgilian authorship, it is hard to see how the term *elementa* can be correctly applied to poems like *Catalepton* IX and XIV. Sommer infers from the peculiar use of the word and from the non-Virgilian form *Homereus* that this epilogue is distinctly post-Augustan.

Galletier notes the striking resemblance between this epigram and a late epitaph given by the grammarians:

> Sicanius vates silvis, Ascraeus in agris,
> Maeanius bellis ipse poeta fui.

This epitaph he regards as the model used for the epilogue. On the other hand, Carcopino looks upon the epilogue as the model for the epitaph. Even so, he notes certain parallels in thought and expression in Martial, Statius, and Juvenal, which lead him to refer the composition of the epilogue to a poet of the Flavian era. Galletier, however, would assign it to some grammarian of the third or fourth century (see *Revue de Philologie*, XLVI (1922), 160, and L (1926), 159).

INDEX

The references are to books and lines in the Latin text. Abbreviations: *A.* = Aeneid; *Ca.* = Catalepton; *Ci.* = Ciris; *Co.* = Copa; *Cu.* = Culex; *D.* = Dirae; *E.* = Eclogues; *G.* = Georgics; *L.* = Lydia; *M.* = Moretum; *P.* = Priapea; also *adj.* = adjective; *fem.* = feminine; *plur.* = plural; *sing.* = singular; *subst.* = substantive. References to the following names are not given in full on account of their frequency: Achates, Aeneas, Anchises, Apollo, Ascanius, Ausonius, Bacchus, Danai, Dardanius, Dido, Graius, Italia, Italus, Iulus, Iuno, Iuppiter, Latinus, Latium, Laurens, Manes, Mars, Nympha, Pallas (3), Phoebus, Phrygius, Priamus, Romanus, Rutulus, Teucrus, Troia, Troianus, Troilus, Tros, Turnus, Tyrius, Tyrrhenus, Venus.

Abaris, member of Turnus' army, *A.* IX. 344

Abas: (1) early king of Argos, *A.* III. 286; (2) companion of Aeneas, *A.* I. 121; (3) an Etruscan, *A.* X. 170, 427

Abella, town in Campania, *A.* VII. 740

Abydus, city on the Hellespont, *G.* I. 207

Acamas, son of Theseus, *A.* II. 262

Acarnan, *adj.* of Acarnania, a province of central Greece, *A.* V. 298

Acca, friend of Camilla, *A.* XI. 820, 823, 897

Acerrae, town of Campania, *G.* II. 225

Acesta, town of Sicily, also called Egesta and Segesta, *A.* V. 718

Acestes, Sicilian king, son of Crinisus, *A.* I. 195, 550, 558, 570; V. 30, 36, 61, 73, 106, 301, 387, 418, 451, 498, 519, 531, 540, 573, 630, 711, 746, 749, 757, 771; IX. 218, 286

Achaemenides, deserted companion of Ulysses rescued by Aeneas, *A.* III. 614, 691

Achaicus, and Achaius, *adj.* Achaean, Greek, *A.* II. 462; V. 623; *Ca.* V. 2

Achates, trusty squire of Aeneas, *A.* I. 174, &c.

Achelois, a water-nymph, *Co.* 15

Acheloius, *adj.* of Achelous, a river of central Greece, used for water in general, *G.* I. 9

Acheron, a river of the lower world; hence, that world itself, *G.* II. 492; *A.* V. 99; VI. 107, 295; VII. 91, 312, 569; XI. 23

Achilles, hero of the *Iliad*, *E.* IV. 36; *G.* III. 91; *A.* I. 30, 458, 468, 484, 752; II. 29, 197, 275, 476, 540; III. 87, 326; V. 804; VI. 89, 168, 839; IX. 742; X. 581; XI. 404, 438; XII. 352, 545

Achivi, Achaeans, Greeks, *A.* I. 242, 488; II. 45, 60, 102, 318; V. 497; VI. 837; X. 89; XI. 266

Acidalia, term applied to Venus from a fountain in Boeotia, *A.* I. 720

Acmon, companion of Aeneas, *A.* X. 128

Acoetes, armour-bearer of Evander, *A.* XI. 30, 85

Aconteus, a Latin warrior, *A.* XI. 612, 615

Acragas, town in Sicily, now Girgenti, *A.* III. 703

Acrisione, daughter of Acrisius, *i.e.* Danaë, *Ca.* IX. 33

Acrisioneus, *adj.* of Acrisius, *A.* VII. 410

Acrisius, king of Argos, father of Danaë, *A.* VII. 372

543

INDEX

Acron, a Greek, *A.* x. 719, 730

Actaeus, *adj.* of Attica, Attic, Athenian, *E.* II. 24; *Ci.* 102

Actias, *adj.* of Acte, earlier name for Attica, *G.* iv. 463

Actius, *adj.* of Actium, promontory and town of Greece on the Ambracian Gulf, where Octavius defeated Antony in B.C. 31, *A.* III. 280; VIII. 675, 704

Actor, a Trojan, *A.* IX. 500; XII. 94, 96

Adamastus, father of Achaemenides, *A.* III. 614

Admetus, king of Pherae in Thessaly, and husband of Alcestis, who died that he might live, *Cu.* 264

Adonis, a youth loved by Venus, *E.* x. 18

Adrastea, daughter of Necessity, a goddess who punishes pride, *Ci.* 239

Adrastus, a king of Argos, only survivor of the Seven against Thebes, *A.* VI. 480

Aeacides, son of Aeacus. The term is applied to Peleus and Telamon, *Cu.* 297; to Achilles, son of Peleus, *A.* I. 99, VI. 58; to Ajax, son of Telamon, *Cu.* 322; to Pyrrhus, son of Achilles, *A.* III. 296; and to Perseus, a remote descendant, *A.* VI. 839

Aeacus, *adj.* of Aea; applied to Circe, who came from Aea in Colchis to the Aeaean island off Latium, which later became the promontory known as Mons Circeius (now Monte Circello), *A.* III. 386

Aegaeon, a giant, *A.* x. 565

Aegaeus, *adj.* Aegean, applied to the sea between Greece and Asia Minor, *A.* XII. 366; *Cu.* 355; also to Neptune, *A.* III. 74; *Ci.* 474

Aegina, island in the Saronic Gulf, *Ci.* 477

Aegle, a Naiad, *E.* VI. 20, 21

Aegon, a shepherd, *E.* III. 2; v. 72

Aegyptius, *adj.* of Egypt; applied to Cleopatra, *A.* VIII. 688

Aegyptus, Egypt, *G.* IV. 210, 292; *A.* VIII. 687, 705

Aeneades, descendant of Aeneas; used of those associated with Aeneas, as the Trojans, *A.* I. 157, 565; III. 18; v. 108; VII. 284, 334, 616; VIII. 341, 648; IX. 180, 235, 468, 735; x. 120; XI. 503; XII. 12, 186, 779

Aeneas, hero of the *Aeneid*

Aeneius, *adj.* of Aeneas, VII. 1; x. 156, 494

Aenides, son of Aeneas, *i.e.* Ascanius, *A.* IX. 653

Aeolia, country of the winds, a group of islands off the west coast of Italy (now Lipari), *A.* I. 52; x. 38

Aeolides, son of Aeolus; applied to Misenus, *A.* VI. 164; to Ulysses, *A.* VI. 529; and to Clytius, *A.* IX. 774

Aeolius, *adj.* of Aeolus, *A.* v. 791; VIII. 416, 454

Aeolus: (1) god of the winds, *A.* I. 52, 56, 65, 76, 141; (2) companion of Aeneas, *A.* XII. 542

Aequi Falisci, a town of Etruria, *A.* VII. 695

Aequiculus, *adj.* of the Aequi, an Italian people on both sides of the Anio, *A.* VII. 747

Aethiops, an Ethiopian, *E.* x. 68; *G.* II. 120; *A.* IV. 481

Aethon, a horse of Pallas, *A.* XI. 89

Aetna, the famous Mt. Etna in Sicily, *G.* I. 472; IV. 173; *A.* III. 554, 571, 579, 674

Aetnaeus, *adj.* of Etna, *A.* III. 678; VII. 786; VIII. 419, 440; XI. 263; *Cu.* 332

Aetolus, *adj.* of Aetolia, in central Greece, *A.* x. 28; XI. 239, 308, 428

Afer, *adj.* African, *E.* I. 64; *G.* III. 344; *A.* VIII. 724; *Ca.* IX. 51; *Ci.* 480; *M.* 32

Africa, *A.* IV. 37

Africus, *adj.* African, *A.* I. 86; *D.* 39

Agamemnonius, *adj.* of Agamemnon, king of Mycenae and commander-in-chief of the Greek forces before Troy; used with *res* "cause," *A.* III. 54; with *Mycenae, A.* VI. 838; with *phalanges, A.* VI. 489; of Orestes, son of Agamemnon *A.*

INDEX

IV. 471; of Halaesus, VII. 723; in this last case it may mean "of the house of Agamemnon"

Aganippe, a fountain in Boeotia, haunt of the Muses, *E.* X. 12

Agathyrsus, *adj.* As a plural, a Scythian people who stained their bodies, *A.* IV. 146

Agaue, or Agave, daughter of Cadmus, wife of Echion, king of Thebes, who in the madness of Bacchic rites tore her son Pentheus to pieces, *Cu.* 111

Agenor, founder of the Phoenician kingdom, and ancestor of Dido, *A.* I. 338

Agis, Lycian warrior, *A.* X. 751

Aglaie, one of the Graces, *Ca.* IX. 60

Agrippa, *i.e.* M. Vipsanius Agrippa, son-in-law of Augustus, *A.* VIII. 682

Agyllinus, *adj.* of Agylla, Greek name of Caere, now Cervetri, *A.* VII. 652; VIII. 479; XII. 281

Ajax, Ajax, son of Oileus; on the night of Troy's fall, he offered violence to Cassandra in Minerva's temple, *A.* I. 41; II. 414

Alba, *i.e.* Alba Longa, said to be the mother city of Rome, *A.* I. 271; V. 597; VI. 766, 770; VIII. 48; IX. 387

Albanus, *adj.* of Alba, *A.* I. 7; V. 600; VI. 763; VII. 602; VIII. 643; IX. 388; XII. 134, 826

Albula, ancient name of the Tiber, *A.* VIII. 332

Albunea, a forest or grove near Lavinium, *A.* VII. 83

Alburnus, a mountain in Lucania, in Italy, *G.* III. 147

Alcander, a Trojan, *A.* IX. 767

Alcanor: (1) a Trojan, *A.* IX. 672; (2) a Latin, *A.* X. 338

Alcathous: (1) founder of Megara, *Ci.* 105, 106; (2) a Trojan, *A.* X. 747

Alcestis, wife of Admetus, *Cu.* 262

Alcides, descendant of Alcaeus, used especially of his grandson Hercules, *E.* VII. 61; *A.* V. 414; VI. 123, 392, 801; VIII. 203, 219, 249, 256, 363; X. 321, 461, 464

Alcimedon, a carver in wood, *E.* III. 37, 44

Alcinous, king of Homer's Phaeacians, *G.* II. 87

Alcippe, a female slave, *E.* VII. 14

Alcon, a sculptor or engraver, *Cu.* 67; *E.* V. 11 (here perhaps an archer)

Aletes, companion of Aeneas, *A.* I. 121; IX. 246, 307

Alexis, a slave-boy, loved by Corydon, *E.* II. 1, 6, 19, 56, 65, 73; V. 86; VII. 55

Allecto, one of the three Furies, *A.* VII. 324, 341, 405, 415, 445, 476; X. 41

Allia, a branch of the Tiber six miles from Rome, where the Gauls defeated the Romans July 16, 390 B.C., *A.* VII. 717

Almo, a Latin, *A.* VII. 532, 575

Aloidae, descendants of Aloeus, Otus and Ephialtes, giants, *A.* VI. 582

Alpes, the Alps, *G.* I. 475; III. 474; *A.* X. 13

Alphesiboeus, a herdsman, *E.* V. 73; VIII. 1, 5, 62

Alpheus, river of Elis, which was fabled to reappear in Sicily, *G.* III. 19, 180; *A.* III. 694; X. 179

Alpinus, *adj.* Alpine, *E.* X. 47; *A.* IV. 442; VI. 830; VIII. 661

Alsus, a Latin, *A.* XII. 304

Amaryllis, a rustic girl, *E.* I. 5, 30, 36; II. 14, 52; III. 81; VIII. 77, 78, 101; IX. 22

Amastrus, a Trojan, *A.* XI. 673

Amata, wife of Latinus, *A.* VII. 343, 401, 581; IX. 737; XII. 56, 71

Amathus, a town of Cyprus, *A.* X. 51

Amathusia, *i.e.* Venus, *Ci.* 242

Amazon, an Amazon, *A.* XI. 648, 660. Also Amazonides, *A.* I. 490; Amazonius, *A.* V. 311

Amerinus, *adj.* of Ameria, a town of Umbria, now Amelia, *G.* I. 265

Aminaeus, *adj.* of Aminaea, a district of Picenum, *G.* II. 97

Amiternus, *adj.* of Amiternum, a Sabine town, now San Vittorino, *A.* VII. 710

Amor, son of Venus, and god of love, Cupid, *E.* VIII. 43, 47; X. 28, 29, 44, 69; *G.* III. 244; *A.* I. 663, 689; IV. 412; X. 188; *Ca.* XIV. 10; *Co.* 20

545

INDEX

Amphion, king of Thebes, and husband of Niobe, *E.* II. 24

Amphitrite, wife of Neptune and goddess of the sea, *Ci.* 73, 486

Amphitryoniades, son or descendant of Amphitryo, *i.e.* Hercules, *A.* VIII. 103, 214

Amphrysius, *adj.* of Amphrysus, *A.* VI. 398

Amphrysus, a river of Thessaly, near which Apollo fed the flocks of Admetus, *G.* III. 2

Ampsanctus, a lake in Samnium, east of Naples, *A.* VII. 565

Amyclae: (1) a town of Latium, *A.* X. 564; (2) a town of Laconia in Greece, hence Amyclaeus, *adj. G.* III. 89, 345; *Ci.* 376, 489

Amycus: (1) a Trojan, *A.* I. 221; IX. 772; X. 704; XII. 509; (2) a king of the Thracian Bebryces, *A.* V. 373

Amyntas, a shepherd, *E.* II. 35, 39; III. 66, 74, 83; V. 8, 15, 18; X. 37, 38, 41

Amythaonius, *adj.* of Amythaon, father of Melampus, and son of Cretheus, *G.* III. 550

Anagnia, a town of Latium, now Anagni, *A.* VII. 684

Anchemolus, son of Rhoetus, king of the Marsians, *A.* X. 389

Anchises, son of Capys and father of Aeneas, *A.* I. 617, etc.

Anchiseus, *adj.* of Anchises, *A.* V. 761

Anchisiades, son of Anchises, *i.e.* Aeneas, *A.* V. 407; VI. 126, 348; VIII. 521; X. 250, 822

Ancus, Ancus Martius, fourth king of Rome, *A.* VI. 815

Androgeos: (1) son of Minos, king of Crete, slain by the Athenians, *A.* VI. 20; (2) a Greek chief at Troy, *A.* II. 371, 382, 392

Andromache, wife of Hector, *A.* II. 456; III. 297, 303, 319, 482, 487

Angitia, a sorceress, sister of Medea and Circe, honoured by the Marsi, *A.* VII. 759

Anienus, *adj.* of the Anio, *G.* IV. 369

Anio, a tributary of the Tiber, now Teverone, *A.* VII. 683

Anius, a king of Delos, priest of Apollo, *A.* III. 80

Anna, sister of Dido, *A.* IV. 9, 20, 31, 416, 421, 500, 634.

Antaeus, a Latin, *A.* X. 561

Antandros, a town of Mysia, at the foot of Mt. Ida, *A.* III. 6

Antemnae, a Sabine town on the Anio, *A.* VII. 631

Antenor, a Trojan, founder of Patavium, now Padua, *A.* I. 242; hence Antenorides, son of Antenor, *A.* VI. 484

Antheus, a Trojan, *A.* I. 181, 510; XII. 443

Antigenes, a shepherd, *E.* V. 89

Antiphates, son of Sarpedon, *A.* IX. 696

Antonius, the triumvir, Marcus Antonius, defeated by Octavius at Actium, 31 B.C., *A.* VIII. 685

Antores, an Argive with Evander, *A.* X. 778, 779

Anubis, an Egyptian, dog-headed god, *A.* VIII. 698

Anxur, a Rutulian, *A.* X. 545

Anxurus, *adj.* of Anxur, old name of Terracina, *A.* VII. 799

Aones, *adj.* Aonian, Boeotian, *E.* VI. 65

Aonius, *adj.* Aonian, Boeotian, with *vertex* (= Mt. Helicon), *G.* III. 11; also Aonie, *E.* X. 12

Aornos, Lake Avernus, now Lago d'Averno, *A.* II. 242

Aphaea, an epithet of Britomartis, *Ci.* 303

Aphidnus, a Trojan, *A.* IX. 702

Apollo, son of Jupiter and Latona, and twin-brother of Diana, *E.* III. 104, etc.

Appenninus, the Apennines, the main mountain-range of Italy, *A.* XII. 703; also Appenninicola, dweller in the Apennines, *A.* XI. 700

Aquarius, the water-bearer, a sign of the Zodiac, *G.* III. 304

Aquiculus, a Rutulian, *A.* IX 684

Aquilo, the North wind, or the North, *G.* I. 460; II. 113, 261, 334, 404; III. 196; *A.* I. 102, 391; III. 285; IV. 310; V. 2; VII. 361; *Ci.* 145

Arabs, an Arab, *G.* II. 115; *A.* VIII. 706; and Arabus, *adj. A.* VII. 605; *Ci.* 238

546

INDEX

Aracynthus, a mountain between Attica and Boeotia, *E.* II. 24

Arae, rocky islets between Sicily and Africa, *A.* I. 109

Araris, a river of Gaul, now the Saône, *E.* I. 62

Araxes, a river of Armenia, *A.* VIII. 728

Arcadia, a district in the interior of the Peloponnesus, *E.* IV. 58, 59; X. 26; *G.* III. 392; *A.* VIII. 159; X. 429; also Arcadius, *adj.* Arcadian, *G.* IV. 283; *A.* V. 299; VIII. 573; X. 425; XII. 272; and Arcas, *adj.* with plural, as substantive, the Arcadians, *E.* VII. 4, 26; X. 31, 33; *A.* VIII. 51, 102, 129, 352, 518; X. 239, 364, 397, 452, 491; XI. 93, 142, 395, 835; XII. 231, 281, 518, 551.

Arcens, a Sicilian, *A.* IX. 581, 583

Arcetius, a Rutulian, *A.* XII. 459

Archippus, an Umbrian, *A.* VII. 752

Arctos, the constellation of the Great and Little Bear, or the North, *G.* I. 138, 245, 246; *A.* VI. 16

Arcturus, the brightest star in Boötes, whose rising and setting are attended by bad weather, *G.* I. 68, 204; *A.* I. 744; III. 516

Ardea, capital of the Rutulians, *A.* VII. 411, 412, 631; IX. 738; XII. 44

Arethusa: (1) a fountain near Syracuse, *A.* III. 696; (2) the nymph of the fountain, *G.* IV. 344, 351; (3) a Sicilian Muse, *E.* X. 1

Argi, city of Argos, capital of Argolis in the Peloponnesus, sacred to Juno, and representative of Greece in general, *A.* I. 24, 285; II. 95, 178, 326; VI. 838; VII. 286; X. 779, 782; also Argivus, *adj.* of Argos, with masc. plur. the Greeks, *A.* I. 40, 650; II. 254, 393; III. 547; V. 672; VII. 672, 794; XI. 243; XII. 544; *Cu.* 335; Argolicus, *adj.* Argive, Greek, *A.* II. 55, 78, 119, 177; III. 283, 637; V. 52, 314; VIII. 374; IX. 202; X. 56; *Cu.* 303

Argiletum, a street in Rome connecting the Forum with the Subura, *A.* VIII. 345 (where see note on the word)

Argitis, a vine with *white* grapes (cp. argentum), *G.* II. 99

Argo, the ship in which Jason sailed to Colchis for the golden fleece, *E.* IV. 34; hence Argous, *adj.*, *Cu.* 137

Argus: (1) the hundred-eyed keeper of Io, slain by Mercury, *A.* VII. 791; (2) a fabled guest of Evander, *A.* VIII. 346

Argyripa, a town of Apulia, founded by Diomedes of Argos, later called Arpi, *A.* XI. 246

Aricia, a town of Latium, now Riccio, *A.* VII. 762 (where the reference *may* be to a nymph of the place)

Arion, of Methymna in Lesbos, a semi-legendary poet and musician. When sailing home from Sicily with treasure, he leapt into the sea to escape from murderous sailors and was rescued by a dolphin, *E.* VIII. 56

Arisba, a town of the Troad, *A.* IX. 264

Aristaeus, son of Apollo and Cyrene, and a god of shepherds, *G.* IV. 317, 350, 355, 437

Ariusius, *adj.* of Ariusia, a district in Chios, *E.* V. 71

Armenius, *adj.* Armenian, *E.* V. 29

Arna, a town of Lycia, *Cu.* 14

Arpi (*see* Argyripa), *A.* X. 28; XI. 250, 428

Arquitenens, *adj.*, holding a bow; as subst. the Archer-god, *i.e.* Apollo, *A.* III. 75

Arruns, an Etruscan, *A.* XI. 759, 763, 784, 806, 814, 853, 864

Asbytes, a Trojan, *A.* XII. 362

Ascanius: (1) a river in Bithynia, *G.* III. 270; (2) a son of Aeneas and Creusa, called also Iülus, *A.* I. 267, etc.

Ascareus, *adj.* of Ascra, a town in Boeotia, where the Greek poet Hesiod, author of *Works and Days*, was born, *E.* VI. 70; *G.* II. 176; *Cu.* 96

Asilas, an Etruscan, *A.* IX. 571; X. 175; XI. 620; XII. 127, 550

Asius, *adj.* of Asia, originally a town of Lydia; hence, of the

547

INDEX

region round about, *G.* I. 383; IV. 343; *A.* VII. 701; in a wider sense, of the province of Asia, with the fem. as a noun, Asia, *G.* II. 171; III. 30; *A.* I. 385; II. 193, 557; III. 1; VII. 224; X. 91; XI. 268; XII. 15; *Ca.* III. 4

Asius, a Trojan, *A.* X. 123

Assaraci, two Trojans, *A.* X. 124

Assaracus, son of Tros, and father of Capys, *G.* III. 35; *A.* I. 284; VI. 650, 778; IX. 259, 643; XII. 127

Assyrius, *adj.* of Assyria, *E.* IV. 25; *G.* II. 465; *Ci.* 440; *Cu.* 62

Asteria, *i.e.* Delos, so named from Asteria, daughter of the Titan Coeus, who was here thrown into the sea, *Cu.* 15

Astyanax, son of Hector, *A.* II. 457; III. 489

Astyr, an Etruscan, *A.* X. 180, 181

Asylum, the depression between the two summits of the Capitoline hill in Rome, which Romulus made a place of refuge, *A.* VIII. 342

Athenae, Athens, *Ci.* 22, 469

Athesis, a river in Venetia, now the Adige, *A.* IX. 680

Athos, a mountain in Macedonia on the Strymonian Gulf, now Monte Santo, *G.* I. 332; *A.* XII. 701; *Cu.* 31

Atii, a Roman *gens*; the mother of Augustus was Atia, *A.* V. 568

Atilius, *Ca.* XII. 5

Atina, a town of the Volscians, *A.* VII. 630

Atinas, a Latin, *A.* XI. 869; XII. 661

Atlantis, a daughter of Atlas, *A.* VIII. 135; *plur.* the Pleiades, his daughters, a constellation, *G.* I. 221

Atlas, son of Iapetus, father of Electra and Maia, changed by Perseus, through the help of Medusa's head, into Mount Atlas, in northern Africa, *A.* I. 741; IV. 247, 248, 481; VI. 796; VIII. 136, 140, 141

Atrides, son of Atreus: Agamemnon, *Cu.* 334; Menelaus, *A.* XI. 262; *plur.* of both sons, *A.* I.
458; II. 104, 415, 500; VIII. 130; IX. 138, 602

Attalicus, *adj.* of Attalus, the name of several kings of Pergamos. One of these, Attalus III., left his enormous wealth to the Roman people, *Cu.* 63

Atticus, *adj.* of Attica or Athens, *Ca.* II. 3; *Ci.* 115

Atys, a young Trojan, *A.* V. 568, 569

Aufidus, a river of Apulia, now Ofanto, *A.* XI. 405

Augustus, imperial title of Octavius Caesar, *A.* VI. 792; VIII. 678

Aulestes, an Etruscan, *A.* X. 207; XII. 290

Aulis, a town of Boeotia, whence the Greeks sailed for Troy, *A.* IV. 426

Aunus, a Ligurian, *A.* XI. 700, 717

Aurora, goddess of the morning, daughter of Hyperion, wife of Tithonus, and mother of Memnon; used for the eastern world, the East; *G.* I. 249, 447; IV. 544, 552; *A.* I. 751; III. 521, 589; IV. 7, 129, 568, 585; V. 65, 105; VI. 535; VII. 26, 606; VIII. 686; IX. 111, 460; X. 241; XI. 1, 182; XII. 77; *Cu.* 44; *L.* 72

Auruncus, *adj.* of Aurunca, an old town of Campania; *plur.* Aurunci, the oldest inhabitants of Italy; *A.* VII. 206, 727, 795; X. 353; XII. 94

Ausonia, land of the Ausones (Ausonidae or Ausonii), ancient name of the people of southern Italy; hence, Italy, *A.* III. 477, 479, 496; VII. 55, 623; IX. 136; X. 54, 356; XI. 58

Ausonidae (*see* Ausonia), *A.* X. 564; XI. 297; XII. 121

Ausonius, *adj.* Ausonian, Italian, *G.* II. 385; *A.* III. 171, etc.

Auster, the south wind; *plur.* winds in general; *E.* II. 58; V. 82; *G.* I. 241, 333, 418, 462; II. 188, 333, 429; III. 278, 357; IV. 261; *A.* I. 51, 536; II. 111, 304; III. 61, 70, 357, 481; V. 696, 764; VI. 336; VIII. 430; IX. 670

INDEX

Automedon, charioteer of Achilles, *A.* II. 477

Aventinus: (1) a son of Hercules and Rhea, *A.* VII. 657; (2) the Aventine, one of Rome's seven hills, *A.* VII. 659; VIII. 231

Avernus, *adj.* of Avernus, a lake near Cumae in Campania, in an old volcanic crater. It was said that birds flying over it were killed by the fumes rising up, and popular etymology connected the name with ἄορνος, birdless (see *A.* VI. 242). Tradition placed near this an entrance to the lower world, hence the word (both as adj. and subst.) is used of the lower world itself; *G.* II. 164; IV. 493; *A.* III. 442; IV. 512; V. 732, 813; VI. 118, 126, 201, 564, 898; VII. 91

Baccheius, *adj.* of Bacchus, *G.* II. 454

Bacchus, son of Jupiter and Semele, god of wine and of poets; also used figuratively for the vine and of wine; *E.* V. 69; *G.* II. 113, 380, etc.

Bactra, capital of Bactriana, a remote district between Hindoo Koosh and the Oxus, now Balkh, in Afghanistan, *G.* II. 138; *A.* VIII. 688

Baiae, a town of Campania, a favourite seaside resort of the Romans, *A.* IX. 710

Balearis, *adj.* Balearic, of the Balearic Islands Majorca and Minorca, whose people were famous for the use of the sling, *G.* I. 309

Barcaei, Barcaeans, or people of Barce, in Libya, *A.* IV. 43

Battarus, *D.* 1, 14, 30, 54, 64, 71, 97

Batulum, a town of Campania, *A.* VII. 739

Bavius, a poetaster, contemporary with Virgil, *E.* III. 90

Bebrycius, *adj.* of Bebrycia or Bithynia, a province of Asia Minor, *A.* V. 373

Belgicus, *adj.* Belgian, or of the Belgae, a Gallic tribe which, like the Britons, used warchariots, *G.* III. 204

Belides, son of Belus, or descended from Belus, *A.* II. 82

Bellona, sister of Mars, and goddess of war, *A.* VII. 319; VIII. 703

Belus: (1) founder of Dido's royal line, *A.* I. 729, 730; (2) father of Dido, *A.* I. 621

Benacus, one of the Italian lakes, near Verona, now Lago di Garda, *G.* II. 160; *A.* X. 205

Berecyntius, *adj.* of Berecyntus, a mountain in Phrygia, sacred to Cybele, *A.* VI. 784; IX. 82, 619

Beroe: (1) one of the Oceanidae, or ocean nymphs, *G.* IV. 340; (2) wife of Doryclus, *A.* V. 620, 646, 650

Bianor, founder of Mantua, *E.* IX. 60

Bisaltae, a Thracian tribe on the Strymon, *G.* III. 461

Bistonius, *adj.*, and Bistonis, *adj. fem.* Bistonian or Thracian, the Bistones being a people of Thrace, *Ci.* 165; *Cu.* 252

Bitias: (1) a Tyrian noble, *A.* I. 738; (2) a Trojan, *A.* IX. 672, 703; XI. 396

Bocchus, a king of Mauretania, cp. *Cu.* 406

Boethus, a famous sculptor and engraver on silver, *Cu.* 67

Bola, a town of Latium, *A.* VI. 775

Bootes, Boötes, a constellation, to which Arcturus belongs; it sets from Oct. 29 to Nov. 2, *G.* I. 229

Boreas, the North wind, *E.* VII. 51; *G.* I. 93, 370; II. 316; III. 278; *A.* III. 687; IV. 442; XII. 365; *D.* 37; also, personified as Boreas, son of the river-god Strymon, and wedded to Orithyia, *A.* X. 350

Briareus, a hundred-armed giant, *A.* VI. 287

Britanni, the Britons, *E.* I. 66; *G.* III. 25

Britomartis, a daughter of Jupiter and Carme. Being wooed by Minos, she fled into the sea, but was rescued by Diana. In Crete she was worshipped under the name Dictyna, *Ci.* 295, 296

Brixia, a town in Gallia Cisalpina, now Brescia, *Ca.* X. 5

549

INDEX

Bromius, another name for Bacchus, *Co.* 20

Brontes, a Cyclops in Vulcan's smithy, *A.* VIII. 425

Brutus, *i.e.* L. Junius Brutus, who expelled the Tarquins, and was first consul, *A.* VI. 818

Bumastus, a species of grape, *G.* II. 102 (cp. *Cu.* 407)

Busiris, an Egyptian king, who sacrificed strangers, and was slain by Hercules, *G.* III. 5

Butes: (1) son of Amycus, king of the Bebrycians, *A.* V. 372; (2) armour-bearer of Anchises, and guardian of Ascanius, *A.* IX. 647; (3) a Trojan, perhaps the same as the preceding, *A.* V. 372

Buthrotum, a city of Epirus, now Butrinto, *A.* III. 293

Byrsa, citadel of Carthage, *A.* I. 367

Cacus, a son of Vulcan, a fabulous monster once dwelling in a forest on the Aventine, *A.* VIII. 194, 205, 218, 222, 241, 259, 303

Cadmeus, *adj.*, and **Cadmeis,** *adj. fem.*, of Cadmus, founder of the Cadmea, or citadel of Thebes; hence, Theban, *Cu.* 254; he was the father of Agave, *Cu.* 111

Caeculus, a son of Vulcan and founder of Praeneste, *A.* VII. 681; X. 544

Caedicus: (1) an Etruscan, *A.* X. 747; (2) friend of Remulus, *A.* IX. 362

Caeneus: (1) a Thessalian girl named Caenis, transformed into a boy by Neptune, and later restored to her original sex, *A.* VI. 448; (2) a Trojan warrior, *A.* IX. 573

Caerateus, *adj.* of Caeratus, a small river of Crete, near Cnossus, now Kartero, *Ci.* 113

Caere, an ancient city of Etruria, once called Agylla, now Cervetere, *A.* VIII. 597; X. 183

Caerulus, an owner of a lodging-house, *Ca.* X. 7

Caesar, a family name in the Julian *gens*; hence (1) C. Julius Caesar, the renowned general, statesman and dictator, assassinated by Brutus and Cassius 44 B.C., *E.* IX. 47; *G.* I. 466; *Ca.* XIII. 9; (2) C. Julius Caesar Octavianus, also called Augustus when emperor, grand-nephew of the dictator, who adopted him as his son and heir; (in the *Aeneid* Caesar is always Augustus); *G.* I. 25, 503; II. 170; III. 16, 47, 48; IV. 560; *A.* I. 286; VI. 789, 792; VIII. 678, 714; *Ca.* XIV. 11

Caicus: (1) a river of Mysia, now the Mandragora, *G.* IV. 370; (2) a Trojan, *A.* I. 183; IX. 35

Caieta: (1) a town of Latium, now Gaeta, *A.* VI. 900; (2) the nurse of Aeneas, *A.* VII. 2

Calaber, *adj.* of Calabria, a district of lower Italy, *G.* III. 425

Calchas, son of Thestor, and the most famous seer among the Greeks at Troy, *A.* II. 100, 122, 176, 182, 185

Cales, a town of Campania, now Calvi, *A.* VII. 728

Calliope (-ea), Calliope, chief of the Muses, *E.* IV. 57; *A.* IX. 525; *Ca.* XV. 4

Calybe, priestess of Juno among the Rutuli, *A.* VII. 419

Calybita, perhaps a common, not proper, noun, *Co.* 25

Calydon, a town of Aetolia, home of Oeneus, father of Tydeus, and grandfather of Diomedes, *A.* VII. 306, 307; XI. 270

Camena, pure Latin name of the Greek Μοῦσα, Muse, *E.* III. 59; *Ca.* V. 11, 12

Camerina, a town on the south coast of Sicily, near which was a marsh which an oracle had forbidden the citizens to drain. However, they did drain it, whereupon their enemies, crossing the dry land thus formed, captured the city, *A.* III. 701

Camers, a Rutulian, *A.* X. 562; XII. 224

Camilla, a Volscian heroine, *A.* VII. 803; XI. 432, 498, 535, 543, 563, 604, 619, 657, 689, 760, 796, 821, 833, 839, 856, 868, 892, 898

Camillus, *i.e.* M. Furius Camillus, who took Veii, and freed Rome

INDEX

from the Gauls, 390 B.C., *G.* II. 169; *A.* VI. 825; *Cu.* 362

Campanus, *adj.* of Campania, *A.* X. 145

Canopus, a town on the western mouth of the Nile, *G.* IV. 287

Capēnus, *adj.* of Capena, a town in Etruria, *A.* VII. 697

Caphereus, a promontory of the island Euboea, *A.* XI. 260; *Cu.* 354

Capitolium, the Capitol hill in Rome, *A.* VI. 836; VIII. 347, 653; IX. 448

Capreae, now Capri, an island just outside the Bay of Naples, *A.* VII. 735

Capua, chief city of Campania, now Santa Maria, *G.* II. 224

Capys: (1) a companion of Aeneas, said to have founded Capua, *A.* I. 183; II. 35; IX. 576; X. 145; (2) the eighth king of Alba, *A.* VI. 768

Car (*plur.* Cares), a Carian, of Caria in Asia Minor, *A.* VIII. 725

Carme, daughter of Phoenix, and mother of Britomartis, *Ci.* 220, 278, 285

Carmentalis, *adj.* of Carmentis, *A.* VIII. 338

Carmentis, mother of Evander, *A.* VIII. 336, 339

Carpathius, *adj.* of Carpathus, an island in the Aegean, now Scarpanto, *G.* IV. 387; *A.* V. 595; *Ci.* 113

Casmilla, mother of Camilla, *A.* XI. 543

Casperia, a Sabine town, *A.* VII. 714

Caspius, *adj.* of the Caspii, a nation of Media; Caspian, *A.* VI. 798

Cassandra, daughter of Priam and Hecuba, beloved of Apollo, and gifted by him with prophecy; though she proclaimed the downfall of Troy, she was believed by no one, *A.* II. 246, 343, 404; III. 183, 187; V. 636; X. 68

Cassiopēa, wife of Cepheus, and mother of Andromeda; she finally became a constellation, *Ca.* IX. 28

Castalia, a fountain of Parnassus, sacred to Apollo and the Muses, *G.* III. 293; *Cu.* 17

Castor: (1) son of Tyndarus and Leda, brother of Helen and Pollux, identified with the constellation Gemini, served as a guide to sailors, *Ca.* X. 25; (2) a Trojan, *A.* X. 124

Castrum Inui, Fort of Inuus, a town of the Prisci Latini, in Latium, *A.* VI. 775

Catilina, i.e. L. Sergius Catiline, who conspired for the downfall of Rome, *A.* VIII. 668

Catillus, one of the founders of Tibur, *A.* VII. 672; XI. 640

Cato: (1) M. Porcius Cato, the Censor, a stern moralist, *A.* VI. 841; (2) M. Porcius Cato, called Uticensis, because he killed himself at Utica, *A.* VIII. 670

Caucasius, *adj.* of Caucasus, where an eagle devoured the liver of the enchained Prometheus, *E.* VI. 42; *G.* II. 440

Caucasus, a mountain-range between the Black and Caspian Seas, *A.* IV. 367

Caulon, a town on the east coast of Bruttium in southern Italy, *A.* III. 553

Caurus (or Corus), the north-west wind, *G.* III. 278, 356; *A.* V. 126; *Ci.* 460

Caystros, the Cayster, a river of Ionia, now the Little Meander, *G.* I. 384

Cea, the island of Ceos, in the Aegean, *G.* I. 14

Cecropidae, the Athenians, so-called because Cecrops was the fabled founder of Athens, *A.* VI. 21

Cecropius, *adj.* of Cecrops, Athenian, Attic, *G.* IV. 177, 270; *Ca.* IX. 14

Celaeno, one of the Harpies, *A.* III. 211, 245, 365, 713

Celemna, a town of Campania, *A.* VII. 739

Celeus, a king of Eleusis, father of Triptolemus, *G.* I. 165

Centauri, fabled monsters with human heads and equine bodies, *G.* II. 456; *A.* VI. 286; VII. 275; also Centaureus, *adj. Cu.* 29

Centaurus, name of a ship, *A.* V. 122, 155, 157; X. 195

551

INDEX

Ceraunia, a mountain-range in Epirus, now Monti della Chimaera, *G.* I. 332; *A.* III. 506

Cerberus, the three-headed dog that guarded the entrance to the lower world, *G.* IV. 483; *A.* VI. 417; *Cu.* 220, 270

Cerealis, *adj.* of Ceres, wheaten, *G.* I. 212; II. 517; *A.* I. 177; VII. 111

Ceres, goddess of agriculture; used by metonomy of corn, bread, flour; *E.* V. 79; *G.* I. 7, 96, 147, 297, 339, 343, 347, 349; II. 229; *A.* I. 177, 701; II. 113, 714, 742; VI. 484; VII. 113; VIII. 181; *Ci.* 230; *Co.* 20; *Cu.* 135; *D.* 15; *M.* 27, 43, 55

Cethegus, a Rutulian, *A.* XII. 513

Chalcidicus, *adj.* of Chalcis, chief city of Euboea, *E.* X. 50; also, of Cumae, a colony of Chalcis, *A.* VI. 17

Chalcodonii, the people near the Chalcodonian Mount in Thessaly, now called Karadagh, *Cu.* 264

Chalybes, a people of Pontus, famous for their iron and steel, *G.* I. 58; *A.* VIII. 421; X. 174; (cp. *A.* VIII. 446)

Chaon, a Trojan, brother of Helenus, *A.* III. 335

Chaonia, a district of Epirus, *A.* III. 335

Chaonius, *adj.* of Chaonia; also, of Dodona, a city of Epirus, famous for its oracle of Jupiter; *E.* IX. 13; *G.* I. 8; II. 67; *A.* III. 293, 334

Chaos, the Lower World; also, the god of that world, father of Erebus and Nox, *G.* IV. 347; *A.* IV. 510; V. 265

Charon, a god of the Lower World, son of Erebus and Nox, and ferryman of the Styx, *A.* VI. 299, 326; *Cu.* 216

Charybdis, a whirlpool in the straits of Messina, *A.* III. 420, 558, 684; VII. 302; *Cu.* 332

Chelae, the claws of Scorpio, a constellation, *G.* I. 33

Chimaera: (1) a monster in Lycia, in front a lion, in the hinder part a dragon, and in the middle a goat, *A.* VI. 288; VII. 785;

(2) one of the ships of Aeneas, *A.* V. 118, 223

Chimaereus, *adj.* of the Chimaera, *Cu.* 14

Chiron, a Centaur, son of Saturn and Phillyra, skilled in medicine, *G.* III. 550

Chloreus: (1) a Phrygian, *A.* XII. 363; (2) a Trojan, priest of Cybele, *A.* XI. 768

Chromis: (1) a young Satyr, *E.* VI. 13; (2) a Trojan, *A.* XI. 675

Cicones, a Thracian tribe, *G.* IV. 520; *Cu.* 330

Cilix, *adj.* Cilician, of Cilicia, a province in southern Asia Minor, *Cu.* 401

Ciminus, a lake of Etruria, now Lago di Ronciglione, with a mountain-forest near by, *A.* VII. 697

Cimmerius, *adj.* Cimmerian, the Cimmerii being a Thracian people in the Crimea, *Cu.* 232

Cinna, *i.e.* C. Helvius Cinna, a Roman poet, *E.* IX. 25

Cinyphius, *adj.* Cinyphian or Libyan, Cinyps being a river of Libya, *G.* III. 312

Cinyrus, or Cinyras, a Ligurian hero, *A.* X. 186

Circe, a daughter of the sun, said to have gone from Colchis to Circeii in Italy. She was famous as a sorceress, *E.* VIII. 70; *A.* III. 386; VII. 20, 191, 282; also Circaeus, *adj.* of Circe, *A.* VII. 10, 799

Cisseus: (1) a king of Thrace, father of Hecuba, who is therefore called Cisseis, *A.* V. 537; VII. 320; X. 705; (2) a Latin warrior, *A.* X. 317

Cithaeron, a mountain in Boeotia, *G.* III. 43; *A.* IV. 303

Clanius, a river of Campania, *G.* II. 225

Clarius, *adj.* of Claros, a town of Ionia, famous for its temple and oracle of Apollo, *A.* III. 360

Clarus, a Lycian, *A.* X. 126

Claudius, *adj.* Claudian. There were two famous Claudian *gentes*, one patrician, the other plebeian, *A.* VII. 708

INDEX

Clausus, a Sabine, *A.* VII. 707; x. 345

Clio: (1) the muse of history, *Ca.* IV. 10; (2) a daughter of Oceanus, *G.* IV. 340

Clitumnus, a river of Umbria, *G.* II. 146

Cloanthus, a Trojan, *A.* I. 222, 510, 612; V. 122, 152, 167, 225, 233, 245

Cloelia, a Roman maiden who escaped from Porsenna, and swam the Tiber, *A.* VIII. 651

Clonius, a Trojan, *A.* IX. 574; x. 749

Clonus, a sculptor or engraver, *A.* x. 499

Cluentius, a Roman gentile name, *A.* V. 123

Clusium, a town of Etruria, now Chiusi, *A.* x. 167; also Clusinus, *adj.* of Clusium, *A.* x. 655

Clymene, a daughter of Oceanus, *G.* IV. 345

Clytius, a Trojan, *A.* IX. 774; x. 129, 325; XI. 666

Cocles, *i.e.* Q. Horatius Cocles, who, in the war with Porsenna, guarded the bridge over the Tiber until it was hewn down, *A.* VIII. 650

Cocytus, a river of the Lower World, *G.* III. 38; IV. 479; *A.* VI. 132, 297, 323; VII. 562; with Cocytius, *adj.* of Cocytus, infernal, hellish, *A.* VII. 479

Codrus, a poet hostile to Virgil, *E.* V. 11; VII. 22, 26

Coeus, a Titan, the father of Latona, *G.* I. 279; *A.* IV. 179

Colchis, *adj.* Colchian, of Colchis, a district east of the Black Sea, now Mingrelia, *Cu.* 249

Collatinus, *adj.* of Collatia, a town of Latium, *A.* VI. 774

Colophoniacus, *adj.* of Colophon, a city of Ionia, north-west of Ephesus, one of several places claiming to be the birthplace of Homer, *Ci.* 65

Conon, a Greek astronomer of the third century B.C., *E.* III. 40

Cora, a town of Latium, *A.* VI. 775

Coras, an Argive, *A.* VII. 672; XI. 465, 604

Corinthus, Corinth, a famous city of Greece, destroyed by Mummius 146 B.C., famous for its old works in bronze, and as the place where Medea had lived with Jason and afterwards murdered her own children, *A.* VI. 836; also Corinthius, *adj. Ca.* II. 1

Coroebus, a Phrygian, to whom Cassandra was betrothed, *A* II. 341, 386, 407, 424

Corus (*see* Caurus)

Corybantius, *adj.* of the Corybantes, priests of Cybele, *A.* III. 111

Corycius, *adj.* Corycian, of Corycus, a place in Cilicia, *G.* IV. 127; *Ci.* 317

Corydon, a shepherd, *E.* II. 1, 56, 65, 69; V. 86; VII. 2, 3, 16, 20, 40, 70

Corynaeus: (1) a Trojan priest, *A.* VI. 228; IX. 571; (2) a Rutulian, *A.* XII. 298

Corythus: (1) a town of Etruria, Cortona, *A.* III. 170; VII. 209; x. 719; (2) its legendary founder, *A.* IX. 10

Cosae, a city of Etruria, now Ansedonia, *A.* x. 168

Cossus, *i.e.* A. Cornelius Cossus, consul 428 B.C., who won the *spolia opima* by slaying the king of Veii, *A.* VI. 841

Cotyttia, the festival of Cotytto, a Thracian goddess, whose worship was celebrated with great indecency, *Ca.* XIII. 19

Crataeis, mother of Scylla, *Ci.* 66

Cremona, a town of Cisalpine Gaul, whose lands were confiscated by Augustus, *E.* IX. 28; *Ca.* VIII. 6; x. 12

Cressius, *adj.* Cretan, *A.* IV. 70; VIII. 294; with Cressus, *G.* III. 345; *A.* V. 285; *Ci.* 384; and Crataeus, *A.* III. 117; XII. 412; *Ci.* 115

Creta, the island of Crete, *E.* I. 65; *A.* III. 104, 122, 129, 162; V. 588; with Cretes, the people of Crete, *A.* IV. 146

Cretheus: (1) a warrior-bard, *A.* IX. 774, 775; (2) a Greek in the Trojan army, *A.* XII. 538

Creusa, a daughter of Priam, and wife of Aeneas, *A.* II. 562, 597.

553

INDEX

651, 666, 738, 769, 772, 778, 784; IX. 297

Crinisus, a river of Sicily, *A.* V. 38

Crustumeri, a town of the Sabines, *A.* VII. 631; with Crustumius, *adj. G.* II. 88

Cumae, a town of Campania, founded by Greeks from Chalcis in Euboea, *A.* VI. 2; with Cumaeus, *adj. E.* IV. 4; *A.* III. 441; VI. 98

Cupavo, a Ligurian chieftain, *A.* X. 186

Cupencus, a Rutulian, *A.* XII. 539

Cupido, Cupid, Love, son of Venus, *A.* I. 658, 695; with Cupidineus, *adj. Cu.* 409

Cures, a town of the Sabines, *A.* VI. 811; VIII. 638; X. 345

Curetes, ancient inhabitants of Crete, afterwards priests of Jupiter, *G.* IV. 151; *A.* III. 131

Curius, a Roman general, conqueror of Pyrrhus, *Cu.* 367

Curtius, a youth who leaped into a newly-formed chasm in the Roman Forum, and after whom the spot was called the *lacus Curtius*, *Cu.* 363

Cybēbe, another name of Cybele, *A.* X. 220

Cybĕle: (1) a Phrygian goddess, the Magna Mater of the Romans, *Ci.* 166; (2) the mountain on which the goddess dwelt, *A.* III. 111; also called Cybelus, *A.* XI. 768

Cyclades, a group of islands around Delos in the Aegean, *A.* III. 127; VIII. 692; *Ci.* 471

Cyclops, one of the Cyclopes, one-eyed giants, who worked for Vulcan, *G.* I. 471; IV. 170; *A.* III. 569, 617, 644, 647, 675; VI. 630; VIII. 418, 424, 440; XI. 263; *Cu.* 332; with Cyclopius, *adj. A.* I. 201

Cycnus, father of Cupavo, *A.* X. 185

Cydippe, a nymph, *G.* IV. 339

Cydon: (1) a Latin, *A.* X. 325; (2) *adj.* Cydonian, of Cydonia in Crete, used for Cretan, *A.* XII. 858; also Cydonius, *E.* X. 59

Cyllarus, the horse of Pollux, *G.* III. 90

Cyllene, a mountain of Arcadia, the birthplace of Mercury, *A.* VIII. 139; with Cyllenius, *adj.* of Cyllene, *G.* I. 337; *A.* IV. 252, 258, 276; *Ci.* 108

Cymodoce, or Cymodocea, a nymph, *G.* IV. 338; *A.* V. 826; X. 225

Cymothoe, a nymph, *A.* I. 144

Cynthus, a mountain in Delos, where Apollo was born, *A.* I. 498; IV. 147; with Cynthius, *adj.* of Cynthus, *i.e.* Apollo, *E.* VI. 3; *G.* III. 36; *Ca.* IX. 60

Cyprus, the island of Cyprus, sacred to Venus, *A.* I. 622; hence Cyprius, *adj.* of Cyprus, *i.e.* Venus, *L.* 68

Cypselides, son of Cypselus, *i.e.* Periander, tyrant of Corinth, *Ci.* 464

Cyrenae, a Greek city in Africa, *Ca.* IX. 61

Cyrene, mother of Aristaeus, *G.* IV. 321, 354, 376, 530

Cyrnēus, *adj.* of Cyrnus, *i.e.* Corsica, *E.* IX. 30

Cythēra, an island south of Greece, now Cerigo, sacred to Venus, *A.* I. 680; X. 51, 86; hence, Cytherēa, *fem. adj.* the Cytherean, *i.e.* Venus, *A.* I. 257, 657; IV. 128; V. 800; VIII. 523, 615; *Ca.* XIV. 11

Cythnos, one of the Cyclades islands, now Thermia, *Ci.* 475

Cytōrus, a mountain in Paphlagonia, *G.* II. 437; with Cytorius, *adj.* of Cytorus, *Ca.* X. 10

Dacus, *adj.* Dacian, of the Daci, a people on the north bank of the Danube, *G.* II. 497

Daedalus, the mythical artist who built the Labyrinth in Crete, *A.* VI. 14, 29

Dahae, a Scythian tribe, east of the Caspian, in modern Daghestan, *A.* VIII. 728

Damoetas, a shepherd, *E.* II. 37, 39; III. 1, 58; V. 72

Damon, a goatherd, *E.* III. 17, 23; VIII. 1, 5, 16, 62

Danaë, daughter of Acrisius, king of Argos, and founder of Ardea, *A.* VII. 410

Danaus, *adj.* of Danaus, an

INDEX

Egyptian king who settled in Argos; hence, Greek, *A.* III. 602. The plural Danai, the Greeks, *A.* I. 30, and often

Daphnis, a mythical Sicilian shepherd, *E.* II. 26; III. 12; v. 20, 25, 27, 29, 30, 41, 43, 51, 52, 57, 61, 66; VII. 1, 7, 8, 68, 72, 76, 79, 81, 83, 84, 85, 90, 93, 94, 100, 102, 104, 109; VIII. 83; IX. 46, 50

Dardania, the Trojan land, Troy, *A.* II. 281, 325; III. 52, 156; VI. 65; VIII. 120; *Cu.* 323

Dardanides, son of, or descendant of, Dardanus; especially Aeneas; in plur. the Trojans, *A.* I. 560; II. 59, 72, 242, 445; III. 94; V. 45, 386, 576, 622; VI. 85, 482; VII. 195; IX. 293, 660; x. 4, 263, 545; XI. 353; XII. 549, 585, 622, 775

Dardanis, a daughter of Dardanus, *i.e.* a Trojan woman, *A.* II. 787

Dardanius, *adj.* of Dardanus, *i.e.* of Troy, Trojan, *E.* II. 61; *A.* I. 494, and often; also Dardanus, *A.* II. 618; IV. 662; V. 119; VI. 57; VII. 219; XI. 287

Dardanus, son of Jupiter and Electra, founder of the house of Priam and Aeneas, *A.* III. 167, 503; IV. 365; VI. 650; VII, 207, 240; VIII. 134

Dares: (1) a Trojan boxer, *A.* V. 369, 375, 406, 417, 456, 460, 463, 476, 483; (2) a Trojan warrior, *A.* XII. 363

Daucius, *adj.* of Daucus, a Rutulian noble, *A.* X. 391

Daulis, *adj.* Daulian, of Daulis, a city in Phocis, *Ci.* 200

Daunus, a mythical king of Apulia, *A.* X. 616, 688; XII. 22, 90, 934; with Daunius, *adj.* of Daunus, *A.* VIII. 146; XII. 723, 785

Decii, two Romans, both named P. Decius Mus, who devoted themselves to death for their country, one at the battle of Veseris, the other at that of Sentinum, *G.* II. 169; *A.* VI. 824; *Cu.* 361

Deiopea, a nymph, *G.* IV. 343; *A.* I. 72

Deiphobe, a priestess of Apollo, *A.* VI. 26

Deiphobus, a son of Priam, *A.* II. 310; VI. 495, 500, 510, 544

Delia, a girl, *E.* III. 67; *see* Delius

Delos, an island in the Aegean, birthplace of Apollo and Diana, *G.* III. 6; *A.* IV. 144; *Ci.* 473; with *adj.* Delius, Delia, of Delos, used of Apollo and Diana, *E.* VII. 29; *A.* III. 162; VI. 12; *Cu.* 110

Democodus, an Arcadian, *A.* X. 413

Demoleos, a Greek, *A.* V. 260, 265

Demophoon: (1) a Trojan, *A.* XI. 675; (2) son of Theseus, *Cu.* 131, 133

Dercennus, an ancient Latin king, *A.* XI. 850

Deucalion, a son of Prometheus, who with Pyrrha survived the flood, *G.* I. 62 (*cf. E.* VI. 41)

Diana, sister of Apollo, and goddess of the moon, *A.* I. 499; III. 681; IV. 511; VII. 306, 764, 769; XI. 537, 582, 652, 843, 857; *Ci.* 297

Dictaeus, *adj.* of Dicte, a mountain in Crete, in a cave of which Jupiter was born, *E.* VI. 56; *G.* II. 536; IV. 152; *A.* III. 171; IV. 73; *Ci.* 300; *Cu.* 275

Dictyna, another name of Britomartis, *Ci.* 245, 305

Dido, founder of Carthage, *A.* I. 299; IV. 60, etc.

Didymaon, a worker in metal, *A.* V. 359

Dindyma, a mountain in Mysia sacred to Cybele, *A.* IX. 618; X. 252

Diomedes, son of Tydeus, famous as a Greek hero at Troy; founder of Argyripa, *A.* I. 752; VIII. 9; X. 581; XI. 226, 243

Dionaeus, *adj.* of Dione, the mother of Venus, *E.* IX. 47; *A.* III. 19

Diores, a Trojan, *A.* V. 297, 324, 339, 345; XII. 509

Dioxippus, a Trojan, *A.* IX. 574

Dira, properly *adj. fem.* of *dirus*, a Fury, *A.* XII. 869; plur. Dirae, Furies, *A.* IV. 473; VIII. 701; XII. 845

Dircaeus, *adj.* of Dirce, a fountain

INDEX

near Thebes; hence, Theban, *E.* II. 24

Dis, god of the lower world, Pluto, *G.* IV. 467, 519; *A.* IV. 702; V. 731; VI. 127, 269, 397, 541; VII. 568; VIII. 667; XII. 199; *Cu.* 271, 273, 275, 286, 372; *D.* 66

Discordia, Discord (personified), *A.* VI. 280; VIII. 702

Dodona, a place in Epirus, famous for its oak grove and oracle of Jupiter, *G.* I. 149; with Dodonaeus, *adj.* of Dodona, *A.* III. 466

Dolichaon, a Trojan, *A.* X. 696

Dolon, a Trojan, who, for the promised reward of the chariot and horses of Achilles, undertook to explore the Greek camp by night, but, falling into the hands of Ulysses and Diomedes, met death at the latter's hands, *A.* XII. 347; *Cu.* 328

Dolopes, a people of Thessaly, *A.* II. 7, 29, 415, 785

Donysa, a small island in the Aegean, east of Naxos, now Denusa, famous for its green marble, *A.* III. 125; *Ci.* 476

Doricus, *adj.* of the Dorians; more generally of the Greeks, *A.* II. 27; VI. 88; also Doris, *fem. adj.* Doric, Greek, *Cu.* 336

Doris, a sea-nymph, wife of Nereus, used of the sea itself, *E.* X. 5

Doryclus, a Trojan, husband of Beroe, *A.* V. 620, 647

Doto, a sea-nymph, *A.* IX. 102

Drances, a Latin, opposed to Turnus, *A.* XI. 122, 220, 336, 378, 384, 443; XII. 644

Drepanum, a town on the west coast of Sicily, now Trapani, *A.* III. 707

Drusus, a famous Roman name; especially M. Livius Drusus, conqueror of Hasdrubal, and Tiberius Drusus Nero, son of Livia, the wife of Augustus, *A.* VI. 824

Dryades, the Dryads, or Wood-nymphs, *E.* V. 59; *G.* I. 11; III. 40; IV. 460; *Cu.* 116

Drymo, a sea-nymph, *G.* IV. 336

Dryope, a nymph, *A.* X. 551

Dryopes, an early people of Greece,
living between the Ambracian and Malian gulfs, *A.* IV. 146

Dryops, a Trojan, *A.* X. 346

Dulichium, an island near Ithaca, *A.* III. 271; with Dulichius, *adj.* of Dulichium, and so, of Ulysses, *E.* VI. 76; *Ci.* 60

Dymas, a Trojan, *A.* II. 340, 394, 428

Ebysus, a Trojan, *A.* XII. 299

Echidna, mother of Scylla, *Ci.* 67

Echionius, *adj.* of Echion, who aided Cadmus in building Thebes; hence, Theban, *A.* XII. 515

Edōnes (or Edoni), a people of Thrace, *Ci.* 165; with Edōnus, *adj.* Thracian, *A.* XII. 365

Egeria, a nymph of Latium who became the wife of Numa, *A.* VII. 763, 775

Egestas, Want (a personification), *A.* VI. 276

Electra, daughter of Atlas, *A.* VIII. 135, 136

Eleusinus, *adj.* of Eleusis, a city in Attica, where Demeter (Ceres) was worshipped, *G.* I. 163

Elis, a district in the western Peloponnesus, famous for its city Olympia, where the Olympic games were held, *A.* III. 694; VI. 588; with Elēus, *adj.* Elean, Olympian, *G.* III. 202; and Elias, *fem. adj. G.* I. 59

Elissa, a name of Dido, *A.* IV. 335, 610; V. 3

Elysium, the abode of the blest in the lower world, *A.* V. 735; VI. 744; with Elysius, *adj.* Elysian, *G.* I. 38; *A.* VI. 542; *Cu.* 260

Emathia, a part of Macedonia, *G.* I. 492; IV. 390; with Emathius, *adj., Ci.* 34

Emathion, a Rutulian, *A.* IX. 571

Enceladus, a giant, killed by a thunderbolt of Jupiter and buried under Mt. Etna, *A.* III. 578; IV. 179

Enipeus, a river of Thessaly, *G.* IV. 368

Entellus, a Sicilian boxer, *A.* V. 387, 389, 437, 443, 446, 462, 472

INDEX

Epēos, Epeus, inventor of the Trojan horse, *A.* II. 264

Ephialtes, a son of Aloeus and brother of Otus, killed by Apollo when storming heaven, *Cu.* 235

Ephyre, a nymph, *G.* IV. 343

Ephyrēius, *adj.* of Ephyra, an ancient name of Corinth, *G.* II. 464

Epidaurus, a city of Argolis in Greece, *G.* III. 44

Epirus, a district of Greece bordering on the Adriatic, *G.* I. 59; III. 121; *A.* III. 292, 513

Epulo, a Latin, *A.* XII. 459

Epytides, guardian of Ascanius, *A.* V. 547, 579

Epytus, a Trojan, *A.* II. 340

Erato, one of the Muses, *A.* VII. 37

Erebus, the god of darkness; the lower world, *G.* IV. 471; *A.* IV. 26, 510; VI. 247, 404, 671; VII. 140; with Erebous, *adj. Cu.* 202

Erechthēus, *adj.* of Erechtheus, a fabled king of Athens, *Ci.* 22

Eretum, a Sabine city on the Tiber, now Cretona, *A.* VII. 711

Ericetes, a Trojan, *A.* X. 749

Erichthonius: (1) an ancient king of Athens, *G.* III. 113; with Erichthonius, *adj.* Athenian, *Cu.* 30; (2) a son of Dardanus, king of Troy; hence Erichthonius, *adj.* Trojan, *Cu.* 336, 344

Eridanus, Greek name for the Padus, or Po, *G.* I. 482; IV. 372; *A.* VI. 659

Erigone, a daughter of Icarius, who became the constellation Virgo, *G.* I. 33

Erinys, a Fury, *A.* II. 337, 573; VII. 447, 570; *Cu.* 246

Eriphyle, wife of Amphiaraus, and mother of Alcmaeon, who betrayed her husband for a golden necklace, *A.* VI. 445

Erulus, a king of Praeneste, *A.* VIII. 563

Erymanthus, a mountain in Arcadia, *A.* V. 448; VI. 802

Erymas, a Trojan, *A.* IX. 702

Eryx: (1) a son of Venus and king of Sicily, killed by Hercules in a boxing-match, *A.* I. 570; V. 24, 392, 402, 412, 419, 483, 630, 772; *Ca.* IX. 6; (2) a mountain and town of Sicily, *A.* XII. 701; hence Erycinus, *adj.* of Eryx, Sicilian, *A.* V. 759; X. 36

Etruria, the country of the Etruscans, in Italy, *G.* II. 533; *A.* VIII. 494; XII. 232

Etruscus, *adj.* Etruscan, *A.* VIII. 480, 503; IX. 150, 521; X. 148, 180, 238, 429; XI. 598

Euadne, wife of Capaneus, who burned herself on her husband's funeral-pile, *A.* VI. 447

Euandrus or Euander, the king of Pallanteum who welcomed Aeneas, *A.* VIII. 52, 100, 119, 185, 313, 360, 455, 545, 558; IX. 9; X. 148, 370, 420, 492, 515, 780; XI. 26, 31, 45, 55, 140, 148, 394, 835; XII. 184, 551; with Euandrius, *adj.* used of Evander's son, Pallas, *A.* X. 394

Euanthes, a Phrygian in the Trojan force, *A.* X. 702

Euboicus, *adj.* of Euboea, the island east of Attica and Boeotia, *A.* VI. 2, 42; IX. 710; XI. 260; *Cu.* 355

Eumedes, a Trojan, *A.* XII. 346

Eumelus, a Trojan, *A.* V. 665

Eumenides, the Furies, *G.* I. 278; IV. 483; *A.* IV. 469; VI. 250, 280, 375

Euneus, a Trojan, *A.* XI. 666

Euphrates, a river of Asia, used also of the nations dwelling near it, *G.* I. 509; IV. 561; *A.* VIII. 726

Europa, Europe, *A.* I. 385; VII. 224; X. 91

Eurōtas, a river of Lacedaemon, flowing by Sparta, *E.* VI. 83; *A.* I. 498

Eurus, the south-east wind; used also of wind in general, *G.* I. 371, 453; II. 107, 339, 441; III. 277, 382; IV. 29, 192; *A.* I. 85, 110, 131, 140, 383; II. 418; VIII. 223; XII. 733; *Ci.* 25; *D.* 38; with Eurōus, *adj.* Eastern, *A.* III. 533

Euryalus, a Trojan, friend of Nisus, *A.* V. 294, 295, 322, 323, 334, 337, 343; IX. 179, 185, 198, 231, 281, 320, 342, 359,

557

INDEX

373, 384, 390, 396, 424, 433, 467, 475, 481

Eurydice, wife of Orpheus, *G.* IV. 486, 490, 519, 525, 526, 527, 547; *Cu.* 268, 287

Eurypylus, a Greek, *A.* II. 114

Eurystheus, a king of Mycenae, the enemy of Hercules, *G.* III. 4; *A.* VIII. 292

Eurytides, son of Eurytus, *i.e.* Clonus, *A.* X. 499

Eurytion, a Trojan, *A.* V. 495, 514, 541

Fabaris, a tributary of the Tiber, *A.* VII. 715

Fabius, a famous name in Roman history; especially of Q. Fabius Maximus, the famous general opposed to Hannibal, *A.* VI. 845; *Cu.* 361

Fabricius, the conqueror of Pyrrhus, *A.* VI. 844

Fadus, a Rutulian, *A.* IX. 344

Falernus, *adj.* Falernian, of the Falernian territory, in Campania, *G.* II. 96

Falisci, a people of Etruria; *see* Aequi

Faunus, son of Picus, and father of Latinus; also identified with the Greek Pan, and (in *plur.*) with the Satyrs, *E.* VI. 27; *G.* I. 10, 11; *A.* VII. 47, 48, 81, 102 213, 254, 368; VIII. 314; X. 551; XII. 766, 777

Feronia, an Italian goddess, related to Tellus, to whom several groves were dedicated, *A.* VII. 800; VIII. 564

Fescennīnus, *adj.* of Fescennia, a town of Etruria, *A.* VII. 695

Fidēna, a town of Latium, five miles north of Rome, now Castel Giubileo, *A.* VI. 773

Flaminius, *Cu.* 368 (see note)

Flavinius, *adj.* Flavinian, of some part of Etruria, *A.* VII. 696

Fortuna, Fortune (personification), *A.* VIII. 578

Foruli, a Sabine town, *A.* VII. 714

Fucīnus, a lake of Latium, now Lago Fucinô, *A.* VII. 759

Fuga, Flight (personification), *A.* IX. 719

Furia, Fury (personification), a goddess of vengeance, *G.* III. 37; *A.* III. 251, 331; VI. 605; VIII. 669

Gabii, a town of Latium, *A.* VI. 773; with Gabīnus, of Gabii, Gabine, *A.* VII. 612, 682

Gaetūlus, Gaetulian, of the Gaetuli, an African people, in Morocco, *A.* IV. 40, 326; V. 51, 192, 351

Galaesus: (1) a river of Calabria, *G.* IV. 126; (2) a Latin, *A.* VII. 535, 575

Gallia, Gaul, *i.e. Gallia Cisalpina*, in the north of Italy, *Ca.* X. 12; with Gallicus, *adj.* Gallic, applicable to Gaul in general, *Ca.* II. 4

Gallus: (1) a Gaul, *A.* VI. 858; VIII. 656, 657; (2) the poet C. Cornelius Gallus, who, as a member of the land-commission, helped Virgil to recover his farm. Later he became the first prefect of Egypt, *E.* VI. 64; X. 2, 3, 6, 10, 22, 72, 73

Gangaridae, a people near the Ganges in India, *G.* III. 27

Ganges, the famous river of India, *G.* II. 137; *A.* IX. 31

Ganymedes, youthful son of Laomedon, carried off to heaven by an eagle to become Jove's cup-bearer, *A.* I. 28

Garamantes, a people of Libya, *E.* VIII. 44; *A.* VI. 794, with Garamantis, *adj.* of the Garamantes, Libyan, *A.* IV. 198

Gargānus, a mountain-range of Apulia, *A.* VI. 247

Gargara, *plur.*, Gargarus, mountains of the Ida range in Mysia, *G.* I. 103; III. 269

Gela, a city, now Terra Nuova, by a river of the same name, on the south coast of Sicily, *A.* III. 702; with Gelōus, *adj.* Geloan, *A.* III. 701

Gelōnus, one of the Geloni, a Scythian people, *G.* III. 461; *plur. G.* II. 115; *A.* VIII. 725

Germania, Germany, *E.* I. 62; *G.* I. 474, 509

Geryon, and Geryones, Geryon, a

558

INDEX

mythic three-bodied monster in Spain, whose oxen were carried off by Hercules, *A.* VII. 662; VIII. 202

Getae, a Thracian tribe on the Danube, *G.* III. 462; IV. 463; *A.* VII. 604; with Geticus, *adj.* Getic, *A.* III. 35

Giganteus, *adj.* of the Giants, fabled sons of Earth and Tartarus, smitten by the bolts of Jupiter, *Ci.* 30; *Cu.* 28

Glaucus: (1) a sea-deity, *G.* I. 437; *A.* V. 823; VI. 36; (2) a son of Antenor, *A.* VI. 483; (3) a son of Imbrasus, *A.* XII. 343

Gnosius, *adj.* of Gnosus, the ancient capital of Crete, *G.* I. 222; *A.* III. 115; V. 306; VI. 23, 566; IX. 305; *Ci.* 299

Gorgo, a snaky-haired daughter of Phorcus, one of three sisters, the chief one being Medusa, *A.* II. 616; VI. 289; VIII. 438; with Gorgoneus, *adj. A.* VII. 341 (where *venena* refers to the venom of the snakes)

Gortynius, *adj.* of Gortyna, a city of Crete, *E.* VI. 60; *A.* XI. 773; *Ci.* 114

Gracchus, a Roman family of the Sempronian *gens*, especially Tiberius and Gaius, the reformers, *A.* VI. 842

Gradivus, the *strider*, a name of Mars, *A.* III. 35; X. 542

Graecia, Greece, *G.* I. 38; III. 20; *A.* XI. 287; *Ci.* 412; *Cu.* 34; with Graecus, *adj.* Greek, *Co.* 1

Graiugena, one born a Greek, *A.* III. 550; VIII. 127

Graius, *adj.* Greek, *G.* II. 16, etc. (36 instances)

Graviscae, a town of Etruria, *A.* X. 184

Gryneus, *adj.* of Grynia, a town of Aeolis where Apollo was worshipped, *E.* VI. 72; *A.* IV. 345

Gyaros, an island of the Aegean, now Calairo, *A.* III. 76

Gyas: (1) a Trojan, *A.* I. 222, 612; V. 118, 152, 160, 167, 169, 184, 223; XII. 460; (2) a Latin, *A.* X. 318

Gyges, a Trojan, *A.* IX. 762

Gylippus, an Arcadian, *A.* XII. 272

Hadriacus, *adj.* of the Adriatic, *A.* XI. 405, where the reference is to a river flowing back to its source, a perversion of nature's laws.

Haemon, a Rutulian, *A.* IX. 685; with Haemonides, son of Haemon, *A.* X. 537

Haemus, a Thracian mountain-range, now Great Balkan, *G.* I. 492; II. 488

Halaesus: (1) a son or follower of Agamemnon, *A.* VII. 724; (2) a Rutulian, X. 352, 411, 417, 422, 424

Halius, a Trojan, *A.* IX. 767

Halys, a Trojan, *A.* IX. 765

Hamadryades, Wood-nymphs, *E.* X. 62; *Cu.* 95

Hammon, a Libyan god identified with Jupiter, *A.* IV. 198

Harpalyce, a female warrior of Thrace, *A.* I. 317

Harpalycus, a Trojan, *A.* XI. 675

Harpyia, a Harpy, a monster with a human head, but the body of a bird, *A.* III. 212, 226, 249; VI. 289

Hebrus: (1) a river of Thrace, now Maritza, *E.* X. 65; *G.* IV. 462, 523; *A.* I. 317; XII. 331; *Cu.* 117; (2) a Trojan, *A.* X. 696

Hecate, a goddess of the lower world and sister of Latona, identified with Diana on earth, and Luna in heaven, and therefore represented with three heads, *A.* IV. 511, 609; VI. 118, 247, 564

Hector, eldest son of Priam, chief hero of Troy, slain by Achilles, *A.* I. 99, 483, 750; II. 270, 275, 282, 522; III. 312, 319, 343; V. 371; VI. 166; IX. 155; XI. 289; XII. 440; *Cu.* 308, 317; with Hectoreus, *adj.* of Hector, Trojan, *A.* I. 273; II. 543; III. 304, 488; V. 190, 634; *Cu.* 324

Hecuba, wife of Priam, *A.* II. 501, 515

Helena, wife of Menelaus, carried off by Paris, *A.* I. 650; VII. 364

Helenor, a Trojan, *A.* IX. 544, 545

Helenus, a son of Priam, *A.* III. 295, 329, 334, 346, 369, 380, 433, 546, 559, 684, 712

559

INDEX

Heliades, daughters of Helios and sisters of Phaethon, changed into poplars, *Cu.* 129

Helicon, famous mountain in Boeotia, abode of the Muses and haunt of Apollo, *A.* VII. 641; X. 163

Hellespontus, Hellespont, now Dardanelles, *Ci.* 413; *Cu.* 33, with Hellespontiacus, *adj.* of the Hellespont, *G.* IV. 111; *Cu.* 338

Helōrus, a city and river in S.E. Sicily, *A.* III. 698

Helymus, a Sicilian, *A.* V. 73, 300, 323, 339

Herbēsus, a Rutulian, *A.* IX. 344

Hercules, the mythical hero, son of Jupiter and Alcmena, renowned for his "Labours," *A.* III. 551; V. 410; VII. 656; VIII. 270; X. 319, 779, with Herculeus, *adj.* of Hercules, *G.* II. 66; *A.* VII. 669; VIII. 276, 288, 542

Herminius, a Trojan, *A.* XI. 642

Hermione: (1) daughter of Menelaus and Helen and wife of Orestes, *A.* III. 328; (2) a town of Argolis, now Kastri; hence Hermioneus, *adj. Ci.* 472

Hermus, a river of Lydia, *G.* II. 137; *A.* VII. 721

Hernicus, *adj.* of the Hernici, a people of Latium, *A.* VII. 684

Hesiodus, Hesiod, poet of Ascra in Boeotia, *Ca.* XV. 1 (*cf. G.* II. 176)

Hesione, a daughter of Laomedon, sister of Priam, and wife of Telamon, *A.* VIII. 157 (*cf. Cu.* 300)

Hesperia, Hesperia ("Western land"), Italy, *A.* I. 530, 569; II. 781; III. 163, 185, 186, 503; IV. 355; VII. 4, 44, 543; VIII. 148; XII. 360

Hesperides, daughters of Hesperus, keepers of a garden of golden apples in the West, *E.* VI. 61; *A.* IV. 484; VIII. 77; *Ca.* IX. 25

Hesperus, evening star, evening, *E.* VIII. 30; X. 77; with Hesperius, *adj.* of Hesperus, *Ci.* 352 (*sidus* being understood); Hesperian, Italian, *A.* III. 418; VI. 6; VII. 601

Hiberus, *adj.* Iberian, Spanish, *A.* VII. 663; IX. 582; XI. 913; *masc. plur.* Spaniards, *G.* III. 408

Hicetāonius, son of Hicetaon, *A.* X. 123

Hiemps, Storm, or god of the storm (personification), *A.* III. 120

Himella, a tributary of the Tiber, now the Salto, *A.* VII. 714

Hippocoon, companion of Aeneas, *A.* V. 492

Hippodame, daughter of Oenomaus, won by Pelops in a chariot-race, *G.* III. 7

Hippolyte, an Amazon, wedded to Theseus, *A.* XI. 661

Hippolytus, son of Theseus and Hippolyte, who was loved by Phaedra his stepmother, but rejected her love. Being falsely accused by her, he was cursed by Theseus, and slain by a bull sent by Poseidon. Aesculapius restored him to life and Diana hid him in the grove of Aricia under the name of Virbius (*quasi vir bis,* Servius); *A.* VII. 761, 765, 774

Hippomenes, son of Megareus, who in a foot-race won Atalanta as his wife, *Ca.* IX. 26

Hippotades, son of Hippotas, *A.* XI. 674

Hisbo, a Rutulian, *A.* X. 384

Hister, the river Danube, *G.* II. 497; III. 350

Homerus, the Greek epic poet, *Ci.* 65; with Homereus, *adj.* of Homer, *Ca.* XIV. 2

Homole, a mountain in Thessaly, *A.* VII. 675

Horatius, *adj.* of Horatius, *i.e.* Horatius Cocles, who, in the war with Porsenna, defended the Sublician bridge single-handed, *Cu.* 361

Hyades, the Hyades, "daughters of rain," seven stars in Taurus, *G.* I. 138; *A.* I. 744; III. 516

Hybla, a mountain in Sicily, *E.* VII. 37; with Hyblaeus, *adj. E.* I. 54

Hydaspes: (1) a river of India, *G.* IV. 211; (2) a Trojan, *A.* X. 747

560

INDEX

Hydra: (1) a fifty-headed monster in the lower world, *A.* VI. 576; (2) a seven-headed snake, killed by Hercules, *A.* VII. 658

Hylaeus, a Centaur, *G.* II. 457; *A.* VIII. 294

Hylas, a youthful companion of Hercules in the Argonautic expedition, who was carried away by fountain-nymphs, *E.* VI. 43, 44; *G.* III. 6

Hylax, name of a dog, *E.* VIII. 107

Hyllus, a Trojan, *A.* XII. 535

Hymen, god of marriage, *Cu.* 247

Hypanis: (1) a river of Scythia, now Boug, *G.* IV. 369; (2) a Trojan, *A.* II. 340, 428

Hyperboreus, *adj.* of the far North, *G.* III. 381; IV. 517

Hyperion, father of the Sun, then the Sun himself, *Cu.* 101

Hyrcānus, *adj.* of the Hyrcani, a people of Asia near the Caspian Sea, *A.* IV. 367; VII. 605; *Ci.* 308

Hyrtacides, son of Hyrtacus: (1) Hippocoon, *A.* V. 492, 503; (2) Nisus, *A.* IX. 177, 234, 319, 492, 503

Hyrtacus, a Trojan, *A.* IX. 406

Iacchus, Iacchus, a name of Bacchus, *E.* VII. 61; *G.* I. 166; also of wine, *E.* VI. 15

Iaera, Iaera, a wood-nymph, *A.* IX. 673

Ianiculum, the Janiculum, a hill at Rome on the west side of the Tiber, *A.* VIII. 358

Ianus, a two-faced Italian deity, *A.* VII. 180, 610; VIII. 357; XII. 198

Iapetus, one of the Titans, *G.* I. 279

Iapys, *adj.* of the Iapydes, an Illyrian people, at the head of the Adriatic, *G.* III. 475

Iapyx, *adj.* Iapygian, or Apulian, *A.* XI. 247, 678; as *subst.* (1) Iapyx, a wind blowing from Iapygia toward Greece, *A.* VIII. 710; (2) son of Iasus, *A.* XII. 391, 420, 485

Iarbas, a Gaetulian king, son of Jupiter Ammon, *A.* IV. 36, 196, 326

Iasides, son of Iasus, *A.* V. 483; XII. 392

Iasius, brother of Dardanus, and son-in-law of Teucer, *A.* III. 168

Icariotis, daughter of Icarius, the son of Oebalus, king of Sparta, *i.e.* Penelope, *Cu.* 265

Icarus, son of Daedalus, who, flying through the air with his father, fell into the sea, *A.* VI. 31

Ida: (1) a mountain of Crete, *A.* XII. 412; hence, Idaeus, *adj.* of Ida, *G.* II. 84; *A.* III. 105; *Ci.* 168; (2) a mountain of Phrygia, near Troy, *G.* IV. 41; *A.* II. 801; III. 6; V. 252, 254, 449; IX. 79; X. 158; XII. 546; *Cu.* 311, 312; hence Idaeus, *adj.* of Ida, *G.* III. 450; *A.* II. 696; III. 112; VII. 139, 207, 222; IX. 111, 617, 669; X. 230, 252; XI. 285; (3) the mother of Nisus, *A.* IX. 177

Idaeus, Idaeus, Priam's charioteer, *A.* VI. 485

Idalius, *adj.* Idalian, *A.* V. 760; X. 52; *Ca.* XIV. 2; hence, *fem. subst.* Idalia, a town and grove of Cyprus, *A.* I. 693; *neut. subst.* Idalium, with same meaning, *A.* I. 681; X. 86

Idas: (1) a Trojan, *A.* IX. 575; (2) a Thracian, *A.* X. 351

Idmon, a Rutulian, *A.* XII. 75

Idomeneus, a Cretan hero at Troy, *A.* III. 122, 401; XI. 265

Idumaeus, *adj.* of Idume (Edom), a district of Syria, *G.* III. 12

Ilia, Ilia, or Rhea Silvia, mother of Romulus and Remus, *A.* I. 274; VI. 778

Ilione, a daughter of Priam, *A.* I. 653

Ilioneus, a Trojan, *A.* I. 120, 521, 559, 611; VII. 212, 249; IX. 501, 569

Ilithyia, goddess of childbirth, daughter of Juno, *Ci.* 326

Ilium, Ilium (*i.e.* Troy), city of Ilus, *A.* I. 68; II. 241, 325, 625; III. 3, 109; V. 261, 756; VI. 64; hence Ilius, *adj.* Trojan, *A.* I. 268; IX. 285; XI. 245; and Iliacus, *adj.* Trojan, *A.* I. 97, 456, 483, 647; II. 117, 431; III. 182, 280, 336, 603;

561

INDEX

IV. 46, 78, 537, 648; V. 607, 725; VI. 875; VIII. 134; X. 62, 335, 635; XI. 255, 393; XII. 861; and Iliades, *adj. fem. plur.* Trojan women, *A.* I. 480; II. 580; III. 65; V. 644; VII. 248; XI. 35

Illyricus, *adj.* of Illyria, N.W. of Greece, on the Adriatic, *E.* VIII. 7; *A.* I. 243

Ilus: (1) son of Tros, and king of Troy, *A.* VI. 650; (2) an earlier name of Iülus, *A.* I. 268; (3) a Rutulian, *A.* X. 400, 401

Ilva, Elba, an island off the coast of Etruria, *A.* X. 173

Imaon, a Rutulian, *A.* X. 424

Imbrasides, son of Imbrasus, *A.* X. 123; XII. 343

Imbrasus, a Lycian, *A.* XII. 343

Inachus: (1) first king of Argos, father of Io, *A.* VII. 372; (2) a river of Argolis, now Banitza, *A.* VII. 792; hence Inachius, *adj.* of Inachus, *A.* VII. 286; or Argive, *G.* III. 153; *A.* XI. 286; also Inachis, *fem. adj.* Argive, *Ca.* X. 33

Inarime, an island in the Tuscan Sea, now Ischia, *A.* IX. 716

India, India (to be understood as extending from the Indus to China), *G.* I. 57; II. 116, 122; with Indus, *adj.* Indian, *A.* XII. 67; *Cu.* 67; also as *subst.* an Indian, *G.* II. 138, 172; IV. 293, 425; *A.* VI. 794; VII. 605; VIII. 705

Indigetes, native heroes who after death are deified, Heroes of the land, *G.* I. 498; *sing.* Indiges, *A.* XII. 794

Inous, *adj.* of Ino, daughter of Cadmus, changed to a sea-goddess, *G.* I. 437; *A.* V. 823

Insidiae, personification, Craft, Ambush, *A.* XII. 336

Inuus, a name of the god Pan; see *Castrum Inui*

Io, Io, daughter of Inachus, loved by Jupiter and changed by Juno's craft into a heifer, *A.* VII. 789

Iolciacus, *adj.* of Iolcus, a town of Thessaly, associated with Jason; hence, Thessalian, *Ci.* 377

Iollas: (1) a shepherd, *E.* II. 57; III. 76, 79; (2) a Trojan, *A.* XI. 640

Ionius, *adj.* of Ionia, a maritime district of Asia Minor, Ionian, *G.* II. 108; *A.* III. 211 (*sc.* mare), 671; V. 193

Iopas, a Carthaginian minstrel, *A.* I. 740

Iphitus, a Trojan, *A.* II. 435

Irae, personification, Anger, *A.* XII. 336

Iris, Iris, goddess of the rainbow, daughter of Thaumas and Electra, and messenger of the gods, *A.* IV. 694, 700; V. 606; IX. 2, 18, 803; X. 38, 73

Ismarus: (1) a mountain of Thrace, also called Ismara, *E.* VI. 30; *G.* II. 37; *A.* X. 351; (2) a Lydian, *A.* X. 139

Isthmos, the Isthmus of Corinth, *Ci.* 463

Italia, Italy, *G.* II. 138; *A.* I. 2, etc. (44 instances in the *Aeneid*); with Italus, *adj.* Italian, *A.* I. 109 (43 instances in *A.*), and Italides, *fem. pl.* Italian women, *A.* XI. 657

Italus, eponymous hero of Italy, *A.* VII. 178 (*cp. A.* I. 533)

Ithaca, the island Ithaca, off the west coast of Greece, *A.* III. 272, 613

Ithacus, *adj.* of Ithaca, home of Ulysses, *A.* II. 104, 122, 128; III. 629; *Cu.* 125, 265, 326

Ituraeus, *adj.* of Ituraea, a district of Syria, *G.* II. 448

Itys: (1) a Trojan, *A.* IX. 574; (2) son of Tereus and Procne. He was killed by his mother, and served up to his father for food, upon which he was changed into a pheasant, the mother into a swallow, and the father into a hoopoe, *Cu.* 252 (*cp. E.* VI. 78)

Iulius, *adj.* Julian, the name of the *gens* to which Caesar belonged, *G.* II. 163 (see Lucrinus); as *subst.* Julius, *A.* I. 288 (where the reference is to Augustus, whose full name was Caius Iulius Caesar Octavianus Augustus)

Iulus (trisyllabic), Iülus or As-

INDEX

canius, son of Aeneas, *A.* I. 267, 288, etc. (35 instances in *A.*)

Iuno, Juno, daughter of Saturn, wife of Jupiter and queen of the gods, *G.* III. 153, 532; *A.* I. 4, 15, etc. (56 instances in *A.*); *Ci.* 139, 157; *L.* 64; with Iunonius, *adj.* of Juno, *A.* I. 671; in *A.* VI. 138 Iuno Inferna is Juno of the lower world, *i.e.* Proserpina

Iuppiter, Jupiter, son of Saturn and king of the gods, identified with the Greek Zeus, *E.* III. 60, etc. (113 instances in Virgil). For Iuppiter Stygius see *Stygius*

Iustitia, Justice (personification), *G.* II. 474

Iuturna, a nymph, sister of Turnus, *A.* XII. 146, 154, 222, 244, 448, 468, 477, 485, 798, 813, 844, 854, 870

Ixion, king of the Lapithae and father of Pirithous; he was fastened to an ever-revolving wheel in Tartarus, because he had insulted Juno, *G.* III. 38; *A.* VI. 601; with Ixionius, *adj.* of Ixion, *A.* IV. 484

Karthago, Carthage, city of north Africa (near modern Tunis), *A.* I. 13, 298, 366; IV. 97, 224, 265, 347, 670; X. 12, 54; *Cu.* 371

Labici, Labicians, people dwelling in Labicum, a town of Latium, *A.* VII. 796

Labyrinthus, the Labyrinth, a building at Cnosus in Crete, the work of Daedalus, wherein dwelt the Minotaur, *A.* V. 588 (*cp.* VI. 27)

Lacaenus, *adj.* Laconian or Spartan, *G.* II. 487; in *fem.* Lacaena, the Spartan woman, *i.e.* Helen, *A.* II. 601; VI. 511

Lacedaemon, Lacedaemon or Sparta, *A.* VII. 363; with Lacedaemonius, *adj.* Spartan, *A.* III. 328

Lacinius, *adj.* of Lacinium, a promontory of southern Italy, *A.* III. 552, now Capo Colonna

Lades, a Lycian, *A.* XII. 343

Ladon, an Arcadian, *A.* X. 413

Laertius, *adj.* of Laertes, father of Ulysses, *A.* III. 272; *Cu.* 327

Laestrygones, a savage people that once dwelt near Formiae in Campania, and later in Sicily, *Cu.* 330

Lageos, Lagean wine, *G.* II. 93

Lagus, a Rutulian, *A.* X. 380

Lamus, a Rutulian, *A.* IX. 334

Lamyrus, a Rutulian, *A.* IX. 334

Laocoon, priest of Neptune at Troy, *A.* II. 41, 201, 213, 230

Laodamia, wife of Protesilaus, who killed herself on learning of her husband's death at Troy, *A.* VI. 447

Laomedonteus, *adj.* of Laomedon, father of Priam and king of Troy, who broke his compact with Apollo and Neptune, when they built a wall around his city, *G.* I. 502; *A.* IV. 542; also Laomedontius, *adj.* Trojan, *A.* VII. 105; VIII. 18; and Laomedontiades, son or descendant of Laomedon; hence, Priam, *A.* VIII. 158, 162; in *plur.* the Trojans, *A.* III. 248

Lapithae, a Thessalian people, famous for their battle with the Centaurs, *G.* II. 457; III. 115; *A.* VI. 601; VII. 305, 307; *Cu.* 29

Lar, the tutelar deity of the hearth, *A.* V. 744; VIII. 543; IX. 259

Larides, a Rutulian, *A.* X. 391, 395

Larina, a companion of Camilla, *A.* XI. 655

Larissaeus, *adj.* of Larissa, a town of Thessaly, *A.* II. 197; XI. 404

Larius, a lake of Cisalpine Gaul, now Lake Como, *G.* II. 159

Latagus, a Trojan, *A.* X. 697, 698

Latinus: (1) Latinus, king of Latium, whose daughter Lavinia became the wife of Aeneas, *A.* VII. 45, etc. (44 instances in *A.*); (2) *adj.* of Latium, Latin, *A.* I. 6; V. 568, 598, etc. (61 instances in *A.*)

Latium, the plain between the lower Tiber and Campania, *A.* I. 6, etc. (31 instances in *A.*)

563

INDEX

Latona, mother of Apollo and Diana, *A.* I. 502; XII. 198; *Cu.* 11, 237; with Latonius, *adj.* of Latona, *G.* III. 6; *A.* IX. 405; XI. 557; *fem.* Latonia, daughter of Latona, Diana, *A.* XI. 534

Laurens, *adj.* **Laurentine (see App. on *A.* VIII. 1): with *masc. pl.* Laurentes, the Laurentines, *A.* v. 797, etc.; with Laurentius, *adj. A.* x. 709**

Laurentum, *i.e.* **Laurentum,** *A.* **VIII. 1, but see App. on the verse**

Lausus, son of Mezentius, *A.* **VII. 649, 651; X. 426, 434, 439, 700, 775, 790, 810, 814, 839, 841, 863, 902**

Lavinia, daughter of Latinus, *A.* **VI. 764; VII. 72, 314, 359; XI. 479; XII. 17, 64, 80, 194, 605, 937**

Lavinium, a town of Latium founded by Aeneas, *A.* I. 258, 270; VI. 84; now Pratica

Lavinius, *adj.* of Lavinium, *A.* I. 2; IV. 236

Leda, mother of Helen, as well as of Castor and Pollux, *A.* I. 652; *Ci.* 489; with Ledaeus, *adj. A.* III. 328; VII. 364

Leleges, an early people of Asia Minor and Greece, *A.* VIII. 725

Lemnius, *adj.* of Lemnos, the Aegean island upon which Vulcan fell from heaven; hence, of Vulcan, *A.* VIII. 454

Lenaeus, *adj.* of the wine-press, of Bacchus, *G.* II. 4, 7; III. 510; *A.* IV. 207; as *subst.*, Bacchus, *G.* II. 529

Lerna, a marsh near Argos, where Hercules slew the hydra, *A.* VI. 287, 803; XII. 518; with Lernaeus, *adj.* of Lerna, *A.* VIII. 300

Lesbos, a famous island of the Eastern Aegean, *G.* II. 90

Lethaeus, *adj.* of Lethe, the river of forgetfulness in the lower world, *G.* I. 78; IV. 545; *A.* v. 854; VI. 705, 714, 749; *Cu.* 140, 215

Letum, Death (personification); also, the world below; *G.* IV. 481; *A.* VI. 277, 278; x. 319; XI. 172, 830; XII. 328

Leucaspis, a Trojan, *A.* VI. 334

Leucates, Leucata, a promontory at the south end of Leucadia, near the coast of Acarnania, *A.* III. 274; VIII. 677

Leucothea, the name given to Ino after she was transformed into a sea-goddess, *Ci.* 396

Liber, the same as Bacchus, *E.* VII. 58; *G.* I. 7; *A.* VI. 805

Libethrides, *plur. adj. fem.* of Libethra, a fountain and cave on Helicon, *E.* VII. 21

Liburni, a people of Illyricum near the head of the Adriatic, *A.* I. 244

Libya, a country of North Africa, *G.* I. 241; III. 249, 339; *A.* I. 22, 158, 226, 301, 384, 556, 577; IV. 36, 173, 257; VI. 694, 843; *Cu.* 406; with Libycus, *adj,* Libyan, *G.* II. 105; *A.* I. 339, 377, 527, 596; IV. 106, 271, 320, 348; v. 595, 789; VI. 338; VII. 718; XI. 265; *Ci.* 179; *Cu.* 371; *D.* 53; also Libys, *adj. Ci.* 440; and Libystis, *adj. A.* v. 37; VIII. 368

Lichas, a Latin, *A.* x. 315

Licymnia, a slave, *A.* IX. 547

Ligea, a nymph, *G.* IV. 336

Liger, a Latin, *A.* IX. 571; x. 576, 580, 584

Ligus, *adj.* and *subst.* Ligurian, *G.* II. 168; *A.* x. 185; XI. 701, 715. The Ligurians lived in Cisalpine Gaul, about modern Genoa

Lilybeïus, *adj.* of Lilybaeum, the western promontory of Sicily, *A.* III. 706

Linus, the musician who taught Orpheus and Hercules, *E.* IV. 56, 57; VI. 67

Lipare, Lipara, now Lipari, one of the Aeolian Islands, *A.* VIII. 417

Liris, a Trojan, *A.* XI. 670

Locri, a Greek people who settled in southern Italy, *A.* III. 399; XI. 265

Longa, see *Alba*

Lucagus, a Latin, *A.* x. 575, 577, 586, 592

Lucas, a Latin, *A.* x. 561

Lucetius, a Latin, *A.* IX. 570

Lucienus, *Ca.* XIII. 35

564

INDEX

Lucifer, the morning star, *E.* VIII. 17; *G.* III. 324; *A.* II. 801; VIII. 589

Lucina, the name of Diana as protectress of women in childbirth, *E.* IV. 10; *G.* III. 60; IV. 340

Lucrinus, the Lucrine Lake, near the coast of Campania, which Agrippa provided with a ship-channel from the sea and breakwater and united with an inner lake, that of Avernus. Thus he secured for the Roman fleet a protected harbour, which he called Julian in honour of Augustus, *G.* II. 161

Luna, Luna or Diana, the moon-goddess, *G.* I. 396; III. 392; *A.* IX. 403; *Cu.* 283; *L.* 41, 42.

Lupercal, a grotto on the Palatine, sacred to Lupercus or Pan, *A.* VIII. 343

Luperci, priests of Lupercus or Pan, *A.* VIII. 663

Lyaeus: (1) *subst.* same as Bacchus, *G.* II. 229; *A.* IV. 58; (2) *adj.* Bacchic, *A.* I. 686

Lycaeus, a mountain of Arcadia, *E.* X. 15; *G.* I. 16; III. 2, 314; IV. 538; with Lycaeus, *adj.* Lycaean, *A.* VIII. 344

Lycāon: (1) a Cretan worker in metals, *A.* IX. 304; (2) a king of Arcadia, *G.* I. 138

Lycaonius, *adj.* of Lycaon, *A.* X. 749

Lycia, a country on the S.W. coast of Asia Minor, *A.* IV. 143; VII. 721; X. 126; XII. 344, 516; with Lycius, *adj.* Lycian, *A.* I. 113; IV. 346, 377; VI. 334; VII. 816; VIII. 166; X. 751; XI. 773

Lycidas, a shepherd, *E.* VII. 67; IX. 2, 12, 37

Lycisca, a dog, *E.* III. 18

Lycorias, a sea-nymph, *G.* IV. 439

Lycōris, a girl, *E.* X. 2, 22, 42

Lyctius, *adj.* of Lyctos, a city of Crete; hence, Cretan, *E.* V. 72; *A.* III. 401

Lycurgus: (1) a king of Thrace, *A.* III. 14; (2) name of a soldier, *D.* 8

Lycus: (1) a river of Colchis, *G.* IV. 367; (2) a Trojan, *A.* I. 222; IX. 545, 556

Lydia: (1) Lydia, a country in Asia, *G.* IV. 211; hence, Lydius, *adj.* Lydian, and, as the Etruscans were supposed to be of Lydian origin, Etruscan, *A.* II. 781; VIII. 479; X. 155; Lydi, *plur. subst.*, Etruscans, *A.* IX. 11; (2) name of a girl, *D.* 41, 89, 95; *L.* 4

Lynceus, a Trojan, *A.* IX. 768

Lyrnēsus, a town of Troas, *A.* XII. 547; with Lyrnesius, *adj.* of Lyrnesus, *A.* X. 128

Machāon, a Greek physician, son of Aesculapius, *A.* II. 263

Maeander, a river of Lydia famous for its windings; hence, a winding border, *A.* V. 241

Maecenas, the great patron of Virgil, friend of Augustus, *G.* I, 2; II. 41; III. 41; IV. 2

Maenalus, or Maenala, a mountain of Arcadia, *E.* VIII. 22; X. 15, 55; *G.* I. 7; with Maenalius, *adj.* of Maenalus, Arcadian, *E.* 21, 25, 28a, 31, 36, 42, 46, 51, 57, 61; *Co.* 9

Maeon, a Rutulian, *A.* X. 337

Maeonia, old name of Lydia, and therefore used for Etruria, *A.* VIII. 499

Maeonidae, Lydians or Etruscans, *A.* XI. 759

Maeonius, *adj.* Maeonian or Lydian, *G.* IV. 380; *A.* IV. 216; IX. 546; X. 141; *Ci.* 62

Maeōtius, *adj.* of the Maeotians, a Scythian people, dwelling about Lake Maeotis, now Sea of Azov, *G.* III. 349; *A.* VI. 799

Maevius, a poet hostile to Virgil, *E.* III. 90

Magus, a Rutulian, *A.* X. 521

Maia, mother of Mercury, and daughter of Atlas; she was one of the Pleiades, *G.* I. 225; *A.* I. 297; VIII. 138, 140

Malea, a promontory at the S.E. of the Peloponnesus, *A.* V. 193

Mānes, the spirits of the departed, the gods below, or the lower world in general, *G.* I. 243; *A.* III. 63; VI. 896; *Ca.* XI. 7;

565

INDEX

Cu. 214, etc. (30 instances in Virgil)

Manlius, *i.e.* M. Manlius Capitolinus, who saved the Capitol from the Gauls, *A.* VIII. 652

Manto, a prophetess, wedded to the Tiber-god, *A.* X. 199

Mantua, a city of Gallia Transpadana, near Virgil's birthplace, *E.* IX. 27, 28; *G.* II. 198; III. 12

Marcellus, a family name in the Claudian *gens*; especially, M. Claudius Marcellus, who opposed Hannibal and conquered Syracuse, and M. Marcellus, nephew and adopted son of Augustus, who died in 23 B.C., *A.* VI. 855, 883

Mareotis, *adj.* of Mareotis, a district of Egypt, *G.* II. 91

Marica, a nymph, *A.* VII. 47

Marius, Marius, conqueror of the Cimbri and Jugurtha; in *plur.* men of his stamp, *G.* II. 169

Marpesius, *adj.* of Marpesus, a mountain of the island Paros. *A.* VI. 471

Marruvius, *adj.* of Marruvium, a city of Latium, capital of the Marsi, now S. Benedetto, *A.* VII. 750

Mars, the god of war, *E.* X. 44; *G.* I. 511; *A.* I. 4, etc. (42 instances); with Martius, *adj.* of Mars, warlike, *E.* IX. 12; *G.* IV. 71; *A.* VII. 182; IX. 566; XI. 661

Marsus, *adj.* of the Marsi, a Sabellian tribe in Italy, *A.* VII. 758; *plur. subst.* Marsi, the Marsians, *G.* II. 167; *A.* X. 544

Massicus: (1) *adj.* of Mt. Massicus, a mountain on the borders of Latium and Campania, *G.* II. 143; III. 526; *A.* VII. 726; (2) an Etruscan, *A.* X. 166

Massȳlus (1) of the Massyii, a people of North Africa, *A.* IV. 132, 483; *plur. subst.* the people themselves, *A.* VI. 60

Maurusius, *adj.* of the Mauri, Moorish, *A.* IV. 206

Mavors, another name of Mars, *A.* VI. 872; VIII. 630, 700; X. 755; XI. 389; XII. 179, 332; *L.* 69; with Mavortius, *adj.* of Mars, martial, *G.* IV. 462; *A.* I. 276; III. 13; VI. 777; IX. 685

Maximus, *i.e.* Q. Fabius Maximus, *A.* VI. 845

Media, a country of Asia, south of the Caspian, *G.* II. 126; with Medus, *adj.* Median, *A.* IV. 211; *plur. subst.* Medi, Medes, *G.* II. 134, 136; also Medicus, *adj.* Median, *G.* I. 215

Medon, a Trojan, *A.* VI. 483

Megaera, one of the Furies, *A.* XII. 846

Megara, chief city of the Megarid, a district of the Isthmus between the Saronic and Corinthian Gulfs, *Ci.* 105, 388

Megarus, *adj.* of Megara (in Sicily), *A.* III. 689

Melampus: (1) a famous seer and physician, *G.* III. 550; (2) a Latin, *A.* X. 320

Meliboeus: (1) a shepherd, *E.* I. 6, 19, 42, 73; III. 1; V. 87; VII. 9; *Ca.* IX. 18; (2) *adj.* of Meliboea, a town of Thessaly, from which came Philoctetes, *A.* III. 401; V. 251

Melicerta, son of Ino and Athamas, changed into a sea-god, *G.* I. 437

Melite, a sea-nymph, *A.* V. 825

Mella, a river of Cisalpine Gaul flowing through Brescia, *A.* IV. 278

Memmius, a Roman gentile name, *A.* V. 117 (where Virgil seems to assume that Μνησθεύς was assimilated to the Latin *meminisse*, and so became *Memmius*)

Memnon, son of Tithonus and Aurora, and king of the Ethiopians. His armour was made by Vulcan, *A.* I. 489

Menalcas, a shepherd, *E.* II. 15; III. 13, 58; V. 4, 64, 90; IX. 10, 16, 18, 55; X. 20

Menelaus, son of Atreus, brother of Agamemnon, and husband of Helen, *A.* II. 264; VI. 525; XI. 262

Menestheus, a Trojan, *A.* X. 129

Menoetes: (1) a Trojan, *A.* V. 161, 164, 166, 173, 179; (2) an Arcadian, *A.* XII. 517

INDEX

Mercurius, Mercury, son of Jupiter and Maia, and messenger of the gods, *A*. IV. 222, 558; VIII. 138

Meropes, a Trojan, *A*. IX. 702

Messalla, a Roman surname; especially M. Valerius Messalla Corvinus, patron and friend of Tibullus, *Ca*. IX 40 (see introductory note), *Ci*. 54

Messapus, the eponymous hero of Messapia or Iapygia (at the heel of Italy), represented by Virgil as leading a force from southern Etruria, *A*. VII. 691; VIII. 6; IX. 27, 124, 160, 351, 365, 458, 523; X. 354, 749; XI. 429, 464, 518, 520, 603; XII. 128, 289, 294, 488, 550, 661

Metabus, a Volscian, father of Camilla, *A*. XI. 540, 564

Methymnaeus, *adj*. of Methymna, a city of Lesbos, *G*. II. 90

Metiscus, a Rutulian, charioteer of Turnus, *A*. XII. 469, 472, 623, 737, 784

Mettus, *i.e.* Mettus Fuffetius, dictator of Alba, who for his treachery was torn asunder by horses, *A*. VIII. 642

Metus, Fear or Dread (personification), *G*. III. 552; *A*. VI. 276

Mezentius, an Etruscan king, *A*. VII. 648, 654; VIII. 7, 482, 501, 569; IX. 522, 586; X. 150, 204, 689, 714, 729, 742, 762, 768, 897; XI. 7, 16

Micon, a shepherd, *E*. III. 10; VII. 30

Milesius, *adj*. of Miletus, a city of Ionia in Asia Minor, *G*. III. 306; IV. 334

Mimas, a Trojan, *A*. X. 702, 706

Mincius, the Mincius, now the Mincio, a river of Cisalpine Gaul, *E*. VII. 13; *G*. III. 15; *A*. X. 206

Minerva, a Roman goddess, patroness of arts, handicrafts, and science, identified with Pallas Athene, *G*. I. 18; IV. 246; *A*. II. 31, 189, 404; III. 531; V. 284; VI. 840; VII. 805; VIII. 409, 699; XI. 259; *Ci*. 23

Minio, a river of Etruria, *A*. X. 183

Minos, a king of Crete, whose capital was Cnosus. After death he became a judge in the lower world, *A*. VI. 432; *Ci*. 111, 132, 272, 286, 287, 301, 367, 414, 421, 454; *Cu*. 374. Hence **Minois**, daughter of Minos, *i.e.* Ariadne, *L*. 49; and **Minoius**, *adj*. of Minos, *A*. VI. 14

Minotaurus, the man-bull, the Minotaur, killed by Theseus, *A*. VI. 26

Misenus: (1) a Trojan, trumpeter of Aeneas, *A*. III. 239; VI. 162, 164, 189, 212; (2) a promontory north of the Bay of Naples, now Miseno, *A*. VI. 234

Mnasyllos, a young Satyr, *E*. VI. 13

Mnestheus, a Trojan, *A*. IV. 288; V. 116, 117, 184, 189, 194, 210, 218, 493, 494, 507; IX. 171, 306, 779, 781, 812; X. 143; XII. 127, 384, 443, 459, 549, 561

Moeris, a shepherd, *E*. VIII. 96, 98; IX. 1, 16, 53, 54, 61; *Ca*. IX. 18

Molorchus, the entertainer of Hercules when he killed the Nemean lion; hence, *luci Molorchi*, the haunt of the lion, *G*. III. 19

Molossus, *adj*. of the Molossi, a people of eastern Epirus, *G*. III. 405; *Cu*. 331

Monoecus, a promontory of Liguria, now Monaco, *A*. VI. 830

Mopsus, a shepherd, *E*. V. 1, 10; VIII. 20, 29

Morini, a Belgic people of western Gaul, *A*. VIII. 727

Mors, Death (personification), *A*. XI. 197; *Cu*. 188

Mucius, a Roman hero, *Cu*. 365 (where see note)

Mulciber, a name of Vulcan, *A*. VIII. 724

Murranus, a name of Latin kings, *A*. XII. 529, 639

Musa: (1) a Muse, *A*. I. 8; usually *plur.*, the Muses, *E*. IV. 1; VI. 69; VII. 19; *G*. II. 475; III. 11; IV. 315; *A*. IX. 77, 774, 775; *Ca*. IX. 60; (2) Octavius Musa, a poet and friend of Virgil and Horace, *Ca*. IV. 6, 8

Musaeus, an ancient Greek bard, *A*. VI. 667

Mutusca, a Sabine town, *A*. VII. 711

INDEX

Mycene (or -ae), Mycenae, city of Agamemnon in the Peloponnesus; also of Greece in general; *G.* III. 121; *A.* I. 284, 650; II. 25, 180, 331, 577; V. 52; VI. 838; VII. 222, 372; IX. 139

Myconos, one of the islands of the Cyclades in the Aegean, *A.* III. 76

Mygdonides, son of Mygdon, *A.* II. 342

Myrmidones, a tribe of Thessaly, *A.* II. 7, 252, 785; XI. 403

Myrrha, daughter of Cinyras, *Ci.* 238

Mysia, a district of Asia Minor, *G.* I. 102; also Mysus, *adj.* of Mysia, *G.* IV. 370

Nais, a Naiad, a water-nymph, *E.* II. 46; VI. 21; X. 10; *Cu.* 19, 117

Napaeae, the wood-nymphs, *G.* IV. 534

Nar, a river in Sabine territory, tributary of the Tiber, *A.* VII. 517

Narycius, *adj.* Narycian of Naryx, a Locrian city on the Euboean Sea, *G.* II. 438; *A.* III. 399

Nautes, a Trojan, *A.* V. 704, 728

Naxos, an island of the Cyclades, *A.* III. 125

Neaera, a rustic girl, *E.* III. 3

Nealces, a Trojan, *A.* X. 753

Nemeus, *adj.* Nemean, of Nemea, a district of Argolis, *A.* VIII. 295

Neoptolemus, a name of Achilles' son Pyrrhus, *A.* II. 263, 500, 549; III. 333, 469; XI. 264

Neptunus, Neptune, god of the sea; hence, the sea itself; *G.* I. 14; III. 122; IV. 29, 387, 394; *A.* I. 125; II. 201, 610; III. 74, 119; V. 14, 195, 360, 640, 779, 782, 863; VII. 23; VIII. 699; IX. 145; *Ci.* 474, 509; *D.* 50, 58, 63

Nereus, a sea-god, *E.* VI. 35; *G.* IV. 392; *A.* II. 419; VIII. 383; X. 764; hence Nereis, daughter of Nereus, a Nereid, *A.* III. 74; V. 240; *Ci.* 474; *Cu.* 300, 345; and Nereius, *adj.* of Nereus, *A.* IX. 102; also Nerine, daughter of Nereus, *E.* VII. 37

Neritos, Neritus, an island near Ithaca, *A.* III. 271

Nersae, a city of the Aequi, *A.* VII. 744

Nesaee, Nesaea, a nymph, *G.* IV. 338; *A.* V. 826

Nilus, the Nile, *G.* III. 29; IV. 288; *A.* VI. 800; VIII. 711; IX. 31

Niphaeus, a Rutulian, *A.* X. 570

Niphates, a snowy mountain in Armenia, *G.* III. 30

Nisus: (1) a king of Megara, betrayed by his daughter Scylla, and robbed of a lock of hair upon which depended his life; he was changed into a hawk; *E.* VI. 74; *G.* I. 404, 408; *Ci.* 112, 124, 191, 207, 378, 411, 540; also Niseius, *adj.* of Nisus, *Ci.* 390; (2) a young Trojan, *A.* V. 294, 296, 318, 328, 353, 354; IX. 176, 184, 200, 207, 223, 230, 233, 258, 271, 306, 353, 386, 425, 438, 467

Noctuinus, *Ca.* VI. 2; XII. 1, 3, 4, 8

Noëmon, a Trojan, *A.* IX. 767

Nomades, the Numidians, *A.* IV. 320, 535; VIII. 724

Nomentum, a Sabine town, *A.* VI. 773; VII. 712

Noricus, *adj.* of Noricum, a mountainous country of modern Austria, north of the Alps, and south of the Danube, *G.* III. 474

Notus, the South Wind, *G.* I. 444; *A.* I. 85, 108, 575; II. 417; III. 268; V. 242, 512; VI. 355; VII. 411; X. 266; XI. 798; XII. 334

Nox, Night, a personification, mother of the Furies, sister and wife of Erebus, *A.* III. 512; V. 721, 738, 835; VII. 138; XII. 846; *Cu.* 202

Numa: (1) Numa Pompilius, second king of Rome, *A.* VI. 808; (2) a Rutulian, *A.* IX. 454; X. 562

Numanus, a Rutulian, *A.* IX. 592, 653

Numicius or **Numicus**, a stream in Latium, *A.* VII. 150, 242, 797. See note on *A.* VII. 150 in Appendix

Numidae, Numidians, a people of North Africa, *A.* IV. 41

Numitor: (1) a king of Alba,

568

INDEX

grandfather of Romulus and Remus, *A.* VI. 768; (2) a Rutulian, *A.* X. 342

Nursia, a town of the Sabines, now Norcia, *A.* VII. 716

Nyctelius, *i.e.* νυκτέλιος (νύξ), the nightly one, a name given to Bacchus because of his festivals by night, *Cu.* 111

Nympha, a nymph or muse, *E.* II. 46; *G.* IV. 334, etc. (42 instances).

Nysa: (1) a girl, *E.* VIII. 18, 26; (2) a mountain and city of India, *A.* VI. 805

Oaxes, a river of Crete, *E.* I. 65

Oceanitides, daughters of Ocean, *G.* IV. 341

Oceanus, Ocean (personified), *G.* I. 246; II. 122, 481; III. 359; IV. 233, 381, 382; *A.* I. 287, 745; II. 250; IV. 139, 480; VII. 101, 226; VIII. 589; XI. 1; *Ca.* IX. 54; *Ci.* 392; *Cu.* 103

Ocnus, founder of Mantua, *A.* X. 198

Octavius: (1) the later Augustus, *Cu.* I. 25; (2) Octavius Musa, friend of Virgil and of Horace, *Ca.* XI. 1

Oeagrius, *adj.* of Oeagrus, king of Thrace, father of Orpheus; hence, Thracian, *G.* IV. 524

Oebalius, *adj.* of Oebalus, king of Sparta, the founder of Tarentum, *G.* IV. 125

Oebalus, a king in Campania, *A.* VII. 734

Oechalia, a town of Euboea, *A.* VIII. 291

Oenides, son of Oeneus, *i.e.* Meleager; or perhaps grandson of Oeneus, *i.e.* Diomedes, *Ca.* IX. 6

Oenotrus, and Oenotrius, *adj.* of Oenotria, the southern part of Italy, *A.* VII. 85; in *plur.* Oenotri, the people of Oenotria, *A.* I. 532; III. 165

Oeta, a mountain range of Thessaly, *E.* VIII. 30; *Ci.* 350; *Cu.* 203

Ogygius, *adj.* Ogygian, of Ogygus, founder of Thebes, *Ci.* 220

Oileus, father of Ajax, *A.* I. 41

Olearos, an island of the Cyclades, now Antiparos, *A.* III. 126

Olympiacus, *adj.* of Olympia, the city of Elis where the Olympic games were held, *G.* III. 49

Olympus: (1) a mountain in the north of Thessaly, *G.* I. 282; *Ci.* 34; (2) the heavens, sky, *E.* V. 56; VI. 86; *G.* I. 96, 450; III. 223; IV. 562; *A.* I. 374; II. 779; IV. 268, 694; V. 533; VI. 579, 586, 782, 834; VII. 218, 558; VIII. 280, 319, 533; IX. 84, 106; X. 1, 115, 216, 437, 621; XI. 726, 867; XII. 634, 791; *Ca.* XIV. 11

Onites, a Rutulian, *A.* XII. 514

Opheltes, a Trojan, *A.* IX. 201

Opis: (1) a nymph, *G.* IV. 342; (2) a companion of Diana, *A.* XI. 532, 836, 867

Orcus, a god of the lower world, Death; also, the lower world itself, *G.* I. 277; IV. 502; *A.* II. 398; IV. 242, 699; VI. 273; VIII. 296; IX. 527, 785

Oreades, mountain-nymphs, *A.* I. 500

Orestes, son of Agamemnon and Clytemnestra. He killed his mother and was driven mad by the Furies, *A.* III. 331; IV. 471

Oricius, *adj.* of Oricum, a town of Epirus, *A.* X. 136

Oriens, the Dawn or East, *G.* I. 250; *A.* I. 289; V. 42, 739; VIII. 678; *Cu.* 30

Orion, a fabled hunter placed in the heavens as a constellation, *A.* I. 535; III. 517; IV. 52; VII. 719; X. 763; *Ci.* 535

Orithyia, a daughter of Erechtheus, king of Athens, *G.* IV. 463; *A.* XII. 83

Ornytus, an Etruscan, *A.* XI. 677

Orodes, a Trojan, *A.* X. 732, 737

Orontes, a Trojan, *A.* I. 113, 220; VI. 334

Orpheus, a mythic bard, whose skill won his wife Eurydice back from the lower world. He was torn to pieces by the Thracian women, *E.* III. 46; IV. 55, 57; VI. 30; VIII. 55, 56; *G.* IV. 454, 494, 545, 553; *A.* VI. 119; *Cu.* 117, 279, 292

Orses, a Trojan, *A.* X. 748

569

INDEX

Orsilochus, a Trojan, *A.* XI. 636, 690, 694

Ortinus, *adj.* of Orta, a town of Etruria on the Tiber and Nar, *A.* VII. 716

Ortygia: (1) the island of Delos, *A.* III. 124, 143, 154; (2) an island in the harbour of Syracuse, *A.* III. 694

Ortygius, a Rutulian, *A.* IX. 573

Osci, the Oscans, an early people of Campania, *A.* VII. 730

Osinius, a king of Clusium, *A.* X. 655

Osiris, a Rutulian, *A.* XII. 458

Ossa, a mountain of Thessaly, *G.* I. 281, 282; hence Ossaeus, *adj.* of Ossa, *Ci.* 33

Othryades, son of Othrys, *A.* II. 319, 336

Othrys, a mountain in Thessaly, *A.* VII. 675

Otos, Otus, twin brother of Ephialtes, *Cu.* 234

Pachynus, Sicilian promontory at the south-east of the island, now Capo di Passaro, *A.* III. 429, 699; VII. 289; *Ci.* 88

Pactōlus, a river of Lydia, *A.* X. 142

Padus, the river Po of North Italy, *G.* II. 452; *A.* IX. 680

Padusa, one of the mouths of the Po, *A.* XI. 457

Paeonius, *adj.* of Paeon (god of medicine); hence medical or healing, *A.* VII. 769; XII. 401

Paestum, a city of Lucania, once called Posidonia, now Pesto, *G.* IV. 119

Pagasus, an Etruscan, *A.* XI. 670

Palaemon: (1) son of Athamas and Ino, changed to a sea-god, *A.* V. 823; *Ci.* 396; (2) a shepherd, *E.* III. 50, 53

Palaepaphius, *adj.* of Old Paphos, referring to Venus, who had a famous temple in Paphos, *Ci.* 88

Palamedes, a Greek hero, *A.* II. 82

Palatium, the Palatine hill, on which Augustus had his residence, *G.* I. 499; hence Palatinus, *adj.* of the Palatine, *A.* IX. 9

Pales, a shepherd goddess, *E.* V. 35; *G.* III. 1, 294; *Cu.* 20, 77

Palīcus, the name of twin sons of Zeus (Jupiter) by Thalia, worshipped in Sicily, *A.* IX. 585

Palinurus, the Trojan pilot of Aeneas, *A.* III. 202, 513, 562; V. 12, 833, 840, 843, 847, 871; VI. 337, 341, 373, 381

Palladium, a statue of Pallas, especially that stolen from Troy by Ulysses and Diomede, *A.* II. 166, 183; IX. 151

Palladius, *adj.* of Pallas, *i.e.* Athene or Minerva, *G.* II. 181; *Ci.* 29; *M.* 113

Pallantēus, *adj.* of Pallas (2), *A.* IX. 196, 241; *neuter*, as *subst.* Pallantēum, the city built by Evander, *A.* VIII. 54, 341

Pallas: (1) an epithet of the Greek goddess Athene (= Minerva), *E.* II. 61; *A.* I. 39, 479; II. 15, 163, 615; III. 544; V. 704; VII. 154; VIII. 435; XI. 477; *Cu.* 329; (2) an ancient king of Arcadia, forefather of Evander, *A.* VIII. 51, 54; (3) son of Evander, killed by Turnus, *A.* VIII. 104, 110, etc. (41 instances)

Pallene, a peninsula of Macedonia, on the Thermaic Gulf, *G.* IV. 391

Palmus, an Etruscan, slain by Mezentius, *A.* X. 697, 699

Pan, a son of Mercury, and god of woods and of shepherds; in *plur.* gods resembling Pan, *E.* II. 31, 32, 33; IV. 58, 59; V. 59; VIII. 24; X. 26; *G.* I. 17; II. 494; III. 392; *A.* VIII. 344; *Cu.* 94, 115

Panchaia, an island or district of Arabia famous for frankincense, *G.* II. 139; hence Panchaius, or Panchaeus, *adj.* of Panchaea, *G.* IV. 379; *Cu.* 87

Pandarus: (1) a Trojan, son of Lycaon, *A.* V. 496; (2) a Trojan, son of Alcanor, *A.* IX. 672, 722, 735; XI. 396

Pandionius, *adj.* of Pandion, king of Athens, father of Procne and Philomela, *Cu.* 251; hence, Athenian, *Ci.* 101

Pangaea, *plur.* a mountain-range between Macedonia and Thrace, now Pilaf Tepeh, *G.* IV. 462

570

INDEX

Panopēa, a sea-nymph, *G.* I. 437; *A.* V. 240, 825

Panopes, a Sicilian, *A.* V. 300

Pantagias, a river of Eastern Sicily, now Fiume di Porcari, *A.* III. 689

Panthus, a Trojan, priest of Apollo, *A.* II. 318, 319, 322, 429

Paphos (-us), a city of Cyprus, famous for its temple of Venus, *A.* I. 415; X. 51, 86; *Ca.* XIV. 2; hence, Paphius, *adj.* of Paphos, *G.* II. 64

Parcae, the Fates, identified with the Μοῖραι (Clotho, Lachesis, and Atropos), *E.* IV. 47; *A.* I. 22, III. 379; V. 798; IX. 107; X. 419, 815; XII. 147, 150; *Ci.* 125, 270

Paris, son of Priam and Hecuba. Having adjudged Venus to be more beautiful than Juno or Minerva, he won Helen as his prize, and thus brought on the Trojan war, *E.* II. 61; *A.* I. 27; II. 602; IV. 215; V. 370; VI. 57; VII. 321; X. 702, 705; *Cu.* 325

Parnasus, a mountain in Phocis, haunt of the Muses, *E.* X. 11; *G.* III. 291; hence, Parnasius, *adj.* of Parnassus, *E.* VI. 29; *G.* II. 18; *Cu.* 15

Paros, one of the Cyclades islands famous for its white marble, *A.* III. 126; *Ci.* 476; hence, Parius, *adj.* Parian, *G.* III. 34; *A.* I. 593

Parrhasius, *adj.* of Parrhasia, a town in Arcadia; hence, Arcadian, *A.* VIII. 344; XI. 31

Parthenius, *adj.* of Parthenius, a mountain in Arcadia, *E.* X. 57

Parthenius, a Trojan, *A.* X. 748

Parthenopaeus, son of Meleager and Atalanta, and one of the seven chieftains in the Theban war, *A.* VI. 480

Parthenope, the ancient name of Naples, *G.* IV. 564

Parthus, *adj.* Parthian, of the Parthians (a nation living north-east of the Caspian Sea); also used as a substantive, *E.* I. 62; X. 59; *G.* III. 31; IV. 211, 314; *A.* VII. 606; XII. 857, 858; *Ci.* 299

Pasiphae, wife of Minos, king of Crete, and mother of the man-bull, the Minotaur, *E.* VI. 46; *A.* VI. 25, 447

Patavium, a city of Cisalpine Gaul, now Padua, *A.* I. 247

Patron, an Arcadian, *A.* V. 298

Pegasides, the Muses, so called from Pegasus, the winged horse of the Muses, who with a blow of his hoof caused Hippocrene, fountain of the Muses, to spring from Mount Helicon, *C.* IX. 2

Pelasgus, *adj.* Pelasgian; hence, Greek (the Pelasgians having been the ancient inhabitants of Greece), *A.* I. 624; II. 106, 152; IX. 154; *Cu.* 309; hence, Pelasgi, as *subst.*, the Pelasgians, *A.* II. 83; VI. 503; VIII. 600

Pelethronius, *adj.* Pelethronian or Thessalian (so called from Pelethronius, a forest on Mount Pelion), *G.* III. 115

Peleus, son of Aeacus, also husband of Thetis, and father of Achilles, *Cu.* 297

Pelias, a Trojan, *A.* II. 435, 436

Pelides, son or descendant of Peleus; hence, of Achilles his son, *A.* II. 548; V. 808; XII. 350; and of Neoptolemus his grandson, *A.* II. 263

Pelion, a mountain of Thessaly, now Zagora, *G.* I. 281; III. 94

Pellaeus, *adj.* Pellean, of Pella (the Macedonian town where Alexander the Great was born); hence, Alexandrian, of Alexandria (the Egyptian city founded by Alexander), *G.* IV. 287

Pelops, son of Tantalus, who served him up to the gods at a feast. He was restored to life, and provided with an ivory shoulder in place of the one eaten. He won his wife Hippodameia by defeating her father Oenomaus in a chariot-race, *G.* III. 7; hence, Pelopēius, *adj.* of Pelops, Peloponnesian or Greek, *A.* II. 193

Pelorus, a promontory of north-east Sicily, now Capo di Faro, *A.* III. 411, 687

Pelusiacus, *adj.* of Pelusium, a

571

INDEX

town of Egypt; hence, Egyptian, *G.* I. 228

Penates, the Penates, household gods, or gods of the state considered as a household (often used in the sense of *home*); *A.* I. 68, 378, 527, 704; II. 293, 514, 717, 747; III. 12, 15, 148, 603; IV. 21, 598; V. 62, 632; VII. 121; VIII. 11, 39, 123, 543, 679; IX. 258; XI. 264; *Ca.* IX. 35; *Ci.* 331, 419

Peneleus, a Greek, *A.* II. 425

Penēus, a river of Thessaly, flowing through Tempe, now the Selembria, *G.* IV. 355; hence, Penēius, *adj.* of the Peneus, *G.* IV. 317

Penthesilea, queen of the Amazons, *A.* I. 491; XI. 662

Pentheus, king of Thebes, torn in pieces by his mother Agave and her companions because he had mocked at the rites of Bacchus, *A.* IV. 469

Pergama (also Pergamum and Πέργαμος in Greek), the citadel of Troy, therefore Troy itself, *A.* I. 466, 651; II. 177, 291, 375, 556, 571; III. 87, 336, 350; IV. 344, 426; VI. 516; VII. 322; VIII. 37, 374; X. 58; XI. 280; hence, Pergameus, *adj.* Trojan, *A.* III. 110, 476; V. 744; VI. 63

Pergamea, Pergamea or Pergamum, the name given by Aeneas to his city in Crete, *A.* III. 133

Peridia, mother of Onites, *A.* XII. 515

Periphas, a Greek, *A.* II. 476

Permessus, a river of Boeotia flowing from Helicon, a haunt of the Muses, *E.* VI. 64

Persae, the Persians, *Cu.* 34

Persephone, the Greek form of the name Proserpina, *Cu.* 261

Persis, Persia. The name is used loosely by Virgil so as to include Arabia and Syria, *G.* IV. 290

Petelia, a town of the Bruttii, *A.* III. 402, now called Strongoli

Phaeāces, the Phaeacians, mythic inhabitants of Corcyra (the Scheria of the *Odyssey*), *A.* III. 291

Phaedra, wife of Theseus, and daughter of Minos, *A.* VI. 445

Phaëthon: (1) Helios, the Sungod, *A.* V. 105; (2) more commonly, a son of Helios, who attempted to drive his father's steeds, but losing control of them was destroyed by Jove's thunderbolt, *A.* X. 189; *Cu.* 128

Phaëthontiades, the sisters of Phaëthon, who, when mourning over their brother's fate, were changed into alders (or, according to some, poplars), *E.* VI. 62

Phanaeus, *adj.* of Phanae, a promontory of Chios, noted for its wine, *G.* II. 98

Pharus, a Rutulian, *A.* X. 322

Phasis, a river of Colchis, emptying into the Euxine, now Rion, *G.* IV. 367

Phegeus, a Trojan, *A.* V. 263; IX. 765; XII. 371

Pheneus, a town of Arcadia, *A.* VIII. 165

Pheres, a Trojan, *A.* X. 413

Philippi, a town of Macedonia, now Filibi, where Brutus and Cassius were defeated by Octavius and Antony, *G.* I. 490

Phillyrides, son of Philyra, nymph beloved by Saturn. Their son was the centaur Chiron, *G.* III. 550

Philoctetes, son of Poeas, king of Meliboea, in Thessaly. From Hercules he inherited the poisoned arrows without which Troy could not be taken, and with which he slew Paris. After the war he founded Petelia in Italy, *A.* III. 402

Philomela, daughter of Pandion, and sister of Procne. Tereus, the latter's husband, did violence to her and cut out her tongue, whereupon the sisters slew Tereus' son Itys and served him up at a feast. All three were changed into birds, Philomela becoming a nightingale, Procne a swallow, and Tereus a hoopoe, *E.* VI. 79

Phinēius, *adj.* of Phineus, son of Agenor and king of Thrace, who was struck blind by the gods and tormented by the Harpies for

572

INDEX

putting out the eyes of his sons, *A.* III. 212

Phlegethon, a river of fire in Tartarus, *A.* VI. 265, 551; *Cu.* 272, 374

Phlegra, a country of Macedonia, afterwards called Pallene, where the gods and giants fought, *Cu.* 28

Phlegyas, a son of Mars, and father of Ixion. He was punished in the world below for the impious act of burning Apollo's temple at Delphi, *A.* VI. 618

Phoebe, a name of Diana, as moon-goddess, *G.* I. 431; *A.* X. 216

Phoebigena, son of Phoebus, *i.e.* Aesculapius, *A.* VII. 773

Phoebus, a name of Apollo, *E.* III. 62; *A.* I. 329, etc. (54 instances); hence Phoebēus, *adj.* of Phoebus, *A.* III. 637; IV. 6

Phoenīces, the Phoenicians, *A.* I. 344

Phoenissa, *fem. adj.* Phoenician, *A.* I. 670; as *subst.* a Phoenician woman, *A.* I. 714; IV. 348, 529; VI. 450

Phoenix: (1) son of Amyntor and companion of Achilles, *A.* II. 762; (2) a son of Agenor, brother of Cadmus and Europa, *Ci.* 220

Pholoē, a slave-woman, *A.* V. 285

Pholus: (1) a Centaur, who entertained Hercules, but was accidentally killed by one of his guest's arrows, *G.* II. 456; *A.* VIII. 294; (2) a Trojan, *A.* XII. 341

Phorbas, a Trojan, *A.* V. 842

Phorcus: (1) a sea-god, *A.* V. 240, 824; (2) a Latin, *A.* X. 327

Phrygius,*adj.* Phrygian, of Phrygia, a country of Asia Minor, in which lay Troy; hence Trojan; also Phryx, *adj.* with *plur.* Phryges, Phrygians or Trojans. The *fem. sing.* Phrygia is also used as a *subst.*, *G.* IV. 41; *A.* I. 182, 381, etc. (31 instances of Phrygius and 13 of Phryx)

Phthia, a district of Thessaly, home of Achilles, *A.* I. 284

Phyllis: (1) a rustic girl, *E.* III. 76, 78, 107; V. 10; VII. 14, 59, 63; X. 37, 41; *Cu.* 132; (2) daughter of Sithon, king of Thrace, and betrothed to Demophoön, son of Theseus; *cf. Cu.* 131

Phyllodoce, a Nereid, *G.* IV. 336

Picus, son of Saturn and father of Faunus; he was changed by Circe into a wood-pecker, *A.* VII. 48, 171, 189

Pierides, the Muses, so called from their haunt Pieria in Thessaly, *E.* III. 85; VI. 13; VIII. 63; IX. 33; X. 72; *Ci.* 94; also Pierius, *adj.* Pierian, Thessalian, *Cu.* 18

Pilumnus, son of Daunus and ancestor of Turnus, *A.* IX. 4; X. 76, 619; XII. 83

Pinarius, *adj.* of the Pinarii, a family who with the Potitii first assisted at the rites of Hercules, *A.* VIII. 270

Pindus, a mountain in Thessaly, a seat of the Muses, now Mezzara, *E.* X. 11

Piraeeus, the Piraeus, the celebrated port of Athens, *Ci.* 468

Pirithous, son of Ixion, king of the Lapithae, companion of Theseus, with whose aid he attempted to carry away Proserpina from the home of Pluto, *A.* VI. 393, 601

Pisa, a city of Elis, near the river Alpheus, *G.* III. 180

Pisae, Pisa, a town of Etruria, supposed to be a colony from Pisa in Elis, *A.* X. 179

Pleias (Plias), one of the Pleiades, the seven daughters of Atlas who were changed into a constellation, *G.* I. 138; IV. 233

Plemyrium, a promontory of Sicily near Syracuse, *A.* III. 693

Pluton, Pluto, brother of Jupiter and king of the lower world, *A.* VII. 327

Podalirius, a Trojan, *A.* XII. 304

Poenae, Punishments (personification), goddesses of vengeance, identified with the Furies or Fiends, *Cu.* 377

Poenus, *adj.*, Phoenician, Carthaginian, *E.* V. 27; *Ci.* 135; with Poeni, *subst.*, the Phoenicians or

573

INDEX

Carthaginians, *A.* I. 302, 442, 567; IV. 134; VI. 858; XII. 4

Polites, a son of Priam, *A.* II. 526; v. 564

Pollio, C. Asinius Pollio, a distinguished statesman and writer, a friend and patron of Virgil, *E.* III. 84, 86, 88; IV. 12

Pollux, brother of Castor. As son of Jove, he was immortal, and on the death of Castor he was allowed to share his immortality with his brother on alternate days, *G.* III. 89; *A.* VI. 121

Polyboetes, a Trojan, priest of Ceres, *A.* VI. 484

Polydōrus, son of Priam, slain in Thrace by Polymnestor, *A.* III. 45, 49, 55, 62

Polyhymnia, one of the Muses, *Ci.* 55

Polyïdos, a priest, *Ci.* 112

Polyphēmus, a Cyclops of Sicily, whose eye was put out by Ulysses, *A.* III. 641, 657

Pometii, a Volscian town, also called Suessa Pometia, *A.* VI. 775

Pontus: (1) the Euxine or Black Sea, *G.* I. 58; (2) the region south of the Euxine, *E.* VIII. 95, 96

Populonia, a city on the coast of Etruria, *A.* X. 172

Porsenna, a king of Etruria, who attempted to restore the banished Tarquins, *A.* VIII. 646

Portūnus, the god of harbours, Greek Παλαίμων, *A.* v. 241

Potitius, one of the family who, along with the Pinarii, assisted at the rites of Hercules, *A.* VIII. 269, 281

Potniae, *adj.* of Potniae, a town of Boeotia, the residence of Glaucus, son of Sisyphus, whose horses went mad and tore their master in pieces, *G.* III. 268

Praeneste, an ancient city of Latium, now Palestrina, *A.* VII. 682; VIII. 561; with Praenestīnus, *adj.* of Praeneste, *A.* VII. 678

Priamides, son of Priam, *A.* III. 295, 346; VI. 494, 509

Priamus: (1) Priam, son of Laomedon and king of Troy, *A.* I. 458, etc. (38 instances); hence Priameius, *adj.* of Priam, *A.* II. 403; III. 321; VII. 252; (2) son of Polites, and grandson of (1), *A.* v. 564

Priapus, a god of gardens, protecting them against thieves and birds. His image served as a kind of scarecrow, *E.* VII. 33; *G.* IV. 111; *P.* III. 17, 20

Pristis, name of a ship (Seadragon), *A.* v. 116, 154, 156, 187, 218

Privernum, a town of the Volsci, in Latium, *A.* XI. 540

Privernus, a Rutulian, *A.* IX. 576

Procas, a king of Alba, *A.* VI. 767

Prochyta, an island off the coast of Campania, now Procida, *A.* IX. 715

Procne, wife of Tereus and sister of Philomela, changed into a swallow; hence used of the swallow itself, *G.* IV. 15; *Ci.* 410

Procris, wife of Cephalus, who shot her accidentally while hunting, *A.* VI. 445

Proetides, the daughters of Proetus, king of Tiryns, whom Juno changed into cows, *E.* VI. 48

Prometheus, son of Iapetus. He stole fire from heaven, *E.* VI. 42

Promolus, a Trojan, *A.* IX. 574

Proserpina, daughter of Ceres and wife of Pluto, who stole her from her mother, *G.* I. 39; IV. 487; *A.* IV. 698; VI. 142, 402, 487

Proteus, a sea-god, shepherd of the sea-calves of Neptune. His dwelling was in the island of Pharos or Carpathus, and he was associated with Egypt. He had the power of changing himself into all kinds of forms, *G.* IV. 388, 422, 429, 447, 528; *A.* XI. 262

Prytanis, a Trojan, *A.* IX. 767

Publicola, a surname of the Messallae, *Ca.* IX. 40

Punicus, *adj.* Punic, Carthaginian, *A.* I. 338; IV. 49

Pygmalion, Dido's brother, who killed her husband, *A.* I. 347, 364; IV. 325

Pyllus, *adj.* of Pylos, in southern

INDEX

Elis, where Nestor lived, *Ca.* IX. 16

Pyracmon, a Cyclops, *A.* VIII. 425

Pyrgi, a town of Etruria, *A.* x. 184

Pyrgo, the nurse of Priam's children, *A.* V. 645

Pyrrha, wife of Deucalion, who after the deluge repeopled the earth by casting stones behind her, *E.* VI. 41

Pyrrhus, the son of Achilles; also called Neoptolemus. After the Trojan war he founded a kingdom in Epirus, *A.* II. 469, 491, 526, 529, 547, 662; III. 296, 319

Quercens, a Rutulian, *A.* IX. 681

Quinctio, a servile name, *Ca.* X. 8

Quirinus, the name given to the deified Romulus, *G.* III. 27; *A.* I. 292; VI. 859; hence Quirinalis, *adj.* of Quirinus, *A.* VII. 187, 612

Quirites, the Quirites or Roman citizens, *G.* IV. 201; *A.* VII. 710

Rapo, a Rutulian, *A.* X. 747

Remulus, a Rutulian, *A.* IX. 360, 593, 633; XI. 636

Remus: (1) brother of Romulus, *G.* II. 533; *A.* I. 292; (2) a Rutulian, *A.* IX. 330

Rhadamanthus, a son of Jupiter, brother of Minos, and a judge in the lower world, *A.* VI. 566

Rhaebus, the horse of Mezentius, *A.* X. 861

Rhaeticus, *adj.* of the Rhaeti, a nation dwelling in the Tyrol and eastern Switzerland, *G.* II. 96

Rhamnes, a Rutulian, and augur of Turnus, *A.* IX. 325, 359, 452

Rhamnusius, *adj.* of Rhamnus, the most northern town of Attica, *Ci.* 228

Rhea, a priestess, mother of Aventinus, *A.* VII. 659

Rhenus, the Rhine, *E.* X. 47; *A.* IX. 727

Rhesus, a king of Thrace, whose horses were captured by Ulysses and Diomedes, *G.* IV. 462; *A.* I. 469; *Cu.* 328

Rhodius, *adj.* of Rhodes, an island in the eastern Mediterranean, *G.* II. 102

Rhodope, a mountain-range of Thrace, now Despoto Dogh, *E.* VI. 30; VIII. 44; *G.* I. 332; III. 351, 462; hence Rhodopeius, *adj. G.* IV. 461

Rhoeteius, *adj.* of Rhoeteum, a promontory of the Troad; hence Trojan, *A.* V. 646; XII. 456

Rhoeteus, a Rutulian, *A.* III. 108; VI. 505; *Cu.* 313

Rhoetus: (1) a centaur, *G.* II. 456; (2) a Rutulian, *A.* IX. 344, 345; (3) a king of the Marsi, *A.* X. 338

Riphaeus, *adj.* Riphaean, of the Riphaei, a mountain-range of Scythia, *G.* I. 240; III. 382; IV. 518

Ripheus, a Trojan, *A.* II. 339, 394, 426

Roma, Rome, *E.* I. 19, 26; *G.* I. 466; II. 534; *A.* I. 7; V. 601; VI. 781; VII. 603, 709; VIII. 635; XII. 168; *Ca.* III. 5; IX. 37; *Cu.* 360; hence, Romanus, *adj.* Roman, *G.* I. 490; *A.* I. 33, etc. (32 instances)

Romulus, the mythical founder of Rome, *G.* I. 498; *A.* I. 276; VI. 778; VIII. 342; also as *adj.*, of Romulus, *A.* VI. 876. Hence, Romuleus, *adj.* of Romulus, *A.* VIII. 654, and Romulidae, sons or descendants of Romulus, *A.* VIII. 638

Roseus, *adj.* of Rosea, a district in Central Italy near the Veline Lake, *A.* VII. 712

Rufrae, a town of Campania, *A.* VII. 739

Rutulus, *adj.* Rutulian, of the Rutuli, a people of Latium, whose capital was Ardea; the *plur.* Rutuli is used as a *subst.*; *A.* I. 266; VII. 318, etc. (64 instances)

Sabaeus, *adj.* of Saba (Sheba) in Arabia Felix; the *masc. plur.* Sabaei is used as a *subst., G.* I. 57; II. 117; *A.* I. 416; VIII. 706

Sabellus, *adj.* Sabellian or Sabine, of the Sabelli or Sabini, *G.* II.

INDEX

167; *A.* VII. 665; VIII. 510; also Sabellicus, *adj.*, *G.* III. 255

Sabinus: (1) *adj.* Sabine, of the Sabines, a people of Central Italy, also in Latium and Southern Italy, with *plur. subst.* Sabini, the Sabines, *G.* II. 532; *A.* VII. 706, 709; VIII. 635; *Cu.* 404; (2) the mythical ancestor of the Sabines, *A.* VII. 178; (3) the name of a muledriver, *Ca.* X. 1, 8, 14

Saces, a Rutulian, *A.* XII. 651

Sacranus, *adj.* of the Sacrani, a people of old Latium, *A.* VII. 796

Sacrator, a Rutulian, *A.* X. 747

Sagaris, a Trojan, *A.* V. 263; IX. 575

Salamis, the famous island in the Saronic Gulf, once the home of Telamon, *A.* VIII. 158; hence, Salaminius, *adj. Ci.* 470

Salii, the twelve dancing priests of Mars, *A.* VIII. 285, 663

Salius: (1) an Acarnanian, *A.* V. 298, 321, 335, 341, 347, 352, 356; (2) an Etruscan, *A.* X. 753

Sallentīnus, *adj.* of the Sallentini, a people of Calabria in Italy, *A.* III. 400

Salmoneus, a son of Aeolus, ruling in Elis, punished for his impiety in imitating the thunder and lightning of Jupiter, *A.* VI. 585

Same, an island in the Ionian Sea, the later Cephallenia (now Cephalonia), *A.* III. 271

Samos: (1) an island off the coast of Asia Minor, now Samo, *A.* I. 16; (2) another name for Samothracia, *A.* VII. 208

Samothracia, an island off the coast of Thrace, now Samothraki, *A.* VII. 208

Sapientia, Wisdom, or Philosophy (personification), *Ci.* 14

Sardonius, *adj.* Sardinian, of Sardinia, famous for bitter herbs, *E.* VII. 41

Sarnus, a river of Campania, now the Sarno, *A.* VII. 738

Sarpēdon, a son of Jupiter, king of Lycia, killed before Troy, *A.* I. 100; IX. 697; X. 125, 471

Sarrānus, *adj.* of Sarra, ancient name of Tyre; hence, Tyrian, *G.* II. 506

Sarrastes, a people of Campania, about Sorrento, *A.* VII. 738

Saticulus, *adj.* of Saticula, a town in the hills of Campania, *A.* VII. 729

Satura, a lake in Latium, *A.* VII. 801

Saturnus, a fabled and deified king of Latium, identified with Κρόνος; in his time fell the golden age, *G.* I. 336; II. 406, 538; III. 93; *A.* VI. 794; VII. 49, 180, 203; VIII. 319, 357; XII. 830; hence, Saturnius, *adj.* of Saturn, applied to children of Saturn, as Jupiter, Neptune and Juno; and Saturnia, *fem. subst.*, Juno, *E.* IV. 6; VI. 41; *G.* II. 173; *A.* I. 23, 569; III. 380; IV. 92, 372; V. 606, 799; VII. 428, 560, 572, 622; VIII. 329, 358; IX. 2, 745, 802; X. 659, 760; XI. 252; XII. 156, 178, 807

Satyri, Satyrs, deities of the woods, represented with goats' legs and horns, *E.* V. 73; *Cu.* 116

Scaeus, *adj.* Scaean, name of the western (left) gate of Troy, facing the sea, *A.* II. 612; III. 351

Scipiadae, the Scipios, one of the most famous families of Rome, *G.* II. 170; *A.* VI. 843; *Cu.* 370

Sciron, a noted robber on the coast between Megara and Athens, slain by Theseus, *Ci.* 465

Scorpios, the constellation Scorpion, *G.* I. 35; *Ci.* 535

Scybale, name of an African woman, *M.* 31, 50, 119

Scylaceum, a town of southern Italy, on the coast of Bruttium, now Squillace, *A.* III. 553

Scylla: (1) a sea-monster dwelling on one side of the Strait of Messene, *A.* III. 420, 424, 432, 684; VI. 286; VII. 302; *Ci.* 65; *Cu.* 331; (2) a daughter of Nisus, who betrayed her father to Minos and was changed to a bird, *E.* VI. 74; *G.* I. 405; *Ci.* 49, 91, 130, 131, 209, 386, 410, 455, 493; (3) name of one of Aeneas' ships, *A.* V. 122

INDEX

Scyllaeus, *adj.* of Scylla, *A.* I. 200; *Ci.* 57

Scyrius, *adj.* of Scyros, an island north-east of Euboea, now Skyro, *A.* II. 477

Scythia, Scythia, the country north of the Black Sea, *E.* I. 65; *G.* I. 240; III. 197, 349

Sebethis, a nymph, *A.* VII. 734

Selinus, a town on the south-western coast of Sicily, now Pileri, *A.* III. 705

Selius, a rhetorician, *Ca.* v. 3

Semele, daughter of Cadmus, and mother of Bacchus by Jupiter, *Ca.* IX. 33

Senectus, Age (personification), *A.* VI. 275

Seres, a people of Eastern Asia (including probably the Chinese), *G.* II. 121

Serestus, a Trojan, *A.* I. 611; IV. 288; v. 487; IX. 171, 779; X. 541; XII. 549, 561

Sergestus, a Trojan, *A.* I. 510; IV. 288; v. 121, 184, 185, 203, 221, 272, 282; XII. 561

Sergius, *adj.* of Sergius, the name of a Roman *gens*, *A.* v. 121

Seriphus, a small island among the Cyclades in the Aegean, now Serfo, *Ci.* 477

Serranus: (1) a cognomen of the famous Regulus, who was ploughing when told of his election as consul, *A.* VI. 844; (2) a Rutulian, *A.* IX. 335, 454

Sevĕrus, a mountain in the Sabine territory, *A.* VII. 713

Sextus Sabinus, name of a youth, *Ca.* v. 6

Sibylla, a Sibyl, prophetess; especially the Cumaean, who guided Aeneas to the world below, *A.* III. 452; v. 735; VI. 10, 44, 98, 176, 211, 236, 538, 666, 752, 897

Sicanius and Sicānus, *adj.* Sicanian, of the Sicani, an old race of Sicily, *E.* X. 4; *A.* III. 692; v. 24; VIII. 328, 416; XI. 317; with Sicani, *subst.* the Sicilians, *A.* v. 293; VII. 795; and Sicani, *fem. subst.* Sicily, *A.* I. 557

Sicelis, *fem. adj.* Sicilian, *E.* IV. 1

Siculus, *adj.* Sicilian, *E.* II. 21; X. 51; *A.* I. 34, 549; III. 410, 418, 696; v. 702; VII. 289

Sicyonius, *adj.* of Sicyon, a city of the Peloponnesus, now Vasiliko, *G.* II. 519; *Ci.* 169

Sidicinus, *adj.* of the Sidicini, a people of Campania, *A.* VII. 727

Sidon, a city of Phoenicia, now Saida, *A.* I. 609; hence, Sidonius, *adj.* Sidonian or Phoenician; also Tyrian, because Sidon was the mother-city of Tyre, *A.* I. 446, 613, 678; IV. 75, 137, 545, 683; v. 571; IX. 266; XI. 74; *Ci.* 387

Sigeus, *adj.* of Sigeum, a promontory of the Troad, *A.* II. 312; VII. 294; *Cu.* 307

Sila, a forest in Bruttium, *G.* III. 219; *A.* XII. 715

Silarus, a river between Lucania and Campania, now Sele, *G.* III. 146

Silenus, an old Satyr, chief attendant of Bacchus, *E.* VI. 14

Silvanus, a woodland god, *E.* X. 24; *G.* I. 20; II. 494; *A.* VIII. 600

Silvia, a Latin maid, daughter of Tyrrhus, *A.* VII. 487, 503

Silvius: (1) a son of Aeneas, *A.* VI. 763; (2) Silvius Aeneas, a king of Alba, *A.* VI. 769

Simois, a river of the Troad, now Mendere Tchai, *A.* I. 100, 618; III. 302; v. 261, 634, 803; VI. 88; X. 60; XI. 257; *Cu.* 307

Simylus, a rustic, *M.* 3, 53, 121

Sinon, the Greek spy, through whose craft the wooden horse was taken into Troy, *A.* II. 79, 195, 259, 329

Sirenes, the Sirens, fabulous creatures, half maiden, half bird, living on rocky islands near the Campanian coast, and with their songs enticing sailors to their destruction, *A.* v. 864

Sirius, the Dog-star, whose rising is associated with extreme heat, *G.* IV. 425; *A.* III. 141; X. 273

Siron, Siro, an Epicurean philosopher, teacher of Virgil, *Ca.* v. 9; VIII. 1

Sithonius, *adj.* of the Sithonii, a Thracian tribe, *E.* X. 66

577

INDEX

Sol, the Sun (personified), *G.* II. 321; IV. 51; *A.* I. 568; IV. 607; VII. 11, 100, 218, 227; XII. 164, 176

Somnia, Dreams (personification), *A.* VI. 283

Somnus, Sleep, the god of sleep, son of Erebus and Nox, *A.* V. 838; VI. 893

Sophocleus, *adj.* of Sophocles, the great Attic tragedy-writer, *E.* VIII. 10

Sopor, Sleep (personification), *A.* VI. 278

Soracte, a mountain in Etruria, not far from Rome, now S. Oreste, *A.* VII. 696; XI. 785

Sparta, the capital of Laconia; also called Lacedaemon, *G.* III. 405; *A.* II. 577; X. 92; with Spartanus, *adj.* Spartan, *A.* I. 316, and Sparticus, *adj.* Spartan, *Cu.* 400

Spercheos, a river of Thessaly, now the Ellada, *G.* II. 487

Spio, a sea-nymph, *G.* IV. 338; *A.* V. 826

Steropes, a Cyclops, *A.* VIII. 425

Sthenelus: (1) a Greek, charioteer of Diomedes, *A.* II. 261; (2) a Trojan, *A.* XII. 341

Sthenius, a Rutulian, *A.* X. 388

Stimichon, a shepherd, *E.* V. 55

Strophades, two islands of the Ionian Sea, south of Zacynthus, to which the Harpies were driven by the sons of Boreas, now Strofahia, *A.* III. 209, 210

Strymon, a river of Macedonia, near Thrace, now Struma, *G.* IV. 508; with Strymonius, *adj.* of the Strymon, *G.* I. 120; *A.* X. 265; XI. 580; *Cu.* 328

Strymonius, a Trojan, *A.* X. 414

Styx, a river of the lower world, *G.* I. 243; IV. 480; *A.* VI. 154, 439; with Stygius, *adj.* Stygian or infernal, *G.* III. 551; IV. 506; *A.* III. 215; IV. 638, 699; V. 855; VI. 134, 252, 323, 369, 374, 385, 391; VII. 476, 773; VIII. 296; IX. 104; X. 113; XII. 91, 816; *Cu.* 240; also Stygialius, *adj.* Stygian, *Ci.* 374

Sucro, a Rutulian, *A.* XII. 505

Sulmo, a Rutulian, *A.* IX. 412; X. 517

Sunias, *adj.* of Sunium, a promontory of Attica, where a temple of Aphrodite stood; now known as Capo Colonna, *Ci.* 472

Surisca, Syrisca, an inn-keeper, *Co.* 1

Surrentinus, *adj.* of Surrentum, now Sorrento, a town of Campania, *Ca.* XIV. 12

Sybaris, a Trojan, *A.* XII. 363

Sychaeus, husband of Dido, *A.* I. 343, 348, 720; IV. 20, 502, 632; VI. 474; also as *adj.*, *A.* IV. 552.

Symaethius, *adj.* of the Symaethus, a river at the east end of Sicily, near Catina, *A.* IX. 584

Syracosius, *adj.* of Syracuse, chief city of Sicily and home of Theocritus, *E.* VI. 1; *Ca.* XV. 1

Syrius, *adj.* of Syria; used freely of all the country at the east end of the Mediterranean, *G.* II. 88; *Ci.* 512

Syrtis, the name of two shallow bays on the north coast of Libya, now the Gulf of Sidra and the Gulf of Cabes, *A.* IV. 41; V. 51, 192; VI. 60; VII. 302; *D.* 53; (cf. *A.* I. 111, 146; X. 678)

Taburnus, a mountain of Campania on the borders of Samnium, now Monte Taburno, *G.* II. 38; *A.* XII. 715

Taenarius, *adj.* of Taenarus, a promontory at the south extremity of Laconia, with a cave fabled to be an entrance to the world below, *G.* IV. 467

Tagus: (1) a Latin, *A.* IX. 418; (2) a river of Lusitania (Portugal and Western Spain), *Ca.* IX. 52

Talos, a Rutulian, *A.* XII. 513

Tanager, a river of Lucania, now Tangro, *G.* III. 151

Tanais: (1) a river of Scythia, now the Don, *G.* IV. 517; (2) a Rutulian, *A.* XII. 513

Tantaleus, *adj.* of Tantalus, father of Pelops, grandfather of Atreus, and great-grandfather of Agamemnon and Menelaus, *Cu.* 334

Tarchon or Tarcho, an Etruscan,

INDEX

A. VIII. 506, 603; X. 153, 290, 299, 302; XI. 184, 727, 729, 746, 757

Tarentum, a city of Calabria on the Gulf of Tarentum, now Taranto, *G.* II. 197; *A.* III. 551

Tarpeia, a maiden, companion of Camilla, *A.* XI. 656

Tarpeius, *adj.* Tarpeian, a name applied to the rock of the Capitol, *A.* VIII. 347; with *arx*, of the Capitol itself, *A.* VIII. 652

Tarquinius, Tarquinius Superbus, or Tarquin, the last king of Rome, *A.* VIII. 646; in *plur.*, the Tarquins, the family generally, *A.* VI. 817, or Tarquinius Superbus and his father Tarquinius Priscus, *Ca.* IX. 36

Tarquitius, a rhetorician, *Ca.* V. 3

Tarquitus, a Latin hero, *A.* X. 550

Tartarus, the abode of the wicked in the lower world, *G.* I. 36; II. 292; IV. 482; *A.* IV. 243, 446; V. 734; VI. 135, 543, 577; VIII. 563; IX. 496; XI. 397; XII. 14, 205; *Cu.* 274, 294, 333; with Tartareus, *adj.* Tartarean, infernal, *A.* VII. 295, 395, 551; VII. 328, 514; VIII. 667; XII. 846

Tatius, Titus Tatius, king of the Sabines, with whom Romulus shared his kingdom, *A.* VIII. 638

Taygete, one of the Pleiades, *G.* IV. 232

Taygetus, a mountain-range of Laconia, *G.* II. 488; III. 44

Tegeaeus, *adj.* of Tegea, a town of Arcadia; hence, Arcadian, *G.* I. 18; *A.* V. 299; VIII. 459

Telamonius, *adj.* of Telamon, son of Aeacus, brother of Peleus and father of Ajax and Teucer, *Cu.* 297, 315

Teleboae, a people dwelling in some islands between Leucadia and Acarnania, whence came the early settlers of Capri, *A.* VII. 735

Tellus, Earth (personification), *A.* IV. 166; VII. 137

Telon, a king of the Teleboae, *A.* VII. 734

Tempe, a valley in Thessaly, famous for its beauty, now Lykostomo, *G.* II. 469; IV. 317; *Cu.* 94

Tempestates, goddesses of the weather or storm, Tempests, *A.* V. 772

Tenedos, an island in the Aegean, near the Troad, still so called, *A.* II. 21, 203, 255

Tereus: (1) a king of Thrace, husband of Procne the sister of Philomela, and father of Itys, *E.* VI. 78; (2) a Trojan, *A.* XI. 675

Terra, Earth (personification), *G.* I. 278; IV. 178; VI. 580, 595; XII. 176, 778

Tethys, a sea-goddess, wife of Oceanus, and mother of all waters, *G.* I. 31; *Ci.* 392

Tetrica, a mountain in the Sabine territory, *A.* VII. 713

Teucer and Teucrus: (1) first king of Troy, father of Batea, who married Dardanus, *A.* I. 235; III. 108; IV. 230; VI. 500, 648; hence Teucri, *subst.* the Teucrians or Trojans, *A.* I. 38, 89; II. 252, etc. (130 instances); also Teucrius, *adj.* Teucrian or Trojan, *Cu.* 306, with Teucria, *subst.* the Teucrian or Trojan land, *A.* II. 26; (2) a son of Telamon and Hesione, half-brother of Ajax, and founder of Salamis in Cyprus, *A.* I. 619

Teuthras, an Arcadian, *A.* X. 402

Teutonicus, *adj.* of the Teutones, a tribe of Germany, *A.* VII. 741

Thaemon, a Lycian, *A.* X. 126

Thalassio, an ancient salutation to a bride at her wedding, possibly of Etruscan origin. One explanation, given by Livy (I. 9), is that at the time when the Sabine women were carried off by the Romans, one woman of great beauty was taken by the attendants of a certain Thalassius, and to the frequent inquiry for whom she was intended the answer given was *Thalassio*, *i.e.* "for Thalassius," *Ca.* XII. 9; XIII. 16

Thalia: (1) a Muse, usually assigned to Comedy, *E.* VI. 2; *Cu.* 1. (2) a sea-nymph, *A.* V. 826

Thamyrus, a Trojan, *A.* XII. 341

579

INDEX

Thapsus, a city and peninsula on the eastern coast of Sicily, now Magnisi, *A.* III. 689

Thasius, *adj.* of Thasos, an island in the north Aegean, now Thaso, *G.* II. 91

Thaumantias, *fem. adj.* daughter of Thaumas, Iris, *A.* IX. 5

Theano, a Trojan woman, *A.* X. 703

Thebae, Thebes, capital of Boeotia, now Thiva, where the scene of the *Bacchae* of Euripides is laid, *A.* IV. 469; hence Thebanus, *adj.* Theban, *A.* IX. 697

Themillas, a Rutulian, *A.* IX. 576

Thermodon, a river of Pontus, along which dwelt the Amazons, now Termeh Tchaï, *A.* XI. 659

Theron, a Latin, *A.* X. 312

Thersilochus, the name of two Trojans, *A.* VI. 483; XII. 363

Theseus, an early king of Athens, slayer of the Minotaur. Along with Pirithous he attempted to carry Proserpina from the lower world, and in punishment was made to sit on a rock for ever, *A.* VI. 122, 393, 618; *Ci.* 102; hence Thesidae, sons of Theseus, *i.e.* Athenians, *G.* II. 383

Thessandrus, a Greek, *A.* II. 261

Thestylis, a rustic woman, *E.* II. 10, 43

Thetis, a sea-nymph, one of the Nereids, mother of Achilles, *G.* I. 399; *A.* V. 825 (*cf.* VIII. 383); also of the sea itself, *E.* IV. 32

Thoas: (1) a Greek, *A.* II. 262; (2) a Trojan, *A.* X. 415

Thraca, Thrace, *A.* XII. 335; also Thraces, Thracians, *A.* III. 14; Thracius and Threicius, *adj.* Thracian, *E.* IV. 55; *A.* III. 51; V. 312, 536, 565; VI. 120, 645; VII. 208; IX. 49; XI. 659; with Thraex, *adj.* Thracian, *D.* 37; and Threicii, *subst.* Thracians, *A.* X. 350; also Threissa, *fem. adj.* Thracian, *A.* I. 316; XI. 858

Thronius, a Trojan, *A.* X. 753

Thucydides, famous Greek historian, *Ca.* II. 3

Thule, a supposed island at the north-east of Europe, beyond Britain, discovered by Pytheas, *G.* I. 30

Thybrinus, *adj.* of the Tiber, *A.* XII. 35

Thybris: (1) a king of the Etruscans, *A.* VIII. 330; (2) same as Tiberis, *A.* VIII. 331, etc.

Thyias, a Thyiad, a female worshipper of Bacchus, a Bacchante, *A.* IV. 302

Thymber, a Rutulian, *A.* X. 391, 394

Thymbraeus: (1) *adj.* of Thymbra, a town of the Troad, in which was a temple of Apollo, *G.* IV. 323; used as *subst.* god of Thymbra, Apollo, *A.* III. 85; (2) a Trojan, *A.* XII. 458

Thymbris, a Trojan, *A.* X. 124

Thymoetes, name of two Trojans, *A.* II. 32; X. 123; XII. 364

Thyrsis, a shepherd, *E.* VII. 2, 3, 20; VII. 16, 69

Tiberis or Thybris, the river Tiber, now Tevere, *G.* I. 499; *A.* II. 782; III. 500; V. 83, 797; VI. 87; VII. 151, 242, 303, 436, 715; VIII. 64, 72, 86, 331, 540; X. 421; XI. 393; *Ca.* XIII. 23; hence, Tiberinus, *adj.* of the Tiber, *A.* I. 13; X. 833; XI. 449; used as *subst.* the river-god Tiber, *G.* IV. 369; *A.* VI. 873; VII. 30, 797; VIII. 31; IX. 125

Tibur, an ancient town of Latium on the Anio, twenty miles northeast of Rome, now Tivoli, *A.* VII. 630; hence Tiburs, *adj.* of Tibur, *A.* VII. 670; IX. 360; with *plur.* Tiburtes, as *subst.* the Tiburtines, *A.* XI. 757

Tiburtus, an Argive, one of the mythic founders of Tibur, *A.* VII. 671; XI. 519

Tigris: (1) the famous river of Asia, *E.* I. 62; (2) name of a ship, *A.* X. 166

Timavus, a small river in Istria, between Aquileia and Trieste, *E.* VIII. 6; *G.* III. 475; *A.* I. 244

Timor, Fear or Terror (personification), *A.* IX. 719

Tiphys, pilot of the Argo, *E.* IV. 34

Tirynthius, *adj.* of Tiryns, an ancient city of Argolis, where Hercules was reared; hence, as *subst.* the Tirynthian, Hercules

INDEX

A. VII. 622; VIII. 228; *fem. subst.* Juno, *Ci.* 161

Tisiphone, one of the three Furies, *G.* III. 552; *A.* VI. 555, 571; X. 761; *Cu.* 218

Titan, one of the six sons of Caelus and Terra; also a name of the sun-god, who was son of Hyperion, *A.* IV. 119; hence Titanius, *adj.* Titanian, of the Titans, *A.* VI. 580, 725

Tithōnus, son of Laomedon, husband of Aurora, and father of Memnon, *G.* I. 447; III. 48; *A.* IV. 585; IX. 460; with Tithonius, *adj.* of Tithonus, *A.* VIII. 384

Tityos, a giant, son of Jupiter, slain by Apollo for offering violence to Latona, *A.* VI. 595; *Cu.* 237

Tityrus, a shepherd's name, common in bucolic poetry, *E.* I. 1, 4, 13, 18, 38; III. 20, 96; V. 12; VI. 4; VIII. 55; IX. 23, 24; *G.* V. 566

Tmaros, a mountain in Epirus, *E.* VIII. 44; hence, Tmarius, *adj.* of Tmaros, *A.* V. 620

Tmarus, a Rutulian, *A.* IX. 685

Tmolus, a mountain in Lydia, famous for its vines, now Kisilja Mousa Dagh, *G.* I. 56; with Tmolius, *adj.* of Tmolus, *Cu.* 75; as *subst.* (properly Τμώλιος οἶνος), Tmolian wine *G.* II. 98

Tolumnius, a Rutulian augur, *A.* XI. 429; XII. 258, 460

Torquatus, a surname of Titus Manlius, who wore the collar of a Gaul whom he had slain in single combat. In his consulship B.C. 340, he put his son to death for disobedience, *A.* VI. 825

Trinacria, Sicily (so called from its three promontories), *A.* III. 440, 582; V. 393, 555; *Ca.* IX. 20; *D.* 9; with Trinacrius, *adj.* of Sicily, Sicilian, *A.* I. 196; III. 384, 429, 554; V. 300, 450, 530, 573

Triptolemus, son of Celeus, and inventor of agriculture, *Cu.* 136 (*cf. G.* I. 19)

Triton: (1) a sea-god, son of Neptune, who blows a shell at the bidding of his father, *A.* I. 144; VI. 173; in *plur.* sea-gods, *A.* V. 824; (2) name of a ship, with the figure-head of a Triton, *A.* X. 209

Tritonis, Pallas or Minerva, so called because of her birth (according to Egyptian fable) near Lake Triton in Africa, *A.* II. 226; with Tritonius, *adj.* Tritonian, *A.* II. 615; V. 704; XI. 483; with *fem. subst.* Tritonia, Tritonia or Minerva, *A.* II. 171

Trivia, an epithet of Diana or Hecate, whose images were placed at the intersection of roads (properly, those of the three ways), *A.* VI. 13, 35, 69; VII. 516, 774, 778; X. 537; XI. 566, 836

Troades, Trojan women, *A.* V. 613.

Troia: (1) the city of Troy, *E.* IV. 36; *G.* I. 502; II. 385; *A.* I. 24, etc. (92 instances); (2) a city founded by Helenus in Epirus, *A.* III. 349, 497; (3) part of the city Acesta in Sicily, *A.* V. 756; (4) a game of Roman boys, *A.* V. 602; with Troius, *adj.* Trojan, *A.* I. 119, etc. (22 instances), and Troianus, *A.* I. 19, etc. (46 instances)

Troilus, a son of Priam, *A.* I. 474.

Troiugena, a Trojan (Trojan in birth), *A.* III. 359; VIII. 117; XII. 626

Tros: (1) son of Erichthonius, father of Assaracus, and king of Phrygia, *G.* III. 36; (2) *adj.* Trojan; or *subst.* a Trojan, *A.* I. 30, 129, etc. (35 instances)

Tryphon, a muleteer, *Ca.* X. 6

Tucca, *i.e.* Plotius Tucca, one of Virgil's friends and literary executors, *Ca.* I. 1

Tulla, an attendant of Camilla, *A.* XI. 656

Tullus, *i.e.* Tullus Hostilius, the third king of Rome, *A.* VI. 814; VIII. 644

Turnus, the son of Daunus and the nymph Venilia, king of the Rutulians, who, as suitor for the hand of Lavinia, resisted the

INDEX

settlement of Aeneas. (The word may be a contraction from *Tyrrhenus*.) *A.* VII. 56, 344, etc. (152 instances)

Tuscus, *adj.* of Etruria, Etruscan or Tuscan, with *subst. plur.* Tusci, Etruscans or Tuscans, *G.* I. 499; *A.* VIII. 473; X. 164, 199, 203; XI. 316, 629; XII. 551

Tydeus, son of Oeneus, father of Diomedes, and one of the "Seven against Thebes," *A.* VI. 479; hence Tydides, son of Tydeus, Diomedes, *A.* I. 97, 471; II. 164, 197; X. 29; XI. 404; XII. 351

Tyndaridae, sons of Tyndareus (or Tyndarus), viz., Castor and Pollux, by Leda. As Pollux was really the son of Jupiter, he was immortal, but after Castor's death he shared his immortality on alternate days with his brother, *Ci.* 399. The *sing.* Tyndaris, daughter of Tyndareus, is used of Helen, really the daughter of Jupiter, who had taken the form of a white swan, *A.* II. 569, 601; *Ca.* IX. 27

Typhoeus, son of Earth and Tartarus, also called Typhon, who had a hundred heads and breathed fire. He was slain by lightning and buried under Aetna or Ischia, *G.* I. 279; *A.* VIII. 298; IX. 716; hence Typhoeüs, *adj.* of Typhon, *A.* I. 665

Typhon, another name for Typhoeus, *Ci.* 32

Tyres, an Arcadian, *A.* X. 403

Tyros, Tyre, the chief city of Phoenicia, famous for its purple dye, *A.* I. 346; IV. 36, 43, 670; hence Tyrius, *adj.* of Tyre, or of Carthage (colonised from Tyre); also used as a *subst.* a Tyrian or a Carthaginian, *G.* III. 17, 307; *A.* I. 12, 20, etc. (28 instances)

Tyrrhenus: (1) an Etruscan, *A.* XI. 612; (2) *adj.* Etruscan or Tuscan; also used as a *subst.* *G.* II. 164, 193; *A.* I. 67, etc. (34 instances)

Tyrrhus or Tyrrheus, a Latin, herdsman of Latinus, *A.* VII. 485, 508, 532; hence Tyrrhidae, the sons of Tyrrhus, *A.* VII. 484; IX. 28

Ucalegon, a Trojan, *A.* II. 312

Ufens: (1) a small river of Latium, now Ufente, *A.* VII. 802; (2) a Rutulian, *A.* VII. 745; VIII. 6; X. 518; XII. 460, 641

Ulixes, Ulysses, the hero Odysseus of the Odyssey, *E.* VIII. 70; *A.* II. 7, 44, 90, 97, 164, 261, 436, 762; III. 273, 613, 628, 691; IX. 602; XI. 263; *Ci.* 58

Umber, *adj.* Umbrian, of the Umbri, a tribe of Northern Italy; used as *subst.* (*sc. canis*), an Umbrian hound, *A.* XII. 753

Umbro, a Marsian, ally of Turnus, *A.* VII. 752; X. 544

Valerus, an Etruscan, *A.* X. 752

Varius, an epic poet, friend of Virgil, for whom he was a literary executor, *E.* IX. 35; *Ca.* VII. 1

Varro, a rhetorician, probably not the famous and versatile M. Terentius Varro, *Ca.* V. 3

Varus, L. Alfenus Varus, who succeeded Pollio in Cisalpine Gaul and had charge of the confiscation of lands in Virgil's district, *E.* VI. 7, 10, 12; IX. 26, 27

Velinus: (1) *adj.* of Velia, a town on the coast of Lucania, now Castellamare della Bruca, *A.* VI. 366; (2) a lake in the Sabine territory, *A.* VII. 517, 712

Venilia, a nymph, mother of Turnus, *A.* X. 76

Venulus, a Latin, messenger of Turnus, *A.* VIII. 9; XI. 242, 742

Venus, goddess of love and beauty, daughter of Jupiter and Dione; identified with the Greek Aphrodite, *E.* III. 68; VII. 62; VIII. 78; *G.* III. 267; *A.* I. 229, etc. (53 instances); often used as a synonym for *amor*, *G.* II. 329; III. 64, 97, 137, 210; IV. 199,

INDEX

515; *A*. IV. 33; VI. 26; XI. 736; *M*. 86

Vergilius, the poet Virgil, *G*. IV. 562.

Vesaevus, Vesuvius, the famous volcano in Campania, *G*. II. 224

Vesper, evening, the evening star (Hesperus); also the West, *E*. VI. 86; *G*. I. 251; IV. 186, 434, 474; *A*. I. 374; VIII. 280; *Cu*. 203; (*cf*. also *G*. I. 461; III. 336; *A*. V. 19)

Vesta, goddess of the hearth and household, emblem of family life. In her temple, on the hearth of the Roman state considered as a family, her fire was kept always burning, *G*. I. 498; IV. 384; *A*. I. 292; II. 296, 567; V. 744; IX. 259; *Co*. 26; *M*. 52

Vesulus, a mountain in Liguria, now Monte Viso, *A*. X. 708

Victoria, Victory (personification), *A*. XI. 436; XII. 187

Virbius: (1) a name given to Hippolytus on his return to life, *A*. VII. 777; (2) a son of Hippolytus, *A*. VII. 762

Virtus, Valour (personification), *Cu*. 299

Volcanus, Vulcan, god of fire, son of Jupiter and Juno, also used for fire itself, *G*. I. 295; IV. 346; *A*. II. 311; V. 662; VII. 77, 679; VIII. 198, 372, 422, 729; IX. 76, 148; X. 543; XI. 439; *M*. 52; *D*. 52; *L*. 70; hence, Volcanius, of Vulcan, of fire, *A*. VIII. 422, 535; X. 408; XII. 739; *Cu*. 320

Volcens, a Latin, *A*. IX. 370, 375, 420, 439, 451; X. 563

Volscus, *adj*. Volscian, of the Volsci, a people who once occupied a considerable part of Latium, *A*. VII. 803; *plur*. *subst*. Volsci, the Volscians, *G*. II. 168; *A*. IX. 505; XI. 167, 432, 463, 498, 546, 800, 898

Volturnus, a river of Campania, now Volturno, *A*. VII. 729

Volusus, a Rutulian, *A*. XI. 463

Xantho, a Nereid, *G*. IV. 336

Xanthus: (1) a river of the Troad, *A*. I. 473; III. 497; V. 634, 803, 808; VI. 88; X. 60; *Cu*. 14, 307; (2) a stream in Epirus, named from (1), *A*. III. 350; (3) a river in Lycia, haunt of Apollo, *A*. IV. 143

Zacynthos, an island in the Ionian Sea, now Zante, *A*. III. 270

Zanclaeus, *adj*. Zanclaean, of Zancle (older name of Messana, or Messina, in Sicily), *Cu*. 332

Zephyrus, god of the west wind, son of Astraeus and Aurora; also the west wind itself, *E*. V. 5; *G* I. 44, 371; II. 106, 330; III. 134, 273, 322; IV. 138, 305; *A*. I. 131; II. 417; III. 120; IV. 223, 562; V. 33; X. 103; XII. 334; *Ci*. 25